THE AMERICAN CONGRESS

★ ★ ★

The AMERICAN CONGRESS

THE BUILDING OF DEMOCRACY

Julian E. Zelizer, Editor

Houghton Mifflin Company
BOSTON • NEW YORK
2004

Visit our Web site: www.houghtonmifflinbooks.com.

Library of Congress Cataloging-in-Publication Data

The reader's companion to the United States Congress / edited by Julian E. Zelizer.
p. cm.
Includes index.
ISBN 0-618-17906-2
1. United States. Congress — History. I. Zelizer, Julian E.
JK1041.R43 2004
328.73 — dc22 2004040511

PRINTED IN THE UNITED STATES OF AMERICA

QUM 10 9 8 7 6 5 4 3 2 1

TO

LOUIS GALAMBOS

One of the History profession's great editors
and most talented mentors

Contents

Contributors

RICHARD BENSEL Cornell University
EDWARD D. BERKOWITZ George Washington University
DONALD T. CRITCHLOW Saint Louis University
JANE DAILEY The Johns Hopkins University
ROBIN L. EINHORN University of California, Berkeley
WILLIAM DEVERELL California Institute of Technology
DANIEL FELLER University of Tennessee
LOUIS FISHER Congressional Research Service
JOANNE BARRIE FREEMAN Yale University
ALONZO L. HAMBY Ohio University
DONALD R. HICKEY Wayne State College
MICHAEL F. HOLT University of Virginia
K. AUSTIN KERR Ohio State University
DAVID E. KYVIG Northern Illinois University
JOHN LAURITZ LARSON Purdue University
FREDRIK LOGEVALL Cornell University
PATRICK MANEY University of South Carolina
JOSEPH A. McCARTIN Georgetown University
PAUL C. MILAZZO Ohio University
MARK E. NEELY, JR. The Pennslyvania State University
ALISON M. PARKER State University of New York, Brockport
JEFFREY L. PASLEY University of Missouri
ERIC PATASHNIK University of Virginia
THOMAS R. PEGRAM Loyola College in Maryland
L. A. POWE, JR. The University of Texas
JACK N. RAKOVE Stanford University
ERIC RAUCHWAY University of California, Davis
DONALD A. RITCHIE U.S. Senate Historical Office

ELIZABETH SANDERS Cornell University
MICHAEL SCHUDSON University of California, San Diego
BRUCE J. SCHULMAN Boston University
JOEL H. SILBEY Cornell University
BROOKS D. SIMPSON Arizona State University
BARBARA SINCLAIR University of California, Los Angeles
BARTHOLOMEW H. SPARROW The University of Texas at Austin
ALAN TAYLOR University of California, Davis
TIMOTHY N. THURBER Virginia Commonwealth University
DANIEL J. TICHENOR Rutgers University, New Brunswick
RANDALL BENNETT WOODS University of Arkansas

Biographical sidebars by John Sisson

Acknowledgments

I would like to begin by thanking the Dirksen Congressional Center for providing me with a generous grant that helped make this book possible. The Dirksen Congressional Center has been a wonderful and indispensable addition to the community of scholars interested in congressional history. In an era where research support for studying Congress is scarce, the Dirksen Congressional Center has been an invaluable asset. The Center has offered the financial support that scholars need to conduct research into the legislative branch, while it has been instrumental to the organization of conferences, workshops, web-based initiatives, and teaching programs that greatly further our knowledge of congressional history. Frank Mackaman, who currently directs the Center, has been a source of support for those of us who want to grapple with this complex, fragmented, and tumultuous institution.

Professor Alan Brinkley initially suggested that I would be the right man for this job. I am deeply appreciative of his confidence in my scholarship, and I hope that this book fulfills the high standard that he set with *The Reader's Companion to the American Presidency.*

Houghton Mifflin has been an absolute delight to work with. Gordon Hardy is the kind of editor writers are rarely fortune enough to encounter. He is intelligent, efficient, enthusiastic, and highly supportive. Throughout this process, he has also offered the kind of tough and constructive criticism that we all seek, at the same time that he gave me the intellectual breathing space that I needed to pull off my vision for this book. He has constantly pushed me as an editor to get the most that I could out of my authors, and he has always kept me thinking about the reader — not just the writer — on whose table this book will ultimately sit. Judy Moore and Wendy Holt have been helpful throughout this process. Judy Moore's skillful work on finding the illustrations was integral to the quality of the final product. Wendy Holt's editing helped bring this book through the final stages of production.

The authors in this volume are the heart and soul of the project. When editors approach scholars to contribute essays to a big volume, it is always hard to know what to expect. I have been very fortunate, and want to thank the team behind this book. Each author has produced an outstanding piece that went far beyond the call of duty. They put together original, well-written, and insightful interpretations on subject matter that has not been thoroughly examined. The authors have also tolerated my editing — and constant stream of gentle reminders — since the invitations went out. This is a volume that I am proud to be an editor of, given the caliber of the work that the contributors produced.

My wife, Nora, as always, is a source of endless encouragement. She never doubted that I could pull off this project, and she has always helped me work through some of the challenges that emerged. Our daughter Sophia found great amusement in playing with the stack of papers on my floor that constituted the draft chapters of this book, suggesting this will be fun for people to read (or at least to play with!). She is everything to me, and I hope that one day she can enjoy this book. Our son, Nathan, born as this book came to completion, is also too young to give me his thoughts on the volume. But his constant stream of smiles created a wonderful aura within which to finish this work. Nathan's a great son, and I can't wait to sit down at the dinner table and talk politics with his sister and him.

Finally, this book is dedicated to Louis Galambos, my mentor at the Johns Hopkins University. As anyone who has worked with him knows, Lou is a great editor. He has tremendous skill at getting the best scholarship out of an author, pushing him or her to their limits, while never editing in such a fashion as to impose his own views on the piece. He taught me to always engage the authors on their own terms, rather than my own. There are many historians in this business who have been the beneficiaries of his skilled editorial hand. While at graduate school, and ever since, I learned most of what I know about editing from Lou, and I hope that one day I can begin to have the same effect on other scholars as he had on me. Most important, I hope that he is proud of this book.

Introduction

When the Texan Sam Rayburn served as Speaker of the House of Representatives during the 1940s and 1950s, he met with select Democrats every late afternoon and early evening in what observers called "the Board of Education." The Democrats assembled in a former committee room tucked away under the Speaker's lobby on the ground floor of the Capitol. Approximately twelve feet square with an elaborately decorated ceiling, the walls were covered with signed photographs of famous politicians, a formal portrait of Rayburn, the flags of Texas and the United States, and a few of Rayburn's favorite cartoons. Sitting in an oversized chair that stood behind a long desk, the taciturn Rayburn would loosen up as he talked with the Democratic colleagues who made up his inner circle. They ranged in age and ideology from the abrasive and aggressive Georgian Eugene Cox—a staunch anti–New Deal conservative who nonetheless helped Rayburn as a powerful Democrat on the House Rules Committee—to the populist Texan Wright Patman, who was so trusted that he received a personal key to the room. Even though he was physically small and unassuming, Rayburn commanded enormous respect by relying on informal relationships to influence decisions in an era when southern committee chairs dominated the chamber. Lewis Deschler, the House Parliamentarian whose immense knowledge of parliamentary procedure made him an invaluable asset to Rayburn, was a fixture at these gatherings. A few trusted news reporters attended, but only under the strict understanding that conversations were off the record. While drinking bourbon and playing cards on the long leather couch and eight chairs that filled the room, Democrats debated the nation's biggest issues.

The Board of Education is a landmark in congressional history. Scholars of Congress speak about this room with the same respect shown when presidential experts discuss the Oval Office. It was in this room that a deeply divided Democratic party hashed out difficult compromises on controversial issues ranging from Cold War foreign policy to civil rights for African Americans. This was where Vice President Harry Truman received the call to become president in 1945 when Franklin Roosevelt passed away and where the young Lyndon Johnson strove to ingratiate himself with the

Speaker's drinking circle. In many ways it was like the closed rooms of other congressional eras: a place where senators and representatives could meet and do the hard business of a legislature: discuss, deal, compromise, and finally agree to act on the nation's problems.

Yet the Board of Education, and the individuals who met there, have generally escaped historical attention. Overshadowed by presidents and social movements, legislators remain ghosts in America's historical imagination. Tourists visiting Washington, D.C., enter the White House with a strong sense of the history of the presidents who lived there. Many Americans are familiar with the lineage linking George Washington to George W. Bush. Although the Supreme Court is less familiar, a popular narrative centers on the Chief Justices. Unlike the presidency and Supreme Court, however, Congress remains much of a mystery. While many Americans know about a handful of prominent representatives and senators, few have been exposed to a history of the institution as a whole. Most individuals are likely to think of Congress as an amorphous, messy, and chaotic body. At worst, many envision the Congress as depicted in the film *Bulworth,* in which Warren Beatty plays a senator who once marched for civil rights but who had been morally destroyed by an institution dominated by corrupt individuals and crooked interest groups. Some experts lament that Congress is not what it used to be, but they seem to have little sense of what those times were actually like.

This lack of knowledge is unfortunate. Congress is the heart and soul of our democracy, the arena where politicians and citizens most directly interact over pressing concerns. Frequently, commentators joke that legislation resembles sausage: the taste may be good, but people do not want to see how it was made. The very messiness of congressional decisions, which is often lamented by commentators, reflects the diversity and richness of the nation. As the Democratic presidential candidate Adlai Stevenson once argued: "Government is like a pump and what it pumps up is just what we are, a fair sample of the intellect, the ethics, and the morals of the people — no better, no worse." In Congress, grand policy proposals are created by politicians responding to the nation's economic, social, sectional, cultural, and political interests. Its members attempt to placate diverse portions of the population and broker complicated compromises between the myriad of voices to find concrete solutions to the nation's most pressing problems. The histories of the House and Senate demonstrate the great virtue of the legislative process is, namely, its ability to create innovative policies through difficult compromise. Yet Congress has also been the source of democracy's greatest vices, plagued by scandal, insular deliberations, rampant corruption, and bitter partisanship.

The size, messiness, virtues, and vices that make Congress so interesting also create enormous barriers to our understanding the institution. Unlike the presidency, Congress is difficult to conceptualize, with up to 535 members who are constantly rotating in and out. In many respects, moreover, the House and Senate are two distinct institutions, each with its own story. In contrast to the presidency, where the succession of individual leaders creates its own chronological narrative, the structure of Congress makes the crafting of a coherent history challenging.

Furthermore, there are many histories of Congress. For example, there is the internal development of the legislative process (committees, seniority, norms, etc.), as well as the relationship between internal process and external forces. There is also the question of leadership, in its many forms. For example, one study might focus on the history of party leaders in Congress, but another could center on the formidable and independent role played by committee chairs or independent mavericks. As a result, historians have focused on specific legislators and on critical conflicts at different moments in congressional history.

Given all these complications, we believe the best way to understand congressional history is to study the institution in action and what has emerged from that action. Because its job is to make law, the successes and failures of Congress can best be understood by examining seminal moments, when legislators had to make important decisions. Written by thirty-nine of the nation's leading historians and political scientists, the chapters in *The American Congress* therefore revolve around events, not individuals, although each chapter also covers a broad range of legislators, procedural issues, and policies that defined Congress at different moments. Thus, the collective nature of Congress, rather than the individual-centered history that is more appropriate for the presidency, is underscored. Seen from this legislative perspective, many of the events with which we are most familiar — such as the Constitutional Convention, slavery, or the New Deal — look quite different.

Despite the diverse issues and approaches that make up the history of Congress in this volume (and the conflicting interpretations among the authors), several themes recur. One is the changing relationship between the legislative, judicial, and executive branches, which has been a defining tension in American politics. We see how Congress evolved from the time it was the central institution in government to the period when legislators fought for power with an expanded executive branch in the twentieth century, as well as an assertive judiciary that was willing to interfere in legislative business. Another theme, just as significant, will be the importance of the internal structure of the House and Senate to legislative history. In Congress, policy and process have always been intertwined, and changes in the internal structure have been dramatic.

A third theme is the changes in the intermediary institutions—the vital organizations such as political parties, civic associations, interest groups, and the mass media—through which citizens and politicians have communicated. Since the American Revolution, the nature and power of these organizations have shifted, and the story of Congress has shifted with them.

Another theme is political power. We will show that Congress has not been a solely reactive institution, entering the political fray only after the president, courts, or events have initiated action. Rather, Congress has always played an active role in shaping politics, government policy, and public life.

A fifth theme is that Congress has been an active force. Many historians have downplayed the role of Congress because they see it as a passive institution whose members usually react to the pressure bearing down on them. To understand the prime movers in American political history, historians have looked to the White House, experts, or to social movements. But in fact, although Congress is extraordinarily sensitive to democratic pressure, the members of Congress have also been able to initiate their own policy proposals, develop their own agendas and interests, and form their own distinct institutional identity. Indeed, the search and evolution of this identity have been at the heart of congressional history.

Sixth, many of the essays touch on an ongoing controversy about the nature of representative government everywhere: should legislators simply voice directly the desires of the citizens they represent, or should they decide what policies would be best for the nation and its citizens? This vexing issue, which dates back to at least the sixteenth- and seventeenth-century English debates over the role of Parliament, has been a constant source of controversy that plays out in battles over the institutional structure of Congress and the legislation it passes.

A final question is one of historical framework. How shall we describe the different eras of congressional history? Surely today's Senate and House are very different from those of the 1790s, and each has gone through a process of evolution. Yet, as most of the essays in this collection reveal, congressional time does not follow the more familiar rhythms of American politics, which center on individual leaders, dominant ideologies and parties, major public policies, or social movements. Making matters more complicated, the elections of legislators are staggered, the institution is composed of two distinct chambers, there is no titular head or unified leadership in a split body with hundreds of members, and Congress handles an enormous number of issues that are often unrelated except for the process through which they travel. So, how to think of the lifetime of Congress?

I believe that historical periods in America's Congress are best defined by the changing nature of the legislative process itself. The periods of congressional history gain their flavor from the formal and informal "rules of the game," the process and the structures through which all participants operate and all decisions are made. The legislative process of any given congressional era has been much more than a "technical backdrop" to the real political action. The way in which the nation's elected officials have structured Congress to solve problems says a great deal about the character of the nation's representative democracy.

In this context, it is helpful to think of Congress as an automobile. While drivers of various skills can take the automobile in different directions on various types of roads, the internal machinery of the vehicle plays a crucial role in determining how smooth the drive will be, as well as how far and fast the driver can go. Each particular process, moreover, favors certain types of policies. Each generation of legislators and their leadership become closely identified to the legislative process through which they worked.

There have been four major eras in American congressional history: the formative era (1790s–1820s); the partisan era (1830s–1900s); the committee era (1910s–1960s); and the contemporary era (1970s–today). In this book, the procedural framework is meant to be much broader than the relative power of committees and caucuses. It includes the political environment in which legislators governed, such as the structure of the news media, interest groups, social movements, and political parties. In the introductions to the sections of this book, we shall look in detail at the nature of each era. It is important to note that the eras did not begin and end with any type of precision. Rather, each evolved gradually, usually built on top of the previous one, rather than replacing wholesale what came before. As a result, the process that shaped each era contained remnants of what preceded it.

So let us begin our exploration of the American Congress. I hope that once readers have completed this book, Sam Rayburn's Board of Education won't seem so foreign and its place in the trajectory of congressional history will seem much more familiar. Given the vast size of the institution and the lengthy amount of time that is covered in this collection, it is of course not a complete history of Congress. Many personalities and events could not be included. Regardless, we believe the breadth of the essays captures many of the major issues that the legislative branch has confronted and the struggles that took place within its halls. We begin this exciting excursion during the writing of the Constitution, when the nation's Founders struggled over what role the legislative branch should have in the national polity, and we end with recent decades, when a grass-roots conservative movement tried to take advantage of a legislative institution dominated by partisanship and scandal. In the end, we hope to show that, with all of its vices and flaws, Congress has been a critical institution in this nation's history; it has given life to the meaning of democracy and offered an arena in which to tackle some of our greatest challenges.

—Julian E. Zelizer

Part I

THE FORMATIVE ERA

1780s–1820s

Federal Hall, the seat of Congress in New York City, 1789

WHEN THE UNITED STATES CONGRESS came into being, its future was unclear. The colonial and revolutionary eras left two contradictory legacies for the creators of the new country. On the one hand, the eras generated tremendous respect for, and extensive experience with, representative institutions. Every English colony (except Newfoundland) had embraced legislative government in the seventeenth century. Colonial assemblies amassed significant power, including control over the purse, and restrained the influence of governors who were the voices of the English crown. To be sure, there were limits to the power of assemblies. England retained a tight grip on foreign policy, international trade, and many other important issues. In contrast to the English Parliament, moreover, colonial assemblies had few administrative responsibilities. Nonetheless, since assemblies defined the political experience of most English colonists, the nation's founders anticipated a central role for Congress in the new republic. Under the Continental Congress in place between 1774 and 1776, delegates from the colonies were able to respond to England and orchestrate a war against the motherland.

On the other hand, the colonial and revolutionary eras inspired grave fears about the dangers of excessive legislative power. England had moved from a state of royal absolutism in the sixteenth century toward one of parliamentary dominance by the end of the Glorious Revolution of 1688; the emergent conception of the King-in-Parliament stipulated that all sources of power were concentrated in a single body, namely, the Parliament. The forcefulness of Parliament convinced many colonists that a collective body could be as tyrannical as a monarch. The Continental Congress, a body that was often internally divided and unable to raise sufficient revenue, likewise hinted at the challenges assemblies would face when trying to govern effectively. The fears about legislatures were evident in the states after the Revolution. Rather than recreating parliamentary hegemony, state constitutions mandated legislative bodies that were forced to respond to the electorate through regular elections and where power was checked in many cases by bicameral structures. Despite these built-in mechanisms, however, state legislatures were frequently perceived as excessively dominant.

The unsuccessful government under the Articles of Confederation added to these conflicting legacies, motivating the Founding Fathers as they struggled to define the structures of America's Congress during the Constitutional Convention. But even after the creation of Congress, these tensions were never laid to rest. In the first three decades of the American experience, the character of Congress remained uncertain as legislators tried to determine how it would actually operate. There were no clear rules about how decisions should be made. Although the major procedures that are still used by legislators emerged during this formative era — including standing committees, political parties, and the rules governing the relationship between the majority and minority — none of them was well defined until the 1830s, and there was little certainty about which would dominate or survive. Instead, the legislators engaged in experimentation and transformation. For example, when President George Washington came to the Senate for advice and consent on Indian treaties in 1789, the senators were not sure what they were supposed to do. When they decided to postpone discussion on what Washington saw as an urgent matter, the president decided that he would not seek their advice ever again. The upper chamber itself would gain greater stature relative to the House as time progressed and legislators such as John C. Calhoun, Daniel Webster, and Henry Clay brought prestige to the Senate.

Moreover, elected officials did not know which rules would guide informal and formal interactions among colleagues and with constituents. These rules were important. Since their institutional environment was in flux, legislators relied on personal character to judge those with whom they interacted. Legislators quickly abandoned any expectations about elite, aristocratic personal behavior as they descended into the nitty-gritty of bargaining. This confusion was not surprising since it was a period when most elites were not even confident about whether the republic would survive. The newness of all the political institutions rendered any procedure incapable of achieving much stability.

There was no honeymoon period for Congress. In foreign affairs, Congress soon had to provide the means for waging war even though everyone had hoped the nation could avoid being drawn into the wars of Europe. After the ratification of Jay's Treaty (which France perceived as an aggressive action, since it eased America's relations with their adversary Great Britain) — and after the French foreign minister tried to extort money from a delegation sent by President John Adams — the United States engaged in a "quasi-war" with its erstwhile ally. Although Congress did not formally declare war, the government recruited troops, appropriated money for the navy, and engaged in a few naval battles. The war generated suspicion of subversion and fueled emerging partisan divisions, resulting in the infamous Alien and Sedition Acts. Seventeen years later, the United States was at war once again, but this time against Britain, who carried the war to the nation's own soil. The War of 1812 aggravated the deep divisions among Republican legislators and necessitated a military mobilization that strained the underdeveloped capacity of the government.

Domestically, Congress played an important role in the expansion of an administrative government. In addition to waging war, administrative government was needed to deal with such issues as transportation, tariffs and trade, banking and currency, and internal communication. Territorial expansion was arguably the biggest project undertaken by Congress. President Thomas Jefferson negotiated a deal with France, the Louisiana Purchase, which was approved by the Senate in 1803, doubling the size of the nation through the acquisition of the land between the Rocky Mountains and the Mississippi River. But after presidents acquired land, Congress was responsible for handling a wide variety of problems, including relations with Native Americans, the treatment of foreign nationals, the distribution of public lands, the establishment of territorial government, and the admission of new states. In all these matters, congressional policy was neither consistent nor unified, as legislators varied in how they treated similar issues across geographic spaces. There were many other tasks for the legislators. In what was largely an agricultural and rural nation, all levels of government helped to create roads and canals for travel and trade. Federally imposed tariffs protected American goods such as fur hats, cotton, and iron. Congress also spent a good deal of its time responding to petitions, which they received in numbers far greater than in the colonial era.

During this formative era, members of Congress also had to figure out how their institution would actually work. Despite the Founders' aversion to political parties, a party system clearly started to emerge in the 1790s that pitted Federalists against Democratic-Republicans. Sometimes Congress found itself deciding on matters related to other branches of government. It determined the outcome of two deadlocked presidential elections, in 1800 and 1824. Furthermore, Congress passed the Judiciary Act of 1789, which created a three-tiered legal system, including the Supreme Court. The Court became powerful in this period. The principle of judicial review was firmly established in *Marbury v. Madison* (1803), a case that enabled the justices to strike down acts of Congress and turned the Court into the ultimate voice on constitutional questions. Meanwhile, Presidents George Washington, John Adams, Thomas Jefferson, James Madison, James Monroe, and John Quincy Adams — all of whom are considered among the nation's greatest leaders — struggled to define the role of the executive in this republic and to understand its relationship to Congress. Men such as James Monroe, in his legendary battles with the House Speaker Henry Clay of Kentucky, found that this institutional relationship could be explosive.

And always during the formative era, the issue of slavery lurked beneath the surface. The American Revolution had shaken the institution of slavery. Thousands of slaves had escaped from their masters, and the northern states took steps toward abolishing the institution between 1774 and 1804. Congress banned the importation of slaves in 1807. Even when the issue was not being explicitly discussed, most politicians understood that they needed to be extremely sensitive, given the role of African American slaves in the southern economy. Every issue that Congress touched — from taxes to war to territorial expansion — was understood in this context. Even the internal organization of Congress, including the formation of party caucuses and the emergence of a standing committee system, was linked to the protection of slavery.

These are just a handful of the bewildering issues Congress faced during its first historic era. The combination of the contradictory legacies of the colonial and revolutionary experiences, the evolving and uncertain procedural framework under which the legislators worked, and the monumental issues facing the young nation made this one of the most tumultuous periods in congressional history.

1

From the Old Congress to the New

A FEW WEEKS AFTER the First Continental Congress adjourned, Edmund Burke — then a member of the House of Commons and agent for the colony of New York, later the French Revolution's harshest critic — delivered his famous speech to his electors at Bristol in which he offered his classic definition of Parliament and the duties of its members. "Parliament is not a *congress* of ambassadors from different and hostile interests; which interests each must maintain, as an agent and advocate, against other agents and advocates," Burke declared. Rather, it was "a *deliberative* assembly of *one* nation, with *one* interest, that of the whole; where, not local purposes, nor local prejudices, ought to guide, but the general good, resulting from the general reason of the whole." Burke's definitions found curiously mixed echoes in the representative assemblies that Americans soon began to form in the mid-1770s, as events drove them from resistance to revolution and the formation of republican governments in the states. At the national level, the institution that directed the Revolution chose to describe itself as the United States in Congress Assembled, implying that its members were indeed delegates from thirteen more or less sovereign entities. Or as John Adams observed a decade later, Congress was essentially "a diplomatic assembly" rather than a real legislature or a true government. Yet if Congress was indeed a congress as Burke used the term, the imperatives of revolutionary unity placed a great premium on just the forms of deliberation that Burke also idealized. The Revolution began as "the common cause," and the alliance held firm even after eight years of warfare taxed American patriotism more severely than anyone had anticipated during the heady moments of 1775.

American ideas about representation and deliberation were not formed exclusively at the national level of government, however. They drew as well on the legacy of a century and a half of colonial self-government, and they were expressed far more vividly in the state constitutions that were framed concurrently with the decision for independence. The state legislatures were what John Adams had in mind when he suggested, in his influential *Thoughts on Government* (1776), that an American assembly should be a miniature of the larger society — that one should be able to look at a representative assembly and see therein a "mirror" or "portrait" or "transcript" of the larger society. This metaphor evoked a degree of precision that British commentators, like Burke, would have found strange. In Britain, the fiction that the people as a whole were somehow represented in the House of Commons begged fundamental questions of scale, proportion, and inclusion that the defenders of the restrictive suffrage and gross malapportionment of the Georgian constitution were loath to pursue. In America, however, Adams's metaphor became almost a commonplace.

When the framers of the federal Constitution set out to design a new national Congress in 1787, these standards of representation and deliberation shaped the context for discussion. Adams's metaphor was invoked more than once, but so was the Burkean ideal of deliberating for the common good. The framers hoped to avoid making the new Congress a replica of the old one, but they were equally mindful of the shortcomings of legislative government in the states. Indeed, the agenda that James Madison succeeded in imposing on the Constitutional Convention was grounded in his critical observations of the failings of the state legislatures, whose performance he had closely monitored as a member of both the Continental Congress and the Virginia legislature.

The Old Congress

The First Continental Congress, which met at Philadelphia in September–October 1774, was called to frame a common strategy of resistance to the Coercive Acts that Parliament had imposed on the troublesome colony of Massachusetts. By the time its successor, the Second Continental Congress, convened in Philadelphia the following May, war had erupted, and the returning delegates immediately found themselves acting as a national government. Determining exactly what form of government it was to be, however, was not an urgent concern. In appearance, Congress resembled a legislative assembly, and its proceedings generally followed the familiar practices of the colonial assemblies. But its most important responsibilities — over war and foreign affairs — were generally regarded, in eighteenth-century separation of powers thinking, as executive tasks. British constitutional doctrine treated war- and treaty-making as royal prerogatives, tempered by parliamentary power over taxation and appropriations. Nor did Congress possess the power to legislate. It could not enact statutes binding either individuals or states. Rather, its decisions took the form of resolutions and requisitions, which it conveyed to the states to implement in good faith, and they generally tried to do so. But the fact remained that Congress could not legislate in the ordinary sense of the term.

The early meetings of Congress were well attended, but as the war dragged on, attendance lagged. Even during the Revolution, politics remained more an avocation than a professional occupation, and delegates repeatedly balanced their public responsibilities against their family obligations. On any given day, two to three dozen delegates might be present, individual states sometimes went unrepresented, and many members found it difficult to attend for more than a few months at a time. The resulting patterns of attendance and membership did not promote the efficiency that wartime demanded. Routine administrative business was assigned to small committees and consumed a fair share of the delegates' time, but these committees in turn reported to the full body. The members' ability to act as true delegates from their states was also impaired by erratic communications with their governors and legislatures at home.

Its initial success in coordinating the American resistance in 1774–1776 gave Congress a reserve of popular support that it continued to tap, with diminishing results, during the war. In June 1776, Congress appointed a committee to draft articles of confederation and union, and its proposed plan was extensively debated in July and August. Three issues proved particularly intractable. One was the allocation of votes in Congress. Here the small states clung to the one state, one vote, rule that the First Congress had adopted in 1774, while the delegates from the more populous states argued for some other rule of apportionment. The absence of reliable data on the population and wealth of different states, as well as the revolutionary pressure to reach decisions by consensus, gave the advantage to the small states. A second problem involved agreeing on a rule for apportioning the common expenses of the war among the states: by population, by acreage under cultivation, or by an assessment of the value of improved lands. A third problem concerned the disposition of the unappropriated western lands. A bloc of "landless" states (Maryland, Delaware, New Jersey, Rhode Island, Pennsylvania), whose colonial charters left them without claims to the interior, favored giving Congress jurisdiction over the trans-Appalachian West as a national resource to defray the mounting expenses of the war. A rival bloc of "landed" states, led by Virginia, clung to their claims, at least until the various conditions they wanted to impose on their eventual cession were met. Disagreement over these three issues delayed the final draft of the Articles of Confederation until November

1777, and then opposition from the landless bloc, which had lost its key points, further delayed their ratification until February 1781.

In the meantime, many national leaders came to recognize that the Articles were already inadequate, not least by failing to give Congress independent sources of revenue. Congress submitted its first amendment to the states, seeking the authority to collect an impost (or tax) on imported goods, just as the Articles were taking effect. But Rhode Island rejected this proposal, and subsequent amendments fared no better. In 1783, after months of debate, Congress submitted new revenue amendments to the states, and in 1784 it sought the authority to regulate foreign commerce. None of these proposals received the required unanimous approval by the state legislatures.

By the mid-1780s, then, the reputation and authority of Congress contrasted sharply with its power and stature a decade earlier. For a while, it operated as an itinerant institution, moving from Philadelphia to Princeton to Annapolis to Trenton before finding a permanent home in New York City (where a number of its bachelors soon found brides among the daughters of the city's merchant elite). Maintaining a quorum proved increasingly problematic. In 1786, a dispute over the policy toward Spain and American rights to the free navigation of the Mississippi River divided Congress into northern and southern factions, leaving some to wonder whether the Union might devolve into two or three regional confederacies. Congress and the Confederation it embodied were frequently faulted for their "imbecility," but with the unanimity rule blocking the path to amendment, there were no obvious solutions to its problems.

Framing the Madisonian Agenda

By 1785, James Madison was emerging as the most thoughtful student and critic of what he called the "vices of the political system of the United States," by which he particularly meant the abuse of legislative authority in the states and the debilitating dependence of the national government on those same legislatures. The eldest son of the largest landowner in Orange County, Virginia, and a graduate of the College of New Jersey at Princeton, Madison was one of those young men whom the Revolution awakened to a political career. After serving in the state government of Virginia, he had entered Congress in March 1780, a time when it was desperately trying to induce the states to support the war effort more vigorously, and he served for three and a half uninterrupted years before the term-limits provision of the Articles of Confederation forced him to retire to Virginia. As a delegate, Madison flirted with the idea of authorizing

Congress to use coercive force against delinquent states. He also played a leading role in framing the proposed impost amendment of 1781 and the revenue amendments in 1783, while helping to negotiate the cession of Virginia's western land claims to Congress. Once back home, Madison was quickly elected to the Virginia legislature, where he repeatedly urged his colleagues to adopt measures that supported Congress.

Madison's experience profoundly shaped his constitutional thinking. His service in Congress alerted him to the difficulties of framing coherent policies for states with competing interests and convincing them to comply with national decisions; his observations of Virginia lawmakers drove him to reflect on the deeper problems of republican government. By 1785, he believed that the constitutions adopted a decade earlier were seriously flawed, especially when measured by the lack of "*wisdom* and steadiness" in state legislation. Madison thought that the legislatures needed to have genuine senates capable of checking the impulsive measures favored by the lower houses and that all legislators needed to be insulated from their own constituents. These concerns led him in turn to reflect further on the sources and implications of legislative misrule.

Madison recognized, in the first place, that in a republican government, the real business of a legislature was not, as Whig constitutional thinking would have it, to check a dangerous executive branch, always seeking to aggrandize its power. Rather, it was to make law in the positive sense. This perception was derived, in part, from the extraordinary amount of legislation that the states had to adopt to wage the Revolution and deal with its aftermath. "Among the evils then of our situation may well be ranked the multiplicity of laws from which no State is exempt," Madison observed in the spring of 1787. "The short period of independency has filled as many pages" in the statute books "as the century which preceded it." This perception also reflected the realization that republican legislators were far more likely to act as the agents of their immediate constituencies than were the British parliamentarians whom Edmund Burke idealized. Second, Madison concluded that the active inspiration for this lawmaking came not from the legislators themselves, but rather from interests, passions, and opinions swirling through the larger society. With annual elections the norm, legislators were likely to be all too responsive to the concerns of their constituents. But mere majority opinion could not always discern the true public good that legislators should pursue; the challenge was to encourage legislators to deliberate while preventing popular majorities from asserting their naked interests to the detriment of minority rights and the general public good. Third, it could hardly be expected that either citizens or their elected representatives could form enlightened ideas about national policy. To leave Congress dependent on the voluntary compliance of the states, Madison concluded, was a formula for preventing national government from ever becoming effective.

Before the fall of 1786, however, it was difficult to imagine how or when this critique of the defects of federal and state government could be acted on. Madison, James Monroe, John Jay, Charles Thomson, and other leaders initially favored a piecemeal approach to the reform of the Confederation, hoping that the adoption of single amendments would eventually encourage more comprehensive change. That strategy collapsed at the Annapolis convention of September 1786, when only a dozen delegates from five states managed to appear at a meeting called by Virginia to discuss giving Congress authority over foreign commerce. Rather than adjourn without doing anything, the commissioners — including Madison and Alexander Hamilton, a former Continental army officer and delegate to Congress, now retired to a lucrative legal practice in New York — issued a call for a general convention to meet at Philadelphia in May, there to consider the general problems of the Articles of Confederation.

Madison was eligible to return to Congress in 1787, and in the early spring, he pulled together his plans for the coming convention. Other delegates from the twelve states that agreed to attend (only Rhode Island stayed away) may also have been preparing for the meeting, but none as thoroughly as Madison. Five elements of his program had a major impact on the convention's deliberations about the reconstitution of a national congress. First, Madison concluded that any system of federalism requiring the voluntary compliance of the state legislatures with national measures was doomed to fail. The new government had to be empowered to enact, execute, and adjudicate its own laws, and this meant creating a bicameral legislature, because most Americans opposed vesting legislative power in a single chamber. Second, in place of the rule giving each state an equal vote in the Continental Congress, Madison favored applying principles of proportional representation to both houses of the new legislature. In part, this notion rested on a political calculation that the populous states would reject any system that preserved the old rule. But Madison also believed that the equal state vote was fundamentally unjust because citizenship and property, rather than statehood or corporate identity, were the sole legitimate bases for political representation.

How powerful should such a legislature be? Here, in the third place, Madison's position was more ambiguous. On the one hand, much of his constitutional theory sought to find ways to limit the scope of lawmaking authority, which was inherently expansive because the very authority to make rules that legislatures enjoyed gave them important advantages over the weaker branches of the executive and judiciary. Calculating lawmakers could always deploy "an infinitude of legislative expedients" to disguise their insidious purposes as legitimate exercises of their power. On the other hand, Madison also believed, at least initially, that it was better to err on the side of a broad national legislative power than to risk giving the new government less authority than it needed to secure the collective public good. Fourth, by insulating the new Congress from the populist pressures of the state legislatures and the people at large, he hoped to create conditions of deliberation that would enable it to legislate far more wisely than the state assemblies had managed to do. This in turn could be used to justify perhaps the single most radical proposal that Madison carried to Philadelphia: to empower Congress to exercise a negative (or veto) over state laws, not only to protect the national government from the interference of the states, but also to enable it to intervene in the states to protect minorities against unjust state laws favored by popular majorities. Yet he was not completely confident that a national legislature could be wholly immune to the impulsive lawmaking he had witnessed in the states. Accordingly, in the fifth place, he wanted to give the executive and judiciary some security against Congress, preferably by joining them in a council of revision armed with a limited negative over national laws. With such a power, the weaker branches could not only defend themselves against legislative "encroachments" (one of the most loaded words in the eighteenth-century republican vocabulary, routinely used to describe and disparage the efforts of one branch of government to subvert the just authority of another); they could also improve the quality of legislation, giving it a "perspicuity" it otherwise lacked.

These ideas transformed the basic terms in which the whole problem of national government had been framed. Before 1787, would-be reformers of the Confederation favored adding powers incrementally to those already enjoyed by the Continental Congress. Now Madison was proposing radical alterations in the powers and structure of the national legislature, in its relations to the states and their citizens, and also to its coordinate branches in the national government. Short of abolishing the states themselves, it would be difficult to imagine a more radical agenda.

Designing the New Congress

Madison's agenda was largely incorporated in the plan that the Virginia delegation drafted while waiting for the convention to muster a quorum. Two weeks after the appointed date of May 14, the convention finally convened a quorum of seven states and organized itself for business. Serious discussion began on May 29, when Governor Edmund Randolph introduced the Virginia Plan. Among other provisions, it called for a bicameral legislature, with a lower house elected by the people and an upper chamber selected by the lower from nominations made by the state legislatures. Representation in both houses would be "proportioned" among the states either by their contributions to the national treasury or by "the number of free inhabitants." Rather than specify particular legislative powers, the Virginia Plan authorized this new Congress "to legislate in all cases to which the separate States are incompetent, or in which the harmony of the United States may be interrupted by the exercise of individual legislation," as well as to exercise a negative on all state laws contravening "the articles of Union." This last provision represented Madison's favored solution to the problem of excessive and unjust lawmaking in the states, indicating how much influence he exercised over a delegation that included George Mason, one of the state's most distinguished and learned public servants, and George Wythe, perhaps its leading legal authority.

The first days of debate on the Virginia Plan, conducted in committee of the whole, quickly set the conflict that dominated the deliberations until mid-July. Delegates from the less populous states insisted on retaining the equal vote rule of the Articles of Confederation in at least one house of the legislature. They also favored deferring the contentious debate over voting until the convention had first decided what powers the legislature should exercise. But Madison and his allies insisted on settling the principles of representation first. If justice was not done on this point, they argued, the large states would never assent to giving the Union the powers it needed.

The small states had effective spokesmen of their own, however: John Dickinson of Delaware, the principal framer of the Articles of Confederation; William Paterson of New Jersey, who had built a flourishing legal career on his service as state attorney general; Oliver Ellsworth of Connecticut, who later became the leading author of the Judiciary Act of 1789; and his colleague Roger Sherman, who had attended the Stamp Act Congress of 1765 and signed both the Declaration of Independence and the Articles of Confederation. The small states gained an early victory on June 7, when the convention voted to allow the state legislatures to elect the upper house. Although that did not preclude states sending different numbers of senators, it did imply that they would be represented as equal corporate entities. Madison and one of his allies, James Wilson of Pennsylvania, took this as a significant reverse, but they did not change course. Through June and into July, they tried to wear down the small states in debate, pressing them to explain why an unjust rule of representation should be preserved when there was no plausible reason to assume that legislators from the large states would ever unite to dominate the government. The most populous states would have a common stake only when the issue was the rule of voting itself. On all other occasions, their representatives would vote in accord with the interests of their constituents, and those interests would have nothing to do with the size of their states but with all the characteristics that made the societies of Virginia, Pennsylvania, and Massachusetts so different from one another.

The delegates from the small states rarely answered these arguments directly. Rather, they argued that their constituents could not be expected to forfeit the equal vote that they enjoyed under the Confederation, especially if the legislature exercised the discretionary power the Virginia Plan proposed. "Can it be expected that the small states will act from pure disinterestedness," one Delaware delegate asked, when the large states were "evidently seeking to aggrandize themselves at the expense of the small?" In response, the small states rallied behind the New Jersey Plan introduced by Paterson in mid-June, which retained a unicameral Congress with the equal state vote and a modest increase in power. This alternative seemed so inadequate that it was easily turned aside, but the animus behind it persisted.

On July 2, the Convention deadlocked, five states each, on Ellsworth's motion to give each state an equal vote in the upper house. This stalemate led to the appointment of a "grand committee" of one delegate from each state to seek a compromise. Such a committee was elected with the entire body of the convention voting for a member from each state; revealingly, while the small states were represented by their stalwarts, the members chosen by the large states were those who seemed to favor compromise. Madison and Wilson objected that a committee could only replicate the basic divisions in the larger body, and on the whole, the committee's deliberations proved them right. Yet the members, once assembled, felt they had to do something. Prodded by the great sage Benjamin Franklin, they adopted a report giving each state an equal vote in the upper house, apportioning seats in the lower house among the states by population, and requiring appropriation bills to be introduced in the lower house and not subject to amendment in the Senate — seemingly a concession to the populous states.

The advocates of proportional representation in both houses thought this a compromise in name only. The restriction on appropriations was meaningless, they argued. As long as the upper house was free to reject appropriation bills, it could always make its wishes felt. The committee's good work had changed nothing.

At this point, with the deadlock unresolved, the committee shifted its attention to the lower house. The delegates had agreed all along that popular election of the more numerous chamber was a requisite of republican government, echoing John Adams's sentiment of 1776 that a representative body should resemble the society at large. The convention had previously endorsed the formula to apportion seats among the states on the basis of their free population, enabling slaveholding states to count their African American population at a ratio of three to five. (Madison had first proposed that coefficient in 1783, as a rule for allocating the common expenses of the Union.) Now, however, it had to return to this issue in light of the efforts of two successive committees to agree on the initial apportionment of seats in the first Congress to meet once a constitution was adopted.

The committees produced figures (first for an initial house of fifty-six members, later increased to sixty-five) that alarmed the Southerners by reminding them of their minority status in the Union. That alarm deepened when Gouverneur Morris suggested that the seaboard states, north and south, should unite to ensure that they would enjoy a permanent majority in future Congresses, even after the distribution of the American population acquired a predictable western, interior bias. "In time the Western people wd. outnumber the Atlantic States," Morris observed on July 10. "He wished therefore to put it in the power of the latter to keep a majority of votes in their own hands." Determining when and how reapportionment should occur, Morris concluded, were questions best left to the later discretion of the legislature itself. But the southern delegates believed that the westward movement of the population would favor their region, bringing it closer to population parity with the North. Accordingly, they had an incentive to secure a constitutional mandate that reapportionment take place. Moreover, to compensate for their current inferiority in population, they also wanted to factor slaves into the rule of representation.

Why should slaves be represented at all? the northern delegates asked. As a matter of principle, representation was conceived as a substitute for the collective deliberations of the people at large, made necessary in large societies by the inconvenience and impossibility of assembling the whole civic population in the manner of ancient Athens. Because slaves had no legal rights and would never act as citizens or participate in deliberations, they were irrelevant to the process of representation and hence should go uncounted. "If such a meeting of the people was actually to take place," William Paterson asked, "would the slaves vote?" Of course "they would not." The southern delegates replied that the slaves contributed materially to the national prosperity, that government was about the protection of property as well as the personal rights of citizens, and that their region would be foolish to enter the Union as a minority bloc if its voting strength was not augmented by including slaves in the rule of apportionment. In the end, the northern delegates agreed, voting not only to accept the three-fifths rule but also to require a decennial census to provide the data for reapportionment.

Madison had attempted to use the problem of factoring slaves into the rule of representation as a means of demonstrating why the disputes between large and small states need *not* be treated similarly. For better or worse, the presence of slavery was a true interest that would have to be accommodated if a permanent union was to be secured. By contrast, the division between large and small states was an ephemeral one that would never again define the real interests of the voters and their representatives. But the legitimation of one minority interest through the three-fifths clause may have confirmed that the minority interests of the small states also merited constitutional protection. Once one accepted that the protection of one minority — those unfortunate enough to live in the least populous states — was a valid interest deserving constitutional protection, it was hard to deny a similar claim on behalf of the southern states, which would enter the new Union as a minority region as well.

The critical vote came on July 16. Five states voted to give the states equal representation in the Senate, four states voted against, and one state, Massachusetts, was divided when Elbridge Gerry and Caleb Strong accepted the rationale of "compromise" by siding with the small states. Had either of these delegates voted with the minority — which they arguably should have done on the basis of their state's population — the convention would have remained deadlocked. The Great Compromise or Connecticut Compromise, as it is known, was in reality a defeat for one bloc and a victory for the other. Save for those of Gerry and Strong, few minds had been changed or positions altered, Madison's and Wilson's best efforts notwithstanding.

This decision initially left the advocates of the Virginia Plan uncertain how to proceed. They had continued to believe that somehow they would prevail, but the small states had called their bluff. When Randolph suggested that the convention should adjourn overnight, to allow the small states to ponder the consequences of their victory, Paterson replied that the convention should indeed adjourn for good, so that Americans could discover what it had been doing behind closed doors. Randolph hastily apologized, saying that his meaning had been mistaken, and tempers cooled. When the delegates from the large states caucused the next morning, they could not agree on how to redeem their lost position. In effect, they consented to proceeding with a legislature that would retain the "vicious" principle of an equal state vote.

The consequences of this crucial decision took some weeks to unfold. One important change, however, took place immediately: the convention rejected the proposed negative on state laws. Over the next ten days, the delegates debated the perplexing topic of the presidency. Then they adjourned for another ten days while a committee of detail converted the resolutions adopted thus far into a working draft of a constitution. Its report of August 6 effected a significant change in the convention's idea of the legislature by replacing the Virginia Plan's open-ended definition of the scope of legislative authority with a list of the particular powers to be vested in Congress (as the legislature was again to be called). Because the convention had not previously discussed this change, the question arises: was the committee adventurously substituting its own judgment for that of the convention or simply acting on a tacit understanding shared by the delegates generally? In the absence of any recorded objection to this facet of its report, it is reasonable to conclude that the committee acted on the second principle.

The change was nonetheless momentous. The original language of the Virginia Plan was consistent with the general doctrine of legislative power that had informed Anglo-American constitutional theory since the Glorious Revolution of 1688. In that view, legislative power was virtually unlimited, and no object of human activity lay beyond the purview of legislative regulation. The state constitutions replicated that view by vesting a general lawmaking authority in the legislatures rather than delegate particular powers. The federal Constitution, however, sharply modified that model. Congress would possess substantial powers over war, taxation, commerce, the militia, and other matters; but those powers were nonetheless confined to particular objects. In part, this limitation was a byproduct of the facts of federalism and the belief that the regulation of the daily activities of Americans was primarily a matter of state law and local custom. But it also reflected the deeper conception of the limited nature of constitutional government that had emerged since 1776. The principle that all power was a grant from the people implied that the people might withhold certain powers from government more generally. The closest the report came to acknowledging the discretionary authority of Congress was a clause permitting it "to make all laws necessary and proper for carrying into execution the foregoing powers" already delegated.

During the month of August, the convention slightly revised the committee's list of powers without challenging its underlying concept of legislative authority. On August 17, for example, it altered the clause empowering Congress "to make war" by substituting "declare" for "make." To the original clause conveying the power to regulate foreign and interstate commerce, it added "and with the Indian Tribes" as well, thereby correcting the remarkably ambiguous corresponding clause in the Confederation. It resisted the efforts of several southern delegates to require a two-thirds majority for "navigation acts" — that is, laws regulating foreign trade. Much of the convention's final tinkering with the list of legislative powers took place in committee. There is little evidence to suggest that the delegates found anything controversial in the provisions that ultimately became Article I, Section 8, of the Constitution.

The delegates also resisted efforts to impose significant qualifications on either members of Congress or the electorate. Some delegates thought that restrictions on membership or suffrage could be used to protect the rights and interests of property. But in practice it was impossible to make a uniform constitutional rule that would be equally effective across the disparate societies of the expanding republic. The only qualifications mandated for members of Congress involved age, citizenship, and residency in their states. As for suffrage, the framers provided that the House of Representatives would be chosen by the same electorate that selected the lower houses of the state legislatures. Similarly, rather than specify how state electorates should be organized for choosing representatives — statewide, by district, or by a statewide electorate selecting a member from each district — the framers left this question to be determined by the state legislatures, thereby assuring that the decennial exercise in redistricting would often be conducted in highly politicized circumstances.

The framers' conception of the legislature was also reflected in their discussion of the executive branch, a subject that perplexed them throughout their deliberations. In early June, they had reached agreement on two main points: to vest the executive power in a single person, and to arm him with a limited negative over legislation. The Virginia Plan had proposed vesting the negative in a joint executive-judicial council of revision, but a majority of the framers felt that judges should not be allowed to act in so political a capacity. A few may have imagined that the executive could wield the veto on behalf of his own political aims, but most probably regarded it as a weapon with which the executive branch could defend itself against legislative "encroachments." The state constitutions had generally stripped the executive branch of its monarchical prerogatives — including the veto — and any means of influencing legislative deliberations. Even so, the restoration of the negative illustrated how much the dangers of an unchecked legislature concerned the framers.

Through July and into August, however, the election of the executive and other questions related to his tenure (length of term, eligibility for reelection, methods of removal) continued to vex the convention. The general expectation was that critical powers that might be considered executive — the power to make appointments or negotiate treaties — should be vested in the Senate. But in August, a reaction against the Senate set in, and the president (as the office was eventually called) emerged as the beneficiary, gaining powers not previously contemplated by the convention. The chief recommendations were made by a committee on postponed parts, which presented its major report on September 4.

The critical question was how to elect the president. Each of the methods proposed was vulnerable to significant objections. Popular election seemed impractical in a polity likely to remain highly decentralized for decades to come; the people were likely to scatter their votes among many favorite provincial candidates. By contrast, election by the legislature would result in a highly informed choice, but unless the executive was made ineligible for reelection, it could well produce a president subject to manipulation by a dominant congressional faction. Election by a body of electors could also produce much favorite-son voting, and no one had a good idea of how to choose the electors or whether they would be qualified for the task.

The committee's report proposed instead to create an electoral "college" (as it much later came to be known, though its faculty would never meet on one campus but simply vote in their separate states and adjourn). Should the electors not produce a majority for one candidate, the contingent election would fall to the Senate — which many framers expected would be the usual practice. Electors would be allocated among the states on the basis of their total membership in Congress. This arrangement had the advantage of replicating the decisions over representation that the delegates were now more willing to regard as a compromise than they had been in July. The large states would have the edge in promoting candidates, but if the electors failed to make a decisive choice, the small states would have the advantage in the second, final round. But this solution proved objectionable because the committee report also proposed that the president exercise the appointment and treaty powers jointly with the Senate. This suggestion raised the possibility that the executive would once again be reduced to a position of subservience to another branch. It took three days of debate and a flash of inspiration from Roger Sherman to hit upon the ingenious solution of allowing the House, voting by states, to elect the president when the electors failed in their task.

Like the restoration of the veto, these final decisions about the presidency offer an important insight into the framers' thinking about Congress. Their genuine uncertainty in imagining the political dimensions of executive power in a national republic explains why the matter of election proved so vexing. But one principle remained constant: most of the framers were intent on making the executive as politically independent of Congress as possible. They shared the concern that Madison expressed first in the convention and again in *Federalist* 48 when he warned that the legislature was necessarily the dominant branch of a republican government and had an alarming tendency to absorb "all power into its impetuous vortex." Whether the executive could be an effective counterweight remained to be tested, but the reaction against the excesses of legislative misrule in the states had produced a new concept of the importance of imposing constitutional restraints on the legislature.

The Ratification Debates

The Anti-Federalist opponents of the Constitution doubted that these constraints would prevent the national government from exercising its legislative powers so vigorously that the state governments would soon atrophy for want of business and resources. A handful of dissenting members of the Federal Convention — including George Mason, Elbridge Gerry, and Luther Martin of Maryland — played important roles in mobilizing early opposition, and they were joined by some of the most distinguished early leaders of the Revolution, such as Samuel Adams of Massachusetts, George Clinton of New York, and Richard Henry Lee and Patrick Henry of Virginia. The Anti-Federalists remained faithful to the deep suspicion of the aggrandizing nature of all forms of political power that had figured so prominently in the ideology that drove the colonists from resistance to revolution after 1765. In their view, ominous clauses seemed to lurk everywhere in the Constitution. Two provisions of Article I (the legislative article) seemed especially dangerous. The Necessary and Proper Clause promised to undermine the limited enumeration of legislative powers in Article I, Section 8, by allowing Congress to judge what further measures were required "for carrying" those powers "into execution." Similarly, the Supremacy Clause, first introduced as a weak alternative to the negative on state laws, then quietly but powerfully enhanced, would enable Congress to trump any efforts by state governments to resist doubtful national measures. Other powers were susceptible to equally grim analysis: the general power over taxation, the authority over the militia, even Congress's authority to alter state laws for the election of representatives.

The Anti-Federalists reinforced these criticisms of the formal legislative powers of Congress by attacking the political character of representation in both houses. At Philadelphia, the framers had repeatedly invoked the conventional American wisdom that said, as James Wilson put it, that "the legislature ought to be the most exact transcript of the whole Society." The Anti-Federalists objected that a House that would initially number only sixty-five could never meet that standard. Representatives would lack the requisite "sympathy" that would enable them to recall the real burden that legislation, especially taxation, would place on their constituents. The Senate seemed dangerous for other reasons. Even though senators would be elected by the state legislatures and therefore be sensitive to protecting state interests, the Senate seemed likely to evolve into an aristocracy, especially because it violated the fundamental tenets of the separation of powers by exercising all three forms of power: the lawmaking authority it shared with the House, the executive power over appointments and treaties that it shared with the president, and the judicial power to try impeachments brought by the House, which it could arguably use to shield its lackeys in the executive from punishment for unscrupulous acts.

Much of the Federalist response to these criticisms took a predictable form. The Federalists repeatedly argued that the particular powers granted were reasonable, that the Necessary and Proper Clause did not license a general superintending legislative authority, and that a Constitution that did not establish the legal supremacy of national acts risked returning the Union to its parlous state under the Articles of Confederation. Without the Supremacy Clause, Madison observed in *Federalist* 44, "the world would have seen for the first time, a system of government founded on the inversion of the fundamental principles of all government; it would have seen the authority of the whole society every where subordinate to the authority of the parts; it would have seen a monster in which the head was under the direction of the members." They also argued that the charges leveled against the political inadequacy of representation under the Constitution required relying on the worst possible assumptions about the motives of legislators and the vigilance of voters.

Beyond these conventional responses, however, Madison and Hamilton, the main authors of *The Federalist,* offered additional arguments that probed the case for national legislation and representation more deeply. Several of these arguments merit particular mention. In the celebrated *Federalist* 10, now often described as the principal statement of the underlying theory of the Constitution, Madison presented two main arguments for defending the national government in general, as well as Congress. In a national government representing so many different interests, he argued, it was far less likely that improper coalitions could form, inimical to liberty, than would be the case within the smaller compass of the states. Moreover, he hypothesized, the larger electoral districts from which representatives would be chosen would be far more likely to produce a superior class of lawmakers, "representatives whose enlightened views and virtuous sentiments [would] render them superior to local prejudices and to schemes of injustice." In later essays, both Madison and Hamilton suggested that legislators should possess other qualities than "sympathy" for constituents. In their thinking, and that of other Federalists, it was no less important to recruit lawmakers whose experience, intelligence, and capacity for deliberation would enable them to frame public measures with an enlarged view of the public good rather than a parochial loyalty to local interests.

Of course, all of the statements about the future character of political representation and lawmaking were merely predictions: the Federalist ideal of improving the character of deliberation and representation as much as the Anti-Federalist concern about a haughty aristocracy riding roughshod over the true interests of their constituents. The Constitution established the institutional framework within which these hopeful and gloomy expectations would be tested. But the outcome of that test depended, as Madison and Hamilton soon learned, on the vicissitudes of politics and events that both sought to influence and neither could control.

— JACK N. RAKOVE

BIBLIOGRAPHICAL NOTES

Edmund C. Burnett, *The Continental Congress* (New York, 1941), is the standard narrative history of the Continental Congress. Important interpretive studies of this institution include H. James Henderson, *Party Politics in the Continental Congress* (New York, 1974); Merrill Jensen, *Articles of Confederation: An Interpretation of the Social-Constitutional History of the American Revolution, 1774–1781* (Madison, Wisc., 1941); Jerrilyn Greene Marston, *King and Congress: The Transfer of Political Legitimacy, 1774–1776* (Princeton, N.J., 1987); and Jack N. Rakove, *The Beginnings of National Politics: An Interpretive History of the Continental Congress* (New York, 1979). For the constitutional debates of 1787–1788, see Jack N. Rakove, *Original Meanings: Politics and Ideas in the Making of the Constitution* (New York, 1996). For broader discussions of the constitutional theory of the revolutionary era, Gordon S. Wood, *The Creation of the American Republic, 1776–1787* (Chapel Hill, N.C., 1969), and Willi Paul Adams, *The First American Constitutions: Republican Ideology and the Making of the State Constitutions in the Revolutionary Era*, trans. by Rita and Robert Kimber (expanded edition, Lanham, Md., 2001), are essential.

James Madison

March 5, 1751–June 28, 1836

James Madison

Revered as "the father of the Constitution," discounted for his role as the nation's fourth president, James Madison influenced the course of the new nation for decades, from the contentious debates that shaped the federal government to the nullification crisis that threatened to split the Union in the 1830s.

As a public servant, the Virginia native toiled to help shape the federal system, contributing to *The Federalist Papers* and using his political acumen and legislative skill to further civil and religious liberty, government accountability, and federal supremacy. His efforts were crucial in ensuring that the fledgling government would endure. Throughout his career, Madison showed political flexibility — garnering support for a Bill of Rights he didn't favor, even justifying Thomas Jefferson's Louisiana Purchase, although he had several concerns about the measure. Some interpret these actions as policy reversals, but others credit Madison with enough pragmatism to balance his stubborn constitutional views. Looking at Madison's presidency, one could say Thomas Jefferson was a tough act to follow. Modern rankings of presidents give Madison an average rating, mostly for his handling of the diplomatic and economic issues that led up to the War of 1812 and for his management of the war effort. Perhaps, however, his political contributions during four decades of public service should overshadow his presidency, not the other way around.

Madison was born on March 16, 1751, in King County, Virginia, the eldest of ten children in a slave-owning family. His father was a leading planter, vestryman, and justice of the peace who could afford to provide his oldest son with a thorough education. Madison graduated from the College of New Jersey in Princeton in 1771, a time of rising American patriotism. However, he was frail and sickly and considered himself unfit for a military career. He briefly continued his studies at Princeton after graduation, considering, then deciding against, a career in the ministry. He returned home, worried about his health and uncertain about his prospects. During the 1770s Madison became active in Virginia politics, and in 1779, when he was selected as Virginia's delegate to Congress, he was known for his mastery of legislative business.

Madison was a bachelor until 1794. At the age of forty-three, after a four-month courtship, he married an attractive young widow, Dolley Payne Todd, who went on to establish several national traditions, including the Inaugural Ball and the White House Easter Egg Roll. As the White House hostess for Jefferson, a widower, Dolley Madison shaped the social scene of Washington, D.C. — at that time an unpolished city. She helped Jefferson establish egalitarian standards of dress and etiquette and became the most important woman in Washington society even before her husband became president, in 1809. Creating the role of first lady as republican hostess, she was admired for being elegant but with a simple and unaffected manner. She is also remembered as the heroine of the War of 1812 for saving, among other treasures, the portrait of George Washington from the British army.

After Madison's term in the White House ended in 1817, the couple retired to the family farm in Orange County, Virginia. Madison stayed active in his retirement, serving as rector of the University of Virginia and as a delegate to Virginia's Constitutional Convention in 1829–1830. He compiled his notes on the debates and speeches of the Continental Congress and managed the large (and increasingly unprofitable) family plantation. When he died in 1836, Madison had outlived every other signer of the Constitution. Dolley Madison returned to Washington, where she spent the rest of her life as a distinguished member of political society. She had known personally the first twelve presidents by the time she died in 1849.

References

Banning, L. 2000, February. Madison, James. *American National Biography Online.* Retrieved June 30, 2003, from http://www.anb.org/articles/03/03-00303.html.

Brief Biography of James Madison from *James Madison: His Legacy.* The James Madison Center of James Madison University. Retrieved July 14, 2003, from http://www.jmu.edu/madison/biography/index.htm.

Shulman, H. C., and D. B. Mattern, 2002. *The Dolley Madison Project.* Virginia Center for Digital History. Retrieved July 14, 2003, from http://moderntimes.vcdh.virginia.edu/madison/editors.html.

2

Opening Congress

Slow Beginnings

WHEN THE AMERICAN REPUBLIC sprang to life in the spring of 1789, many people were disappointed. Compared with the members of the Continental Congress, the roughly one hundred men assembled in the national capital seemed none too impressive. "The appointments in general are not so good," thought Georgia's Representative Abraham Baldwin; the members were less "heroic" than those in previous congresses, agreed Representative Fisher Ames of Massachusetts.

There was good reason for such concern, because the new Congress *was* different from those that had come before, representative in membership and mission in a way that no former intercolonial or interstate congress had been. The First and Second Continental Congresses (1774–1781) had been focused on the heroic task at hand: organizing and winning a revolution. The Confederation Congress (1781–1789) had been the administrative center of a league of independent states, its members more like appointed diplomats than representatives. But the new Congress was a permanent body devoted to the often tedious business of politics-as-usual, representative of the American people in an entirely different way. Aware that their congressmen would be the lone advocates of their interests in this new arena, legislators and voters throughout the states had selected true representatives: men of influence, to be sure, but not necessarily the patriot-heroes of the "old congress."

The result was a body of men who were solid and hard-working — up to the task at hand but a far cry from the Roman senators and "demigods" that many had expected. Middle-aged merchants, lawyers, and leisured gentlemen, some with wigs, some without, they were practical men of sober manners (with the exception of a few hotheaded Southerners). More than half had shouldered arms during the Revolution. Nearly all had been legislators in the Continental or Confederation Congress, the Federal Convention, or, most likely, their state assemblies. They were men of fine oratory and impressive appearance, accustomed to power and leadership, though on a different stage. Their portraits reveal a gallery of well-fed and watchful faces, keenly alert to their interests and standing.

The members congregated in Federal Hall, at the corner of Wall and Nassau Streets in New York City, Congress's meeting place until the government moved to Philadelphia in 1790. (The building that stands on the site today was not constructed until well into the nineteenth century.) Originally New York's City Hall, the building was refitted for Congress in an elegant style by Pierre L'Enfant. The first floor housed the octagonal House chamber, the members seated in two semicircular rows in front of the Speaker. One floor up was the Senate chamber, the vice president's chair on an elevated platform with a crimson canopy overhead. The third floor included a room for the New York Society Library, the first library of Congress. Outside and inside, the building was an impressive sight. "No pains have been spared by the inhabitants of this place to provide for the reception of Congress," observed Senator Oliver Ellsworth of Connecticut. The building did "honor to the city & surpasses in elegance any building in the Country."

There were figures of note in both houses. In the House, James Madison of Virginia (1751–1836) was the unquestioned leader and a chief adviser of President Washington. His colleague Roger Sherman of Connecticut (1721–1793) is notable for his presence at the drafting of every founding federal document in the revolutionary era: the Association of 1774, the Declaration of Independence, the Constitution, and the Bill of Rights. Fisher Ames (1758–1808) was second only to Madison and a famed orator as well. In the Senate, Virginia's Richard Henry Lee (1732–1794) was noteworthy as one of the leading opponents of the Constitution during the ratification debates. Charles Carroll of Maryland (1737–1832) was said to be the wealthiest man in America. Pennsylvania's William Maclay (1737–1804) also made his presence known — to posterity rather than to his contemporaries; his voluminous diary offers an invaluable insider's view of the workings of the First Congress.

In lifestyle as well as talents and desires, the First Congress was a sampling of the nation's ruling elite — to many, an alarming realization. The collective sigh of disappointment at the First Congress resulted from the discovery that the new American nation, assembled in representative form, was not as spectacular as expected. If, as William Maclay suggested, the new government was supposed to contain "the collected Wisdom and learning of the United States" ("We hear it ever in Our Ears," he complained), what were the implications of its mediocrity? Fisher Ames was philosophical in his disappointment. Having "reflected coolly" after his initial disillusionment, he decided that "the objects now before us require more information, though less of the heroic qualities, than those of the first Congress. . . . [I]f a few understand business, and have, as they will, the confidence of those who do not, it is better than for all to be such knowing ones; for they would contend for supremacy; there would not be a sufficient principle of cohesion." Mediocrity was a virtue in a deliberative body, for an assemblage of demigods could never manage the mutual dependence that got work done.

The initial spirit of the proceedings was no more encouraging. Although the government opened on March 4, 1789 — the date set by the Confederation Congress for the First Congress to meet — it took almost a month to achieve the required quorum of thirty in the House and five days more to collect the requisite twelve senators. Many blamed bad traveling conditions, but there were also more substantial reasons. Some states had not set the gears of national governance in motion, and their congressional elections were still pending. Other states may have been acting according to precedent, for during the Confederation Congress delegates had drifted in and out on a regular basis, some states not being represented for months and even years at a time. "I am inclined to believe that the languor of the old Confederation is transfused into members of the new Congress," bemoaned Ames. "This is a very mortifying situation. . . . We lose £1,000 a day revenue. We lose credit, spirit, every thing. The public will forget the government before it is born." On April 1, the House finally garnered enough members to proceed to business, and the government got under way.

Creating a Government

Once Congress got under way, it faced a seemingly endless series of precedent-setting tasks, many of them issues of etiquette, rules, and procedure. Clerks, secretaries, and doorkeepers had to be chosen; practical considerations had to be defined, such as the proper means of communicating between houses or with the executive. Some of these decisions concerned the relative status of the House and Senate. Some people conceived of the two bodies as American Houses of Lords and Commons, with the Senate the upper house of superior rank and privilege, like the House of Lords. Predictably, considering his high-toned politics, Secretary of the Treasury Alexander Hamilton assumed as much, suggesting that Washington grant special access to senators. Others took a similar view. Elbridge Gerry considered his election to the House rather than the Senate "a degradation." As he explained it, he had spent "the flower of my life . . . in the arduous business" of politics, only to see preference given to men who had "endured very few toils of the revolution." He could only conclude that "republican governments never were remarkable & probably never will be for gratitude." The debate over congressional salaries in late August 1789 raised the issue again, questioning whether senators should earn a higher salary than representatives. Within the first few years of national governance, this question would be relatively settled, senators and representatives deemed effective equals.

But there was at least one crucial difference between the protocol and procedures of the two houses. The House, seemingly the more democratic branch of Congress, decided to open its doors to the public; the Senate, like previous national congresses and the Federal Convention, met in private. The Senate's privacy was controversial, and there were several failed attempts to change matters. Opponents of the practice worried that the Senate's closed doors hid its proceedings from the vigilant eye of the public, destroying the accountability at the heart of republican governance. As Maclay put it, he was fully convinced "at the propriety of Opening our doors. I am confident some Gentlemen would have been ashamed to have seen their Speeches of this day, reflected in a News paper of tomorrow." Despite such worries, the Senate's doors remained closed. Over the course of the 1790s, newspapers would help to bridge such gaps of accountability by displaying congressional proceedings to the nation at large. There is a reason that Jefferson considered newspapers a "curb on our functionaries."

After establishing its own operational mechanisms, Congress had to breathe life into the other two branches of government, for in many ways the Constitution was little more than a skeletal outline. Distrusting executive power as exemplified by their former monarch, King George III, the drafters of the Constitution had entrusted the new national legislature with the task of launching the new government. Congress was responsible for installing the new president, creating the different departments of the executive branch, structuring the federal judiciary, and devising a revenue system. Its initial duties and responsibilities had such central importance that at least one onlooker dubbed it "a second [Federal] Convention."

One of the first things Congress addressed was the appointment of a national executive and vice president. Counting the electoral votes, they determined, as expected, that George Washington had been elected president and John Adams, vice president, and riders were dispatched to inform each man of his victory. Almost immediately, Congress turned to the question of federal revenue. The costs of government, the management of the Revolutionary War debt, and the new nation's credit all rested on the government's ability to find a source of income. So important was the issue that it took precedence over the establishment of executive departments and the drafting of constitutional amendments, including what would come to be known as the Bill of Rights. By August, Congress had formulated the basis of the federal revenue system: a combination of imposts, tonnage fees, and procedures for collection and enforcement.

With a revenue system established, Congress could now focus on constitutional amendments, an issue that James Madison had first raised in May. Eager for action, state ratifying conventions had submitted more than two hundred recommended amendments to the First Congress. Despite such support, Madison faced stiff resistance. Some members (such as Connecticut's Roger Sherman) saw no need for such paper reassurances; most state governments had a bill of rights, and the constitutional limits of the federal government would prevent it from violating such rights. As the First Congress scholars Charlene Bangs Bickford and Kenneth R. Bowling point out, even some Anti-Federalists opposed amendments, fearful that minor concessions might rule out major revisions at a later date. After heated debate, on August 24, the House approved seventeen amendments and sent them to the Senate. Some differences of opinion in the Senate led to a conference between House and Senate committees, after which the House approved twelve amendments on September 24 and the Senate followed suit the next day. Congress then sent the twelve amendments to the states. Ratified by eleven of the fourteen states by the end of 1791, ten of these twelve amendments would come to be known as the Bill of Rights.

At the same time, Congress turned to the establishment of the executive departments. The Department of State (initially Foreign Affairs) was established on July 27, the War Department on August 7. But the creation of the Treasury Department proved particularly problematic. Fearful that placing a single individual in charge of the nation's finances would invite corruption and powermongering, many members favored a three-man Treasury board. But others, led by James Madison, preferred a single secretary of the treasury, presuming the inefficiency of a council or board. Urged on by Madison, on September 2, 1789, Congress passed the Treasury Bill, creating the Treasury Department, to be headed by a single secretary. Loath to surrender control of the nation's purse strings to an already powerful executive branch, Congress specified that the secretary of the treasury would make reports directly to Congress rather than to the president, unlike the other executive departments. Congress protected itself as well. Concerned that the secretary of the treasury might have undue influence over Congress, representatives closely monitored the phrasing of the Treasury Bill, voting, for example, that the secretary should "digest and prepare" plans rather than "digest and report" them, the latter suggesting that he would defend his measures on the floor, in person. The bill also gave Congress the right to demand information and documentation from the secretary without going through the president first.

Over the course of his tenure as secretary of the treasury (1789–1795), Alexander Hamilton would use his department's ambiguous connection with both the executive and legislative branches to full advantage. His ability to report to Congress gave him a voice and presence in the House and Senate, enabling him to propose policy and further his own agenda. His status as an executive officer enabled him to limit congressional investigations through invoking what we now call executive privilege (with the administration's backing) — a policy that was worked out through practice. As Hamilton expressed it during a 1792 cabinet meeting, "as to his departmt the act constituting it had made it subject to Congress in some points, but he thot himself not so far subject as to be obliged to produce all papers they might call for. They might demand secrets of a very mischievous nature." The result was a vital stronghold for Hamilton's controversial financial policies. Indeed, his connection with Congress was so clearly his primary source of power that, beginning in 1791, his enemies tried repeatedly (and unsuccessfully) to cut it off. "Congress may go home," Maclay fumed in 1791. "Mr. Hamilton is all powerful and fails in nothing which he attempts."

Shortly after the passage of the Treasury Bill, Congress turned to another branch of government: the judiciary. Controversy over this judiciary bill centered on prevailing fears that a federal judicial system would swallow state courts in the same way that the federal government threatened to subsume the states; the cost of providing federal judges with permanent salaries also raised some concern. After debate in both houses, Congress passed the Judiciary Act on September 21, creating a limited federal judiciary system (a Supreme Court and federal circuit courts and district courts); judicial power was thus distributed between the federal government and the states. The new government's laws and taxes could now be enforced.

Further structural issues would arise for years to come. Each time an aspect of the Constitution was tested, it raised new questions about procedure and precedent. Washington's first attempt to seek the advice and consent of the Senate is one noteworthy example. On Saturday, August 22, 1789, the president entered the Senate with some proposals respecting Indian treaties. After having them read aloud, along with a supporting document, he repeated the first proposal and asked for the Senate's consent. There was an awkward pause. Some senators had not even heard him due to the noise of passing carriages; Maclay noted in his diary that "I could tell it was something about indians, but was not master of one Sentence of it." Washington reread the article. There was "a dead pause." Finally, several senators asked for time to inform themselves on the subject and the related documents, ultimately passing a motion to postpone further discussion to Monday. Washington, who sought immediate consent, was not pleased; he had been glowering with an expression of "stern displeasure" all the while. The postponement was the breaking point. As Maclay noted, the president "started up in a Violent fret. *This defeats every purpose of my coming here*," he fumed. Although he returned on Monday to settle the matter, he never sought senatorial advice in person again, setting a precedent that continues to the present day.

Shaping the Tone of Governance

Of course, before all such debates about the framework of the new government, Congress had to install Washington as president. So, immediately upon counting the electoral votes and notifying Washington and Adams of their victories, it began to plan the president's inauguration, a topic that raised a host of questions about the tone of national governance. The debate over Washington's inauguration, joined with the month-long debates over ceremonial matters — such as the proper title for the president — highlight the precedent-setting nature of the First Congress.

The best witness to these discussions is Senator William Maclay, who recorded his observations in his diary. On April 30, 1789, the date of Washington's inauguration, Maclay described the debate in the Senate. On "the great important day," both houses of Congress would receive Washington in the Senate chamber to administer the oath of office — a seemingly simple ceremony that raised a multitude of questions. When the president arrived in the Senate chamber, what would be Vice President Adams's precise status and title? Would there be two presidents in the Senate? After consulting the Constitution, Senator Oliver Ellsworth of Connecticut reported ominously, "I find Sir, it is evident & clear Sir, that wherever the Senate is to be, then Sir you must be at the head of them. but further Sir, (here he looked agast, as if some tremendous Gulph had Ya[w]ned before him) I, shall, not, pretend, to, say."

Should the senators rise in respect to a superior or sit as before an equal? The answer risked casting the president as a monarch or the Senate as a House of Lords, prompting an extended debate. Richard Henry Lee testified that during the king's speech, the House of Lords sat and the House of Commons stood, an observation that seemed to have deep political significance until another senator made "this sagacious discovery, that the Commons stood because they had no seats to sit on . . . being arrived at the Bar of the House of lords." An interruption from the House clerk sparked yet another discussion: how should the clerk be received? Should he be admitted into the Senate chamber or should the sergeant at arms (complete with ceremonial mace) receive his communication at the door? It was, Maclay sighed, "an Endless business."

Comical as this debate may seem, it highlights a primary concern of the First Congress: the tone of republican governance. The problem was the lack of precise standards. As good republicans, Americans considered themselves everything that their corrupt European forebears were not — egalitarian, representative, straightforward, and virtuous in spirit, public-minded in practice. Republican leaders were supposedly exceptional as well, a natural elite of the talented and worthy who lived modestly, dressed practically, and behaved forthrightly in a spirit of accommodation. Yet though most people agreed on such generalities, concepts like simplicity, virtue, and public-mindedness were entirely relative, meaningful in comparison with European luxury and corruption but lacking any intrinsic meaning. This ambiguity seemed dangerous in a new republic of unformed character. High-toned trappings might push the new government toward monarchism and warp the soul of the republic. As many congressmen well realized, falling back into the habits of America's monarchical past was the path of least resistance.

This fundamental ambiguity raised troubling questions about the status of national representatives. In general, republicanism encouraged a leveling of social distinctions when compared with the aristocratic Old World; the people reigned supreme. But what of their representatives? Should they be superior men of wealth and standing or should they mirror the body politic? What props of authority were appropriate for this new social rank? Foreign relations complicated matters, presenting yet another judgmental audience with different standards. Somehow, national leaders had to uphold their authority among foreign dignitaries without succumbing to monarchical excess. In devising a national model of leadership, politicians were determining their standing and reputation as a ruling elite.

The Life of a Congressman

This debate over leadership and national character did not take place in a serene and orderly legislative chamber. Populated by ambitious and aggressive lawyers and merchants, the floor of Congress was a challenging stage. Performing before one another as well as their constituents back home (through letters and newspapers), the congressmen felt compelled to display their talents and establish their reputations. Congressional oratory was critical to such self-promotion. Well aware of the importance of their performances, many politicians prepared them in advance, scribbling notes on bits of paper that could be hidden in their hat or the palm of their hand; they were actors who needed a script. Given the competitive nature of oratory and the vulnerability of reputations, oratorical attacks had a peculiar power: they could tear a man to pieces before the face of the public.

Of course, galvanizing the attention of either the House or Senate was virtually impossible, given their routine pandemonium. Rarely were all the members seated, their attention politely focused on the speaker at hand. Some wrote letters to family and friends; others conversed or read. Members wandered into antechambers to propose bargains and devise legislative strategies. They stood in small clusters in hallways and corners or, in winter, around the stoves, whispering and laughing. Clerks came and went, the rustle of papers accompanying their passage. The thumping of boots on wood floors or the rumble of passing carriages drowned out speakers, as they did when Washington, seeking senatorial advice and consent, erupted into a presidential temper tantrum. Orators who bellowed to be heard above the din only made matters worse. Despite being on different floors of the same building, the House and the Senate were within earshot of each other, and a loud speaker in one compelled the other to shut its windows. As Maclay himself described his surroundings on one particularly chaotic day, "As well might I write . . . the Vagaries of a pantomine, as attempt to Minute the Business of this Morning. What with the Exits And the entrances of our [Secretary] Otis. The Announcings the Advancings Speechings drawings & Withdrawings of [House secretary] B[e]ckley & [executive secretary] Lear And the comings & goings of our Committees of Enrollment &c. And the consequent running of Doorkeepers opening and Slaming of doors the House seemed in a continual Hurricane. Speaking would have been Idle. for nobody would or could hear."

Maclay considered the House even worse than the Senate. The representatives have "certainly greatly debased their dignity," he wrote on March 22, 1790. "Using base invective indecorous language[,] 3 or 4 up at a time. Manifest signs of passion. The most disorderly Wandering, in their speeches, telling Stories, private anecdotes &c. &c." He knew for a fact that they enjoyed passing one another poems and lampoons ridiculing their most renowned colleagues — men who deserved a strong dose of humility. John Adams, a favorite target, often watched from the visitors gallery, oblivious to the nature of the goings-on below. Maclay guessed that the representatives must spend their nights devising their creations "in Order to pop them on the Company to the greater advantage." It was difficult to politick in such confusion.

Maclay and his colleagues spent four to five hours each day in this maelstrom. Rising early at scattered boardinghouses and visiting a few colleagues in preparation for the day's proceedings, they arrived at Federal Hall shortly before matters got under way at eleven o'clock. Business came to an end at three o'clock, an earlier adjournment raising "the same flutter of Joy among the Members. that I have seen among Children in a School on giving leave," Maclay groused. By four o'clock, the evening's activities had begun. Often they involved a dinner party, many lasting as long as six hours. For many legislators, dinners followed a weekly schedule. For example, every Thursday, Washington held a "public dinner" for eighteen to thirty guests, often attended by both husbands and wives. Held for ceremonial reasons rather than social desire, they were usually somber affairs featuring endless toasts ("such a buz of health sir and health Madam, & thank You sir and thank You Madam. never had I heard before," Maclay noted on one occasion) and long, awkward silences, punctuated by the tap of Washington's silverware as he glumly banged it against the table "like a drumstick." As many congressmen did, Maclay spent one night each week with his state delegation, enjoying food and wine, smoking cigars, and telling the occasional off-color joke as they consulted on their state's interests. Other days featured receptions or levees, Martha Washington, Abigail Adams, and a number of other women each claiming one night of the week to hold her own. George Washington's levees met on Tuesdays at three o'clock; ceremonial and somewhat formal affairs, they were restricted to national officeholders and dignitaries. While no one attended all such affairs — nor could they, given their sheer number — public figures had daily social obligations. Attendance was not mandatory but recommended, for social events were hubs of political influence and standing that forged networks, strengthened bonds, and established a person's presence. In addition, there were meetings to attend and letters to write; politicians could accumulate backlogs of thirty, forty, or even fifty letters. In essence, Maclay and his colleagues were politicking from morning till night.

Lines of Conflict

Politicking both on and off the floor of Congress came to a head during the most heated debate of the First Congress; not surprisingly, it involved the controversial Treasury Department and its equally controversial head,

Alexander Hamilton. On January 14, 1790, Hamilton presented the first phase of his financial program, what would come to be known as the Funding Act. The act proposed that the national government would pay off the states' debts remaining from the Revolution, making creditors beholden to the national government and thereby enhancing its power and prestige, one of Hamilton's core goals. The Southerners, who had largely extinguished their debts through heavy taxes, resented this seeming reward to laggard Northerners. Others thought that the plan would benefit money men and speculators. In fact, that was part of Hamilton's intent: he wanted to bolster the weak national government with the moral and financial support of the wealthy and powerful. The failure of this fundamental proposal would mean the end of Hamilton's plan, his almost certain resignation, and to many, the collapse of the government, so debate was fierce and lengthy, and alliances soon emerged. On April 12, 1790, the House defeated Hamilton's assumption plan, much to the chagrin of Hamilton and his supporters, who were not ready to surrender.

The permanent location of the national capital was the other major controversy of the congressional session. New York and Pennsylvania were vying for the profitable and prestigious station, while Southerners looked farther south. By mid-June 1790, after months of debate, the issue was at a standstill, as were much of the workings of government. With the government barely more than a year old, many feared the collapse of the Union. As Bickford and Bowling note, tensions were so fierce that Madison even considered adjourning Congress to allow tempers to cool.

Not surprisingly, as the gears of government ground to a halt over the Funding Act and the national capital, the two issues became entwined, devolving into an ongoing series of private bargains between champions of assumption and those who wanted the national capital in their home state. Given that republican governance was grounded on public accountability and open debate and compromise, this outburst of private bargaining seemed to set a dangerous precedent. Many men were unsettled by the "negotiations, cabals, meetings, plots & counterplots" that had "more influence on the public business than fair argument & an attention to the general good." In the end, it was just such a private bargain — forged between Hamilton and Madison at Jefferson's dinner table in June 1790 — that settled the matter. In the "Compromise of 1790," Madison agreed to withdraw his opposition to the Funding Act, Hamilton agreed not to block the relocation of the national capital south, to the banks of the Potomac River, and the debates came to a close. On July 16, Congress adopted a bill that placed the capital in Philadelphia until 1800, when it would move to its permanent location, and on August 4, Hamilton's assumption plan passed. The legislative storm had been weathered. But the regional, partisan, and personal clashes that it provoked plagued national governance for years to come.

— JOANNE BARRIE FREEMAN

BIBLIOGRAPHICAL NOTES

On the First Federal Congress, the supreme authority is the First Federal Congress Project at George Washington University, the ongoing documentary edition of the papers of the First Federal Congress. In addition, see Charlene Bangs Bickford and Kenneth R. Bowling, eds., *Birth of the Nation: The First Federal Congress 1789–1791* (Washington, D.C., 1989); Kenneth R. Bowling and Donald R. Kennon, eds., *Inventing Congress: Origins and Establishment of the First Federal Congress* (Athens, Ohio, 1999). Also invaluable is the National Gallery exhibition catalogue, Margaret C. S. Christman, *The First Federal Congress, 1789–1791* (Washington, D.C., 1989), which includes portraits of members of the First Congress. More general studies that touch on the First Congress include John C. Miller, *The Federalist Era, 1789–1801* (New York, 1960); Stanley Elkins and Eric McKitrick, *The Age of Federalism* (New York, 1993); and Leonard D. White, *The Federalists: A Study in Administrative History* (New York, 1948).

A number of studies address specific aspects of the First Congress. On the first federal elections, see R. B. Bernstein, "A New Matrix for National Politics: The First Federal Elections, 1788–1790," in *Inventing Congress: Origins and Establishment of the First Federal Congress,* ed. Kenneth R. Bowling and Donald R. Kennon (Athens, Ohio, 1999). For the documents relating to the passage of the Bill of Rights, see *Creating the Bill of Rights: The Documentary Record from the First Federal Congress,* ed. Helen E. Veit, Charlene Bangs Bickford, and Kenneth R. Bowling (Baltimore, 1991). On Alexander Hamilton's relationship with Congress, see Joanne B. Freeman, "'The Art and Address of Ministerial Management': Secretary of the Treasury Alexander Hamilton and Congress," in *Neither Separate nor Equal: Congress and the Executive Branch in the 1790s* (Athens, Ohio, 2000). On the compromise of 1790, see Kenneth R. Bowling, *The Creation of Washington, D.C.: The Idea and Location of the American Capital* (Fairfax, Va., 1991). For an alternate view of the 1790 "dinner deal," see Jacob E. Cooke, "Compromise of 1790," *William and Mary Quarterly* 27 (1970): 523–45. See also Kenneth R. Bowling (with a rebuttal by Cooke), "Dinner at Jefferson's: A Note on Jacob E. Cooke's 'The Compromise of 1790,'" *William and Mary Quarterly* 28 (October 1971): 629–48; and Norman K. Risjord, "The Compromise of 1790: New Evidence on the Dinner Table Bargain," *William and Mary Quarterly* 33 (April 1976): 309–14.

More cultural studies of early congresses and the tenor of national politics are included in Joanne B. Freeman, *Affairs of Honor: National Politics in the New Republic* (New Haven, Conn., 2001); Kenneth R. Bowling and Donald R. Kennon, eds., *Neither Separate Nor Equal: Congress and the Executive Branch in the 1790s* (Athens, Ohio, 2000); Kenneth R. Bowling and Donald R. Kennon, eds., *The*

House and Senate in the 1790s: Petitioning, Lobbying, and Institutional Development (Athens, Ohio, 2002); and James Sterling Young, *The Washington Community: 1800–1828* (New York, 1966).

On William Maclay and his diary, the authoritative edition is Kenneth R. Bowling and Helen E. Veit, eds., *The Diary of William Maclay and Other Notes on Senate Debates* (Baltimore, 1988). On Maclay, see also Heber G. Gearhart, "The Life of William Maclay," *Proceedings of the Northumberland County Historical Society* 2 (May 1930): 46–73.

3

Democracy, Gentility, and Lobbying in the Early U.S. Congress

The Natural Aristocracy

ACCUSTOMED as modern Americans are to the grinning, baby-kissing, constituent-serving congressmen of the early twenty-first century, they often have a difficult time grasping the rather distant and condescending nature of an early American politician's relationship with his constituents. While the young United States had a broader distribution of land and wealth than anywhere else in the world at the time and granted its citizens far more expansive political rights, it also possessed a clear elite, men who (along with their families) enjoyed social and economic preeminence over their neighbors: planters in the rural South; merchants in the coastal cities; the manor lords and large-scale landowners of the rural Northeast; eminent clergymen in New England; and leading attorneys everywhere. Contemporaries might have spoken of "the better sort" or "the most respectable part" of the community, and historians sometimes refer to them as "the gentry." Certainly the gentility or refinement of their manners, speech, and style of living was one of the most important ways that the elite distinguished themselves from more ordinary Americans.

Conforming, albeit in a less rigid fashion, to the political theory and practice of societies the world over, American men of wealth and status also held the reins of political power. It had been true in colonial times, and the founders hoped it would remain true in their new nation, with appropriate modifications. The fifty-five delegates who created the new government at Philadelphia in 1787 comprised a cross section of the revolutionary political elite. Thirty-four were lawyers, and the rest were wealthy merchants or planters, with some combining more than one of these roles. Thirty were creditors of the Confederation government; twenty-six were college graduates — at a time when there were only a handful of colleges on the continent and far less than 1 percent of Americans were able to attend them.

The Constitution these men devised did not impose the wealth or property qualifications on congressional candidates that some of the framers had favored, opting instead for relatively mild requirements respecting age (twenty-five and thirty years old for the House and Senate, respectively) and citizenship (seven and nine years). The only other stipulation was a residency requirement: "When elected," members of Congress had to be inhabitants of the state they were to represent. Nevertheless, it was expected, as James Madison put it, that those who "will have been distinguished by the preference of their fellow citizens . . . will be somewhat distinguished also." John Adams and Thomas Jefferson alike spoke highly of a "natural" aristocracy, based on accomplishments and character, as opposed to an "artificial" aristocracy, rooted in noble titles and inherited wealth. America was thought to have purged the bad sort of aristocrat during the Revolution; her natural aristocrats *deserved* their preeminence. It seemed both unavoidable and desirable that natural aristocrats hold power in the United States, as long as the constitutional system prevented them from gaining excessive power.

A more complicated question than who served in Congress, and one to which the Constitution provided even fewer answers, was how these natural aristocrats were supposed to relate to the people that elected them. The modern democratic answer — to keep in close touch with their constituents, faithfully doing their will and representing their interests before the government — was not the one the founders gave. (The residency requirement was a departure from the British practice that theoretically kept members somewhat closer to their constituents, but the difficulties of late-eighteenth-century travel alone ensured that most members would not be rushing back home for consultations during the session.)

The Constitution was at least partly born out of a reaction against the "excess of democracy" that many natural aristocrats felt plagued the new nation in the 1780s. The egalitarian rhetoric and participatory experience of the Revolution had led many ordinary Americans to assert themselves much more readily. Deferential social customs, like tradesmen and laborers removing their hats in the presence of a gentleman, fell out of fashion. In politics, ordinary citizens proved much more likely to vote their own interests, for instance, supporting measures (or men who supported measures) that protected farmers in danger of losing their property to creditors during the economic depression of the '80s.

What was worse, the people's new respect for themselves often seemed to translate into disrespect for their leaders. "It would seem to be a maxim of democracy to starve the public servants," fumed a future vice president, Elbridge Gerry, who was outraged by calls for a legislative pay cut back in Massachusetts. James Madison and others made it clear that the people's representatives should have a much higher purpose than constituent service. "The aim of every political Constitution is or ought to be first to obtain for rulers, men who possess most wisdom to discern, and most virtue to pursue the common good of the society," Madison wrote in *Federalist* 57, "and in the next place, to take the most effectual precautions for keeping them virtuous, whilst they continue to hold their public trust."

Elections were no more than the proper republican means of accomplishing these goals, and to some extent, the motivation to be a virtuous representative stemmed from a sense of having been elevated above their fellow citizens. Madison argued hopefully that every man possessed "a sensibility to marks of honor, of favor, of esteem, and of confidence, which, apart from all considerations of interest, is some pledge for grateful and benevolent returns." If representatives were tempted to use their position for personal gain or to join forces with those who might want to oppress their constituents in some way, the next election would force them "to anticipate the moment when their power is to cease, when their exercise of it is to be reviewed, and when they must descend to the level from which they were raised; there for ever to remain."

Madison was not talking about daily or weekly monitoring of the legislator's fealty to his constituents' wishes. The expectation was that representatives would be sent off to the seat of government and have their performance reviewed every two to six years. Congressional elections were haphazardly organized in the early decades: many states had to pass a new electoral law for every contest, calling the election and settling basic questions, such as whether representatives were to be elected in districts or statewide. Campaigns were often comically short by modern or even late-nineteenth-century standards, only a few weeks or a few days. The political mores of the time often dictated that the candidate never even speak on his own behalf, though in 1788 Madison himself did have to rush home and "make it convenient to see the people" when it looked as if he might not even be elected to the Congress he had helped to create.

Neither the Constitution nor the early congresses made much provision for the constituents' monitoring of representatives once the election was over. The proceedings were not required to be open, and the reporting of debates was privately conducted and often incomplete or highly telescoped in the early years. The main provision was for the publication of the results of congressional action — that is, the statutes that were actually passed — in newspapers around the country. A few of the more proactive representatives wrote open letters back home on what they were doing in Congress, but there is little evidence that this practice was very widespread. With the rise of political parties, some congressional elections and some members of Congress received close scrutiny in the press, but most went by virtually unnoticed.

Philadelphia: The Gentleman's Club and Its Lobby

Isolated by many days' or weeks' travel from the places that elected them, members of Congress were left more or less on their own in Philadelphia, as far as their constituents were concerned, and hence Congress usually operated like a gentleman's club that happened to make laws. Certainly, its members often behaved like gentlemen of leisure, making a quorum sometimes difficult to achieve. "These idle, lazy, six dollars per day men," complained one visitor with business before a congressional committee, "cannot rise in the morning, sip their coffee, and dismiss their barbers early enough to attend Congress at eleven o'clock."

While it often involved activities and habits we no longer associate with work, being a gentleman in the late eighteenth century was in fact a deeply serious business. As Richard Bushman has shown, gentility was a complex code that the early American elite (and those who wanted to join it) strove to follow. From George Washington on down, the founding generation studied, sweated, and spent to meet standards that applied to every conceivable aspect of life: architecture, home furnishings, table manners, body movements, cleanliness, conversation, penmanship, clothing, even bowel habits.

Americans learned many of these rules from so-called courtesy books, instruction manuals for proper, genteel living that were mostly adapted from advice written for European courtiers in earlier times. One of the most popular courtesy books in the English-speaking world was based on the letters written by Lord Chesterfield, a British courtier and politician, for the instruction of his illegitimate son; others bore such titles as *The School of Good Manners* and *Youth's Behaviour, or Decency in Conversation among Men.* The books preached the need to show elaborate respect for others and present a smooth, beautiful appearance by controlling one's bodily movements, speech, and mind at all times. The young George Washington had to copy out a courtesy book as a school exercise and listed rules against touching your private parts, rinsing your mouth, or humming in public, among other prohibitions. Americans who could afford it went beyond these self-help books, hiring writing masters to teach their children the fashionable round, or Italian, hand and dancing masters to teach them the complex group dances they were expected to navigate as well as the genteel approach to the most basic movements of everyday life: how to stand, how to sit, how to walk, how to enter a room.

Gentility was essentially a performance, and everyone else in the room was a critic. In their letters and diaries, members of the founding generation constantly assessed the performances they witnessed, often harshly, determining whether an individual should be adjudged "the better sort" or the worse. However, much more was riding on a person's ability to project gentility than mere social prestige. In a world without credit bureaus, background checks, or official identification, properly genteel attire, speech, and behavior determined where a person could go, whom he could see, and how he was judged in every area, from creditworthiness and personal integrity to professional competence and innate intelligence. Members of Congress dealt constantly with people they knew little about and from places they had never been, both their fellow members and others who tried to influence their deliberations from the outside. Often genteel appearances, and perhaps a family name or a cursory letter of introduction, were all they had to go on when deciding whether to take a contact seriously.

By all accounts, the early congresses were well integrated into polite New York and then Philadelphia society, where their courtesy book learning was constantly put to use. Ensconced in fashionable rented homes, as houseguests, or in upscale boardinghouses with fellow members, congressmen's lives were dominated by a social schedule of receptions, balls, dinner parties, and concerts, in addition to the controversial presidential levees and less formal socializing with other members in taverns and coffeehouses. It could be a strenuous life, as a visiting Massachusetts clergyman, Manasseh Cutler, wrote home to his wife: "The constant routine of four and five o'clock dinners at the most sumptuous tables almost kills me. I had infinitely rather sit down with you to a piece of salt junk at one o'clock than be tormented with the parade and delay of Philadelphia entertainments." Congress Hall itself became a place of fashionable resort for the ladies and gentlemen of Philadelphia, giving rise to the first known political use of the term "lobby" on the floor of Congress.

While this early "lobby" had relatively few paid agents of special interests, it was nonetheless felt to wield a potent political influence, one that sometimes seduced otherwise faithful rural representatives to "sacrifice agriculture at the shrine of . . . commerce." When proposals were made in 1808 to move the seat of government back to Philadelphia from its muddy encampment on the Potomac, Republican congressmen squawked that such hated Hamiltonian policies as the Bank of the United States and the Jay Treaty had been carried through the efforts of Philadelphia's high society lobby. "Congress were almost overawed by the population of that city; measures were dictated by that city," Representative Matthew Lyon of Kentucky complained. A rough-hewn Irish printer by background, Lyon himself had suffered in Philadelphia's high-toned atmosphere. Blue-blooded Federalists had ostracized and taunted him, and the Connecticut Federalist Roger Griswold had finally taken a cane and beaten him savagely on the floor of the House. (Lyon had spat on Griswold, and corporal punishment was considered the appropriate way for a gentleman to redress an insult from an inferior.) Even then, it was Lyon who found himself facing censure for having insulted his gentleman assailant and defending himself with a pair of fire tongs. In most cases, Maryland's Philip Barton Key pointed out, the social influences on Congress were much more subtle than Griswold's cudgel. The Philadelphians would work through "good dinners and handsome entertainments, operating on our prejudices and taking advantage of unguarded moments [and] insensibly bias our better judgment."

If this was the age-old tale of innocent country boys being corrupted by life in the big city, such fears were hardly unfounded. Members of Congress do tend to be influenced by their social milieu in ways that subtly change their personal sympathies and may in the long run shape their political decisions. By socializing frequently with wealthy Philadelphia merchants and financiers, some members almost certainly came to share at least partly in their concerns. At the same time, early national Philadelphia was that era's "Athens of America" and included some of the nation's leading scientists, artists, and writers. The typical rural congressman doubtless had much to learn from these cosmopolitan, well-informed people. He also might learn to think twice before expressing a view that could get him excluded from his new social circle. The control of Congress that Hamilton and the Federalists enjoyed for much of the 1790s was doubtless aided by the Philadelphia "lobby."

This genteel social milieu also fostered (and concealed) the first known examples of the classic modern type of congressional lobbying, by businesses seeking protection and favors. Gentility provided what all lobbyists and other political supplicants need most, even today: access to important legislators and policymakers. In the early Republic, a lobbyist whose manners, clothing, and speech seemed to mark him as a gentleman had virtually unlimited access to any member of Congress. Gentility created a kind of imaginary club, and one of the principal benefits of membership was the right to be treated hospitably, as a friend, an equal, and an honored guest, by other gentry wherever one happened to go. Once acknowledged as a fellow gentleman, a lobbyist could not only see congressmen but also join fully in their social life at the seat of government, providing all sorts of unofficial settings where contacts could be built and sensitive business matters discussed discreetly and effectively.

Undoubtedly the most successful early lobbyist was the aforementioned Reverend Manasseh Cutler, both an agent and member of the Ohio Company of Associates, a group of New England investors. Chosen by his colleagues to represent them before the government, the smooth-tongued Cutler descended on the old Congress in New York in July 1787. Through a few weeks of socializing with congressmen and a side arrangement with the head of the Treasury Board, William Duer, Cutler worked a deal to purchase 1.5 million acres of land in the Northwest Territory for the discounted price of one dollar per acre, payable in depreciated government securities. When better economic conditions and Indian wars sucked the profit out of the original deal, Cutler went back to the new Congress for long stints of lobbying in 1790 and 1792 and got the terms radically altered: 750,000 acres for the equivalent of around twelve cents per acre. (In contrast, the price for federal lands sold to the public was set at two dollars per acre.)

Some New England clergymen criticized gentility as it took hold in America during the eighteenth century, but Manasseh Cutler, resplendent in his black velvet suit and silver shoe buckles, was a thoroughgoing, self-conscious practitioner of it. "A man of consummate prudence in speech and conduct," a relative remembered, "of courtly manners" that made him "a favorite in [the] drawing room," Cutler was the type of lobbyist who could make influence and dealmaking seem nothing more than a friendly dinner conversation. The courtesy books called conversation "the Cement and Soul of Society," and Cutler, an amateur scientist and parlor *philosophe* like so many gentlemen of his generation, could weave fantastically lucrative proposals in and around discussions of botany, wine, politics, and the classics without ever appearing the crass manipulator or greedy boodler. Cutler could even get a little contemptuous about how easy it was to have his way with "their High Mightinesses" of Congress. "It is not easy to conceive," he wrote to his wife, "how much a very *little being* may, if disposed, work upon their caprice and whims."

It would be wrong to claim that Congress was somehow more lobby-ridden or corrupt in the early days than later. Once the railroads and other big businesses got into the act in the mid-nineteenth century, Congress became a veritable fleshpot of bribes, blackmail, and flesh, if the Gilded Age accusations of prostitute-lobbyists are believed. The corruption was usually not so flagrantly criminal, but by any standard the midcentury Congress was overrun by business lobbyists, influence peddlers, and "borers" of all sorts. An angry Walt Whitman lumped "lobbyers" in with "bribers" and "sponges" and "monte-dealers . . . men, scarred inside from the vile disorder, [but] gaudy outside with gold chains made from the people's money . . . crawling, serpentine men, the lousy combings and born freedom sellers of the earth."

On the other hand, there were some "crawling, serpentine men" in and around the early Congress, and in those days they did not have to crawl. The culture of gentility in which the institution was embedded provided a wide latitude for dealings that in retrospect seem shot through with conflict of interest, corruption, and sometimes conspiracy.

While eighteenth-century gentlemen often evaluated one another's characters, they were almost exclusively external and superficial in their standards. Gentry were evaluated by how successfully they performed the outward qualities of gentility; gentlepeople were really what they ate and wore, how well they danced, wrote, and spoke. They were essentially actors, onstage before the rest of society. The "characters" they played were not exactly false, but they were very much masks, to be taken at face value. In a sense, the generation of American gentlemen who founded the United States was especially superficial. Having abandoned older, more objective and inflexible standards of gentility such as membership in a titled nobility — you either were the earl of Shaftesbury or not, no matter how you behaved — American gentry were left to rely exclusively on outward, learned characteristics.

The most serious problem with this outlook in terms of government was that the American gentry who served in Congress and the executive offices did not know they were being superficial. Their assumption was that the genteel mask really did reflect the inner person or else that the beast within had been effectively repressed. Genteel standards of taste and beauty were all about imposing smoothness, order, and harmony on rough nature, about putting an overlay of beautiful serenity on the harsh, chaotic realties of human life, about valuing and believing in those exteriors rather than the things they covered. Bushman writes that "gentility hid what it could not countenance and denied whatever caused discomfort." Gentility assumed integrity, but it did not necessarily teach honesty, which could be extremely unconducive to gentility's primary purposes of pleasing others and creating social harmony. Samuel Johnson growled that Lord Chesterfield's letters, one of the bibles of gentility, taught "the morals of a whore, and the manners of a dancing master."

This type of thinking caused problems when used by men in power and those who wanted things from them: if a man had been accepted by society as a gentleman, he was assumed to be a man of honor and integrity and therefore was safe to put in office. There was no need for close oversight or regulation of such a man's official conduct, because his gentlemanly regard for his own character would automatically preclude any misbehavior. To question an official gentleman's integrity or even appear to doubt it was to question his social standing in a fundamental way, along with that of everyone who had acknowledged it. That was the kind of insult duels were fought over. So a gentleman's integrity was rarely questioned, and safeguards or even strong taboos against conflicts of interest were rare. It took overwhelming, absolutely incontrovertible evidence of a legislator's or official's criminality — documents indicating a treasonous conspiracy or a lengthy prison stay — for the genteel world to admit that its standards of character judgment had failed.

Corruption in Velvet: Jonathan Dayton and the Miami Purchase

Several examples of how this system could be abused leap out from the history of another Ohio land deal, the Symmes or Miami Purchase. In 1788, John Cleves Symmes of New Jersey, a former delegate to the old Congress, parlayed his extensive connections there into a contract for one million acres of land on the Great Miami River, the present Cincinnati area, at roughly 66⅔ cents an acre. Symmes moved to the Northwest Territory, got himself appointed a territorial judge, and set about the business of selling farms and town lots to migrants. His partner and agent in the venture was the illustrious Jonathan Dayton, a 1776 graduate of Princeton, a war hero, the youngest member of the 1787 Constitutional Convention, and a member of the new Congress from 1791 to 1805, including two terms as Speaker. Though the purchase was eventually doomed by Indian wars, rising land prices, and proprietary incompetence, Dayton kept it alive through the 1790s despite growing congressional and public hostility, stopping early attempts to repeal the contract and heading off numerous actions that might have harmed Symmes's interests. In 1789, having been narrowly defeated in the first New Jersey congressional elections, Dayton acted as an incredibly well-connected private lobbyist and used his influence with former colleagues now in the First Congress to preserve Symmes's judgeship during the transition to the new government. Then he arranged for troops to protect the Miami settlement during the flaring Indian wars. A member himself, beginning with the Second Congress, Dayton spent much of his time "counteracting & frustrating" plans to open a land office that would sell federal lands in the Northwest Territory to individual settlers; he feared the government's prices would be lower than what Symmes was asking.

Dayton's greatest service to the Miami Purchase probably came in 1792. Out in the Northwest Territory, Symmes had been selling overlapping plots and land outside his boundaries while falling far behind in his payments to the government; his whole claim to the land grant fell into question. But Dayton, now a rising congressional star on his way to the Speaker's chair, was on the case. In the midst of sabotaging yet another land office bill in the spring of 1792, he introduced resolutions in favor of Symmes, got himself appointed chair of the committee to frame a bill, and this committee soon reported a measure confirming Symmes's title (along with his own) and establishing a liberal interpretation of the purchase's disputed boundaries. He then muscled the bill through both houses of Congress. Dayton's personal stake in the Symmes purchase was well known to his fellow congressmen but caused little concern. In fact, he claimed to have won some senators over with the assurance that he, rather than the erratic Symmes, would handle the final payment details.

Dayton had fallen out with Symmes by the time he became Speaker in 1795 but continued to amass a record of ethically challenged behavior much like that of his friend Aaron Burr. Other large-scale land speculations also benefited from his political connections. (In fairness, insider land-jobbing was a way of life for many of the Founding Fathers, including President Washington himself.) Politically malleable, Dayton was a critic of the Federalists' Jay Treaty in Congress but later cooperated with a Federalist maneuver to elect him Speaker despite the party's lack of a majority in the House. As a result, Dayton became the first seriously partisan Speaker, using the power of the once-impartial office to stack committees and influence the votes of wavering members. He also managed to run $18,000 behind in his congressional accounts, having mixed public money with his own (as gentleman officials were allowed to do), and probably used it for land speculation. Dayton's arrearage was exposed in 1800, but he was allowed to pay the money back without interest. Elected to the Senate in 1798, Dayton almost simultaneously accepted an army appointment during the French war crisis without resigning from Congress. In 1803 he switched his allegiance again and supported the Louisiana Purchase. The string ran out only when he was arrested as a member of Aaron Burr's conspiracy in 1807. An investor rather than a soldier in the venture, Dayton was charged with treason but never tried. Nevertheless, he was finished as a major political figure.

The Miami Purchase found other friends besides Dayton. Congressional action on Symmes's claims was increasingly unfavorable after his break with Dayton, but around 1800 Symmes got some help from another member of Congress, William Henry Harrison, a delegate from the Northwest Territory and the new husband of Symmes's daughter. The scion of a great Virginia family — he was born at the famous Berkeley Plantation, overlooking the James River — Harrison was only twenty-seven years old and an instant star in Philadelphia. The future president, appointed chair of a committee to consider the Symmes case, crafted a bill giving his father-in-law one more chance to acquire the lands he had sold outside his boundaries, the purchasers of which were suing him in droves. The Symmes relief bill passed the House but got postponed in the Senate, despite Harrison's Herculean efforts that extended even to testifying before the committee himself. The loyal son-in-law admitted to his constituents that these activities placed him in a "most delicate situation" but assured them that his "whole conduct was meant to be guided by moral integrity." Harrison had such impeccable credentials that it would have been almost impossible to challenge this statement without recourse to the field of honor.

The Petition Process and the Limits of Early Congressional Democracy

Gentleman's club though it was, Congress was by no means immune to democratic forces in the early days, even before the rise of political parties. The United States was a small place in the early decades, with only 3.9 million people in the first census, about the size of South Carolina today. It was fairly easy to know a state's or district's economic interests, and from the beginning, senators and representatives pursued these special interests avidly. In one of Congress's very first policy debates, over the first U.S. tariff, members wasted no time in pleading for their local industries: Pennsylvanians argued for duties high enough to protect their state's manufacturers, but not so high or so strict that they would hurt Philadelphia's merchants; New Englanders fought against the proposed molasses duty because it would hurt Massachusetts rum distillers.

Of course, promoting local business interests hardly qualifies the early Congress as a paragon of representative democracy. Several of the members making these arguments had personal connections to the industries they were speaking for, and their ability to defend these interests was greatly enhanced by Congress's incestuous tendency to appoint the members most interested in a particular measure to the ad hoc committee charged with considering it. (There was only one standing committee in the First Congress, the House committee on elections, and the formal committee system of conducting congressional business did not develop until the nineteenth century.) Merchants were the group most directly affected by import duties, so the House select committee appointed to draft the impost (tax) bill was made up of a Philadelphia merchant, a Massachusetts merchant, and a New York attorney described in Senator Maclay's diary as "a mere tool for British Agents & factors."

At least one form of democracy was much more effective in the gentleman's congress than it would be later. Though left out of the Constitution by the Philadelphia convention (along with the colonial practice of formally instructing legislators how they should vote), the right of citizens to petition Congress was guaranteed in the Bill of Rights. With roots deep in British history, petitions were taken very seriously by the early Congress and treated as legal documents requiring action rather than mere expressions of public opinion. Petitions could be sent by individuals or groups; once received, they were introduced on the House or Senate floor, where they were usually given serious consideration and often referred to a select committee for recommendations. The early House rules required that each petition be read in full on the floor. Many petitions were in essence lobbying appeals by business interests, such as the merchants of Philadelphia, but others were appeals from relatively ordinary citizens, such as the fishermen of Marblehead, Massachusetts, the farmers of Orange County, New York, and the blacksmiths of Boston, the latter two groups asking compensation for work and supplies commandeered by the armies during the Revolutionary War. A host of individual soldiers and officers sent petitions seeking, though not always finding, pensions, back pay, or a settlement of their accounts.

Petitions were the chief constitutional mechanism for popular participation in the legislative process, but they were also a very limited mechanism. Very few petitions addressed public policy matters other than the tariff or war debts, and on one of the few occasions on which petitioners presumed to canvass a larger question, the reaction from Congress was defensive. This was the 1790 campaign against slavery by Quakers in Philadelphia and New York City. An "embassy" of eleven Philadelphia Quaker leaders spent several weeks in New York, using every possible means of pressuring Congress to abolish or restrict slavery and the slave trade. The lobbyists wrote supplemental briefs for the committee considering their petition, accosted members outside the doors of Congress, visited them at their lodgings, and invited them for meals, all the while making themselves conspicuous in the House galleries, looming over the proceedings like the specters of a guilty national conscience. At the same time, their petitions were published in the newspapers, and New York seemed suddenly awash in antislavery pamphlets and broadsides.

This campaign proved to be the exception that helped establish an unwritten rule against such concerted, policy-oriented lobbying of Congress. The onslaught of politicking by such a wealthy and well-connected group left the southern congressmen infuriated and suspicious. They resented being pressured by men who were not even their constituents and questioned the constitutionality of the whole procedure. The eventual House committee report declared that the federal government had no power to emancipate slaves or (for twenty more years) prevent their importation; even mild committee resolutions affirming the right of Congress to lay taxes on imported slaves (along with the general principle that slaves should be educated and treated well) were struck down by southern votes.

After the Quaker lobbying ended, the editors of *The Documentary History of the First Federal Congress* write, "Congress took steps to prevent a repeat of the episode," and there is little evidence of anything similar until well into the nineteenth century. Those citizens looking to settle claims or secure particular economic benefits had all the democracy they needed, but those hoping to effect broad changes in government policy were largely denied direct access to Congress.

Democratization and the Democratic Republicans

Statistically, it is impossible to argue that Congress underwent any very thorough democratization during the early Republic. The levels of wealth, education, and legal training among its members always far exceeded that of the general population, and business interests would always be better represented than the policy preferences or best interests of the general citizenry. The rate of congressional turnover did increase between the War of 1812 and the Civil War, but even in the 1790s, the rate was many times higher than it is today — in the 30–50 percent range for the House of Representatives. As the turnover rate climbed from that point, it became more and more likely that departing members would be defeated for reelection or forced out by local party customs of "rotation in office" rather than simply retiring.

Yet if statistically measurable change occurred slowly, the pressure in Congress grew rapidly under the influence of international crises and rising partisanship. Bitter criticism of the Washington and Adams administrations, and of some proceedings in Congress, poured in from the newspapers, and some (though probably not all or most) state and congressional elections turned into partisan battles over national issues. Members not only began to feel this pressure but generate some of it, too. The practice of sending open letters and copies of speeches back to constituents developed during the Adams administration, especially among Democratic-Republican members from the South and West.

The supporters of Washington, Hamilton, and Adams bristled at these changes. No act could be lower than "to find fault, abuse and write infamous insinuations to degrade our own Government," snarled Representative William Barry Grove of North Carolina, and it was worse that it was "sent throughout the Country to Poison the People." Much more prone than the Republicans to considering themselves and administration officials a naturally and appropriately aristocratic elite, the Federalists perceived what would later be seen as the normal give-and-take of politics as intolerable assaults on the honor of gentlemen, the greatest of whom would avoid public service rather than "abandon the source of their glory and pride," their reputations. "Our wisest and best public officers have had their lives embittered," complained the Pennsylvania Federalist judge Alexander Addison, "and have been driven from their stations by unceasing and malignant slander." Partisan elections and the unlimited freedom of political expression gave "base, factious, and wicked men" "without virtue or talents" an advantage over gentlemen who had reputations to protect.

Confirmation of these fears seemed to come in the form of Matthew Lyon, first elected to the House from Vermont in 1796. An Irish immigrant who had been a printer and an indentured servant, Lyon was one of the first artisans elected to Congress and possibly the very first former servant. Drawing on his printing background and the labor of his son, also a printer, Lyon had used the press to elevate himself into consequence, just as the Federalists feared such "base" men would. Lyon and his son had founded the Rutland *Farmer's Library* "as a means of saving the district" from "the overpowering flood of anti Republicanism," and it promptly put the father in Congress over a more eminent Federalist.

In Philadelphia, Federalist congressmen and the lobby mocked Lyon's ethnicity and accent during House debates and carefully froze him out of polite society, treating him as "a meer beast and the fool of the play" and fomenting the brawl described earlier. Significantly, the argument between Lyon and Roger Griswold had begun as a discussion of the new, more public and democratic politics that Federalists found so threatening. Frustrated over the hard-line Federalism of the Connecticut delegation, Lyon had theorized to the Speaker, Jonathan Dayton, that the people of Connecticut, where he once lived, were misrepresented in Congress. He said he was certain that if he were to set up a newspaper there, even for a few months, he could "effect a revolution" in public opinion and turn out all the present delegation at the next election. Griswold overheard Lyon's boast and angrily contradicted his analysis, telling Lyon he "could not change the opinion of the meanest hostler in the state." From there, it was surprisingly few steps to sputum, walking sticks, and fire tongs.

The Federalists designed the Alien and Sedition Acts to shut down the political culture that had produced Matthew Lyon, and Lyon himself was one of those jailed. In the long term, the strategy blew up in their faces, leading to Jefferson's election in 1800 and the permanent installation on the American political scene of such features as political parties, campaigns, and aggressively partisan newspapers. These factors would make it difficult for the "natural aristocracy" to run the country as independently, or in as genteel a fashion, as they had once hoped. The 1800 elections also marked the first obvious and decisive shift in party control of Congress, making it relatively clear that the institution could not remain truly elevated above the larger political nation.

A changed environment drove the new democratic tendencies as much as changed values. Once Congress was set up at the muddy rural construction site on the Potomac, Philadelphia's glittering lobby must have seemed very far away. The legislature was still attended by throngs of people, but now it was a highly utilitarian and unavoidably egalitarian place where no lobbying gentleman was likely to go unnoticed. Benjamin Henry Latrobe, the surveyor of public buildings, estimated that four hundred to five hundred persons brought their business to Washington during each session of Congress; for them and many Washington residents, including servants, laborers, and tradesmen, the Capitol's interior "afforded the only shelter during the severity of winter." It was impossible to tell who belonged in the building, and the literal lobbies of the House chamber were often so loud and crowded with visitors, loiterers, and even food vendors that legislative business was sometimes interrupted. What was worse, from Latrobe's point of view, was that "idle and dissolute persons ranged the whole building," defacing the walls "with obscenity and . . . libels" and stealing "the public furniture and utensils."

Many of Jefferson's Republican supporters, including Matthew Lyon, found these much more chaotic and democratic surroundings preferable to the lobby they knew in Philadelphia, and some members sharply criticized Latrobe when he tried to regulate access to the House and its galleries. "In a speech of some length," David R. Williams of South Carolina condemned the "outrageous audacity" of the surveyor of public buildings "in lately altering the arrangement of the Representative Hall in respect to the entrance to the galleries."

Though the upper-class ladies of Washington City, along with the remaining Federalists and not a few of the more polished Republicans, did their best to build a polite society around Congress, their efforts were slowed and often defeated in the early decades. President Jefferson delighted in populist gestures that involved selective violations of the code of gentility, such as throwing "pell-mell" dinner parties, banning the formal receptions for Congress that had taken place under Washington and Adams, dressing down to receive guests, and eagerly participating in the occasional "efflorescence" of democratic enthusiasm. On New Year's Day

1802, for instance, Jefferson threw open the White House to the bearers of a twelve-hundred-pound "Mammoth Cheese," a gift from admiring Baptists in Cheshire, Massachusetts. Receiving some Federalist congressmen, who had come "determined" to keep up the old social nicety "of waiting on the President with the compliments of the season" and thus flouting the new informality, Jefferson amused himself by inviting the visitors to come in and eat a chunk of the massive dairy product, which they regarded as a "monument of human weakness and folly."

Two years later, just as the great cheese was finally being polished off and removed from what Jefferson referred to as the Mammoth Room (now the East Room), the president gave his blessing to another culinary stunt that took the festivities directly to Congress's door. The navy's bakers created a "Mammoth Loaf," made from an entire barrel of flour and baked in a specially built oven. On March 26, 1804, the loaf was covered in white linen and carried on the shoulders of decked-out bakers to the Capitol, where it was placed in a committee room off the Senate chamber along with plenty of roast beef, hard cider, wine, and whiskey. A wild public party ensued, with (as one disapproving observer put it) "people of all classes & colors from the President of the United States to the meanest vilest Virginia slave" crowding into the Senate to enjoy the victuals and offend gawking New England Federalists. Jefferson himself was there "in the midst of the motley crew," reportedly eating beef and bread off his pocketknife and doing some justice to the liquor as well. Shocked Federalists claimed to have heard the president "sneeringly" compare "the unhallowed bread and wine" at "this disgraceful entertainment" to the elements of the Christian Communion, which rumor was hotly debated in the press.

Nor was Jefferson's comment the only political event of the day. Some members of the crowd brought large prints caricaturing certain senators who had proposed moving the government out of the city, and a large number of the partygoers lingered loudly in the chamber for the rest of the afternoon. The sergeant at arms was initially unable to eject them, and when he was at last successful, the revelers only moved to the public gallery. At one point, Senator James Jackson of Georgia paused in the middle of a speech to threaten the unruly citizens of Columbia with violence if they ever behaved so badly again: "You shall be punished — I will inflict it — The navy shall be brought up & kill you outright."

Political Life Lessons: The First Congressional Pay Raise

This sort of public bacchanal did not become the norm of congressional life just yet. The truth is that the personnel and outlook dominating Congress, even after 1800, was far from plebeian and relatively little changed despite the more relaxed atmosphere. About the only real changes in the social structure was a decline in the class of lawyer who was elected and an incoming trickle of printers and newspaper editors, who followed in the footsteps of Matthew Lyon by using the press as a springboard to political power. One of the earliest and most powerful newcomers, at home if not in Congress, was New Jersey's James J. Wilson, who was elected senator in 1814 after becoming his state's virtual dictator on the strength of his Trenton *True American*, New Jersey's leading Republican journal. More than a hundred printers, editors, and journalists would be elected to Congress between Wilson's time and the Civil War; while they definitely helped make political life there more democratic, their presence was not enough to make much of a statistical dent in Congress's social profile.

It must also be noted that the dream of an independent, gentlemanly Congress made a strong comeback just after the War of 1812, only to die very hard and perhaps not even permanently in the 1816 elections. With the Federalist party atrophied because of wartime misbehavior and new, expansive notions of the federal government's role in American society uniting many former congressional enemies, the Democratic Republicans in Congress were able to work relatively insulated from partisan pressures and showed an increasing tendency to conduct themselves as a leadership class (that old natural aristocracy again) to which a certain status and income were due.

Whereas, under Jefferson, the ruling gentlemen had shown at least some cosmetic respect for popular sensibilities, the Fourteenth Congress openly disregarded those sensibilities by voting itself a pay raise. Complaining of high living costs and a depreciated currency, the House and Senate took only two weeks in March 1816 to pass a bill converting members' six-dollar-per-diem to a $1,500 salary. The expanded physical size and population of the country had increased the "weight and responsibility" of members, explained one congressional supporter of the Compensation Act. It was impossible to "live in the style of a gentleman" (two horses, a servant, and residence in a genteel boardinghouse) on the current allowance, complained another. The possibility of adverse public reaction was brushed aside. Voters would never have the "poorness of spirit" to demand that their representatives "degrade themselves . . . or . . . sacrifice their private property" in order to serve, Samuel W. Dana of Connecticut assured his colleagues.

Though some Compensation Act advocates argued that higher pay would allow politicians of more modest means to serve, the bill was clearly an effort to gentrify Congress, not democratize it. Representative John C. Calhoun of South Carolina, a planter blue blood educated at Yale and the Litchfield Law School, made this clear in mounting an elaborate defense of the pay raise. The "best materials for politics," Calhoun argued, meaning young men of property who had obtained liberal educations and pursued learned professions, were avoiding Congress in favor of the executive branch, government, or private life. A genteel income would improve the "tone of parties" in both Congress and the country at large. "Make a seat in Congress what it ought to be, the first post in the community," Calhoun predicted, "and men of the greatest distinction . . . will seek it."

Significantly, one of the few senators to speak up against the original bill was the only Republican printer in Congress at the time, James J. Wilson; he was also likely one of the poorer men in Congress, having abandoned his many New Jersey sinecures in order to serve. Wilson noted the terrible political timing of the pay raise, "at the very close of a very expensive war, when many of the internal taxes and high impost duties are yet continued." All outstanding claims from the war ought to be paid and the war taxes repealed, he argued, before Congress even considered rewarding itself. The editor-senator asked his colleagues to consider the matter from the viewpoint of politicians and ordinary citizens outside Washington. In his own state, Wilson explained, no official except the governor made any amount close to the proposed new salary.

The next Republican editor to arrive in the Senate, William Hendricks from the new state of Indiana, was more explicit on this point when the issue was reopened in December 1816. Living in an area that was only tenuously connected to the national market, where "the sources of wealth, means of procuring money, were few and narrow," and families sustained themselves by exchanging goods and subsistence farming, the citizens of Indiana held "ideas of expenditure . . . very unlike those of all the Eastern cities. Six dollars per day sounded large enough to them." Indeed, the new $1,500 salary was more money than a frontier family would see over a period of years and many times the income of a typical urban artisan. Wilson and Hendricks were making elementary points of democratic politics — gauging how the voters would perceive the government's actions — but the statesmen in Congress apparently needed the new editor-politicians to explain them.

In retrospect, the sequel to the Compensation Act does not seem surprising, though at the time it came as a tremendous shock for many gentleman congressmen. Political editors everywhere denounced the act or avoided defending it if a local political ally happened to have supported the pay raise. Denunciation quickly escalated into concrete action. Protest meetings were held all over the country and heavily publicized in the newspapers. Several state legislatures passed resolutions instructing their representatives to reverse the pay raise. Having failed to stop the bill in Congress, Senator Wilson planned to hold several apostate Republicans accountable in the fall election. The incumbent representative Lewis Condict would be dropped from the congressional ticket outright for voting for the bill, Wilson decided, and others would be disciplined: "Some are even for dismissing the entire delegation on the grounds that the receiver [of the pay raise] is as bad as the thief." The protests achieved stunning results. Even in the remotest frontier settlements, it was reported, "there was scarcely a man . . . who had not heard [of] and reprobated the law."

The displeasure translated directly into votes. More than two-thirds of the Congress that passed the Compensation Act were not reelected in 1816, including more than four-fifths of the members who had voted for it. Many of the remaining fifth had to work hard to survive, sometimes abasing themselves before the voters. The bill's sponsor, Representative Richard Mentor Johnson of Kentucky, went out stumping in its defense but found his constituents' opposition so intense that "after a passionate speech in favor of the measure," he would often "conclude by promising to vote for its repeal, because such was the will of the people."

The voters' outrage and Congress's rush to placate them inspired some disturbed reflections about the much more directly democratic polity that the Republic was turning out to be. When the Compensation Act was first considered, and especially during the long, bitter debates over its repeal, many supporters made no secret of their contempt for a politics that forced leaders to regulate themselves according to the values of ordinary voters. When it was suggested that members consult their constituents before proceeding with the pay raise, Virginia's John Randolph snorted, "Consult them for what?" John C. Calhoun and several other speakers in the repeal debates cited Edmund Burke as they attacked the whole notion that Congress should consider itself bound by voter preferences. "Have the people of this country snatched the power of deliberation from this body?" Calhoun cried, frustrated over the repudiation of a Congress he had led through bold new departures in national policy. Though he never directly mentioned it, this experience may have helped launch Calhoun on his way to becoming America's great antidemocratic political theorist.

Full, direct democracy, social equality, and social justice were not among the achievements or goals of the early Congress, nor were they part of its experience. Nevertheless, popular political forces ensured, from very early on, that members of Congress could never really ascend too far or too openly above the level from which they were raised. For better or worse, the Founders' vision of a conclave of natural aristocrats, deliberating in peace and returning to the voters occasionally to have their virtuous conduct ratified, was one of many constitutional expectations that quickly dissipated in the heat of democratic politics.

— Jeffrey L. Pasley

BIBLIOGRAPHICAL NOTES

The essential work on the culture of gentility in which early America's "natural aristocracy" steeped itself is Richard L. Bushman, *The Refinement of America: Persons, Houses, Cities* (New York, 1993). George Washington's "Rules of Civility & Decent Behaviour In Company and Conversation," copied from a contemporary courtesy book as a school exercise, has been published many times, perhaps most prominently in Richard Brookhiser, ed., *Rules of Civility: The 110 Precepts That Guided Our First President in War and Peace* (New York, 1997). The George Washington Papers project has also published the rules on the Internet at http://gwpapers.virginia.edu/civility/index.html.

Though there has been a long tradition of studying the rise of political parties in Congress, most recently synthesized in James Roger Sharp, *American Politics in the Early Republic: The New Nation in Crisis* (New Haven, Conn., 1993), historians and political scientists have written surprising little about how the early Congress interacted with its constituents. Some raw materials about such interactions have been published in Noble E. Cunningham Jr., *Circular Letters of Congressmen to Their Constituents, 1789–1829,* 3 vols. (Chapel Hill, N.C., 1978); Merrill Jensen, Robert A. Becker, Gordon DenBoer, and Lucy Trumbull Brown, eds., *The Documentary History of the First Federal Elections, 1788–1790,* 4 vols. (Madison, Wisc., 1976–1989); and volumes 7 and 8 of *The Documentary History of the First Federal Congress of the United States of America;* and Kenneth R. Bowling, William Charles diGiacomantonio, and Charlene Bangs Bickford, eds., *Petition Histories: Revolutionary War–Related Claims* (Baltimore, 1997) and *Petition Histories and Nonlegislative Official Documents* (Baltimore, 1998).

The only secondary work to cover lobbying and petitioning in the early years of Congress is Kenneth R. Bowling and Donald R. Kennon, eds., *The House and Senate in the 1790s: Petitioning, Lobbying, and Institutional Development* (Athens, Ohio, 2002), a collection of articles that just scratches the surface of its subject. Some sections of this chapter draw on the present author's contribution to the volume, "Private Access and Public Power: Gentility and Lobbying in the Early Congress," 57–99. The antislavery petition campaign mounted by Quakers during the First Congress is recounted in William C. diGiacomantonio, "'For the Gratification of a Volunteering Society': Antislavery and Pressure Group Politics in the First Federal Congress," *Journal of the Early Republic* 15 (1995): 169–97. The rampant lobbying and corruption that characterized the mid-nineteenth-century Congress are described in two books by Mark Wahlgren Summers: *The Plundering Generation: Corruption and the Crisis of the Union, 1849–1861* (New York, 1987), and *The*

Era of Good Stealings (New York, 1993). A more benign view is taken in what seems to be the only historical monograph on nineteenth-century lobbying, Margaret Susan Thompson, *The "Spider Web": Congress and Lobbying in the Age of Grant* (Ithaca, N.Y., 1985).

Writing about congressional life in early Washington, D.C., James Sterling Young, in *The Washington Community, 1800–1828* (New York, 1966), suggested that members were almost completely isolated, to the point that their boardinghouses determined voting blocs more than partisanship or region. This thesis was debunked in Allan G. Bogue and Mark Paul Marlaire, "Of Mess and Men: The Boardinghouse and Congressional Voting, 1821–1842," *American Journal of Political Science* 19 (1975): 207–30, and belied by the tremendous public backlash against the first congressional pay raise in 1816, as detailed in G. Edward Skeen, "*Vox Populi, Vox Dei:* The Compensation Act of 1816 and the Rise of Popular Politics," *Journal of the Early Republic* 6 (1986): 253–74.

Nevertheless, several recent books have emphasized the way that the genteel society surrounding Congress created a political culture quite distinct from the earthier and more partisan atmosphere that seems to have existed in communities around the country. Inside the early Republic's "beltway," some members of the natural aristocracy used duels, gossip, and other forms of political gamesmanship to jockey for a better position in the history books, and some elite women were able to convert their control over the capital's social life into significant political influence. See Joanne B. Freeman, *Affairs of Honor: National Politics in the New Republic* (New Haven, Conn., 2001), and Catherine Allgor, *Parlor Politics: In Which the Ladies of Washington Help Build a City and a Government* (Charlottesville, Va., 2000).

For the specifics of congressional circumstances in the "Athens of America" during the 1790s, see Russell F. Weigley, ed., *Philadelphia: A 300-Year History* (New York, 1982), 155–257, and the old but still useful account of Philadelphia high society, Rufus Wilmot Griswold, *The Republican Court; or, American Society in the Days of Washington,* new ed. (New York, 1867).

Historical trends in the recruitment of congressmen and the turnover in membership are analyzed in Nelson W. Polsby, "The Institutionalization of the U.S. House of Representatives," *American Political Science Review* 62 (1968): 144–68; Allan G. Bogue, Jerome M. Clubb, Carroll R. McKibbin, and Santa A. Traugott, "Members of the House of Representatives and the Processes of Modernization, 1789–1960," *Journal of American History* 63 (1976): 275–302; Morris P. Fiorina, David W. Rohde, and Peter Wissel, "Historical Change in House Turnover," in Norman Ornstein, ed., *Congress in Change: Evolution and Reform* (New York, 1975), 24–49; and Samuel Kernell, "Toward Understanding 19th Century Congressional Careers: Ambition, Competition, and Rotation," *American Journal of Political Science* 21 (1977): 669–93.

On Manasseh Cutler, the early Republic's champion lobbyist as well as a clergyman, botanist, and connoisseur of fine living, see Louis W. Potts, "Manasseh Cutler, Lobbyist," *Ohio History* 96 (1987): 101–23; and Janice Goldsmith Pulsifer, "The Cutlers of Hamilton," *Essex Institute Historical Collections* 107 (1971): 335–

408. Much of Cutler's lobbying activity can be followed in William Parker Cutler and Julia Perkins Cutler, eds., *Life, Journals, and Correspondence of Rev. Manasseh Cutler, LL. D.* (1888; reprint, Athens, Ohio, 1987).

No full biography of Jonathan Dayton has ever been written, but his role in making the speakership political is covered in Norman K. Risjord, "Partisanship and Power: House Committees and the Powers of the Speaker, 1789–1801," *William and Mary Quarterly,* 3d ser., 49 (1992): 628–51. His land dealings with, and lobbying for, John Cleves Symmes can be followed in Beverley W. Bond Jr., ed., *The Correspondence of John Cleves Symmes, Founder of the Miami Purchase* (New York, 1926).

Land speculation was the favorite pastime of the early Republic's political insiders and the focus of many dealings that modern standards would consider highly corrupt. For muckraking accounts of these deals, see A. M. Sakolski, *The Great American Land Bubble: The Amazing Story of Land-Grabbing, Speculations, and Booms from Colonial Days to the Present Time* (New York, 1932), and Daniel M. Friedenberg, *Life, Liberty, and the Pursuit of Land: The Plunder of Early America* (Buffalo, N.Y., 1992). A more scholarly account of federal land policy is Malcolm Rohrbough, *The Land Office Business: The Settlement and Administration of the American Public Lands, 1789–1837* (New York, 1968).

Aaron Burr

February 6, 1756–September 14, 1836

Aaron Burr

The life of Aaron Burr has all the elements of a tawdry television miniseries. The captivating New Jersey native was a spontaneous leader, an impertinent officer, a successful lawyer, a killer, and a womanizer whose lust for adventure and unbridled ambition produced both his rise and fall. His political career carried him from a distinguished upbringing to national power, then to notoriety, exile, and eventual decline.

Looking back across two centuries of evolving democracy under the federal government, today's students of history may view American independence as preordained. From that perspective, Burr is an aberrant villain. How else can one explain a former U.S. vice president advocating the secession of territories from the United States? No doubt, Burr's actions were treasonous. However, in the early years of a fledgling country, when the United States held title to neither Florida, California, nor the expansive Louisiana Territory, Burr — who had lived through the uncertainties of the Revolutionary War — may have fancied himself an entrepreneur.

Born in Newark, New Jersey, Burr came from a respectable family. His grandfather and father had both been religious leaders. The family moved to Princeton, where the Reverend Burr became the second president of the prestigious College of New Jersey, but the young Burr was orphaned at a young age and raised by an uncle. Known as intelligent and ambitious, Burr graduated from the college with distinction but decided to study law, having become disenchanted with religious studies. Despite his intellect, Burr was also known for being distractible, with a fondness for adventure that gave him a somewhat wayward reputation. Tradition has it that the intrigue of the Revolutionary War, more than patriotism, motivated Burr to request a commission in the Continental army. Turned down by General George Washington, Burr later fought under General Benedict Arnold and Major General Israel Putnam, earning a reputation for vigilance, military discipline, and womanizing.

In 1777 he began wooing Theodosia Prevost, ten years Burr's senior and the wife of a British officer who was frequently away on duty. When she was widowed four years later, Burr married her within nine months.

It is believed that Burr, a veritable Don Juan before and after his marriage, was not unfaithful to his wife; she died in 1796. The couple had one child, a daughter, Theodosia, in 1783, to whom Burr was zealously devoted until her death at sea in 1812.

Burr had resigned from the army in 1779 and began studying law with William Paterson, whom he'd known in college. He began practicing law in 1782 in New York, where he gained a solid reputation for the clarity and conciseness of his legal arguments, although they were admired more for dexterity than sound judgment or logic. Burr was unsuccessful in his attempts to enter New York politics, which were then controlled by two factions, one headed by Burr's professional rival, Alexander Hamilton, and the other by Governor George Clinton. After Burr made inroads with the Clinton machine, he was appointed the state's attorney general in 1789 and sent to the U.S. Senate in 1791. He made several national contacts during these years but was not really accepted into either of the political parties being formed and had accomplished no memorable legislation by the time he was turned out of office six years later. He returned to New York and built up his own political machine, which, with the machinations of Tammany Hall and despite heavy campaigning by Hamilton, enabled his rise to vice president under Thomas Jefferson in 1800. Burr's relations with the Jefferson administration were strained, and he was not included on Jefferson's winning ticket four years later.

Then came the infamous duel with Hamilton, which Burr had tried to avoid. After mortally injuring Hamilton in July 1804, Burr fled for his own safety. The event destroyed what little political base in New York he had left. This, coupled with four years of frustration under Jefferson, may have led Burr to think of recouping power through some nefarious land-grabbing schemes in Spanish territories. Although his exact intentions are debated, his actions — leading an armed force to separate territories from the United States — were treasonous. Acquitted for his actions, Burr was nonetheless a political pariah. He wandered through Europe, instigating England and France to seize U.S. territories, but was considered a crank. He was not allowed to return to the United States until 1812, financially destitute and in poor health. Burr rebuilt his legal practice in New York, but, having never been good with money, he depended on the charity of family and friends. His marriage to a wealthy and much younger widow in 1833 soon ended in divorce when it became apparent that Burr planned to run through her fortune. After a series of strokes left him paralyzed, Burr died in 1836.

Throughout his life, Burr was brazen, ambitious, and naive. His charisma and intelligence found many supporters, who, like Burr himself, believed he was entitled to lead. But his transparent lust for power raised the hackles of his opponents who were rightfully suspicious of his intentions.

Reference

"Aaron Burr." *Dictionary of American Biography Base Set.* American Council of Learned Societies, 1928–1936. Reproduced in *Biography Resource Center.* Farmington Hills, Mich.: The Gale Group. 2003. Retrieved December 10, 2003, from http://galenet.galegroup.com/servlet/BioRC.

4

The Alien and Sedition Acts

PROBABLY NO AMERICAN CONGRESS suffers from a worse reputation than the Fifth (1797–1799), owing to the notorious Alien and Sedition Acts of 1798: the Naturalization Act (June 18); the Alien Act (June 25); the Alien Enemies Act (July 6); and the Sedition Act (July 14). Passed at the height of a war scare with France, the laws delayed and complicated the naturalization of aliens, authorized the executive branch to deport or arrest aliens suspected of political activity, and promoted the prosecution of domestic critics for seditious libel. The four acts represented both Federalist fears, of internal subversion, and Federalist hopes, of perpetuating their political power by discrediting as anti-American the opposing Republicans (not to be confused with today's party of the same name, which dates only from the 1850s). In June of 1798, Alexander Hamilton eagerly predicted that the Republicans could be reduced to "a station in the public estimation like that of the Tories of our Revolution." Instead, the Alien and Sedition Acts proved so unpopular that they contributed to the Federalists' crushing defeat in the pivotal national election of 1800.

Because the Federalists never recovered, the election of 1800 validated the Republicans' interpretation of the Alien and Sedition Acts as unconstitutional follies, dangerous to civil liberties and to the survival of the American republic. By assailing this legislation, the Republicans made the case for the more generous definitions of free speech and a free press that are (usually) honored in our own day. Although the Republicans posed as defenders of liberties established by the Bill of Rights, in 1789, the freedoms of speech and the press were, in fact, ambiguous and limited until fully debated during the controversial life of the Alien and Sedition Acts.

Crisis

During the 1790s, the new American republic seemed to teeter between future greatness or imminent collapse. Unlike Americans today, the leaders of the early republic could not comfort themselves with a long, successful history of free and united government. Instead, the new nation seemed both potentially powerful and immediately fragile. Although endowed with an immense potential for economic and demographic growth, the United States was also relatively weak in a world of more powerful empires (principally the British and the French). Moreover, the American revolutionaries gambled their future on what was then a risky form of government: a republic in which elections determined leadership.

Fortunately, the new nation possessed a consummate generation of political leaders, subsequently known as the Founding Fathers. They had rescued the United States from the impotence of its original constitution (the Articles of Confederation) by crafting and ratifying the federal Constitution of 1787. But during the early 1790s, the Founders became bitterly polarized into rival political parties. This development shocked them all, for they had designed the Constitution to discourage organized partisanship. Led by George Washington, John Adams, John Marshall, and Alexander Hamilton, the Federalist party initially dominated the country. Their opponents, who called themselves Republicans, emerged under the leadership of Thomas Jefferson, James Madison, Albert Gallatin, George Clinton, and Aaron Burr.

Hostile to the concept of political parties, neither group accepted the legitimacy of the other. Each believed that its party alone represented the public will and defended the public good. Consequently, their opponents had to be insidious conspirators, determined to destroy both freedom and union. The partisans were so shrill because the stakes seemed so high: nothing less than the survival of free government in the United States, deemed the last, best hope for liberty in the world.

The parties differed ideologically over the proper degree of democracy needed to sustain the republic. The Federalists insisted that the United States primarily needed a stable and respectable government that was secure in the public esteem. The common people should, they argued, elect and sustain a cohesive political elite defined by their superior education, wealth, and status — as well as by their commitment to the federal union, to a republican form of government, and to civil liberties. Once elected, such republican rulers should govern free from "licentious" criticism, which could erode their public esteem. For if the government lost respectability, the nation would spiral downward, beginning with the triumph of demagogues, leading to anarchy and civil war, and culminating in military tyranny. The Republican leaders, however, waxed democratic to celebrate their own subordination to public opinion — and their vigilance in exposing the Federalists as crypto-monarchists and would-be aristocrats plotting to subvert the republican form of government.

The internal debate over democracy and stability became entangled in the great foreign policy crisis of the 1790s: the globe-spanning warfare between France and Great Britain that imperiled American commerce on the high seas. Both powers pressured the neutral United States for assistance. The British relied on America's economic dependence on British imports and its vulnerability to the superior might of the British navy. The French expected American gratitude for their help in defeating the British in the War of the American Revolution, securing American independence. After 1789, when the French Revolution toppled the monarchy and established a republic, the French also enjoyed the Americans' identification with their cause. The British, in contrast, were associated in American minds with monarchy, aristocracy, and the corruption of public liberties.

Initially pervasive, the American sympathy for France weakened during the mid-1790s, when the French revolutionaries initiated a Reign of Terror that killed thousands. Thereafter, the Federalists concluded that France was a perversion of republicanism and a greater threat than the British to the neutrality — and to the survival — of the United States. The Federalists insisted that they alone could defend the nation against France's deluded partisans, both within and without the United States. Although sobered by the French bloodshed, American Republicans still hoped that their fellow republic would survive its war with Europe's monarchs and aristocrats. And in the new Federalist enthusiasm for British victories, the Republicans detected a revival of the Toryism that threatened America's own experiment in republican government.

Although both parties favored neutrality, each suspected the other of covertly tilting toward one belligerent or the other. In 1794 the Washington administration negotiated Jay's Treaty, which resolved trade and border disputes with Great Britain. The Republicans, however, agreed with the French that the new treaty violated the Franco-American treaty of alliance. To bring pressure on the Americans, in 1796 the French unleashed their privateers to seize hundreds of American ships on the high seas.

In early 1797 that crisis fell to a new president, John Adams, who succeeded Washington by narrowly prevailing over Thomas Jefferson in the election of 1796. As the second-place candidate, Jefferson became vice president — to the discomfort of both parties. To ease the foreign crisis, Adams sent three envoys to negotiate with the French. But when French officials demanded bribes and an American loan to France — which would have ruptured America's neutrality — the offended envoys broke off negotiations and sent dispatches to the president. On March 19, 1798, Adams alerted Congress and requested preparations for war. When suspicious Republican congressmen demanded to see the dispatches, Adams happily complied. Newspapers published the insulting particulars, which outraged most of the American public and embarrassed the Republicans.

During the Second Session of the Fifth Congress, the Federalists had firm control of the Senate and a narrow edge (55–51) in the House. The partisan distribution of congressmen revealed a sectional divide, with the Federalists prevailing in the northern states (40 of 57 seats) and the Republicans in the southern (34 of 49 seats). Because of the close margin in the House and the moderation of some of its Federalists, the hard-line leaders often had to temper their most extreme proposals. Senator Theodore Sedgwick of Massachusetts lamented that Federalist measures had to be "graduated by the feelings and opinions of the most cool and feeble friends." During May, Congress fell just short of formally declaring war by suspending the treaty of alliance, curtailing commerce with France, expanding the army, fortifying the seaports, establishing a navy, and authorizing attacks on French privateers and warships.

With good cause, Republican leaders suspected the Federalists of maximizing the crisis for political advantage. Congressman Albert Gallatin of Pennsylvania charged that the Federalists were "led away by imaginary fears, or wished to improve the temporary alarm they had themselves created, for the purpose of assuming and exercising arbitrary power." The Republicans believed that reconciliation with France was still feasible — if they could slow the Federalists' drive to provoke a war.

Appalled by the Republican criticism, the Federalists depicted their opponents as French partisans who were undercutting American unity. Alarmed by the French victories in Europe, the Federalists noted France's skill at using agents and dissidents to subvert Italy, the Netherlands, and Switzerland from within, inviting French invasion from without. During the spring of 1798, the Federalists were especially troubled by news of another uprising against British rule in Ireland. Known as the United Irishmen, the rebels looked to France for inspiration and aid. Surely, the Federalists reasoned, the French meant similarly to subvert the United States with Irish immigrants and Republican sabotage. On April 20, 1798, Congressman John Allen of Connecticut announced: "I believe there are men in this country, in this House, whose hatred and abhorrence of our Government leads them to prefer another, profligate and ferocious as it is." For evidence, the Federalists made much of the brutal boasts by French officials that they possessed a "French party in America" that would undermine the administration if it did not meet their demands.

The Federalists also bristled at the criticism in the Republican newspapers, especially the Philadelphia *Aurora,* published by Benjamin Franklin Bache. In the 1790s American newspapers were small operations that ordinarily appeared only once or twice a week and depended on an entrepreneur who was at once editor, printer, publisher, and bookseller (and sometimes postmaster). To make a profit, most newspapers needed government contracts to print laws and legislative proceedings. This need drove ambitious printers increasingly to champion one political party or the other in order to get, or keep, state or national patronage. As rival editors grew ever more shrill, they earned the animus of the leaders in the opposing party.

The Federalists insisted that an unregulated and irresponsible press favored obscure and venal demagogues by driving from politics the respectable people who cherished their reputations. Although there were many more Federalist than Republican newspapers in 1798, Allen complained, "A flood of calumny is constantly poured forth against those whom the people have chosen as the guardians of the nation." Considering such criticism seditious, Federalist congressmen prepared legislation to intimidate Republican editors and congressmen.

The Federalist leaders found models in the alien and sedition acts that Parliament had passed to suppress French support in Great Britain. Beginning in 1793, the British administration of William Pitt (the Younger) systematically prosecuted and suppressed political agitators who had sympathized with the French Revolution and demanded republican reforms at home. In the most famous case, jurors condemned in absentia the British-born American revolutionary Tom Paine for publishing his *Rights of Man* in England. By 1798, both Paine and the French Revolution had also become horrific points of reference for American Federalists, who no longer blanched from identification with Britain. Indeed, Federalist congressmen openly praised the British alien and sedition acts. On June 19, Robert Goodloe Harper of South Carolina warned, "Unless we follow their example, we shall not like them, escape the scourge which awaits us." Of course, that open admiration for British repression confirmed the Republicans' suspicions of a Federalist plot to eviscerate the American republic.

The prime architects and spokesmen for the Alien and Sedition Acts were three especially voluble and aggressive congressmen: John Allen (1763–1812) of Connecticut, Robert Goodloe Harper (1765–1825) of South Carolina, and Harrison Gray Otis (1765–1848) of Massachusetts. All were lawyers, relatively young (in their thirties) and new to Congress (arriving in 1795 or 1797). Given the rapid turnover of legislators and the lack of permanent committees, seniority mattered less than personal charisma, social connections, and eloquent discourse. A tall, imposing, grim man, Allen was a former military officer; he was the most virulent congressman in his hatred of Republicanism and the most impatient of constitutional restraints. He assured Congress, "Liberty of the press and of opinion is calculated to destroy all confidence between man and man; it leads to the dissolution of every bond of union." Compared to Allen, Harper was only a bit less intemperate but significantly more handsome, eloquent, dapper, and conceited. A skilled if irresponsible politician, he mastered a folksy style that secured his election by the farmers of his rural southern district. The scion of a wealthy and distinguished Boston family, Otis was the most elegant, eloquent, and self-assured of the three. Although skilled at electioneering, he privately expressed contempt for the public, disdaining "the duped and deluded mob whose hosannas and execrations are as much mechanical and responsive as the pipes of an organ." Ambitious young politicians, the three men saw the crisis of 1798 as their opportunity to advance by perpetuating Federalist power. Instead, their identification with the Alien and Sedition Acts would soon blight their prospects as it undermined their party.

The first of the controversial laws was the Naturalization Act of June 18, 1798, which expressed the Federalist distrust of immigrants. During the 1790s, immigrants came primarily from Ireland and rallied to the Republican party, which better expressed their democratic aspirations and their animus toward the British Empire. Moreover, in this decade (and culminating in 1798), Irish radicals staged a spate of violent but failed uprisings against British rule; hundreds of defeated radicals sought refuge in the United States, where they exercised their formidable political abilities for the Republicans. Persuaded that the Irish were uncivilized and turbulent, the Federalists longed to discourage their arrival and frustrate their participation in politics.

Initially, the hard-line Federalists proposed banning further immigration and denying to those who had already arrived, but not yet been naturalized, both the vote and the right to hold office. In the House on May 1, Harper insisted, "The time is now come when it will be proper to declare that nothing but birth shall entitle a man to citizenship in this country." But his proposal lost by a 2–1 margin when moderate Federalists balked. The Federalists instead settled for a bill that extended the period for naturalization to fourteen years from the previous five. The bill also proposed a system for registering immigrants, requiring them to report to the district court within forty-eight hours of entry; resident aliens had six months to do the same after the bill became law. The bill passed the House by a single vote, 41–40.

As a permanent wartime statute enacted with bipartisan support, the Alien Enemies Act was the wild card among the Alien and Sedition Acts. Most Republicans reluctantly agreed with the Federalists on the need to authorize the executive branch to regulate, arrest, or deport resident aliens from an enemy power *in the event of war.* With relatively little debate, the House passed the bill on June 26; the Senate concurred on July 3; and the president signed it into law on July 6. Because the conflict with France never became an overt, declared war, the United States never applied this act during the crisis of 1798–1800.

The Federalists invested greater energy in the more controversial Alien Act. Although temporary (limited to two years), it applied to all foreign-born and persons not yet naturalized even without a declaration of war. Unlike the other alien acts, this measure began in the Senate in late April. It immediately gave the president authority to expel any alien whom he judged "dangerous to the peace and safety of the United States" — without a hearing (much less a trial) and without even specifying charges. If the person failed to depart within his assigned time, the president could force his deportation or prosecute him. If convicted, the alien faced up to three years in prison and could never become a citizen.

Passed by the Senate on June 8, the bill went to the House, where it faced a more vigorous Republican opposition led by Albert Gallatin (1761–1849) of Pennsylvania and Edward Livingston (1764–1849) of New York. The Federalists derided Gallatin, a Swiss immigrant of modest means, for his foreign origins, French accent, and frontier residence. But he repeatedly turned the tables with his incisive mind, debater's tenacity, keen timing, and mastery of public finance. By contrast, Livingston could rely on wealth, connections, and the social graces garnered by birth into a leading family of landlords, by his education at Princeton, and by his success as a lawyer in New York City. Known as "Beau Ned" for his elegance in manner and attire, Livingston should have been, the Federalists insisted, one of their own. Instead, he earned their enmity as a traitor to gentility for shrewdly preferring the Republican party as the better long-range bet for his political career.

Gallatin and Livingston denounced the Alien Act as an unconstitutional encroachment on the right of states to control aliens and on the right of individuals against arbitrary procedures. They emphasized the Tenth Amendment (part of the Bill of Rights), which stated that all rights not delegated to the federal government belonged to the states (unless specifically prohibited to them). They noted that the Constitution granted the federal government no specific power to banish or remove aliens. In debate on June 26, Livingston bluntly exposed the arbitrary nature of the bill:

> A careless word, perhaps misrepresented, or never spoken, may be sufficient evidence; . . . no innocence can protect, no circumspection can avoid the jealousy of suspicion; surrounded by spies, informers, and all that infamous herd which fatten under laws like this, the unfortunate

stranger will never know either of the law, or of the accusation, or of the judgment, until the moment it is put in execution.

Led by Otis and Harper, the Federalists countered with a broad construction of the Constitution as empowering the federal government to take all measures necessary for its own survival and to defend the Union. And they insisted that aliens had no rights under the Constitution except those extended as a matter of courtesy. On June 21, by a bare margin of 6 votes, the House passed the act, which proved largely inconsequential. Feeling scrupulous, President Adams never applied it. The Alien Act expired in June 1800 without a single alien deported or imprisoned — although some nervous French immigrants left of their own accord.

Of the four laws, the most contentious, initially efficacious, and ultimately disastrous (to the Federalists) was the Sedition Act. Whereas the three alien acts pinched the immigrant minority, the Sedition Act affected the citizen majority. It became a federal crime to utter or publish "any false, scandalous, and malicious writing or writings against the government of the United States or the President of the United States, with intent to defame . . . or to bring them into contempt or disrepute." The guilty faced penalties of up to $2,000 and two years in prison.

The congressional and press debates over the act revealed, as never before, a divergence within the American elite over the meaning of "free speech." The Federalists championed a relatively limited but time-honored definition rooted in the prerevolutionary English common law, while the Republicans developed a new, more expansive definition, the one usually recognized today.

The common law tradition maintained that speech was free when its initial publication was not impeded, but that it was subsequently liable for prosecution as "sedition" if the words undermined public respect for the government. Under English common law, truth was no defense against a charge of sedition; indeed, a "true" statement was more likely to affect the government. Founded on a pessimism about human nature, the law of seditious libel held that the erosion of the majesty of government was the slippery slope to anarchy and civil war.

After the lapse of official censorship in 1694, the British government relied on the intimidating power of prosecution after publication. The consummate interpreter of the common law, Sir William Blackstone, explained that the law of seditious libel was fully compatible with a proper notion of a free press: "The *liberty of the press* is indeed essential to the nature of a free state; but this consists in laying no *previous* restraints upon publications, and not in freedom from censure for criminal matter when published. . . . Thus the will of individuals is still left free; the abuse only of that free-will is the object of legal punishment." Of course, the prospect of subsequent prosecution encouraged self-censorship, achieving approximately the same end as the former system of government licensing.

Before 1798, the American Founders said surprisingly little to define what they meant by "freedom of speech" or "freedom of the press." Neither at the Constitutional Convention nor even in passing the Bill of Rights (which included the First Amendment barring federal — but not state — interference with a free speech and a free press) did the members debate or specify their intent. When the Founders did attempt a definition, their statements usually echoed Blackstone.

Consequently, the Federalist congressmen of 1798 insisted that their Sedition Act defended traditional liberty by subsequently punishing only "licentious speech" without burdening responsible "free speech" with prior censorship. Indeed, the Federalists congratulated themselves for liberalizing the common law of sedition in three ways. First, their act mandated that juries, rather than judges, would determine whether words were seditious. Second, they required courts to accept truth as a legal defense against sedition. Third, prosecutors had to prove that the defendant maliciously intended to undermine respect for the government. Of course, these concessions fell short of today's libertarian conviction that words are not criminal unless they directly exhort a crime and that the burden of proof should fall on the prosecutor rather than the defendant.

The Sedition Act provoked the Republicans to begin to formulate a broader definition of freedom of speech and the press — and to narrow the power of government over them. But rather than recognize (or concede) the novelty of their definition, the Republicans argued that they were simply defending the Bill of Rights. They insisted that the First Amendment already barred the federal courts from applying the common law of sedition. (Generally, however, the Republicans accepted that state courts could and should apply that law.)

The Republicans insisted that subsequent prosecution for sedition was every bit as chilling as prior censorship in suppressing the free circulation of ideas that was essential to a republic. In the House of Representatives on July 10, John Nicholas of Virginia warned that printers "would be afraid of publishing the truth, as, though true, it might not always be in their power to establish the truth to the satisfaction of a court of justice." And without a truly free press, elections could not be free and fair. James Madison explained:

> [In] competitions between those who are and those who are not members of the Government, what will be the situation of the competitors?

> Not equal: because the characters of the former will be covered by the Sedition Act from animadversions exposing them to disrepute among the people, whilst the latter may be exposed to the contempt and hatred of the people without a violation of the act. What will be the situation of the people? Not free: because they will be compelled to make their election between competitors whose pretensions they are not permitted by the act equally to examine, to discuss and to ascertain. And from both these situations will not those in power derive an undue advantage for continuing themselves in it, which, by impairing the right of election, endangers the blessings of the Government founded upon it?

Despite the Republicans' opposition, Federalist majorities passed the Sedition Act in the Senate on July 4 (18–6) and in the House on July 10 (44–41). President Adams signed the bill into law on July 14. A temporary law, it would expire on March 3, 1801, along with the term of the president. John Marshall was the only Federalist leader perceptive enough to see that the Alien and Sedition Acts were politically foolish because they were "calculated to create, unnecessarily, discontents and jealousies."

In contrast to the Alien Act, the administration did not neglect to enforce the Sedition Act. Secretary of State Timothy Pickering, the most extreme Federalist in the Cabinet, took the lead in promoting arrests by federal marshals and coordinating prosecutions by federal district attorneys. Federal judges cooperated by charging grand juries with their duty to identify and indict offenses against the Sedition Law. Often federal officials responded to pressure from Federalist newspaper editors, who were especially keen to punish and ruin their Republican competitors. Dependent on juries for conviction, prosecutors secured indictments only in districts where Federalism enjoyed strong support. They pressed sixteen cases in the northern states, where it was more popular, and only one — that of the journalist James Thomson Callender — in the South, where the party was weaker.

As the Republicans predicted, the Federalist concessions in the Sedition Act proved hollow. In practice, the "truth" of political opinions could not be proven, putting an unfair and expensive burden on defendants, who lost the customary presumption of innocence. And because federal marshals slanted the selection of juries, they often demonstrated as much partiality as judges for the party in power. Federal authorities also applied the Sedition Act to punish only critics of the administration, despite the greater venom of Federalist papers against Republican legislators and editors.

The law's first victim was a congressman, Matthew Lyon, who stood for everything the Federalists despised and feared in Republicans. A poorly educated immigrant from Ireland, Lyon had risen from indentured servitude through sharp dealing and a fortunate marriage to become a wealthy land speculator and ironworks owner in Vermont. He served as a militia officer in the Revolution, but his reputation suffered from charges of cowardice, which the Federalists subsequently hurled at him at every opportunity. After the war, Lyon became a populist politician and was elected in 1796 to Congress, where his crude manners and bombastic speech thoroughly offended the Federalists. In January 1798 Roger Griswold of Connecticut, a Federalist, insulted Lyon's war record. In response, Lyon spat in Griswold's face. The Federalists tried to expel Lyon but lacked the necessary two-thirds majority. Taking his own vengeance in the House, Griswold attacked Lyon with a hickory cane while Lyon fought back with fire tongs — a violent scene that symbolized the political rancor of the decade.

The Sedition Act gave the Federalists a new opportunity to ruin Lyon when he published a blunt attack on President Adams, saying he was driven by "an unbounded thirst for ridiculous pomp, foolish adulation, or selfish avarice." Although Federalist newspapers routinely said far worse about Lyon, he faced prosecution; they did not. Unable to prove the truth of his opinions to a jury dominated by Federalists, Lyon was convicted of sedition that October. The federal judge sentenced him to four months in jail and fined him $1,000. Rendered a political martyr for Republicanism, Lyon won reelection from his prison cell by twice the margin of his previous victory. Republican newspapers spread his story, and Republican politicians conspicuously paid his fine. Perhaps because of the political consequences, the federal authorities prosecuted no other congressman under the Sedition Act, instead targeting Republican journalists.

In the short term, however, Lyon's reelection was a conspicuous exception, as the war fever remained sufficiently strong for the Federalists to strengthen their hold on the House of Representatives in the election of 1798 (which in some states occurred in early 1799). When the Sixth Congress convened in 1799, the Federalists held 63 seats in the House to the Republicans' 43. The most striking development was the weakened sectional distinction between the parties as the Federalists lost a few northern seats but captured many more in the South.

In part, the Federalists scored electoral gains by exploiting a Republican miscalculation. In late 1798, the Republican state governments of Kentucky and Virginia adopted resolutions denouncing the Alien and Sedition Acts as unconstitutional. They further hinted that states could and should nullify the enforcement of such laws within their bounds — a states' rights challenge to federal supremacy. The other state legislatures, however, blanched at the doctrine of nullification and rejected the Kentucky and Virginia resolves, which proved a political liability for the Republicans in the approaching election.

Thereafter, however, the Federalists lost popularity as the Republicans masterfully exploited the news of further Sedition Act convictions and linked them to the increased federal taxes to fund the expanding army and navy. Jefferson shrewdly predicted the rapid decline of popular support for the Federalists: "This disease of the imagination will pass over, because the patients are essentially republican. Indeed, the Doctor is now on his way to cure it, in the guise of a tax gatherer." Averse to paying taxes, the public rallied to the Republican suggestions that the Federalists were plotting to ruin the common people and the republic.

And a growing network of Republican newspapers defied the Sedition Act to spread the party message, often by highlighting Federalist abuses of the law. Designed to suppress the small but vocal Republican press, the Alien and Sedition Acts backfired, as more newspapers became defiant partisans of the opposition party. The historian Jeffrey L. Pasley calculates that by 1800 the nation had 85 partisan Republican papers, a dramatic increase from the 51 of 1798. In August 1800 the Federalist senator Uriah Tracy of Connecticut complained that the Republicans were "establishing Democratic presses and newspapers in almost every town and county of the country."

Meanwhile, the war fever cooled, despite American naval victories in the undeclared "quasi-war." Responding to positive French signals, Adams sent another diplomatic delegation to Paris to seek peace during the fall of 1799. And he rejected Hamilton's advice to use military force to confront Virginia over its resolutions against the Alien and Sedition Acts. Instead, during the spring of 1800, Adams demobilized most of the army. This action infuriated Hamilton and the other staunch Federalists, who wished to prolong the crisis as a political boon. The rancorous division in the ranks of the Federalists and the public dismay at their record helped Jefferson to defeat Adams in the presidential election that fall. The Republicans also captured a split in the Senate and clear control of the House: 65–41 seats. Soon, news arrived that on October 3, 1800, the American and French diplomats had negotiated a settlement, preserving America's neutrality and ending the crisis.

The election of 1800 was pivotal, for the Federalists thereafter declined into political irrelevance. The Republicans interpreted their victory as a mandate for free speech and a free press — free at least from interference by the federal government. Although Federalist congressmen stubbornly tried to renew the expiring Sedition Act, the Republicans ensured its demise, and the new president pardoned the men convicted under that law. In his first inaugural address, Jefferson eloquently argued: "If there be any among us who would wish to dissolve this Union or to change its republican form, let them stand undisturbed as monuments of the safety with which error of opinion may be tolerated where reason is left free to combat it." This defense of public debate also implicitly legitimized political parties, which depended on open, indeed aggressive, criticism of officeholders. Previously regarded as threats to the republic, parties became grudgingly accepted as unavoidable — and perhaps even necessary — in a republic.

In practice, however, Jefferson and his fellow Republicans proved less than consistent civil libertarians. In 1804 the new president assured Abigail Adams, "While we deny that Congress have a right to controul the freedom of the press, we have ever asserted the right of the states, and their exclusive right to do so." Indeed, Jefferson urged Republican governors to prosecute the most vociferous Federalist printers in their state courts. The most famous case occurred in 1804, when the Republican administration of New York State indicted Harry Croswell, editor of the Federalist newspaper *The Wasp*. The state supreme court convicted him of seditious libel for printing the story — which was true — that Jefferson, in the 1790s, had subsidized the scandalmongering journalist James Thomson Callender. The republican judge, Morgan Lewis, dismissed Croswell's defense on the grounds that, according to state law, truth was irrelevant against a charge of seditious libel. A belated convert to freedom of the press, Alexander Hamilton was Croswell's lawyer.

Jeffersonian Republican inconsistency attests that no matter how venerable, no constitutional right survives without continuous definition and defense by the living against the powerful. In 1918 and again in 1940 Congress adopted new, albeit temporary, sedition acts to restrict speech and publication. The contest over the Alien and Sedition Acts was but the first of many and ongoing battles to define the intertwined freedoms of speech and the press.

— Alan Taylor

BIBLIOGRAPHICAL NOTES

For congressional debates during the 1790s, the primary source is United States Congress, *Debates and Proceedings in the Congress of the United States, 1789–1825,* 42 vols. (Washington, D.C., 1834–56). Scholarly convention abbreviates this compilation as the *Annals of Congress.*

For treatments of the Alien and Sedition Acts and the crisis with France, see Alexander DeConde, *The Quasi-War: The Politics and Diplomacy of the Undeclared War with France, 1797–1801* (New York, 1966); John C. Miller, *Crisis in Freedom: The Alien and Sedition Acts* (Boston, 1951); and James Morton Smith, *Freedom's*

Fetters: The Alien and Sedition Laws and American Civil Liberties (Ithaca, N.Y., 1966).

For the political practices and ideologies of the era, see Doron Ben-Atar and Barbara Oberg, *Federalists Reconsidered* (Charlottesville, Va., 1998); Aleine Austin, *Matthew Lyon: "New Man" of the Democratic Revolution, 1749–1822* (University Park, Pa., 1981); Richard Buel Jr., *Securing the Republic: Ideology in American Politics, 1789–1815* (Ithaca, N.Y., 1972); Michael Durey, *Transatlantic Radicals and the Early American Republic* (Lawrence, Kans., 1997); Stanley Elkins and Eric McKitrick, *The Age of Federalism* (New York, 1993); David Hackett Fischer, *The Revolution of American Conservatism: The Federalist Party in the Era of Jeffersonian Democracy* (New York, 1965); and James Roger Sharp, *American Politics in the Early Republic: The New Nation in Crisis* (New Haven, Conn., 1993).

For the early American press and civil liberties, see Leonard W. Levy, *Legacy of Suppression: Freedom of Speech and Press in Early American History* (Cambridge, Mass., 1964), and Jeffrey L. Pasley, *"The Tyranny of Printers": Newspaper Politics in the Early American Republic* (Charlottesville, Va., 2001).

For Congress during the 1790s, see Kenneth R. Bowling and Donald R. Kennon, eds., *Neither Separate nor Equal: Congress in the 1790s* (Athens, Ohio, 2000); Bowling and Kennon, eds., *The House and Senate in the 1790s: Petitioning, Lobbying, and Institutional Development* (Athens, Ohio, 2002); and David P. Currie, *The Constitution in Congress: The Federalist Period, 1789–1801* (Chicago, 1997).

5

The Early Impact of Slavery

SLAVERY WAS RELATIVELY rarely the subject of specific legislation in the early congresses, but it was always a divisive issue looming over the legislative process. The Revolution had affected slavery in two crucial ways. First, in its rhetoric it had reinforced the idea, already widespread in the colonial era, that slavery was a moral abomination — as in the reference in the Declaration of Independence to the "self-evident" truth that "all men are created equal." Second, the Revolution had caused the northern states to abolish slavery, some during the war itself and others in "gradual abolition" schemes that were not complete until the 1840s. The Revolution also weakened slavery in the South, although this effect turned out to be temporary. It promoted a wave of manumissions, especially in the states of the Upper South, and it provided opportunities for large numbers of African Americans to seize their own freedom through military service, by self-purchase, and particularly by escaping from their owners. In the late colonial era, slavery had been a marginal institution in the North and there had been vocal critics of its immorality everywhere. In the early republic, however, slavery was more fully sectional and a palpable violation of the ideals for which Americans had ostensibly fought the Revolutionary War.

The early congresses reflected both legacies. No matter how hard the congressmen tried to ignore slavery — and they tried very hard — they could never avoid the fact that it was a major institution in the American political economy. The 700,000 enslaved African Americans in 1790 made up nearly one-fifth of the U.S. population: 2 percent of the northern population and 33 percent of the southern. The 2.5 million enslaved African Americans in 1840 made up 15 percent of the U.S. population and 44 percent of the southern population. There were still 1,100 slaves in the North in 1840, but they were part of a total northern population of 9.7 million. These figures only begin to suggest slavery's impact on the American economy, society, and culture, although they clearly demonstrate its sectional nature. Congress could not help but be influenced by an institution of this magnitude. The legislators could not talk about taxes, foreign policy, or the expansion of U.S. territory unless they reckoned with the impact of slavery. Even when they did not discuss slavery directly, they knew that their decisions affected the power and security of an extremely influential "interest group." From 1788 to 1850, the president was a slaveholder 80 percent of the time, while 18 of the 31 Supreme Court justices owned slaves. In the House of Representatives, the Speaker was a slaveholder 66 percent of the time, and the Ways and Means chairman, 68 percent of the time. Many of the rank-and-file congressmen also owned slaves. The members of this "slave power" generally demanded protection for slavery. When they could not win protection, they demanded silence about it.

Slavery shaped many aspects of the early congresses: their basic organization, the kinds of issues they could tackle, and the ways in which they handled a range of issues far broader than those concerning slavery itself. In particular, slavery made it hard for congressmen to consider anything that required them to reckon with the structure of the economy. The early congresses experienced relatively few of the bitter sectional conflicts that became familiar in the antebellum decades, such as the gag rule to table abolitionist petitions without reading them, the Compromise of 1850 with its infamous Fugitive Slave Law, and the Kansas-Nebraska Act, which introduced slavery into territory north of the Missouri Compromise line. In the early republic, few southern congressmen were prepared to defend slavery as directly and openly as they later would. In fact, surveying the legislation restricting the slave trade, Don Fehrenbacher has recently concluded that the early congressional policies were "vigorously abolitionist." This may be an exaggeration, although Congress did ban the importation of slaves into the United States in 1807 — not only by a landslide vote (113–5), but with the ban taking effect at the first moment allowed by the Constitution's slave trade clause (January 1, 1808). Nevertheless, it is incorrect to date the "appearance" of slavery as a divisive issue in Congress to the Missouri debates of 1819–1820, as generations of historians have done. The Missouri debates were a culmination of earlier history every bit as much as they were the start of something new (Thomas Jefferson's "fire bell in the night"). Slavery — or the fact that the United States was, as Lincoln later said, "half slave and half free" — influenced the early congresses in many ways.

The composition of the early congresses was determined by the compromises embedded in the Constitution — though not in precisely the way the framers had intended. "Equal" representation of states in the Senate had been expected to favor the North especially by boosting the power of the small New England states. Meanwhile, proportional representation in the House of Representatives, using the three-fifths rule to count slaves, had been expected to favor the South by boosting the power of the states with large slave populations, as indeed it did. Under the three-fifths clause, seats in the House were apportioned to the states by what was called their "federal populations": their free populations plus three-fifths of their slave populations. Today, the three-fifths clause is often interpreted as an insulting definition of enslaved African Americans as "three-fifths of a person." It was actually much worse. Because it granted the South extra seats in the House for slaves — whose interests were in no sense "represented" — it enhanced the power of the owners of slaves to defend the institution of slavery.

As it turned out, both "compromises" actually favored the southern states in Congress. The Senate part of the original deal was undone almost immediately. Another "small" New England state, Vermont, was added in 1791, but then two "small" southern states were admitted — Kentucky in 1792 and Tennessee in 1796. After the admission of Ohio (1803), Congress maintained a "balance": Louisiana (1812), Indiana (1816), Mississippi (1817), Illinois (1818), Alabama (1819), and then the formal trade of Maine (1820) for Missouri (1821). The three-fifths ratio, meanwhile, failed to create southern majorities in the House. European immigrants avoided the slave South but flocked in large numbers to the free North. As a result, House apportionments for the growing northern free population overwhelmed the so-called slave representation of the three-fifths clause. Yet the "extra" southern seats were still decisive in close votes. One of the most famous examples, although not the first, came at the end of the Missouri debates: the 1820 vote on whether to insist that Missouri abolish slavery as a condition of statehood. Introduced by James Tallmadge Jr., a Republican from New York, in the House and championed by Rufus King, a Federalist from New York, in the Senate — King had helped to frame the three-fifths clause in the first place as a member of the 1787 Philadelphia convention — Missouri abolition lost in 1820 by three votes (90–87) in a House where "slave representation" accounted for 17 of the southern seats. *Every* southern member voted to perpetuate slavery in Missouri. Although 14 northern members voted with them, these "doughfaces" ("northern men with southern principles") could not have swung the decision to the South without the "slave representation" of the three-fifths clause.

As Leonard Richards has shown, the "slave representation" also boosted southern power in the House in another way. The founders had not anticipated the emergence of the national political parties. As it happened, the structure of these parties amplified the effects of the three-fifths clause. In the "caucus" system, which the parties began to elaborate in the early 1790s, the members of each party met regularly to determine legislative priorities, tactics, and committee assignments, as well as to nominate presidential candidates. A Federalist newspaper complained in 1802 about this "economical plan of making laws" by the Republican (Jeffersonian) majority. "All business is to be settled in *caucuses* before it comes before the House; and the arguments or motives be given in *newspapers* afterwards. The federal [Federalist party] members are to be treated as nullities." Through the Republican caucus, southern members were able to control the House agenda despite the northern majority of total House seats. The power of a state delegation in the caucus rested on the number of party members it elected. While the northern states elected more congressmen, the southern states elected more Republican (Jeffersonian) congressmen, as they later elected more Democratic (Jacksonian) congressmen. Thus, the South held a majority in the caucus of what was almost always the majority party. Because of the caucus's amplification of the three-fifths clause, Southerners controlled the House. They chose Speakers, chaired the major committees, and forged legislative agendas. Northern Republicans sometimes abandoned the decisions of their party caucus on important sectional votes (with the attempt to abolish slavery in Missouri again a good example), but Southerners ran the House.

Southerners wanted to control the speech of Northerners on the floor. In particular, they wanted to prevent speeches against slavery. In the Missouri debates, when Northerners condemned slavery at length, Southerners argued that Congress had no right to talk about slavery at all, since speeches against slavery would encourage slave rebellions. Edward Colston, a Federalist from Virginia, charged that the northern speakers were actually "endeavoring to excite a servile war." This charge seemed to be confirmed when state officials in South Carolina noticed that Denmark Vesey had a copy of Rufus King's Missouri speeches. (Vesey was the rebel leader whose plan to subvert the slave regime by force in Charleston was betrayed shortly before it was set to begin in 1822.)

Yet the effort to silence the debate about slavery did not start with Missouri; Southerners had been trying to enforce such a silence since the very creation of the United States. They wanted to avoid confrontations like the one that occurred in the Second Continental Congress on July 30, 1776, three weeks after the adoption of the Declaration of Independence, when Thomas Lynch of South Carolina threatened to destroy the new nation to protect the wealth of his constituents. "If it is debated, whether their slaves are their property," Lynch had warned, "there is an end of the Confederation." In 1790, in the first House of Representatives under the Constitution, James Madison of Virginia led an effort to make the silencing strategy explicit. Under his management, the House responded to petitions to end the slave trade before the date specified in the Constitution (1808) with a report stating its intention to silence debate about slavery forever — by calling congressional action unconstitutional. "The Congress," this resolution said, "have no authority to interfere in the emancipation of slaves, or in the treatment of them within any of the States." It was a remarkable statement. President George Washington saw it as a cause for relief that "the slave business has at last [been] put to rest and will scarce awake."

The nature of Madison's victory becomes even clearer if we compare the final language, that Congress could not interfere in the emancipation or treatment of slaves, with the draft that it replaced. Acting in "committee of the whole," Congress had adopted a report that was much too explicit for southern tastes, declaring that Congress could not ban the slave trade before 1808 and that, "by a fair construction of the Constitution," it was "equally restrained from interfering in the emancipation of slaves, who already are, or who may, within the period mentioned, be imported into, or born within, any of the said States." Then it went further:

> That Congress have no authority to interfere in the internal regulations of particular States, relative to the instructions of slaves in the principles of morality and religion; to their comfortable clothing, accommodations and subsistence; to the regulation of their marriages, and the prevention of the violation of the rights thereof, or to the separation of children from their parents; to a comfortable provision in cases of sickness, age, or infirmity; or to the seizure, transportation, or sale of free negroes; but [Congress] have the fullest confidence in the wisdom and humanity of the Legislatures of the several States, that they will . . . promote the objects mentioned . . . and every other measure that may tend to the happiness of slaves.

This, of course, was a bill of particulars against the institution of slavery. Madison's victory was in replacing it with the terse ban on any form of congressional interference.

The 1790 slave trade debate and the 1819–1820 Missouri debates represented dramatic breakdowns of this silencing strategy. It became so bad in 1790 that William Loughton Smith of South Carolina demanded to know, in reference to antislavery Quakers, whether "any of them [had] ever married a negro, or would any of them suffer their children to mix their blood with that of a black?" The Missouri debates created similarly intense moments. "How long will the desire of wealth," Arthur Livermore, a Republican from New Hampshire, cried, "render us blind to the sin of holding both the bodies and souls of our fellow men in chains!" The successes of the silencing strategy were far less dramatic, but they may well have been more significant. As the antebellum gag rule conflict suggests, one place to look for these successes in the early congresses is in the rules governing debate — and especially in the burst of House rules reform that began in 1811, when Kentucky's Henry Clay, a Republican, became the first powerful Speaker of the House. The early speakers had served primarily as moderators of debate; they were not party floor leaders. Clay, however, combined the roles of Speaker and leader of the majority party, creating a powerful position that could shape the House agenda.

More important, under Clay's leadership the House shifted much of its deliberative work from "committee of the whole" to standing committees that the Speaker appointed. "Committee of the whole" was a device to facilitate relatively free debate. One of its crucial features was that when the House voted in "committee of the whole," no printed roll calls identified the positions of individual members. Thus, for the 1790 slave trade debate, we do not know who voted for or against the draft with the bill of particulars against slavery. When "committee of the whole" was the primary mode of framing legislation, select and standing committees served merely as adjuncts for technical jobs such as investigating details and drafting bills as instructed by the larger House. Only in 1815 did standing committees receive a blanket authorization to originate legislation on their own. Starting in 1819, the Ways and Means Committee framed appropriation bills and submitted them to the floor rather than submitting lists of spending objects containing "blanks" for the dollar figures — to be filled through debate in "committee of the whole." This tighter organization, with the composition of committees determined by the Speaker, enhanced the power that Southerners could mobilize through their base in the Republican party caucus.

Historians and political scientists used to explain these rules changes as accommodations to a growing workload. Committee authority, it was argued, made the House a more efficient body, able to cope with its own increasing size and the increasing claims on its time from a larger and more complex agenda. Committee members became experts in the subject areas of their responsibilities and decided complex matters before they moved to the floor. Recently, political scientists have replaced the workload interpretation with one based on partisanship. The changes that "streamlined" House operations provoked loud resistance from its members, especially minority members, who considered them antidemocratic efforts to silence opposition. A study of the 1811 adoption of the "previous question" motion in the House, for example, shows that partisan considerations outweighed workload considerations in the decision. The "previous question" motion allowed the majority to silence the minority by producing an immediate vote on a bill. The Republicans won its adoption not only on an almost straight party-line vote but after 2 A.M. — and with no warning to the minority (Federalist) members that the vote would be taken. Because most of the Federalist members were Northerners, and because the Republican caucus amplified the power that the South enjoyed as a result of the three-fifths clause, this partisan analysis implies a sectional corollary, connecting the rules changes to the Southerners' efforts to control the speech of Northerners on the floor.

Still, "the slave business" could never be "put to rest" entirely. Slavery was relevant to all manner of other issues because it was a major institution in the American political economy. This fact became clear in the first session of the First Congress — and in relation to the first piece of legislation it considered: the tax bill that, as Madison proclaimed, would prove that the Constitution had enabled the country to escape the "imbecility" of the Articles of Confederation, which had required the unanimous consent of the state legislatures for a national tax. Madison is most often remembered today for activities other than his management of the first House of Representatives. We think of him as a leader in the Philadelphia convention that framed the Constitution, as the Publius who wrote the most important *Federalist* essays, and as the president who had to flee when British troops burned Washington during the War of 1812. Yet Madison, who was one of the most influential members of the Confederation Congress under the Articles, also made huge contributions as the floor leader of the first House. He introduced and managed critical legislation: the constitutional amendments that became the Bill of Rights; the creation of the executive departments of Foreign Affairs (State), Treasury, and War; and the first national tax, on imports. Madison later became the Republican leader in the House. In the First Congress, however, he was the floor manager whose leadership was acknowledged universally.

Madison's experience in the Confederation Congress had taught him that debates about the economy inevitably led to divisive debates about slavery. He therefore tried to persuade his colleagues to enact a tax bill without talking about the economy! He introduced a bill with the simple rates devised by the Confederation Congress and urged that it be adopted with minimal discussion. But this attempt to pass a simple tax law by acclamation failed immediately. Seizing the role they played for the next century, the Pennsylvania members demanded a protectionist schedule to promote manufacturing, launching the first of what became the depressingly long series of tariff debates. The members insisted on evaluating the economic impact of individual provisions on their constituents, with the Southerners claiming that their region would bear a disproportionate burden as consumers. Protective tariffs, Theodorick Bland of Virginia complained, taxed "the whole community, in order to put the money in the pockets of a few." Thomas Tudor Tucker of South Carolina called the tariff "a burthen on agriculture . . . big with oppression, and tending to burthen particular States." In the First Congress, the Northerners would have none of it. Slavery reduced the consumption of imported goods in the South because slaveholders enforced low consumption levels on their slaves in order to extract more profits from their labor. Thomas Fitzsimons of Pennsylvania "never could conceive that the consumption of those articles by the negroes of South Carolina would contribute to the revenue as much as that of the white inhabitants of the Eastern States." Fisher Ames of Massachusetts agreed: "Admitting the people of New England to live more moderate than the opulent citizens of Virginia and Carolina, yet they have not such a number of blacks among them, whose living is wretched, consequently the average consumption per head will be nearly the same."

Arguments like this, of course, struck at the southern pretension that slaveholders treated their slaves well — that African Americans, as James Jackson of Georgia asserted, "were better off in their present situation than they would be if they were manumitted." Madison tried to head off such debates. When Southerners offered moralistic temperance arguments to defend a high duty on molasses, the raw material for New England's rum industry, George Thatcher of Massachusetts lost his temper: "If the pernicious effects of New England rum have been justly lamented, what can be urged for negro slavery?" Madison assured his fellow Southerners that Thatcher had not expressed "either the deliberate temper of his own mind or the good sense of his constituents." Yet Madison was even more effective with a different tactic: presenting himself as the Southerner (and slaveholder) who condemned slavery as loudly as any Northerner.

Madison used this second tactic when Congress turned to the question of whether to tax the slave trade. Members from the Deep South such as South Carolina's Tucker demanded silence. Rhetoric against slavery, he argued, would "excite a great degree of restlessness in the minds of those it is intended to serve [i.e., the slaves], and that [restlessness] may be a cause for masters to use more rigor [i.e., violence] towards them than they might otherwise exert." Madison, however, knew what he was doing when he condemned not only the slave trade but slavery itself — the "evil," as he phrased it, of "considering the human race as a species of property." This tactic paid a high dividend for slaveholders when Madison used it to kill the $10 tax on imported slaves that the slave trade clause of the Constitution permitted Congress to enact. As a result of his effective management of the first House of Representatives, the forty thousand Africans sold into slavery in the United States before 1808 entered the country enslaved but "duty free."

Eight years later, when Congress turned to a "direct tax" on property, slaveholders found even more cause for alarm, for slaves were a huge fraction of the "property" that was owned in the South. Two clauses of the Constitution protected Southerners against heavy slave taxes: the three-fifths clause ("Representatives and direct taxes shall be apportioned . . .") and the direct tax clause ("No capitation, or other direct tax, shall be laid, unless in proportion to the census" taken according to the three-fifths clause). These mandates forced Congress, if it was going to levy a direct tax at all, to find a way to tax different forms of property — commercial wealth in the North, slaves in the South, agricultural land everywhere — within the rubric of apportionment. Congress managed to do this only twice before the Civil War: in 1798, during the "quasi-war" with France, and in 1813 and 1815, during the War of 1812. The framers had intended that the power to levy direct taxes would be used in precisely these situations, wartime emergencies. They had also intended that the direct taxes would be levied primarily on land and slaves. But the founders had not thought through the problem of how apportioned property taxes would work in practice.

The House figured out one way to make them work in 1798. After intense maneuvering by Northerners, Southerners, Federalists, and Republicans in various combinations, the House framed a tax whose complexity is impressive even to our own jaundiced age. The 1798 direct tax (1) set quotas for the states by their "federal" populations; (2) levied 50 cents on each slave aged 12 to 50; (3) levied a progressive tax on houses, exempting those worth less than $100, then setting brackets ranging from 0.2 to 1.0 percent; and (4) levied an *ad valorem* tax on land — but only in states where the slaves and houses failed to raise the total state quotas and at rates set independently in each state to make up the difference. The idea here was that the house tax would tap the wealth of northern merchants, on the assumption that they owned expensive houses. Yet this tax also reflected the rare circumstance of 1798: Federalist control of the House created an unusual opportunity for northern members to shape legislation. Virginia's Abraham Venable, a Republican, understood what the Federalists had done: if the "houses [were] taxed as the representatives of other property" in the North, the house tax worked in the South as "a double tax" because "the large slaveholders" who paid the slave tax also "generally occupied the largest houses." Northern merchants paid for their houses, southern planters paid for their slaves and their houses, and ordinary "yeoman farmers" paid only enough to meet their state quotas after the rich had paid their due.

The slaveholders had lost this political battle, but the Jeffersonian "Revolution of 1800" changed the political equation. Congress did not levy another direct tax until the War of 1812. By then, the Republican caucus had won control of the House, with the newly powerful Speaker in place and the beginning of the shift of power to the standing committees. This time, Congress dispensed with the details of the 1798 direct tax. Now the tax was apportioned to the states and then levied on land, houses, and slaves "at the rate each of them is worth in money." Despite what the law said, this Congress hoped that federal collectors would not have to assess the "value" of each individual slave. The 1813 direct tax offered the states 15 percent discounts if they opted to "assume" their quotas, using their own tax systems to raise the money. Most southern state tax systems charged flat rates per slave rather than attempting to assess an individual "value." If a state did not "assume" its quota, however, this Jeffersonian tax charged "yeoman farmers" a proportional burden — without a prior assessment of the property of the rich. The real lesson was the difficulty of framing direct taxes under the Constitution's apportionment rule. No matter how hard it was to enact tariffs — and no matter how much the Southerners resented having to pay for the tariff's protectionist subsidies to northern industries — direct taxes brought slavery to center stage in an intolerable way. Slavery made it almost impossible for Congress to levy any broad-based tax but the tariff.

Other issues also necessarily brought slavery onto the floor of Congress. From Jay's Treaty and the Haitian revolution in the 1790s through the Texas revolution in the 1830s and the Mexican War in the 1840s, foreign policy issues often required considerations of slavery. Jay's Treaty (1794) was a settlement with Britain of issues left outstanding from the Revolution, particularly U.S. trade access to the West Indies and British evacuation of military posts in the Northwest. It was controversial for many reasons, but one of its political problems was that it abandoned an American claim based on the initial Treaty of Paris (1783), which ended the Revolutionary War. That treaty stipulated that British troops would leave the United States without "carrying away any Negroes or other Property of the American Inhabitants." In fact, they "carried away" thousands of slaves, many to freedom and some to a new slavery in the West Indies. After the Senate ratified Jay's Treaty in 1795 by a bare two-thirds majority (20–10), Madison led an attempt to kill it in the House — to usurp the ratification power from the Senate. With the help of his new Republican lieutenant, Albert Gallatin of Pennsylvania (who had been elected to the House after his local leadership in the Whiskey Rebellion of 1794), Madison hit on the strategy of rejecting the appropriation to implement the treaty on the constitutional ground that the Senate could not originate a money bill in the guise of a treaty. The House's power to appropriate money, he argued, "may be viewed as co-operative with the Treaty power." When the House was asked to fund a treaty, it could give "due weight to the reasons which led to the Treaty, and to the circumstances of the existence of the Treaty" — in other words, it could kill an already ratified treaty.

The ensuing legislative battle was complex, but Madison ultimately failed to kill Jay's Treaty, largely because President Washington favored it. His main opponent in the House was Fisher Ames, the Federalist from Massachusetts. Looking very ill (he had been absent throughout the session) and having advertised his appearance effectively enough to pack the galleries, Ames showed up dressed in black to make a dramatic speech for an hour and a half, without notes, leaving many in his audience in tears. Ames did not deign to notice the objection Madison had articulated — Jay's Treaty's "very extraordinary abandonment of the compensation due for the Negroes." Rather, Ames stressed that the treaty was already ratified. "Reasons of policy, if not morality, dissuade even Turkey and Algiers from breaches of Treaty in mere wantonness of perfidy." Breaking the treaty "would not merely demoralize mankind" but would replace American patriotism with "a repulsive sense of shame and disgust." It also would cause Indian wars on the frontier. Jay's Treaty committed the British to evacuate their northwestern posts so that they no longer would be able to help Indians resist American encroachments. If the House killed the treaty, they would be murdering frontier settlers. Ames continued:

> In the day time, your path through the woods is ambushed; the darkness of midnight will glitter with the blaze of your dwellings. You are a father: the blood of your sons shall fatten your corn-field! You are a mother: the war-whoop shall wake the sleep of the cradle! . . . I fancy that I listen to the yells of savage vengeance, and the shrieks of torture. Already they seem to sigh in the West wind: already they mingle with every echo from the mountains.

That undoubtedly helped. The prospect of western settlers being "roasted at the stake" overcame the South's demand to be compensated for the slaves "carried off" by the British. In the final vote, Madison had the support of all but four of the southern members, but he needed two more. The House voted the funds and Jay's Treaty survived, 51–48. The House failed to usurp the power to ratify a treaty from the Senate. Nor were the slaveholders ever compensated for their 1783 losses — although when the War of 1812 created the same problem, the United States managed to wring an indemnity from the British.

Then there was Haiti. In 1791 the slaves of the French colony of St. Domingue rose in rebellion, killing many of the planters, resisting French efforts to reenslave them, and, in 1804, establishing an independent black republic under the leadership of Toussaint L'Ouverture. The United States refused to recognize Haiti, though Congress did not have to take action directly on that decision. U.S. policy was framed by the administrations of John Adams (which largely supported L'Ouverture) and Thomas Jefferson (which supported France). The Haitian liberation struggle terrified slaveholders in the United States, particularly when it was echoed in 1800 in Richmond, Virginia, by the Gabriel Conspiracy. This revolt, like the later Denmark Vesey revolt in South Carolina, involved a plan that was betrayed shortly before it would have begun. Haiti, meanwhile, influenced Congress indirectly. When Napoleon gave up his effort to take back Haiti, he decided he no longer needed Louisiana as a breadbasket for the sugar colony he had lost. The result was the Louisiana Purchase (1803), which did so much to structure the lengthy struggle in Congress over slavery in the territories. (The story of this conflict is covered elsewhere in this volume.) Much was at stake, since the territories would turn into additional slave states or free states. Yet it is often forgotten that this conflict began long before Missouri applied for statehood. It began as it would later end, in debates about whether to permit slaveholders and slaves to enter areas during the territorial phase, with slavery winning in 1798 for the Mississippi territory and in 1804 for the Orleans (Louisiana) territory.

Even the abolition of the slave trade in 1807 was more controversial than it seemed from the final roll call. The problem was not whether to abolish the slave trade but what to do when traders were caught trying to smuggle slaves into the United States illegally. Southerners demanded, and won, a provision that the traders would forfeit the slaves to the U.S. government, which then would sell them at auction. This meant, of course, that the slaves would be imported into and enslaved in the United States. Northerners proposed that the bill grant freedom to any person forfeited by an illegal slave trader, pointing out that the alternative would turn the federal government itself into a slave trader at the auction. Pennsylvania's Republican John Smilie asked the basic question: "Shall we . . . while we are attempting to put a stop to this traffic, take upon ourselves the odium of becoming slave traders?" The answer was yes. Southerners refused to permit any action that put the federal government in the position of having to liberate slaves. Peter Early, a Republican from Georgia, added a violent threat. If the federal government freed slaves and allowed them to settle in the South, "not one of them would be left alive in a year." An amendment proclaiming "that no person shall be sold as a slave by virtue of this act" produced a 60–60 tie vote, which the Speaker (Nathaniel Macon, a Republican from North Carolina) broke to defeat it. Without the "slave representation" of the three-fifths clause, this outcome would have been different.

For slaveholding congressmen, one very personal issue was the location of the national capital. The choice of the Potomac site is often explained by noting its "central" location, but its southern location was significant. In the 1790 debates, every Southerner favored the Potomac, while the Northerners were divided between the merits (and interests) of New York City and Philadelphia. Hence the victory of the Potomac, although the fact that George Washington favored it carried weight as well. Shortly before the government moved from New York to Philadelphia in 1790, William Loughton Smith of South Carolina complained of harassment by New York abolitionists. Although slavery was still perfectly legal in New York, abolitionist agitation was also both legal and safe — New York being a northern state after all. "A gentleman can hardly come from [the South] with a servant or two, either to this place or Philadelphia," Smith protested, "but there are persons trying to seduce his servants to leave him." In the decade that the government spent in Philadelphia, Pennsylvania law reigned. Temporary residents could keep slaves for up to six months at a time, but slaves who were kept longer would be freed. George Washington shuttled his own slaves back and forth between Philadelphia and Mount Vernon. Slaveholders would not face these inconveniences and embarrassments in Washington, D.C. Congress adopted a slave code for the capital in 1801 by deciding that the laws of Maryland and Virginia would govern the District of Columbia.

Slavery was a huge institution in the American economy and society in the early republic. The Constitution designed a House of Representatives in which the southern states gained "extra" seats because of their large slave populations and a Senate in which the power to help or hinder slavery rested on decisions about the admission of new states. The first party system, through the Republican caucus, enhanced the power of the southern slaveholders by amplifying the effects of the three-fifths clause. The victorious Republicans then used this power to tighten the rules governing speech on the floor. For these reasons, Congress became a body racked by serious sectional conflicts, but not one that could forge political solutions. Simply put, the slaveholders had too much power because they had been able to shape the organizational structure of Congress itself. The solution to the problem of governing a nation that was "half slave and half free" would not emerge from Congress. It would emerge on bloody battlefields instead.

— Robin L. Einhorn

BIBLIOGRAPHICAL NOTES

The most useful works on the early impact of slavery on Congress are Leonard L. Richards, *The Slave Power: The Free North and Southern Domination, 1780–1860* (Baton Rouge, La., 2000); Don E. Fehrenbacher, *The Slaveholding Republic: An Account of the United States Government's Relations to Slavery* (New York, 2001); Joseph J. Ellis, *Founding Brothers: The Revolutionary Generation* (New York, 2000), chap. 3; and Donald L. Robinson, *Slavery in the Structure of American Politics, 1765–1820* (New York, 1971). On the early congresses more generally, see Stanley Elkins and Eric McKitrick, *The Age of Federalism: The Early American Republic, 1788–1800* (New York, 1993), and James Sterling Young, *The Washington Community, 1800–1828* (New York, 1966). On the rules changes, Ralph Volney Harlow, *The History of Legislative Methods in the Period Before 1825* (New Haven, Conn., 1917), remains indispensable. See also Sarah A. Binder, "Partisanship and Procedural Choice: Institutional Change in the Early Congress, 1789–1823," *Journal of Politics* 57 (1995): 1093–1118; Evelyn C. Fink, "Representation by Deliberation: Changes in the Rules of Deliberation in the U.S. House of Representatives, 1789–1844," *Journal of Politics* 62 (2000): 1109–25; and Joseph Cooper, "Congress and Its Committees: A Historical and Theoretical Approach to the Proper Role of Committees in the Legislative Process" (Ph.D. diss., Harvard, 1960). On the tax debates, see Robin L. Einhorn, "Slavery and the Politics of Taxation in the Early United States," *Studies in American Political Development* 14 (2000): 156–82.

Rufus King

March 24, 1755–April 29, 1827

Rufus King

Rufus King was one of the United States' most important Federalist politicians. From his contributions at the Continental Congress (1784–1787) and the Constitutional Convention of 1787 to his two decades of service in the Senate, he was an influential proponent of enlarged powers for the federal government and one of the earliest politicians to voice opposition to slavery. He also led many successful negotiations as minister to Great Britain (1796–1803, 1825–1826).

Born in Scarborough, Massachusetts (now part of Maine), King was the son of a Tory merchant but was caught up in the drive for independence. He graduated from Harvard College in 1777 at the head of his class and began studying law. He was admitted to the bar in 1780 and became a justice of the peace the following year. With a successful career and a rising reputation, King entered politics as a delegate to the Massachusetts General Assembly in 1783. His denunciations of slavery date from 1785, when he drafted a bill that prohibited that institution in the Northwest Territories. Renowned as a speaker and a strong advocate for the ratification of the Constitution, King moved his family to Long Island, New York, in 1788 and was elected to the Senate the following year. During his seven years as a senator, he was a solid Federalist and a supporter of Alexander Hamilton's financial plans. Along with his political influence, King expanded his legal and commercial interests and became one of the wealthiest men in New York.

Resigning as minister to Great Britain in 1803, King was selected as the Federalist candidate for vice president in 1804, but Thomas Jefferson's administration was reelected. He was nominated for vice president again in 1808 but again lost. After the declaration of war in 1812, King was elected to the Senate, where he opposed both James Madison and Madison's disunion opponents. In 1816 King became the last Federalist candidate for president. He was soundly beaten by James Monroe and remained in the Senate, where he served until 1825. Except for John Marshall, King was the only original member of the Federalist party who remained an influential leader despite refusing to join the Republican party. He spoke out against the Missouri Compromise of 1820, both because of his opposition to slavery and because he feared it would increase the South's political power. In his sixties King suffered from gout, which led him to retire from the Senate. He reluctantly accepted a second appointment from President John Quincy Adams to serve as minister to Great Britain in 1825 but returned the following year, having achieved little success in his negotiations and still suffering health problems. He died in New York within a year of returning home.

Reference

Siry, S. E. 2000, February. "King, Rufus." *American National Biography Online.* Retrieved June 30, 2003, from http://www.anb.org/articles/03/03-00262.html.

6

The War of 1812

In late 1811, shortly after the first session of the Twelfth Congress — known to history as the War Congress — had convened, Henry Clay was chosen Speaker of the House. Clay was only thirty-four years old and a first-term congressman, but already he was known as "the Western Star." Although his friends had high hopes for the talented young Kentuckian, no one anticipated the stellar performance that he would deliver as Speaker. Shortly after assuming the chair, Clay gave a hint of things to come. When John Randolph of Roanoke, the eccentric, irascible, and acid-tongued congressman from Virginia, brought one of his dogs into the House, Clay immediately ordered the doorkeeper to remove it. Never before had anyone so directly challenged the prerogatives of the much-feared Randolph. Clay's forcefulness showed that he would not simply preside over the House, like past speakers, but he would manage it as well. "Such was the man," the Federalist Josiah Quincy later commented, "whose influence and power more than that of any other produced the War of 1812."

Congress in this war exerted more power than it had in other wars for several reasons. The legislature was still considered the most important branch of government. Although some presidents, such as George Washington and Thomas Jefferson, exercised considerable influence over Congress, the imperial presidency was still more than a century away, and most presidents deferred to Congress on a host of important issues. Although every president had a legislative agenda, the norm was for a strong, though often fractious, Congress to chart its own course.

In addition, James Madison, the president during the War of 1812, was not a strong leader. A gifted student of constitutional principles and international law, he had played a seminal role in forging the nation's Constitution in the Philadelphia Convention of 1787 and later in securing the adoption of the Bill of Rights. After helping Jefferson establish the Republican party in the early 1790s, Madison had served loyally and effectively for eight years as Jefferson's secretary of state and succeeded to the presidency in 1809. But he lacked Jefferson's sure hand with Congress. As a matter of principle, he was often inclined to defer to the legislative branch. Moreover, he had neither the dominant personality nor the political savvy needed to tame the factionalism that racked Congress in this era. Throughout the war, Congress repeatedly ignored or defeated presidential initiatives while pursuing its own agenda, sometimes in open defiance of the president. Congress also left a record of unruliness unmatched in any other foreign war.

The Impact of the Napoleonic Wars

Before the War of 1812, both the president and Congress seemed to flounder as they searched for a way to win greater respect for American rights in the Napoleonic Wars (1803–1815), a worldwide contest that pitted Great Britain against France in a fierce struggle for dominance in Europe. The two belligerents and their allies frequently interfered with American trade, and the British encroached on a host of other maritime rights as well. Britain and the United States found themselves on a collision course as the former sought to use its naval power to deprive its enemies of neutral commerce while the latter sought to make a profit by trading in a war-torn world. Two issues in particular bedeviled Anglo-American relations: the Orders in Council, British regulations that restricted American trade with the Continent; and impressment, the Royal Navy's practice of removing seamen — presumably, but not always, British subjects — from American merchant vessels to keep its own warships manned.

To force the European belligerents to show greater respect for America's neutral rights, the Jeffersonian Republicans had resorted to economic coercion in 1806, and for the next six years the United States used its trade as an instrument of foreign policy. The restrictive system, as the various measures were called, consisted of a series of nonimportation and nonexportation laws, designed to extort concessions on neutral rights from one or both of the European belligerents. But instead of winning the desired concessions, the restrictive system undermined American prosperity and reduced government revenue. By 1811, the bankruptcy of the restrictive system was widely recognized, although neither President Madison, who was both a cautious man and a devoted restrictionist, nor the Eleventh Congress, which held its last session that year, could find any palatable alternative. In truth, there were only two options: dropping the restrictive system and admitting failure, which could invite defeat at the polls, or raising the stakes by going to war, which could risk the very survival of the new nation and its republican experiment.

War was particularly risky given the state of the American military establishment. Ever since assuming power in 1801, the Republicans had expected to rely heavily on militia and privateers, at least at the outset of any war, and thus had refused to spend the money needed to maintain the military organization they had inherited from the Federalists. The Republicans had weakened the army by filling the officer corps with political hacks, which had so demoralized the rank and file that the Republican Nathaniel Macon of North Carolina had suggested publicly in 1810 that the army might as well be disbanded. The men hated their officers so much, they could not be counted on to obey them in a crisis. The Republicans also had gutted the navy, consigning most of the ships to port, where they rotted due to a lack of attention. If the nation were ever to undertake war, especially against a great power, it would first have to rebuild its military forces.

War Preparations

When the Twelfth Congress convened for its first session in November 1811, there was a note of expectation in the air, not simply because it was a new congress but also because the Republicans shared a sense that Anglo-American relations had reached a critical stage. "Never did the American Congress assemble under circumstances of greater interest and responsibility," commented the Republican Boston *Chronicle.*

The two-party system had emerged in the mid-1790s, so by 1812 it was well established. By modern standards, however, it was still immature. There were no party whips to keep members in line, and party attachments were weak. Most members of Congress prided themselves on their independence. In fact, few actually acknowledged that they belonged to a party or that their votes were ever influenced by party considerations. By convention, most members spoke not of fellow Federalists or Republicans but rather of "their friends in Congress" or "those in Congress with whom they were accustomed to acting." Most, in other words, continued to pay lip service to the fiction that parties did not exist.

In the Twelfth Congress, the Republicans controlled 75 percent of the House seats and 82 percent of those in the Senate. Although this meant that they would control all the standing committees, the committee system was much weaker than it is today. Committee chairs had little real power, and they did not determine which legislation reached the floor for action. Any member of Congress could introduce a resolution or bill by merely giving notice, and proposals might be referred to an ad hoc committee or even to a committee of the whole rather than to one of the standing committees. It was possible for members to secure a vote on a resolution or a bill that had very little support. In short, dissidents had considerably more influence on congressional business than they do today.

In addition, the Republican party was racked by divisions. "Factions in our own party," lamented Jonathan Roberts of Pennsylvania, "have hitherto been the bane of the Democratic administration." An identifiable group of regular Republicans could usually be counted on to support the administration. But their votes were never guaranteed on any issue, and other Republican factions were either unreliable or openly hostile.

Among the other factions were the Old Republicans, headed by John Randolph, the beardless and soprano-voiced Virginian who had never matured properly because of a hormone deficiency. Once Jefferson's floor leader in the House, Randolph never found the role congenial and had taken a small band of his followers into opposition at the end of 1805 after concluding that the administration had failed to live up to the ideals of the Republican party. These Old Republicans were southern agrarians who served as the conscience of the party. They upheld economy in government, states' rights, and a strict construction of the Constitution, all of which they feared might be compromised by a major foreign war.

The Old Republicans might be dismissed as a minor splinter group, but the northern commercial Republicans were more numerous and posed a greater threat to Republican unity. This group consisted mostly of backbenchers who had grown weary of the cavalier way that the Virginia dynasty (Jefferson, Madison, and James Monroe) had treated American commerce and the defense establishment. Disillusioned with the restrictive system, they favored building a navy to protect the nation's trade. Although without a clear floor leader in Congress, many in this group took their cue from New York's powerful Clinton family, headed by the elderly George (who served as vice president until his death in April 1812) and his nephew De Witt (who nearly unseated Madison in the presidential election later that year and subsequently gained fame as the father of the Erie Canal).

Yet another Republican group was the Smith faction or Senate "Invisibles," headed by Samuel Smith of Maryland. A successful merchant, Smith was the Republican political czar of Baltimore, then the third-largest city in the republic and known as "mobtown" because its large and hard-drinking working-class Republican majority often resorted to violence to silence its Federalist foes. This small but pivotal group disliked Madison and positively hated Secretary of the Treasury Albert Gallatin and his parsimonious policies, which had starved the navy for so many years. In the small Senate of the day (there were only 34 members in 1812), the Invisibles showed a talent for blocking administration measures.

The most visible and implacable of the administration's opponents in Congress were the Federalists, headed by two Massachusetts leaders, Josiah Quincy in the House and James Lloyd in the Senate. Quincy, who later had a distinguished career as mayor of Boston and president of Harvard College, was especially strong-willed and vocal. Never reticent or intimidated, he showed a talent for infuriating Republicans with his sharply worded critiques of the administration's personalities and policies. Lloyd, a Boston merchant of broad experience, was more moderate but often gave the major Federalist speeches in the Senate.

Representing mainly New England, which had a rich maritime tradition and a deep interest in commerce, the Federalists had openly denounced the direction of Republican foreign policy ever since Jefferson had refused to ratify the Monroe-Pinkney Treaty of 1806 and had opted instead for trade restrictions. With some justice, the Federalists argued that had it been ratified, this commercial treaty would have reforged the Anglo-American accord of the 1790s and taken the nation down the road to peace and prosperity instead of the one that led to trade restrictions and war. Although the Federalists controlled only about a quarter of the votes in Congress, by joining the dissident Republican groups, they could sometimes defeat administration measures, especially if they could peel off some regular Republican support.

The Twelfth Congress also had a new group of Republicans, perhaps ten in number, who were quickly dubbed "War Hawks." Headed by Henry Clay, this group was too young to remember the horrors of the last British war and thus not afraid to risk a new war to uphold American rights. Clay's role was particularly important. A rising star in the West, Clay was a hard-drinking gambler who practiced law in Lexington and had made a name for himself in the Kentucky legislature, where he had served as speaker. He had also twice served in the U.S. Senate to fill vacancies (1806–1807, 1810–1811) but, finding the "solemn stillness" of that chamber uncongenial, had successfully stood for election to the House in 1810. By this time Clay had made it clear that he preferred war "with all of its calamities and desolation to the tranquil and putrescent pool of ignominious peace." Chosen Speaker of the new House, a post that heretofore had been largely ceremonial, Clay genially but firmly molded the office into a position of power. By packing important House committees with War Hawks, by interpreting the rules to block obstructionists, by acting forcefully behind the scenes, and by frequently leaving the chair to speak on the issues, Clay ensured that the war movement gained and retained its momentum.

President Madison appeared to share the War Hawks' position. In his opening address to Congress on November 5, 1811, he denounced British encroachments on American rights and recommended that the nation be put into "an armor and an attitude demanded by the crisis." After Secretary of State James Monroe privately assured the War Hawks that the president would not shrink from war, the House passed six resolutions that called for putting the nation on a war footing by expanding the regular army, raising a corps of short-term volunteers, authorizing the use of militia, fitting out the navy, and permitting merchant vessels to arm for defense. The resolutions were adopted by large majorities, ranging from 75 to 112. Even the most timid Republicans could support them, both because they did not actually commit the nation to war and because it was widely believed that the mere threat of war might win concessions from Great Britain. The Federalists also supported the resolutions, not because they favored war, but because they had always championed military preparedness and they also wished to avoid the old and groundless but politically effective charge of "British gold" (that is, that they were British partisans whose votes were bought and paid for by the British government).

But it was one thing to endorse military preparedness in principle and quite another to forge a consensus on specific measures. Although Congress adopted a number of war preparations between December 1811 and April 1812, no one was entirely happy with the results, least of all the administration. Madison had hoped to wage war in 1812 with short-term volunteers and militia, but instead Congress (with Clay's support) had insisted on raising a large and costly body of long-term regulars. Even though Congress agreed to authorize the volunteers that the president requested, it gave the states the power to appoint the officers, and state officials proved so dilatory that the law was effectively nullified. Congress also balked at the administration's requests to purchase arms for the militia and to divide it into several classes so that younger men could be trained separately and developed into a more effective fighting force.

Worse yet, when Secretary Gallatin proposed taxes to finance the war, House Republicans were so furious that they refused to print his report, and Robert Wright of Maryland accused him of trying "to chill the war spirit." Gallatin's internal taxes were particularly obnoxious because these very duties had contributed to John Adams's defeat in the presidential election of 1800. The Republicans' decision to repeal the internal taxes in 1802 had been very popular, especially in the West. Only fierce lobbying by Clay and the administration finally carried the day for the tax resolutions. Even then, the taxes were not to be adopted until after war had been declared, and some Republicans, confident of a quick victory, insisted that they would never be needed. "I cannot think it will be necessary at present to resort to *direct taxes & stamp acts*," said William Plumer of New

Hampshire. "That was the very course that proved fatal to John Adams' administration."

If the administration was not entirely happy with the war program, neither were the commercial Republicans or their Federalist allies, whose proposals for naval expansion were voted down in both houses. Although Clay surprised western opponents of the navy by speaking from the floor for the House proposal, the measure was lost. "We cannot contend with Great Britain on the ocean," said his opponent Adam Seybert of Pennsylvania. "Our vessels will only tend to swell the present catalogue of the British navy." The majority made it clear that it planned to use the nation's limited resources, not to protect commerce and assault British power and property on the high seas, but to launch a land war against British Canada instead.

The Declaration of War

Once the war program was in place, Congress marked time until the USS *Hornet* returned with the latest information from Europe. Anticipating the worst, Clay persuaded the president to recommend a short-term embargo as a prelude to war. Congress complied with Madison's request in early April. Clay also had to contend with a movement to authorize a congressional recess. The session had dragged on long past the usual March adjournment date, and there was no end in sight. A short recess appealed to many weary congressmen. The War Hawks argued that it was absurd to recess if the nation were serious about war, and Clay helped defeat two resolutions from the Senate for a recess of three and five weeks, respectively.

The *Hornet* finally arrived in New York on May 19. The news it brought suggested that the British were standing firm on the Orders in Council — although in fact they were on the verge of retreat. Shortly thereafter, John Randolph sought to force a public debate on the merits of war by raising the issue in a rambling speech. Invoking several obscure rules, Clay said that Randolph could not continue unless he offered a written resolution on the subject, that his resolution would have to be seconded, and that it could not be debated until the House voted to consider it. Randolph offered a resolution asserting that it was inexpedient to go to war against Great Britain, but the House immediately voted not to consider it. Silenced, the enraged Randolph had to sit down.

Since the *Hornet* had brought no news of British concessions, Clay and his fellow War Hawks agreed that war must be declared. Although the Constitution entrusted the decision to Congress, the War Hawks wanted the president to take the lead. Hence on June 1, 1812, President Madison sent a war message to Congress. It was a momentous occasion. Although Congress had earlier authorized hostilities against Indians (the early 1790s), France (1798), and Tripoli (1801), it was the first time that a president had ever asked for a formal declaration of war.

The House quickly passed a war bill. Since the proceedings were conducted in secret session, the Federalists refused to deliver their speeches against the war and instead contented themselves with expressing their views with their votes. The bill was then sent to the Senate, where it nearly foundered. At first, the Senate approved an amendment to limit the war to the high seas. Only later was this decision reversed when the president pro tem's vote forced a tie, which killed the amendment.

In the end, the war bill passed essentially unchanged. It declared war against "the United Kingdom of Great Britain and Ireland and the dependencies thereof" and authorized the president "to use the whole land and naval force of the United States to carry the same into effect, and to issue private armed vessels of the United States commissions of marque and general reprisal." The vote on the bill, however, was relatively close: 79–49 in the House and 19–13 in the Senate. Never has the nation undertaken a major war against so much opposition. Every Federalist in Congress voted against the bill, as did almost 20 percent of the Republicans. Although it is impossible to quantify public opinion in this era, it seems likely that the war vote roughly matched the views of the American people, with just over 60 percent supporting the decision and just under 40 percent opposing it.

Although the War Hawks and their Republican allies hoped that the decision for war would unify their own party and silence the opposition, it had neither effect. Congress continued to be racked by divisions and outright opposition to the war policy. The House narrowly defeated a proposal to repeal the nonimportation act of 1811, which prohibited all British imports and was the last major coercive measure adopted before the war. Although the Republicans had always defended the restrictive system as an alternative to war, the retention of this measure made it clear that the majority still planned to wage economic war against Great Britain. As Henry Clay put it, "If persisted in, the restrictive system, aiding the war, would break down the present [British] ministry, and lead to a consequent honorable peace." Congress also adopted an enemy trade act that revealed deep fissures within the Republican party over the wisdom of cutting off all British trade.

Even more divisive was the tax issue. Although the Republican majority increased the customs duties, the internal taxes that Gallatin had said were essential and that Congress had promised earlier in the session were now postponed indefinitely. "It was admitted by the ruling party in debate," said the Federalist James Breckinridge of Virginia, "that to impose them now would endanger their success at the next election." To meet the anticipated revenue shortfall, Congress authorized treasury notes, short-term interest-bearing notes that were used throughout the war to pay government bills.

The Rage of Debate

The military campaign of 1812 ended in disaster for the United States. One army surrendered at Detroit, a second was defeated on the Niagara frontier, and a third made little more than a demonstration on the St. Lawrence front before retreating to the safety of New York. "Our aff[a]irs," confided the barely literate senator Thomas Worthington of Ohio to his diary at the end of 1812, "is [in] a miserable way[,] defeated and disgraced[,] the revenue extravagantly expended[,] the war not man[a]ged at all." Though generally a loyal Republican, Worthington had voted against the war, and with good reason, since his own state's northwest frontier was now exposed to Anglo-Indian depredations. The only redeeming feature of the year's campaign was a series of strategically insignificant but morale-boosting victories on the high seas, where several American frigates and smaller vessels had defeated British warships in single-ship duels.

No doubt the failure of the military campaign had an effect on the elections of 1812. In those days, there was no nationwide election day. Each state followed its own timetable, and the results drifted in over the fall and early winter. In the presidential election, Madison barely defeated De Witt Clinton, who had the support of many northern Republicans as well as the Federalists. The difference was Pennsylvania, where fat government war contracts promoted prosperity and thus support for Madison and his allies. The Federalists, however, made significant gains in Congress and increased the number of states they controlled from three to six (out of eighteen). The elections revealed that the Republicans were vulnerable to charges of mismanaging the war and that opposition to the war itself was often a winner at the polls, especially in New England.

The failed military campaign coupled with the close election results did nothing to reduce factionalism in the Twelfth Congress when it convened for its second and last session on November 2, 1812. The House Federalists set the tone when they launched a full-scale assault on the war, delivering the speeches they had written but never presented the previous session, when the war bill was under consideration. This led to an extended and often bitter debate that raged for two weeks, consuming valuable time and postponing the adoption of necessary war legislation. The most provocative speech was delivered by the Federalist leader Josiah Quincy, who claimed that for twelve years the nation's affairs had been mismanaged by "two Virginians and a foreigner" (Jefferson, Madison, and Gallatin) and that they were abetted by "toads or reptiles [New England Republicans], which *spread their slime in the drawing room*" — language so offensive that Quincy deleted the passage before publishing his speech. The Republicans responded in kind, accusing the Federalists of subverting the war effort and threatening the future of the Union.

Congress enacted most of the president's recommendations for upgrading and expanding the army in this session, although the Senate killed administration bills to arm and classify the militia and to authorize the enlistment of minors eighteen or older without the consent of an elder. Congress also significantly expanded the navy. The spectacular naval victories of 1812 had turned many Americans, including Madison, into naval advocates. In addition, Congress adopted as a basis for ending impressment the administration's proposal to bar British subjects from American ships, although this measure was sharply criticized by members of both parties, one Republican claiming that it was tantamount to "begging for peace."

Administration proposals on tax and trade policy ran into more trouble. Many merchants had shipped their property home from Great Britain in direct violation of the nonimportation law, and when sympathetic judges ordered the merchandise released, the administration was left holding $18 million in penal bonds. Normally, the Treasury might have prosecuted for the full value of the bonds, but Gallatin decided to remit half their value. The merchants found this unsatisfactory and persuaded Congress to remit the entire value. This pleased the mercantile community but made a mockery of the nonimportation law and deprived the administration of $9 million in revenue.

The Senate also killed bills recommended by the president that would have barred the used of foreign (that is, British) licenses and prohibited American exports in foreign bottoms (which were suspected of being British ships in disguise). Nor was Congress sympathetic to proposals, which had Gallatin's support, to modify the nonimportation act to generate more revenue. Despite the nation's deteriorating finances, Congress also rejected Gallatin's proposals for new taxes. More than six months after war began, the Republicans were still unwilling to risk their popularity by confronting the need for additional tax revenue to finance the war.

Taxes and Trade

To deal with the nation's growing financial problems, President Madison summoned the Thirteenth Congress to a special session on May 25, 1813. The new Congress, however, was unlikely to be any more cooperative than the old one. The Federalists had improved their position in the recent elections, increasing the proportion of seats they held from 25 to 37 percent in the House and from 18 to 22 percent in the Senate. Moreover, Madison was unable to provide effective leadership; most of the session he was so ill from dysentery that his very life was despaired of. The unruliness and divisions in the new Congress prompted one War Hawk, John C. Calhoun of South Carolina, to comment that "party spirit is more violent than I ever knew."

The Senate blocked two of Madison's diplomatic appointments, refusing to confirm Jonathan Russell as the U.S. minister to Sweden or Albert Gallatin as a member of the peace delegation appointed in the wake of a Russian mediation initiative. Russell's nomination was defeated because he was suspected of mismanaging earlier diplomatic assignments and because many senators doubted that a full-fledged minister was needed in Sweden. Gallatin's nomination was voted down partly because he had not given up his Treasury portfolio and partly because his stingy spending policies had alienated a number of senators, particularly the Smith faction.

The House added to the president's embarrassments by adopting resolutions that forced the administration to acknowledge that it had no real proof that France had repealed its restrictions on neutral trade, even though that was the basis for the nonimportation act of 1811 and ultimately the declaration of war in 1812. "I declare confidently and boldly," said the Federalist Harmanus Bleecker of New York, "*that Napoleon has inveigled us into the war.*" The debate over these resolutions further embittered party relations when the Republican Felix Grundy of Tennessee characterized the Federalist opposition to the war as "moral treason," a charge that the Federalists hotly denied but that dogged them for the rest of the conflict.

The Republican majority finally faced the need for new taxes, although, as one Federalist put it, they "approach the subject with *fear & trembling.*" The Republicans closed ranks to enact a broad range of internal taxes, although they put off the effective date until the end of the year. Congress also agreed to the president's longstanding request to ban the use of foreign licenses, but only after a federal court had outlawed them.

Madison's other recommendations for trade restrictions fell on deaf ears. He proposed an embargo on all ships and goods to put pressure on the British and to end enemy trade; the House overruled its own Foreign Relations Committee to adopt the measure, but it was killed by the Senate. The House, for its part, rejected presidential proposals to expand the scope of enemy trade legislation and to prohibit the export of provisions and naval stores in foreign bottoms. Congress adopted another proposal, favored by Secretary of the Navy William Jones but opposed earlier by Secretary of the Treasury Gallatin, that reduced the duties on prize goods.

Throughout this session, the Senate was particularly obstreperous. In fact, by the end of the session the administration considered this body so unreliable that Vice President Elbridge Gerry refused to follow custom and vacate the chair. He thereby ensured that the line of succession would bypass the Senate and that House Speaker Henry Clay would succeed to the presidency if both the ailing Madison and the elderly Gerry died in office.

The Last Embargo

By the time the Thirteenth Congress convened for its second session on December 6, 1813, there was a note of apprehension in the air. In the campaign of 1813, the United States enjoyed success in the Creek War in the Southwest and in the war against Great Britain and its Indian allies in the Northwest, but the nation was no closer to the conquest of Canada. "In spite of some gleams of success," said the Federalist William Hunter of Rhode Island, "we are further off our object than at first."

More ominously, the tide of the war in Europe appeared to be turning. If Great Britain won in Europe before it lost in America, the United States could find itself alone in the field against a formidable enemy. The only good news was that although the British had rejected the Russian offer of mediation, they had agreed to direct negotiations with the United States.

Since Clay had resigned from Congress to serve on the peace delegation, the House had to elect a new Speaker, and it chose Langdon Cheves of South Carolina over Felix Grundy of Tennessee. Both were strong War Hawks, but Cheves was more widely respected for his talents, and as a known enemy of the restrictive system, he had the support of many commercial Republicans as well as the Federalists. Moreover, the opposition of the Federalists in this session was as implacable as ever. "There is every appearance," said Jonathan Roberts, "that the minority will contest every inch of ground."

The Federalists sought to halt offensive operations against Canada pending the outcome of the peace negotiations, which led to yet another round of long-winded speeches that prevented any immediate action on war legislation. The debate raged for weeks and even spilled over into routine appropriation bills, prompting the veteran congressman Nathaniel Macon to comment that this was "the [most] talking legislature that I have ever seen."

Congress adopted a number of measures for fighting and financing the war, although it dismissed Secretary of War John Armstrong's proposal to draft militia into the regular army. Congress also refused to comply with the administration's request for more taxes.

To reduce the growing incidence of enemy trade and increase the pressure on Great Britain, President Madison, ever confident of the efficacy of economic coercion, submitted a message to Congress calling for a broad range of new restrictions. Although Congress finally gave him the embargo he wanted, it rejected his proposals for curtailing imports, limiting the access of foreign ships to American ports, and banning the ransoming of captured American ships (often a cover for enemy trade).

Even the embargo proved short-lived. When news arrived of the allied victory over Napoleon at Leipzig, thus opening all of northern Europe to British trade, even Madison could see the futility of pursuing economic coercion and so called for the repeal of the embargo as well as the nonimportation act of 1811. Despite the bitter opposition of die-hard restrictionists, Congress complied with Madison's request in April 1814, although it refused to adopt a companion measure that would have banned the export of specie. Congress also refused to act on two other presidential recommendations that would have continued some of the taxes beyond the end of the war and opened American ports to French warships and privateers.

The Crisis of 1814

When the Thirteenth Congress met for its third and last session in the fall of 1814, the military campaign of that year was winding down, and the nation's situation had become desperate. Napoleon had been defeated the previous spring, and for the first time in a decade there was peace in Europe, meaning that the British could shift their military and naval assets to the American war. Great Britain was now able to threaten the United States on a number of fronts from the Canadian frontier to the Gulf Coast. The British were particularly successful in the Chesapeake, where they occupied the nation's capital and burned the public buildings (including the Capitol and the White House). This humiliation was undoubtedly the Americans' low point in the war.

For the United States, the war was now both more defensive and more dangerous. Moreover, the problems associated with waging the war had all gotten worse. The nation could not raise the men and money it needed, trade with the enemy had escalated to huge proportions, and internal opposition continued to mount. In addition, deteriorating economic conditions, brought on mainly by a British blockade that sealed off the entire coast, made it even more difficult to manage these problems.

This desperate plight prompted President Madison to summon Congress to an early meeting on September 19, 1814. Everyone agreed that a crisis was at hand, but once again there was no agreement on how to meet it. The Republicans were unable to close ranks behind many measures, and most Federalists soon concluded that supporting Republican proposals would only prolong the war. Thus, despite considerable talk of presenting a united front and adopting forceful measures, this Congress proved as divided and unruly as its predecessors.

The first issue that Congress took up separated members along not party lines but sectional lines. The British destruction of much of Washington the previous summer led to an attempt by the North to move the capital to a city that was more defensible and more comfortable. The Southerners were able to block this step, but the president had to threaten a veto and lobby northern Republicans to muster the needed votes.

Congress also passed two bills recommended by the new secretary of war, James Monroe, that authorized the enlistment of minors over eighteen without the consent of their elders and provided for raising volunteer troops both for local defense and for another campaign against Canada. But the centerpiece of Monroe's program — a scheme to raise additional regulars by conscription — had little chance, and even a substitute proposal, to draft militia for two years of service, went down to defeat when the two houses could not agree on the details. Similarly, Congress accepted Secretary of the Navy William Jones's recommendations to reform the navy and build additional warships, but it rejected his proposals for naval conscription and a naval academy.

There was no consensus, even in the administration, about how to cope with the nation's financial problems. The government's position had collapsed in 1814. The Treasury had been unable to fill its loan for the year, leaving it far short of the funds it needed to cover the escalating cost of the war. The solutions proposed ranged from issuing paper money to establishing a national bank. The new secretary of the Treasury, Alexander J. Dallas, persuaded Congress to enact a new and sweeping round of taxes and to authorize additional Treasury notes (even though by this time most government contractors and banks would no longer accept them).

Once again, however, the centerpiece of the administration's program — a national bank — met with resistance. Instead of establishing a large bank that the government could use as a source for loans, Congress authorized a small autonomous bank that would provide the Treasury with little financial relief. When Madison vetoed the bill, Congress appeared ready to give the administration the kind of bank it wanted, but news of peace killed the proposal.

On only one issue did Congress give the administration everything it wanted. Trade with the enemy, not only across the Canadian border but also in American waters, had reached scandalous proportions. In August 1814 the governor general of Canada reported that "two-thirds of the army in Canada" was "eating beef provided by American contractors, drawn principally from the states of Vermont and New York." Congress responded with a new enemy trade act that gave customs officials more sweeping powers than they had ever enjoyed, even under the enforcement acts that had followed the embargo of 1807. But this law never received a fair test; it expired two weeks after it was adopted, when peace was restored.

News that the Treaty of Ghent had been signed reached Washington on February 13, 1815, while the Thirteenth Congress was still sitting. Three days later, the Senate unanimously approved it. Madison's own approval later that day completed the ratification process, thus ending hostilities. When the instruments of ratification were exchanged with a British representative on February 17, the treaty became operative and the war officially ended. By this time the nation was rejoicing, and the atmosphere of crisis had abated. Even during the crisis, however, Congress had proved remarkably resistant to administration measures. Its two most important proposals — conscription, deemed essential to waging the war, and a national bank, deemed essential to financing the war — both went down to defeat.

Conclusion

Throughout the War of 1812, Congress had shown an independent streak rare in times of national crisis. The Republicans blamed the Federalists for blocking many essential measures, and it is certainly true that the Federalists voted with remarkable unity during the war, opposing almost all proposals to raise men and money or to restrict trade with the enemy, supporting only measures to increase the navy or construct coastal fortifications (which they considered a long-term investment worthy of support even during a war they opposed). The Federalist opposition to administration measures during this war went significantly further than partisan opposition in any other war. And yet, far from prolonging the war (as the Republicans repeatedly charged), the Federalist opposition probably had the opposite effect, helping to persuade the administration to give up its war aims and agree to restore peace on the basis of the *status quo ante bellum.*

The Republicans needed to look closer to home to explain why so many administration measures went down to defeat. The Federalists, after all, never controlled more than 37 percent of the seats in the House or 22 percent in the Senate. The Republicans could easily brush aside Federalist opposition if only they closed ranks. But they rarely did. The Old Republicans, northern commercial Republicans, and Invisibles often broke with the regular Republicans, and even the regular Republicans divided over some issues.

In truth, honest people could disagree over how best to fight and finance this war, and there was no guarantee that the administration actually knew best. In fact, there was a good case for denying the administration the untrained, short-term troops it wanted at the beginning of the war or the untrained conscripts it sought at the end. Nor was there any reason to believe that indulging Madison's obsession for ever more trade restrictions would have brought the nation any closer to victory.

Congress can be censored in this war mainly for its lack of fiscal responsibility. The Republicans repeatedly postponed internal taxes, partly because they hoped for a quick war and partly because they feared the political consequences. But these taxes were essential. Gallatin can be faulted for relying too heavily on loans to finance the war, but congressional Republicans also bore a share of the responsibility for the collapse of public credit in 1814.

Yet even if Congress had given the administration everything it asked for, the United States probably would not have fared much better in the war. The war effort failed not so much because of a recalcitrant Congress but because, in the field, the nation was saddled with incompetent officers and untrained men who had to contend with insuperable logistical problems while facing a determined and capable foe. Despite all the talk that the conquest of Canada would be, in the words of Jefferson, "a mere matter of marching," it proved no easy task to defeat veteran British troops led by experienced officers and aided by large bodies of Indians on a distant frontier.

In the end, it is unlikely that congressional independence and factionalism had much effect on the outcome of the war. However frustrating Congress's behavior might have been to the administration, it did not torpedo the war effort nor did it reflect any sinister attempt to discredit the government or its policies. Rather, it was simply a reflection of honest differences of opinion among the nation's leaders and the inability of an immature party system to resolve them. Moreover, those differences mirrored the views of the American people at large on the merits of the war and how best to bring it to a conclusion. If the war effort suffered, it was a victim of American democracy.

For all the chaos that it seemed to cause, the War of 1812 had surprisingly little effect on the institutional history of Congress. The only significant change was Henry Clay's transformation of the speakership, but even this was not quite as far-reaching as it might appear. There were precedents for some of Clay's actions; he simply went further and acted more energetically than his predecessors. Moreover, not all of his successors followed his lead. Some preferred to treat the speakership as more ceremonial, to preside over rather than to manage the House. But Clay's precedents were on record for those who did wish to go further, and in time the more ambitious of his successors would build on these precedents to create an even more powerful speakership.

— Donald R. Hickey

BIBLIOGRAPHICAL NOTES

The classic study of the domestic history of the War of 1812 is Henry Adams, *History of the United States [during the Administration of Jefferson and Madison]*, 9 vols. (New York, 1889–91), vols. 6–9, although one must take the author's judgments with a grain of salt because they are often unfair, yet are disguised as widely held views. (Adams was fond of using phrases such as: "No one would deny" or "All intelligent men could agree.") J.C.A. Stagg does a fine job of developing the Republican side of the story in *Mr. Madison's War: Politics, Diplomacy, and Warfare in the Early American Republic, 1783–1830* (Princeton, N.J., 1983), while Donald R. Hickey tries to do justice to the Federalists in *The War of 1812: A Forgotten Conflict* (Urbana, Ill., 1989).

For Madison's role, one should consult the last volume in Irving Brant, *James Madison*, 6 vols. (Indianapolis and New York, 1941–61), which is comprehensive but heavily biased in favor of the president, and Robert A. Rutland, *The Presidency of James Madison* (Lawrence, Kans., 1990), which is more limited in scope but also more balanced. Also useful are Bernard Mayo, *Henry Clay: Spokesman of the New West* (Boston, 1937); Henry Adams, *The Life of Albert Gallatin* (Philadelphia, 1879); and Samuel Eliot Morison's study of one of the leading New England Federalists, *Harrison Gray Otis, 1765–1848: The Urbane Federalist* (Boston, 1969).

To understand the factionalism in the war congresses, one should look at Norman K. Risjord, *The Old Republicans: Southern Conservatism in the Age of Jefferson* (New York, 1965); Noble E. Cunningham Jr., "Who Were the Quids?" *Mississippi Valley Historical Review* 50 (September 1963): 252–63; John S. Pancake, "The 'Invisibles': A Chapter in the Opposition to President Madison," *Journal of Southern History* 21 (February 1955): 17–37; and Steven E. Siry, "The Sectional Politics of 'Practical Republicanism': De Witt Clinton's Presidential Bid, 1810–1812," *Journal of the Early Republic* 5 (Winter 1985): 441–62.

Henry Clay

April 12, 1777–June 29, 1852

Henry Clay

Known as both a hot-headed partisan and a skilled pacificator, Henry Clay rose from a successful legal career on the Kentucky frontier to serve a central role in Congress for much of five decades. Although he failed, in several attempts, as a presidential candidate, he is remembered as "the Great Compromiser" for his role in securing the Missouri Compromise, one milestone of many in his work to preserve the Union against the competing interests of slaveholding and free states.

Born in Hanover County, Virginia, Henry Clay claimed the American Revolution as his cradle. As a three-year-old, he watched the British troops ransack his family home. The following year his father, a Baptist minister, died, leaving his mother to remarry. And it was with his stepfather's influence that the fifteen-year-old Clay was hired as a clerk in the state chancery office in Richmond, where he was taken under the wing of Chancellor George Wythe, whose pupils included Thomas Jefferson and John Marshall. After being admitted to the Virginia bar in 1797, however, Clay decided to follow his family to Kentucky. He settled in Lexington, opened a law office, and became known as a talented orator.

In 1799 he married Lucretia Hart, the daughter of one of Kentucky's eminent families, and became a major landowner, livestock breeder, and farmer. But his family life became a lonely one, punctuated by tragedy. His wife disliked the social life of Washington, refused to travel with him, and rarely, if ever, wrote to him. Of the couple's eleven children, all six daughters died at an early age. Their eldest son was committed to a "lunatic asylum," another suffered mental breakdowns, a third wrestled with alcoholism, and Henry Jr. was killed in the Mexican War.

Clay had a stellar political life, however. In 1803 he was elected to the Kentucky General Assembly and, within a few years, became known as the most promising young politician in Kentucky. Before he arrived in the House of Representatives in 1811, he had already earned national recognition, having served out the unfinished terms of two senators from Kentucky. Clay had earned the support of a group of young congressmen known as War Hawks, who believed that he could lead the government to declare war on Great Britain. By a large majority, the House selected the freshman congressman as its Speaker. Under Clay's command, the office of the Speaker became the political leader of the House and the second most powerful position in the government. Serving longer than any other Speaker in the nineteenth century, Clay strictly enforced House rules and the flow of legislation.

In the contested presidential election of 1824, Clay ran against three other candidates. Since no one received a majority of the electoral votes, the choice fell to the House of Representatives, where the Speaker exercised enormous influence. Clay threw his support behind John Quincy Adams, with the tacit understanding that Adams would appoint him secretary of state, a position that traditionally led to the presidency. Opponents called the appointment a "corrupt bargain." The charge haunted Clay, and when he ran for the presidency in 1832 against the popular Andrew Jackson, he suffered a crushing defeat. He ran again in 1844, as a Whig, against the Democrat James K. Polk and lost by a narrow margin, probably because of his opposition to the Mexican War.

Clay is best remembered for his role in pacifying sectional interests in order to shepherd the Missouri Compromise through the House in 1821. His work as "the Great Compromiser" continued for decades, overcoming the nullification crisis of 1832–1833 and engineering the Compromise of 1850, which arguably postponed southern secession by a decade. But Clay is also remembered for his "American System," through which he defined the role of the federal government in domestic affairs. His efforts helped lead to the development of the National Road, federal aid for other internal improvements, tariff protection of American industries, and the chartering of the Second National Bank of the United States. Clay's political compromises may have unraveled after his death, but his "American System" did strengthen the bonds that tied the nation together.

References

Clark, T. D. *Henry Clay.* Retrieved on July 26, 2003, from http://www.henryclay.org/hc.htm.

Remini, R. V. 2000, February. "Clay, Henry." *American National Biography Online.* Retrieved June 30, 2003, from http://www.anb.org/articles/03/03-00100.html.

7

Congress, Internal Improvement, and the Problem of Governance

At the time of the American Revolution, government was recognized across the English-speaking world as a legitimate provider of services required for the general welfare. Even Adam Smith, the high priest of government noninterference, devoted a section of *Wealth of Nations* (1776) to the legitimate duties of the sovereign, which included roads, bridges, canals, public schools, and security forces to defend the nation. Thus, when *sovereignty* was placed in the hands of the people by our revolutionary forefathers, it was not just legal restraint but also positive action that was charged to Congress. From the first day, these "duties of the sovereign," bundled loosely in the rubric of "internal improvement," appeared prominently on congressional agendas; and from the first day, because of their local nature and the peculiar division of labor in America's federal system, internal improvements sparked bitter arguments about the power of government and the character of Congress itself.

The Problem Is Born

As soon as the First Congress took up the post office system, the "problem" of internal improvement began to appear. The Constitution obligated Congress to "establish" post roads for the distribution of information throughout the Union, but this charge left unanswered questions: Did this grant imply the mere designation of existing roads, or did it include the authority to build new roads at federal expense? If Congress could build roads, could it also seize private property, divide a man's farm, build up or tear down the business of a town without regard for the interests of its population? Should federal post roads run straight and true, or should they meander from village to village, encompassing the largest number of citizens? Finally, if Congress were to build (as Virginia's Congressman James Madison urged in 1796) a great Maine–Georgia post road, would federal authorities acquire sovereignty along such a right-of-way, or did the states retain the right to tax and govern the land and prosecute highwaymen that lurked about the national turnpike?

These debates sound ridiculous to modern ears, and even at the time they often seemed pedantic. But the Constitution was vague, and everything done by the first several congresses set precedents for the future. Maritime custom, for example, gave Congress control of the saltwater coast, but did the federal erection of coastal lights and batteries justify similar installations on freshwater streams such as the Hudson, Delaware, Potomac, and James Rivers? Behind these concerns lay the question of patronage. How deep was government's purse? And for whose benefits might it be opened?

Common to all these questions was the expenditure of the whole people's money on public works that were fixed to the ground *in some particular place.* Internal improvements might serve the general good, but they could do so only by improving transportation and trade in particular locales — and not in others! The genius of popular government was supposed to be equal treatment for all citizens, yet roads and canals unavoidably favored some over others. To prevent such preferential treatment, some denied that Congress had the authority to act. Others, who desired a strong central government, seized on the utility of roads and canals to stretch the "elastic clauses" in the Constitution — the charges to promote the "general welfare" and do anything "necessary and proper" to carry out the enumerated duties. Still others, largely unreconciled Antifederalists, insisted that enumerated powers were the *only* grants to Congress and resisted every effort to construe the Constitution broadly. Thus internal improvement, important enough in its own right, also became a bellwether issue regarding liberty, power, and the line of separation between state and national authority.

The Federalist Agenda and the Rise of Opposition

Among the first major projects seeking public assistance was the Potomac Canal, a hobby of George Washington's to open navigation on the river that promised to pour the commerce of the Ohio Valley into the new federal city. The sums requested were not large, but American governments were deeply in debt from the Revolution and lawmakers everywhere were chary of taxation (with or without representation). In the case of the Potomac Canal, Virginia and Maryland already had approved it, and Congress enjoyed a unique, singular power over the federal district; still, the friends of New York and Philadelphia resisted spending federal money on an upstart commercial rival (Pennsylvania's acid-tongued senator William Maclay called the new capital city a "dirty speculation"), while even some Virginians feared the new federal district would be "the ambush from which the masked monarchy of the Constitution was to spring upon the people."

By 1791 Treasury Secretary Alexander Hamilton's fiscal program, including import and excise taxes, funding and assumption, and a national bank (this last a necessary and proper innovation), had sparked a states' rights backlash against all "loose construction." In the next few years, opposition congressmen made "strict construction" the central tenet of a new partisan creed, Republicanism. Strongest in Virginia and rural Pennsylvania, among planters, farmers, and small tradesmen, the Republicans became so suspicious of their urban, mercantile, loose-construction Federalist opponents that even a project as logically compelling as the Potomac Canal could not rally support in Congress.

By the late 1790s, the Federalists had overplayed their centralizing hand in so many ways that the Republican opposition, led by James Madison and the presidential candidate Thomas Jefferson, swept the elections of 1800 with a promise to restore limited government, strict construction, and maximum states' rights. Rallying around these principles (called "the Spirit of '98"), some Republicans opposed internal improvements on local or practical grounds while others condemned them simply as examples of the Federalists' reach for unlimited power. Either way, cheap, inactive government prevailed, and legislative discourse acquired the character of a musical duet: one singer pleading the cause, the other harmonizing on constitutional implications and the fear of corruption.

Jefferson's creed of little government close to home undercut the Maine–Georgia post road, the grand Federalist navy, and many supporting fortifications. His partisans in Congress spoke against federal aid to piers in the Delaware River: strictly local installations, they believed, masquerading as national improvements. Strict construction and frugality guided Jeffersonians steadily toward less, not more, energy in government — that is, until the rising revenue from trade and a number of attractive possibilities caused the president himself to relax and dream of doing more positive good. As the Federalists (he called them "monarchists") retreated, Jefferson and the Republicans in Congress found that governing called for more than negative reactions.

The first test came in 1802, when Congress adopted a provision in Ohio's Enabling Act to build a national Cumberland Road through the wilds of Maryland and northern Virginia toward the first new state north of the Ohio River. Then in 1803, with no shred of constitutional authority,

Jefferson purchased Louisiana from the French because it was so unmistakably good for the country. Compelling in the president's mind, these exceptions fueled hair-splitting arguments in Congress over federal power and the merits of every other turnpike, canal, pier, buoy, lighthouse, or gun emplacement that had ever been turned down on grounds of strict construction. Roger Griswold from Connecticut (still a Federalist stronghold) found laughable the Republicans' claim of "national significance" for a road to Ohio: it served primarily Virginia, the president's home state! At the other extreme, Virginia's Christopher Clark (the one who called Washington City the "ambush" of monarchy) urged not one but three separate roads to Ohio in order to spread federal money widely. Another strict constructionist from Old Dominion, John G. Jackson, insisted (absurdly) that the plural noun "*roads*" in the Ohio bill rendered Congress powerless to adopt just one. To quiet this cacophony, Jefferson recommended in his Second Inaugural Address (1805) that Congress amend the Constitution to include internal improvements. Then, he hoped, Congress could direct the surplus that mounted because of booming trade with war-torn Europe to this "useful class of activities" without damaging the federal system.

"What is the amendment alluded to?" asked Madison. Many friends of improvement (including Madison) believed that the elastic clauses adequately covered works of national importance. No amendment was needed, and many thought it unsafe to tamper with the boundaries of federalism for fear of reigniting desperate battles from the ratification of the Constitution. Others such as North Carolina's Nathaniel Macon and Virginia's John Randolph — staunch enemies of federal power and literal advocates of strict construction and states' rights — proclaimed their opposition to any amendment that allowed outsiders to turn one spadeful of earth in their states. Nobody quite saw it yet, but a gauntlet had been thrown.

That gauntlet found coherent articulation three years later in Treasury Secretary Albert Gallatin's *Report on the Subject of Public Roads and Canals* (1808). Using firsthand reports of all the roads, canals, bridges, and river improvements under way in the United States, Gallatin drew up an exquisitely balanced package of coastal waterways and interregional trunk-line canals and turnpikes that formed a national communications backbone. Cost, local jealousies, and the difficulties of interstate cooperation made these projects impossible except through the patronage of Congress: "The national legislature alone," he concluded, "embracing every local interest, and superior to every local consideration, is competent to the selection of such national objects."

The Gallatin Plan reached Congress in April 1808, just as opposition was cresting to the embargo of American trade passed the previous December in an effort to stay out of the European war. Jefferson's political support collapsed. The Federalists fumed, New England's Republicans sulked in embarrassment, and stricter states' rights radicals south of Washington — led by Randolph, Macon, and James Monroe — slashed away at the administration's drift toward nationalism. Fearing that Jefferson and Madison had grown too fond of federal power and the interests of other states, these radicals or "Old Republicans" sought a fundamental adherence to the Spirit of '98. The implacable John Randolph refused to report out of committee the internal improvement amendment Jefferson requested; meanwhile, special interests all over the country seized Gallatin's invitation to proceed wherever states acquiesced. As a result, after 1808 Congress was besieged with requests for aid — requests that proved what the ideological radicals suspected, that a venal people would trade their freedom for a few miles of turnpike.

In 1811, as the United States stumbled toward a second war with England, New York's congressman Peter B. Porter and Kentucky's senator John Pope introduced a bill that required the government to purchase one-third of the stock of any company chartered to carry out the projects named in the Gallatin Plan. But President Madison refused to endorse the bill, and it slipped beneath the tide of the oncoming war. Three years later the British withdrew, not without burning both the Capitol and the president's mansion, but also suffering an ignominious drubbing by Andrew Jackson at New Orleans.

Postwar Economic Nationalism

The Congress that returned to Washington in 1815 — where the newly painted White House gleamed in defiance — exhibited a whole new outlook on governance. Young men such as Henry Clay of Kentucky and John C. Calhoun of South Carolina seized the opportunity to claim a more ambitious role for the government of the Union. A jealous disregard for national integrity had brought the country to the brink of disaster during the war, and the postwar Congress seemed determined not to undermine the budding nationalism that sprang from the battle of New Orleans. Madison asked for and got a national bank to manage the national finances. Manufacturers asked for and got protective tariffs to encourage home markets and industrial independence, lest we became so reliant on England for calico and cooking pots we could not assert our sovereignty. Riding this wave in 1816, Calhoun and Clay introduced what they thought of as the third leg of a national program: a bill to use the "bonus" from the national bank (a one-time $1.5 million payment in exchange for the new bank's charter) to start a fund for national works of internal improvement.

"Let us bind the republic together," proclaimed Calhoun. "Let us conquer space" and knit together a people so happy and interdependent that no "low, sordid, selfish, and sectional spirit" would allow them to cherish local interests over liberty within the Union. The case was not easily made; "Old Republicans" railed against what they perceived as a dangerous new campaign to enlarge federal power. Special interests hungry for "pork" conspired to maximize subsidies while deflecting any sense of control or central design. In the end, Calhoun and Clay accepted a compromise bill that doled out money in proportion to population (not transportation) needs and required state assent to any national roads and canals; but at least they got the Bonus Bill passed just days before the end of Madison's second term.

To everyone's astonishment, on his last day in office in March 1817 James Madison vetoed the Bonus Bill. After having pressed for internal improvements since at least the 1790s and after accepting a national bank and protective tariffs (both anathema to strict construction Republicans), he suddenly demanded the amendment he had never before required. Why? Clay and Calhoun had crafted the Bonus Bill precisely, they thought, to suit Madison's delicate balance between states' rights and national supremacy. But Madison saw in the bill an alarming potential for horse-trading congressmen to plunder the Treasury — not to mention the Constitution — as long as everybody got his share. Without a blueprint like the Gallatin Plan or Jefferson's amendment to restrain them, Madison feared that members of Congress would use the Bonus Bill to buy up popularity with roads and canals until nothing was left of states' rights or federal limitations.

The Attack of the Neo-Antifederalists

If Madison feared consolidated power in the hands of a pork barrel Congress, he failed to see a countervailing threat from a neo-Antifederalist movement centered on Virginia's Old Republicans. Drawing moral and rhetorical energy from the former president Thomas Jefferson and his Spirit of '98, the Richmond editor Thomas Ritchie, Virginia's Justice Spencer Roane, the agricultural writer and political philosopher John Taylor of South Carolina, and Congressman John Randolph, together with North Carolina's Nathaniel Macon and a host of lesser players, seized upon the Bonus Bill veto as an invitation to recover states' rights ground lost to the Constitution (lost to Madison himself) during the ratification debates of 1788.

Feral particularists, political conservatives, antimoderns, and eccentric personalities (Randolph and Macon), these neo-Antifederalists dug in their heels against anything that threatened the order of things as they stood in the Tidewater South in 1800. Macon (next to Randolph the quirkiest of the lot, living in a coldwater cabin with his hounds and his African servant) enjoyed seniority on committees, served for a term as Speaker of the House, and made his reputation by opposing all legislative encroachments on the rights of the landholding, slaveholding, independent gentry. Together with Randolph, Philip Pendleton Barbour of Virginia, and a number of other southern members, Macon anchored the radical wing of Old Republicans as they struggled to reverse Madisonian "liberalism" and the drift toward consolidation.

In 1817 the Virginian James Barbour (a moderate Republican) introduced exactly the amendment demanded by Madison, only to have it die without debate in the Senate. In the House, more radical Virginians launched a determined campaign to roll back "consolidation." Internal improvement belonged to the states, argued Alexander Smyth, and federal exceptions like the Cumberland Road provided no precedent because they were not legal! Philip Barbour (James's brother but a radical) repeated this conviction: no error in the past could truly alter the original meaning of the Constitution. Speaker Clay tried to rescue the Constitution from the "water-gruel regimen" Virginians now fed it, but his efforts relied on quoting Washington, who now was tainted and dismissed as a dupe of monarchist conspirators. Younger men (fearing that their states were losing prominence in the Union) followed Macon and Randolph in an all-out attack on national authority. North Carolina's Lemuel Sawyer dared national roadmakers to "tear at the virgin bosom" of his country: he, at least, would fight until the "flesh were hacked from my bones." Virginia's Hugh Nelson rallied fellow members to the "last battle" for the Spirit of '98, the "triumph of the States over the Federal Constitution."

The friends of improvements marveled at these rhetorical excesses, but their enemies could see no end to the enlargement of federal power if the utilitarians ever started stacking precedent upon precedent. (Legislation was like shingling a house, quipped Macon: "the first row is useless unless you go on lapping one row over another to the top.") An amendment seemed the logical way to limit the impact on the Constitution; but if an amendment were proposed and defeated, the power of Congress to make roads and canals, now inferred, immediately became proscribed!

Many in Congress, especially Henry Clay, knew the neo-Antifederalists could add to their minority opponents of particular routes, several votes from New England (where the Federalists still opposed all things brought forward by Republicans), New Yorkers (who just that year began their own state-funded Erie Canal and opposed federal aid to their competitors), and other doubtful strays enough to defeat any plan — or an amendment making one lawful. In 1817 Nathaniel Macon first circulated privately a blood-chilling argument that John Randolph in 1824 declaimed on the floor of the House: if Congress could make these roads and canals, it could with better right emancipate the slaves! Therefore, more was riding on this issue than mere partisanship, discrete economic interests, or even cherished principles of government. Internal improvements could not go forward without stirring up the unfinished business at the heart of the American Union.

Well aware of the dangers ahead, John C. Calhoun, who headed the War Department in James Monroe's administration (1817–1825), tried to advance internal improvements as a matter of national defense. Meanwhile Henry Clay, now Speaker of the House, lined up a series of motions that would test the support for any new version of the Bonus Bill. Did Congress have the power to appropriate money for internal improvements? Make roads for defense or the postal service? Make canals for defense or the postal service? Build roads and canals for commerce? To Clay's chagrin, only one of the four propositions passed at all — and that well short of a veto-proof two-thirds majority. With no consensus in Congress, to proceed with an amendment seemed suicidal; the friends of internal improvement thus turned their attention to finding ways to package a program of national aid that could be justified by the artful constructions of existing powers and the elastic clauses in the Constitution.

The Birth of the American System

During the first years of Monroe's administration, events played into the hands of local interests, political factions, and libertarian enemies of the "consolidation" of national power. Jealous partisans in Pennsylvania and New York demanded that the Virginians surrender their control of the White House and the Republican party. Rival factions jockeyed to name presidential candidates to succeed Monroe. In 1819 the booming land market collapsed, and the resulting panic exposed corruption in the national bank. The Supreme Court, still led by the Federalist John Marshall, struck down, in *McCulloch v. Maryland,* a state law taxing banknotes issued by the federal Bank of the United States. Marshall's extremely nationalistic ruling sent states' rights conservatives into paroxysms of fury. Finally, in the House, New York's Congressman James Tallmadge stirred up sectional tensions by proposing to ban slavery in the new state of Missouri. By the time Henry Clay restored order in 1820 with the so-called Missouri Compromise, fewer politicians than ever trusted the federal government to exercise doubtful powers for the benefit of anybody.

Into this climate of uncertainty Clay stepped with a series of speeches outlining an "American System" of policy he hoped would rally the fragmenting nation. Public lands rested at the base of this program, the sale of which brought in revenue while encouraging frontier development and economic growth. (This alternative to taxes appealed to the South and the West.) To prevent an unhealthy dependence on cotton and grain exports, he added protective tariffs to enhance urban prosperity and guarantee national security in case war cut off the sources of European imports. (New England and the Middle Atlantic states appreciated this feature.) A national banking system would foster trade and investment inside the domestic national economy, helping to ease the local discomforts that accompanied the transition to market-based production. Finally, Clay would pour a steady stream of money into national roads and canals to facilitate domestic trade and transportation, circulate money and information, and cultivate bonds of friendship among the people of the disparate sections of the country. (The capital-starved West and Southwest stood to gain while northeastern merchants hoped to profit from dramatically improved internal commerce.)

While it grew naturally out of Republican postwar economic nationalism, Clay's American System envisioned an energetic role for government — especially the national government — that reminded conservative and radical Republicans of the centralizing, class-biased policies of Alexander Hamilton. While Clay labored to effect a marriage of interests among voters in the new West, the South, and the old Northeast, the states' rights and radical Republicans consolidated their power in Virginia, New York, and Pennsylvania. National investments in roads and canals obviously served Clay's peripheral coalition better than this old Jeffersonian core, so once again strategy and ideology converged.

The issue of extending the National Road through Ohio, Indiana, and Illinois surfaced in the early 1820s as a test of Congress's ability to pursue any national program of economic consolidation. Even this true-blue Jeffersonian policy came in for heavy criticism by neo-Antifederalist Republicans, who openly called it a mistake and blamed it on special interests. (Even Madison now "remembered" it had been passed in haste late at night near the end of a session.) Voters in the West howled at the thought of being stranded in the wilderness as Virginians lost interest in their welfare. A majority in Congress agreed; but the rapid deterioration of the heavily used older sections of the road, together with the failure of the original funds set aside to pay all the costs of construction (let alone upkeep), gave the enemies of public works new reasons to attack the only living example of a national internal improvement. Extension squeezed through the Sixteenth Congress in 1820, and in 1822 the Seventeenth Congress narrowly passed a bill erecting toll gates on the National Road to fund repairs and perpetual maintenance. But this innovation stirred the executive's wrath, and Monroe's veto message came with a 25,000-word memo explaining what was wrong with federal efforts to build roads and canals in the states.

Monroe's pedantic review of the issues notwithstanding, he proposed nothing new. Amend the Constitution: nothing less would render internal improvements legal. Citing the popular demand for public works, Pennsylvania's Joseph Hemphill introduced a General Survey Bill designed to use the Army Corps of Engineers to survey public works in the states, but the opposition to "consolidation" and federal initiatives grew ever more intractable and bitter. Silas Wood of New York denounced the practice (the "cant of the day") of calling every useful objective a "national subject." Soon enough, speculated Rollin Mallary of Vermont, the government would seize all the roads as well as the new Erie Canal. Nevertheless, in 1824 the internal improvers in Congress finally passed Hemphill's General Survey Act, providing at least design advice and engineering expertise for improvements of national importance. Apparently satisfied that the scheme preserved his constitutional scruples, Monroe signed the survey bill, a weak foundation for erecting a national framework of public works but the strongest measure possible — and, it turns out, the high-water mark in the long campaign for a national system of roads and canals.

The General Survey Act was followed closely by the flawed election of 1824, making it difficult to separate cause and effect from obstruction and intrigue during the administration of John Quincy Adams. Vice President John C. Calhoun thought he saw a scheme designed to bar him from the White House; the day of Adams's election in the House of Representatives (February 9, 1825), Calhoun reversed his support for internal improvement, purged his correspondence, and launched a determined opposition to his president. Andrew Jackson charged Adams with stealing the election through "bargain and corruption" with the new secretary of state, Henry Clay. From the first day, Adams labored against the widespread presumption that he had not been elected properly.

With such a shadow on his own legitimacy, the president could only bring dishonor to programs he genuinely favored — such as national support for roads and canals. By temperament stiffly moralistic and self-destructive, he seized the fact of his own unpopularity to lecture the nation on what it needed (public works) and how to get them (by letting the government exercise authority). His infamous First Annual Message to Congress, in 1825, called for energetic national programs of science, education, and internal improvement. Trumpeting his notion that "Liberty *is* power," Adams dared Congress not to be cowed by the ignorant penury of common voters. When the most despotic nations in Europe excelled in their support for roads, canals, universities, scientific expeditions, and astronomical observatories, it would be a shame, he concluded, if we were to "fold up our arms and proclaim to the world that we are palsied by the will of our constituents." That disastrous turn of phrase marked him (unfairly) as a thorough elitist, an unreconstructed "son of the father" New England Federalist. Given such an opening, Andrew Jackson spent four years laying claim to the entire Jeffersonian legacy — the Spirit of '98 and the "true" principles of little government, local home rule, and real democratic self-government.

In Congress during these years, the General Survey Act set off a flurry of requests for federal attention to every river, creek, and sandbar for which some scrap of "national significance" could be imagined. With acid sarcasm, Virginia's William Cabell Rives, a bitter Jackson partisan, belittled such "great national objects" as the Androskoggin River and the Ammonusuck, Oliverian, and Gardiner canals, and he despaired even of finding in Morse's *Gazetteer* the location of Lake Memphremagog or Winnipisscogee — both in the wilds of northern New England. Charles Wickliffe of Kentucky complained that under the Act of 1824 "it was only necessary to get up a town meeting to ask for a survey of a road or canal, and the Surveyors were sent there." The pork barrel banquet had begun — just as Madison had feared; but under a cloud as he was, Adams found it hard to say no to any petitioner. Professionals in the Army Corps of Engineers, he hoped, would distinguish good from bad projects, but no engineer could match the pressures that politicians leveled at this otherwise sensible procedure. Even the catholicity of his approach was used against Adams: his surveys, said detractors such as Rives, "excited false hopes" as the president attempted to purchase the "favor of the People with their own money."

Three basic positions appeared in the Nineteenth and Twentieth Congresses on the question of internal improvements. First, those opposed to any federal aid for roads and canals included Old Republicans (neo-Antifederalists), centered in Virginia, die-hard provincial New Englanders, tax-wary slaveholders, and New Yorkers eager to protect their state-owned Erie Canal. Second, National Republicans, American System advocates like Henry Clay, continued to press for a coherent program of aid and a rational, national design. Finally, local interests, especially in the undeveloped new western states, scrambled to support any and all bills that might bring federal dollars into their cash-strapped frontier economies.

Complicating the legislative process were the ideological postures of strict construction and states' rights, reinforced now by righteous indignation over the "corrupt bargain" that supposedly had given office to Adams and Clay. Jockeying for advantage became transparent and sometimes comic. In 1825 Indiana's Jonathan Jennings objected to spending so-called 2 percent land revenues on the National Road in Ohio: the money was earmarked for roads to Indiana. But how, others asked in astonishment, was one to build a road to Indiana without going through Ohio? Friends of Andrew Jackson worked both sides of the street, trying to scatter funds in constituencies likely to support Old Hickory while discrediting Adams's pretensions, Clay's designs, and all forms of broad or loose construction of the Constitution.

Major initiatives that survived this legislative predation included the extension of the Cumberland Road to St. Louis, the Chesapeake & Delaware Canal, the Chesapeake & Ohio (the old Potomac) Canal, stock subscriptions for the Dismal Swamp (Virginia) and Louisville & Portland (Kentucky) Canals, and land grants to the Wabash & Erie and Illinois & Michigan Canals in Indiana and Illinois, respectively. But in the end, every dollar spent convicted Adams of "corrupting" the nation with patronage, while every project rejected proved his hostility to that particular region, interest group, or political clique. Perhaps because Americans experienced a steady rise in spending for roads and canals, they allowed the politicians to attack the legitimate platform on which such spending relied; in 1828 they overwhelmingly transferred their allegiance to Andrew Jackson, who said nothing at all about internal improvements but promised to restore "democracy" and end "corruption" in Washington.

Jackson Strikes Back

Initially, Jackson did not oppose roads and canals per se, nor was he truly an enemy of national power or energetic government. Still, he was convinced that Adams and Clay had conspired to deprive him of his victory in 1824 and so stood guilty of ignoring the will of the people. The first of a long line of political "innocents" elected on an "outside the beltway" platform, Jackson hoped to quiet both sectional and partisan quarreling by taking the federal government out of the business of delivering advantages to any one place, interest, or industry. This policy, he thought, would eliminate the dangers that accompanied all the arguments about public lands, national banks, protective tariffs, slavery, and internal improvements. Jackson's strategy, orchestrated by New York's Martin Van Buren, fused together in common cause the radical Virginia neo-Antifederalists (although Jackson never shared their visceral hatred of the national government), New York and Pennsylvania Republicans who simply distrusted Clay and Adams, and southern cotton producers who saw protective tariffs as a scam by the federal government to tax slaveholding planters on behalf of northern (free-labor) manufacturers and western (free-soil) farmers.

For strategic purposes, Van Buren urged Jackson to hang back on internal improvements (they continued to be popular, especially in the West) until some egregiously local project passed through Congress, then pounce on it with full fury. As luck would have it, the perfect case involved a turnpike in Kentucky running practically through Henry Clay's plantation. In 1830 Jackson struck at the "purely local character" (Van Buren probably penned the words) of the Maysville Turnpike and called for an end to the ad hoc approach to internal improvement until the scope of federal power was clarified by an amendment to the Constitution. The current practice, Jackson argued, distributed benefits unequally and stirred up resentment and agitation against the government. Congress seemed unable to resist the temptation to court favor (and harvest votes) by distributing legislative patronage, and Jackson denied utterly that the approval of people — even a great majority of them — could legitimate federal actions that he thought contradicted the original intentions of the Founders.

Whether Jackson's fears about internal improvements, limited government, and legislative corruption were sincere or not, the Maysville Veto marked a retreat from grand systems of policy and, in the absence of the elusive amendment, established a test that only the president seemed able to apply. The veto hammer would fall on anything not clearly national in character, which chilled the efforts of system builders like Clay. At the same time, pork barrel projects with wide partisan backing in Congress might slip through unnoticed without setting precedents. By some undocumented sense of understanding, the Jackson Democrats continued to press for aid to popular projects, especially in the West, favoring roads and river improvements over canals and chartered corporations. In this way the Jacksonians stayed in the swamps of interest group politics and enjoyed the high ground of principle simultaneously. Henry Clay tried to find a way to the White House by combining the reduction of the price of public lands with a scheme of distributing surplus revenue to the states for internal improvements according to population (Jackson's gold standard of fairness). Senator Thomas Hart Benton of Missouri preferred to see the price of western lands drastically reduced, and he positioned himself as an alternative Democratic leader to Clay and the nationalists (now called Whigs). Thus, as the 1832 presidential campaign hove into view, land policy and the distribution of the surplus replaced both the Gallatin Plan and the General Survey Act as the legislative vehicle for systematic internal improvement.

For the next twelve years, the opposition to internal improvements by the federal government could not be separated from the opposition to Clay's persistent campaigns for president. Jackson Democrats practiced a kind of ideological purity even while majorities in Congress pumped an ever-wider stream of money into local roads and river improvements. An administration clone of Clay's distribution bill, drawn up and promoted by South Carolina's Calhoun, passed in 1836, "loaning" the federal surplus to the states proportionally but reserving the right to recall the money. Jackson signed it unenthusiastically, and in 1836 Van Buren campaigned against any further aid to internal improvements (real spending having almost tripled in the previous three years). Clay tried again in 1840 and 1844 to rally the nation around positive government and national economic policies, but as long as people got much of what they wanted without conceding power to Congress or the White House, the Jacksonian approach to internal improvements prevailed. Finally, in 1846, the Tennessee Democrat James K. Polk, long a Jackson henchman in Congress, ascended to the presidency and took Old Hickory's veto hammer to a bloated rivers and harbors bill. Federal aid to internal improvement would proceed by way of an amendment — or not at all!

Railroads and Federal Land Grants

Two new variables changed the terms of the internal improvement debates from the Polk veto through the balance of the nineteenth century. The first was the triumph of railroad technology, which, by the early 1850s, was emerging from its experimental infancy. The second, closely related, was the rise of a private capital market and a national enterprise system capable of building and operating railroads as private businesses with only a helping hand from government. In part because of so much public support for canals before 1840, railroads had been forced in most cases to develop as private corporations. The financial panic and depression of 1837–1844 laid waste to the public works programs in several important states. During the inevitable backlash against public spending, maturing railroad corporations — with their higher speeds, all-weather service, geographical flexibility, and relative economy (compared with canals) — stepped forward to lead a new era. Their presence changed the congressional debates about the transcontinental railroad and led to the private control of critical structures in the marketplace.

As early as 1844, Congress entertained dreams of a railroad to the Pacific; it was first promoted by Asa Whitney as a land grant scheme to be built by private enterprise. At the time, congressmen still worried deeply about the wisdom of farming out the nation's public works to private parties — monopolists, they feared — who might hold everybody hostage in the future. Thomas Hart Benton, for one, found his libertarian Jacksonian perspective virtually reversed when he thought about the transcontinental route: "We own the country from sea to sea; we can run a national central road through and through the whole distance, under our flag and under our laws." Trapped in this contest over public versus private initiative, as well as sectional conflicts about location, Pacific railroad debates sputtered repeatedly throughout the 1840s and 1850s, with a dozen different schemes finding their way into the pages of the *Congressional Globe.* What emerged in the last several congresses before the Civil War was a fundamental shift away from national public works toward capital subsidies — especially land grants — to private corporations that could take the risk, do the work, and insulate the lawmakers from any unanticipated negative consequences.

Precedents abounded for this arms-length approach from earlier subscriptions to turnpike and canal companies by both Congress and state governments. In addition, Congress had experimented as early as 1827 with land grants to major canals, and in 1850 lawmakers applied the device to the Illinois Central Railroad. The Pacific railroad debates brought these pieces together in final form by 1854, but the sectional crisis made it impossible to select a route until the southern Democrats removed themselves from Congress in 1861. The following year, legislation authorized the Union Pacific and Central Pacific companies to begin building toward each other from Council Bluffs, Iowa, and San Francisco, respectively. The famous checkerboard land grants subsidized both corporations — although it took some innovative, and often fraudulent, financing to turn the arid lands in Nebraska and Wyoming into money for shovels, timbers, and rails. In 1869, at Promontory Point in Utah, a golden spike completed the first transcontinental railroad; the same moment effectively marked the end of the internal improvement issue in Congress.

In the end, the twisting story of national internal improvements is more about governance than transportation. Dreams of power and integration had animated visions of a national system — from George Washington's private musings on the Potomac route to Albert Gallatin's 1808 blueprint for a land and water network before the rise of industry. The same dreams of power and integration frightened people in the states that cherished decentralized authority and did not wish to see consolidation. The early debates about confederation and consolidation exposed the profoundly unfinished nature of the Union as set down in the Constitution of 1787. The efforts of Congress to do the nation's business — with one eye on the framers' intentions and the other on the possible impact of each step as a precedent — proved uneven at best. Sometimes members worked with the care of surgeons, probing the intricate organism of a living Constitution; at other times they thrashed and stamped upon the creature so recklessly, it is a wonder the government survived. This particular story is not especially heroic: the results were neither expected nor desired by the principal actors, and the tactics used often seemed knavish and disingenuous. But the story does reveal in epic terms the homely ways in which deliberative government can function (or fail to function) to shape both itself and the nation.

— John Lauritz Larson

BIBLIOGRAPHICAL NOTES

For a book-length treatment of the story sketched briefly here, see John Lauritz Larson, *Internal Improvement: National Public Works and the Promise of Popular Government in the Early United States* (Chapel Hill, N.C., 2001). On a closely related question, see Richard R. John, *Spreading the News: The American Postal System from Franklin to Morse* (Cambridge, Mass., 1995). For the important link between constitutional law and markets, see James Willard Hurst, *Law and Markets* (Madison, Wisc., 1982).

On the Federalist era, see Stanley Elkins and Erik McKitrick, *The Age of Federalism* (Oxford, 1993), and James Roger Sharp, *American Politics in the Early Republic* (New Haven, Conn., 1993). For the Jeffersonians, see two books by Noble Cunningham: *The Jeffersonian Republicans* (Chapel Hill, N.C., 1957) and *The Jeffersonian Republicans in Power* (Chapel Hill, N.C., 1963). The best introduction to the Jacksonian era is Harry L. Watson, *Liberty and Power* (New York, 1990), although George Dangerfield, *The Awakening of American Nationalism* (New York, 1965), is still entertaining. Drew R. McCoy, *The Last of the Fathers: James Madison and the Republican Legacy* (Cambridge, Mass., 1989), offers important insights. Finally, Merrill D. Peterson, *The Great Triumvirate: Webster, Clay, and Calhoun* (Oxford, 1987), places Henry Clay in the rich context of antebellum politics.

For the roads and canals themselves, see Ronald E. Shaw, *Canals for a Nation* (Lexington, Ky., 1990), Carol Sheriff, *The Artificial River: The Erie Canal and the Paradox of Progress* (New York, 1996), Forest G. Hill, *Roads, Rails, and Waterways: The Army Engineers and Early Transportation* (Norman, Okla., 1957), Edward C. Kirkland, *Men, Cities and Transportation* (Cambridge, Mass., 1948), and George Rogers Taylor, *The Transportation Revolution* (New York, 1951). For the larger context of economic development, see the first half of Alfred D. Chandler Jr., *The Visible Hand* (Cambridge, Mass., 1977).

John C. Calhoun

March 18, 1782–March 31, 1850

John C. Calhoun

Much like Henry Clay, John C. Calhoun rose from a legal career on the American frontier to national political prominence. Unlike Clay, however, who ventured from Virginia as a young lawyer to find his fortune on the Kentucky frontier, Calhoun was a native of the frontier and remained loyal to that agrarian way of life.

The third son of a prosperous South Carolina slaveholder, Calhoun was considered striking if not handsome, with piercing eyes and obvious intellect. In the course of his career, he served as a representative, a senator, the secretary of war, the secretary of state, and vice president to two administrations. Even his political foes commended his intelligence, graciousness, and integrity, although he was said to have no sense of humor and few interests beyond politics.

Calhoun was a fervent nationalist, especially in the wake of the War of 1812, but his allegiances were tested when federal tariffs favoring the more industrial North threatened the agricultural economy of his and other southern states. In decades of public service, Calhoun worked as both a politician and a political theorist to lead the nullification efforts that asserted state sovereignty in the face of rising federal power. If, after his death, Calhoun was adopted as the intellectual forefather of the Confederacy, he never advocated secession. His "Exposition and Protest" and other papers were constitutional arguments defending a way of life that he refused to compromise. Unlike Clay, perhaps Calhoun did not anticipate the calamitous results of sectional strife.

Calhoun graduated from Yale College in 1804, studied law, and was admitted to the bar in South Carolina while pursuing a career as a planter. He was elected to the state legislature in 1808 and was swept into Congress two years later, along with many other southern and western politicians who favored expansion and war with Great Britain. Before taking office, Calhoun married his cousin Floride Colhoun, a Charleston belle, who, beyond love, provided him with wealth and status in the tidewater aristocracy. The Calhouns were people of political and social convictions, which, when coupled with John's strict sectional views, may have undermined many of his political prospects. In 1829, as Andrew Jackson's vice president, Calhoun supported his wife when she ostracized Peggy Eaton, the outspoken and allegedly promiscuous wife of the secretary of war, leading to an irreparable division in Jackson's cabinet and fairly well destroying Calhoun's chances of attaining the presidency.

Although Calhoun's positions may have shifted over the course of his legislative career, his convictions never waned. On March 4, 1850, Calhoun sat in the Senate, emaciated and too ill to speak, while a colleague read his speech denouncing Clay's compromise and arguing for the legislature to restore the sectional equilibrium being jeopardized by abolitionists and the Northern majority's unmitigated rule. He died within weeks.

Calhoun was a proficient executive of the War Department and an intelligent man of convictions for which he was both respected and disliked. Perhaps he is best remembered as a political theorist who struggled to protect minority rights under majority rule with arguments that have influenced both liberal and conservative thinkers.

References

"Calhoun, John C." 1994. *Historic World Leaders.* Retrieved June 30, 2003, from http://www.galenet.com/servlet/BioRC.

Niven, J. "Calhoun, John C." *American National Biography Online* (February 2000). Retrieved June 30, 2003, from http://www.anb.org/articles/03/03-00081.html.

Part II

THE PARTISAN ERA

1830s–1900s

The United States Capitol in Washington, D.C., ca. 1846, with its first dome.

POLITICAL PARTIES were the most important institutions of nineteenth-century American politics. Although the Founding Fathers had abhorred the concept of parties, fearing that they would undermine the unity of the nation through factionalism, clear partisan divisions had taken full shape by the middle of the century, and parties became the primary institutions of American politics. Politicians frequently followed the dictates of party leaders, the press was thoroughly partisan in its orientation and ownership, and average Americans often attended partisan rallies, torchlight parades, barbecues, marches, and picnics. When white male Americans went to exercise their right to vote, they found that parties controlled the ballot box and used a variety of mechanisms to keep track of who voted for whom. "We work through one campaign," complained one politician, "take a bath and start in on the next."

Sectionalism was always a force that threatened to divide the nation, and it resulted in a brutal Civil War. But before and after the Civil War, political parties were able to overcome the threat of sectionalism. There were several reasons for it. The increase in the number of white males who were eligible to vote strengthened the electoral foundation of this political system. Voter participation reached unprecedented levels, with the turnout in presidential elections averaging almost 80 percent in the late nineteenth century and between 60 and 80 percent for nonpresidential-year, congressional elections. Election day was a major public event akin to entertainment. In addition to slavery, moreover, there were enough policy differences among Northerners and Southerners that the parties could create cross-sectional alliances. Although many Americans were involved in partisan activities only because of raw political intimidation or outright bribery and the major parties often feared the threat posed by third parties, political parties were nonetheless integral to defining the character of the democratic process. The parties also adapted when confronted with threats. As a result of congressional legislation in 1842, for example, the states were required to use single-member districts. Previously, the states had total control over election practices, and many had relied on statewide at-large districts. This practice helped parties easily gain control over the entire state delegation. After 1842, parties were forced to fight for the control of state government, which would determine the creation of district lines. While this step was a big change in how congressional elections were to be conducted, the major parties quickly adapted.

Parties defined the second congressional era, which lasted from the 1830s to the 1900s. Membership was unstable: turnover was high and long incumbency rare. At any given time, a large number of legislators were serving their first term, and frequently served only one term. Congressmen floated in and out of many political jobs. A person might be a governor one year, a senator a few years later, and then a representative. Since elections were competitive, few legislators counted on winning their seats in the next session.

There were several ways in which parties asserted themselves in Congress during this time. Although the formal mechanisms of party leadership within Congress were very weak until after the Civil War — and it was impossible to speak of centralized party bodies in Congress — the parties nonetheless saturated almost every nook and cranny of the American polity. Highly partisan electorates and state legislatures kept a close eye on their representatives and senators. In the House and Senate, informal norms discouraged maverick behavior, such as Senate filibusters. Some formal procedural rules were important: Speakers made committee assignments on the basis of party loyalty, and parties punished those who deviated from the party line. In 1833, for example, the Whig leader Henry Clay removed a large number of financial bills from the jurisdiction of the Senate Finance Committee to ensure that the panel remain loyal to the party agenda and to emasculate its chairman. In 1845 the Senate party caucuses took over the responsibility of making standing committee assignments. In 1858 the Senate Democrats stripped Senator Stephen Douglas of Illinois of his chairmanship of the Committee on Territories because he had taken a strong public stand against President Buchanan's position on the handling of the Kansas Territory. In the House, the Speaker scheduled and controlled the floor debate to protect his party's interests. Most important, parties distributed patronage to their supporters. Many prominent political leaders in state government ran for the Senate to gain access to federal jobs that they could then control. This is not to say that the parties were always victorious. There were many situations in which sectionalism or localism triumphed. Overall, however, the parties' power was impressive, as shown by the high rates of partisan voting on most issues.

Between the 1830s and 1850s, partisan warfare pitted the Whigs —

who championed national programs for economic growth, protective tariffs, a national bank, and moral reform — against the Democrats, who backed the southern slaveholding economy, strong presidential power, aggressive territorial expansion, and the primacy of local and state over federal power in domestic affairs. Certainly, some issues, such as subsidizing railroad and canal construction, elicited strong bipartisan support, given the commonality of certain local interests. But they were exceptions. The centrality of parties was also evident, for even those on the margins of the political system formed third parties to express their views, including the Anti-Masons, the Liberty Party, and the Know-Nothings.

The party system flourished in a period when America was undergoing dramatic changes. The "manifest destiny" of the United States to expand offered an ideology that legitimated the drive to secure western land in Texas, Oregon, Mexico, and elsewhere. Canals, turnpikes, and railroads improved transportation and commerce. Immigrants arrived from Ireland, China, and Germany, slowly transforming urban landscapes and the nation's Anglo-Saxon social fabric. All the while, moral reform organizations sprang up to fight against social inequities, from slavery to a woman's inability to vote. Abolitionism was the most threatening ideology of all. Under the leadership of such individuals as William Lloyd Garrison and Frederick Douglass, the abolitionist movement opened a fierce assault on the heart and soul of the southern economy and culture: slavery.

Despite their success and power until the 1850s, the mass political parties could not resolve the conflict between the South and the North over slavery. Each time that the federal government acquired a territory, legislators were forced to determine whether slavery would be allowed on the new soil. By the mid-1850s, sectional breakdown seemed inevitable, although partisan voting continued on many issues and legislators never fully abandoned their partisan identities. The situation reached the boiling point with the Kansas-Nebraska Act of 1854, as the Whigs and Democrats crumbled along sectional lines. The tensions in Congress became painstakingly clear in May 1856, when South Carolina's Representative Preston Brooks viciously beat Senator Charles Sumner of Massachusetts with his walking stick on the Senate floor. Sumner fell to the ground, bleeding from his head. Brooks was livid about a speech that Sumner, who was against slavery, had made about his uncle, Senator Andrew Butler, with regard to slavery.

The Supreme Court aggravated the situation with the Dred Scott ruling in 1857, declaring that slaves did not have the rights of a citizen even when they lived in a free state and that no free black could be a citizen. The case rendered the Missouri Compromise unconstitutional. Congress, the Court proclaimed, could not ban slavery since slaves were property. Southerners rejoiced. Members of the new Republican party lambasted the decision as hope for a peaceful solution faded in the North.

The Civil War of 1861–1865 was a trauma unprecedented in American history. The secession of the southern states and the departure of the southern politicians was followed by years of mounting carnage on the battlefield. The Battle of Gettysburg, for example, lasted only a few days but caused more deaths than the American Revolution and the War of 1812 combined. And yet the terrible war solved the slavery crisis by ending it. The Thirteenth Amendment, approved by the Senate in 1864 and the House the following year, was ratified by the states in 1865. The amendment abolished slavery, ensuring that it would never again "exist within the United States."

Remarkably, the party system did not end, despite the Civil War. Republicans replaced Whigs and Southerners seceded from the Union, yet parties remained the primary institution, shaping political activity at all levels. During the Civil War, a truncated Congress dominated by Republicans and the president did not stop making domestic policy rooted in the party's commitments, even as they worked with Abraham Lincoln on the military effort. Partisanship returned in full force during the Civil War. Under Republican rule, and without the southern Democrats around, Congress ended slavery, created the Pacific Railway Act, launched land grant colleges, and established a national income tax and banking system. Congressional partisanship did not always equal support for the president, as evidenced by congressional Republican investigations into military defeats, a task that would normally fall to an opposition party.

During the reconstruction of the South after the war, the federal government experimented with unprecedented types of intervention to achieve social and economic change. Some of the initiatives required constitutional changes. Congress passed, and the states ratified, the Fourteenth Amendment, which guaranteed due process and equal treatment before the law to all Americans; the Fifteenth Amendment protected the right of every male citizen to vote regardless of race. Other initiatives centered on agencies. The Freedmen's Bureau offered former slaves food, education, and other forms of assistance. African Americans themselves played a central role in Reconstruction by building social and political institutions while serving at all levels of government, including Congress. When President Andrew Johnson tried to capitalize on the divisions between moderate and radical Republicans to block aggressive Reconstruction proposals, his strategy backfired. Resurgent partisanship among Republicans led to his impeachment in 1868.

After Reconstruction, the major parties were better organized than ever before. Both Republicans and Democrats secured support among different social constituencies who believed that one or the other party represented their cultural outlook about the role of public institutions. Each party also attracted a particular economic constituency by defending different visions of industrial policy. Republicans thrived in the northern industrial sector by promoting national economic markets, a gold standard, and national tariffs to fund generous Civil War pensions. Democrats attracted southern agriculture, among other areas, by supporting assistance to farmers, inflationary monetary policy, free trade, and states' rights. Democrats and Republicans were also divided over racial issues, with the GOP more willing to address the condition of African Americans, albeit in limited fashion after Reconstruction, while Democrats firmly resisted any challenges to white supremacy. Within Congress, the parties expanded their procedural weapons. In the Senate of the early 1890s, for example, the party steering committees emerged as formal tools that caucus leaders could develop to promote their agendas. Meanwhile in the House, the Republican Speaker, Thomas Bracket Reed of Maine, had pushed through reforms in 1890 that empowered the majority party to block notorious obstructive tactics by the House minority. Most important, the political parties doled out jobs, making patronage the lifeblood of the party system. From the local to the national level, parties gave positions to their loyal supporters. One of the prime areas of patronage was the post office system, for legislators controlled the post office appointments in their districts and states. Political appointees were not only loyal to the party but were also major campaign contributors.

Neither party was able to gain supremacy: Republicans tended to control the Senate and Democrats the House between 1875 and 1895. Majorities were razor thin. An important change in election practices passed by Congress in 1872 dictated that elections for the House would all be held on the same day in November. Previously, states had conducted congressional elections without any apparent rhyme or rhythm on scattered days anywhere between August and November. With the new legislation, political parties were able to rely on common issues in House elections to produce dramatic national sweeps. Opponents of the status quo, moreover, continued to form third parties. Most notably, the Populists gained strength in both Congress and state politics during the 1890s by promising economic and financial assistance to small farmers burdened by chronic debt.

Each region had a different experience after Reconstruction. The North emerged as the booming hub of industrial activity, with the manufacturing and financial sectors in cities such as New York and Chicago. Immigration from eastern and southern Europe provided the urban labor force. The South, however, was economically devastated. The overall framework of the region was in shambles, and race relations deteriorated as states and localities (often aided by U.S. congressmen) enacted Jim Crow laws, which disenfranchised African Americans and created a racially segregated society. The West continued to expand. The transcontinental railway brought new populations into the territory while the discovery of gold and silver stimulated floods of adventurers seeking instant wealth. Throughout the nation, economic divisions grew starker with the solidification of a class of wealthy Americans, such as John D. Rockefeller, Cornelius Vanderbilt, Andrew Carnegie, and J. P. Morgan. Meanwhile, skilled workers were organized through the American Federation of Labor.

Throughout this entire era, before and after the Civil War, Congress was highly visible on the public stage. Indeed, Congress was the primary political institution of the nineteenth century. The executive branch remained underdeveloped both as an institution and because of the long string of mediocre leaders who held the office. Most presidents, with the exception of Andrew Jackson and Abraham Lincoln, shied away from the public eye and on most matters deferred to Congress to initiate the agenda.

The partisan era faded by the late 1880s and 1890s. While parties remained an extremely important component of American political life, their influence diminished greatly. Electoral reforms such as the Australian Ballot (which ensured that voting would be conducted in secret and that every candidate's name would appear on a single ballot paid for by the public) increased the prevalence of split-ticket voting and precluded many of the tactics that parties had traditionally used to influence voters one way or the other. National and state civil service reforms, such as the Pendleton Act of 1883, gradually if haltingly curtailed the parties' ability to ensure loyalty through patronage. Moreover, both parties were forced to compete with organized interest groups, whose leaders promised that they could deliver solid votes and ample campaign assistance. The partisan press disintegrated as a new medium arose, a system of professional journalists with an adversarial outlook who maintained weaker allegiances to elected officials. Americans did not vote as much, and electoral politics lost its salience with many citizens, who were more enthralled by amusement parks than political campaigns.

In Congress, concrete signs showed that parties were weakening by the 1890s. A series of dramatic Gilded Age scandals had brought disrepute to both parties. The frequency of partisan roll call votes declined. Ironically, it happened in the Senate just as the majority and minority parties were defining leadership positions. The high turnover on which parties thrived diminished as rates of incumbency increased and legislators started to conceive of the House and Senate as full-time careers. Congress adopted the model of seniority, whereby legislators obtained the best committee assignments by remaining in office for the longest amount of time rather than by showing party loyalty. Committees themselves gained greater autonomy, procedurally and informally. Even the size of the House and Senate became stable. Finally, although most of the new policies in this period were weak, the congressional parties agreed to delegate some of their authority to federal commissions, such as the Interstate Commerce Commission (1887), which would be run by nonpartisan experts. Within decades, the partisan era faded into American memory.

8

Congress in a Partisan Political Era

> Congress has always been and must always be the theatre of contending opinions; the forum where the opposing forces of political philosophy meet to measure their strength, where the public good must meet the assaults of local and sectional interests; in a word, the appointed place where the nation seeks to utter its thought and register its will.
>
> — CONGRESSMAN JAMES A. GARFIELD, 1877

THE 242 MEMBERS of the House of Representatives and the 48 senators who gathered on Capitol Hill at the opening of the Twenty-first Congress in December 1829 had much in common. Most were lawyers, with a sprinkling of businessmen and farmers. Almost all of them had been involved in politics at the local and state levels, as legislators, as members of the executive branch, or as judges. At the same time, in each new session of Congress in this era, a significant proportion of its members, usually about 40 percent of the House, were new to the institution; in 1843 two-thirds of the congressmen were serving their first term. Most of the senators were also newcomers when each session began. While some members did serve for more extended periods, they were exceptions to the reality that the national legislature was not a long-term career in the middle of the nineteenth century.

There were several reasons for this high turnover. One was the frequent close elections, in which incumbents were often defeated. More critical, the appeal of other offices removed many before they had long been on Capitol Hill. Congress was a fertile recruiting ground for cabinet members, presidential candidates, federal judges, and envoys to foreign countries. Other members left to take up what they considered more attractive positions in their home states.

Those who did arrive in Washington each December found their surroundings daunting. The national capital was small and woefully undeveloped, built on swampy ground and subject to problematic weather at the best of times. Congressmen lived in boardinghouses dotting the

Capitol Hill area and with others along Pennsylvania Avenue toward the White House. Few of these accommodations offered more than the barest comforts, a bed-sitting room, a common parlor, and the dining room. Given their low pay (at first, eight dollars a day while Congress was in session, only slightly better later) and the lack of domestic comforts, many congressmen did not bring their families with them. There was some social life: dinner parties and receptions held by the president, the diplomatic corps, and by the congressmen themselves. There were also many saloons, gambling halls, and other means of diversion from the cares of state.

Inside the Capitol, the accommodations were inadequate and uncomfortable. Congressmen shared the building with both the Supreme Court and the Library of Congress, each of which took up scarce room. Members had neither their own offices nor support staff. They worked at their desks on the floor of their chamber, in the library when they could find space, or in the few committee rooms available. They frequently complained about the heat, inadequate lighting, drafts of foul air, and, particularly, the noise of the many conversations that were always under way. Until 1871 smoking was allowed on the floor of the House, giving "the air a grayish hue." Outside each chamber, vendors sold food and drink. A great deal of liquor was consumed on and off the floor, adding to the general tumult and disarray. Few places were available where the men could retire to and find quiet. Even when the Capitol was significantly enlarged in the 1850s and each house moved into new chambers, conditions improved only marginally. One journalist remarked that the new House of Representatives had better acoustics than the old, but otherwise was "less well lighted and ventilated and [was] far inferior in dignified appearence to the old one."

In short, Congress was quite a chaotic institution. The behavior of individual members did not alleviate the situation or smooth operations. Visitors complained about the "rudeness, insolence, and vulgarity" shown by the members on the floor. The members often got into heated exchanges among themselves that went beyond the bonds of civility, and occasional duels and other outbreaks of violence took place both inside the chamber and elsewhere. The historian Roy F. Nichols refers to "the floor fights in which everything from epithets to cuspidors was hurled." Some members, like the shocked visitors, were themselves disheartened by the tenor of the proceedings. Levi Lincoln, who represented Massachusetts in the House in the late 1830s, lamented that "the labors are as thankless, as they are arduous, and after the best exertions, and at the utmost stretch of endurance, one has often the humiliation of seeing and *feeling,* that an important portion of his life has passed without profit to himself or advantage to others."

Although a relatively light amount of business was conducted, Congress's internal organization did not improve matters. (At the outset, the Twenty-first Congress considered almost 900 measures. The number increased to about 1,600 per Congress in the 1850s and 1860s, and then spiraled upward. In the Forty-sixth, and last, Congress of this era, just over 10,000 measures were introduced.) Each chamber had adopted standing rules to facilitate its activities, but there were always plenty of procedures that could be used to block action if desired. In the 1840s the House restricted the length of members' speeches in order to expedite its business. A one-hour rule in 1841 was shortened to a five-minute limit for each speech in 1847. The smaller Senate had no such restriction.

Congress's deficiencies and disarray underscored the need for effective leadership to make the institution work. In the House after 1830, the Speaker selected the chairs of the committees in which legislation originated or was refined, determined who was called on in debate, and had great influence on the policy agendas. (The presiding officer of the Senate, either the vice president or the president pro tempore, had more limited power.) But speakers were, like their colleagues, often relatively new to the House. And there was a high turnover among them: only three of the fourteen speakers between 1825 and 1860 served more than one term. They moved on to other offices, lost an election, or were replaced when a new majority party took over. The presiding officers of the Senate also changed frequently for similar reasons.

This limited level of experience was not restricted to the men presiding over each chamber. The chair of the most important House committee in the early years of the era, Ways and Means, a person who was usually close to the Speaker, was unlikely to be around long. Such discontinuity also affected the committee rosters. In such a situation, where leadership was always changing, the officeholders had little experience with or time to develop effective skills to direct and control any fractious member determined to go his own way in committee or on the floor. Some of the leaders did well despite these limitations; many of the rest, however, succumbed to the pressures encouraging disarray and confusion.

A Partisan Political Nation

Political parties were the glue that held this underdeveloped and seedy situation together. In the late eighteenth century, congressional contentiousness had been largely shaped by the two great combatants for national power, the Federalists and the Republicans. But after 1815, these battles became much more fragmented as the Federalists collapsed and the Republicans atrophied, leaving behind factional chaos. There continued to be a range of highly charged local and sectional battles in the nation at large over financial policy, government funding of internal improvements, and the admission of new states. Many of them reached the floor of Congress in all their bitter, and often uncontrolled, divisiveness.

In the 1820s and 1830s, a new breed of leaders, the party builders, arose, led by Senator Martin Van Buren of New York. Van Buren was a talented politician who had risen through the ranks of his own state's ferocious factional conflicts, and he sought to order the political landscape in ways that would transcend the intense and fragmenting local and regional divisions — the "violence of faction" so tellingly warned against by James Madison in 1787 — that threatened, as he and his colleagues saw it, to tear the nation apart. In the contentious tumult of Andrew Jackson's presidency after 1829, they succeeded. New national parties emerged, first the Democrats, then the Whigs, each made up of like-minded individuals in every section of the Union who were willing to submerge parochial interests as much as possible in order to work together on behalf of a broader program that they shared in common. They tried to harness the uproar and organize the contentious, narrow, unfocused, pluralism permeating national politics.

The coming of party coalitions marked a significant change in the nation's political values. Earlier, such organizations had been unacceptable to many Americans, condemned as corrupting to the political process and dangerous to the Republic. Some of these feelings remained. But there was now an increased acceptance of the importance of political parties in the life of the nation. As Representative Churchill Cambreleng of New York put it in a speech on the House floor in 1826, parties were not dangerous and unwelcome but, rather, "indespensable [sic], . . . essential to the existance of our institutions." As that notion sank in, the Democrats and Whigs grew in strength and influence throughout the nation. Parties, party identification, and partisan commitment became a natural part of the political environment.

Congress reflected this new reality. These years on Capitol Hill are remembered as a time of great oratory by some of the ablest statesmen in American history, such as Daniel Webster, John C. Calhoun, Henry Clay, and Thomas Hart Benton. But beyond the drama that their words invoked lay the more mundane legislative world of political partisanship. In the years after 1830, most congressmen rose through the ranks of their party, were elected as partisans, carried their party identification and outlooks with them when they arrived on Capitol Hill, and reflected this commitment in their subsequent activities. They thought in partisan terms, accepted partisan discipline, and spoke in the rhythms of party warfare. As a result, the power of the political parties gave each chamber's activities shape and focus — in the organization of both houses, in the day-to-day behavior of the members, and in the formulation, drafting, and implementation of legislation.

This growing partisan wave had a significant ideological focus. The clash of competing ideas, different values, and distinct attitudes toward governance led to the promotion of different policies by each party. In the 1830s and 1840s, Congress was largely preoccupied by economic issues: tariffs, banking, the federal financing of road and canal construction, and the role of the central government in shaping the emerging, market-driven economic order. The uproar set off during Andrew Jackson's presidency over these matters hardened thereafter into two distinct ideological complexes and policy agendas.

In contrast to the twentieth century, the Democrats fostered the notion of weak central government that had become firmly rooted in American political culture. They wanted, as one of them declared, to bring the national government back "to its primitive simplicity." They greatly feared the Whig (and later, Republican) notions of strong government involvement in American life. Democrats in every part of the Union fervently resisted federal intervention in the economy, opposed a national bank, and fought against high tariffs and most federal appropriations for building roads, canals, or railroads. They also opposed government intervention to reform society and supported the president's emerging role as "the tribune of the people," because Jackson had claimed that that office protected the people's rights and liberties against the threat of aggressive government power.

The Whigs, in contrast, favored a much stronger central government. They never wavered in their view that the power of the state was crucial to the nation's development. To Whigs, "the hand of governance never touches us, but to promote the general good." They wanted a national bank, a protective tariff, and more commercial involvement in national policy as a means of fostering economic growth. They were also willing to use government authority to foster social improvements and better behavior among the citizenry. Unlike the Democrats, they put legislative authority first in governing America and were deeply suspicious, therefore, of presidential power, particularly as wielded by Jackson, who was willing to use the veto over congressional bills more than any president before him.

As time passed and new issues appeared, partisan confrontation intensified. In the 1840s the parties divided over territorial expansion, with the Democrats articulating an aggressive continentalism against Mexico and Great Britain, and the Whigs expressing much more caution about acquiring more territory. Each party made its differences on these and other issues repeatedly clear in their speeches, in committee, and on the floor. The Whigs, responding to the great Democratic economic and expansion policy successes under President James K. Polk in 1846 — the passage of a lower tariff, the acquisition of Oregon and California, the veto of an extravagant (to Democrats) federally financed rivers and harbors bill — unsurprisingly lamented that "cursing and not blessing has fallen to the lot of the country." Even during major national crises, such as the devastating economic downturns after 1837 and 1857, partisan behavior remained the central reality of congressional life.

Despite the parties' sharp contrast, there were few formal mechanisms in Congress to promote partisan control. Party caucuses made up of all the members of each party functioned as coordinating institutions. They met at the beginning of each session and at other times as business and need dictated. Each sought to harmonize agendas, overcome internal squabbles, establish priorities, and guide the behavior of its members in committee and on the floor. They chose the membership of the various committees and gave them their marching orders — although they had little coercive authority except the shared values and commitments of its members. The latter paid off; most congressmen loyally accepted and followed caucus decisions in their behavior on the floor of each house.

At the same time, some rules evolved in both chambers to strengthen the ability of partisan majorities to work their legislative will. As party lines hardened, speakers became more partisan in deciding who to recognize to speak. The opposition howled at some of the choices and the way debate was controlled on behalf of the majority party. But they could do little about it. They retained some procedural means of confronting and obstructing the majority, but these measures declined over time. The Speaker could always call on his loyal partisan colleagues if he was challenged by the opposition. That support was always a powerful factor in the partisan era.

The leaders of the Senate could call on similar support from their partisan allies, even though there were more assertions of independence of party dictation in the Senate than in the House. The Senate changed its rules in 1845 so that committee members were no longer chosen by secret ballot but, as in the House, by the party caucuses. The change obviously gave great impetus to one party's domination of the chamber. Nevertheless, some senators continued to see themselves as individual statesmen, outside the reach of partisan command. But such maverick behavior, never widespread (except, perhaps, rhetorically), usually gave way when necessary to advance a party purpose or defend a partisan bastion against enemy assaults.

In this partisan atmosphere, a number of individuals emerged as particularly powerful leaders. Some of them, such as Representative James K. Polk of Tennessee, who was the Speaker of the House in the late 1830s, held an important congressional office; others, such as Senator Henry Clay a few years later, were recognized by party colleagues as their leader regardless of their formal position. None of these men was hesitant about using whatever opportunities he had for partisan purposes — committee investigations, speeches, and agendas. All partisan activities were accepted as the congressional norm.

A divided government, when it existed, intensified partisan warfare. Opposition senators, for example, used their advise-and-consent authority to further partisan goals or to prevent the president from achieving his. There was great hostility between Andrew Jackson and Congress early in the partisan era, with the Senate refusing to confirm a number of presidential appointments. The same tensions appeared when President Polk faced a Whig House of Representatives in 1847 in which the first-term, and highly partisan, congressman Abraham Lincoln of Illinois made a name for himself as a particularly persistent baiter of the president in powerful speeches challenging Polk's domestic and foreign policy initiatives.

Voting the Party Line

Most critical, party dominance became clear when congressmen voted. Strong party cohesion on the many roll calls characterized Congress from the 1830s on. Such agreement on questions of organizing each house — who was to be Speaker, clerk, or official printer — was to be expected. They were procedural matters. In the 1840s, however, when the two major parties had settled in, partisan unity on policy was very high in both houses. On tariff and banking bills and other economic legislation, on questions of territorial expansion, and on most new issues added to the mix, each party was able to mobilize the mass of its members to vote the party line.

Party discipline was never perfect. There was always a range of tension and disagreement within each party over its policy priorities and the specifics of the legislation before them, as well as constituency pressures that sometimes ran counter to a party's stance. Nor did everyone welcome the emergence of powerful, disciplined parties. Dissenters and independent thinkers continued to resist the pressures of party identification as hostile to the nation's political tradition, to its well-being, and to interests that they wished to defend. For one, a persistent sectional contrarianism remained strong among some southern congressmen, led in the 1830s and 1840s by the nation's most defiant opponent of partisan politics, Senator

John C. Calhoun of South Carolina. Calhoun felt that the growing power of party bosses and party discipline was an unacceptable threat to the needs of his own state and to the South in general. Given his great power at home, the two-party system never took root in South Carolina.

As a result of such problems and challenges, partisan unity was higher on some issues than others. It was particularly strong on those matters around which the parties had originally come together, Jacksonian economic policies, as well as on the question of territorial expansion. It was less strong on issues with a high local or regional content, such as federal financing of roads, canals, and railroads, which caused difficulties for otherwise loyal partisans.

The party leaders worked hard to control the differences among their members and subsume them within the larger penumbra of party loyalty and discipline. They were usually successful. Even when the parties occasionally sagged in the face of challenges, they proved strong enough to regain their footing and reassert their dominance over congressional affairs. Most of the time, party members could be counted on to stick together against the threat posed by their opponents. Whatever internal differences existed over specific policies, Democrats tended to cluster at one end of the roll call responses, their opponents, Whigs or Republicans, at the other.

The reason for this commitment was clear. Congressmen came out of partisan networks in their own communities and constantly refreshed their links to them. They returned home when they were not in session, spoke to their loyal supporters, and campaigned strenuously on behalf of their party and themselves. Whig and Democratic campaign rallies were frequent, noisy, and colorful; they etched into the minds of their participants what was at stake in the partisan conflict that engulfed them. To help get the message across, senators and representatives sent copies of their speeches back to their districts and provided their local party newspapers with useful official documents, such as committee reports, to use as campaign weapons. One senator sent more than 17,000 copies of the important speeches of one session back to his constituents. The members listened as well. Correspondence and petitions from demanding individuals and groups at home were quickly answered.

All of these actions reinforced the partisan bonds between constituents and their legislators, bonds based on shared beliefs and values. Congressional voting squared with the partisan speeches, pamphlets, and editorials being heard and read in the election campaigns throughout the country. As the Massachusetts congressman Caleb Cushing told the House in 1839, while their constituents sent them to Washington as free agents, they also "sent us from a previous conviction of the harmony of [our] sentiments with their sentiments, and, in our votes here, we must represent their sentiments, otherwise we are not their representatives."

Sectional Outbursts

Sectional differences had always existed in American public life but rarely in a sustained way. From the 1830s onward, both parties worked hard to control them in the interest of the cross-sectional unity they prized. Occasionally they failed, and Congress was beset by intense sectional arguments, as in the duel over abolitionist petitions in the House of Representatives in the late 1830s. But these confrontations were usually brought under control by the reigning power of nonsectional impulses. As one newspaper editor, frustrated in his efforts to forge sectional unity among southern congressmen, complained, "The antipathies of Whig and Democrat are too strong in Washington and their exercise forms too much the habit of men's lives there."

In the late 1840s, however, bitter sectional battles over the expansion of slavery into the new western territories severely challenged the partisan imperative. A confrontation between the North and South replaced the former partisan norms. After a period of tumult, they were contained, however, through legislative compromise and the reassertion of party loyalties. But that containment was brief. In the mid-1850s, as the North-South confrontation over slavery in the territories intensified, sectional battles moved to center stage, disrupted the existing parties, and overwhelmed the traditional policy agenda. The Whigs ultimately collapsed and disappeared, the Democrats suffered severe reversals in the North, and a new Republican party emerged as a largely northern coalition determined to resist southern territorial expansionism.

Nevertheless, the organization of Congress, its policymaking impulses, and its voting behavior in both House and Senate remained encased in traditional partisan commitments. Whatever sectional pressures existed in the 1850s, the memories of past partisan battles continued to affect many congressmen. The Democrats still fought for their vision of the limited authority of the central government, not only over issues about the expansion of slavery, but over other aspects of the emerging Republican agenda that were rooted in the old Whig centralizing approach.

Even on the new, divisive sectional issues, it often proved difficult for members from the same section to work together comfortably. Northern Democrats were much less sectionally focused than were their Republican opponents. Similarly, southern Whigs proved to be less committed than their Democratic opponents to the sectional division of American politics. As a result, an interplay of sectional differences within a still relevant partisan framework became commonplace in congressional politics — until the end of the 1850s, when the issues between North and South proved too intractable. In the end, the partisan impulse, whatever its staying power, could not hold the nation together.

During the Civil War, Congress greatly expanded its legislative reach. Both senators and representatives played a crucial role in assembling the nation's human, financial, and industrial resources to fight the war and in shaping the peace settlement afterward. Congress also legislated new national responsibilities, such as the Land Grant College Act and the transcontinental railroad bill.

At first, an overwhelming sense of national unity resulted in attempts to blur partisan divisions and create a bipartisan union party. But partisan conflict was never far below the surface and, soon enough, returned to its central place in congressional affairs. Ideological differences persisted as both the issues spawned by the war — the limits of the central government's authority over individuals — and the continued relevance of the old economic agenda were focal points of bitter partisan confrontation. The Republican majority passed a protective tariff and national banking legislation and forcefully pushed other policies that they, as the Whigs before them, had championed in the past. They also taxed individuals to an unprecedented degree — and then fundamentally transformed American society by ending slavery.

The Democrats responded vigorously. Given the history of partisan differences in the United States, it came as no surprise. The Democrats' commitment to states' rights and the limited use of federal authority was sharpened by their wartime experience. Any efforts made to tone down such confrontation in the interest of national unity were futile. The continuity of the issues, the fears, and the partisan habits of a lifetime made it impossible.

In contrast, the Confederate Congress played a less significant role in its nation's policymaking. Familiarly, however, when southern legislators dealt with the matters before them, they too often evinced partisan reactions, even though a formal two-party system did not exist in the wartime South. Memories of past battles remained a potent force among many of the South's leaders.

Into the Gilded Age

Parties remained integral to Congress after the Civil War despite some major changes in the institution. Senators and representatives in the Gilded Age legislated for a nation that had undergone profound changes since the onset of the party system in the 1830s. In the aftermath of the war, their burden of work did not return to its earlier levels. Matters concerning veterans, reconstructing the South, and the growing use of the federal government to deal with individual and group needs created by surging economic change contributed to the intensification of the work rhythms of Congress. (As noted above, Congress now considered an average of 10,000 measures annually.)

As Congress sought to deal with its larger domain, political corruption also became an issue of much concern. The Credit Mobilier scandal, involving the bribing of congressmen on behalf of the Pacific railroad legislation, and a number of similar outrages against the public interest blemished the names and careers of some prominent congressmen and brought the institution, and the political parties, into public disrepute in ways quite worrisome to their leaders. Reformers challenged the partisan imperative and the structure of Congress, which, they argued, allowed the corrupt excesses that were now so visible. They demanded significant changes in procedures, behavior, and the quality of the candidates offered to the voters.

Nevertheless, the internal dynamics of legislative life in Washington changed very little. Congress remained, as always, a reservoir of different interests and commitments organized into two contending partisan armies. In the early 1870s, close electoral competition returned, along with the readmission of the southern states. A growing bloc of Democratic representatives and senators swelled the party's depleted ranks and brought strong party consciousness to their tasks. Once again, Republican power on Capitol Hill, and its use to push specific legislation, infuriated its frustrated and fearful opponents. Convinced, more than ever, of the Republicans' extremism and malignity, the Democrats pushed unstintingly against their misdeeds in the South and elsewhere.

Their outrage was returned with full force. The Republicans viewed the Democrats with disgust because of their allegedly anti-Union behavior during the war and unquestioning support for southern interests afterward. Like their opponents, the Republicans were convinced of the malignity of the other side and fearful of its growing strength. They ferociously thundered the charge of treason against the resurgent Democrats years after the war had ended. As a result, the floors of Congress were awash in the most bitter and intense partisan rhetoric.

Roll call voting echoed the inflamed rhetoric. Most of the issues under consideration reflected the same strong pulls of partisanship displayed in the members' rhetoric. On the many issues that arose concerning Reconstruction and the civil and political rights of African Americans, for example, Democratic and Republican unity on the recorded votes was as high as it had been in the early decades of the partisan era. To be sure, these partisan lineups were never perfect. The Republicans, in particular, were split on how far they were prepared to go on behalf of extending and defending the rights of African Americans. Most of the time, however, despite their internal differences, when they cast their votes, they separated themselves from the position of most of the Democrats in this area.

Congress also had to deal with a variety of national economic issues. Some, such as tariffs and the federal financing of transportation projects, were familiar. Others, including currency reform and labor rights, were new, and they provoked dissenting behavior on roll call votes at a higher level than usual. Minor parties, many of them advocating an economic program that went beyond the plans of the major parties, increased in number, and some of them occasionally elected congressmen. (The Greenback party had 11 members in the House of Representatives in the Forty-sixth Congress, at the end of the 1870s.) Once there, they joined in the partisan brawl, directing their fire against both major parties. Nevertheless, despite the third-party noise, as well as some fragmentation among both Democrats and Republicans, these splits should not be overstated. In general, the differences between the two parties remained central to congressional actions in these years.

The Forty-sixth Congress ended in early March 1881. The House now had 290 members, while thirty-eight states sent 76 senators to the other side of the expanded Capitol, now crowned by a magnificent dome. The Democrats had just regained control of both houses for the first time since the Civil War. (They first won back the House of Representatives in 1874.)

The city of Washington was now larger and more developed. A more vigorous executive branch, with more support personnel than it had fifty years earlier, had moved into quarters near the White House. In the 1870s a great deal of street paving, sewer construction, and new construction occurred, somewhat improving the city's comforts. The great landscape architect of Central Park, Frederick Law Olmsted, was brought in to develop a plan for the muddy and worn Capitol grounds.

Although congressional careers were still relatively short, signs of more extended incumbency were beginning to develop in some parts of both chambers. Each house was no longer "a temporary way station" where members "stopped over on their way to other careers." The institution functioned somewhat better as well as time passed. The number of committees increased and became more specialized in order to meet the growing responsibilities of a continental nation. (The House had had twenty-seven in 1830; it now had forty-six.) More clerks were hired for all these committees as their work increased.

Nevertheless, at the end of the period, as at the beginning, the institutional and environmental settings in which congressmen worked remained at a level of comfort and support well below those of the capitals of other nations. Congressmen were used to poor conditions, but as the 1880s began, they seemed to add to a increasing sense of crisis. The extraordinary growth of new kinds of legislative responsibilities, the need for more focused information to deal with these issues, and the rise of many nonpartisan pressure groups seeking legislative assistance all began to raise the question of whether the existing structure of Congress could still meet America's needs. Congressmen still had few weapons — information, staff, or expertise — with which to deal with the new issues. When they tried to act, there were logjams. After the war, there were too many committees competing for time on the floor, too many different pressures, and no good procedures for handling the onrush of business. And to critics, partisan rhetoric and responses no longer seemed able to deal with this greatly expanded and more complex legislative universe.

The consequences of these problems would ultimately manifest themselves in far-reaching changes in the political world of the nineteenth century. Political parties remained important for some time to come, but they were increasingly weakened by constant assaults on their corruption and their failure to master the new world as effectively as they had the old. Organizational shifts in Congress itself would contribute to loosening the dominant hold of the parties. As time passed, the Democrats and Republicans would no longer command the political landscape on Capitol Hill or elsewhere with the strength that they had once enjoyed. A unique partisan era had run its course.

— JOEL H. SILBEY

BIBLIOGRAPHICAL NOTES

Thomas P. Alexander, *Sectional Stress and Party Strength: A Computer Analysis of Roll-Call Voting Patterns in the United States House of Representatives, 1836–1860* (Nashville, Tenn.,1967); Joel H. Silbey, *The Shrine of Party: Congressional Voting Behavior, 1841–1852* (Pittsburgh, 1967); and Michael Les Benedict, *A Compromise of Principle: Congressional Republicans and Reconstruction* (New York, 1974), delineate Congress's partisan voting behavior from the 1830s to the end of the 1860s. The sectional impulse and its interrelationship with political parties is traced in William Freehling, *The Road to Disunion: Sectionalists at Bay, 1776–1854* (New York, 1990).

Other aspects of congressional history are explored in Sarah Binder, *Minority Rights, Majority Rule: Partisanship and the Development of Congress* (Cambridge, Mass., 1997); Allan G. Bogue, *The Earnest Men: Republicans of the Civil War Senate* (Ithaca, N.Y., 1981) and *The Congressman's Civil War* (New York, 1989); and Margaret Susan Thompson, *The "Spider's Web": Congress and Lobby-*

ing in the Age of Grant (Ithaca, N.Y., 1985); David Rothman, *Politics and Power: The United States Senate, 1869–1901* (Cambridge, Mass., 1966); and Morton Keller, *Affairs of State: Public Life in Late Nineteenth Century America* (Cambridge, Mass., 1977).

Much of Congress's history can be traced in the biographies of its members. Among the most useful are Charles Wiltse, *John C. Calhoun,* 3 vols. (Indianapolis, 1944–51); Robert Remini, *Henry Clay: Statesman for the Union* (New York, 1991); Charles Grier Sellers Jr., *James K. Polk, Jacksonian, 1795–1843* (Princeton, N.J., 1957); William N. Chambers, *Old Bullion Benton, Senator from the New West, 1782–1858* (Boston, 1956); Glyndon G. Van Deusen, *William Seward* (New York, 1967); Robert Johannsen, *Stephen A. Douglas* (New York, 1973); Hans Trefousse, *Thaddeus Stevens, Nineteenth Century Egalitarian* (Chapel Hill, N.C., 1997); David Donald, *Charles Sumner,* 2 vols. (New York, 1960, 1970); David Lindsey, *"Sunset" Cox: Irrepressible Democrat* (Detroit, 1959); David M. Jordan, *Roscoe Conkling: New York's Voice in the Senate* (Ithaca, N.Y., 1971); and Allan Peskin, *Garfield: A Biography* (Kent, Ohio, 1978).

9

The Bank War

On April 10, 1816, President James Madison signed into law "an act to incorporate the subscribers to the Bank of the United States." The passage of this bill was intended to settle a question that had plagued the American government almost since its inception. Instead it ignited a new round of controversy that finally culminated in the Bank War of Andrew Jackson's presidency in the mid-1830s. Overall, no issue Congress faced in its first half century proved more intractable than banking. The subject often dominated politics and twice prompted the creation of national parties, pitting first Alexander Hamilton against Thomas Jefferson and James Madison, and later Andrew Jackson against Henry Clay. The banking question engaged Congress in all its functions — as an investigative and legislative body, as a check on presidential authority and prerogative, as a reflector of popular opinion, and in dialogue and rivalry between its two constituent branches of House and Senate. In the end, Jackson's Bank War served to redefine the place and power of Congress within the American political system.

Government and Banking in the Early Republic

From the beginning, government and banking were entwined in the United States by the need to provide an everyday currency and a source of business credit for a rapidly developing yet severely underfunded national economy. The country had no great private banking houses like the Barings of London or the Rothschilds of Europe, and it suffered chronic shortages of gold and silver specie, the only legal money. Banking in America therefore grew by the forced hand of government. State and federal legislatures enacted charters that incorporated banks and authorized them to lend their own credit in the form of banknotes. Ostensibly redeemable in specie, these notes passed in lieu of coin in daily exchange — in practice, though not in law, as money.

Necessary as it was to prosperity and growth, the banking system also bred distrust. Despite its vast economic potential, the early republic was still mainly agricultural. To the farmers who made up most of the citizenry, the exotic mysteries of credit and finance seemed strange and threatening. Even the men who directed banks had often only a rudimentary understanding of them; many had entered banking not in order to invest but to borrow. Frequent mismanagement, malfeasance, and scandal resulted. Americans had used paper money since colonial days, but they were wary of its abuses. When issued in excess, as during the Revolution, paper depreciated in value, and its fluctuations opened a door to speculation and profiteering.

Beyond this, the role of legislatures in granting charters, and of well-connected insiders in procuring them, invited suspicions of exclusive privilege and a moneyed "aristocracy." The banks' quasi-public character made them inescapable objects of censure, the targets of envy during prosperity and of blame in hard times. Corporations themselves were a novel form of business organization, not yet standardized or widely used; and to skeptics the creation of such artificial entities and their endowment with great financial powers by legislative fiat seemed a kind of malign wizardry. To many Americans, the union of government with banking corporations recalled the hated British financial system of monopoly and corruption. Former president John Adams, though no foe of commerce or credit, condemned chartered banking in 1813 as a giant swindle, a "Sacrifice of public and private Interest to a few Aristocratical Friends and Favourites." His correspondent, former president Thomas Jefferson, heartily agreed.

Add the deep fears and jealousies of an overpowerful central government, and it is not surprising that federal involvement in the banking system was controversial from the first. In 1781 the Confederation Congress incorporated the Bank of North America in Philadelphia. This bold step was taken under the exigency of stabilizing the country's chaotic wartime finances. Still, it represented a doubtful extension of federal authority, and the bank soon covered its bets by accepting and operating under an alternative charter from the state of Pennsylvania.

The First Bank of the United States

The U.S. Constitution says nothing about the power of Congress to charter corporations or about banking in general. Nonetheless, at the urging of Treasury Secretary Alexander Hamilton, the first federal Congress in 1791 passed an act to incorporate the Bank of the United States (BUS) for a period of twenty years. Patterned on the Bank of England, it was to be a private institution serving public needs. It would be the government's own banker, receiving, storing, transmitting, and disbursing its funds and brokering its loans. The United States had a one-fifth share in the Bank's ownership and direction, and securities of the federal debt made up part of its $10 million in authorized capital. With its headquarters in Philadelphia, the Bank could establish branches in the states, making it America's only truly national financial entity. Its notes, redeemable in specie, were legal tender and would provide a uniform currency.

The debate over Hamilton's project aired all the objections — financial, political, constitutional — against banks, against the union of government with moneyed interests, and against chartered corporations and monopolies. In the House of Representatives, the opposition's floor leader, James Madison of Virginia, who had collaborated with Hamilton at the Constitutional Convention and in writing the *Federalist* essays, denied Congress the constructive power to create corporations. In President Washington's cabinet, Secretary of State Thomas Jefferson seconded Madison's objections, while Hamilton defended the charter as pursuant to the congressional authority to collect taxes, borrow money, and regulate trade. The bank debate thus brought forth the "strict construction" and "implied powers" principles of constitutional interpretation that would duel throughout American history. In Congress, the contest over Hamilton's bill furthered the division into administration and opposition camps, which would soon become the Federalist and Democratic-Republican parties. The charter passed the Senate on an unrecorded vote and the House of Representatives by 39–20, with the commercial Northeast in favor and the agricultural South opposed.

The first Bank of the United States fulfilled all its proponents' hopes. Stabilizing the country's credit and currency, it helped invigorate economic growth and restore soundness to American finances. But its success did not quiet the hostility of many Jeffersonian Republicans, who after 1800 controlled both the presidency and Congress. Indeed, the Bank's cool efficiency merely confirmed some men's dread of its concentrated financial power. In 1811 its twenty-year charter ran out. James Madison, now president, had become convinced of the Bank's indispensability and favored renewing the charter. So did Treasury Secretary Albert Gallatin, the Republicans' financial wizard and Hamiltonian counterpart, and the administration's floor leader Senator William Harris Crawford of Georgia. But many congressional Republicans did not agree, including veteran strict constructionists like William Branch Giles of Virginia and a young hotspur from Kentucky, Henry Clay. A new rival to the Bank appeared in the form of state-chartered banks, whose numbers had grown in two decades from three to ninety. By collecting and presenting their notes for redemption in specie, the BUS effectively curbed their lending. State bankers both resented this restraint and thirsted to inherit the Bank's government business. After a debate that largely recapitulated the constitutional arguments of 1791, Congress in 1811 refused, by a one-vote margin in each house, to renew the charter. The Bank was forced to wind up its affairs and dissolve.

Within months, many found reason to regret this decision. The War of 1812 again plunged federal finances into chaos. Suddenly the administration needed to raise large sums on short notice and move them quickly around the country, two functions of the old BUS that no state bank could perform well. As the American armies suffered demoralizing reversals, the government's credit went into rapid decline. Lenders refused their funds, discount rates soared, soldiers and suppliers went unpaid, and the United States for the first time under the Constitution came near to defaulting on its debt. Meanwhile, the states rushed to fill the gap left by the federal bank's demise by chartering scores of new banks. These flooded the country with notes and then suspended specie payments, collectively refusing to redeem their own obligations in coin. Though their unconvertible paper was of doubtful worth, it was now the only currency available.

The Second Bank of the United States

With the coming of peace, Congress moved to restore order. In December 1815, President Madison recommended a new bank to ensure a "uniform national currency," renouncing his old constitutional objections as overruled by events. In the House of Representatives, a bill was produced by John C. Calhoun of South Carolina, one of a new generation of nationalist politicians sprung to prominence by the war. Speaker Henry Clay, confessing that experience had taught him wisdom, pledged his support. With the constitutional issue mooted and the need for a bank made plain by circumstance, the opposition was listless. Curiously, much of it came from New England Federalists led by the young New Hampshire congressman Daniel Webster. Traumatized by their years out of power, the Federalists had retreated into a naysaying parochialism, practically reversing the stance of the two parties. The charter for a new Bank of the United States passed the House, 80–71, and the Senate, after amendment, 22–12. Madison signed it without a qualm.

Like its predecessor, the second BUS was quartered in Philadelphia, with power to establish branches throughout the country. Its capital, paid in gold, silver, and certificates of the federal debt, was set at $35 million. Of this, the United States owned one-fifth, and the president, with the

Senate's consent, annually appointed five of the Bank's twenty-five directors. The Bank's books were open to government inspection, and its paper was legal tender for all payments to the United States. It was to transport and disburse federal funds without charge and to receive all the government's own deposits unless placed elsewhere by the secretary of the Treasury, who in such case had to report his reasons immediately to Congress. Congress pledged to establish no competing bank during the charter's duration, which was again set for twenty years, to expire on March 3, 1836. In return for these "exclusive privileges and benefits," the Bank, once under way, was to pay the government a bonus of $1.5 million.

Though chartered with little stir, the second BUS was soon awash in controversy. It opened for business in January 1817, amid the gathering momentum of a feverish postwar boom. Congressional architects had intended the Bank to rein in the note issues of the state banks. Instead, it merely added its own. Under its president, William Jones (chosen under the charter by vote of the directors), the Bank became a giant freebooting machine, lending profligately and recklessly, with some branches cannibalizing others to sustain their speculations. In 1819 a House committee chaired by John C. Spencer of New York, after scouring the books and taking sworn testimony, reported rampant stockjobbing and preferential lending among the Bank's officers. At its Philadelphia headquarters there was gross malfeasance; at the Baltimore branch, outright fraud.

Jones resigned in disgrace just as the country's inflated prosperity imploded in the calamitous Panic of 1819. Only two years in existence, the Bank was in thorough disrepute and overextended nearly to the point of insolvency. Under the circumstances, the Supreme Court's decision in early 1819 in *McCulloch v. Maryland,* affirming the Bank's constitutionality and immunity from interference by state governments, only added to the public fury — the McCulloch on the winning side of the case being the embezzling cashier of the Baltimore branch. To restore confidence, the Bank's directors chose Langdon Cheves of South Carolina, a former Speaker of the House of Representatives, to succeed Jones. Cheves took charge in the depths of the panic. He began a rigorous contraction that rescued the BUS from failure, but only by pressing debtors to the wall. Business failures left the Bank holding large swaths of forfeited commercial property. As one critic, William Gouge, acidly put it, "the Bank was saved and the people were ruined."

It took years of prudent management to restore confidence in the Bank and repair its devastated reputation. This was in time accomplished under the suave and discreet supervision of Nicholas Biddle, who followed Cheves as president in 1823. Under Biddle, the Bank functioned much as its creators had envisaged, smoothly handling the government's business while gently steadying the supply of credit and the pace of trade. Its own notes were everywhere as good as gold. By the end of the 1820s, the Bank had won broad acceptance as a vital cog in the American financial and governmental system. Its efficiency was unquestioned, and the issue of its constitutionality was as settled as precedent, experience, and adjudication could make it.

Jackson versus the Bank

Yet one who was not convinced was General Andrew Jackson. Like many Americans, Jackson did not understand banking very well, and what he did not understand he intuitively mistrusted. He also saw himself as a Jeffersonian strict constructionist, anointed to restore the government to its original republican purity. In 1828, on his second try, Jackson was elected president of the United States, defeating the incumbent, John Quincy Adams. The Bank went unnoticed in the campaign. But in his first message to Congress in 1829, Jackson startled everyone by challenging its constitutionality and expediency, denying the stability of its notes, and urging Congress to explore alternatives.

The House Ways and Means Committee and the Senate Finance Committee, chaired, respectively, by George McDuffie of South Carolina and Samuel Smith of Maryland, duly inquired. Their reports triumphantly upheld the Bank, declaring its currency the soundest ever known and the constitutional question to be "forever settled and at rest." Jackson, unfazed, repeated his criticisms to Congress in 1830 and 1831. He found a Senate champion in Thomas Hart Benton, a former Tennessean who had once served as a colonel under Jackson, fought him in a street brawl in 1813, and subsequently fled to Missouri. Now reconciled with Jackson, he delivered powerful speeches, painting the Bank as an illicit and alien force that stole Americans' prosperity and contaminated their politics with its concentrated financial power. "All the flourishing cities of the West are mortgaged to this money power," Benton cried. "They may be devoured by it at any moment. They are in the jaws of the monster! A lump of butter in the mouth of a dog! One gulp, one swallow, and all is gone!"

Jackson privately termed the Bank a "hydra of corruption" and "dangerous to our liberties." Nicholas Biddle attempted to placate him with attentions and favors, and two of Jackson's cabinet, Secretary of State Edward Livingston and Treasury Secretary Louis McLane, urged a compromise on recharter. But Jackson's hostility to the Bank — indeed, as he told Biddle, to all chartered banks — was unshakable.

His attacks forced the Bank into partisan politics, where President Biddle had heretofore astutely forborne to tread. Despairing of mollifying

Jackson, Biddle decided to seek an extension of the charter from Congress before the 1832 presidential election on the advice of Jackson's prospective opponent, Senator Henry Clay, and Senator Daniel Webster. Now of Massachusetts, Webster had shed his youthful obstructionism to join Clay as a nationalist spokesman and champion of broad federal powers. Both men were also well-paid Bank attorneys. Assuming that most Americans understood the Bank's merits, they believed Jackson would not dare veto a recharter just before the election. If he did, they would make an issue of it.

In January 1832 the Bank formally solicited Congress to renew its charter. Jacksonians controlled the House of Representatives, but Jackson had not yet drawn a party line against the Bank even in his cabinet, and the opponents' ranks were not firm. In a delaying strategy crafted by Thomas Hart Benton, Representative Augustin Clayton of Georgia moved an investigation of the Bank's affairs by a select committee of the House, a demand its friends could not refuse. Speaker Andrew Stevenson named an anti-Bank majority to the committee, which was headed by Clayton. Their report duly charged it with malfeasance and corruption. The pro-Bank minority demurred, and former president John Quincy Adams, now a maverick Massachusetts congressman, filed his own scathing dissent.

For all the furor, the Bank's supporters, including some Jackson men, still numbered a majority in Congress. A bill to renew the charter with slight modifications passed the Senate, 28–20, on June 11, and the House, 107–85, on July 3. Jackson vetoed it one week later.

This veto defined Jackson's presidency and laid the foundation for a new political party. Jackson attacked the Bank on every front. He denied its constitutionality, claiming a right to judge that question independently of Congress or the courts. He appealed to the rights of the states, undermined by the presence within their borders of an alien corporate power they could neither tax nor regulate. He condemned the Bank as an agent of foreign influence, citing the ownership of its stock by British investors (who in fact were barred by the charter from partaking in management or even voting their shares). He accused the Bank of subverting the freedom of elections by wielding its vast resources to cow or buy off opponents. Above all, he branded the Bank as a bastion of monopoly and privilege. Counterposing its "rich and powerful" stockholders against "the humble members of society — the farmers, mechanics, and laborers," Jackson struck the tone on which he would henceforth proceed to reshape his diffuse following into a new party, the Democrats.

Jackson's veto challenged a tradition that went back to the Revolution, of circumscribing executive authority and regarding the legislative branch as the true embodiment of the public will. Abandoning his predecessors' deference to Congress, Jackson cast himself as the whole people's sole defender against the mere jumble of special interests represented by congressmen. To Jackson's supporters the veto was a rallying cry; to critics it seemed both a stunning affirmation of unbridled executive power and a reckless invitation to class war. In the Senate, Clay attacked it as at odds with "the genius of representative government" while Webster assailed Jackson's "claim to despotic power." Benton responded warmly, and the session closed on a fiery shouting match between him and Clay.

The vote to override the veto failed in the Senate, as all knew it would, 22–19. In the fall campaign, both the Jackson and Clay camps circulated copies of the veto. Biddle, now wholly engaged, used Bank funds to print and distribute documents supporting recharter and opposing Jackson. Nonetheless, Jackson beat Clay handily in the November election. Whether the Bank issue actually gained or cost him votes is uncertain.

The Removal of the Deposits

Jackson read his victory as a mandate to continue warring on the Bank. Its existing charter had three years to run, and the campaign had fortified his belief in its malign political influence. Supporters still hoped for recharter. So Jackson determined to strip the Bank's power by withdrawing federal funds from its control. In his first message to Congress after the election, in December 1832, he intimated that the government deposits were unsafe in the Bank and should be removed. The House of Representatives answered in March 1833 by voting resoundingly, 109–46, that the deposits were safe and should remain where they were.

Congress adjourned the next day, and Jackson took matters into his own hands. The Bank's charter allowed the secretary of the Treasury to remove federal deposits from its keeping, provided he promptly report his reasons to Congress. This provision of the charter contemplated the secretary as a separate agent, answering to Congress rather than the president. It reflected Americans' habitual wariness of concentrating the power of the purse in the executive.

Yet Jackson, seeing himself as the people's tribune, regarded his official subordinates, the Treasury secretary included, as mere instruments of his will. After the House vote, Jackson polled his cabinet on removing the deposits. Nearly all were opposed, including Treasury Secretary Louis McLane, who had hoped for recharter. But Jackson got the support and arguments he needed from Attorney General Roger Taney, a vociferous Bank opponent who had helped draft the veto. Since the government's money needed to be held somewhere, Jackson dispatched a subordinate Treasury official, Amos Kendall, to recruit state-chartered banks to receive it. To dispose of McLane, he elevated him to secretary of state and replaced him in the Treasury with William John Duane, a foe of the Bank and the son of an old Jeffersonian editor from the party's early days. In the cabinet on September 18 Jackson read a memorandum, drafted by Taney and afterward released to the press, announcing his intent to withdraw federal deposits from the Bank of the United States. He then ordered Duane to execute the removal.

To Jackson's astonishment, Duane refused. Jackson dismissed him and put Taney in his place. Taney promptly ordered federal revenues to be placed henceforth in selected state banks, while expenditures would be met by drawing down the government's balances in the Bank of the United States. Through this device, the federal deposits were removed from the Bank, presenting Congress with a fait accompli by the time it reconvened in December 1833.

There open revolt threatened. Many congressmen, including even some foes of the Bank, believed that Jackson's highhanded action defied not only financial prudence but the very letter of the law; his assertions of presidential power smacked of naked royal prerogative. He had, on no shred of proper authority, removed the government's money from the responsible, congressionally sanctioned hands of the Bank of the United States to an untried, unregulated, and perhaps thoroughly irresponsible collection of state banks, selected on political criteria of friendliness to his own administration. In the Senate, Clay, seconded by Webster and John C. Calhoun, denounced Jackson's "open, palpable, and daring usurpation" as pointing toward "a total change of the pure republican character of the government, and to the concentration of all power in the hands of one man." Senators Benton and Silas Wright and Chairman James K. Polk of the House Ways and Means Committee defended Jackson and assailed the Bank. "The question," said Polk, is "whether we shall have the republic without the bank, or the bank without the republic."

Jackson's relations with the Senate had always been stormy, even when he enjoyed a nominal majority there. Party ties developed in slow stages during his presidency; and senators, their sense of independence reinforced by long terms of office and indirect means of election, especially cherished their freedom from outside dictation. Jackson had begun his administration by nominating a slew of rabidly partisan editors like Isaac Hill of New Hampshire and Amos Kendall of Kentucky — "electioneering skunks," John Quincy Adams called them — to high government posts. Several were rejected, a few by huge margins, with even such Jackson stalwarts as Thomas Hart Benton joining the majority. Hill was defeated, 33–15, Kendall confirmed only by the vice president's tiebreaking vote. These early scrapes inaugurated a running warfare over appointments, with the Senate rejecting more nominees than ever before. Jackson fought back by renominating his defeated candidates or their close relations and by keeping men in office through interim appointments even after the Senate had rejected them.

In the Congress that met at the end of 1833, Jackson held a shaky majority in the House. There, after heated debate, resolutions sustaining the deposit removal were duly passed. But in the Senate, the anti-Jackson coalition of Clay, Calhoun, and Webster ruled. The Senate began by demanding a copy of the cabinet memorandum of September 18. Jackson declined, claiming what would later be called "executive privilege," though the paper in question had already been published at his own behest. The Senate next refused Jackson's renomination of four incumbent government directors of the Bank of the United States. Jackson sent the names back in, claiming that the men had provided essential service by informing on the Bank's illicit dealings. Again they were rejected, by a larger margin than before. For good measure, the Senate rejected Taney for Treasury secretary, the first cabinet nominee it had ever refused.

On March 28, 1834, for the first and only time in its history, the Senate formally censured the president himself. The resolution, sponsored by Henry Clay, stated that Jackson "in the late Executive proceedings in relation to the public revenue, has assumed upon himself authority and power not conferred by the Constitution and laws, but in derogation of both." It passed, 26–20.

Jackson replied with a long and angry protest, denying the right of the Senate, a body "not elected by the people and not to them directly responsible," to pass judgment on "the direct representative of the American people" in this extrajudicial manner. As Jackson pointed out, the Senate's censure aspired to the moral weight of an impeachment without any of its procedures: no specification of charges, no vote by the House, no trial or chance for defense, and passage by a simple majority instead of two-thirds. Further, four senators who voted for the censure were under instructions from their own state legislatures to oppose the Bank and support Jackson's policy. The Senate refused to record Jackson's protest as an affront to its own freedom of expression.

Speaking in the Senate in April, Henry Clay christened the new anti-Jackson coalition with the name of Whigs. A British term hallowed for Americans by its use in the Revolution, it signified opponents of royal prerogative. The Whig label united the nationalist, mainly northern followers of Clay and Webster with southern states'-righters already angered by Jackson's handling of the South Carolina nullification crisis of 1832–1833. Northern and southern Whigs had disagreed on the protective tariff and federal transportation spending, which commanded center stage through the 1820s; but they mostly favored the Bank, and at any rate could all join in reprobating Jackson's highhanded actions against it. Spreading out from Congress, the Whig fold gathered in all who for one reason or another found fault with Andrew Jackson. For the next several years, the party's organization proceeded in tandem with that of Jackson's Democrats.

The Bank itself had answered the removal of deposits by sharply curtailing its loans, causing distress in business circles. Ostensibly the diminution of assets necessitated this contraction, but in fact Biddle, his prudence unhinged, was determined to force a recharter even if he had to manufacture a panic to do it. An orchestrated campaign flooded Congress in 1833–1834 with more than 100,000 signatures urging the restoration of the deposits. But in the end, Biddle's naked manipulation only weakened the Bank by vindicating Jackson's warnings of its capricious power. No recharter came to a vote, and the Senate Whigs, having censured Jackson, could do no more. Recognizing its futility, Biddle eased his pressure as the session closed.

Legacies

The rest was anticlimax. The Bank continued quietly for two more years and, at the expiration of its federal charter in 1836, accepted a new one from the state of Pennsylvania. It later became involved in cotton speculations and failed, discredited, in 1841. Meanwhile, just as in 1811, the central bank's demise triggered a frenzy of state banking, note issue, and speculation, culminating in a spectacular collapse and depression that began just as Jackson left office in 1837. The Whigs blamed the disaster on Jackson's folly in destroying the Bank; they continued to agitate into the 1840s for some kind of suitably tamed federal substitute. The Democrats blamed the state banks and carried their war against banknotes and corporate charters into state legislatures and constitutional conventions. At the federal level, Democratic policy settled on divorcing the government from banking altogether and returning to a "hard money" currency of gold and silver. This drive found expression in the Independent Treasury bill, giving the federal government sole custody of its own funds. Enacted under the Democratic president Martin Van Buren in 1840, it was repealed by a Whig Congress the next year and recreated under James K. Polk in 1846. Banking remained a potent party issue and ideological marker until it was swept away by the growing slavery controversy in the 1850s.

Meanwhile, Jackson and the Senate had fought their final round. No sooner was censure voted on Jackson in 1834 than Benton moved to expunge the record of it from the Senate's official journal. This resolution, reintroduced year after year, became the symbol of Jackson's vindication and the instrument for a party purge of the Senate. Acting on orders from Washington, state Democratic legislators offered resolutions instructing their senators to vote to expunge the censure. Legislative attempts to control senators through instruction were not in themselves new. Hitherto used nearly at random, they had been sometimes heeded and sometimes not; for instructions carried no legal weight and contradicted the senators' own conception of their role as autonomous arbiters of the nation's fortunes.

Jackson and the Democrats condemned senatorial independence as aristocratic. For years, Jackson had bridled at his inability to control senators like John Tyler of Virginia, who had called himself a Jackson man yet voted against the president's nominees and policies whenever his conscience dictated. Against such men, the Democrats wielded Benton's expunging resolution as a disciplinary tool. Instructions to support it were jammed through state legislatures, forcing recalcitrant senators to comply or resign. Rather than submit, several, including Tyler, relinquished their seats. By 1837 the Democrats had procured a Senate majority, and of a new kind — not a band of individuals exercising free judgment but a cadre of agents bound to do their party's bidding. Near midnight on January 16, just six weeks before Jackson's term expired, Benton's expunging resolution passed, 24–19. While Clay, Calhoun, and Webster decried the "foul deed" of desecration, the original manuscript journal of 1834 was retrieved and the record of censure blotted out by the clerk. Hisses and moans arose, and Benton roared to clear the galleries of the "bank ruffians."

The economic consequences of the Bank War have been much debated, but its political effect was unmistakable. It shaped the new Whig and Democratic parties and reshaped the balance of power within the federal government. Throughout his early presidency, Andrew Jackson had sought a means to convert his untouchable personal popularity into an effective instrument of governance. The Bank War gave him both an ideological standard and a tool for purging mavericks and malcontents. It became the instrument for defining the membership of the Democratic party at the same time that it cemented the unity of Jackson's opponents under the new Whig umbrella.

The presidency itself emerged from the Bank War with its stature enhanced and with that of Congress, especially the Senate, correspondingly diminished. Their powers have waxed and waned since, but in the Bank War Congress lost a preeminence it would never fully regain, and presidents gained a prerogative they would never fully lose. The new balance was made plain in 1841, when the death of new Whig president William Henry Harrison brought his vice president, the former renegade Jacksonian John Tyler, into office. As the first man to hold the presidency by succession instead of election, Tyler's authority was uncertain. Yet by repeated vetoes, he succeeded in blocking the enactment of banking legislation that formed the centerpiece of the program of the Whigs who had put him in office. In severing his ties to his party, Tyler doomed himself to oblivion at the next election. But he was not impeached or censured, and his vetoes stood. Jackson's claim to represent the people against Congress, new and outlandish when first pronounced, had become a routine assertion, made even by presidents who could show no electoral mandate.

— DANIEL FELLER

BIBLIOGRAPHICAL NOTES

Robert V. Remini, *Andrew Jackson and the Bank War* (New York, 1967), is a brisk and balanced account. The Bank War takes center stage in Arthur M. Schlesinger Jr., *The Age of Jackson* (Boston, 1945), a riveting and panoramic study that votes emphatically for Jackson. Bray Hammond, *Banks and Politics in America from the Revolution to the Civil War* (Princeton, N.J., 1957), erudite and witty, takes the side of the Bank. The most thorough history of the Bank is Ralph C. H. Catterall, *The Second Bank of the United States* (Chicago, 1902).

M. St. Clair Clarke and D. H. Hall, eds., *Legislative and Documentary History of the Bank of the United States* (Washington, D.C., 1832; reprinted 1967), compiles congressional proceedings from 1780 to the eve of Jackson's veto. Presidential papers, including messages to Congress and Jackson's cabinet memorandum of 1833, are gathered in James D. Richardson, ed., *A Compilation of the Messages and Papers of the Presidents, 1789–1897* (Washington, D.C., 1896–99). On Jacksonian politics generally, see Harry L. Watson, *Liberty and Power: The Politics of Jacksonian America* (New York, 1990), and Donald B. Cole, *The Presidency of Andrew Jackson* (Lawrence, Kans., 1993). On the Senate gladiators Webster, Clay, and Calhoun, see Merrill D. Peterson, *The Great Triumvirate* (New York, 1987).

Daniel Webster

January 18, 1782–October 24, 1852

Daniel Webster

Born in Salisbury, New Hampshire, Daniel Webster was not well suited to the demands of farming the 225 acres of land in the upper Merrimack Valley that his father, Ebenezer, had been allotted for his service in the colonial militia. The second-youngest of ten children, the young Webster was frail, with a head seemingly large for his body and a complexion so dark, he was often mistaken for an American Indian. Shy and self-conscious through adolescence, Webster came into his own at Dartmouth College. He graduated in 1801 and went on to become a legendary orator, one of the highest-paid lawyers of his time, and an influential politician during the roiling debates over slavery and state sovereignty in the decades before the Civil War.

After his father's death in 1807, Webster moved to Portsmouth to begin his legal practice. He married Grace Fletcher, the daughter of a New Hampshire clergyman, on May 29, 1808. The union was a happy one, and the couple had ten children together. But Webster outlived all but one of them; his wife died just as he ascended to the Senate. He remarried in 1829, this time to a merchant's daughter who gave him entry into the lavish hospitality of New York high society, where he increasingly indulged in food and drink and became, over time, portly. Webster's appetite for wealth would lead him to land speculation, but his careless financing and the 1830s depression would cause him to remain debt-ridden the rest of his life.

As a young lawyer on the rise, Webster was a staunch Federalist, like his father, but the party was in serious decline, and his several campaigns for election to the state legislature were unsuccessful. Still, Webster prevailed as a champion of the New England shipping interests against foreign acts of oppression, paving his way into Congress in 1812 with the support of voters who had had enough of Thomas Jefferson's 1807 embargo and James Madison's fruitless diplomacy with Britain and France. In two congressional terms, Webster distinguished himself in debates over the chartering of the national bank by demonstrating a great understanding of fiscal policy — his own personal finances notwithstanding.

Webster left Congress and New Hampshire to open a lucrative law practice in Boston, arguing several landmark cases before the Supreme Court, including *McCulloch v. Maryland* (1819) and *Gibbons v. Ogden* (1824). But he could not stay away from politics. Massachusetts elected him to Congress three times in the 1820s. In 1827 he was elected to the Senate, where he served for two decades. He became famous as an orator for his constitutional debates in 1830 with Robert Y. Hayne, a stand-in for the southern leader John C. Calhoun, and with the firebrand Calhoun himself in 1833. He threw his support behind Henry Clay's compromise measures of 1850, arguing to both Southern secessionists and Northern abolitionists that disunion was a greater evil than slavery while keeping one eye on the 1852 presidential campaign.

But Webster's presidential aspirations came to naught. As a Whig candidate for president in 1836, Webster won the electoral votes of only Massachusetts, and he died before the 1852 contest. Regardless, he is still respected for his public service, both as an elected official and as secretary of state under three presidents. Moreover, his legendary stature as an orator has survived him. As depicted in "The Devil and Daniel Webster" (1926), a story by the American poet Stephen Vincent Benét, and its motion picture adaptation (1941), Webster represents the oratorical stature of another era when he is called to the aid of a New Hampshire farmer caught in a Faustian bargain with the devil.

References

Baxter, M. G. "Webster, Daniel." *American National Biography Online* February 2000. Retrieved June 30, 2003, from http://www.anb.org/articles/03/03-00525.html.

"Webster, Daniel." 1998. *Encyclopedia of World Biography,* 2nd ed. 17 vols. Retrieved June 30, 2003, from http://www.galenet.com/servlet/BioRC.

10

Territorial Expansion

EARLY IN 1844 Senator Sidney Breese of Illinois spoke of the promise of the United States: "Our confederacy is peculiarly adapted to expansion, and any number of states can be added to it, strengthened by their number, until its circumference shall embrace all the territory of this continent." Breese, his fellow Illinois senator, Stephen Douglas, and other Democrats in Congress wanted a physically larger United States, one that spanned the continent, with an extended arena for economic action and personal freedom. It was precisely because the United States had ample room for expansion, moreover, that allowed its rise as a world power. Since Europe had a concentrated population in a land with no room for expansion, many legislators (and journalists) saw it as being in decline. For Breese and other Jacksonian Democrats, it was obvious that Congress and the government needed to acquire the land necessary for the emergence of the nation as a world power.

With the congressional Democrats supporting the expansionism of the war against Mexico and the policies of President James K. Polk, himself a Jacksonian Democrat, the Democratic vision of an extended United States would come to pass in a continuation of the path started by the Louisiana Purchase. Only the expansion was not quite how the Democrats had envisioned it.

The actual acquisition of new territory was principally achieved through the actions of a handful of presidents rather than by Congress, given the opportunities of the period and the practical realities of the American political system. Thus did Thomas Jefferson orchestrate the Louisiana Purchase in 1803, notwithstanding his own qualms about its constitutionality, and thereby manage to double the area of the United States. President James Madison acquired West Florida in 1813 and the port of Mobile, by seizing what had been Spanish territory, and secured East Florida (Florida) from Spain in 1819.

In 1846 President Polk provoked war with Mexico in anticipation of gaining California, and then, with the 1848 Treaty of Guadalupe Hidalgo, acquired not only California but almost all of what is now the southwestern and western United States — thereby adding another 1.2 million square miles to the country (the Mexican Cession, Oregon, and Texas). Later, in 1853, the Pierce administration bought a wide strip of land from Mexico in what is now southernmost Arizona in order to build a transcontinental railroad line. The United States thus came to extend from the Atlantic to the Pacific, gaining strategically important ports and access to vital transportation routes: New Orleans and the Mississippi Valley, West Florida and the port of Mobile, East Florida and the sea route from the Caribbean to Europe, San Francisco Bay and the West Coast, Oregon (now Oregon, Washington, and Idaho) and the Pacific Northwest, and the Gadsden Purchase and the path of the transcontinental railroad in southern Arizona.

Yet the actual absorption of these new regions into the United States proper did require congressional action, just as Senator Breese had proposed. Territorial expansion did not just happen through the transfer of land from one nation-state to another. Rather, it required that the new region stay attached to, indeed become part of, the homeland.

Two members of Congress besides Henry Clay in the House and John Calhoun and Daniel Webster in the Senate were of special importance in the westward expansion of the United States. One was Senator Thomas Hart Benton, a Democrat from Missouri and the father-in-law of John C. Frémont. The tall, rugged, and well-spoken Benton served in the Senate from 1821 to 1851 and in the House of Representatives from 1853 to 1855. He constantly advocated what he thought to be the western point of view, one that moderated between the North and the South and endorsed an expansive view of the United States. Although a slaveowner and from a slaveholding state, he wanted the country to extend to the Pacific, with northern free states and slave states both. He also opposed the Nullifiers (those who supported South Carolina's claim of being able to nullify U.S. legislation). Although Benton was a firm opponent of paper money, he opposed giving the surplus federal money to the states in the "land distribution" — the revenues from land sales being distributed to the separate states — as advocated by Clay and other members of Congress.

Another important legislator was Stephen A. Douglas of Illinois, a representative from 1843 to 1847 and a senator from 1847 until his death in 1861. Called "the Little Giant" because of his large head and stocky frame, Douglas is most famous for his three-hour debates with Abraham Lincoln in 1858. As a senator, Douglas was the chairman of the Committee on Territories and orchestrated the passage of the Compromise of 1850 as well as the Kansas-Nebraska Act (1854). He thought that popular sovereignty

— that citizens be left free to decide policy for themselves, slavery included, so long as it was consistent with the Constitution — would be able to bind the northern and southern wings of the Democratic party and settle the slavery issue peaceably. At the same time, he was a strong advocate of Manifest Destiny, which was consistent with his support of the railroads. He declared at one point that the bigger the United States became, the better it could enact its God-given role. This larger United States would include Cuba, since Cuba guarded the entrance to the Mississippi and "naturally" was a part of the American continent. Douglas even suggested that Central America would at some point become part of the United States.

Benton, Douglas, and the other members of Congress faced many different challenges. For one, the territorial expansion of the United States required the suppression, removal, or assimilation of the Indians. The vast lands of the Louisiana Territory and the Mexican Cession were effectively uninhabitable without control over the Indians. Territorial expansion similarly called for the incorporation or absorption of foreign nationals who lived in these new regions. It also demanded a system for the allocation of land to individuals and companies for uses such as farming, mining, the harvesting of timber, and commercial development. It necessitated, too, territorial administration. And for the United States as a federal polity, it meant the eventual inclusion of these territories into the Union as separate states. In these practical dimensions of territorial expansion, Congress set public policy.

The Indians

Congress's Indian policy was an inconsistent mix of strategies, one that reflected political expediency and neglect. As a result, Congress was a party to what students of the American West now refer to as the genocide of the American Indians. This fact does not deny the paternalism or even generosity on the part of the U.S. government and many Americans, but the dominant theme was Indian removal. The white man would replace the red man. Indian removal was "old policy," as Senator Benton noted during the debate over the Removal Act of 1830, which outlined the terms by which the five Indian tribes could be removed from the southeastern United States. Removed they were.

Early public policy toward the Indians was partly based on the hope of civilizing the North American aboriginals (Jefferson's intention, among those of others). In 1793 Congress authorized the U.S. president "to promote civilization among the friendly Indian tribes, and to secure the continuance of their friendship" by providing them with domestic animals, farming implements, and other gifts. (John Calhoun, as secretary of state under President James Madison, recommended intermarriage as a last resort.) And in 1819 Congress budgeted $10,000 annually for the purpose of constructing schools to educate the Indians; by 1832 there were thirty-two such schools in frontier areas.

If education and gifts were two strategies for the civilizing of Indians, a third and more important policy was trade. As George Washington wrote following the Revolutionary War: "I think, if the Indian trade was carried on, on Government Acct., and with no greater advance than what would be necessary to defray the expense and risk, and bring in a small profit, that it would supply with the Indians upon much better terms of than they usually are; engross their Trade, and fix them strongly in our Interest." Once he became president, Washington recommended that Congress establish a system of "trading houses" or "Indian factories."

The factories were to encourage friendship between whites and the Indians (by supplying them with merchandise at reasonable prices), to prevent the Indians from being gouged by private traders (by offering them better terms), and to squeeze out the British, French, and Spanish from the Indian trade (and thereby erode the Europeans' influence on the Indians). In the words of a fellow Virginia congressman, a system of government-led trade with the Indians was needed "to conciliate the affections of a distressed and unhappy people, and as it might prevent the expense of a war with them." As another representative noted, "It was clear as a sunbeam, that the establishment of trade must be the foundation of amity."

A cautious but accommodating Congress appropriated $50,000 worth of Indian goods in 1795. The War Department decided to use the money only for southern Indians at first, two-thirds for a trading house in Georgia and one-third for a trading house in eastern Tennessee. After further debate in early 1796, Congress authorized another $150,000 for President Washington to use for stocking trading houses on the southern or western frontiers or in Indian country. Although there was a lapse in funding at the end of the 1700s (business at the trading houses continued, however, since they lost only a little money each year), Congress renewed its commitment to the system of trading houses in response to Jefferson's initiative. It allocated $100,000 for the factories in 1805, and in 1806 it authorized the appointment of a superintendent of Indian trade to oversee the factories. Although the War of 1812 destroyed five of the factories, the government had established eighteen trading houses by 1818 in the frontier regions of Georgia, Tennessee, Ohio, Louisiana, and in the Alabama, Missouri, Arkansas, Iowa, Minnesota, Illinois, and Michigan Territories.

With foreign competition to American traders ending after the War of

1812, however, fur traders and others who dealt with the Indians, led by John Jacob Astor and the American Fur Company, sought to eliminate their government competition. Senator Benton, who was on the American Fur Company's payroll as a "legal representative," and Representative John B. Floyd, a Democrat from Virginia, spearheaded the effort in the Senate and House, respectively, to take the government out of the Indian trade.

Benton, a member of the Senate Committee on Indian Affairs, used his position in 1820 to launch an investigation of the Indian trading houses. Among those he called on to testify against them were several Indian agents who were personal friends and Ramsay Crooks, one of the top men in Astor's company. In the hearings, Benton used ridicule, sarcasm, and evidence of fraud and bad business practices in the trading houses to argue for an end to the government Indian trade as well as to personally attack the Indian superintendent of trade, Thomas McKenney. In one instance, he mocked the purchase of eight gross of Jew's harps for the Indian factories: the Jew's harps were used by "the superintendent, in reclaiming the savage from the hunter state. The first state after that, in the road to refined life, is the pastoral, and without music the tawny-colored Corydons and the red-skinned Amaryllises . . . could make no progress in the delightful business of love and sentiment." Little matter that the Jew's harps were a standard item of Indian trade.

The factory system was "worse than useless," Benton argued. "The experience of the Indian factory system is an illustration of the unfitness of the federal government to carry on any system of trade, the liability of the benevolent designs of government to be abused, and the difficulty of detecting and redressing abuses in the management of our Indian affairs." After a three-day debate and a third reading, the bill passed the Senate and, soon thereafter, the House. The trading houses were abolished on June 3, 1822.

Ramsay Crooks afterward complimented the senator on his efforts: "The result is the best possible proof of the value to the country of talents, intelligence, & perseverance; and you deserve the unqualified thanks of the community for destroying the pious monster, since to your unwearied exertions, and sound practical knowledge of the whole subject, the country is indebted for its deliverance from so gross and [un]holy an imposition."

Congress also bowed to the traders' demands when it came to regulating the Indian trade. Congress did not enforce the 1832 ban on liquor trade — the "greatest source of difficulty in the Indian trade" as one historian of government relations with the Indians, Francis Paul Prucha, puts it — and neither did the territorial governors Lewis Cass of Michigan or

William Clark of Missouri. Nor did Congress monitor the performance of the Indian agents (under the Bureau of Indian Affairs after 1824; before that, under the War Department), later Indian superintendents, and territorial governors charged with regulating the Indian trade.

Worse, Congress was a party to the taking of Indian land. While the Senate ratified the Indians' land cessions, Congress typically delayed the appropriation of the annuities promised the Indians and made little effort to ensure that the treaty terms were being honored. Members of the House and Senate showed scant interest in guaranteeing the quality of the goods granted the Indians, did not check that the funds for the purchase of Indian goods actually went to their designated place (they were often embezzled or diverted), and did not enforce the withholding of Indian lands from white settlement.

When one Indian agent, William Ward, refused to register Choctaws as heads of household seeking allotments according to the terms of the treaty of 1830, and when speculators rushed into Indian lands, contrary to the terms of the treaty, Congress (and the Jackson administration) looked the other way. And when the Democratic congressman Franklin Plummer of Mississippi warned that his state would not stand for eviction by the War Department of "numerous families of first respectability from Kentucky, Tennessee, Alabama, Georgia, the Carolinas, and older settlements of Mississippi who have . . . settled in the [Choctaw] nation, and pitched their crops for the year" — contrary to terms — Secretary of War Lewis Cass reassured Plummer that President Jackson did not intend to enforce the provisions of the treaty.

Nor did Congress ever pass legislation (such as the Territorial Bill of 1838) that would have established an organized "Indian Territory" in the Old Northwest, Great Plains, mountain west, or far west — even though it is what "Indian Territory" might seem to imply. Indian country was thus ever evolving, an area not yet settled by or controlled by whites but not yet organized into a territory; it was Indian Territory by default. So Congress ended up making portions of the Great Plains — what Colonel Stephen Long early on referred to as "the Great American Desert" — the eventual home for almost all the Indian reservations.

Throughout the late eighteenth and early nineteenth centuries, Congress mostly ignored Indian affairs — after all, neither the Indians nor the white Americans residing in the territories had voting representation in Congress. It neglected to sufficiently fund and supervise the agents, superintendents, treaty commissioners, clerks, translators, and others involved in Indian affairs. Neither did it coordinate the actions of those same persons. Consider that the Indian superintendents were the superiors of the Indian agents, for instance, but the superintendents could not appoint or fire the agents. Or, that the territorial governors had a military function as much or more than a civilian one — and often had military backgrounds — yet were not a part of the military command.

Perhaps most seriously, Congress was unwilling to authorize the money necessary to maintain an army or police force capable of protecting the Indians from invading whites and prosecuting violations of the law by white men or, for that matter, of protecting the white settlers and prosecuting Indian raiding parties. Indian policy was ultimately about military control and thus the province of the War Department and territorial governors, but to stop this frontier terrorism would have been expensive. So white Americans encroached and marauded, the Indians stole and raided, and both retaliated — often horrifically.

As a result of Congress's inattention, others, mostly unscrupulous persons, had a disproportionate influence on U.S. policy. Yet Congress's behavior reflected the dominant American attitudes of the eighteenth and nineteenth centuries: Indians were inferior and uncivilized persons who did not merit equal treatment. Most Indians preferred to keep to their own customs anyway and to interact with whites only for the purpose of commerce in furs, metal products (particularly guns), liquor, blankets, and other goods. And if the Indians did not want to become part of white America, then those who did not die from disease had to be moved. For the great majority of Americans, it scarcely mattered that Congress allowed white traders to get wealthy from the Indian trade, denied Indians their due, and sanctioned the whites' occupation and settlement of land that had been formally ceded to the Indians. Congress was just carrying out Americans' intentions.

Foreign Nationals

After the Louisiana Purchase, Congress had for the first time to contend with the incorporation of foreign nationals into the United States. With the new territory came a polyglot (mostly French) mixture of persons in New Orleans, on the Mississippi, and spread out over the western half of the Mississippi River valley. Not only were many of them not familiar with the English language and of different cultures and legal traditions (e.g., the Napoleonic Code), but they fell under the sovereignty of the United States involuntarily, through the actions of their government.

The Territory of New Orleans attracted about 10,000 immigrants in 1804 and 1806 and 4,000 more in 1807–1808, many of whom were refugees from Haiti. The census of 1810 showed about 75,000 whites and thousands more slaves who worked the plantations for cotton, sugar, and other crops. Since many of them had French or Spanish as their principal language and were Catholic — and thus of questionable fitness for self-rule — President Jefferson took the precaution of installing a military governor for the territory. As Representative William Eustis of Louisiana, a Federalist, told his fellow congressmen: "The principles of liberty can not suddenly be grafted on a people accustomed to a regimen of directly opposite hue. The approach of such a people to liberty must be gradual. I believe them at present totally unqualified to exercise it." Yet not long after, in 1812, Congress admitted the Orleans Territory as the state of Louisiana — over the objections of New England Federalists.

Senator John C. Calhoun of South Carolina similarly worried during the Mexican War about the effects of an annexation of Mexico on white racial purity. In Calhoun's words:

> We have conquered many of the neighboring tribes of Indians, but we never thought of holding them in subjection — never of incorporating them into our Union . . .
>
> [W]e have never dreamt of incorporating into our Union any but the Caucasian race — the free white race. To incorporate Mexico, would be the very first instance of incorporating an Indian race; for more than half of all the Mexicans are Indians, and the other is composed chiefly of mixed tribes. I protest against a union as that! . . . The greatest misfortunes of Spanish America are to be traced to the fatal error of placing these colored races on an equality with the white race . . .
>
> Are we to associate with ourselves as equal, companions, and fellow citizens, the Indians and mixed race of Mexico?

The Polk administration resolved Calhoun's worries somewhat by annexing only the most northwestern part of Mexico in the aftermath of the Mexican War.

Still, Congress was hardly generous with the non-Anglo inhabitants of the Mexican Cession. The 1848 Treaty of Guadalupe Hidalgo drafted by the Polk administration stated, in Article VIII, that the Hispanics in the new territory "shall be considered to have elected to become citizens of the United States" and that according to Article IX, Mexicans were to be "*admitted as soon as possible, according to the principles of the Federal Constitution, to the enjoyment of all the rights of citizens of the United States* (italics mine). In the meantime, they shall be maintained and protected in the enjoyment of their liberty, their property, and the civil rights now vested in them according to the Mexican laws." But the Senate redrafted the article to read, "The Mexicans . . . shall be incorporated into the Union of the United States and be admitted, *at the proper time* (*to be judged by the Congress of the United States*) (italics mine) to the enjoyment of all the rights of the citizens of the United States according to the principles of the

Constitution." Congress could now determine the timing of the Mexicans' participation as full citizens. The reason for this change was land.

The Senate similarly deleted Article X from the treaty; its original form had it that Mexican land grants would be considered valid as long as they had been valid under Mexican law. With the deletion, Congress granted itself the authority to establish tribunals for the settlement of land disputes; the Mexicans absorbed into the Union were not to be treated equally under the law. The U.S. Congress was to dictate U.S. land policy. As Calhoun rationalized, "It is impossible for us to prevent our growing population from passing into an uninhabited county, where the power of the owners is not sufficient to keep them out." Calhoun and other members of Congress believed that the Mexicans would have to sell their lands and move away, to make room for a more "industrious and civilized race."

Congress's discriminatory treatment of those foreign nationals who were to become U.S. nationals, or U.S. citizens, would be repeated in different ways shortly before the turn of the last century upon the territorial annexations of Puerto Rico, Guam, Hawaii, American Samoa, and the Philippines.

The Land

Congress had to decide how all these new public lands — the trans-Appalachian West, Florida, and the trans-Mississippi West — were to be sold, allotted, or otherwise disposed.

The Land Ordinance (passed first while Congress was operating under the Articles of Confederation) established a national system of land sales that divided the public domain into six-mile-square townships, each composed of thirty-six sections, one square mile in area. The ordinance further specified that land was to be auctioned at a minimum of one dollar per acre, that one section per township be dedicated to schools, and that townships be sold alternately whole and in sections. Congress subsequently passed laws in 1796, 1800, 1804, 1820, 1821, 1830, and 1841 to reduce the minimum auction price per acre, shrink the minimum lot size on sale, and/or ease the terms of land purchases. Indeed, in eleven separate laws enacted between 1824 and 1834, Congress provided relief for settlers in arrears on their debts.

There was much to be disposed. Of the 1.2 billion acres once owned by the government, 29 percent was sold in cash to individuals and companies, 27 percent was granted to homesteads, 22 percent was ceded to the states, 9 percent was allocated for military bounties and private land claims, and another 9 percent was turned over to the railroads. Although some of this disposition followed the Homestead Act of 1862 and while many of the railroad land grants came after the Civil War, Congress's antebellum land policy allocated much of the more valuable land and set a precedent for later congressional behavior.

Congress was split on land policy. The Democrats wanted cheaper land, lower interest rates, provisions for preemption, and, of course, further territorial expansion. The Whigs called for a distribution of land revenues to the states for their own internal improvements, sought to limit western expansion, wanted land sold at higher prices, and desired protection for creditors. Congressional votes in the 1830s and 1840s expressed these party differences, with both the House and Senate clearly split into Whigs and Democrats.

With the Democrats in Congress usually holding the upper hand during the Jeffersonian and Jacksonian eras, however, U.S. policy favored the frontier almost from the beginning. From 1809 through the 1810s, when the first buyers of land on credit were defaulting on their loans, Congress refused to hold the line. Rather than having those buyers forfeit their lands and thereby set a firm precedent for future land sales, Congress provided relief. The Jeffersonian Republicans (and the White House) agreed to the petitions of the distressed settlers and speculators, who were faced with losing their land and any improvements they had made, and passed a series of additional bills providing credit relief. Congress passed legislation to help the debtors of Illinois in 1813, for instance, assist pioneers in the Missouri territory, and aid settlers and speculators in the Florida Territory.

Later legislation on preemption — the Preemption Act of 1830, the Renewal Act of 1832, and a two-year extension of the preemption law passed in 1834 — further protected frontiersmen from their financial responsibilities. In 1838, for instance, when Congress began selling land in Iowa, more than 15,000 persons already occupied the land, persons who could thus lay claim to their holdings, who did not have to go through the auction process, and who could buy their land at the minimum price per acre. Much of this land was the best available, of course, and much of it was held by persons acting on behalf of others. Senator Henry Clay called the squatters "a lawless rabble."

Although Democrats such as Senator Benton favored preemption as helpful to the West and to rural populations, and Whigs opposed it as policy that rewarded individuals for violating the law, the western Whigs teamed up with the Democrats to support preemption and easy land policy. Congress reached the ultimate conclusion of subsidizing land ownership with the Homestead Act of 1862, which gave Americans one quarter-section of land (160 acres) so long as they stayed on the land for five years.

Although similar legislation had been proposed earlier, in 1846, 1850, and 1852, it took the Civil War Republicans to get the bill through.

In fact, Congress for several reasons did not want to support an efficient, well-paid land office able to survey the lands under public domain and put them up quickly for auction — a fine arrangement for disposing of the public lands as expediently as possible. Congress did not budget enough money to hire and retain clerks and other Land Office personnel to monitor or enforce the land policy; it preferred what amounted to a catch-as-catch-can system instead. As a result, it let others effectively determine land policy.

One reason for such a policy was that members of Congress enjoyed the support of those who benefited from the existing system. Since Congress never made it illegal for land officers, surveyors, and inspectors to buy and trade land on their own account, government employees often viewed the Land Office business as a means to financial success. Then again, government officeholders also frequently acted on behalf of other individuals and companies interested in opening up the new land: squatters, investors, mining operators, timber harvesters, and railroad companies.

Another reason was that many congressmen themselves either owned or invested in the western lands and thus had little incentive to police or regulate what land policy historians concede was a fraud-filled and opportunistic practice. Such men as Daniel Webster of Massachusetts, Stephen Douglas of Illinois, John Tipton of Indiana, and Simon Cameron of Pennsylvania were among the senators of the early and mid-nineteenth century who had speculative interests in western lands.

Then, too, a more haphazard system of land disposal was almost certainly faster, given the amount of land. Congress let individuals themselves take on the risks and receive the rewards of settlement, despite the risk of illegality (occupying Indian, British, Spanish, or Mexican land not yet a part of the United States or available for purchase) and the ethically dubious results (debtors being let off of their overly ambitious financial obligations, squatters achieving ownership of their ill-gotten lands, and government officials and members of Congress themselves profiting from their land policies).

Territorial Government

Then, too, the new lands had to be governed. Congress had to divide them into administrative units and decide what form of government they were going to have. In its administration of the territories, Congress exercised its authority much as that of parents over children.

The Northwest Ordinance (1787), originally drafted by Thomas Jefferson in 1784, redrafted by James Monroe, and then passed by Congress under the Articles of Confederation, provided a template for territorial government. It established a three-stage process whereby the territories of the Old Northwest were to become states: the "district" phase, which required a population of at least 5,000 white males where the territory was to be ruled by a governor and territorial judges; a second phase with an elected legislature; and a third phase, which required a constitution, republican government, and a population of 60,000. Congress had to approve of the change in phase of territorial government at each step and then determine when and under what terms to admit the third-stage territories as states.

Yet Congress only partly followed the model of the Northwest Ordinance (which was passed again by Congress without debate in 1789). Just nine territories went through the district stage, the last being Florida in 1819. Congress then abandoned the district stage because territories so defined resisted proceeding to the second stage, in which they had to elect a legislature. They resisted because the election of territorial legislatures almost surely meant higher taxes (to support of higher levels of government service) and the political dominance of the territories by the more populated areas. And since the territories were typically controlled by oligarchies, persons whose standing would have been threatened by a transition to second-stage government, they further resisted the move.

But as the populations in the territories grew and their administration became more complex, Congress increasingly came to view the autocratic district stage as unworkable and ill suited to territorial government. (A second version of district government was the establishment of a military government, as happened in Orleans and Florida, although for only a few months in each instance, as well as in California and New Mexico for several years.) Congress therefore eliminated the district phase — although the military government form would be revived in the territorial governments of Hawaii, the Philippines, Guam, Puerto Rico, and the Virgin Islands (only Alaska was spared military administration).

Then, beginning with Alabama in 1818 and followed by Arkansas in 1819 and Wisconsin in 1834, Congress had the territories proceed directly to the second stage with bicameral legislatures, skipping the first stage altogether. (Congress established unicameral legislatures in the Orleans Territory from 1804 to 1805, in Florida from 1822 to 1838, and in Michigan from 1824 to 1838.) After the Wisconsin Organic Act of 1834, all U.S. territories in continental North America (except Alaska) went directly to a modified second-stage government. The territorial governors, who were appointed by the president, were to oversee the apportionment of the territory and the first elections.

Congress also subsidized the territories, especially those of the trans-Mississippi West. For one, it established postal service. Almost every town in a territory had a post office and a postmaster, a situation that also provided a source of patronage for the territorial delegate. Congress further subsidized them by providing U.S. marshals, courts of law, and the protection of the army — as spotty as the law enforcement and criminal justice system may have been. Beginning in 1822, too, Congress subsidized the territorial assemblies by providing per diem allowances, covering travel expenses for territorial legislators, and paying the salaries of territorial governors and judges. In addition, Congress began to make the formation of legislatures easier by lowering the qualifications for voting and holding public office. Land grants, whether to military veterans, the railroads, or educational purposes, were another way by which Congress encouraged the settlement and development of the territories (these were subsidies, of course, since the government would thus be forgoing the revenues from land sales).

Congress enjoyed near total authority over the administration of the territories. It decided on the actual boundaries, as when it divided the Old Northwest in 1803 and split off the Alabama Territory from the Missouri Territory in 1817; it determined their commercial development, as when it forbade the territories from creating banks or other institutions without its expressed permission; and it protected and otherwise facilitated the development of the territories through the budgets and personnel of the federal government.

The territories and their inhabitants can thus be seen as serving in a kind of pupilage or guardianship under Congress. Until 1825 Congress and the presidency had almost full authority over the government of the territories. After 1825 Congress allowed the territories to be governed more by their own legislatures and their local oligarchies. In both instances, though, the government's authority was again like that of a parent over a child: Congress helped and ruled the territories, yet once it admitted the territory as a state and lost its plenary authority, the benevolence ended. The subsidies stopped, and the former territory stood on equal footing with the existing states, with senators and a representative or representatives of its own.

Statehood

Congress could decide, too, when it wanted to admit new states. The Federalist Senate delayed the admission of Tennessee in 1796, for instance, but the Republican House approved its admission and the Senate later capitulated in conference committee. Likewise, the Republican Congress of

1800 agreed to the wishes of the Republican delegate from the Ohio Territory to make Ohio a state, despite the opposition of the Federalist governor Arthur St. Clair. Congress overruled the powerful but unpopular St. Clair, admitted Ohio, and divided up the rest of the Northwest Territory.

The admission of Tennessee, orchestrated by its former governor and new senator, William Blount, was the exception that proved the rule. Blount apportioned Tennessee while it was still a territory, scheduled the election of representatives, and convened a general assembly in the autumn of 1794. He also had a census taken (which determined that Tennessee had well in excess of the 60,000 inhabitants it needed to become a state), initiated a referendum on statehood (it passed by almost a 3–1 margin), and scheduled the election of a constitutional convention. Blount, who had almost half of the convention delegates under his control, managed from behind the scenes to draft a constitution that provided for a strong executive and a bicameral legislature, had low taxes, and abolished property qualifications for voting. The first legislature met in March 1794, less than three months after the beginning of the convention.

Blount then went to Philadelphia to secure from Congress Tennessee's admission to statehood. But the two chambers split along party lines, with the Republican House favoring Tennessee's immediate admission and the Federalist Senate wanting another census. In conference committee, however, Aaron Burr replaced one of two senators who resigned, and Blount succeeded in obtaining from him the committee's favorable recommendation on statehood (with the caveat that Tennessee have only one U.S. representative).

Blount successfully seized the moment to organize for statehood, given that Tennessee was the first territory to be so annexed (Kentucky had not been a territory; Vermont had been independent) and that his situation had no legal or congressional precedent. But the Federalists in the House and Senate as well as others raised questions of the legality of Tennessee's admission, since Congress had not previously passed an Enabling Act to authorize Blount to initiate the change to statehood. After Tennessee, then, territories had to petition Congress to authorize the organization of state government, and it was up to Congress to do the apportioning, set the rules and dates for the election of delegates to a convention, and ensure that the delegates poll themselves on the question of statehood. California (1850), Oregon (1859), and Kansas (1861) were, however, later exceptions to the rule, as they all organized as territories without a congressional Enabling Act.

Whereas majorities in Congress sought the quick admission of Tennessee, Ohio, California, and then Nevada, they delayed the admission of other states, among them Texas, Colorado, Utah (with its Mormon population), New Mexico, and Arizona (both included in the territory of New Mexico and with large proportions of Hispanics). Other states Congress admitted in pairs, given their impact on the Senate (the North, with its population advantage, would always be favored in the House of Representatives). Thus Congress matched Maine (1820) with Missouri (1821), Michigan (1837) with Arkansas (1836), and Iowa (1846) with Florida (1845).

Congress also admitted as states three territories that had fewer than 60,000 persons at the time of their petitions — Illinois (1819), California (1850), and Nevada (1864); new states had on average 133,000 inhabitants when admitted. The admission of Nevada was the result of the Republican Congress of the Civil War years, though, and Congress granted California early admission because of its rapid population growth following the gold rush, its valuable access to the Pacific Ocean, and the Compromise of 1850. And Illinois was admitted early as a result of the tacit pairing of free and slave states (Alabama also being admitted in 1819).

Congress further decided how many House representatives each state would have; it usually granted the minimum of one delegate per state until a new census could determine the proper number. Congress allotted Louisiana (1812) and Missouri (1821) only one representative each, notwithstanding that both qualified for more on the basis of the census. And it allowed Iowa (1846), Wisconsin (1848), California (1850), and Minnesota (1858) just two representatives each, although they qualified for more. Later, Congress granted Oklahoma (1907) five representatives; it qualified for only four.

Policymaking and the West

The territorial expansion of the United States is overdetermined. Any of several reasons may explain how the United States grew from thirteen Atlantic states to encompass the combination of states and territories that by 1848 spanned an entire continent: a quest for national security, a thirst for wealth, a wish for racial-ethnic hegemony, and a belief in Christianity as the only true religion.

The virtue of "manifest destiny" was the indeterminate nature of the phrase. Which destiny was being made evident by American territorial expansion: a greater United States as world power? a greater United States as economic juggernaut? a greater United States as liberal democratic nation? a greater United States as a Christian or white nation? Members of Congress, the Democrats especially, voiced each of these reasons in the debates over western expansion.

All the rhetoric notwithstanding, I would argue that the crucial part of territorial expansion came *after* the government's acquisition of new regions. Whatever the size of the larger United States, Congress had to handle the devilish details of the new areas: what to do with the aboriginal population, how to treat foreign nationals, how to organize and manage the millions of square miles, how much to invest in order to make the land accessible for settlement, how much to protect and defend them, and under what terms and when new states should be allowed as equals in the Union. These were more than details, of course; they were the core, practical realities that determined the effectiveness of the United States' territorial expansion.

An overview of the process of territorial expansion offers several lessons.

One is that Congress was cheap. Whether controlling the Indians, enforcing federal laws, disposing of the public domain, administering the territories, or budgeting for other functions demanded by territorial expansion, Congress did not provide sufficient funds. By default, then, it allowed individuals and private interests to dominate public policy.

A second is that there was no single, unified system of territorial development. Instead, Congress used its discretionary authority to treat the Indians inconsistently, to discriminate against foreign nationals to varying degrees, to alter frequently the size and terms of land sales, to vary the means by which territories were administered, and to decide when and how to annex the territories as states. Any generalization about western expansion has to be tempered by recognizing the great variation in congressional policies and over time with respect to any one policy domain.

A third lesson is Congress's casual attitude toward universal law. Congress made little effort to enforce federal law as it applied to Indians, the incorporation of foreign nationals, the treatment of debtors and squatters, or the annexation of new states. Rather than consistently following a single model or particular guideline, the members of Congress used the political process for their own ends.

These ends were predominantly ones of *party* — the Democrats and the Whigs in the antebellum era — and *section* — the North, the South, and the West. Whereas policy at the beginning of the nineteenth century was divided on the basis of political faction or party, this division became increasingly replaced by sectional differences as the century progressed. By the 1840s, congressional votes on Oregon, the admission of Texas, the Mexican War, internal improvements, as well as other issues evidenced sectional identity, even as party and sectional affinities frequently overlapped. Not surprisingly, northern Democrats and southern Whigs were most subject to these cross-cutting pressures and were thus more likely to vacillate between their partisan and sectional affinities when voting.

Rarely, though, were votes on territorial expansion simply votes on a larger United States. Were that the case, expansion would not have been nearly as controversial as it was. Instead, the extension of slavery and the question of whether new states (and territories) would be free or slave were almost always implicit in the issue under discussion, so that by the 1850s sectional differences took the upper hand as shown by votes on fugitive slaves, the many votes over the Wilmot Proviso (1846), and the admission of California together with the Compromise of 1850. Sectional issues came to dominate both houses of the Thirty-first Congress, in fact, even if partisanship in roll call votes was still very much in evidence.

For all of this increasing sectional division, there were still some institutional distinctions between the House and Senate. For one, the Senate was more obstructionist, given its authority to review appointments (and treaties). It opposed Albert Gallatin, the Swiss-born proponent of internal development, as secretary of state for James Madison and imposed Robert Smith instead. Even Andrew Jackson, who effectively ran the House while he was president, faced a Senate that was willing to thwart his personnel appointments. Later, during the Polk administration, the Senate challenged Colonel John Stephenson's western mission and refused to appoint Senator Benton as supreme commander for the Mexican-American War. (Benton sought the command as a steppingstone to the presidency.)

Another difference was that sectional loyalties were more obvious in the House than in the Senate, as shown by analyses of congressional roll call votes in the 1840s and 1850s. The House was less willing to compromise on sectional differences, perhaps because of the larger number of representatives and their shorter average tenure in office.

Still, the sectional issues raised by western expansion — the Wilmot Proviso, the Kansas-Nebraska Act, the fugitive slave laws, the Compromise of 1850, and the Dred Scott ruling (1857) — overwhelmed the differences between the House and Senate and increasingly tore the nation apart. Sectional loyalties came to overwhelm partisan affiliations until the point that political party — first the Free-Soil party and then the Republican party — became identical to section. Then, the election of Abraham Lincoln — an election made possible by the allied votes of the western and northern states — led to the secession of South Carolina and the rest of the South.

The remarkable career of the presidential aspirant Senator Stephen Douglas epitomizes the split in the Democratic party caused by the geographic expansion of the antebellum era. After the Mexican Cession of 1848, Congress had to decide how to handle the issue of slavery in the new territories. And it was Douglas who worked tirelessly toward the Compromise of 1850, which immediately admitted California as a free state, made New Mexico and Utah organized territories (delaying their admission as states), reduced Texas's extravagant boundary claims, prohibited the slave trade in Washington, D.C., and established new fugitive slave laws. The composite nature of the Compromise of 1850 was its genius: only 4 senators and 28 representatives voted for all its measures, even as Douglas was nonetheless able to find majorities on each of the individual votes (6 votes in the Senate and 5 in the House).

Ever the pragmatist, Douglas was ready to replace the Missouri Compromise (which could not extend to the Pacific) with popular sovereignty (what his opponents called "squatter sovereignty"): the idea that the territories could decide for themselves if they were to be free or slave. This idea was the premise of the controversial and vaguely worded Kansas-Nebraska Act of 1854 and Douglas's Freeport Doctrine. But the Kansas-Nebraska Act wreaked havoc on the congressional Democrats as the historian Don Fehrenbacher reports: they lost more than 70 percent of their free-state seats, and only 7 of the 44 Democrats who had voted for the bill won reelection.

At the same time, though, Douglas honored Chief Justice Taney's ruling in *Dred Scott* — finding that slaves transported to free states and free territories were not free by virtue of the due process clause. A slaveholder's private property was to be protected, and the Missouri Compromise was unconstitutional. Douglas thereby came under attacks from Abraham Lincoln and other Republicans who, with considerable justification, saw his position as legally and philosophically weak. But Douglas also supported the Republicans in their attack on Kansas's proslavery Lecompton constitution, which alienated the southern Democrats. Between Douglas's defection from the Democrats on Kansas and the fact that for most territories Douglas's popular sovereignty meant no slaves, the southern Democrats came to despise Douglas. He was guilty of "flagrant inconsistency and patent double dealing." Although he would be narrowly reelected by the Illinois legislature to the Senate in 1858, President Buchanan had him stripped of his committee chairmanship. And while he still had Democratic supporters in Congress, given his political skills, past leadership, and pragmatism, his run for the presidency in 1860 did not go far, and he died in the Senate chamber shortly thereafter.

A house divided could not stand, as Lincoln warned.

The expansion of the United States, Ralph Waldo Emerson observed, was like taking arsenic: the nation could swallow the territory, but the territory would unavoidably consume the nation. Not until after the horror of the Civil War would the expansion of the United States continue.

— Bartholomew H. Sparrow

BIBLIOGRAPHICAL NOTES

General studies of U.S. territorial expansion in the antebellum era are Ray Allen Billington, *Westward Expansion: A History of the American Frontier* (New York, 1960); Donald S. Meinig, *Continental America 1800–1867, The Shaping of America,* Vol. 2 (New Haven, Conn., 1986); Samuel Eliot Morison, Henry Steele Commager, and William E. Leuchtenburg, *The Growth of the American Republic,* Vol. 1 (New York, 1969); Albert K. Weinberg, *Manifest Destiny: A Study of Nationalist Expansionalism in American History* (Chicago, 1963 [1935]); and especially Thomas R. Hietala, *Manifest Design: Anxious Aggrandizement in Late Jacksonian America* (Ithaca, N.Y., 1985).

For congressional policies, see Leonard S. White, *The Jeffersonians: A Study in Administrative History, 1801–1829* (New York, 1951) and *The Jacksonians: A Study in Administrative History, 1830–61* (New York, 1954). In particular, see Francis Paul Prucha, *The Great Father: The United States Government and the American Indians,* Vols. 1 and 2 (Lincoln, Neb., 1995); Ronald N. Satz, *American Indian Policy in the Jacksonian Era* (Norman, Okla., 2001); Herman J. Viola, *Thomas L. McKenney: Architect of America's Early Indian Policy: 1816–1830* (Chicago, 1974); Malcolm J. Rohrbough, *The Land Office Business* (New York, 1968); Everett Dick, *The Lure of the Land* (Lincoln, Neb., 1970); Paul W. Gates, *Fifty Million Acres: Conflicts over Kansas Land Policy, 1854–1890* (Ithaca, N.Y., 1954); and Paul W. Gates, *History of Public Land Law Development* (Washington, D.C., 1968).

For territorial government, see Peter S. Onuf, *Statehood and Union: A History of the Northwest Ordinance* (Bloomington, Ind., 1987); Jack Erickson Eblen, *The First and Second United States Empires: Governors and Territorial Government, 1784–1912* (Pittsburgh, 1968); and John W. Smurr, "Territorial Constitutions: A Legal History of the Frontier Governments Erected by Congress in the American West, 1787–1900," Vols. 1 and 2, Ph.D. thesis (Bloomington, Ind., 1960).

For the politics of expansion, see David Potter, *The Impending Crisis, 1848–1861* (New York, 1976); Michael F. Holt, *The Rise and Fall of the American Whig Party* (New York, 1999); Don Edward Fehrenbacher, *The Dred Scott Case, Its Significance in American Law and Politics* (New York, 1978); and Michael A. Morrison, *Slavery and the West: the Eclipse of Manifest Destiny and the Coming of the Civil War* (Chapel Hill, N.C., 1997).

For congressional roll call votes, see Thomas B. Alexander, *Sectional Stress and Party Strength* (Nashville, Tenn., 1967), and Joel H. Silbey, *The Shrine of Party* (Pittsburgh, 1967).

Stephen Douglas

April 13, 1813–June 3, 1861

Stephen Douglas

Imbued with a New Englander's love of individual liberty and the romantic spirit of the American West, Stephen Arnold Douglas had the aggressive nature worthy of a Napoleon complex and a deep love of Jacksonian democracy. He would die in his adopted home state of Illinois six weeks after the Confederate bombardment of Fort Sumter, in Charleston, South Carolina, made manifest the violence that had been brewing for decades and destroyed Douglas's hopes that a political compromise could save the Union.

Born in Brandon, Vermont, the young Douglas was enthralled by Andrew Jackson's presidential campaign of 1828. He left his apprenticeship to a Middlebury cabinetmaker and moved with his family to upstate New York, where he studied at Canandaigua Academy. But, impatient, he left the academy in early 1833 to study law under a local attorney. Impatient again, this time at the long period of preparation required for admission to the New York bar, Douglas left his family and headed west to Illinois, where he was admitted to the bar the following year.

Douglas's middle name could have been Ambition. By 1841, at the age of thirty-seven, he had served as a state attorney, state legislator, register of the Springfield land office, secretary of state, and a justice on the Illinois supreme court. He had also made an unsuccessful run for Congress, in 1838. Douglas ran for the Senate the following year and failed, but he ran for a seat in the House and was elected in 1843. He served a scant two terms before again running for the Senate, where he served until his death. Douglas made two presidential bids, losing the Democratic nomination to James Buchanan in 1856 and losing the election of 1860 to the Republican Abraham Lincoln, whom Douglas staunchly supported when war became inevitable.

Douglas did not marry until 1847, when he was already in the Senate. His bride, Martha Martin, was the daughter of a wealthy North Carolina plantation owner. The union produced two sons and, on his wife's death six years later, left Douglas to manage a 2,500-acre plantation with more than a hundred slaves in Mississippi. Politically, he was neither for nor against slavery, but his opponents in Congress tried, on several occasions, to make an issue of his owning slaves. Douglas married again in 1856, this time to Adele Cutts, an attractive Washington socialite half his age whose great-aunt had been Dolley Madison.

Douglas was a fierce but eloquent debater. Standing only five feet four inches tall, he was so full of nervous energy that colleagues dubbed him "the Little Giant" and "the steam engine in breeches." His series of slavery debates in 1858, which are still studied and reenacted today, launched Lincoln as a figure of national prominence. Douglas was involved with many of the critical debates in the years leading up to the Civil War, most notably for drafting the Kansas-Nebraska Bill of 1854, which repealed the Missouri Compromise, leaving the territories to decide the slavery question for themselves. At the time, Northern abolitionist groups were insisting that the federal government ban slavery throughout the Union while proslavery politicians in the South were demanding federal protection for their institution. Douglas hoped his doctrine of "popular sovereignty" might relieve the sectional strife by relegating the slavery question to the states. The passage of the bill, however, failed to assuage the rising rancor.

Reference

"Douglas, Stephen Arnold." *Encyclopedia of World Biography,* 2nd ed. 17 vols. Gale Research, 1998. Reproduced in *Biography Resource Center.* Farmington Hills, Mich.: Gale Group. 2003. http://www.galenet.com/servlet/BioRC.

11

The Slavery Issue

On May 22, 1856, South Carolina's Democratic representative Preston S. Brooks entered the Senate chamber and beat Massachusetts's Republican senator Charles Sumner into bloody unconsciousness with a gutta percha cane. Brooks attacked Sumner because of his indignation at remarks Sumner had made about South Carolina and its senior senator, Andrew Pickens Butler, two days earlier in a speech denouncing slaveholders' attempts to impose slavery on the new Kansas Territory, which Congress had created in 1854. The assault vividly illustrated how escalating quarrels over slavery in Congress since the mid-1830s had displaced earlier patterns of intersectional cooperation within bisectional political parties with a new party alignment, reflecting instead of bridging the widening sectional chasm over slavery that would provoke the Civil War five years later.

Prior to 1854 and the emergence of the exclusively northern Republican party, partisan loyalty had often acted as an antidote to sectional allegiance when congressmen addressed slavery-related issues. Both northern and southern members of the Whig and Democratic parties usually cooperated to preserve internal party unity instead of joining partisan rivals from the same region. Indeed, they often intentionally differentiated their positions on slavery and other issues from those of partisan foes at home. These shared incentives, however, produced a marked contrast between the Democrats and the Whigs. Northern Democrats were always more likely than northern Whigs to acquiesce in proslavery measures pushed by the South and their southern Democratic colleagues, especially in the Senate, whose members were chosen by state legislatures and were more immune to public opinion at home than representatives. In contrast, southern Whigs were often more prone than southern Democrats to join Northerners in opposing such measures. Sincere fears that sectional strife might escalate into disunion also caused some congressmen to defy opinion at home in order to accommodate demands from the other section. Yet even on those occasions, interparty competition helped produce a recurring pattern. The members of one party from a particular section charged the other party with endangering the Union by its stance on slavery while their foes accused them of betraying the section's interests and rights.

One reason that partisan affiliation and sectional identity had a preeminent influence on how congressmen handled slavery issues is that counterbalancing institutional loyalties and checks within Congress itself were so weak. Because of the high turnover rates in both chambers, seniority was not used to pick members of standing committees. And in any event, much important legislation was shaped in the committee of the whole, specially chosen select committees, or ad hoc caucuses rather than standing committees. Congressmen therefore saw themselves primarily as representing their respective parties and sections, not as members and spokesmen of congressional committees.

The competition between the nationwide Whig and Democratic parties first emerged between 1834 and 1836, but the danger that the slavery issue posed to those intersectional alliances appeared almost instantly when northern antislavery societies petitioned Congress to abolish slavery in the District of Columbia. Primarily concerned first with the presidential campaign of 1836 and then with the prolonged depression between 1837 and 1844, most congressmen considered abolitionist petitions a distracting nuisance, but some indignant Southerners insisted that they be quashed. Starting in the spring of 1836, therefore, the House and Senate adopted procedural rules, popularly known as "gag rules," at the start of each new Congress by which such petitions were formally received and then automatically tabled or instantly spurned.

Congressional votes on these measures produced a decidedly sectional pattern that became more pronounced over time. Almost all Southerners supported them, whereas almost all of the opposition came from Northerners. Yet there was also a discernible partisan influence on debates and votes. To define their own party as the South's most resolute foe of abolition, southern Whigs and Democrats often sought to outdo each other in pushing more extreme versions of gags. More important, year after year northern Whigs, led by John Quincy Adams, Joshua Giddings, and William Slade, solidly opposed the Gag Rule while most northern Democrats, typified by New Hampshire's Charles G. Atherton and New York's Samuel Beardsley, initially supported it.

Over time, the northern Democrats paid an increasingly high political cost at home for this support. The suppression of petitions quickly shifted the northern public's attention away from abolition and the plight of black slaves to the deprivation of white Northerners' freedom of speech and right of petition. Pilloried by the northern Whigs for their slavish subjugation to the southern Slave Power, the Democrats began to lose northern House seats to the Whigs, although the depression primarily caused their defeats. As a result, northern Democratic representatives' support for the Gag Rule declined markedly between 1836 and 1844, and more and more of them joined the northern Whigs against it. Finally, in December 1844, the Gag Rule was defeated, 108–80, when 54 northern Democrats opposed the measure and only 14 joined Southerners in supporting it.

Yet the breakdown of party loyalty over the Gag Rule was not fatal, for its defeat did not unleash constant debates in Congress over abolition. During 1844 attention shifted to the question of slavery extension, which remained the primary issue related to slavery addressed by Congress until the Civil War. In April 1844 President John Tyler presented the Senate with a treaty calling for the annexation of the proslavery Republic of Texas, which had declared its independence from Mexico in 1836. Even though its annexation would vastly expand the area of the country in which slavery was legal and even though Secretary of State John C. Calhoun explicitly defended annexation as a proslavery, prosouthern measure, the annexation of Texas, unlike the Gag Rule controversy, produced a battle primarily along partisan, not sectional, lines in both Congress and the nation at large. Understanding why requires an examination of the proposal's political context.

Elected vice president on the Whig ticket in 1840, Tyler succeeded to the presidency in April 1841 when William Henry Harrison suddenly died. In the 1840–1841 election cycle, the Whigs also won control of both houses of Congress, yet in 1841 and 1842 Tyler, a former Democrat and a Virginian of rigid states' rights, strict construction views, vetoed much of the legislation the Whigs passed to promote economic recovery. Outraged, the congressional Whigs formally read Tyler out of their party, and subsequently they reflexively opposed any proposal he made. In addition, they correctly believed that Tyler intended to run for president in 1844 as an independent, pro-Texas candidate, while their own nominee, Kentucky senator and party founder Henry Clay, publicly opposed immediate annexation on the grounds that it would provoke war with Mexico, which had never recognized Texas's independence, and sectional strife, since Northerners were so averse to the spread of slave territory. Their hatred of Tyler and the need to remain united during the presidential campaign, in sum, largely explain why northern and southern Whigs alike resisted annexation in 1844.

Partisan motivations also largely determined the Democrats' behavior in Congress. To undermine Tyler's independent candidacy and gain an electoral advantage over the anti-annexation Whigs in the South, southern Democrats demanded that the party's 1844 presidential candidate and national platform be committed to immediate annexation. Yet the front-runner for the Democratic nomination, Martin Van Buren, believed that a pro-Texas campaign would be suicidal in the North; like Clay, he also published a letter against immediate annexation before the major parties' national conventions. At the Democratic convention in late May, pro-Texas Southerners and anti–Van Buren Northerners denied him the nomination and gave it instead to the Tennessean James K. Polk while adopting a platform that demanded immediate annexation. The furious Van Buren supporters never forgave the pro-Texas Southerners for engineering this upset.

One week after the Democratic convention, the Senate rejected Tyler's treaty by a crushing vote, 16–35. Every Whig except one Mississippian and eight bitter Van Buren Democrats voted against ratification. Annexation by treaty was clearly dead. But immediate annexation by some means was now a major issue in the presidential campaign, and the opposing Whig and Democratic positions were crystal clear. In November, Polk defeated Clay in an exceptionally close popular vote. Their opposing stands on annexation unquestionably helped Polk in the South, but, importantly, to the extent that Texas shaped voting behavior in the North, it helped the Whigs and embarrassed the Democrats.

That fact proved all-important during the short session of Congress from December 3, 1844, to March 3, 1845, when the lame-duck Tyler implored Congress to annex Texas by a joint resolution, which would require simple majorities in both houses rather than the two-thirds of senators necessary to ratify a treaty. Because annexation was now a party issue, passage by the House, where the Democrats enjoyed a large majority, was a foregone conclusion. Unable to prevent them from prevailing and eager to resolve the Texas issue before the Democrats used it against them again in the South's impending state and congressional elections of 1845, a few southern Whigs, led by Tennessee's Milton Brown, decided to pose as even stronger proslavery champions than southern Democrats by amending the annexation resolution to make it even more beneficial to the South. Like Tyler's treaty, the House resolution called for the annexation of Texas as a territory, not its immediate admission as a state. The southern Whigs' amendment offered Texas immediate admission to Congress as a new slave state, and it stipulated that as many as four additional slave states could be carved out of Texas and that future congresses *must* admit them upon their application for statehood. In short, 8 of the 26 southern Whigs proposed adding five more slave states and ten more slave state senators to the Union, thereby giving the South, as one of the amendment's Tennessee Whig backers put it, "a wonderful increase in political power." The southern Democrats dared not resist this proposal, and they successfully pressured their northern Democratic colleagues to adopt it. The amended bill then passed the House, 120–98. Eighty percent of the Democrats supported it while 90 percent of the Whigs were in opposition.

Passage of the resolution was far more problematic in the Senate, where the Whigs still had a four-seat majority and 8 Democrats had rejected Tyler's treaty the previous June. The southern Whig senators were beseeched by their local politicians to vote for the House measure, but with three exceptions they opposed the bill because they considered it unconstitutional and wanted to preserve their unity with their northern Whig colleagues. Nor were the still bitter Van Buren Democrats willing to support the resolution. By late February, with only a few more days in the session, it faced defeat unless its terms were changed.

To appease the North, the Democratic dissenters wanted to admit only the settled area of eastern Texas as a slave state and to organize its vast unpopulated regions as free territories. They secured the passage of an amendment that gave the president the option of offering Texas statehood in accordance with the House bill or of renegotiating the terms along the lines they demanded. They voted for this measure, moreover, only after they received explicit pledges from Polk, whom they assumed would implement the law, to negotiate terms less favorable to slavery. The amended bill passed the Senate, 27–25. The majority included 3 southern Whigs and all 24 Democrats. All the northern Whigs and 12 of the 15 southern Whigs were in the minority. When the new Senate bill returned to the House, party lines became even sharper. Only a single southern Whig joined all the Democrats in passing the Senate bill over the opposition of every other Whig.

Then, to the shocked fury of the Van Buren Democrats, Tyler on his last day in office offered Texas immediate admission by the terms of the House bill and Polk refused to countermand him, thus betraying his pledge to the northern Democratic senators. Texas accepted the offer in July, and it was admitted by Congress as a slave state in December 1845.

Just as the Whigs had predicted, the annexation of Texas led to war with Mexico in May 1846, ostensibly over a dispute about the boundary between Mexico and Texas. But everyone knew that Polk hoped to force a defeated Mexico into ceding California to the United States. The northern Whigs immediately charged that the Democrats sought to expropriate Mexican territory in order to extend slavery still farther westward, causing worried northern Democrats to seek an occasion to refute the accusation before the congressional elections in 1846. It came in the House in August over Polk's request for an appropriation to fund the negotiations with Mexico. To demonstrate that slaveholders did not dominate the Democratic party, a freshman Pennsylvania Democrat named David Wilmot, acting on behalf of other northern Democrats, introduced an amendment to the bill. Wilmot represented a northern Pennsylvania district where antislavery sentiment was widespread, but the Speaker gave him the floor; earlier in the session Wilmot had supported all the other administration measures without a hint of dissent and was expected to do so on the appropriations bill as well. Famous ever since as the Wilmot Proviso, his amendment stipulated that slavery would be barred from any territory acquired from Mexico.

The Wilmot Proviso utterly shattered both the Whigs and the Democrats along sectional lines from 1846 until 1850, when Congress finally decided what to do with the land the United States ultimately acquired from Mexico in 1848. Repeatedly, bipartisan northern majorities passed the proviso over almost unanimous southern opposition in the House, where Northerners outnumbered Southerners, only to see it buried or defeated in the Senate, where free and slave states had an equal number of seats. By 1850 fourteen of the fifteen northern state legislatures had instructed their U.S. senators and requested their representatives to impose the proviso on any new western territories. Further, on its formation in 1848, the new Free-Soil party made congressional prohibition of slavery from federal territories the centerpiece of its platform. Meanwhile, starting in 1847, increasing numbers of Southerners threatened secession should Congress ever prohibit slavery from federal territories.

The congressmen's own convictions and public opinion in their respective home regions fueled this rancorous standoff. The hostility to the spread of slavery was far more widespread than abolitionist sentiment. Some Northerners opposed the extension of an institution they deemed immoral, but others wanted to preserve the West exclusively for the white race, and still others wanted to prevent any further increase in the South's political power in Congress. Southerners disagreed among themselves about whether slavery could be profitably extended to the Mexican Cession, which included the modern states of California, Nevada, Utah, Arizona, and New Mexico, but they all considered the proviso an insulting and intolerable attempt by the majority North to deprive the minority South of its equal rights in territories. To submit to such dictation was to admit their inferiority and acquiesce to their own enslavement by a tyrannical northern majority. And that Southerners refused to do. "What! acknowledge inferiority!" screamed South Carolina's Calhoun when protesting the proviso in the Senate. "The surrender of life is nothing to sinking down into acknowledged inferiority."

Given this intransigent sectional polarization, both the Whigs and the

Democrats sought alternate positions on slavery in the territories that could preserve their parties' national unity and prevent the disruption of the Union. Between 1847 and 1860, many Democrats advocated popular sovereignty. This formula would remove the decision about slavery in the territories from Congress and consign it to the residents of those territories. To preserve party unity, the Democrats were purposely vague about exactly when those residents could decide to permit or bar slavery. The Democrats' presidential candidate in 1848, Senator Lewis Cass of Michigan, championed popular sovereignty; the Democrats would force its inclusion in the territorial provisions of the Compromise of 1850, and the Democratic senator Stephen A. Douglas would incorporate it into his controversial Kansas-Nebraska bill of 1854.

The Whigs followed a more varied course. Until March 10, 1848, when the Senate ratified the Treaty of Guadelupe Hidalgo, bequeathing the Mexican Cession to the United States, northern and southern Whigs in Congress demanded that no territory whatsoever be taken from Mexico. With no new land into which slavery might expand, the Wilmot Proviso was moot. After March 1848, the Whigs in and outside Congress resorted to advocating the proviso in the North and opposing it in the South, a Janus-faced strategy that helped them elect General Zachary Taylor president in 1848. Between his inauguration in March 1849 and the convening of Congress the following December, Taylor sought to skip the territorial stage altogether and have New Mexico and California (which Taylor hoped would include Utah) apply to Congress for admission as free states.

When he presented this proposal to Congress in January 1850, however, only the northern Whigs were willing to support it. Thus the plan was doomed, since the Democrats had majorities in both the House and Senate. The southern Democrats had won sweeping victories in the state and congressional elections of 1849 by insisting on slavery's extension throughout the Mexican Cession. They savaged Taylor's plan as the Wilmot Proviso in disguise and ranted that California's admission as a free state would upset the Senate's sectional balance. Well aware of the shellacking the Whigs had suffered in the South in 1849, the few remaining southern Whigs in Congress rejected Taylor's plan as providing inadequate political cover at home. The northern Democrats, in turn, while willing to admit California, insisted that the remainder of the Mexican Cession be organized as territories on the basis of popular sovereignty. They and other critics of Taylor's proposal, moreover, justifiably faulted it for failing to address an escalating dispute over the location of the boundary between New Mexico and Texas, which claimed all the land east of the Rio Grande, including Santa Fe, as its own.

With Taylor's plan lacking the votes to pass, Congress formulated its own policy for the Mexican Cession and two other matters that Taylor had ignored: the Southerners' demand for a new fugitive slave law and northern demands for the abolition of public slave auctions in the District of Columbia. Famous ever since as the Compromise of 1850, this policy has usually been attributed to Senator Henry Clay, who in late January 1850 did indeed introduce recommendations for a "great national scheme of compromise and harmony" on the issues concerning slavery. Yet Clay's original proposals garnered very little support, and southern Democrats instantly denounced them as "no compromise at all." Thus the Democratic majority along with dissatisfied southern Whigs amended Clay's proposals to make more concessions to the South. Moreover, even this package of bills would never have passed had not President Taylor suddenly died in July and the new Whig administration of Millard Fillmore pressured a critical number of northern Whigs in the House and Senate to abstain on or vote for these measures.

Encompassing five laws, the Compromise of 1850 admitted California as a free state with its present boundaries; adjusted the border between Texas and New Mexico and compensated Texas for surrendering its claim to all land east of the Rio Grande with a payment of $10 million; organized New Mexico and Utah as federal territories on the basis of popular sovereignty; enacted a new Fugitive Slave Law, which eased the ability of slaveholders to reclaim purported runaways in the North while potentially forcing Northerners to help in their capture; and abolished public slave auctions in the District of Columbia.

The roll call voting coalitions on these measures, and on the procedural motions that allowed them to come up for a vote in the Senate and House, were extraordinary. Unlike the previous consideration of matters concerning slavery, neither sectional nor partisan lines held. Instead, a four-way quadrant, with several notable exceptions from each, prevailed. Southern Whigs and northern Democrats passed the compromise measures; most of the northern Whigs and southern Democrats opposed them, if for very different reasons. Northern Whigs protested that slaveholders had been given too much; southern Democrats fumed that they had gained far too little, that the reduction of Texas, where slavery was legal, and the admission of California rendered the compromise an intolerable northern violation of Southern Rights. Significantly, the same four-way pattern appeared in the northern elections of 1850 and the southern elections of 1851. And, almost everywhere, pro-compromise Democratic candidates in the North and Whig (or Union) candidates in the South won those elections. Heeding this apparently emphatic expression of public opinion, both the Whig and Democratic parties endorsed the compromise as a final settlement of all the slavery issues in their 1852 national platforms.

The Democrats had the better of this shouting match, and they elected Franklin Pierce president in 1852 while crushing the Whigs in the congressional elections of 1852–1853. To the deep and oft-expressed chagrin of bitter antislavery diehards in the North, with the controlling Democrats having pledged never again to allow anything involving slavery to come before Congress, the slavery issue at long last appeared to be dead.

In 1854, Congress, without any popular pressure or presidential prodding, revived the issue with fatal consequences for the intersectional two-party system and ultimately the Union itself. In January of that year, Illinois's Douglas reported a bill from the Senate Committee on Territories to organize all of the remaining unsettled area of the Louisiana Purchase west of Missouri, Iowa, and the Minnesota Territory, from the 36°30′ line north to the Canadian border, into a single Nebraska Territory. Long a champion of western development, the five-foot-four-inch "Little Giant" had two primary motives in presenting the bill at that time, neither of which was directly relevant to slavery. No land in that immense area could be legally sold until it was formally organized, surveyed, and put up for sale by the federal government. Thus Douglas sought to appease potential settlers who clamored for the chance to buy land there and especially to facilitate the construction of a railroad to the Pacific coast with federal land grants. Yet because he expected the few remaining Whigs in Congress to oppose western development, he also hoped that this program would allow the Democrats, who had been bitterly divided by squabbles over Pierce's patronage dispensation since March 1853, to unite behind a discernible Democratic legislative program when their traditional Whig foes opposed it.

Douglas's blueprint for western development and Democratic reunification, however, faced a substantial hurdle. The Missouri Compromise of 1820 had "forever prohibited" slavery from the area he wanted to organize, and Southern Democrats, now intransigent because of the recent quarrels over the Wilmot Proviso, refused to support his bill if that prohibition was retained. Douglas knew that any outright repeal of that ban would infuriate Northerners, so he initially asserted that only the popular sovereignty provisions of the Utah and New Mexico acts of 1850 also applied to the new territory. The Southerners of both parties, but primarily the Democrats, bluntly told him that this concession was not enough; they demanded an outright repeal of the ban on slavery in the designated area. As a result, Douglas revised his bill and, along with the southern Democrats, forced President Pierce to declare it a Democratic measure that all congressional Democrats must support. The final bill created two territories, Kansas and Nebraska, and while avoiding the controversial word "repeal," effectively nullified the 1820 ban on slavery by declaring it "inoperative and void" because the popular sovereignty provisions of the Compromise of 1850 had "superseded" it.

Initially, the Kansas-Nebraska bill portended a renewed partisan conflict between the Whigs and Democrats, for most southern Whig congressmen, like their constituents, doubted that slavery could ever be established in Kansas or Nebraska and were prepared to pillory Democrats for wantonly reigniting sectional rancor. But then the few remaining Free-Soilers in Congress condemned the revised bill as a Slave Power aggression against the North, not a Democratic violation of national harmony. Southerners considered that manifesto so insulting that passing the bill now became a matter of sectional honor. As a result, all but two southern Whigs in the Senate and two-thirds of them in the House voted for the measure. In the Senate, where passage was certain because of the huge Democratic majority, the southern Whig votes only increased the size of the 37–14 margin by which the bill passed in March. But in the House, where half of the northern Democrats along with all the northern Whigs and Free-Soilers voted against the measure, the southern Whig support made all the difference, especially in prying the bill from the bottom of the agenda of the House Committee of the Whole, to which its opponents had consigned it in order to bury it. There the measure finally passed in May, 113–100, and Pierce quickly signed it into law. Thirteen southern Whigs were in the majority and 7 in the minority while 4 abstained. If only 7 more of them had joined the opposition, the bill would have failed.

The Kansas-Nebraska Act is arguably the most consequential law ever passed by Congress, for it launched a chain of events that led to the Civil War. It ignited a prolonged battle between Northerners and Southerners, most of whom were residents of Missouri, for control of Kansas's territorial legislature, a battle that made "Bleeding Kansas" a central issue in the 1856 presidential election in the North. It shattered the Whigs forever along sectional lines, for furious northern Whigs never forgave the southern Whigs for supporting the measure. It provoked a massive voter backlash in the North against the Democrats in the congressional elections of 1854–1855. While hostility to the Kansas-Nebraska Act was hardly the only issue that damaged the Democrats in those contests, they lost 66 of the 91 northern House seats they had held in 1854, and they would not recover that lost ground until 1874. Most important, along with the northern voter realignment against the Democrats came a reconfiguration of the opposition. As early as the fall of 1854, bipartisan anti-Nebraska coalitions had displaced the Whigs in four northern states, and by 1856 they had evolved across the North into a powerful Republican party that carried 11 of 16 free states in that year's presidential election, thereby consigning the Whig party to its grave.

Between the end of May 1854 and November 1856, most of the tumultuous events that engendered these developments occurred outside the halls of Congress. Two incidents in the Capitol, however, immeasurably helped the Republicans' sudden surge to potency in 1856. First, after a prolonged two-month struggle, the House elected a Republican Speaker in January, which signaled that most northern anti-Democratic *politicians* in Congress were now prepared to rally behind the Republican banner. Second, the aforementioned caning of Charles Sumner allowed the Republicans to combine "Bleeding Sumner" with "Bleeding Kansas" as campaign issues; the caning of Sumner did more than anything else that year to convince infuriated anti-Democratic *voters* in the North to join the Republican party.

In the three-way presidential election of 1856 (the anti-Catholic, anti-immigrant American party also had a candidate), the Democrat James Buchanan won despite carrying only 5 of the 16 free states. Once in office, his top priority was to strip the Republicans of the Kansas issue by admitting Kansas to statehood as soon as possible. When Congress assembled in December 1857, with the Democrats once again in control of both chambers, Buchanan urged it to admit Kansas as a slave state under the terms of the Lecompton Constitution. Written at Lecompton, Kansas, in the fall of 1857 by a convention that most northern settlers had boycotted and rejected by a clear majority of Kansas residents, who voted in two separate referendums, the Lecompton Constitution clearly violated the bedrock principle of the Democrats' popular sovereignty formula, namely, that a majority of the actual residents in a territory should make the decision on slavery. Thus, when Buchanan insisted that the Democratic congressional majorities accept it as legitimate, Douglas and many of his northern Democratic supporters rebelled. Breaking openly with the Buchanan administration and southern Democrats, they joined the Republicans in opposing its acceptance. They could not stop the Senate from admitting Kansas as a slave state under Lecompton, but in the House they did. The upshot was a face-saving compromise bill, named after its author, the Democratic representative William H. English of Indiana, which made Kansas's admission as a state contingent on the outcome of yet another Kansas referendum on the Lecompton Constitution. On August 2, 1858, the voters there overwhelmingly rejected it, thereby killing any prospect that Kansas would be a slave state. By 1860 only two slaves remained within its boundaries, and in 1861 the Republicans would admit it as a free state.

These events in Congress once again had powerful reverberations throughout the country. They split the northern Democrats between pro- and anti-Lecompton men and helped the Republicans gain a number of House seats in the 1858 elections. More important, the southern Democrats, aided by a vengeful Buchanan, turned openly against Douglas and his doctrine of popular sovereignty. In Congress, they demanded the enactment of a federal slave code that would legalize slavery in all the territories, and they stripped Douglas of his committee chairmanship. At the Democratic national convention in 1860, they fought Douglas's nomination for president, bolting the convention when his northern supporters refused to accept a platform endorsing a federal slave code. These squabbles resulted in two Democratic presidential candidates in 1860 — Douglas and Buchanan's vice president, John C. Breckinridge — but the Republicans' choice, Abraham Lincoln, would probably have won that year even if the Democrats had united behind a single candidate.

The last time Congress addressed the issue of slavery before the Civil War came when it met between the December after Lincoln's election and his inauguration on March 4, 1861. During those three months, seven Deep South states seceded and the Confederacy was formed. Consequently, Congress's priority was to fashion some compromise on slavery that would slow and then reverse the secession movement. The House created a select Committee of Thirty-three, with one member from each state, and the Senate a select Committee of Thirteen, with an artfully balanced mixture of border state moderates, northern Republicans, and southern Democrats, to find a legislative solution. To reassure the South, this session of Congress actually passed by the necessary two-thirds majorities and sent to the states for ratification a new Thirteenth Amendment to the Constitution. Supported by two-fifths of the Republicans in each chamber and explicitly endorsed by Lincoln in his inaugural address, it forever prohibited the federal government from abolishing slavery in the states where it existed. Yet it was not enough; despite the hyperbolic rhetoric of secessionists, most of the Southerners in Congress understood that the Republicans had no abolitionist designs. Instead, they insisted that the Republicans drop their bedrock opposition to the extension of slavery into all present and future territories. And that Republicans refused to do. The possibility of a compromise failed, and, six weeks after Lincoln's inauguration, war came.

— MICHAEL F. HOLT

BIBLIOGRAPHICAL NOTES

The standard studies of roll call voting in Congress between 1840 and 1861 are Thomas B. Alexander, *Sectional Stress and Party Strength: A Computer Analysis of Roll-Call Voting in the United States House of Representatives, 1836–1860* (Nashville, Tenn., 1967), and Joel H. Silbey, *The Shrine of Party: Congressional Voting Behavior, 1841–1852* (Pittsburgh, 1967). Four books, each of which provides a thorough analysis of Congress on particular issues, offer the necessary general background on the disputes over slavery in these years: Roy F. Nichols, *The Disruption of American Democracy* (New York, 1948); David M. Potter, *The Impending Crisis, 1848–1861* (New York, 1976); William W. Freehling, *The Road to Disunion: Secessionists at Bay, 1776–1854* (New York, 1990); and Michael F. Holt, *The Rise and Fall of the American Whig Party* (New York, 1999).

Leonard L. Richards, *The Slave Power: The Free North and Southern Domination, 1780–1860* (Baton Rouge, La., 2000), and Don E. Fehrenbacher, *The Slaveholding Republic* (New York, 2001), provide useful overviews of the slavery issue in Congress. For more detailed treatments of the episodes covered in this essay, see William Lee Miller, *Arguing about Slavery: The Great Battle in the United States Congress* (New York, 1996); Holman Hamilton, *Prologue to Conflict: The Crisis and Compromise of 1850* (New York, 1964); Mark J. Stegmaier, *Texas, New Mexico, and the Compromise of 1850: Boundary Dispute & Sectional Crisis* (Kent, Ohio, 1996); and Roy F. Nichols, "The Kansas-Nebraska Act: A Century of Historiography," *Mississippi Valley Historical Review* 43 (1956): 187–212.

John Quincy Adams

July 11, 1767–February 23, 1848

John Quincy Adams

The eldest son of the second president, John Quincy Adams was bred for the American political life and became the only son of a president to serve in that office until the year 2000. It is perhaps odd that he found the law tedious and politics distasteful because his entire career was spent serving as an ambassador and politician. He hated being out of office and never retired. At the age of eighty, Adams was working on the floor of the House of Representatives when he suffered a stroke and died two days later in the Speaker's Room. He is remembered as a brilliant statesman whose contributions as a foreign minister, secretary of state, and congressman far outweighed his achievements in his single term as president.

Adams was born in Braintree, Massachusetts, into a distinguished family and was expected, by his hard-working parents, to achieve distinction. At the age of ten, he accompanied his father to Europe on a diplomatic mission and attended schools in France and Holland. Returning to Massachusetts, he graduated from Harvard College, studied law, and began to practice in Boston in 1790. A year later he wrote, under a pseudonym, a series of articles attacking the radical position of Thomas Paine's *Rights of Man.* More articles followed in which Adams defended the neutral positions of President George Washington and his father, then vice president. His conservative writings, his experience in Europe, his intelligence, and, no doubt, his family connections helped Adams begin his political career when Washington appointed him minister to the Netherlands.

On a visit to London, Adams met the daughter of the American consul. He and Louisa Catherine Johnson were married in 1797. When the presidential term of Adams's father ended, the couple returned to Boston. They had three sons and a daughter, naming the first two sons after the nation's first two presidents. In spite of Adams's political appointments in Washington and abroad, his family would remain a Boston institution for the next fifty years.

Despite his stated aversion to politics, Adams was soon elected to the state senate. In 1803 his Federalist colleagues selected him for the Senate, but they were surprised by his independent streak in casting his votes. Adams did not defer to the Federalist leaders, and subsequent conflicts with the Massachusetts legislature led him to resign in 1808. The following year he returned to diplomacy, accepting an appointment as minister to St. Petersburg. He joined the American delegation at the Treaty of Ghent, which ended the War of 1812, served two years as minister to Great Britain, and returned to the United States to serve as secretary of state during the two terms of President James Monroe. Adams shined in this position — then a steppingstone to the presidency — and distinguished himself during the negotiations for the acquisition of Florida in 1819 and the formulation of the Monroe Doctrine, which espoused the primacy of the United States in the Western Hemisphere.

Adams emerged from the contested election of 1824 with the presidency but little popular support. Political maneuvers by the Kentucky congressman Henry Clay, with whom he had sparred since the Treaty of Ghent, guaranteed Adams the presidency, but his appointment of Clay as secretary of state brought down cries of a "corrupt bargain" by the supporters of the popular war hero Andrew Jackson, who had won a plurality of the vote. A hostile Congress opposed many of the administration's proposals, although federal support of internal improvements like canals and roadways met with some success. Drawing on his diplomatic experience, Adams concentrated on foreign affairs and was effective in framing many international trade agreements. In the 1828 presidential race, against Andrew Jackson, Adams refused to campaign for reelection, explaining that "electioneering" went against his principles. Regardless, after his defeat he was miserable in retirement and was reinvigorated when Massachusetts Republicans asked him to run for the House of Representatives.

Adams suited the political vision of an increasingly industrial New England, and he was handily reelected to serve in Congress for seventeen years. He continued to support the "American Plan," the domestic program for internal improvements and tariffs that favored industry. And, because southern interests threatened that plan, he turned against the southern political influence and, consequently, the institution of slavery. He became a champion of that fight, campaigning for nearly a decade against the "gag rule" that prevented antislavery petitions from being introduced, protesting the annexation of Texas, and, before the Supreme Court in 1841, participating in the legal defense of the slaves who seized the Spanish slave ship *Armistad.* Adams was a statesman of the old cloth, steadfast in his political convictions and unwilling to compromise. In spite of this unbending approach, he was respected for using sound judgment in pursuit of reasonable and lasting policies during decades of public service.

Reference

Hargreaves, M.W.M. 2000, February. "Adams, John Quincy." *American National Biography Online.* Retrieved June 30, 2003, from http://www.anb.org/articles/03/03-00002.html.

James Buchanan

April 23, 1791–June 1, 1868

James Buchanan

There is no fan club for President James Buchanan. Although a successful businessman and capable politician, he ascended to the presidency as a result of calamitous forces that quickly turned against him. Nor has history been kind to him. A recent survey of historians ranked him as the worst president in American history — a dismal place for a promising leader. Despite the rest of his political career, Buchanan will always be judged for his presidential term, when his actions pleased neither the North nor the South.

Like Lincoln, Buchanan had been born in a log cabin. His father was a Scottish immigrant who settled near Mercersburg, Pennsylvania. The young Buchanan was educated at a local academy and graduated from Dickinson College in 1809, then studied law in Lancaster and was admitted to the bar in 1812. He was a talented debater and diligent lawyer, prospering both from his trade and through shrewd investments. In 1819, for unknown reasons, his fiancée broke off their engagement. When she died soon after, Buchanan vowed he would never marry and, indeed, remained a bachelor for the rest of his life. He did not make friends easily but was close to his professional and political colleagues.

Buchanan began his political career as a Federalist in the Pennsylvania legislature. Elected to Congress in 1820, when the Federalist party collapsed, he joined the Jacksonians and became a loyal party member and important Democratic leader in Congress. He served a total of ten years in the House of Representatives and four years in the Senate. He broadened his career with international experience as minister to Russia (1832–1834) and Great Britain (1853–1856). And he served as secretary of state (1845–1849) in James Polk's administration.

Buchanan was a tall and stout man, distinguished by his white hair, meticulous dress, and courtly manners. His career in Congress had been productive and he had ambition, so he sought the presidential nomination in 1844, 1848, and 1852. Finally, in 1856, the Democrats nominated Buchanan almost solely because he was out of the country when the Kansas-Nebraska Act besmirched its author, Senator Stephen A. Douglas of Illinois, and President Franklin Pierce, who had signed it. Both men had been vying for the nomination, but Buchanan's reputation was undamaged and his qualifications were more than sufficient. He was diligent and experienced, but unfortunately he was also legalistic, unimaginative, and cautious to the point of being ineffectual. At a moment of sectional crisis, Buchanan lacked the skill to inspire and lead others.

As president, Buchanan inherited the impossible task of suppressing sectional strife and keeping the Union together. To his credit, he was devoted to the Union and well understood the danger it was in. His interpretation of the Constitution supported neither slavery nor emancipation, which incensed the Northern abolitionists and left Southerners feeling betrayed. Buchanan's Southern bias was evident when he violated an earlier pledge and endorsed the admission of Kansas as a slave state. An economic depression that began in 1857 made matters worse. His cabinet was wracked by corruption; a congressional probe uncovered misappropriation of funds, kickbacks, and bribes. Buchanan was not personally liable for any of the transgressions, but he was criticized for failing to uncover the crimes. The abolitionist John Brown's raid at Harpers Ferry in 1859, followed by his execution later that year, did nothing to alleviate sectional differences. By the time of the Democratic convention in April 1860, the administration was in tatters. The party formed two factions, with the Northern Democrats supporting Douglas for president and the Southerners supporting Vice President John C. Breckinridge of Kentucky. During the transition to President Abraham Lincoln's administration, Buchanan worked diligently to preserve the peace in South Carolina. In retirement, he supported the war as a Union Democrat.

References

Gienapp, W. E. 2000, February. "Buchanan, James." *American National Biography Online.* Retrieved June 30, 2003, from http://www.anb.org/articles/04/04-00170.html.

Lindgren, J. "Rating the Presidents of the United States, 1789–2000: A Survey of Scholars in History, Political Science, and Law." Published by the Federalist Society and the *Wall Street Journal.* Retrieved July 14, 2003, from http://www.fed-soc.org/pdf/pres-survey.PDF.

12

The Civil War

IN A 1909 BANQUET ADDRESS honoring Abraham Lincoln's birthday, James S. Ewing, an old Illinois associate of Lincoln's, recalled a story told by Senator John B. Henderson of Missouri. Henderson, who served in Congress during the Civil War, said that during a meeting with Lincoln in the White House, the president looked out the window and saw three Republican members of Congress with reputations as eager promoters of emancipation approaching — Senator Charles Sumner of Massachusetts, Senator Benjamin F. Wade of Ohio, and Representative Thaddeus Stevens of Pennsylvania. Lincoln was reminded of the time when he was in a frontier school and reading aloud from the Bible was a standard part of the curriculum. Naturally, the students counted the number of readers ahead of them to determine the passage they would be called on to read, and one poor scholar was distressed to find that his passage would contain three names he had in the past stumbled over: Shadrach, Meshach, and Abednego. The boy turned in misery and said to Lincoln, "Look! there come them three d——d fellers again."

The story may be apocryphal, but it has enjoyed a long and happy life in subsequent biographies of the Civil War president. Its popularity stands as a monument to the relative reputations of the president and Congress in the Civil War: Lincoln's reputation for greatness is secure, but that of Congress has often stood only a little above ridicule.

It is true that the legislative branch was destined to play but a small and unheroic role in the Civil War. The decade before Lincoln came to office, by contrast, had been marked by presidencies widely regarded as failures and had been bracketed by the exploits of congressional leaders of great reputation — from Henry Clay, whose efforts at compromise of sectional issues ushered in the decade, to Stephen A. Douglas, who died shortly after all the compromises failed and the Civil War began.

Lincoln's political talent and moral vision had much to do with the difference, but so did the Constitution. Its provisions for war made the president the commander in chief. It also gave him a long, four-year term. Since the war began in April 1861 within weeks of Lincoln's inauguration and thus coincided in its forty-eight-month length almost exactly with the presidential term, the role of the executive remained paramount throughout the period; Lincoln enjoyed the political staying power necessary to weather shocking battlefield defeats for the Union and appalling losses of men to enemy fire and camp diseases.

Whatever the fortunes of war, the role of the opposition party in Congress, the Democrats, the oldest political party in the world and, just a few years before, the mightiest, likewise remained insignificant. The departure of the southern Democrats from Congress with secession and the war left the Republicans with overwhelming majorities in both the House and Senate.

The "unwritten constitution" gave the Democrats less power still. Most American politicians knew the lesson of the Federalist opposition to the War of 1812: that party's failure to vote supplies for troops in the field amounted to political suicide for the party. Thus, though the Constitution gave Congress the power to raise and support armies and to make rules for their government and regulation, the powers in this instance were not as great as they seemed. Even the leader of the peace faction in the Democratic party, Clement L. Vallandigham of Ohio, who served in the first of the two Civil War congresses, the Thirty-seventh, was careful to point out near the end of his term:

> I could not, with my convictions, vote men and money for this war, and I would not, as a Representative, vote against them. I meant that, without opposition, the President might take all the men and money he should demand, and then to hold him to a strict accountability before the people for the results. Not believing the soldiers responsible for the war, or its purposes, or its consequences, I have never withheld my vote where their separate interests were concerned. (*Cong. Globe*, 37 Cong., 3 sess., pt. 2, appendix, p. 54.)

Taken all in all, the role of the opposition party proved frustrating and very small. Thus the *New York World*, the organ of the moderate, pro-war wing of the Democratic party — the other pole of opinion from Vallandigham's, pointed out with philosophic resignation on June 15, 1863,

> The last Congress gave the administration the power to raise all the men and all the money it needed to carry on the present war, until the close of its term of office. If the Democratic party unanimously sustained the administration in its war policy they could give it no additional strength,

> and if they were unanimously for peace they could do nothing to stop the war until Mr. Lincoln's term of office expired.

The situation "left to the opposition no choice between submission along with the persistent expression of its views on the one hand, and on the other anarchy" (March 19, 1863). The paper counseled patience and the cynical evasion of issues:

> It is the mission of the Opposition party not to break down or enfeeble the federal government, but to get possession of it and administer it on constitutional principles . . . Why should we encumber ourselves with a positive policy while as yet we have no power to put it in force? (February 19, 1863.)

The Special Session

The first Civil War Congress came together initially on July 4, 1861, in a special session called by the president because of the rebellion. In the eighty days of war preceding, the president had, as the great constitutional historian James G. Randall points out, exceeded his constitutional powers by increasing the army without congressional appropriations, expended funds in other ways than Congress had designated, and used agents for disbursing money who had no legal authorization. At the time, the opposition and a few uneasy Republicans took notice mainly of Lincoln's suspension of the privilege of the writ of habeas corpus, widely regarded as a congressional power. Relying on his knowledge of the Republicans' control of Congress, the president in his message to the special session somewhat blithely acknowledged that

> these measures, whether strictly legal or not, were ventured upon, under what appeared to be a popular demand, and a public necessity; trusting, then as now, that Congress would readily ratify them. It is believed that nothing has been done beyond the constitutional competency of Congress.

Congress, confining itself in the session to war measures, performed as expected.

Otherwise, the session is best known for passing the so-called Crittenden Resolution, pushed by Representative John J. Crittenden of Kentucky, which in its House version read as follows:

> . . . the present deplorable civil war has been forced upon the country by the disunionists of the southern States, now in arms against the constitutional Government and in arms around the capital; . . . in this national

> emergency, Congress, banishing all feelings of mere passion or resentment, will recollect only its duty to the whole country; . . . this war is not waged on their part in any spirit of oppression, or for any purpose of conquest or subjugation, nor for the purpose of overthrowing or interfering with the rights or established institutions of those States, but to defend and maintain the *supremacy* of the Constitution, and to preserve the Union with all the dignity, equality, and rights of the several States unimpaired; and . . . as soon as these objects are accomplished the war ought to cease. (*Cong. Globe*, 37 Cong., 1 sess., p. 233.)

"Established institutions" and "rights of the . . . states" were nothing more than euphemisms for "slavery" here, and the resolution amounted to a promise not to touch the South's peculiar institution in waging the war to a successful conclusion. The resolution passed the House, 117–2, and the Senate, 30–5.

The Democrats were responsible for the continuing fame of the Crittenden Resolution. They pointed to it throughout the war as the original consensus on war aims — no subjugation of the South and no interference with slavery, goals later betrayed by abolitionist Republicans, the Democrats complained. The Republicans generally tried to forget about it, and indeed most modern historians carefully look at the resolution in its context. As the historian James McPherson points out, the resolution was introduced the day after the Bull Run defeat and carried reassurance to the border slave states, where secession sentiment remained a serious threat and whose population and resources would likely have given the Confederacy victory, that the government would not meddle with slavery.

Any agreement on war aims, if it ever existed beyond the situational demands of border state strategy in the wake of battlefield defeat, disappeared quickly, and the Crittenden Resolution failed reaffirmation in the House when it met in regular session before the end of the year. The session, which convened on December 2, 1861, saw partisanship undiminished. No sooner had the initial prayer been spoken and a few organizational formalities acquitted than Senator Lyman Trumbull of Illinois gave notice of his intention to "introduce a bill for the confiscation of the property of rebels and giving freedom to the persons they hold in slavery" — a marked departure from the Crittenden Resolution. Acrimonious debate on confiscation proved a major preoccupation of this Congress.

Republican Goals Realized

As the historian David Potter has pointed out in describing the party preoccupation of the nineteenth-century congresses, the first session of the first Congress of any presidential term was usually the only one to accomplish much; the remaining session of that Congress was focused on off-year elections and the second Congress was absorbed altogether in presidential politicking. The session of the Thirty-seventh Congress that followed its special session accomplished a great deal. Capitalizing on the absence of its Democratic members because of the rebellion, the Republicans managed to legislate the major planks of the Republican platform of 1860.

Sometimes mistaken as an embodiment of the mobilization for "total war," the measures passed in 1862 smacked more of party opportunism. Perhaps the domestic legislation most obviously shaped by the war was financial measures. Many Republicans had to torture their consciences to endorse the Legal Tender Act (February 25, 1862), which, after the war ended, came to be regarded by some as akin to original sin. On the other hand, increasing the tariff, as the Republicans did four times — eventually doubling the duties on some items by war's end — enhanced revenue for the fight. But raising tariff levels also realized a Republican desire for the protection of domestic industries.

The Homestead Act (May 20, 1862), which lured settlers west with the promise of free public land, was surely dysfunctional militarily, but free land had been a plank in the Republican platform for the life of the party. Of no use to immediate military might as well was the Morrill Land Grant Act (July 2, 1862), which aimed to fund colleges with the revenue from the sales of public lands. (It is the foundation of the A&M universities of today, but no college education or research was going to help the war effort in the short run.) The Pacific Railroad Act (July 1, 1862) also exploited public lands to help underwrite the construction of a trunk line from Omaha, Nebraska, to San Francisco, California. In part, at least, it was a long-range measure to cement the Union.

Financial measures continued to be driven by the Treasury Department's needs for war expenditures and by prodding from the secretary of the Treasury, Salmon P. Chase. By 1864 Congress had created a national banking system that would forever replace with a national currency the varieties of paper money issued by local banks before the Civil War. This Treasury Department initiative even brought a brief attempt on the part of Congress to outlaw speculation in gold on the financial markets in 1864. Taxation remained unpopular in the American republic, but war allowed wary congressmen to depart from normal. They imposed a modest graduated income tax (created as early as 1861 and modified in 1864) and numerous taxes on consumer goods like whiskey (the attempt to tax which in the early Republic brought virtual revolution).

The Joint Committee on the Conduct of the War

If the Republicans reaped a harvest of policy advantages from their domination of Congress and the administration during the war, they paid a price as well — the accustomed one of political factionalism, which by war's end sometimes seemed to pit the president against a large faction of his own party in Congress. Over the years, the work of the Joint Committee on the Conduct of the War has stood out as a feature of this factionalism and conflict between the president and Congress. Established in December 1861 to investigate the Union military defeats of the previous season of campaigning, the committee proceeded in its long career to interrogate generals of the army and others and to publish eight stout volumes of reports on military defeats and occasional scandals.

The chair of the committee throughout was Benjamin F. Wade, who set the radical tone for its work. The investigations were highly charged with partisanship and, as the historian Bruce Tap has argued, anything but well informed about modern warfare. Abetted by two other radicals with extravagant opinions vehemently expressed — George Washington Julian, a member of the House from Indiana, and Senator Zachariah Chandler of Michigan — Wade led his committee in investigations and reports that provided the crucial documentation for destroying the military reputation of General George B. McClellan, a Democrat in politics cordially hated by the armchair generals who dominated the committee.

A landmark of the attack came in a speech in the Senate made by Chandler on July 16, 1862, about two weeks after McClellan's army was turned back from Richmond. Using information gleaned from testimony before the committee, Chandler ridiculed the circuitous maneuvering of military "strategy" and scorned the cowardly work of "spades and pick axes" in fortification and entrenchment. Even deaths from camp disease were laid at the general's feet: they were less the products of an inadequate knowledge of public health than of choosing to approach the Confederate capital through swampy land, where unacclimated Union soldiers died uselessly from disease when they should have been attacking Richmond. In its published version, franked to constituents and other Northerners, the speech was called "Conduct of the War."

The domination of the government by one party led to the performance by the Republicans themselves of the investigatory and watchdog functions customarily provided by a loyal opposition party. Other committees made more important exposés, particularly of fraud in the New York Customs House, but the Committee on the Conduct of the War investigated alleged fraud, for example, in providing ice for military hospitals early in 1864. The committee might also be seen as an embodiment of the continuing frustrations of a constitutional presidential system of government rather than a parliamentary one. The military defeats that had provoked the Crittenden Resolution and the establishment of this major investigative committee would likely have led in a parliamentary government to the fall of the administration itself — and Abraham Lincoln would have headed our government for as few as five months and certainly no more than fifteen, being unable to survive, politically, the national trauma of the defeat of McClellan's great army before Richmond at the end of June 1862.

But the Constitution made Lincoln the commander in chief until at least March 1865. The committee thus stood also as yet another monument to the weakness of Congress in wartime, for it could publish reports and destroy reputations but not direct military planning. On the other hand, military historians like Carol Reardon have noted that the work of the committee marked the advent of the modern era of warfare, in which generals had a clear sense of operating with politicians looking over their shoulders and with public opinion following closely behind.

Congress at Work

Despite the polarization of party ideologies and the shrillness of the partisan denunciation that marked this period, congressional debate, unlike stump speeches on the hustings, remained muted by a veneer of courtliness. Traditional customs of formal reference to opposing individuals still marked most debates, though some of them actually dealt with expelling members of Congress. Opponents were routinely, if not sincerely, described as "my friend from" this state or that. The sheer dogged adherence to these customs and rules of debate had the practical effect of muting personal conflict, for the debates were regularly marked, throughout the Civil War period, by indications of laughter among the members.

Students of history will find the polite language, combined with the obscure and byzantine rules of parliamentary order by which Congress strictly operated, slow going. Most careful readers will realize what many members of Congress and congressional observers noted at the time, that the members' minds were rarely changed by debate. The real audience of the speeches was not the listeners in Congress but the constituents back home, and the ultimate purpose of most utterances on the floor was electioneering. That was particularly so because Congress remained a principal organizer and funder of political campaigns through publishing and circulating pamphlet versions of the speeches on the members' franking privileges. At the time of national political campaigns, party congressional committees remained in Washington during the election to direct documents across the country. Thus one of the greatest efforts and contributions of Congress to the outcome of the Civil War lay in work that was in fact extracongressional. The National Union Congressional Committee distributed some six million documents for the election of 1864, nearly three for every vote Lincoln garnered.

Slavery

A bright spot in the history of the Civil War Congress is its record on slavery. Though the legislative branch has long labored under the shadow of the reputation of the Great Emancipator, the record of Congress on slavery always stood as a sort of threat to that reputation. Historians in the past emphasized the degree to which Congress anticipated, pushed, and generally equaled the administration's antislavery measures before the announcement of Lincoln's preliminary Emancipation Proclamation on September 22, 1862. Though the measures showed a will, they did not in fact show the way to practical freedom for most of the slaves emancipated during the war. Freedom came from the executive branch and its armies.

The Constitution, it must be said, greatly complicated the problem of slavery for Congress (as well as the president), and in the end it required a controversial reading of the president's war powers to find the power that was used to emancipate. The Constitution protected slavery without mentioning the word itself, and that widely acknowledged protection limited Congress's ability to eliminate the institution.

Congress passed a Confiscation Act in the special session, on August 6, 1861, depriving masters of their ownership of the slaves used by the Confederate military. On April 16, 1862, Congress abolished slavery in the District of Columbia, which cheered antislavery activists, who interpreted it as a foreshadowing of similar policies. Congress had already forbidden the army (on March 13, 1862) to enforce the Fugitive Slave Act. After much debate, and only shortly after McClellan's defeat in the Seven Days' Battles around Richmond, Congress passed another Confiscation Act (July 17, 1862). Its provisions appeared sweeping. It declared free the slaves of persons who supported the rebellion, but all agree that the legislation had little practical effect because it was not clear where and how to prove such support.

Beginning in 1864, Republicans introduced proposals to amend the Constitution to eliminate slavery forever from the entire country, not merely the parts of the country that came under the Emancipation Proclamation of January 1, 1863, and not merely by the somewhat uncertain authority of a proclamation justified only by the war powers of the commander in chief. They failed to get the two-thirds majority needed for passage in the House of Representatives — 78–62 (February 15, 1864) and 93–65 (June 15, 1864). A Senate vote on April 8, 1864, had easily cleared the measure, 38–6.

Given the rigid partisanship of the nineteenth-century party system, the Republicans were not likely to sway the requisite number of Democrats in the House, certainly not before the 1864 elections. Even the smashing election victory of the Republicans, committed though they were to an antislavery amendment in their 1864 presidential platform, could not conquer the absurd calendar of the nineteenth-century Congress, as the historian Michael Vorenberg reminds us. In fact, it was remarkable that the votes were picked up even in the lame-duck session of Congress that followed the election of 1864.

The new Congress would not meet until December 1865, more than a year after the election, and slaves would languish in bondage an extra year unless the lame-duck session, which met from December 1864 until the presidential inauguration in March 1865, reconsidered the amendment.

Despite the Democratic party's exploitation of the race issue in the recent canvass, a handful of Democrats, some of them encouraged, apparently, by patronage favors from the administration, changed their votes or abstained, and the measure moved on to the states for ratification, 119–56 (January 31, 1865).

Nevertheless, President Lincoln and Congress's Radical Republicans from 1864 until the president's assassination on April 14, 1865, were locked in conflict over the reconstruction of the Confederate states, and especially over the role African Americans would take in the reconstructed societies. The dispute focused on occupied Louisiana but swirled around any occupied Confederate territory. A congressional bill guided through the House by Henry Winter Davis of Maryland and through the Senate by Wade, called the Wade-Davis Bill, required reconstruction to be delayed until half a state's prewar voting population took a loyalty oath to the United States. Then only those who could swear never to have supported the Confederacy would elect a convention to write a new state constitution. That constitution must abolish slavery in the state and repudiate the Confederate debt. Lincoln, who did not think Congress could abolish slavery, who did not want to be committed to only one way of reconstructing the former Confederate states, and who was willing to see as few as 10 percent of the prewar voters form a new government, pocket-vetoed the bill on July 4, 1864. His veto message called the congressional power over slavery into question, and the scorching manifesto issued by Wade and Davis exploited the issue of executive usurpation in so important a task as reconstructing the Union, but in truth the conflict had more to do with visions of the future Union than of the powers of the different branches of government.

The election of 1864 and the need to defeat the Democrats brought a temporary and fragile party unity and cooperation between the administration and the party in Congress. But even with the advance of the Thirteenth Amendment to the states for ratification early in 1865, the dispute over Reconstruction — between Radical Republicans and moderates in Congress and between Radicals and the president — continued, and the case of Louisiana and all the other Confederate states remained completely unresolved at the end of the war.

The Other Congress

Between 1861 and 1865 two "American" congresses operated, one in Washington and the other in Richmond, Virginia (after a brief period when the Confederate capital was Montgomery, Alabama). The question naturally arises, which of them performed better? In general, historians have given the Confederate Congress lower marks.

As in the North, two congresses met during the presidential administration, but since the Confederates had only a provisional congress until the elections in November 1861 for a permanent one, the second (last) congress's role ended abruptly at the end of the war. The elections held in 1863 chose the members of the second Confederate Congress, and they did not convene for the first time until May 1864.

Although political parties never formed in the Confederacy and elections were not contested on party lines, historians generally agree that the second Confederate Congress was not as supportive of President Jefferson Davis and harbored a greater sentiment for peace than the first. The second congress, for example, refused to renew the president's authority to suspend the privilege of the writ of habeas corpus, despite the granting of that authority in February 1862 by the previous congress (its authority expired early in 1863 but was renewed for six months early in 1864) and despite the obviously dire condition of the Confederacy in the late summer of 1864. Perhaps, if the date of consideration had fallen a bit later, after the Union's capture of Atlanta in September, even the recalcitrant second regular congress would have offered the president the authority over civil liberties he sought. As it was, Frank Owsley, the first of the great modern analytical historians of the Confederacy, could write in 1925, "[I]t was no mere coincidence that . . . after August 1, 1864, when the last act suspending the writ had expired, the fortunes of the South never rose again."

There were no parties or even identifiable factions in the congress —

no administration party and no opposition — but historians agree that the congressmen most to be relied on to support the administration's vigorous war measures were those with the fewest constituents. The Confederate Congress, unlike its Union counterpart, had numerous seats occupied by men who represented territory the Confederacy only claimed but never really held, Kentucky and Missouri. As time went on and the Confederacy's fortunes sank and borders shrunk, the men who represented what had once been a part of the Confederacy but was now occupied by Union troops grew more numerous in the congress as well. The members representing these phantom constituencies, because they needed above all else to gain territory by war and because they had few voting constituents who would be taxed, regulated, and even personally sacrificed to make war, were the administration's steadiest reliance for the mobilization, taxation, and authorization of the curtailment of civil liberties.

The printed record of the Confederate Congress does not match that of the North. There is no Confederate version of the *Congressional Globe,* and historians must rely on a *Journal* published in the twentieth century (recording votes and motions) and a reconstruction of the debates based on reports in the Richmond newspapers and compiled over thirty years of the twentieth century in the *Southern Historical Society Papers.* Moreover, the Confederate Congress frequently voted itself into secret session, leaving constituents as well as historians in the dark about what really shaped legislation.

Congress did not prove to be the locus of the leadership of the opposition to President Davis; that came mainly from state governors, most notably Joseph Brown of Georgia and Zebulon Vance of North Carolina, and from Davis's own vice president, the difficult and inflexible ideologue Alexander H. Stephens, also of Georgia. The congress, for its part, passed the legislation one might expect from the central government of a nineteenth-century republic engaged in war, and the measures were not markedly dissimilar from those passed in the North for the war effort. The most striking similarity, of course, and a measure of great unpopularity in both sections of the country, was military conscription, which was first instituted in the Confederacy in April 1862, only months before the Republicans in the North found themselves forced to rely on it.

Ultimately, the same constitutional determinism seems to have operated on the Confederate Congress as on the Union Congress. Both legislatures labored in unheroic obscurity while the president, as commander in chief for a securely long term, conducted the serious business of a country engaged in war for the life or death of a nation.

— MARK E. NEELY JR.

BIBLIOGRAPHICAL NOTES

For the "Shadrach" anecdote, see Isaac N. Phillips, *Abraham Lincoln by Some Men Who Knew Him* (Bloomington, Ill., 1910). On the configurative role of the Constitution, see Arthur Bestor, "The American Civil War as a Constitutional Crisis," *American Historical Review* 69 (1964), 327–52. David M. Potter, *The Impending Crisis, 1848–1861* (New York, 1976), provides essential background. For the actions of the early Lincoln administration, see James G. Randall, *Lincoln the President: Volume I: Springfield to Bull Run* (New York, 1945). Indispensable histories of the war, complete with descriptions in context of congressional legislation, on which I relied heavily, are James M. McPherson, *Battle Cry of Freedom: The Civil War Era* (New York, 1988); J. G. Randall and David Donald, *The Civil War and Reconstruction*, 2nd ed. (Boston, 1961); and Phillip S. Paludan, *"A People's Contest": The Union and Civil War, 1861–1865* (New York, 1988). More specialized studies of Congress are Heather Cox Richardson, *The Greatest Nation of the Earth: Republican Economic Policies during the Civil War* (Cambridge, Mass., 1997); Leonard P. Curry, *Blueprint for Modern America: Nonmilitary Legislation of the First Civil War Congress* (Nashville, Tenn., 1968); Herman Belz, *Reconstructing the Union: Theory and Policy during the Civil War* (Ithaca, N.Y., 1969); Allen G. Bogue, *The Earnest Men: Republicans of the Civil War Senate* (Ithaca, N.Y., 1981); Bruce Tap, *Over Lincoln's Shoulder: The Committee on the Conduct of the War* (Lawrence, Kans., 1998); and Michael Vorenberg, *Final Freedom: The Civil War, the Abolition of Slavery, and the Thirteenth Amendment* (Cambridge, U.K., 2001). On the Democratic party, see Joel Silbey, *A Respectable Minority: The Democratic Party in the Civil War Era, 1860–1868* (New York, 1977).

Essential for the "other" congress are Thomas B. Alexander and Richard E. Beringer, *The Anatomy of the Confederate Congress: A Study of the Influences of Member Characteristics on Legislative Voting Behavior, 1861–1865* (Nashville, Tenn., 1972), and Wilfred Buck Yearns, *The Confederate Congress* (Athens, Ga., 1960), on both of which I also relied heavily. See also Frank L. Owsley, *State Rights in the Confederacy* (Chicago, 1925).

To see the big picture, read Michael Holt, "An Elusive Synthesis," in James M. McPherson and William J. Cooper, eds., *Writing the Civil War: The Quest to Understand* (Columbia, S.C., 1998).

William Henry Seward

May 16, 1801–October 10, 1872

William Henry Seward

William Henry Seward will be perpetually overshadowed by Abraham Lincoln and, despite his other significant political achievements, will too often be remembered solely for engineering the purchase of Alaska. Even the high school in Seward's small hometown is named after someone else: his father, Judge Samuel S. Seward, a prosperous farmer and land speculator who helped develop the town's school system. The son deserves better. He made substantial contributions and harrowing personal sacrifices as a senator and secretary of state during some of the nation's most turbulent years.

Born in the Hudson Valley farm town of Florida, New York, Seward distinguished himself early as a quick student with an independent streak. He graduated from Union College in 1820, studied law with attorneys in New York City and Goshen, New York, and moved upstate to Auburn in 1823 to practice law. The following year he married the daughter of his prominent law partner. Together they had five children, but Seward's wife, whose devout faith influenced his perspective on slavery, did not support his political aspirations, and their union may have grown perfunctory.

Leaving the national Republican party in 1829 to join the growing Antimasonic movement in upstate New York, Seward became friends with Thurlow Weed, a newspaper publisher and behind-the-scenes political adviser, who helped him gain his first elected office. As a state senator, he joined the Whigs and was elected, after his second campaign, as governor of New York. He served two terms, promoting internal improvements and reforms of the state's education and prison systems. With an eye toward national politics, Seward pushed several measures against slavery and discrimination, including jury trials for fugitive slaves and the repeal of repressive voter eligibility laws. Elected to the Senate in 1849, he served for twelve years, quickly establishing himself as a forceful politician in the slavery debates while Weed engineered his reelection by the state legislature.

Despite his provocative speeches against slavery, Seward held out hope for a voluntary and peaceful emancipation, which would include compensation for slaveowners. He joined the Republican party, made up of former Whigs and Democrats, and remained in the public eye as the premier antislavery politician. Some of his colleagues, however, considered him an unprincipled opportunist whose only real goal was the presidency. This perspective may have overlooked one of Seward's two personas. As described by historians, he was both an outspoken champion of righteous causes and an ambitious but pragmatic dealmaker.

Because of his antislavery rhetoric and his stance in favor of immigrants, Seward lost the Republican presidential nomination to Lincoln in 1860, but he became Lincoln's supporter, adviser, and secretary of state. Early in Lincoln's first term, he struggled in vain to find political compromises that would reunite the country as Southern states seceded. After the war began, however, Seward turned to diplomatic chores, preventing European recognition of the Confederacy and securing the right to search British vessels on the high seas. At home, Seward supported Lincoln's Emancipation Proclamation, although with reservations: he feared that the proclamation would be regarded as a confession of Union weakness if issued before the Union had a significant battlefield victory. When the war ended, Seward favored leniency and the rapid readmission of the Southern states, which put him at odds with many of his Republican colleagues in Congress.

Badly injured in a carriage accident in early April 1865, Seward was bedridden on the night of Lincoln's assassination when Lewis Powell, an accomplice of John Wilkes Booth's, broke into his home and attacked him and his son, Frederick, with a knife. The elder Seward was gravely injured but recovered to serve in Andrew Johnson's administration. He worked unsuccessfully to acquire Hawaii, but he did successfully negotiate with Congress for the funds to purchase the Alaska Territory in 1867. "Seward's Folly," as the deal was called, turned out to be a monumental bargain, with the United States paying Russia approximately 25 cents an acre for a huge territory rich in natural resources. Incidentally, the forty-ninth state does have a high school named after Seward. It's two turns off Seward Highway on the north side of the city of Seward.

Reference

Crofts, D. W. 2000, February. "Seward, William Henry." American National Biography Online. Retrieved June 30, 2003, from http://www.anb.org/articles/04/04-00898.html.

Charles Sumner

January 6, 1811–March 11, 1874

Charles Sumner

Charles Sumner, a man of burning intellect, preferred academic pursuits to politics, but he was catapulted into the limelight and the Senate because of his reform views and the popularity of his well-researched orations on education, war, and slavery. He is often remembered as the victim of a violent assault in Congress in 1856, when Representative Preston S. Brooks of South Carolina beat Sumner over the head with a cane until he lay bleeding and unconscious on the floor. Sumner never fully recovered from his injuries, but he returned to the Senate and served until his death, leading a crusade for civil rights even after other legislators had grown weary of the issue.

Sumner was born into a middle-class family in Boston, where he attended Boston Latin School and graduated from Harvard College in 1830 and from Harvard Law School in 1833. Influenced by the antislavery convictions of his father, a lawyer with Unitarian beliefs, Sumner was not as interested in the legal profession. He did not marry until the age of fifty-five, and the union did not survive a year. He preferred intellectual pursuits in a circle of friends that included the poets and writers Henry Wadsworth Longfellow and Ralph Waldo Emerson. He left his legal practice and traveled abroad, studying the systems of government in Europe. When he returned to Boston, he joined other pacifists in opposing the Mexican War and abolitionists fighting against the spread of slavery in the Southwest and discrimination against blacks. Sumner was ahead of his time. In 1849 he argued for civil rights in an unsuccessful court battle for the racial integration of Boston's public schools. Not until a judicial order 125 years later, in 1974, were the city's schools forcibly desegregated.

Dissatisfaction with the 1850 Compromise, especially the provisions of the Fugitive Slave Act, brought about a coalition of the state's Free-Soil and Democratic parties, which together elected Sumner to the Senate in 1852. He was soon known in Washington for his passionate orations against slavery, which did nothing but underline the depth of the nation's sectional differences. The Kansas-Nebraska Act of 1854, which broke the sectional truce, was lambasted by Sumner in one of his most famous orations, "The Crime Against Kansas," in 1856. Heated exchanges between Sumner and

Senator Stephen A. Douglas of Illinois followed, contributing to an unprecedented animosity between legislators. Days later, Brooks attacked Sumner at his desk. For more than three years Sumner's Senate seat remained empty while he recuperated, the Massachusetts legislature choosing not to fill it in protest. Initially lauded for defending the South's position, Brooks died in a Washington hotel room the following year, at thirty-seven, fearing that his violent actions had only undermined his section's interests.

When Sumner returned to the Senate in 1859, now as a Republican, he continued his long diatribes against slavery. When the Civil War erupted, he became one of the first congressional leaders to urge abolition, and he worked tirelessly to convince President Abraham Lincoln to issue the Emancipation Proclamation. Throughout the war, Sumner's legislative efforts were single-mindedly directed toward destroying the institution of slavery. Following the war, he differed with Andrew Johnson, then Ulysses S. Grant, over the handling of Reconstruction. In Sumner's view, the former Confederate states should be treated as conquered territories, and he refused to compromise although his moral stance was considered impractical. Active in the passage of the Civil Rights Act of 1866, which was enacted over the president's veto, Sumner became a ceaseless critic of Johnson's and a leading player in the attempt to impeach the president. He later lost battles with Grant, whose administration caused Sumner to be removed from his coveted Foreign Relations Committee chairmanship. In 1872 Sumner joined the Liberal Republicans, both to continue opposing Grant and to work on civil rights legislation. At the time of his death, he was trying to secure the passage of a far-reaching civil rights bill, which would have prohibited discrimination in schools, transportation, and public accommodations. A watered-down version of this legislation was passed the following year, partly in tribute to the outspoken politician of conscience, but it was soon struck down as unconstitutional by the Supreme Court.

References

Blue, F. J. 2000, February. "Sumner, Charles." *American National Biography Online.* Retrieved June 30, 2003, from http://www.anb.org/articles/04/04-00969.html.

"Sumner, Charles." 1998. *Encyclopedia of World Biography,* 2nd ed. 17 vols. Retrieved June 30, 2003, from http://www.galenet.com/servlet/BioRC.

13

Reconstruction

DURING THE CIVIL WAR and Reconstruction, the U.S. Congress, led by Republicans in both houses, played a major role in providing for the reconstruction of the Union and the emancipation of African Americans. Some critics, both then and more recently, charged that the congressional Republicans went too far, especially in impeaching President Andrew Johnson; others claimed that after the Civil War, Congress, under the control of vindictive and power-hungry radical Republican zealots, was the dominant branch of government, infringed on executive power, and had its way with weak presidents. The real story proves somewhat more complex.

In some sense, Reconstruction began with the debates over compromise proposals during the secession winter of 1860–1861, for many of the propositions advanced would have led to a restructured Union. Once war broke out, however, the Republicans in Congress began to contemplate what a reunited republic would look like — especially without slavery. The initial measures looking to restrict the war to simply a quest for a restored country, epitomized in the Johnson-Crittenden resolutions of July 1861 (which declared that the sole object of the conflict was reunification), soon gave way to a flurry of legislative initiatives looking to confiscate secessionist property (including slaves), abolish slavery in the District of Columbia, and provide for a process of emancipation. While a handful of representatives as well as Tennessee's Senator Andrew Johnson retained their places in Congress, the legislators gave little thought to governing occupied areas or cultivating resurgent loyalty.

The terms of the debate changed in December 1863, when Lincoln outlined a new approach to Reconstruction in his third annual message. He set forth a procedure whereby the citizens of states currently in rebellion could fashion new governments loyal to the Union. Designed in part to sap support from the Confederacy by offering dissatisfied Confederates as well as southern Unionists an alternative to the current Confederate state regimes, Lincoln's plan made readmission relatively painless. Once a mere 10 percent of the eligible electorate in 1860 took an oath of future allegiance to the United States, those people could elect delegates to a state constitutional convention that would be charged with abrogating the ordinances of secession, abolishing slavery, and establishing the institutional and constitutional framework for a new loyal regime.

Having ratified the proposed constitution, voters in each reconstructed state would elect state officials and members of the House of Representatives (state legislatures would select U.S. senators); those congressional delegations would present their credentials to Congress. Lincoln sought to implement this policy, commonly called the Ten Percent Plan, through a pair of proclamations, one outlining a process for individuals to seek "pardon and amnesty" (thus blurring two distinct concepts) and setting forth a process to reconstitute civil governments in the South.

The Republicans in Congress were not happy with this proposal. Many of them wanted to play a larger role in reconstructing southern society and politics along more egalitarian lines and with sufficient safeguards in place against a resurgence of disloyalty. Massachusetts Senator Charles Sumner advanced the notion that in seceding, the states in insurrection had forfeited their status as states and thus could be governed as territories by Congress; Pennsylvania's Representative Thaddeus Stevens argued that the former Confederate states ought to be classified as conquered provinces, giving the federal government (through Congress) a freer hand in dictating terms of reconstruction and readmission.

Neither Sumner nor Stevens took the lead in framing a congressional alternative to the president's plan; that job was left to Ohio's Senator Benjamin F. Wade and Maryland's Representative Henry Winter Davis. They collaborated on a bill that would require half of the electorate in each Confederate state to pledge future loyalty to the United States; however, only those voters who could pledge past as well as future loyalty by taking a so-called ironclad oath could participate in the selection of delegates who also met that stringent qualification. Although the bill's sponsors decided to drop enfranchising blacks as one of the measure's objectives, it did provide for explicit guarantees of equality before the law for the freedmen and women, including the outright abolition of slavery.

Passed just before Congress adjourned for the summer in July 1864, the Wade-Davis Bill offered a stiff alternative to Lincoln's initiative. The president chose to pocket-veto it, claiming that such sweeping emancipation could not be achieved through federal legislation. Wade and Davis crafted a response that blasted the president for intruding in areas they believed were reserved to Congress. While the resulting Wade-Davis Manifesto prefigured later efforts to render debates over Reconstruction policy into a contest between the executive and legislative branches of the government, it faded away during the fall presidential contest as the Republicans realized that Lincoln's reelection was essential to achieving victory and the Republican visions of a reconstructed union.

During the winter of 1864–1865, the president and congressional Republicans failed to reach a compromise that would satisfy both parties, leaving regimes erected in accordance with Lincoln's program awaiting admittance to Congress. However, both the president and Congress cooperated in passing a constitutional amendment abolishing slavery and in establishing the Freedmen's Bureau, which hoped to assist African Americans make the transition from slavery to freedom and hinted at the possible redistribution of confiscated lands to the former slaves. As the war ended, Lincoln contemplated revising his approach to comport with the challenges presented by peace, only to be assassinated before he could outline his plans. Aside from a desire to enfranchise a limited number of southern blacks, Lincoln left little indication what he wanted to do.

At first many Republicans welcomed the arrival of Andrew Johnson as president, convinced that they would find it easier to work with someone who made clear his hatred of treason and his willingness to punish traitors. However, Johnson had no intention of calling on Congress for assistance as he formulated a postwar policy that looked remarkably like Lincoln's wartime efforts, aside from a requirement that those white Southerners who owned $20,000 in taxable property were among the individuals who had to seek special pardons. Johnson rejected the opportunity offered by the Freedmen's Bureau to confiscate and redistribute planter lands, and he set aside black hopes for participation in reestablishing civil governments. What emerged instead was a series of state governments that barely met the president's requirements to nullify secession, abolish slavery, and repudiate the Confederate war debt; new state legislatures passed so-called Black Codes, which established second-class citizenship for blacks, including differentiating punishments for crimes by the race of the convicted. The congressional delegations selected by the voters and legislatures contained an alarmingly large number of former Confederates, leading northern observers to wonder whether the war had been fought in vain.

Meeting in December 1865 as the Thirty-ninth Congress, the Republicans first placed Johnson's policy on hold by refusing to seat the controversial delegations; they then sought a moderate alternative, providing for some safeguards for African Americans, that they hoped would meet with presidential approval. Initially, this took the form of two measures framed in large part by Illinois senator Lyman Trumbull: a bill that extended the life of the Freedmen's Bureau and improved the chances for at least the limited confiscation and redistribution of land and a measure, the Civil Rights Bill, that established equality before the law with the promise of federal intervention should state courts fail to act. Johnson first vetoed the Freedmen's Bureau bill, then delivered a speech lambasting prominent radical Republicans as traitors; he followed with a veto of Trumbull's civil rights measure, although the senator thought he had secured the president's acquiescence. The Republicans in Congress barely failed to override the first veto; however, they united to override the second one, highlighting the break between the president and the majority party.

During the winter and spring the congressional Republicans, through a Joint Committee on Reconstruction, investigated conditions in the South and framed yet another constitutional amendment that would establish civil rights, remedy the challenge posed by the possible augmentation of southern political strength through emancipation (by reducing a state's representation in the House and thus its electoral votes should it deny the vote to any classes of adult male citizens), setting forth restrictions on federal officeholding, and repudiating the Confederate war debt. Much to their enjoyment, Tennessee, controlled by the president's foes, immediately ratified the amendment. The Republicans also passed a second Freedmen's Bureau bill, more limited in scope, that survived an executive veto.

The 1866 midterm elections tested which of these rival concepts of Reconstruction would prevail in the North. Johnson undertook a speaking tour in an effort to secure the election of his supporters, who had coalesced under the label of the National Union movement; however, the "Swing Around the Circle," as it was dubbed, proved a disaster, as Johnson exchanged insults with the crowd and went so far as to compare himself to Jesus Christ. The Republicans, meanwhile, pointed to the outbreak of racial violence, especially in Memphis in May and New Orleans in July, as evidence of white southern recalcitrance and the need for sterner measures toward the South. They managed to secure vetoproof majorities in both houses, much to Johnson's disgust.

With the Republicans now firmly in charge, its leaders tried to fashion a new Reconstruction policy that would undo Johnson's handiwork. The need for action became apparent when rumors circulated that the president was thinking of recognizing a Congress composed of splinter groups and supporters, going so far as to inquire of General in Chief Ulysses S. Grant which Congress the army would sustain. Fantastic as such stories were, the president's actions proved threat enough: the ten remaining legislatures in the former Confederate states followed his advice in rejecting the Fourteenth Amendment; and Johnson used the pretext of the Supreme Court's opinion in *ex parte Milligan* (1866), which ruled that military commissions were unconstitutional where civil courts were open, to strike at the use of those commissions in the South to protect African Americans and their white allies from unjust civil proceedings. Some Republicans had led white Southerners to believe that the ratification of the Fourteenth Amendment might prevent the taking of more drastic steps; however, Tennessee remained the lone complier. So it was back to the beginning for the legislators. Not only did they have to devise a method of establishing new state governments that would satisfy their concerns about loyalty and equality, but they also wanted to shield officeholders and the general in chief from executive obstruction and removal.

What emerged after several months of deliberation was a process that seemed as much designed to prevent executive interference as it was to establish the foundation for lasting loyal governments grounded in biracial political participation. Casting aside suggestions that it was time to manage the South for an indefinite time under federal supervision, the Republicans instead provided for the registration of both black and white adult male voters, to select delegates to new constitutional conventions. To supervise this process and to protect against fraud, violence, or the participation of disqualified white voters, the measure provided for military supervision of the process: the ten remaining former Confederate states would be divided into five military districts, each headed by a major general, who was charged with carrying out Congress's mandates. The process guaranteed black political participation, paving the way for black suffrage and officeholding; the state governments that emerged would be required to ratify the Fourteenth Amendment in order to secure representation in Congress. This done, federal jurisdiction would end. Predictably, Johnson vetoed the measure, called the Reconstruction Act (and sometimes, a bit misleadingly, the Military Reconstruction Act); just as predictably, Congress overrode the veto on March 2, 1867.

The Republicans also framed two additional pieces of legislation to facilitate Reconstruction. To protect officeholders, they crafted the Tenure of Office Act, which required that the Senate concur in the removal of an officeholder appointed with its advice and consent. The details of the act raised questions about whether cabinet officers who had been part of the Lincoln administration were protected (since Johnson had never appointed them): the uncertainty became acute in the case of Secretary of War Edwin M. Stanton, a staunch supporter of congressional initiatives. At the same time, the Republicans, aware that Johnson had tried to displace or circumvent Grant, attached a rider to an army appropriations bill that allowed Grant to establish his headquarters wherever he wanted and required that all orders issued by the president had to go through Grant's office. Grumbling, Johnson accepted these restrictions begrudgingly; his veto of the Tenure of Office Act failed to survive a Republican override.

The Reconstruction Act reflected the Republicans' fundamental ambivalence about expanding federal power. While it set forth a federally supervised process of reestablishing civil governments and mandated black participation in that process, in the end Congress left white and black Southerners to shape their own futures under new civil governments. Gone were notions of prolonged federal occupation or mandated political or economic changes. Moreover, the initial act proved flawed in several respects, leaving loopholes that Johnson and conservative white Southerners were prepared to exploit to the utmost. It was the product of a compromise between moderate and radical Republicans, reflecting the fact that if the two wings of the party did not find common ground, the president and the Democratic minority would play each off against the other.

The Republicans left the choice of which generals would head the military districts to the president; the legislation placed the army at the beck and call of two federal masters who were at odds, with the president holding the trump card of removal. Taking advantage of provisions that required a majority of eligible voters to register to initiate the process, many white Southerners boycotted registration. In two subsequent acts, both passed over vetoes, the Republicans remedied some of these shortcomings, thwarting the obstruction of the registration and election process and insulating district commanders and their subordinates from executive branch efforts at obstruction through the narrow construction of congressional initiatives.

The Republicans ignored Grant's warning that Congress should shield military commanders from executive removal. No sooner had Congress adjourned for the summer at the end of July than the president swung into action, first requesting Stanton's resignation and then suspending him under the term of the Tenure of Office Act; he then took aim at three district commanders, Philip H. Sheridan, John Pope, and Daniel Sickles, who had pleased the Republicans in their implementation of congressional mandates. Grant proved unable to protect his subordinates, although he limited the damage caused by Stanton's suspension by agreeing to take over the War Department on an ad interim basis until Congress reconvened in December.

That fall, in several crucial state elections, the Republicans suffered setbacks when the voters rejected proposals to allow blacks to vote in their home states. These setbacks ate into the Republican Senate majority; among the casualties was Ohio's Benjamin Wade, the president pro tem of the Senate and next in line for the White House, who had been considering a presidential bid. The lesson — that the Republicans were more likely to secure majorities if they reminded voters of wartime alignments and not racial justice — was not lost on them. The voters' rejection of radicalism also meant that the Republicans would turn to Grant to head their ticket in 1868. In January, with the Senate prepared to vote on whether to concur with the president's removal of Stanton, the chief executive failed to secure Grant's cooperation in challenging the Tenure of Office Act, whereupon he turned on the general, alleging a breach of faith. The two engaged in a heated exchange of letters that served largely to assuage any Republican concerns about Grant's commitment to the party. Thwarted in several efforts to seek a replacement for Stanton or to challenge Grant, Johnson finally removed the secretary outright in February. The House of Representatives immediately responded by impeaching him.

It was not the first time the House Republicans had contemplated impeachment. A series of hearings in 1866 and 1867 had probed all sorts of charges, including fantastic claims implicating Johnson in Lincoln's assassination. Despite the enthusiasm of some Republicans to engage in such futile fishing expeditions, a majority of the Republican congressmen rejected such notions, and the judiciary committee failed to frame a single impeachment charge. However, Johnson's outright defiance overcame such reservations; moreover, the Republicans would no longer brook interference with their policy. They had just headed off a possible court challenge to the constitutionality of their program by rescinding the Supreme Court's ability to hear appeals under the Habeas Corpus Act of 1863.

From the start, the effort to convict Johnson proved problematic. Instead of basing a case on the president's obstruction of justice, the House Republicans based articles of impeachment primarily on the president's supposed violation of the Tenure of Office Act, as well as other alleged transgressions (including a rather broad indictment that the president had attacked Congress — not an impeachable offense based on a statutory basis). Whether Stanton was indeed covered by the Tenure of Office Act remained an open question, fostering enough doubt in the minds of several Republican senators who were already questioning the wisdom of replacing Johnson with the lame-duck Wade, whose views on economic policy as well as Reconstruction alarmed the Republican moderates. The president helped his case by maintaining an uncharacteristically low profile and giving assurances that he would temper his opposition to congressional Reconstruction. Just enough Republicans defected to secure Johnson's acquittal by a single vote on May 16, 1868; when another vote failed ten days later, impeachment came to an inglorious end.

The failure of impeachment overshadowed other Republican successes. By the middle of 1868, seven former Confederate states had joined Tennessee in regaining their representation in Congress; the Fourteenth Amendment was ratified. In the fall presidential contest, Grant and his running mate, Speaker of the House Schuyler Colfax, triumphed; the party owed its popular majority to the ballots cast by African Americans, many of whom were participating in their first national election. Aware that black suffrage in the South remained vulnerable to state politics and that efforts to secure the ballot for blacks in the North had proven politically costly, the congressional Republicans decided to frame another constitutional amendment, this time prohibiting race, color, or previous condition of servitude as a barrier to voting.

The measure was politically shrewd — the Republicans knew that what they could not achieve at the polls they could secure through ratification by Republican state legislatures — but it was also limited, because it did not preclude obstructionist whites from devising other means of restricting suffrage that would unduly disenfranchise blacks. The advocates of women's suffrage complained that, as in the case of the Fourteenth Amendment, Congress did not go far enough, for it could have removed gender as well as a barrier to voting. Whether such an amendment could have been ratified at the time was debatable; as Frederick Douglass put it, it was "the Negro's hour come round at last," and perhaps it was prudent not to jeopardize that achievement, which was radical enough at the moment.

At the time of Grant's election in 1868, all but three of the former Confederate states had completed the process outlined by Congress. The new president, in line with his declaration "Let us have peace," facilitated the restoration of civil government by allowing for the separate submission of state constitutional clauses that would have disqualified significant numbers of former Confederates from voting or holding office. Although several congressional Republicans, led by Charles Sumner, managed to tack on a requirement that Virginia, Texas, and Mississippi ratify the Fifteenth Amendment, Congress seated the delegations from all three states in 1870. Georgia proved somewhat more of a challenge. After the elections in April 1868 resulted in the installing of a Republican governor and state legislature, a combination of violence, intimidation, and fraud caused the Republicans in Congress to decide to remand the state to military supervision in an effort to restore order. However, both the president and Congress failed to favor more extreme measures to maintain the state's Republican regime, so that when Congress seated Georgia's congressional delegation in 1871, bringing to a close the process outlined in 1867 and 1868, its Republicans knew that they would not be in control for long.

The ratification of the Fifteenth Amendment and the restoration of civil state governments throughout the South appeared to bring Reconstruction to a conclusion. Many Republicans felt they had done all they could for African Americans; some party leaders hoped their own organization would follow the "New Departure" proposed by the Democrats, who wanted to put the issues of war and Reconstruction behind them. But the escalation of violence against black voters and their white allies led to calls for legislation to stop such political terrorism as practiced by white supremacist groups such as the Ku Klux Klan. Beginning in May 1870, Congress passed a series of laws designed to extend federal protection to targeted groups. The first Enforcement Act provided for the federal supervision of elections and the prosecution of individuals who attempted to interfere with political activity on the basis of race; the Ku Klux Act (April 1871) authorized the president to suspend the writ of habeas corpus and declare martial law to quell such uprisings. Grant invoked the latter measure only once, in the fall of 1871 in upstate South Carolina; his authority to act expired in 1872. Many Republicans felt uneasy about such legislation, and not a few commented that all that could be done for the South and African Americans had been done.

At first President Grant hoped to do more. Reasoning that black Southerners might force white Southerners to respect their rights by threatening to take their labor elsewhere, the president seized on a recurring inquiry about the possibility of annexing the Dominican Republic as a way to give blacks the leverage they needed by providing a place to which they might emigrate. Sumner, already unhappy with the administration's unwillingness to pay him the deference he thought he was due and justifiably alarmed at some of the circumstances behind the negotiation of a proposed treaty, joined Missouri's Senator Carl Schurz and scattered other Republicans as well as the Democratic minority to thwart ratification. Believing that he had been betrayed, Grant battled the Massachusetts senator, mustering a coterie of supporters in the Senate held together as much by patronage as by principle. If it was a blunt weapon Grant forged, he nevertheless wielded it effectively in securing Sumner's removal as chair of the Foreign Relations Committee; however, annexation failed, and the fight fueled the dissident Republicans' opposition to the incumbent and his bid for reelection.

This battle highlighted the continuing presence of rival institutional imperatives as well as policy differences. Coming to office in 1869, Grant challenged the Tenure of Office Act by refusing to name new appointees; eventually he secured a modification of the legislation that removed provisions for restoring removed officeholders. Many senators at first cared little for executive initiative; the new president also bruised some egos in overlooking certain aspiring candidates for cabinet service. For his part, after initially seeking to govern on his own, Grant cobbled together a coalition of supporters, based in the Senate and led by New York's Roscoe Conkling, Indiana's Oliver P. Morton, and Wisconsin's Matt Carpenter, who battled the foes of the administration and passed policy initiatives (although several of them looked askance at Grant's support for civil service reform, with its potential for altering the patronage game). Opponents deplored what they saw as executive interference with legislative matters; in truth, however, Grant enjoyed a better working relationship with Congress during his first six years in office than did either of his predecessors, and the alliances he forged helped him secure reelection in 1872 over an alliance of Democrats and dissident members of his own party, the self-styled Liberal Republicans.

Despite such successes, Grant and the Republicans watched as several southern Republican regimes slipped back into Democratic hands. Republicanism never gained a firm foothold in Virginia; during the president's first term, the party faltered in Tennessee, North Carolina, and Georgia and struggled elsewhere. However, in the election of 1872, outside Louisiana there was a marked decline in political violence; the passage that year of a general amnesty act served as a sign that the Republicans retained an interest in setting aside the hard feelings engendered by the war. The respite proved temporary. In 1873 an economic crisis precipitated by a panic led to several years of a depressed economy. Struggling northern workers were far more interested in their own welfare than in the fate of southern freedmen; the collapse of investment banks crippled any efforts to attract white Southerners to Republican ranks under the banner of economic development, while many southern whites complained that they no longer could shoulder the tax burden required by Republican regimes to finance initiatives in public education that served both races. The Grant administration struggled to provide economic relief, but the president's decision to veto legislation providing for a moderate inflation of the currency angered impoverished debtors in the South and West. Critics of the administration charged that the president was interested in seeking a third term: the Democrats blamed it for the economic downturn; the southern Republicans scrambled to survive in states where they remained in power, attempting to fend off a resurgence in white supremacist terrorism.

The events in Louisiana provided vivid examples of the terrorism against Republican state governments. The contests for the governorship and the state legislature in 1872 resulted in no clear winner, and when Congress failed to resolve the situation, Grant recognized the Republican claimants to office. At that, the Democrats resorted to violence to intimidate and eliminate their opponents. On April 13, 1873, after several days of skirmishing, whites attacked blacks who had sought protection in a courthouse in Colfax, Louisiana. Setting fire to the building, the terrorists then murdered any blacks who attempted to escape; in the end, some one hundred African Americans were killed.

All efforts to prosecute the murderers went awry. In *U.S. v. Cruikshank* (1874), Justice Joseph P. Bradley, acting in his capacity as circuit judge, ruled that critical portions of the Enforcement Acts were unconstitutional; two years later, the Supreme Court concurred. Stripped of the ability to find a legal basis for prosecuting white terrorisms, the Justice Department backed away from protecting black voting rights; meanwhile, conservative white Louisianans kept up their offensive, ambushing and killing several Republican officeholders at Coushatta and twice attempting to overthrow the state government in New Orleans. Outrageous as it might be, more voters were tired of Reconstruction and held the party in power responsible for the economic downturn; in the 1874 midterm elections, the Democrats regained control of the House of Representatives, effectively ending any efforts to pass new legislation to protect the freedmen and their allies.

Grant sought congressional support in his efforts to protect several Republican regimes, but little was forthcoming, leaving him to manage as best he could. Although he quelled protests against the vigorous suppression of Democratic terrorism in Louisiana, he discovered that Congress was not interested in reversing a Democrat triumph in the confusing world of Arkansas politics, and he let Alabama and Texas return to the Democratic column without much protest. By the spring of 1875, the Republicans remained in power, sometimes by the slimmest of margins, in Mississippi, Louisiana, South Carolina, and Florida. A final effort to provide Grant with the ability to adopt tough measures fell through in the dying days of the lame-duck session in the winter of 1875; in such an environment the passage of a new civil rights act, outlawing segregation in public places (but not in schools) faced a difficult future. That summer and fall, as Mississippi's Democrats rallied behind the cry to prevail "peaceably if we can, forcibly if we must," Grant recognized the growing public apathy and politically counterproductive aspect of dispatching federal troops in the absence of widespread violence. The resulting Democratic triumph suggested that the end of Reconstruction was only a matter of time.

The Democratic House of Representatives came to power in December 1875, determined to derail the Republicans' efforts to retain the White House in 1876. A series of hearings and investigations revealed corrupt and questionable activities by members of the Grant administration, forcing the resignation of one cabinet member and casting a dark shadow on the reputation of several others. This strategy complimented the party's decision to nominate New York's Governor Samuel J. Tilden for president on a platform calling for reform, retrenchment, and an end to Reconstruction. The Republicans countered by selecting Ohio's Governor Rutherford B. Hayes, who was more than acceptable to their reform wing, leaving Reconstruction as the major issue distinguishing the parties. In the fall contest, neither candidate secured a clear majority of electoral votes, although Tilden probably won a majority of the popular votes cast (Democratic control of several southern states having depressed African American voting). With 184 electoral votes, Tilden was one shy of a majority; Hayes had won 165 votes, with 20 votes (Louisiana, Florida, and South Carolina, plus an elector in Oregon) in dispute.

Congress wrestled with proposals to resolve the crisis. Finally, after some prodding from President Grant, it crafted a 15-member electoral commission, with 5 members from the House (3 Democrats, 2 Republicans), 5 from the Senate (3 Republicans, 2 Democrats), and 5 from the Supreme Court, where, after the Independent David Davis withdrew to accept a Senate seat from Illinois, the count stood at 3 Republicans and 2 Democrats. With the commission members remaining faithful to their parties, the Republicans carried the day in each of the contested cases; the southern Democrats then filibustered in an effort to make sure that the Republican leaders would keep their promise to withdraw federal support from the Republican state regimes in Florida, South Carolina, and Louisiana. A more elaborate set of promises, involving Republican support for economic legislation for the South and the selection of a former Confederate for the Hayes cabinet in exchange for southern Democratic support to organize the next House under Republican leadership, never amounted to much, and its impact on the outcome of the dispute remains unclear.

Once installed as president, Hayes battled the Senate Republicans over appointments for much of his first two years in office; however, these intraparty foes united in the aftermath of the elections of 1878, when the Democrats attempted to restrict the federal enforcement of voting rights protection. Believing that it was another legislative encroachment on executive power, Hayes issued a series of vetoes, all of which were sustained. However, the impact on reviving Republican fortunes in the South was minimal, and by 1880 the Republicans understood what had first become evident in 1876: that the party could prevail in national elections without the support of a single southern state so long as it solidified its northern base.

During Reconstruction, competing concepts of executive and legislative power overlapped with partisan differences: veto overrides and the passage of the Tenure of Office Act exhibited the strength of the congressional Republicans, while all four presidents protected executive prerogatives and in the case of Grant fashioned a working partnership. Contrary to later stereotypes of a radical-dominated Congress steamrolling over constitutional restraints, most Reconstruction initiatives were the product of compromise and political feasibility, sometimes flawed in draftsmanship, that looked to the rapid restoration of civil government and the honoring whenever possible of traditional federal-state boundaries so long as the states did their part to preserve justice under law for all. Nevertheless, the congressional Republicans did bring forth a constitutional revolution through the passage of three amendments and civil rights legislation, setting forth a promise of equality under law that would be realized a century later.

— BROOKS D. SIMPSON

BIBLIOGRAPHICAL NOTES

Herman Belz, *Reconstructing the Union: Theory and Policy during the Civil War* (Ithaca, N.Y., 1969), *A New Birth of Freedom: The Republican Party and Freedmen's Rights, 1861–1866* (Westport, Conn., 1976), and *Emancipation and Equal Rights: Politics and Constitutionalism in the Civil War Era* (New York, 1978); Michael Les Benedict, *A Compromise of Principle: Congressional Republicans and Reconstruction, 1863–1869* (New York, 1974); Benedict, "Preserving the Constitution: The Conservative Basis of Radical Reconstruction," *Journal of American History* 61 (June 1974): 65–90; Allan G. Bogue, *The Earnest Men: Republicans of the Civil War Senate* (Ithaca, N.Y., 1981); William R. Brock, *An American Crisis: Congress and Reconstruction, 1865–1867* (New York, 1963); David Donald, *The Politics of Reconstruction* (Baton Rouge, La., 1965); Eric Foner, *Reconstruction: America's Unfinished Revolution, 1863–1877* (New York, 1988); William Gillette, *Retreat from Reconstruction, 1869–1879* (Baton Rouge, La., 1979); Joseph B. James, *The Framing of the Fourteenth Amendment* (Urbana, Ill., 1956); Eric L. McKitrick, *Andrew Johnson and Reconstruction* (Chicago, 1960); William E. Nelson, *The Fourteenth Amendment: From Political Principle to Judicial Doctrine* (Cambridge, Mass., 1988); Terry L. Seip, *The South Returns to Congress: Men, Economic Measures, and Sectional Interrelationships, 1868–1879* (Baton Rouge, La., 1983); and Brooks Simpson, *The Reconstruction Presidents* (Lawrence, Kans., 1998).

Thaddeus Stevens

April 4, 1792–August 11, 1868

Thaddeus Stevens

Remembered as an ideologue and powermonger who spearheaded the impeachment of President Andrew Johnson and blamed by historians for many of the failures of Reconstruction, Thaddeus Stevens was indeed a domineering man of rigid principles, but he was also an able legislator who steered a course between his radical convictions and his pragmatism.

Stevens was born into a poor family in Danville, Vermont. His father, a cobbler and surveyor, abandoned the family, and Sarah Stevens worked odd jobs to support her children and pay for their education. The young Stevens, feeble and club-footed, was encouraged to pursue his education. His family and the frontier environment helped form his determination for self-improvement and personal austerity. He graduated from Dartmouth College in 1814, giving the commencement speech, and moved to Pennsylvania, where he passed the bar and established himself as an able businessman and community leader. He acquired significant business and land holdings, was elected to the Gettysburg Council five times, and became active in the Antimason party, which, aligned with the Whigs, fought against the political influence of the exclusive fraternal order.

Stevens never married, and his personal life has been the subject of speculation. He adopted two nephews, to whom he was a demanding guardian, and he shared his parental responsibilities with his housekeeper of twenty years, Lydia Hamilton Smith, who was of mixed white and black ancestry. No evidence exists to either confirm or refute the contemporary assumption that the two were romantically involved.

Throughout his life and political career, Stevens promoted personal self-improvement through equal opportunity and education. In 1835, while serving in the Pennsylvania legislature, he was able to turn the tide of a popular antitax movement that would have abolished the state's first public education statute. Roused by Stevens's oration, his fellow legislators instead strengthened the public education provision. However, his domineering personality and strong-arm tactics also led to "the Buckshot War" of 1838, when Stevens had to escape from an angry mob by crawling out a back window of the capitol. Although he was reelected to the legislature twice, his influence had diminished and his financial situation was untenable. Stevens moved to Lancaster to start over and, with a group of antislavery insurgents, took control of the local Whig party in 1848, becoming its candidate for the House of Representatives; there he served as a Whig until 1853.

In his vigorous support of abolition and civil rights, Stevens's legal interpretations, as well as his actions, were radical for the time. He participated in the Pennsylvania constitutional convention but would not sign the document, saying it disenfranchised free black citizens. He argued against the Compromise of 1850 on the issue of slavery, advancing the view that, according to common law, man is not the subject of property. He gave legal and illegal assistance to runaway slaves. And during the Civil War he argued for immediate emancipation. Stevens's commitment to his convictions often alienated his constituents, as well as members of his own party. For his role as a cocounselor for the defendants in the trial following the Christiana Slave Riot of 1852, Stevens was denied nomination to Congress.

Never one to give up, Stevens helped establish the Republican party in Pennsylvania and in 1858 was reelected to the House, where he served until his death ten years later. Respected, and feared, for his parliamentary skills and demeaning wit, Stevens assumed the powerful chairmanship of the Ways and Means Committee. He used his position to advocate civil rights, internal improvements, and increased federal involvement in the nation's economy. Although he did not get along with Abraham Lincoln, whose wartime actions he considered too moderate, he was a forceful ally of the president's, ensuring the speedy passage of military appropriations and conscription laws and even campaigning for Lincoln's reelection in 1864.

After the war, Stevens wanted to treat the Confederate states as conquered territories subject to congressional control and impose stern requirements for their readmission. As a member of the Joint Committee on Reconstruction, however, he deferred to moderate Republicans to ensure the passage of legislation, such as the 1867 Military Reconstruction Act and the Fourteenth Amendment, portions of which he had written. The amendment might have been the culmination of a life's work advocating equality under the law and equal opportunity for self-advancement. But Stevens's antagonistic relationship with the office of the president, by now held by Andrew Johnson, led to his role in the impeachment proceedings against Johnson. The impeachment failed by a single vote, and Stevens spent his final weeks in an unsuccessful attempt to impeach Johnson again.

Reference

Zeitz, J. 2000, February. "Stevens, Thaddeus," *American National Biography Online.* Retrieved June 30, 2003, from http://www.anb.org/articles/04/04-00953.html.

14

The Press Coverage of Congress: Reporting Johnson's Impeachment

THE IMPEACHMENT of the president in 1868 made for dramatic news coverage, but it profoundly shook the relations between the members of Congress and the reporters who covered them. Andrew Johnson's Senate trial produced the Washington press corps' best writing and most anxious moments. Years later, the reporters swore they would rather cover the Gettysburg campaign again than relive the rough-and-tumble years of Reconstruction, despite its abundance of news. During the months of uncertainty over whether Congress would expel Johnson from the White House, the *Baltimore Sun* reporter Francis Richardson recalled: "There was not a moment when men's passions were not hot; not a moment when rumor and rancor were not in the air; not a moment when hearts did not tremble for the Republic." Correspondents could barely find the time to eat or sleep as they struggled to keep up with events and meet their deadlines. During this period, the common bonds that had been forged between the predominantly northern press corps with the predominantly Republican Congress during the Civil War suffered, as the impeachment raised doubts about legislative motives and disillusioned many journalists. The reporters' shifting attitudes influenced public opinion, contributed to President Johnson's narrow acquittal, and helped erode popular support for the congressional reconstruction of the defeated South. Among the most long-lasting consequences of the impeachment was this shattered harmony between Congress and the Washington press corps, which led to more intense scrutiny and exposure of national politics. The reporting of the impeachment trial provides a window of observation on the operations of the Washington press corps at midcentury and its working relationships on Capitol Hill.

Before the Civil War

A regular Washington press corps had evolved during the decades before the Civil War. The first Washington reporters were actually stenographers employed by Washington's newspapers to record speeches in the Senate and House of Representatives. The *National Intelligencer,* Washington's first major newspaper, founded in 1800, printed congressional debates verbatim and sent copies free of postage to newspapers around the country. Exchange editors would then clip relevant portions to print in their own papers. Their monopoly on Washington's news lasted until the 1820s, when different sectional interests in tariff legislation prompted the merchants of Boston and the planters of South Carolina to hire their own reporters to attend sessions of Congress and provide them with relevant news. Since these reporters mailed their dispatches, they became known as correspondents. Since the reporters of the debate were already producing verbatim texts of speeches, the correspondents were hired to produce commentary, giving them license to criticize and even ridicule congressional behavior — which naturally raised the ire of senators and representatives. (In one celebrated account, a correspondent recorded the daily ritual of an Ohio congressman, who ate a lunch of sausage sandwiches while seated by a window in the House chamber: "These he disposes of quite rapidly, wipes his hands with the greasy paper for a napkin, and then throws it out the window. — What little grease is left on his hands he wipes on his almost bald head which saves any outlay for Pomatum.") Although both houses of Congress allowed reporters of debate access to the floor of their chambers, they rejected the correspondents' requests for parity.

Kentucky's Senator Henry Clay, in his efforts to cultivate the press to further his presidential ambitions, finally arranged in 1841 for the Senate to establish the first press gallery for the correspondents. The Senate reserved ten seats in the gallery above the presiding officer's chair for the small number of correspondents, most of whom reported for several newspapers by using different pseudonyms. In 1844 Samuel F. B. Morse publicly tested the telegraph from the Capitol to Baltimore, and Baltimore's newspapers carried the first telegraphic dispatches of votes in Congress. Within a few years, New York's newspapers had pooled their resources to form the first Associated Press (AP), to provide common telegraphic news dispatches. The AP began offering the basic reports of legislative activities, while the correspondents provided analysis. The number of Washington reporters grew steadily with emotional debates over the extension of slavery into the western territories. Correspondents from the North, South, and West timed their arrival in Washington with the opening of each new session of Congress and left as soon as it adjourned. The executive branch did not generate enough news to justify their staying any longer. When Congress adjourned, the *Boston Journal*'s correspondent Benjamin Perley Poore wrote that Washington became as "silent as a theatre when the performances are concluded and the spectators have gone home."

The Civil War Press

After 1860 the southern reporters seceded along with their states. Their seats in the press galleries were quickly taken by a new generation of journalists, who covered the military and political aspects of the Civil War from Washington. The youthful, free-spirited, hard-drinking, battle-scarred, nose-for-news correspondents styled themselves "a Bohemian Brigade." The white male college graduates who made up the pack of correspondents were always eager for a scoop, but they regularly pooled their efforts, covered for absent colleagues, and fought political harassment, which encouraged a sense of fraternity and a collective press ethic.

The first battle of Bull Run took place only thirty miles from the capital, and the largest share of the war was fought in nearby Virginia, Maryland, and Pennsylvania, enabling the correspondents to make Washington their base of operation. There they could take advantage of the telegraph offices and ready supply of military news and gossip. It was an era of overtly partisan newspapers, when they were subsidized by political factions and even owned and operated by politicians to promote themselves and their parties. Mark Twain (briefly a congressional correspondent himself) commented that "the editor of a newspaper cannot be independent, but must work with one hand tied behind him by party and patrons, and be content to utter only half to two thirds of his mind." With most wartime correspondents reporting for Republican newspapers in northern and western states, they forged lasting friendships with the Union army officers, many of whom would play roles in national politics for the remainder of the century. The reporters, military officers, and politicians achieved nearly "universal accord," wrote the *Cincinnati Gazette* reporter Henry Boynton, "so long as active war was waged along the Union front." At this time, the swelling ranks of correspondents opened bureaus on "Newspaper Row," a string of small buildings along Fourteenth Street between the telegraph office and the leading hotels, close to the White House and accessible to the Capitol by a horse-drawn trolley. At night, members of Congress would drop by Newspaper Row to read the news reports and pass along inside information. With the AP supplying the newspapers with the substance of what happened in Congress, the correspondents needed such inside sources to provide a different slant on the news, geared to local interests, which justified their existence.

Because AP dispatches went to papers of all political hues, its reporters had to avoid making partisan judgments. During the war, Lawrence Gobright, the AP's Washington correspondent from 1846 to 1871, won the respect and confidence of President Lincoln and other high officials, who kept him promptly informed of developments both in the government and on the battlefront. In 1862 Gobright was called before the Joint Committee on the Conduct of the War to explain why his dispatches got past the government censors when so many other journalists had their reports suppressed. "My business is merely to communicate facts," Gobright explained. "My instructions do not allow me to make any comment upon the facts which I communicate. My despatches are sent to papers of all manner of politics, and the editors say they are able to make their own comments upon the facts which are sent to them. I therefore confine myself to what I consider legitimate news." Gobright was defining a style that later generations of reporters would call objective: taking no sides on the issues they reported. Rather than celebrate his impartial reporting, however, he apologized for it, saying: "My despatches are merely dry matters of fact and detail."

When the war ended, many of the correspondents remained in Washington to form the nucleus of a permanent press corps. In addition to their bureaus on Newspaper Row, the Capitol served as their center of operation. Both the House and Senate provided gallery seating, desk space, supplies, and telegraph offices for the reporters' exclusive use. By contrast, the White House had no press room in the nineteenth century, forcing reporters to stand outside on the driveway to interview the president's callers. In addition to work space, congressional patronage provided the correspondents with part-time work to supplement their newspaper salaries. Congress hired committee clerks to handle mail and prepare other documents but paid them only for the months that it met in session, about half of the year. Newspapers similarly paid their Washington correspondents only for the months that Congress was in session. Since the newspapers were openly partisan, there seemed nothing unethical about a working reporter's clerking on the side for a senator or representative from his paper's party. Committee clerkships offered reporters access to the House and Senate floors and inside notice of committee business. In return for this congressional largesse, their patrons expected favorable treatment in the correspondents' dispatches. In 1867, for instance, Lorenzo Crounse of the *New York Times* served as clerk for the House Committee on Banking and Currency; the *Philadelphia Inquirer*'s Uriah Hunt Painter for the

House Committee on Post Office and Post Roads; and Benjamin Perley Poore of the *Boston Journal* for the Senate Printing Committee.

The Reconstruction Era

Following Abraham Lincoln's assassination, the Republicans in Congress and their allies in the press anticipated that his successor, Andrew Johnson, would ally himself with their policies on the Reconstruction of the South and protection of the freedmen. The correspondent David Bartlett, a prewar abolitionist, advised his readers in the *New York Independent* that the new president had repeatedly stated his preference for giving freedmen the right to vote. But Johnson ended this honeymoon abruptly when he vetoed the Freedman's Bureau bill in 1866. Believing that the president had "broken the faith, betrayed the trust," Republican moderates shifted into an alliance with the radical wing of their party. Echoing the same sentiments in the press corps, D. F. Drinkwater, the House correspondent for the United Press Association, decried Johnson's "sympathy with treason and traitors against the loyal and for the disloyal." John Russell Young, a correspondent who left Washington to write editorials for the *New York Tribune,* likewise declared the Johnson administration dishonored.

Siding largely with Congress, the Washington correspondents portrayed Johnson as an implacable, intemperate, and inebriated southern sympathizer. Within the press corps, the president retained the loyalty of only a small circle, including some shady characters who took advantage of his isolation to peddle inside information. William W. Warden, who wrote for the *Boston Post* and other papers, served as the president's personal secretary and as a conduit between the White House and Capitol Hill. In 1867 Johnson's Annual Message was leaked to the press before it reached Congress. When a congressman charged that someone from the White House had sold the message to the papers, reporters in the press gallery exchanged "significant winks." The *Washington Evening Star* confirmed that the correspondent for the *Boston Post* had hawked the message among those reporters willing to pay for advance copies. Soon afterward, William Warden drew laughter and applause at a Washington correspondents' dinner when, in mock seriousness, he urged the assembled crowd to "put a stop to unauthorized or surreptitious publications of official documents" to regain public esteem.

But President Johnson also enlisted the more reputable aid of Joseph McCullagh, an AP reporter known for his evenhanded coverage. At that time, interviews published in question-and-answer format were becoming popular in the press, but until then presidents had never allowed direct attribution of their comments by the press. It took a president under the threat of impeachment to seize the interview as a device for carrying his case directly to the people. Johnson summoned McCullagh to the White House. "I don't want you to take my side," he told him. "I can fight these fellows singlehanded; but put me down correctly." Distributed over the wires and widely published, McCullagh's interviews revealed Johnson as a proud and reasonable man who retained his sense of humor through his ordeal, without the violent intemperance that often slipped out when he confronted hecklers on the stump. Pleased with their collaboration, the president summoned McCullagh back repeatedly. "I want to give these fellows hell," he said, gesturing toward the Capitol, "and I think I can do it better through your paper than through a message, because the people read the papers more than they do messages." Johnson drew criticism from those who considered it undignified for a president to be interviewed, but the method proved so popular with readers that his successors in the White House continued the practice. Members of Congress scrambled to be interviewed as well — some being so accommodating that they prepared the questions as well as the answers.

The nation's most influential newspaper in that era was Horace Greeley's *New York Tribune,* whose weekly edition reached homes across the northern and western states. As publisher, Greeley fielded an aggressive staff of reporters who regularly scooped the rest of the press corps in obtaining closed-door congressional testimony. When the paper's editorials endorsed Johnson's impeachment and removal, Greeley argued unsuccessfully that impeachment was the worst way to settle the differences between the president and Congress. He believed that if left alone, the hot-tempered Johnson would hang himself: "All Andy wants is rope enough and time enough, and he will save us the trouble."

In February 1868 the House Republicans, infuriated with Johnson's opposition to their Reconstruction policies, voted overwhelmingly to impeach him, even though he had just a year left to his term. With the South not yet returned to Congress, the Senate Republicans held more than two-thirds of the seats and therefore felt certain they had enough votes to remove the president. The Senate trial opened in March and ran until May, drawing such large crowds that for the first time the Senate had to issue tickets to its gallery. The men recognized by the press gallery needed no tickets, but the women reporters who used the public galleries had to scramble for admission. Emily Edson Briggs, the Washington columnist for the *Philadelphia Press* under the pen name Olivia, appealed for help from the Senate's president pro tempore, Benjamin Wade, an Ohio Republican: "I hope you will remember me as the Lord did his chosen people in the wilderness, but in place of daily bread, a daily ticket will answer every purpose." With Wade's assistance, Briggs got into the galleries almost daily throughout the trial and provided colorful portraits of the members who most fascinated her. (If New York's red-bearded Senator Roscoe Conkling were a planet, she wrote, it would be Mars, "owing to that precious high-colored ingredient which was used so lavishly in his physical construction.") She especially defended her benefactor, Wade, who stood next in line to succeed to the presidency if Johnson were removed.

Initially, most of the correspondents favored Johnson's conviction and removal from office, but as the trial dragged on for months, their mood shifted. Horace White, a former Washington correspondent turned editor of the *Chicago Tribune,* returned to cover the trial personally. His paper had editorially endorsed impeachment, but White also strongly advocated free trade, and Johnson's removal would elevate the protectionist Wade to the White House. On second thought, therefore, White and the *Tribune* changed course on impeachment. George Alfred Townsend, who corresponded for many papers under the pen name GATH, began his coverage under the assumption that Johnson represented the chief barrier to any settlement of the "Southern question." His certitude eroded as he interviewed members of Congress who seemed less excited over Johnson's Reconstruction policies than over his threat to fire their patronage appointees from the government. Petty concerns to protect postmasters, revenue officers, and brothers-in-law disheartened Townsend and reversed his position on impeachment.

"Impeachment drags on heavily," complain the *Boston Journal*'s Poore, a staunch Republican whose faith in the final result diminished rapidly. In private correspondence with his publisher (the chairman of the Massachusetts Republican party), Poore had at first worried that Johnson's acquittal would allow him to trample down what remained of congressional Reconstruction. But what he viewed as unreasonable behavior among congressional radicals caused Poore to curse the "d——d impeachment squabble." The trial similarly dismayed Henry Boynton, whose dispatches turned increasingly critical. A former Union officer and loyal Republican himself, Boynton concluded that the radicals had made as many corrupt deals as Johnson's defenders, "probably more!"

The president's interviewer, Joseph McCullagh, divided the correspondents between those who opposed impeachment and those who expected some appointment in the new regime. Those who supported impeachment seemed more interested in getting "the ins out and the outs in." The most consistent advocate of impeachment was Uriah Painter of the *Inquirer,* who was also a close adviser to Senator Wade. Painter expected to become "a power behind the throne" in a Wade presidency. His partisanship did not bother his editors in Philadelphia, who shared his views on Reconstruction and impeachment, but he also wrote for the *New York Sun,* whose editor, Charles Dana, condemned the "partiality" of his dispatches. "This is *not* a partisan paper," Dana reminded Painter. "What we want is the facts. The comments, and especially ill-natured ones, we wish to add ourselves." Metropolitan newspapers like the *Sun* no longer needed to count so heavily on political parties for revenue, thanks to the profitability of commercial advertising. The postwar movement toward objectivity, of separating editorial content from news columns, was a way of doing business that veteran correspondents like Painter never mastered.

Until the day of the vote, the impeachers felt confident they could remove the president from office. Wagers ran high in the press gallery, with Johnson's opponents betting heavily on conviction and his few supporters — like William Warden — staking everything on acquittal. When seven Republican senators defected from their party and the president won reprieve by a single vote, Warden collected a small fortune.

The constitutional crisis demolished the political career of Henry J. Raymond, publisher of the *New York Times,* who had won election to the House in 1864 and then allied himself too closely with Andrew Johnson. Other prominent editors and publishers, among them Horace Greeley and Joseph Pulitzer, also served in the House, although each quickly discovered that he had less influence over legislation as a freshman representative than as a newspaper editor. In 1880 the *American* magazine published a long list of senators and representatives with previous experience in journalism, concluding that "many a good journalist has been spoiled in making a poor Congressman." Yet the increasing number of reporters, editors, and publishers entering Congress after the Civil War indicated that a background in journalism was an asset for aspiring politicians. Elected officials who wanted to influence what their colleagues and constituents read needed to cultivate those writing it. Well-placed leaks of confidential information, availability, and quotability all made a congressman popular with the press corps.

Congress's failure to convict Johnson discredited impeachment as a congressional tool against the presidency for another century. Had Johnson been removed, Reconstruction would have been more forcefully implemented, but Congress would have been able to exert greater authority over the presidency, using impeachment as a device similar to a vote of no confidence in a parliamentary system. Not until the Watergate scandal in 1974 would Congress seriously consider the prospect of impeaching another president.

During Johnson's impeachment and trial, rumors spread through

Washington that the Russian ambassador was using some of the money Congress had appropriated to purchase Alaska to pay back critical members of Congress and the press who had promoted the sale. At first, the reporters did not take these stories seriously, assuming that the charges against the congressmen were as spurious as those against themselves. The longer the allegations persisted, however, the more they called into question the journalists' own integrity and the more compelled they felt to uncover the facts and report the story. Henry Boynton lamented that the press itself should have suffered such a public relations blow, "just now when the lobby and corrupt Congressmen are joining hands to fight newspapermen who *will* expose them." Shortly afterward, in 1872, when the news of another congressional bribery scandal, involving the distribution of Crédit Mobilier stock to win votes for building the transcontinental railroad, reporters were quicker to assume the worst. The newspaper coverage of the scandal ruined the reputations of prominent senators and representatives, as well as two vice presidents.

The Gilded Age

The intensive press coverage of these scandals chilled the correspondents' once intimate relations with congressional leaders. "Up until that time Newspaper Row was daily and nightly visited by the ablest and most prominent men in public affairs," wrote Henry Boynton. "Suddenly, with the Crédit Mobilier outbreak, and others of its kind which followed it, these pleasant relations began to dissolve under the sharp and deserved criticism of the correspondents." Years of estrangement followed, diminishing the number of congressional visitors to Newspaper Row, and the members of the press and the Congress adopted "a warlike attitude" toward the other. Exacerbating the problem was Congress's failure to keep lobbyists out of the press galleries. During the Civil War, a number of correspondents had speculated in the stock markets and exploited their advance knowledge of the news for their personal profit. After the war, some of these men branched into lobbying, which raised questions about their motives in seeking and publishing government information. Since the congressional leaders seemed unable or unwilling to distinguish between legitimate journalists and those posing as reporters as a cover for lobbying, the correspondents formally proposed that they take charge of the press gallery membership themselves. Conceding that they had done a poor job of management, and not wishing to further alienate the press, the House and Senate between 1879 and 1884 revised their rules to assign the task of press accreditation to a standing committee of correspondents that the reporters themselves elected. (The rules, relatively unchanged over time, are published annually in the *Congressional Directory*, along with the names of all the accredited correspondents.)

The new rules limited press gallery membership to correspondents who derived their primary salary from journalism and who sent telegraphic dispatches to daily newspapers. They prohibited reporters from lobbying or from serving as clerks in executive agencies (but not congressional committees). As intended, these rules rid the press galleries of lobbyists, but also — whether intentionally or not — eliminated the few women and African American reporters who had previously gained admittance to the press gallery. The women reporters could not meet the criterion of reporting for a daily paper by telegraph, since character sketches and social news did not justify the high telegraph tolls and were mailed to their papers instead. Black reporters could not get jobs at white mainstream newspapers, and the black press consisted entirely of weekly papers throughout the nineteenth century.

The women protested their exclusion, pointing out that the men had reserved seats in the galleries and comfortable places to work, whereas the women, whatever their merit as journalists, had to compete for seats in the public galleries and could find no work space at the Capitol. In 1890 Margaret Sullivan Burke became the first woman to qualify for membership under the new rules. She had been making a living as a stringer, doing work "for the gentlemen of the press that they could not do for themselves." Watching how "the boys" on Newspaper Row took care of one another by exchanging news and covering for colleagues who were ill or otherwise indisposed, she realized that she needed similar support. Signing her dispatches M. S. Burke to disguise her gender, she began to get work from distant editors and publishers. She could not hide her identity from the standing committee of correspondents when she applied for a press pass, but they reviewed her dispatches to the *Philadelphia Item* and ruled that her work met their criteria. "Other women who have applied are engaged in social work," commented one of the men on the committee, "for which they need no such advantage at this building." The men in the press gallery treated her collegially, but when she lost her daily paper after a year they immediately dropped her membership.

However inequitable, the press gallery rules marked the origin of giving the Washington press corps professional status, and they remain in place as a vital legacy. Reporters who cover Congress today still elect standing committees of correspondents to run separate press galleries devoted to newspapers, radio and television, periodicals, and photographers. Standing committees continue to judge the qualifications of those applying for press passes and accreditation, thereby defining legitimate journalism as free from lobbying and political patronage. The rules allowed for the evolution of a more independent, respected, and powerful press corps, whose members scrutinize, analyze, and criticize the legislative process. Just as the journalists' first consciousness of objectivity in reporting dates back to the experiences of the wire services during the Civil War, the origins of the modern adversarial relations between the government and the press can be traced to the reporting on Reconstruction and the impeachment of a president.

— DONALD A. RITCHIE

BIBLIOGRAPHICAL NOTES

General histories reflecting aspects of the nineteenth-century Washington press corps include J. Frederick Essary, *Covering Washington: Government Reflected to the Public in the Press, 1822–1926* (Boston, 1927); F. B. Marbut, *News from the Capital: The Story of Washington Reporting* (Carbondale, Ill., 1971); Donald A. Ritchie, *Press Gallery: Congress and the Washington Correspondents* (Cambridge, Mass., 1991); Culver H. Smith, *The Press, Politics, and Patronage: The American Government's Use of Newspapers, 1789–1875* (Athens, Ga., 1977); and Mark Wahlgren Summers, *The Press Gang: Newspapers and Politics, 1865–1878* (Chapel Hill, N.C., 1994).

Press coverage of the Civil War is described in Louis M. Starr, *Bohemian Brigade: Civil War Newsmen in Action* (Madison, Wis., 1987 [1954]). For the struggle to integrate journalism, see Kay Mills, *A Place in the News: From the Women's Pages to the Front Pages* (New York, 1988), and Donald A. Ritchie, "Race, Rules and Reporting," *Media Studies Journal* 10 (Winter 1996): 133–42.

Gerald J. Baldasty, *The Commercialization of News in the Nineteenth Century* (Madison, Wis., 1992), and Michael Schudson, *Discovering the News: A Social History of American Newspapers* (New York, 1978), shed light on the shift from a partisan press to objective reporting.

The nineteenth-century Washington reporters themselves left personal accounts in books and articles, some of the most useful being Henry Van Ness Boynton, "The Press and Public Men," *Century Magazine* 42 (October 1891); Theron C. Crawford, "The Special Correspondents at Washington," *Cosmopolitan* 12 (January 1892); Lawrence A. Gobright, *Recollections of Men and Things at Washington, during the Third of a Century* (Philadelphia, 1869); Benjamin Perley Poore, "The Capital at Washington," *Century Magazine* 3 (April 1883); and George Alfred Townsend, *Washington, Outside and Inside* (Hartford, Conn., 1873).

15

White Supremacy

A Definition of Terms; Amending the Constitution

An essay entitled "The Congress and White Supremacy" must begin by defining its terms. Readers of this volume can safely define "the Congress" for themselves, but "white supremacy" requires a bit more explication. "More than a slogan and less than a fact" is how Stephen Kantrowitz put it in his recent biography of one of white supremacy's greatest standard-bearers, South Carolina's one-eyed, race-baiting Democratic Senator Benjamin Ryan Tillman (1846–1918). Although white supremacists existed before the Civil War, after emancipation "white supremacy" acquired new meaning and, for its proponents, new urgency. As practiced by men like Tillman, "white supremacy" was both a social argument and a political program, designed to reestablish white men's social and political dominance during and after Reconstruction.

Driven by concerns over African American political and social power, immigration, and the domestic implications of America's new overseas possessions (e.g., Hawaii and the Philippines), white supremacy was at its height in Congress from Reconstruction through the 1920s. Those legislators who sponsored or supported white supremacist agendas were typically motivated by racist ideologies, economic self-interest, partisanship, or a combination of these factors. After considerable legislative achievement (from their perspective), the power of congressional proponents of white supremacy began to wane as a result of African American and immigrant voting power in the North and the rise of national civil rights organizations dedicated to ending public discrimination based on race. Although Congress continued to shelter many men who defended white supremacist ideas and practices long past the 1930s, by the time of the New Deal it was clear that playing the race card held risks as well as benefits.

The Reconstruction Debate

Most accounts of postwar white supremacist politics focus on local events at the state level (particularly southern disenfranchising constitutions), on Supreme Court decisions (especially the momentous 1896 *Plessy v. Ferguson* ruling, which established the "separate but equal" standard), and on terrorist organizations such as the Ku Klux Klan and western anti-Asian mobs. The actions of Congress carry little weight in these interpretations, yet its initial equivocations regarding African American equality during the debates over the Reconstruction amendments to the Constitution paved the way for later assaults on the rights of nonwhite American citizens.

The Union military victory in the Civil War did not free the slaves. Neither did the Emancipation Proclamation, issued as a war measure by President Lincoln in 1863. Abolition was finally accomplished only through the passage and ratification in December 1865 of the Thirteenth Amendment, which outlawed slavery throughout the United States. Emancipation began, rather than ended, a broader political discussion about the contours and meaning of freedom. What was the proper relationship of freedom to equality? Did abolition make all free men and women equal? Congress debated this question intensely. An early version of the Thirteenth Amendment began: "All persons are equal before the law, so that no person can hold another as a slave." When even northern Republican supporters of abolition worried that such language would mean that "before the law a woman would be equal to a man, a woman would be as free as a man," the language — and the question of equality before the law — was dropped.

But the question would not go away. When southern legislatures passed laws known as Black Codes in late 1865, which severely restricted African American movement, freedom of association, and employment, Congress was obliged to expand its understanding of abolition. The task fell to the Illinois senator Lyman Trumbull, who had drafted the Thirteenth Amendment. Elected to the Senate by the Illinois legislature in 1855 over, among other candidates, Abraham Lincoln, Trumbull was one of the first Republicans to see emancipation as a war goal. As Judiciary Committee chair, he sponsored the Second Confiscation Act (1862), which freed all slaves owned by those in rebellion against the United States. Responding now to both white persecution of the freedpeople and the demands of southern blacks for "a republican form of government," Trumbull drafted the Civil Rights Act of 1866. This act, which defined in legislative terms the essence of the freedom granted by the Thirteenth Amendment, was designed to protect the lives and livelihoods of African

Americans through "full and equal benefit of all laws and proceedings for the security of person and property as is enjoyed by white citizens."

When white southern resistance to black rights continued, the Republicans responded with the Fourteenth Amendment (1868), which introduced into the Constitution the concept of equality before the law guaranteed by the national government. This amendment embraced African Americans as citizens, guaranteed "due process of law" and "equal protection of the laws" to every American, and encouraged white Southerners to support black suffrage by threatening to reduce the congressional representation of any state that denied the vote to male citizens aged twenty-one or older.

Although it would, in the long term, be the most powerful constitutional tool for the protection of minority rights in America, in the short term the Fourteenth Amendment failed spectacularly to guarantee the political participation of black men. In 1868 the Georgia legislature dealt with the election of African American representatives by expelling them, prompting Congress to draft its third and final Reconstruction amendment. The Fifteenth Amendment (1870) prohibited both the federal and the state governments from depriving male citizens of the right to vote on racial grounds. It was silent about the right to hold office, and it failed to forbid other forms of suffrage restriction (such as literacy tests and educational and property qualifications), causing Henry Adams to note that the Fifteenth Amendment was "more remarkable for what it does not than for what it does contain." Its omissions may be attributed, as the historian Eric Foner has argued, to the Republicans' desire to protect their party in the South while limiting the right to vote in their own regions. The enfranchisement of Asians in the West would "kill our party dead as a stone," warned California's Senator Cornelius Cole, while the repeal of property qualifications on voting in the East would benefit the Democrats far more than the GOP. Yet despite its limitations, the Fifteenth Amendment enshrined in the nation's fundamental law the principle that every man has the right, as its Senate sponsor William Stewart put it, "to protect his own liberty."

But that liberty was not absolute. The first area to come under pressure was that of sexual right. Linking sexual and political rights, the Democrats charged that the Republicans favored "miscegenation" between blacks and whites. Countering, the Republicans insisted that clear lines could be drawn between political and what became known as "social" rights. During the debate over the Civil Rights Act, Lyman Trumbull was asked if the bill gave a black man the right to marry a white woman. He replied that the chief object of the bill was

> to secure the same civil rights and subject to the same punishment persons of all races and colors. . . . [A state law] forbidding marriages between whites and blacks operates alike on both races. This bill does not interfere with it. If the negro is denied the right to marry a white person, the white person is equally denied the right to marry the negro. I see no discrimination against either in this respect that does not apply to both.

From limits on freedom of marriage and sex were derived limits on other forms of social contact. Public schools, hospitals, trains, streetcars, restaurants, theaters — cemeteries, even — were segregated. Southerners called this system of legal segregation Jim Crow, and it influenced race relations elsewhere in America as well, particularly the West. Freedom of marriage may seem less important than the right to vote, to enter into contracts, or to hold elective office. But because restrictive marriage laws depended on other laws that defined individuals' racial identity, antimiscegenation statutes became the critical legal barrier defining the postwar South's segregated, stratified society. Congress's failure to extend the prohibition of discrimination based on "race, color, or previous condition of servitude" to the question of marriage (and the Republicans' insistence that marriage was not a federal issue) allowed the southern and western states to erect a new segregating state apparatus that classified people according to race and then limited their rights accordingly. It would be another century before Congress and the Supreme Court undid the Jim Crow laws.

Black Suffrage and Congressional Politics

"Congress," of course, is never a static creature: it is an institution peopled by a whole range of individuals, including those who embody the nightmarish visions of others. During the late nineteenth century, South Carolina could be represented in Congress by Robert Smalls, a former slave, and by Smalls's mortal political enemy "Pitchfork" Ben Tillman, who cut his teeth massacring black Republicans in Hamburg in 1876 and went on to become the governor and then, for twenty-three years, a U.S. senator. At the same time Virginia — the very soul of the Confederacy — could send to the Senate William Mahone, a former Confederate general and the leader of an interracial, majority-black third party. Politics after the Civil War was exceptionally fluid across the nation, but particularly in the South, which struggled over how to incorporate newly enfranchised black men into the existing political system. In this context of tremendous political flexibility, congressional intervention or inaction could tip the balance in the struggle over white supremacy.

To the extent that it was an electoral body, Congress had to recognize that black men were, after 1870, part of the electorate and, indeed, part of Congress. The disenfranchisement of former Confederates during Reconstruction strengthened the Republican party in the South, particularly in black majority states like Mississippi, Louisiana, and South Carolina. Twenty-two black men were elected to Congress between 1870 and 1900, including two senators, both from Mississippi. In 1869 Hiram Revels, a free-born minister and educator from North Carolina, became the first African American to serve in the Senate when the Mississippi legislature elected him to fill the seat vacated by Jefferson Davis in 1861. Revels's Mississippi colleague in the House, Blanche K. Bruce, was the first African American to be elected to a full term in Congress (1874–1880). Born a slave in Virginia and educated by private tutors and at Oberlin College, Bruce settled in Bolivar County, Mississippi, during Reconstruction, where he served as sheriff, tax collector, and county superintendent of schools. Like Revels, Bruce defended black rights and championed public education, which southern blacks as well as whites considered a powerful weapon against the white supremacist cause.

With the exception of those African Americans who lived in black majority districts (most of them gerrymandered by the Democrats to artificially concentrate the black vote and limit the Republican party's power), most black voters in the South did not have the option of choosing black congressional candidates. After 1877, with the Republican party in retreat and disarray throughout the South, black voters had two options: accede to Democratic plans to marginalize and contain African American political power, or strike out and form interracial political alliances with the few remaining white Republicans and a larger group of disenchanted white Democrats. These coalition parties did surprisingly well in a political region long regarded as "solid." Between 1865 and the turn of the century, every state south of the Mason-Dixon Line experimented with political alliances that spanned the color line. In two southern states, Tennessee and Virginia, third-party interracial coalitions gained control of the state government during the 1880s. In Alabama, the Greenbackers (supporters of "soft money" who favored the continued circulation of the paper greenbacks issued during the war) successfully combined the votes of white and black coal miners and farmers, while in Mississippi and Georgia, black Republicans joined moderate Democrats in opposing both the GOP and a local Independent movement. The success of each of these parties depended on the ballots of African Americans, who voted in most places throughout the late nineteenth century.

Voter loyalty in this period depended to a considerable degree on the ability of the elected representatives to deliver federal money to support state services and local party organizations. Democrats, Republicans, and Independents alike rewarded their party faithful and starved their opponents through federal patronage. Federal funds meant jobs for one's supporters (for Hiram Revels, it meant black mechanics at the Navy Yard in Washington), money to finance future campaigns, and power to punish political foes. A chief complaint of black Republicans, and a motive for forging interracial third-party alliances, was the unwillingness of the GOP leaders to share the federal patronage with the black electorate. Independents, positioned as they were between the two national parties, were more generous. Virginia's Senator William Mahone, elected by a coalition of white and black Republicans and white Democrats, managed to add 347 new post offices to his state during his six years in office. By using its patronage power in certain ways (such as by supporting interracial third-party movements or, alternatively, denying patronage to African American Republicans), Congress could strengthen white supremacy or work against it.

Probably no individual was more influential at either the state or national level in articulating and policing white supremacist politics than South Carolina's Ben Tillman. Certainly the senator's white supremacist vision shaped congressional politics longer than Mahone's interracialism. Born in 1847 to a slaveholding family in Edgefield County, Tillman was too young to fight in the war but served his race by participating in the bloody campaign that overthrew South Carolina's Reconstruction government in 1876. An ardent opponent of both black education and suffrage, he tried over and over again to repeal the Fifteenth Amendment; when that failed, he recommended violence and fraud, boasting that "in 1876 we shot negroes and stuffed ballot boxes." Tillman reserved a special loathing for white men who cooperated with African Americans. When an alliance between North Carolina's Republican party and white Populists resulted in fusion governments in 1894 and 1896, Tillman recommended revolution through a "shotgun policy" at the next election. North Carolina's Democrats did not disappoint him: when their party lost in November, white supremacists in Wilmington, the state's largest city, seized the city government and murdered at least a dozen black men.

At the time of the massacre, Wilmington was represented in Congress by George White, the last in a line of African American congressmen elected from North Carolina's black majority second congressional district. When the Republican president William McKinley failed to condemn the violence and electoral fraud in North Carolina, White took to the floor of the House to call for "justice — simple justice." Despite this appeal and the efforts of the National Afro-American Council, which met with the president, McKinley remained silent. The Democratic seizure of power in North Carolina went unchallenged; the lesson was clear: "The negro," Tillman explained, "must remain subordinate or be exterminated."

Congress and Disenfranchisement

Tillman's formulation of the problem was characteristically extreme: white supremacists did not imagine that African Americans would voluntarily subordinate themselves. Nor did they consider extermination a real possibility. Instead, racist politicians sought a middle way, and they found it in disenfranchisement. Fusion politics that sent men like George White and William Mahone to Congress were a continuous threat to Democratic power in the South. Hoping to legitimate their racism rather than operate outside the law through violence and fraud, the southern Democrats looked for more legal, and lasting, means to disenfranchise the competition. "There must be devised some legal defensible substitute for the abhorrent and evil methods on which white supremacy lies," insisted one Mississippi newspaper.

The Fifteenth Amendment forbade voter discrimination on the basis of race, color, or previous condition: beyond these broad guidelines, each state could define its electorate on its own terms. Northerners interested in restricting suffrage to the literate had already embraced secret ballot laws. The adoption of the secret (or Australian) ballot in the South during the 1890s eliminated a considerable portion of the electorate, white as well as black. In Louisiana, the number of black registered voters fell from 130,000 in 1894 to 1,342 a decade later; 80,000 white Louisianans lost the vote during the same period. But illiteracy was not necessarily a permanent condition. More effective in the long term was the revision of state constitutions. Beginning in 1890, all eleven states of the former Confederacy rewrote their constitutions to eliminate the votes of black men and those white men misguided enough to support African American political power.

The timing of the southern disenfranchisement campaigns reflected the resurgence of Republican power in Washington after the national election of 1888 and the potential resuscitation of African American political power in the South. Emboldened by their party's control of the White House and both houses of Congress, black Republicans demanded a greater share of federal patronage and a renewed commitment to black suffrage. In Mississippi, African American Republicans moved to contest three of the state's seven recent congressional elections and nominated the first complete Republican ticket since 1876. In a bid to end black voting power once and for all, Mississippi's Democrats called for a constitutional convention to rewrite the state's electoral laws. The new constitution limited black political participation through a combination of complicated registration procedures, a poll tax, a literacy requirement, and what was dubbed "an understanding clause." Its purpose was to guard the interests of illiterate white voters, who, while unable to read the state constitution, could presumably provide a "reasonable interpretation" of it. In 1898 the U.S. Supreme Court ruled in *Williams v. Mississippi* that poll taxes and literacy tests did not violate the Fifteenth Amendment.

The adoption of understanding clauses, in Mississippi and elsewhere, was the clearest indicator that democracy was the chief target of constitutional conventions. Such clauses contributed to fraud rather than eliminated it, because they could be administered in a discriminatory manner against blacks and white Republicans. When this point was raised during the 1902 Virginia constitutional convention, a triumphant Carter Glass, at the beginning of his influential career as a Democratic power broker, congressman, cabinet secretary, and U.S. senator, declared, "Discrimination! Why, that is precisely what we propose; that, exactly, is what this Convention was elected for — to discriminate . . . with a view to the elimination of every negro voter who can be gotten rid of." Glass and his fellow white southern Democrats were direct beneficiaries of the newly truncated southern electorates. The severely circumscribed Virginia electorate sent Glass to Congress for the next forty-four years, during which time he established an expertise in banking and currency questions, writing or coauthoring the most important financial legislation between 1912 and 1933.

The Republican party benefited mightily from black men's votes and, until the 1890s, defended them. Stung into action by "the Mississippi Plan," in 1890 a young Republican representative from Massachusetts, the patrician Henry Cabot Lodge, sponsored a measure that provided for federal supervision of elections in any congressional district on the petition of one hundred or more citizens. The enaction of federal voter protection legislation would have reintroduced competition into southern elections and jeopardized Democratic congressional seats. No call was issued for federal troops or marshals to police the polls, but this did not deter the bill's opponents from denouncing the act as a return to Reconstruction. In 1891 Ben Tillman warned that "the Force Bill" would "make the pyramid stand on its apex and give us back again the negro as a ruler." The bill passed in the House on a strict party vote but ran aground in the Senate when the minority leader, Maryland's Arthur P. Gorman, mounted a Democratic filibuster. The undisputed boss of Maryland's Democrats and the chair of the national Democratic caucus, Gorman was once described by a critic as a master of all the "crafty, treacherous ways of smothering, of emasculating, of perverting legislation." It took all his skill to defeat the Lodge bill, but the stakes were high: southern congressmen, elected over and over by their tiny, segregated electorates, wielded vastly disproportionate power in national politics as heads of congressional committees. The defeat of the Lodge bill shielded their power for another seventy-five years.

Federal protection of voting rights was dangerous for southern Democrats; so too was black education, which had the potential to limit the application of literacy requirements. As illiteracy rates dropped in black majority states like South Carolina, whites began to worry that African Americans might "take advantage of the school houses, get educations and outvote us." The Republicans in Congress magnified these worries in 1889 and 1890 when they proposed significant increases in federal aid to education. The Blair Federal Education bill, which would have vastly increased the federal money available for education but also mandated equal expenditures for white and black children, was, like the Lodge bill, denounced by southern Democrats as unwelcome federal interference in local affairs. As ever, no one was a more vociferous opponent of black education than Ben Tillman, no one more tireless in tying federal power to the cause of black rights. His rhetorical and analytical linking of Washington and black Americans would leave a lasting mark on twentieth-century American politics. As his biographer Kantrowitz notes, Tillman's analysis "nourished a nascent political culture in which . . . white men used the words 'states' rights' as a synonym for 'white supremacy.'"

Faced with a united and vitriolic Democratic opposition to election and education reform, the party of Lincoln began to fray along the seams. A vocal and increasingly influential segment of the party believed that the Republicans' future lay more in managing the nation's emerging industrial economy than in waving the "bloody shirt" war issue of equal rights. In January 1891 a group of eight Republican senators, led by Nevada's William M. Stewart (a chief architect of the Fifteenth Amendment twenty years earlier), agreed to vote against the Lodge bill if the Democrats supported the free coinage of silver. This initiative on behalf of western mining interests was later defeated in the House, but it buried the Lodge bill in the Senate all the same.

The defeat of the Lodge bill, like that of the Blair bill, represented both a generational shift within the GOP and a broader ideological repositioning of the party of Lincoln away from the concerns of emancipation. In case the Republicans changed their minds, the Democrats took advantage of their control of the executive and legislative branches after Grover

Cleveland's election in 1892 to repeal all federal election laws, thereby depriving the federal government of the authority to enforce the Fifteenth Amendment. In repealing these laws, Congress in effect made itself immune to black electoral pressure as long as African Americans remained concentrated in the South. Some Republicans resisted, correctly interpreting repeal as a partisan assault on national authority as well as the franchise; the veteran Massachusetts senator George F. Hoar, who had fought for black men's rights since the 1860s, implored his colleagues that "the nation must protect its own." But most Republicans had by this time abandoned even the pretense of their former commitment to equal rights. Reflecting this shift, the *Washington Post* announced that the Fifteenth Amendment had been a "fateful mistake." The law remained, but it was a dead letter in the South.

"America's Negro Empire": Race and Imperialism at the Turn of the Century

At the turn of the century white supremacy got a boost from an unexpected quarter — overseas — when the Republican establishment went on a binge of imperialist acquisition. Between 1898 and 1915, the United States acquired colonies in the oceans on both sides of the continent. In 1898 Hawaii, the home of many white missionaries and entrepreneurs, was formally annexed. That same year, as part of the Spanish-American War, America seized Cuba, Puerto Rico, Guam, Wake Island, and Manila in the Philippine Islands. (The United States captured the remainder of the Philippines in 1902, after a vicious colonial war.) At the height of the age of steam, these island possessions created a line of coaling stations that made possible the extension of American political, economic, and cultural influence from California to China.

In Congress, opinions on empire broke down along partisan lines, with sharp regional differences. Republicans, influenced by the needs of commerce, generally favored expansion across the globe. But trade was not the only motive for the new imperialists. Republicans like Theodore Roosevelt (the president from 1901 to 1909) believed deeply in the moral obligation of America to spread its civilization beyond its borders and demonstrate that empires can benefit their subjects — especially when those subjects occupied lower rungs on the ladder of racial hierarchy. Democrats, particularly those from the South, resented the influence of eastern financial elites and worried about the injection of so many people of color into the American body politic. The acquisition of what the historian John

Hope Franklin calls "America's Negro Empire" raised crucial questions of citizenship and the future of the Republic. The Stars and Stripes now flew from Cuba to the Philippines. But would the Constitution follow the flag?

Fundamental disagreements about colonial expansion formed along two axes: first, could a republic have colonial subjects? And second, if so, what rights could those subjects expect? When anti-imperialists like Idaho's Senator William Borah argued that the acquisition of an empire would mean the sacrifice of the principles fought for in the Revolution — namely, "that colonies exist for their own benefit, and not for the advantage of the mother country" — expansionists countered with what turned out to be a trump argument: America had been an empire since its birth because the authors of the Declaration of Independence themselves "governed the Indian without his consent." Henry Cabot Lodge — who had only recently fought for black suffrage in the South and now won support for the war in the Senate — explained that the Filipinos would become subjects, not citizens, of the nation and that this represented no break with the past. "The other day . . . a great Democratic thinker announced that a republic could have no subjects," Lodge lectured. "He seems to have forgotten that this Republic not only has held subjects from the beginning, in the persons of those whom we euphemistically call the 'wards of the nation,' but that . . . we not only hold subjects, but have acquired them by purchase [as in Alaska]."

Indian policy provided a precedent for congressional imperialists, who argued that American citizenship did not necessarily accompany American sovereignty. The nation had never dealt generously with the continent's original inhabitants. After the Civil War, facing massive resistance by the western tribes, federal policy toward Indians only hardened. Between 1870 and 1900, Congress gradually restricted native rights and sovereignty. In 1871, pushed by Republicans who considered tribal sovereignty contradictory to the national unity forged in the Civil War, Congress stopped making new treaties with Indians, refusing to recognize any longer the independent nation status of tribes. The Dawes Act of 1887 (named for the Massachusetts senator Henry L. Dawes, who chaired the Senate's Indian Affairs Committee) further eroded tribal identity by breaking up the tribal lands into small parcels to be distributed to individual Indian families or sold to whites. In 1898 Congress ignored tribal governments in the Indian Territory in the interest of an Oklahoma ruled by whites — a process that mirrored the dismissal of Hawaii's native government in favor of a white territorial government. As Henry Dawes summed things up, Indian relations were an excellent template for the nation's new dealings with "other alien races whose future had been put in our keeping" by the Spanish-American War.

It was the alien nature of these new imperial subjects that most disturbed the anti-imperialists and fueled southern Democratic objections to expansion. Worrying about what would happen when Hawaii became a state, Representative Champ Clark of Missouri moaned, "How can we endure our shame when a Chinese Senator from Hawaii, with his pigtail hanging down his back, with his pagan joss in his hand, shall rise from his curule chair and in pigeon English proceed to chop logic with George Frisbie Hoar or Henry Cabot Lodge?" Clark turned out to be wrong in the details but not in the demographics: Hawaii's first senator, elected in 1959, was Hiram Fong, a millionaire graduate (like Cabot Lodge) of Harvard Law School.

Hawaii was annexed without considerable opposition in Congress. Such was not the case for the lands acquired in the war with Spain. President William McKinley and his floor manager for the Treaty of Paris, Henry Cabot Lodge, expected any opposition to the treaty to be confined to those few senators who had opposed the war. However, they underestimated the unifying power of southern Democrats' racial beliefs and the coercive leadership of Maryland's Arthur Gorman. Rather than supporting the administration, the Southerners attacked the treaty with Spain. John W. Daniel of Virginia (who, as the head of the suffrage committee to the 1902 state constitutional convention, had played a leading role in disfranchising his state's black and common white citizens) complained that Americans were being asked to annex a "mess of Asiatic pottage." The ratification of the treaty, he argued, would mean that the Filipinos would inevitably "take up and annex and combine with our own blood and with our own people," to the detriment of the Republic. While some of the opposition saw empire as principally a social problem, others viewed it in political terms. Stanford University's President David Starr Jordan (who considered the tropics "Nature's asylum for degenerates") summed up the problem neatly: "If we govern the Philippines, so in their degree must the Philippines govern us."

Nonsense, countered the expansionists: denied citizenship rights, the Filipinos would no more dominate the nation than the Indians had. And the Filipinos (and the native Hawaiians, and the Puerto Ricans, and the Cubans) would not have citizenship rights because they were not yet capable of using them responsibly. Something had been learned, after all, from Reconstruction. As the Vermont senator Redfield Proctor explained in his speech on annexation, "Let us avoid the criminal blunder made in the past, when we bestowed with unthinking liberty the highest privilege of Anglo-Saxon freedom upon an illiterate, alien race just emerging from bondage." White Southerners who had fought black political power tooth and nail could not now resist pointing out the new imperialists' racial conversion experiences. "Do you acknowledge that you were wrong in 1868?" demanded Ben Tillman in a sarcastic response to the expansionist senator Knute Nelson of Minnesota, a former abolitionist.

White Supremacy and Immigration

Having gone to spectacular lengths to purge the southern electorate of African Americans at the end of the nineteenth century and assured of the subordinate status of the nation's new nonwhite colonial subjects, white supremacists in Congress turned their attention to immigration. By 1910 one-third of the American population was either foreign-born or had at least one foreign-born parent. Congress debated immigration policy incessantly from the 1880s through the 1920s, with the main line of division falling between those who favored mass immigration as an economic stimulus and those who worried about the rising numbers of racially and culturally different foreigners. A series of anti-immigration laws passed between 1917 and 1924 reduced overall immigration by approximately 85 percent and ended nearly all immigration from southern and eastern Europe and Asia. Congress's marking of these groups as racially inferior (and, often, politically radical) encouraged local organizations to police the behavior of Americans who traced their roots to Africa, Asia, or eastern Europe. In the South, the modern Ku Klux Klan policed racial sexual boundaries; in the Midwest it accused Catholics and Jews of communist subversion. In California, Oregon, and Washington, the Native Sons of the Golden West kept a close eye on the business and social habits of the Japanese. The National Origin Act of 1924, which was designed to "confine immigration as much as possible to western and northern European stock," was strongly supported by white supremacist organizations like the Anglo-Saxon League, a eugenicist group dedicated to protecting and improving the white race through state action. At the congressional level, the Anglo-Saxon League fought for restrictive immigration laws; at the state level, it opposed interracial sex and marriage. The link between these two sorts of laws was clear to many in Congress at the time: if miscegenation destroyed the "racial purity" of individuals, immigration — particularly from Asia and southern and eastern Europe — was diluting the old American stock that had made the nation great. As Congressman Fred S. Purnell, a Republican from Indiana, put it during the debate on the immigration act, "There is little or no similarity between the clear-thinking, self-governing stocks that sired the American people and this stream of irresponsible and broken wreckage that is pouring into the lifeblood of America the social and political diseases of the Old World."

This sort of thinking did not go unchallenged, however. Southern and eastern European immigrants found their champions in those congressmen from the industrial Northeast and Midwest who, not coincidentally, received the votes of the nation's newest white citizens. The Republican congressman Richard S. Aldrich of Rhode Island denounced the 1924 immigration act as "absolutely opposed to our American ideas of equality and justice." Pitting patriotism against bigotry, Congressman Nathan D. Perlman of New York entered into the *Congressional Record* the names of every ethnic American soldier who had received the Distinguished Service Cross in World War I. These arguments were on the losing side in 1924. But they revealed the changing political world of the 1920s.

Resisting White Supremacy, 1920–1930

By the late 1920s, a number of pressures were beginning to mount against white supremacy in Congress. Internal migration was part of it: those who could not vote in North Carolina, to give one example, were moving to Harlem, where they could. Combined with European immigration into northern and midwestern cities, the Great Migration of African Americans out of the South shifted these regions' political balance. Suddenly, northern and midwestern congressmen had ethnic white and African American constituencies to please. At the same time, the passage of the Nineteenth Amendment (1920) swelled the voting registers, as women joined their husbands, fathers, and sons in polling booths around the country. New voters meant new issues, and new issues meant congressional change.

One reflection of this change was the rise and sudden influence of a new organization, the National Association for the Advancement of Colored People (NAACP). Founded in 1909 to secure for black Americans their basic constitutional rights, the NAACP gained its earliest successes before Congress when it vigorously opposed a rash of legislation inspired by Woodrow Wilson's expansion of segregation in the capital. Although the very necessity of such an organization reflected the limits of black political power, particularly in the South, its successes woke up northern politicians. Exasperated by Democratic assaults on black rights and Republican pusillanimity, Walter White, assistant secretary of the NAACP, warned the GOP, "Positive action correcting the evils of America is the only thing that can appease colored voters and enlist their support at the polls next November."

In a political world where black votes mattered, Congress had to reconsider its commitment to white supremacy. Congressmen like Emanuel

Celler, first elected from Brooklyn in 1923, would, over time, move easily from defending the interests of the new immigrants to defending those of African Americans. Celler, who served in the House for fifty years, played a critical role in the drafting and passage of the Civil Rights Acts of 1957, 1960, and 1964 and was an important figure in the creation of the Immigration and Nationality Act of 1965, which corrected some of the western European tilt of American immigration law. By the 1950s, white southern congressmen with national ambitions elected under Jim Crow conditions (such as Texas's Lyndon B. Johnson and Tennessee's Albert Gore Sr.) found themselves taking more moderate stands on racial issues. Both Johnson and Gore refused to sign the 1956 "Southern Manifesto," protesting the desegregation of public spaces and institutions.

At the same time, African Americans began to sit in Congress again. In 1928 the first black congressman was elected from a northern district — Chicago's Oscar De Priest. Declaring himself "congressman-at-large" for the nation's twelve million black Americans, De Priest fought for the enforcement of the Fourteenth and Fifteenth Amendments, pensions for surviving slaves, and a federal antilynching bill. His greatest success came in 1933, when he succeeded in passing an amendment barring discrimination based on race, color, or creed to the bill creating the Civilian Conservation Corps.

Although congressional white supremacists were not out yet, the political sands were shifting beneath their feet. When the presence of Oscar De Priest's wife, Jessie, at First Lady Lou Henry Hoover's tea for congressional wives sparked controversy in 1929, De Priest used the publicity to raise funds for the NAACP. That organization, meanwhile, kept up its lobbying efforts, acting in effect as a national political force for African Americans. Although it failed to achieve its long-term goal of a federal bill against lynching, in 1930 it did succeed in blocking the Supreme Court appointment of John J. Parker, a Republican judge from North Carolina, who ten years earlier had dismissed black voters. Anxious not to be tagged as the party of white supremacy, Senate Republicans refused the nomination. Furnifold Simmons, who had masterminded the North Carolina Democrats' white supremacist campaign of 1898, lost his Senate seat that same year. It would take a world war and a domestic civil rights revolution to undo even some of the political damage caused by Simmons and his ilk. Yet if by 1930 the world had not been made safe for either democracy or equality, in America at least it was becoming more dangerous for out-and-out white supremacists.

— Jane Dailey

BIBLIOGRAPHICAL NOTES

Histories of Reconstruction and late-nineteenth-century congressional race politics (including the legal history of marriage) include Steven Hahn, *A Nation Under Our Feet: Black Political Struggles in the Rural South from Slavery to the Great Migration* (Cambridge, Mass., 2003); C. Vann Woodward, *Origins of the New South, 1877–1913* (Baton Rouge, La., 1951); Michael Perman, *Struggle for Mastery: Disfranchisement in the South, 1888–1908* (Chapel Hill, N.C., 2001); Stephen Kantrowitz, *Ben Tillman & the Reconstruction of White Supremacy* (Chapel Hill, N.C., 2000); Heather Cox Richardson, *The Death of Reconstruction: Race, Labor, and Politics in the post–Civil War North, 1865–1901* (Cambridge, Mass., 2001); Michael Vorenberg, *Final Freedom: The Civil War, the Abolition of Slavery, and the Thirteenth Amendment* (Cambridge, Mass., 2001), and Nancy F. Cott, *Public Vows: A History of Marriage and the Nation* (Cambridge, Mass., 2000).

On interracial politics between Reconstruction and 1920, see Jane Dailey, *Before Jim Crow: The Politics of Race in Postemancipation Virginia* (Chapel Hill, N.C., 2000); Michael Hyman, *The Anti-Redeemers: Hill-Country Political Dissenters in the Lower South from Emancipation to Populism* (Baton Rouge, La., 1990); Daniel Letwin, *The Challenge of Interracial Unionism: Alabama Coal Miners, 1878–1921* (Chapel Hill, N.C., 1998); Glenda Elizabeth Gilmore, *Gender and Jim Crow: Women and the Politics of White Supremacy in North Carolina, 1896–1920* (Chapel Hill, N.C., 1996); and David S. Cecelski and Timothy B. Tyson, eds., *Democracy Betrayed: The Wilmington Race Riot of 1898 and Its Legacy* (Chapel Hill, N.C., 1998).

On race, imperialism, and immigration after the turn of the century, see Warren Zimmerman, *First Great Triumph: How Five Americans Made Their Country a World Power* (New York, 2002); Walter L. Williams, "United States Indian Policy and the Debate over Philippine Annexation: Implications for the Origins of American Imperialism," *Journal of American History* 66, no. 4 (March 1980): 810–31; Anders Stephanson, *Manifest Destiny: American Expansionism and the Empire of Right* (New York, 1995); Rubin Francis Weston, *Racism in U.S. Imperialism: The Influence of Racial Assumptions on American Foreign Policy, 1893–1946* (Columbia, S.C., 1972); Nell Irvin Painter, *Standing at Armageddon: The United States, 1877–1919* (New York, 1987); Gary Gerstle, *American Crucible: Race and Nation in the Twentieth Century* (Princeton, N.J., 2001); and Hyung-Chan Kim, ed., *Asian Americans and Congress* (Westport, Conn., 1996).

Hiram Rhoades Revels

September 27, 1822 (or 1827?)–January 16, 1901

Hiram Rhoades Revels

In 1877 Hiram Rhoades Revels became the first African American man sworn into the Senate. But his short and undistinguished career in Washington may be only a footnote to his achievements during a lifetime of public and religious service. The national appointment, to fill the unexpired term of Jefferson Davis, was as much a result of Revels's prominence in Mississippi as an attempt at racial reconciliation after the Civil War.

Revels worked throughout his life as a preacher and educator. Little is known about his family and childhood in Fayetteville, North Carolina, where he was born to free parents. He was educated at a school for black children and worked briefly as a barber before moving to Indiana in 1844 to escape the North Carolina laws that limited educational opportunities for blacks. He enrolled in a Quaker seminary in Liberty, Indiana, but moved to another in Darke County, Ohio, the following year. His preaching career began in the American Methodist Episcopal (AME) Church around this time, and he was confirmed as an elder of the organization in 1849.

For several years Revels traveled and preached throughout Indiana, Ohio, and Illinois. Not publicly known as an abolitionist, he was able to move freely in Missouri, Kansas, Kentucky, and Tennessee. Ostensibly there to preach the gospel to slaves, he later admitted that he also, when possible, assisted fugitive slaves to escape. During this period, he married Phoeba A. Bass, with whom he had six children; they settled briefly in St. Louis in 1853. But Revels seemed unable to stay in one place for very long. After a dispute with the AME bishop, he left the denomination to work for two years as the pastor of a Presbyterian church in Baltimore, Maryland, before entering Knox College in Galesburg, Illinois. Returning to Baltimore and the AME church in 1857, Revels began his career in educational administration when he became the principal of a high school for blacks.

Once the Civil War began, Revels helped organize black work battalions for the Union army. Not long after President Lincoln issued the final Emancipation Proclamation in January 1863, Revels moved back to St. Louis to teach school and help organize the first black regiment from Missouri. He moved to Jackson, Mississippi, within a year of the Confederate surrender of Vicksburg, the last Confederate stronghold on the Mississippi River, and helped establish several schools and churches around Jackson and Vicksburg. Never one to sit still, Revels joined the AME Church North in 1865 and served as a pastor of churches in Kansas, Kentucky, and Louisiana before becoming the presiding elder of a church in Natchez, Mississippi, in 1868.

As a respected orator and one of the most highly educated African Americans in Mississippi, Revels was encouraged to seek public office and easily won election to the state senate in 1869. Although his colleagues considered him their second choice to fill Davis's unexpired term in the Senate, Revels garnered the appointment partly because of his impressive invocation for the legislative session. He arrived in Washington ten days later but could not present his credentials until Mississippi was formally readmitted to the Union. Revels was sworn in and seated after several days of contentious debate. He served for less than two years in the Senate, but his oratorical skills received favorable attention from the national press, and his stance favoring amnesty for white Southerners drew criticism from other blacks.

On Revels's return to Mississippi, Governor James L. Alcorn enlisted him to establish a college for black men halfway between Vicksburg and Natchez. The state legislature recommended that it be named after Revels, but he demurred. Instead, when Alcorn University began offering classes in 1872, Revels served as its first president. He remained involved with the university for ten years before resigning because of his own health problems and the university's financial difficulties. In his later years, Revels continued teaching theology, preaching, and traveling. He died while attending a religious conference.

References

"Revels, Hiram Rhoades." *Notable Black American Men.* Gale Research, 1998. Reproduced in *Biography Resource Center.* Farmington Hills, Mich.: Gale Group. 2003. http://www.galenet.com/servlet/BioRC.

Williams, K. H. 2000, February. "Revels, Hiram Rhoades." *American National Biography Online.* Retrieved June 30, 2003, from http://www.anb.org/articles/04/04-00839.html.

16

The American West

THROUGH THE 1840S AND 1850S, the fate of the territories in the American West, especially regarding their future as slave or free states, played an increasingly tense and critical role in the coming of the Civil War. What would the nation do with the lands seized from Mexico following the brutal war of 1846–1848? Would slavery gain a critical western foothold in the golden land of California? Would the Kansas-Nebraska Territory, so bloodied by one sectional atrocity after another, yank the entire nation into fratricidal combat?

Forced in part by such calamitous questions to pay sustained and close attention to the Far West for the first time in the nation's history (save a few notable exceptions concerning earlier American scientific and expeditionary penetration of the Far West), Congress proved a serious, if ultimately woefully inadequate, student of the region stretching from just east of the Rocky Mountains to the Pacific Ocean. In the end, neither Congress nor the American people could come to a peaceful agreement about the fate of the West (and the fate of slavery within it), and the tragic payback for that failure was the Civil War.

It might be argued that the congressional recognition and knowledge of the West increased after the Civil War, almost as if the legislative body were making amends for its shoddy, tragically inept leadership in the years leading up to the war. There is little doubt that one can define a steep, if erratic, learning curve describing the response of Congress to the American West in the last third of the nineteenth century. But the notion of a chastened Congress intent on not repeating the mistakes of the past offers too much credit to institutional memory and shame. Better, perhaps, merely to suggest that Congress had a great deal to learn about the Far West and its young states and territories in the latter part of the century. With fits, starts, and the growing voice and influence of the western leaders themselves, Congress attempted to answer that pressing need.

Two legislative bookends define this attempt at regional knowledge:

the 1862 Homestead Act and the 1902 Newlands Reclamation Act. These two sweeping pieces of legislation, embodying very different concepts of the West and its development, offer appropriate brackets between which to place an essay exploring Congress and the West after the Civil War. While it is far too simple to claim that these acts represent the full spectrum of complex congressional action focused on the West in this period, they do nonetheless offer an analytically meaningful framework in which to place an overview of the federal government and the region. Between (and through) these two legislative and chronological brackets came the final incorporation of the American West into the political economy of the nation.

One West? The Homestead Act of 1862

The 1862 Homestead Act is a curious piece of legislation. On the one hand, it was an aggressive move by a northern Congress against the South as the nation fell into civil war. At the same time, it was an anachronistic throwback to an earlier period in American history, a memorial of sorts to Thomas Jefferson and his naïve vision of a nation sustained by virtuous and independent yeomen tilling small farms.

For several decades following Jefferson's death in 1826, calls for public grants of land to American workers had come most prominently from laborers on the eastern seaboard, who saw in the West the opportunity to throw off the yoke of wage work and take up independent farming. By the late 1840s, the refrain had been picked up by congressional leaders, many of them proslavery Democrats from the South and the Midwest who had at least some political loyalty to the workers agitating beneath the political banner "Vote Yourself a Farm." Congressional leaders such as the Texan Sam Houston and Stephen Douglas of Illinois championed the idea that the government ought to distribute parcels of public land to those citizens willing to take up and improve that land through farming.

With the heightening of sectional tensions between North and South through the 1850s, the homestead issue became a political football between the parties. Prominent Democrats, Pennsylvania's Galusha Grow in particular, carried the homestead idea into the camps of antislavery Northerners trying to fashion a new political party as civil war loomed. Some, Grow among them, believed that homestead legislation might assist the abolitionist cause by putting a dagger in the heart of slavery. (In 1857 Grow and the South Carolinian Laurence Keitt came to blows on the floor of the House over the future of slavery; their fight precipitated a melee among dozens of their colleagues.) Others viewed the new Republican party's slogan of "free land" as less a statement about the wrongs of slavery and more about preserving the public domain of the West for white workers and their families (not unlike the Democrat's position staked out earlier). In the late 1850s, with the Civil War threatening, the ascendant Republican party reached tacit agreement within its own ranks that "free land" could be a policy both wide and deep enough to accommodate both activists for homesteads and opponents of slavery's expansion. As the historian Henry Nash Smith writes, the homesteading principle, "with its utopian blueprint for developing the trans-Mississippi West," rose to the top of the Republican platform, over and above such issues as slavery's complete abolition.

Congress heard homestead bills a number of times through the late 1850s and early 1860s, but the rising furor between North and South had by then negated any hope of passage. A bill written by Grow passed in the House fairly easily in 1859, but despite fervent support from such Republican stalwarts as Benjamin Franklin Wade of Ohio, it fell far short of passage in the Senate. A year later Congress passed a homesteading bill, thanks in large measure to those western Democrats who broke with their southern party mates in advancing the measure. But the South's strident opposition to the bill, and to accelerated western settlement in general (lest that settlement ensure a free-soil, abolitionist future for the West), tipped the Democratic president James Buchanan's hand in vetoing the bill. Explicit sectional divisions in the Democratic party over homesteading legislation as both tool and symbol of federal policy in the West helped ensure that the Republicans elected Abraham Lincoln president in the fall of 1860. On the eve of his inauguration, Lincoln affirmed his support for legislation "getting the wild lands into small parcels so that every poor man may have a home."

Civil war followed secession in short order, and the North took advantage of a one-sided Congress again to pass the Homestead Act, this time easily and quietly; it was virtually the same proposal that Grow had put forth three years earlier. Lincoln signed the act into law in the spring of 1862, and it took effect on January 1, 1863, the same day as the Emancipation Proclamation. Triumphal, if for a moment, Galusha Grow became Speaker of the House in the Thirty-seventh Congress, only to immediately lose his 1862 reelection bid, the victim less of his hard-fought homestead legislation success than his ahead-of-the-pack stance supporting abolition.

The design of the Homestead Act was simple. It authorized the distribution of public land in up to 160-acre parcels to citizens or intended citizens who paid a minimal filing and registration fee. After five years' residency and the completion of prescribed improvements to the land, the homesteader would receive title. In theory, the Homestead Act confirmed, as its staunch supporter from Kansas, Senator Samuel Pomeroy, voiced in standard rhetoric, the nation's commitment to "the hearts, the bones, the sinews of an independent, loyal, free yeomanry, who have the comforts of home, the fear of a God, the love of mankind, and the inspiration of a good cause." In practice, the law operated in haphazard relationship to such vaunted language. To be sure, the Homestead Act succeeded in important and lasting ways — millions of Americans and new immigrants took up the promise of western farming under its provisions over the course of the next seventy years. But the act's unstated and wishful view of the western environment — that 160 acres in eastern Nebraska was the same as 160 acres in eastern Colorado, for example — imagined rainfall in places where there was little. Homesteading relatively small parcels of land worked far better east of the hundredth meridian than in the West's more arid lands. Other congressional actions — such as those designed to promote railroads, speed the development of colleges and universities, and "extinguish" Native American landholding rights — removed vast amounts of public land from those that homesteaders could claim. Homesteaders also lost out to speculators and corporations, which grabbed great swaths of the best parcels of public domain through inventive, if unscrupulous and illegal, tactics in the West and elsewhere. Corporations quickly found out that they could, for example, use proxy filings by individuals as a way to accumulate chunks of western land; tried and true methods of graft and corruption often proved just as successful.

Passed the same year as the Homestead Act, the Land Grant Act (also known as the Morrill Act for its supporter Justin Morrill, a congressman from Vermont) offered states parcels of public land to use as funding sources for new institutions of higher education. A number of western congressmen opposed the measure, either through an apparent lack of interest in establishing schools or a vociferous hostility to the act's potential loopholes. In the latter category, Senator James H. Lane insisted that the passage of the act would "ruin" his state of Kansas. Morton Wilkinson, a senator from Minnesota, railed against the speculators, "a remorseless class of vampires," whom he was certain would benefit most from the legislation. Despite such opposition, the bill passed, and dozens of educational institutions were created under this act and allied pieces of legislation.

Railroad Grants

The postwar Congress gave railroads nearly as much western land as it gave homesteaders. The United States had been granting parcels of the public domain to railroad projects since well before the war, but the Pacific Railroad Acts of the 1860s put the federal government squarely in the cross-country railroad business and created incentives for the construction of the century's most important industrial and economic facets of western settlement and development. Signed into law by President Lincoln in July of 1862, the first Pacific Railroad Act offered federal support "to aid in the construction of a railroad and telegraph line from the Missouri River to the Pacific Ocean."

Long an ambition of industrial entrepreneurs, dreamy visionaries, and rival sectional and congressional factions, the transcontinental railroad project became real once secession and the establishment of the Confederacy had removed the southern congressional delegations from Washington. Thus unencumbered by North-South debates about the railroads' route and shape, Northerners and Westerners successfully hashed out their differences and emerged with the initial bill. Critical to this effort was California's Senator James McDougall, chair of the special Senate committee designated to tackle the railroad project and a fervent supporter of the measure. Through its extraordinarily generous provisions, the several Pacific Railroad Acts offered infant rail companies a combination of federal land grants and loans to encourage the private construction of the nation's first cross-country rail line. Through successive acts — the initial 1862 legislation laid out congressional ambitions; subsequent actions clarified and even extended federal support — the United States further agreed to extinguish Native American title to those lands needed by the railroads. The 1862 act designated two rail companies as the major actors in the scheme: California's Central Pacific would build east from Sacramento, and Union Pacific track would push west from Omaha, both adhering to Congress's designation of the 32nd parallel as the line of the tracks. Years later, in the spring of 1869, the two rail lines met in northwestern Utah, and the grand effort was complete. The support and backing of Congress had been of the utmost importance, and congressmen, especially western members such as McDougall, congratulated themselves on their sponsorship of the audacious engineering project. Three other transcontinental lines soon followed, each offered similar levels of congressional support in the form of grants of land and loans of money. By century's end, the corporations running the cross-country and affiliated lines had amassed federal land grants totaling nearly 200 million acres of what had formerly been the public domain.

Amid charges that Congress cared more for railroads than struggling homesteaders, Washington clumsily attempted to address the Homestead Act's "one size fits all" naiveté regarding the West's complex environmental realities. The 1873 Timber Culture Act explicitly recognized that the Homestead Act's 160-acre freehold was often unworkable in the arid stretches of the Far West. Under the act's provisions, homesteaders could double their allotment of land if they planted trees on at least a fourth of the new parcel. While recognizing that arid conditions required western farming and ranching to extend over larger parcels of land, the act had an environmental blind spot in requesting that homesteaders plant forty acres of trees on that same dry landscape (Congress later lowered the requirement to ten acres). Nor did the Timber Culture Act contain the necessary preventive measures regarding fraud and the (by now inevitable) actions of speculators, all of which further undercut what democratic intentions may have prompted the legislation. In 1878 Congress did a legislative and forestry about-face, passing the aptly named Timber Cutting Act, which threw open federal lands to private and corporate timber harvesting, with few safeguards blocking environmental degradation or corporate monopolies. Similar actions, through similar acts, defined congressional action related to western mining and mineral rights throughout the period. Congress essentially chose not to interpose itself or the laws of the land between that land and the largely corporate interests exploiting it.

Despite Congress's general adherence to laissez-faire perspectives on western land policy and development, a few voices in Washington actually called for the repeal of all legislation, including railroad land grants, that served corporate interests at the expense of those of the settlers aiming to take up homesteading freeholds. But such proposals gained little purchase in the halls of power. Congress simply kept trying to do two things at once with further legislative acts: appease settlers and powerful interests at the same time. In 1877 Congress passed the ill-advised Desert Land Act, which, on the surface, indicated that the government knew that agrarian practices were different in the West than in the East and that homesteaders needed innovative legal frameworks on which to extend the Republic westward. Under this act homesteaders could, at nominal expense, extend their claims to 640-acre parcels, provided they irrigated that land within three years. The Desert Act may have been right to enlarge western homesteading parcels, but the legislation flew in the face of the Homestead Act's democratic principles, given the obvious obstacles for single-family farm or ranch operations to irrigate such large parcels of land. Speculators, ranching kings, and corporations filled the breach in short order, and the Desert Land Act helped further the maldistribution of western lands from the smaller landholder to the larger.

The Denial of Native American Land Rights

Of course, no western group had more to lose (in land and otherwise) nor lost more than the Native Americans in the period following the Civil War.

Although a flurry of treaties were made with the Indian tribes immediately following the end of the war, it was already clear that a reformulation of Indian policy was at hand. Driven by presidential and congressional policies, this revision of the long-standing federal stance toward Indians had far-reaching consequences across the expanse of "Indian Country," especially in the regions and among the tribes of the West.

At the core, new policies addressing Native Americans were provoked by the federal government's realization that Indian tribes no longer, with some important exceptions, represented the threat to settlement and expansion that they had before the war. The recent examples of tribes allied with the Confederacy during the Civil War also predisposed northern interests (both outside and in the government) to look unfavorably on treaties as acceptable policies. Of perhaps surprising significance in Indian affairs generally, the House of Representatives frequently sought to limit the Senate's ability to make Indian policy through little other than jealousy that the Constitution had left making treaties solely to the upper house.

Through various compromises, Congress agreed in 1871 to make no further treaties while honoring those that existed. A basic phrase in the agreement stated that "hereafter no Indian nation or tribe within the territory of the United States shall be acknowledged or recognized as an independent nation, tribe, or power with whom the United States may contract by treaty."

Such sweeping language aside, the government continued to make agreements with tribes that were, in effect, treaties under other names. The end of making treaties, which can be marked by the passage of the 1871 act, did not mean as much to Indian-government relations and affairs as the transitions that took place shortly thereafter. The supposed abolition of treaties is itself more a symbol of changing legislative attitudes toward Native America in the period. With the eventual embrace of allotment policy as the major coercive tool in Indian affairs, an entirely new era in relations between the United States and the formerly "domestic, dependent nations" was ushered in.

Driven in part by the same republican, agrarian ideals codified in the Homestead Act, the government increasingly addressed Indian relations in the postwar era through the prism of assimilation. As the West rapidly developed, particularly in the decades after the completion of the transcontinental railroad, Congress (and, to a lesser degree, the executive branch) adopted legislative and other methods by which the Indian lands could be brought under the control and authority of the federal government. Assimiliationist ideology — arguments that Native Americans could and should be brought into the mainstream of American society through a variety of means — offered convenient and often morally defensible justifications for the eventual delivery of the Indian lands into the public domain.

The iron fist of assimilation fit uncomfortably into the velvet glove of paternalism. No longer would tribes own land in a communitarian fashion. Individual Native Americans would embrace private property, through assimilation's amalgam of encouragement and coercion, as the keystone of American democracy and, by extension, their own agrarian futures. Following President Grant's late-1860s decision to turn over the operation of most Indian reservations and agencies to missionary and church organizations (Grant's "Peace Policy"), congressional oversight of Indian affairs, for a time, lessened. But Grant's ill-fated scheme provoked nearly as much trouble and distress as previous federal stances toward Native America, and Congress hardly stayed away from intervening in the general arena of coercive assimilation. In an important example, Congress reached across reservation boundaries to insist that federal laws operated even in arenas in which federal or state jurisdiction was murky. Following a murder on reservation land, the Supreme Court ruled that the Indian defendant could not be tried in federal court. Congress leapt to amend a federal act on news of the court's caution, insisting that there were seven major crimes over which the federal courts had unassailable rights to adjudicate.

A Native American Homestead Act?

The legislative foundation on which assimilationist perspectives and policies rested was the congressional allotment program: the distribution of Indian lands to individual Native American titleholders or lessees. Congress had begun to wrestle with various allotment plans in the late 1870s, pushed there in part by the enthusiasm of the two senators from Massachusetts, George Hoar and Henry Laurens Dawes, both of whom, through close identification with the citizenship provisions of the Fourteenth Amendment, argued that Native Americans deserved U.S. citizenship once they accepted homestead allotments carved from Indian lands. Congressmen from the West (especially in the House), far less enamored of allowing Native Americans to become citizens so quickly, helped ensure that early allotment acts never made it out of Congress.

But proponents, backed by the strong support of Indian reform organizations, did not give in easily. Failure in the Forty-sixth, Forty-seventh, and Forty-eighth Congress turned to success with the passage of the General Allotment Act of 1887 (better known as the Dawes Act). This sweeping piece of legislation rises above all other markers on the landscape of postwar Indian affairs. Dawes, a long-time congressman and senator from Massachusetts, had spent much of his legislative life involved in actions related to the American West. He proposed the legislation that made Yellowstone into the nation's first national park in 1872, he lobbied for increased federal spending on various geological surveys of the West, and he played a critical role in the abolition of treaties after the Civil War. But he is best known for chairing the Senate's Committee on Indian Affairs and his long efforts directed toward Native American assimilation. "In its very nature," the reform Indian Rights Association claimed, the Dawes Act "is a new departure on the part of Congress" regarding Native American affairs.

The Dawes Act was a legislative sword that cut at least two ways. It aimed to protect Native Americans from the rapaciousness of western settlement and growth, if not the military antagonism of the federal government. Embracing a naïve Jeffersonian vision of the cultural and political power of freehold parcels not unlike those who eloquently championed the Homestead Act a generation earlier, many supporters of the Dawes Act saw the legislation as a way to bring Native America into the American mainstream. "I do not believe," Senator Joseph Brown of Georgia claimed, "there is any other plan that will solve this Indian question short of their extermination from the continent."

Empowered by the act, the president had the sweeping prerogative to divide (or "allot") surveyed reservation lands into 160-acre parcels for heads of Native American households. Smaller parcels could be granted to other allottees. Though title remained vested in the United States for twenty-five years (time enough, proponents argued, for the Indians to make the transition from tribal to "American" status), those who accepted this arrangement would become immediate U.S. citizens.

Though the underpinnings of the Dawes Act were humanitarian and must be so acknowledged, the paternalism and ethnocentrism of the legislation are manifest. Once they had made their peace with Native American citizenship, congressional representatives from the western states largely supported the Dawes Act, precisely because it promised to open "surplus" Indian lands to non-Indian settlement once the allotments had run their course. An exception to this general support was the strident opposition of Senator Henry Teller of Colorado, who argued vociferously that the assimilationist ideology behind allotment would work if, and only if, white settlers were deliberately and liberally sprinkled onto former Indian lands amid Native Americans from the start. Otherwise, Teller argued, the Dawes Act offered little hope for the lasting integration of Native Americans into mainstream American society.

In hindsight, the results of the Dawes Act were not surprising: Indian lands disappeared from tribal oversight, white settlement accelerated on former Indian lands, and tribal authority and legitimacy weakened accordingly. Within twenty years, Native landholdings in the United States had been halved. The vast bulk of that redistribution occurred in the American West, as places like the former Indian Territory of Oklahoma shrunk in the face of allotment surveys and the creation of new homesteading parcels for white settlers.

The Consequences of Contradiction

Congressional assimilationist policies provoked the century's final eruptions of Native American resistance to coerced incorporation into mainstream America (such as the Ghost Dance revivals' being brutally extinguished at century's end). But concerted discontent with federal acts and actions was not at all limited to Native Americans in the West. The blame for rising discontent among western farmers and workers in the 1880s must be substantially laid at the steps of the Capitol. The legislative flurry of the 1860s and 1870s, which was designed to bring the West, and especially western lands, into national byways of commerce and culture, created, not surprisingly, rising expectations about the promise of western life. The 1880s brought trouble, and Congress had to wrestle with economic and political crises, one after another, until century's end.

Congressional ignorance of the western landscape again played a critical role. Homesteads and ranches obtained through legislation depended, to be sure, on the western climate. Terrible winters in the mid-1880s froze out ranchers and farmers on the Great Plains, and the dryness of the succeeding summers exacerbated and extended the crisis. Railroad monopolies in land, labor, capital, and transport routes — built on the foundations of congressional largesse — had quickly grown to rankle Westerners and Easterners alike. Contradictions in federal land policies, the most glaring of which pitted railroad grants against the principles of the Homestead Act, meant a great deal once crops or livestock froze or dried up. Small farmers stood little chance of watering their crops if irrigation companies held a monopoly on water rights or storage facilities; nor did they have much chance of success if cattle or railroad barons coveted their land. The Westerners made their voices heard, and they proved increasingly willing to elect representatives who could do their share of the shouting.

Congress responded, if somewhat haphazardly, by revising federal land policy in the 1891 General Revision Act and attempting to recoup federal monies loaned to various rail corporations. Other legislation in this period scaled back the Timber Cutting Act's liberal policies that allowed timber harvesting on public land. At the same time, Congress moved quickly to beat back western labor radicalism in the Rocky Mountains and elsewhere, motivated in part by the vehement anti-union stances of not a few western mining moguls with seats in Congress. When western Populists pinned their reform hopes on the Nebraskan William Jennings Bryan ("the Boy Orator of the Platte") in the 1896 presidential election, the contradictions of western discontent were made clear. Not a few Westerners aimed at a sweeping reform of the national economy, hoping that deep federal involvement in such things as price controls, subtreasuries, and crop management would remake the West into the place Jefferson had imagined. But while some western mining elites (and, to a lesser degree, their counterparts in corporate agriculture) may have backed Bryan for his opposition to the gold standard, they were not about to support the more radical wings of the Populist movement. Nor would Bryan: he embraced only the free coinage of silver from the Populist platform. Bryan lost, and would lose again four years later, as the deep discontent of the 1880s and 1890s got pushed beneath the surface of western society.

Learning the West?

By the last decades of the century, numerous western crises focused on land policy and its reform, the railroad monopoly, and widespread labor conflicts (especially in the mines of the Rocky Mountains) made attentive students out of many a congressman previously untutored in the ways of the West. But so too did Congress's establishment of the United States Geological Survey in 1879. Bringing together a number of government surveys, agencies, and individuals, this reorganization of federal scientific inquiry helped ensure that a fairly steady stream of information about the West reached Congress at century's close. Previous scientific surveys — expeditions sent out to explore and study western spaces — included the great geological treks immediately after the war, led by men such as Ferdinand V. Hayden, John Wesley Powell, and Clarence King. When the surveyor John Wesley Powell became the agency's second director, it embarked on an ambitious and far-reaching pedagogical mission to educate Congress, and hence the American public, on the ethnographical, topographical, and geological properties of the American West.

Powell played a critical role in the ways in which Congress approached western topics and western lands from the close of the Civil War until his death in 1902. Already a veteran explorer (and beneficiary of congressional support) by the late 1870s, Powell, with a few other pioneering geologists, helped popularize the western landscape just as Congress rushed through legislation such as the Timber Culture Act and Desert Land Act of the 1870s. His 1878 report to Congress, *Report on the Lands of the Arid Region of the United States,* offered an ambitious, even (according to its opponents) a revolutionary corrective to the ways in which congressional land policies had been circumvented by environmental and other circumstances, speculators, and big corporations. Powell proposed that Congress alter the nation's land laws to bring them more in line with the spirit of democratic access, as embodied in the ideals of the Homestead Act. To do so effectively, however, he recommended sweeping changes in how the arid landscapes of the West ought to be approached through policy, practice, and land law.

Congress moved slowly and reluctantly to embrace Powell's vision of irrigation districts and federal reservoir systems in the West. The Western congressmen in particular, who controlled the House Committee on Public Lands, viewed Powell's proposals as too much of a challenge to the status quo and blocked any significant adoption of his recommendations, cutting his budget at the agency as well. Powell's insistence that vast stretches of western land remain in the hands of the government until the establishment of large federal irrigation schemes ran contrary to western, laissez-faire outlooks. It was not until the year Powell died that Congress moved to adopt many of his recommendations, albeit in a more conservative fashion, through the Newlands Reclamation Act.

Not all action focused on the western landscape in the postwar decades aimed at settlement and a redistribution of the public domain. Educated in part by agencies such as the USGS and students of the West such as John Wesley Powell, Congress had begun as early as the 1870s to support innovative measures designed to preserve parts of the western landscape. This preservation ethos in federal legislation, so at odds with the set of development principles embodied in both homesteading and railroad land grant legislation (which aimed at various forms of land use and development), represents a significant departure from the period's standard practice of quickly rendering public land into private.

Here, the establishment of Yellowstone National Park stands out. Though the bulk of federal actions leading to the protection of large chunks of the American West as parks and natural monuments are largely a phenomenon of the twentieth century, the impulse arose much earlier. Yellowstone, the oldest and largest national park, was created by Congress in the early 1870s. Its enabling legislation, strongly supported by railroad interests sensing a tourist payoff, removed more than two million acres from commercial or agrarian development, in part because Congress did not believe that the protected lands were arable anyway. And though it took Congress nearly another half century to establish the National Park Service (the administration of Yellowstone was initially assigned to the army), a fundamental environmental precedent had been established, almost by happenstance. Congress created California's Yosemite National Park in 1890, as well as the nearby Sequoia National Park of giant redwoods.

Making States from Territories

Congress transferred the governance and supervision of U.S. territories from the secretary of state to the secretary of the interior in 1873. From these territories would come a handful of western states by the turn of the century, including Colorado (1876), Montana, Washington, and both North and South Dakota (1889), Wyoming and Idaho (1890), and Utah (1896). For the most part, the congressional oversight of western territories fell under the realm of "benign neglect."

Affairs in Utah proved the exception. There, the Mormon theocracy had exasperated the federal government since the Mormons' arrival in the 1840s; the Buchanan administration had even launched an odd "war" against them in 1857. By the postwar period, the Mormon practice of polygamy so alienated Congress that a series of laws was passed designed to crush it, if not the Mormon Church itself. This conflict slowed Utah's transition from territory to state; not until the very end of the century did its Mormon leaders convince Congress that Mormonism had effectively policed its own house and that Utah ought to be the nation's forty-fifth state.

A Different West: The Newlands Act of 1902

The political career of Nevada's Francis Griffith Newlands is a case study of the rise of new western voices in Congress in the last years of the nineteenth century. Nevada had been a state only since 1864 when Newlands presided over the passage of his important act. His own political and personal biography touches on much of the maturation of the West after the Civil War. As a young California attorney after the gold rush and, especially, after his marriage to the daughter of a mining baron in 1874, Newlands moved in the elite circles of western society. After moving to Nevada in the 1880s, he quickly built an alliance with the powerful William Stewart, a Nevada senator intimately identified with the state's mining interests and the Far West's Southern Pacific Railroad (his loyalty to the latter earned him the unflattering title "California's third senator"). As a protégé of Stewart's, at least until a bitter breach in the late 1890s, Newlands embraced one of Stewart's key interests: the reclamation of western lands through irrigation projects. In 1901, as a congressman from Nevada (he would be elected to the Senate a year later), Newlands introduced the reclamation bill that would carry his name.

Western irrigation — its practices, legal intricacies, and political ramifications — is itself a hugely complex historical topic. What is critical to our understanding here is how the Newlands Act represented a break from previous congressional action on the western landscape and its development. In many respects, the act and the ideas behind it were perfectly consistent with some of what the western Populists had been aiming for in the preceding ten years. It simply took, in essence, elected leaders longer to figure out that the Populists had been correct in arguing for the need to rethink federal concern with western problems in such areas as resource management. The Newlands Act made the U.S. government a critical, if not the primary, agent of irrigation in the West, and it did so in such a way that it validated some of the Populist movement's insistence on cooperative arrangements and the central organization and distribution of goods and resources. In the case of reclamation, "goods and resources" were but one thing: water.

Like the Homestead Act before it, the Newlands Reclamation Act is a deceptively simple collection of words and ideas with far-reaching consequences. It authorized the federal government, through the secretary of the interior, to build reclamation dams and reservoirs throughout the West. These projects would be funded through the sale of public lands in the western states and territories. In earlier periods, when the status of the West vis-à-vis the East approached a more classical colonial relationship, the monies generated by such sales would have quickly been transported east. But the West had more clout at the end of the century. It still needed federal assistance, massive amounts of it. But western demographic and political power (and there now being more western states that had once been territories) had obviously risen since the Civil War, and public money from the West had a better chance of staying in the West.

The lands watered by federal reservoirs would be available in 160-acre Homestead Act parcels to individual homesteaders, who would receive title after three years, following improvements and payments for construction costs. The act nodded to the Populists by authorizing the federal control of critical irrigation projects, and it also became something of a memorial to Powell in that it accepted his arguments that western lands, if they were to be taken up by small farmers and ranchers, required innovative irrigation practices (which, in terms of scale and expense, only the federal government could provide). Every bit as important as the Homestead Act, the Newlands Act represented a significant break with past land policy. Through its provisions, the federal government — especially the new Bureau of Reclamation — would play an even larger role in the growth, development, and environmental transitions of the twentieth-century West. The Newlands Act became, in the words of the historian Richard White, "a landmark in the larger resurgence of federal power in the West." And again like the Homestead Act, the Newlands Act promised more for the poor, the landless, and the dispossessed than it could deliver.

The Newlands Act likely would not have passed Congress without Theodore Roosevelt's support. In his very first address to Congress as president, Roosevelt insisted that western "irrigation works should be built by the national government." Roosevelt could very nearly be termed a western congressman during his presidency, given his critical support of important western legislation in the shape of what once would have been called "internal improvements." Catapulted into the presidency by William McKinley's assassination, Roosevelt in fact became the prime mover for federal action in the West, often coaxing (or yanking) western congressmen along with him. His ebullient championing of federal reclamation was one such instance of executive enthusiasm.

In looking westward after the Civil War, Congress imagined the great drama of American history playing itself out in glorious fashion. The rhetoric was nothing short of grandiose, if not sheer fancy. Under Congress's legislative guidance, Americans would take up free land and, through virtue and an adherence to republican principles, bring civilization and nationhood to the West. With that view and those settlers on western lands as a foundation, Congress simultaneously set about ensuring the construction of an industrial and corporate framework in short order. Those twin processes, at times mutually supportive, at times plainly contradictory, forced Congress to learn about the West.

This learning came, of course, at a horrible price: the destruction of Native American hunting and gathering societies and, to a large degree, the various ecosystems on which they were based. No other fact is so salient in any consideration of the legislation of the period, and it would be historically irresponsible to avoid it. Nor would it be correct to ignore how Congress, in a somewhat similar fashion, proved all too willing to take up the legislative cudgel of racism to push the West's vicious juggernaut against the Chinese in the 1870s into the realm of national legislation in the 1880s.

Yet the congressional response toward the American West between the Civil War and the end of the nineteenth century had its salutary facets. Through the imperfect Homestead Act and later legislation, millions of Americans, native and immigrant alike, settled on parcels of the public domain and tried to make their land and their lives match those of

Thomas Jefferson's fertile imagination. African Americans, freed slaves as well as others, also took up land and new lives in the West, all of them hoping that the congressional safeguards of life and liberty traveled with them (which they at times did not). Tens of thousands of women also took up homesteads as heads of households in the western lands. And in a region experiencing rapid development and urban growth (a greater proportion of Westerners lived in cities in 1900 than Easterners), Congress proved willing to commit the funds and expertise to support internal western growth, from river and harbor improvements to the subsidization of agricultural research stations, the implementation of irrigation projects, and the establishment of a variety of educational institutions. On the one hand, such profound federal intervention furthered West's dependence on the United States government; on the other, Westerners — voters and those they elected — accepted that role without much kicking.

— William Deverell

BIBLIOGRAPHICAL NOTES

Important and thorough general studies of the West include Richard White, *It's Your Misfortune and None of My Own: A New History of the American West* (Norman, Okla., 1991), and Robert V. Hine and John Mack Faragher, *The American West: A New Interpretive History* (New Haven, Conn., 2000). A rich and distinguished scholarly tradition is devoted to the analysis of federal land policy and land distribution in the American West. Interested readers should begin with the work of Paul Wallace Gates, perhaps especially his volume *The History of Public Land Law Development* (Washington, D.C., 1968). Roy Robbins, *Our Landed Heritage, 1776–1936* (Princeton, N.J., 1947), is similarly rich and insightful. Mary E. Young, "Congress Looks West: Liberal Ideology and Public Land Policy in the Nineteenth Century," in David M. Ellis, ed., *The Frontier in American Development* (Ithaca, N.Y., 1969), is extremely helpful, as is the entire volume in which it is published (a festschrift to Gates from his students). Karen R. Merrill, *Public Lands and Political Meaning* (Berkeley, Calif., 2002), is an examination of the relationship between the western ranchers and the federal government. For insight into the Jeffersonian hold on the American imagination well into the late nineteenth century, with special reference to U.S. congressmen, readers should consult Henry Nash Smith's masterful study *Virgin Land: The American West as Symbol and Myth* (Cambridge, Mass., 1950). Two excellent studies of Native America that explore the post–Civil War period in depth are Brian W. Dippie, *The Vanishing American: White Attitudes and U.S. Indian Policy* (Middleton, Conn., 1982), and Robert M. Utley, *The Indian Frontier of the American West, 1846–1890* (Albuquerque, N.Mex., 1984). Important studies of western electoral politics and the rise of Populism include Paul Kleppner, "Voters and Parties in the Western States, 1876–

1900," *Western Historical Quarterly* 14 (January 1983): 49–68, and James Turner, "Understanding the Populists," *Journal of American History* 67 (September 1980): 354–73. On Senator Francis Newlands, see William Rowley, *Reclaiming the Arid West: The Career of Francis G. Newlands* (Bloomington, Ind., 1996). Donald Worster, *A River Running West: The Life of John Wesley Powell* (New York, 2001), is the definitive study of Powell and his ideas for the federal reorganization of western lands and water.

17

Railroad Policy

In the spring of 1869, at a remote location in the Utah desert, a group of Americans gathered for a ceremony that seemed to mark the highest achievement in the history of the young United States. They represented all sections of the country and occupations ranging from financier to laborer. They met to drive the last spike — a golden spike — to symbolize the completion of the great transcontinental railroad. A special telegraph apparatus sped the mallet blows across the continent as Americans everywhere celebrated the enormous achievement of linking the Atlantic and Pacific with a modern transportation system, the steam railroad. For the celebrants great promise beckoned: the promise of binding the nation together and of promoting economic growth and western settlement.

Politicians were among the celebrants because they had played an important role in the development of the railroads. Congressional action in particular was important. Congress had actively encouraged the construction of railroads, and its support was a critical subsidy for the construction of this transcontinental route, as it would be in the future for lines crossing from the Mississippi River valley to the Pacific coast. Political leaders, however, would face an entirely new set of problems. As the industry matured after 1869, Congress passed the first modern federal regulation of business, the Interstate Commerce Act of 1887. The enactment of both developmental and regulatory policies required political skills in a fractured nation and ingenious arrangements within the American political tradition.

Constructing the Railroads

A railroad craze swept across the nation after 1830. Railroads promised reliable and speedy transportation in all weather, even to remote regions like Utah. Their construction costs were lower than those of manmade canals. The building and successful operation of the railroads, however, faced some special hazards. Where population density was fairly high, as in parts of New England and the eastern states, railroads promised strong and regular profits for private investors. But in sparsely settled country, the profits from railroads appeared too far in the future to guarantee returns on investment. Nevertheless, the railroads promised to facilitate rapid economic development for both commercial agriculture and industry. Because of this great promise, boosters agitated for government subsidies to construct lines across isolated territories where private investors did not see profitable returns. For example, while the Thirtieth Congress (which convened in December 1847) was in session, Representative Abraham Lincoln of Illinois introduced no fewer than twelve requests from his constituents for federal assistance in building railroads in Illinois. The young Lincoln had supported railroad construction from his first days as a politician.

The citizens like Lincoln, who sought assistance in building railroads, did not seek government construction. Americans generally were leery of publicly owned internal improvements after the state-owned canals defaulted on bonds during the business depression of the 1830s. Moreover, obtaining a congressional majority to support the construction of a public railway in a particular locale was difficult simply because so many citizens would bear the expense for the benefit of so few. In the middle of the nineteenth century, congressional advocates of federal help for building railroads found another device, the land grant. The land grant had great potential as a policy that would attract private investors by giving them land as a tangible asset backing construction loans.

Since the earliest days of Congress, leaders in both the executive and legislative branches had called for national programs of government assistance for "internal improvements," the phrase early-nineteenth-century Americans used to describe the opening of the country with roads, canals, river and harbor work, and eventually railroads. Few Americans at the time subscribed to the economic theory of laissez faire (keeping government's hands off the economy). Indeed, the second law enacted by the First Congress in 1789 was a tariff designed to help American manufacturers succeed against British competitors, who enjoyed lower costs. Even this modest measure proved controversial, however; subsidizing internal improvements was even more so. The difficulty was in seeing any particular internal improvement project as national, thereby appropriate for federal action. State and local governments subsidized railroad and other internal improvement projects with grants of land, stock subscriptions, loans, and the like, but each individual project clearly benefited its own locality. In some cases they even built railroads, seen most dramatically in the decision of Cincinnati's municipal government to build a railway to connect the town and its businesses with southern markets. Federal subsidies were controversial, on the other hand; a project such as the Cincinnati Southern Railroad seemed not to command national importance.

Nevertheless, Congress had sometimes supported state projects indirectly, eventually providing the precedent for larger projects. The federal government owned a tremendous acreage of land, but in many places it had little value without transportation facilities. Hence the land grant. Its initial strategy was to give land to states that would, in turn, use it as collateral on mortgages for the construction of internal improvements. During the first half of the century, Congress ceded vast tracts of land for this purpose. This strategy proved especially useful in the first congressional subsidy support for railroad construction, in 1850, a project linking the Gulf of Mexico with Lake Michigan.

By that time, private investors were launching substantial railroad construction projects in the more settled states to the east. Ohio, for example, witnessed the building of a network of railways linking its people with one another and with long east-west routes without direct aid from Congress. Farther west lay problems, however, for the territory was not yet settled enough for private investors to risk their capital without certain prospects for returns. A new senator from Illinois, Stephen A. Douglas, provided the leadership to have federal subsidies ensure railroad development in his state, linking it with other territories to the south and west. Douglas had migrated to Illinois in 1833 as a young man seeking his fortune. He soon realized that connecting the state with railways to markets to the south and west would boost prosperity. Elected to the Senate in 1847, Douglas began working to achieve federal assistance for rail projects. He enlisted the cooperation of Senator Jefferson Davis of Mississippi and other congressmen interested in southern railroad development to have Congress support what they called "a great national thoroughfare," a route through Illinois to the Gulf Coast. A northern leader even expressed the hope that the combined Mobile and Ohio and Illinois Central Railroads, as the lines were called, would bind North and South "together so effectually that the idea even of separation" could not arise.

Douglas's scheme was ingenious both politically and legally. The principal argument against federal land grants held that it was wrong to cede a resource owned by all of the people to a special class, in this case railroad companies. This argument was potentially fatal to Douglas's dreams, for only a few would directly benefit from giving away assets owned by all. The solution to the problem was brilliant. Douglas and his friends arranged for land titles to pass to the railroads, once constructed, in a checkerboard fashion, with the government retaining title to a good portion of the land near the railways. They argued that the acreage retained would substantially rise in value with the provision of transportation services, and this value would benefit all citizens, not just those directly served by the new railroad. Douglas and Davis thus obtained a vote of 26–14 in the Senate and 101–76 in the House. (New England's representatives divided evenly on the issue, but majorities from every other section carried the day for the measure, with support from both Whigs and Democrats.) The 1850 Land Grant Act provided that 3.75 million acres of land go to the states to support the railroad project. By 1857 some 21 million acres of public land were used for railroad construction in the Mississippi River valley.

The 1850 statute set the stage for a much more substantial congressional subsidy, a "Pacific railroad" to link California to the rest of the nation. By 1845 petitions were pouring into Congress, pleading for the construction of such a line, and each Congress thereafter considered some sort of Pacific railroad bill until an agreement was reached in 1862 to support the lines that met in Utah seven years later. Its promoters envisioned great benefits from the Pacific railroad. A House committee in the Thirty-first Congress declared that the Pacific railroad "would make the United States the center and axle of the commerce of the world," where Europe would "bow to Asia, and Asia to Europe, across our bosom." This project would cover many more miles of undeveloped and largely unpopulated terrain, however, than any other venture in the national experience. Nor was the most advantageous path for a new railroad clear, as political and sectional interests clouded the selection of a route. A Wisconsin newspaper put the question "Shall the Upper West or the Lower West be the great avenue of trade and commerce?" With the Union increasingly divided over slavery, no agreement was forthcoming on the transcontinental's eastern terminus.

The Thirty-second Congress, shortly before adjourning in March 1853, decided to approach the issue of a favorable route as objectively as possible. It authorized the secretary of war to conduct surveys to determine the most economical route from the Mississippi River to the Pacific Ocean. Five general routes were proposed, and the army sent out parties to survey each of them. Professional topographical army officers examined the results, and in 1855 Secretary of War Jefferson Davis reported their findings to Congress. Most favorable, in his judgment, was the southernmost route, which followed the Gila River for part of its course. In the meantime, in 1853 the Pierce administration had negotiated the Gadsden Purchase with Mexico, to bring the Gila River into the United States.

This report, and the surveys on which it rested, did not produce an objective decision, however. The partisans of a more northerly route accused

Davis of southern prejudice, calling him a "true son of the South" who had revealed "a little southern proclivity in his report." Northerners looked at the surveys to find support for their own cause. Distrustful of the Pierce administration, northern congressmen insisted on choosing the eventual route or routes through legislation rather than executive action. Senator Douglas, so politically successful in devising the 1850 land grant, tried to assume leadership again. He fervently favored a central route across the West to San Francisco, a route that would obviously benefit Illinois. Other midwestern congressmen, with different local interests, favored a northern route to Puget Sound, while Southerners remained adamant in favor of the southern route. By the middle of the decade, a pattern appeared in which Douglas introduced legislation to fund a central route and tried to obtain a majority by adding to it funds for a southern and a northern route as well. This political strategy, however, foundered on southern opposition to the other routes. Although by 1855 there were congressional majorities in favor of the federal funding of a transcontinental railroad, they simply could not overcome sectional divisions. It was not until the southern states seceded that a clear majority appeared for funding a transcontinental railroad with a northern terminus.

Finally, in 1860 Democrats and Republicans alike campaigned on platforms advocating federal grants to permit private firms to build a railroad. The Republicans asserted "that a Railroad to the Pacific Ocean is imperatively demanded by the interest of the whole country; that the Federal Government ought to render immediate and efficient aid in its construction," while the Democratic convention that nominated Douglas for president observed that "the necessities of the age, in a military, commercial, and postal point of view, [were] speedy communication between the Atlantic and Pacific States" via railroad.

In the spring of 1861, the Thirty-seventh Congress began writing a Pacific railroad bill capable of obtaining majority agreement. Both houses established special committees and eventually reached an agreement on what became the Pacific Railroad Act of 1862. Not surprisingly, compromises were made. The secession of the southern states removed one obstacle to the eastern terminus of the new railroad; it would be in Omaha, Nebraska, which was already reached by a line from Chicago. (The western terminus was San Francisco, then the largest settlement on the Pacific coast.) Still, to achieve the needed votes Congress waffled: potentially, five routes might get help. As the delegate from the territory of New Mexico noted, the advocates of a Pacific railroad would not support any one measure "unless it starts in the corner of every man's farm and runs through all his neighbors' plantations."

Supporters of the compromise saw the favored line as a national project crossing largely unoccupied territory. For instance, the Chamber of Commerce of the State of New York argued that the new line would strengthen "every bond of union between our Atlantic and Pacific coasts" while benefiting the trade of both the state and city of New York. To build westward from Omaha to the California border, the law chartered the Union Pacific Railroad Company, with a capital stock of $100 million. Its fifteen-member Board of Directors included two persons appointed by the president. The government would help finance the road by holding thirty-year bonds. Meanwhile, Congress also agreed on heavy subsidies to allow the Central Pacific to build a line across California, linking the Union Pacific with San Francisco. (When it reached the border from the west well ahead of the Union Pacific's construction from the east, the Central Pacific continued laying track into Utah, where the two lines were joined in 1869.) The Union Pacific was to receive ten sections of public land for every mile constructed. This measure, however, failed to attract sufficient private investors, so the next Congress passed a second Pacific Railroad Act in 1864, with further inducements to attract private investors, the most important of which were the government bonds being held as a second mortgage.

The policy of using land grants to encourage railroad construction ended in 1872. In sum, the railroads received title to 130,401,606 acres of land. Four transcontinental lines — the Union Pacific, the Southern Pacific, the Northern Pacific, and the Santa Fe — received 73 percent of those acres. A fifth line, the Great Northern, was built without benefit of land grants. In return, Congress required some of the carriers receiving the subsidy to haul military shipments at no charge and to transport the mail at favorable rates. Thousands of miles of track were laid as a result. In fact, during the 1880s, American firms built more railroad track than anyone else in a comparable time anyplace in the world.

The Birth of Railroad Regulation

While the promotion of railroads was still under way, Congress turned its attention to regulation. Garnering political support for railroad construction was relatively easy so long as it benefited many districts. Once built, however, the railroads' business practices proved contentious. The interest in regulation by the 1880s, in fact, became so great that it transcended partisan and sectional disputes. Eventually Congress passed the Interstate Commerce Act of 1887, a compromise that created the Interstate Commerce Commission and set the pattern for much of future American policy toward business.

Almost as soon as a railroad was built, its prices and services became controversial. Railroads were a fundamentally different type of business than those to which Americans were accustomed. The capital invested in traditional businesses was usually mobile; a merchant could close shop, sell his real estate, and reinvest his capital to meet changing business conditions. Not so with railroads: the capital invested was, compared to that of any other private enterprise in history, enormous, and it was fixed in rails, rolling stock, and terminals and could not be easily reinvested as conditions changed. The successful operation of the railroads, furthermore, required new managerial systems to coordinate the flow of trains, to develop revenue-producing traffic, and to set passenger and, especially, freight rates in order to produce profits. These economic realities led to a widespread popular suspicion of railroad companies.

Americans in the nineteenth century agreed widely on the virtues of independent, traditional small businesses, ideas that contributed to a myth of democracy and egalitarianism. Central was the notion that an individual should be able to enter business and function autonomously. The government could provide help — the sort of assistance that the land grants entailed, policies that were developmental. Providing land cheaply (or even free) to help independent farmers was part of this myth. Once established, so these ideas ran, businesses should operate independently, without special privileges. Americans were especially hostile toward monopolies, which fettered individual opportunities. They grew suspicious, as the railroads developed, that the carriers were monopolies exercising powers inimical to democracy and individual economic opportunity, a kind of evil force.

Thus the movement for federal regulation emerged to check the power of the railroads and ensure the public interest. In developing a regulatory policy, Congress faced complicated economic and political problems. Economic relationships among communities were a central political concern. Every village, town, and city saw the railroad as bringing the promise of enormous economic benefits. In general, of course, these hopes were realized, as railroad transportation helped spark a boom in American industry and agriculture. As railroad construction lowered transportation costs, which benefited the national economy, lower freight rates also encouraged widespread competition between businesses of all sorts, including farmers, who needed access to regional or national markets. This new competition was unsettling and led to state regulation and, by the 1880s, to widespread pressures for federal regulation of the railroads.

These political pressures did not arise from concerns that the railroads charged too much. In general, after 1870 railroad charges dropped for the rest of the century. The pressures came from the complications of *relative* freight rates, over whether rates discriminated against one community or business in favor of another. For example, when merchants in New York City learned that the trunk lines (as the major east-west railroads were known) were charging somewhat less for shipments to rival ports on the eastern seaboard, they mounted a campaign to have Congress regulate railroad charges by forcing them to place all of the major ports on an equal footing. The New York merchants were powerful men whose grievances commanded public attention, but they were far from alone. Aggrieved oil refiners in Pennsylvania, farmers in remote Texas fields, and Alabama cotton merchants were among those who complained about railroad freight rates.

Part of the problem arose from the nature of the railroad business. American railroads were aggressive in improving their technology and management to reduce their costs. Wherever there was competition among the lines — and those points expanded with the enlarging railroad network — shippers were in a position to bargain for lower rates. Where one shipper, such as the Cleveland oil refiner John D. Rockefeller, was more powerful than his rivals, very favorable rates indeed were obtained. Rates, in other words, were set in part by market conditions, and railway improvements allowed the carriers to lower their charges in response to those conditions.

Another aspect of railroading was more complex, however. Rail executives were pioneers in developing accounting techniques to keep track of their costs. The insights gained by the new science of cost accounting provided opportunities for analyzing and lowering costs. Railroading was a capital-intensive business, meaning that profits came largely from using the trains and tracks to their fullest. Running trains full was important, for a train returning empty freight cars cost almost as much to operate as a full train. And costs were highest in the terminals where cars were loaded and trains made up. Thus the railroads sought to administer freight rates in ways to attract traffic, fill freight cars, and run them for long distances. Per mile, it became cheaper to ship goods a long distance than a short distance. To those shipping goods shorter distances, however, this situation seemed discriminatory, leading to calls for government intervention and the reform of "long and short haul discrimination." The complaints about this discrimination were loudest from agricultural districts in the South and West, where an individual shipper did not enjoy service from competing lines and therefore could not play off one railroad against another.

Competition hurt the railroads, moreover. In the "hard times" of the 1870s, desperate carriers had slashed freight and passenger rates in a vain attempt to attract traffic, ruining some companies like the Baltimore and

Ohio. A bankrupt line worsened competition, for it could slash rates without having to pay interest costs. Rates had become, in the words of the scholar Albro Martin, an "oriental bazaar" of haggling, uncertainty, and unprofitability. Railroad executives responded by trying to build agreements among firms to rationalize prices and divide traffic and revenue to the benefit of all lines. The efforts to avoid ruinous competition and administer rates were called "pooling," for which railroad executives wanted a statutory sanction.

The two men most responsible for federal railroad regulation were John H. Reagan, a Democratic representative from Texas, and Shelby M. Cullom, a Republican senator from Illinois. Reagan had enjoyed a successful political career before the Civil War, having served in Congress and, after secession, as postmaster general of the Confederacy. Imprisoned after the war, Reagan soon returned to Texas to resurrect his career; Texans elected him to the House in 1874. Cullom was also an experienced politician who had served in the House of Representatives and two terms as governor of Illinois before his election to the Senate in 1883. Both men approached the subject of railroad regulation with an agrarian outlook suspicious of large corporations, and they were responsive to the complaints about railroad practices. Then they differed. Reagan saw the railroads as "evil," whereas Cullom took a calmer, less strident approach. In the end, Cullom proved the more influential leader. Republicans, strong in the Far West where shippers and passengers benefited from cheap long-haul rates and in the Midwest and East where shippers benefited from competition, generally favored Cullom's views; Democrats, reflecting the interests of the South and parts of the West, adopted a more hostile approach.

Reagan provided the initiative, however, for federal railroad regulation. Soon after 1874 Reagan, seeking a national reputation, became a magnet for dissatisfaction. He consulted with eastern writers, who condemned powerful businessmen, and listened sympathetically to complaints about rate setting. Reagan voiced a strident negative ideology. He decreed that any long- and short-haul discrimination was simply wrong, that, in effect, all freight rates should be the same per mile. He condemned pooling. Although a number of states had set up commissions to shed light on railroad practices and govern their rates, Reagan rejected that approach. He thought that the railroads would control commission appointments, thereby removing decisions from the popular will. Reagan preferred legislation carefully defining erroneous behavior and forbidding any differentials in price between freight carried short or long distances, and he expected the courts to enforce the law strictly. Anything less, Reagan claimed, would allow the railroads to achieve "complete mastery . . . of all our material interests" and of the government "until a few railroad magnates shall own most of the property of the country," with "the masses of the people . . . reduced to a condition of serfdom, poverty, and vassalage."

Reagan soon became determined to force the railroads to their knees. In 1876 the House Commerce Committee held hearings in which powerful businessmen and their attorneys seemed bent on confusing and delaying any attempts at regulation; eventually the clerk announced that the testimony was lost, and the effort came to naught. Reagan angrily asserted that the records had been stolen. This episode made him all the more determined to chasten the carriers' "powers for evil." Later that year the U.S. Supreme Court, in *Munn v. Illinois,* accepted regulation in principle, a decision that emboldened Reagan to seek legislation providing redress over unfair rates in the courts. In 1878 he introduced a regulatory bill outlawing pooling and requiring rates set on a per-mile basis. Stymied when the Republicans assumed control of the House in 1880, Reagan reassumed his push for regulation in 1883, when the Democrats regained the majority. In 1885 the House passed his bill, 161–75. Its supporters came mostly from the South and West. However, dozens of representatives did not vote; they could not support Reagan's hostile approach, even if they wanted some form of effective railroad regulation.

Senator Cullom, on the other hand, suppressed his ideological instincts about the evils of railroad corporations and set out to inform himself, and the nation, about railroad economics. In 1884 the new senator sponsored the creation of a select committee, which he chaired, to investigate the railroad situation; it held hearings in fourteen cities around the country. The committee listened to railroad executives, who carefully explained the basis for their rates. It listened to shippers, boosters of aspiring communities, and state officials. Cullom also consulted with Judge Thomas Cooley of Michigan, a leading jurist. He, also a Republican, was known for his independence from partisanship. Cooley, who eventually served as the first chairman of the Interstate Commerce Commission, noted that public demands for rate stability and open competition were inconsistent. He suggested that the government should try to encourage rate stability while ending egregious favoritism and discrimination.

Educated by this process, Cullom, who as governor of Illinois had witnessed the operation of its regulatory commission, concluded that an Interstate Commerce Commission was desirable. Such a commission, institutionally removed from the partisan fray and public whims, would be able to learn about railroad economics and public policy, as Cullom had done. Cullom accepted the ideas of Charles Francis Adams, the father of the Massachusetts Railroad Commission and later a railroad president himself, about the importance of revealing railroad practices clearly through uniform accounting and reporting measures. This "sunshine" approach, Cullom and his supporters believed, would have a salutary impact on the industry. The commission, furthermore, provided a place for Americans to air their grievances. Its hearings seemed likely to discourage frivolous complaints while allowing government officials to gain the information required to set wise policies. In the end, one important function of the commission, facing a hugely complex subject, was to advise the Congress on future legislation. The commission thus was at the heart of Cullom's thinking.

Cullom also disagreed with Reagan on a strict ban on long- and short-haul discrimination. A better policy was to allow the carriers to administer freight rates based on their analysis of costs, their need to attract traffic, and on the realities of market conditions, an approach not without sympathy among railroad executives. Again, the commission would supervise this approach to ensure the common good. Railroads wanted the federal sanction of pooling and government supervision of administered rates. Cullom and his colleagues heard testimony from a variety of state officials and business leaders arguing for making it legal to "pool" under government supervision. The bill the Senate finally passed — with only four dissenting votes — was silent on the matter of pooling. It did allow long- and short-haul discrimination under the watchful eyes of the commission.

The differences between the House and Senate bills threatened to kill railroad regulation. Although both bills condemned rebates and required publicity about rates, the House bill forbade pooling and strictly outlawed long- and short-haul discrimination. Reagan continued to reject the idea of the ICC, which Cullom thought was central. Eventually the issues went to a conference committee for resolution.

The compromise in 1887 dissatisfied both houses. As one House member said, it was a bill that "practically no one wants and yet everybody will vote for." Cullom won the creation of the ICC and a phrase limiting a ban on long- and short-haul discrimination to cases where such hauls occurred under "substantially similar circumstances and conditions." This phrase, which was at the heart of the disagreement between Reagan and Cullom, allowed the new commission to permit discrimination based on the realities of railroad economics. On the other hand, the railroads failed to obtain pooling. Although partisans in both houses found the compromises unpalatable, eventually pressure from state legislatures and state regulatory commissions prompted both houses to bring the conference committee bill to a vote. It passed by substantial margins, 50–20 in the

Senate and 231–48 in the House. The federal government thus began a new era in its relations with business.

In this law, Congress set the model for later efforts to regulate business. The Interstate Commerce Commission combined judicial, administrative, and legislative powers. Serving staggered six-year terms and with no one party allowed to dominate membership, the commissioners could develop expertise removed from political whims and the partisan fray. Although the courts soon stripped the commission of any power to set railroad rates, its creation provided an institutional model for later reforms in business regulation. It provided uniform accounting and reporting in the railroad industry, and its hearings and reports shed light on the industry's business practices, two accomplishments Cullom had sought.

Soon after Congress passed the law, the railroads began quietly to administer rates through "traffic associations," private organizations through which the carriers cooperated to set rates administratively, based on an analysis of costs. The ICC lent its tacit permission, and considerable stability in the nation's freight rates ensued. Although shippers were still able to negotiate rates with carriers, the requirement that the ICC be informed about those rates dampened abuses. However, after the passage of the Sherman Antitrust Act in 1890, the Supreme Court, in 1897, ruled that rate-setting by railroad traffic associations was illegal. The carriers' response was to merge, so that by the early twentieth century most railroads were part of seven families of lines connected by interlocking directorates and mergers.

By the end of the nineteenth century, because of congressional initiatives in railway policy, the United States had fundamentally changed legally and institutionally. Although federal support for economic development was present at the start of the century, it grew, through the land grants to railroads as well as other measures, on a massive scale. Federal development policies were firmly established in the fabric of the nation's political life. The regulatory policy that began in 1887 with the Interstate Commerce Act was truly innovative. Although by the end of the twentieth century the ICC would disappear as an agency as part of a widespread movement of deregulation, the underlying principles first enacted in 1887 would remain. Government was to appoint officials capable of rising above the partisan concerns of the moment. And those officials, and the laws that empowered them, were to provide continuing economic interventions intended to make private enterprise function fairly and effectively.

— K. AUSTIN KERR

BIBLIOGRAPHICAL NOTES

Carter Goodrich, *Government Promotion of American Canals and Railroads, 1800–1890* (New York, 1960), is the standard work on land grants and other subsidies; Carlton J. Corliss, *Main Line of Mid-America: The Story of the Illinois Central Railroad* (New York, 1950), is also useful in this regard. Albro Martin provides a vivid explanation of the birth of regulation in "The Troubled Subject of Railroad Regulation in the Gilded Age — A Reappraisal," *Journal of American History* 60 (September 1974): 339–71. Ben H. Procter, *Not Without Honor: The Life of John H. Reagan* (Austin, Tex., 1962), and James W. Neilson, *Shelby M. Cullom, Prairie State Republican* (Urbana, Ill., 1962), are lasting works of scholarship that help explain the birth of railroad regulation. Stephen Skowronek, *Building a New American State: The Expansion of National Administrative Capacities, 1877–1920* (New York, 1982), casts the birth of railroad regulation in the larger framework of the resistance of nineteenth-century Americans to building executive authority. Elizabeth Sanders, *Roots of Reform: Farmers, Workers, and the American State, 1877–1917* (Chicago, 1999), argues the case for agrarian interests as the principal force behind railroad regulation.

18

Industrialization

IN ONE OF THE MOST explosive transformations in history, the United States emerged as the preeminent industrial nation in the world between the end of Reconstruction and the turn of the century. This change was contested in popular politics at almost every level, from the warrens of working-class tenements to the shacks of impoverished sharecroppers throughout the southern cotton belt. These challenges to American industrialization were met by the Republican party, which successfully crafted a political program that could both draw sufficient popular support to win elections and, at the same time, satisfy the market conditions for rapid economic development.

American industrialization was promoted by three broad developmental policies: the expansion of a largely unregulated national market, adherence to the international gold standard, and tariff protection for manufacturing and heavy industry. An unregulated national market enabled the consolidation of industrial production in what Alfred Chandler Jr. has called "the modern business enterprise," which became the distinctive American contribution to the industrialization of the world economy. The gold standard stabilized international exchange rates between the United States dollar and other foreign currencies — most important, the British pound. Stable exchange rates were almost a necessity for any rapidly developing nation because they encouraged the retention of domestic profits and made possible the importation of foreign capital. The protective tariff redistributed wealth from the agricultural to the industrial sectors of the economy, most important, from the export-oriented cotton belt of the South to the manufacturing and heavy industrial regions of the Northeast and the Great Lakes littoral. Taken together, these policies formed the backbone of the Republican program, enabling both the party's electoral success and meeting the necessary requirements for rapid development. Although Congress was not always accommodating, it was the central arena in which the Republicans worked out the mechanics of their program, converting the electoral popularity of the tariff and related policies into the bare minimum of political support for the gold standard and, to a lesser extent, a largely free national market.

The National Market

By striking down the attempts of state and local governments to regulate firms in other states, the Supreme Court was the branch of the national government most responsible for creating the intensely competitive national market that led to the development of the modern corporation. For example, the Court ruled in 1886 (*Wabash Railway v. Illinois*) that states could not regulate railroad rates for goods crossing state lines. Congress could have frustrated the enforcement of judicial doctrines by overturning decisions that constrained state and local regulation of the national market. However, with the exception of alcohol, which was made subject to the states' regulatory authority over interstate transportation, Congress never seriously challenged Court doctrine.

Congress also could have intervened in the national marketplace under the interstate commerce clause of the Constitution. Here Congress was more active, passing the Interstate Commerce Act of 1887 and the Sherman Antitrust Act of 1890. The former created the Interstate Commerce Commission (ICC), an independent federal agency with responsibility for the regulation of railroad rates and enforcing a prohibition on "pools" (organized collusion by competing railroad companies). The most important proponent of this legislation was Congressman John Reagan of Texas. When a Senate bill proposing a regulatory commission with a rather vague mandate came before the House in 1886, Reagan succeeded in substituting his own bill, which contained strict statutory prohibitions on pooling and rate discrimination against short-haul shippers. After the *Wabash* decision made state regulation of most railroad rates impossible, the Senate and House compromised, combining a commission with Reagan's statutory prohibitions.

The Sherman Antitrust Act declared illegal every "contract, combination in the form of trust or otherwise, or conspiracy, in restraint of trade," as well as all attempts "to monopolize . . . any part of the trade or commerce among the several states." It was drafted by Senator John Sherman of Ohio, former secretary of the Treasury and chair of the Senate Finance Committee. Enforcement was primarily the responsibility of the U.S. attorney general, who was empowered to initiate suits against those firms that engaged in monopolistic practices. However, as was also the case with the ICC, the federal judiciary retained the ultimate authority over whether firms would have to comply. The Supreme Court subsequently frustrated the original intent of Congress by seriously limiting the range of economic activity that the laws could regulate. In only one area — the extension of the Sherman Act to the activities of labor unions — did the Supreme Court aggressively extend federal jurisdiction. Of course, by restraining labor unions, the Court *enhanced* the ability of large industrial firms to reorganize their operations in response to competition. For the remainder of the nineteenth century, as the Supreme Court reduced the Interstate Commerce and Sherman Antitrust Acts to little more than wastepaper, an extremely "business friendly" Congress never responded in ways that might have repaired the damage. Years later, looking back on the halcyon years when his giant steel corporation ruled the American industrial economy, Andrew Carnegie remarked, "Nobody ever mentioned the Sherman Act to me, that I remember."

The construction of a national market, along with the continental size and wealth of the United States, allowed American industry to experiment with a wide variety of organizational forms to exploit its advantages of scale in production and distribution. The most important of these advantages came from the centralized processing of raw materials into finished products (e.g., in Carnegie's integrated iron and steel factories or the gathering and refining operations of John D. Rockefeller's Standard Oil Corporation). The modern corporation, with its many specialized divisions, became the most successful of these forms and came to dominate the American economy. Initially formed to coordinate the long-distance transportation of goods and rolling stock over the nation's railroads, the modern corporation spread throughout American industry and commerce after the Civil War. Intense competition in the national marketplace rapidly eliminated most firms that used less efficient modes of production and distribution. The surviving firms steadily reduced the costs of their raw materials, manufacturing operations, and distribution systems as they struggled to dominate their various sectors. Their resulting technological superiority and high productivity vastly increased the international competitiveness of American industry in the last half of the nineteenth century. Transformed from a largely agricultural nation into a major industrial power in the decades following the Civil War, the United States became one of the most advanced economies in the world by 1900.

The Gold Standard

Although Congress had consistently supported the resumption of the gold standard (which occurred in 1879), the national legislature was subsequently far less accommodating than it had been with respect to the construction of the national market. The gold standard fixed the value of one

American dollar equal to .0484 ounces of gold. Other major nations, such as Great Britain, also tied the value of their currency to gold. Together these nations thus created an international gold standard community with fixed exchange rates between the members. Great Britain was the leading financial center in this community, as well as the most important one commercially in the world. It played both roles for the United States, providing much of the capital for the construction of the nation's railroads, financing much of the debt of the state and federal governments, and trading manufactured products for American cotton and other agricultural commodities.

By fixing the American dollar in terms of gold, the United States in effect fixed the exchange rate between the American dollar and the British pound. Fixing the exchange rate, in turn, facilitated the extremely close integration of the London and New York capital markets. This integration expanded the supply of capital that funded American industrial expansion by increasing the confidence with which European investors could participate and the confidence with which American industrialists and financiers could reinvest profits in domestic operations. Then, as now, a developing nation's commitment to fixed exchange rates was a tangible promise to investors that the currency would not be devalued, with all the economic dislocations that would entail.

America's commitment to the gold standard was tangibly demonstrated by its ability to redeem, upon demand, every paper or silver dollar with the equivalent in gold. To do this, the day-to-day operations of the Treasury had to be managed with a discretionary judgment that Congress could not have exercised, so the administrative responsibility for maintaining gold payments became the duty of the executive branch, which also became the major defender of the gold standard.

During Reconstruction, many southern states were either outside the Union or represented in Congress by Republicans. As a result, Congress was relatively friendly to "hard money," as gold was often called, and granted the president broad legislative authority to control Treasury operations. Under this authority, the executive branch was able to maintain gold payments between 1879 and 1900, when industrialization became self-sustaining as a political project. In the intervening years Congress, particularly the Senate, became openly hostile to gold. This change was primarily caused by the return of southern Democrats to Congress, many of whom were inflationists, along with the admission into the Union of what became "soft money" states from the western plains and mountains. Led in the House of Representatives by Richard "Silver Dick" Bland, a plain-spoken Missouri farmer whose fervent commitment to the soft-money cause was far more impressive than his oratory, they fought to replace gold with silver as the nation's monetary standard for more than twenty years. Although the Senate Republicans under William Allison managed to curb the western demands for free silver, the Bland-Allison Act of 1878 still mandated Treasury purchases and the subsequent coinage of that silver into millions of silver dollars. The Sherman Silver Purchase Act of 1890 increased these mandatory purchases, again heading off even more threatening western demands. This congressional campaign almost brought about the abandonment of gold payments in the early 1890s when a financial crisis engendered one of the deepest depressions in American history. In the end, President Grover Cleveland was able to save the gold standard, thus preventing an exodus of investment from the United States that would have scuttled further industrial development.

The Tariff

Congress played the central institutional role in the protective tariff in the late nineteenth century. A tariff is essentially a tax on the imports of goods or commodities from foreign countries. It usually raises the domestic prices of those goods, regardless of whether they are manufactured or raised by domestic producers. For example, during this time the United States placed heavy duties on iron and steel imports. Since many of these imports were made in Great Britain, the tariff raised the price of these products in America. By protecting domestic producers from foreign competition, the tariff also raised the price of iron and steel made in the United States. However, the duties placed on products that the United States ordinarily exported had little or no impact on the prices that the American producers received because the international market determined their prices. For example, because the market for American cotton was heavily oriented toward international consumers, a tariff had no impact on its price.

At this time, most American imports were manufactured goods, and most exports took the form of agricultural commodities, particularly cotton, wheat, and meat. As a result, tariff protection could only raise the price of manufactured products and thus work to the advantage of industrial producers. For most American farmers, the tariff was simply irrelevant to the income they received for their harvests. However, farmers had to buy manufactured products (such as tools, clothing, and household furnishings) with the proceeds from their crops. Since the prices of those goods were artificially raised by tariff protection while the sale of their crops and livestock were set by market competition, tariff protection redistributed the wealth from agricultural producers to the industrial sector. Members of Congress aligned themselves accordingly, with Democratic representatives and senators from the southern cotton belt voting against almost all the Republicans and many of the Democrats from the northeastern and midwestern manufacturing region. Since industrial state delegations dominated Congress during the last quarter of the century, opponents of tariff protection were never very successful.

Almost all attempts at executive branch intervention failed, most notably President Cleveland's efforts to legislate a "free trade" reform of import duties in 1888 and 1893–1894. The one exception, proving the rule, came in 1897 when the Republican president William McKinley proposed and Congress enacted the highly protectionist Dingley Tariff. In fact, congressional Republicans had been holding hearings on a new tariff bill for months before McKinley's inauguration. When the new president called Congress into special session for that purpose, Nelson Dingley of Maine, chairman of the House Ways and Means Committee, promptly reported a revision to the full chamber, passing the bill only two weeks after the opening of the new legislative session. As a member of the House of Representatives, McKinley had been the principal architect of what became known as the McKinley Tariff in 1890. As a congressional veteran, he was well aware that executive branch intervention in assembling a new tariff schedule would not be appreciated, aside from public support for higher rates, and he stood aside as the House and the Senate worked their will.

The crafting of tariff legislation usually involved two very different types of deliberation. On the one hand, most of the detailed schedules on minor products and commodities were decided in a free-wheeling deliberative process in which individuals and small blocs of members bargained with one another in what were often classic examples of legislative log-rolling. On the other hand, tariff protection was also a complex system in which several major policies had to be centrally coordinated. As part of a policy system, the tariff combined protection for industrial manufacturing, wool growers, and producers of raw sugar. In political terms, the duties on iron and steel enlisted strong support from congressmen representing Pennsylvania, Ohio, and Illinois and thus provided the most important single bloc supporting the tariff. The most prominent spokesman for this bloc was probably Congressman William Kelley of Philadelphia, whose support for higher duties was so notorious that he earned the sobriquet "Pig Iron" during his fifteen terms of service between 1861 and 1890. The construction of a new tariff always began by reassuring iron and steel producers that their interests would be protected.

The most important nonindustrial tariff schedules protected raw wool and sugar. Unlike almost all other agricultural commodities grown in the United States, raw wool could be raised more cheaply abroad and, in the absence of duties, could be readily imported. Tariff protection was thus an effective means of raising the income of wool growers. Duties were imposed because almost all the northern and western farmers raised at least a few sheep. By extending trade protection in this way, the tariff gained many supporters in Congress from rural districts outside the South, and the sheer breadth of the sheep-raising interest in the United States led many observers to call the tariff on raw wool "the keystone in the arch of protection." However, duties on raw wool also raised the cost of the primary commodity used in the production of woolen goods. In order to make certain that woolen manufacturers were not damaged by foreign competition, compensating duties were placed on clothing and carpets made from wool. The wool schedules, in addition, had to be carefully calibrated so that consumers would not shift from woolens to cotton goods (as a potentially cheaper substitute). All of these considerations made the wool schedule one of the most complicated and contentious items in any revision of the tariff. Revenue needs were usually met by manipulating rates on the importation of sugar, since demand was fairly inelastic and consumption was relatively high. In most years, the sugar schedule was thus one of the primary revenue sources for the national government.

The Federal Budget and the Gold Standard

The tariff, along with internal excise taxes on alcohol and tobacco, was one of the revenue mainstays of the Treasury. Like most taxes, tariff revenue tended to oscillate with the business cycle of the domestic economy. When times were good, the nation imported more goods and revenue rose; when times were bad, demand for foreign goods fell and revenue declined. Government expenditures, however, tended to remain fairly constant from year to year. Both surpluses and deficits could threaten the Treasury's ability to keep the nation on the gold standard. Because a revenue surplus brought into the Treasury more money than was spent, an expanding economy tended to withdraw gold from the banking system, stockpiling the metal in Treasury vaults. This withdrawal made it more difficult for the nation's banks to maintain adequate reserves for their own currency issues (national banknotes). This difficulty, in turn, would lead banks to call in short-term loans, thus tightening the money market, raising interest rates, and, ultimately, restricting liquidity and lowering prices on capital markets for stocks and bonds. A deficit worked in the opposite direction, with the potential inability of the federal government to redeem its currency in gold (thus abandoning the gold standard).

By the 1880s, surpluses in the federal budget had become a serious threat to both the gold standard and the protective tariff. In response, the Republican party supported the expansion of federal pensions paid to

Union veterans from the Civil War. By making more veterans eligible and increasing the size of pensions, this expansion eliminated the budget surplus by spending it. The political impact was even more significant. The Grand Army of the Republic, composed of Union Civil War veterans and one of the largest private organizations in the nation, became the primary interest group pressing for more generous pensions. Because the Republican party supported both tariff protection and Union pensions, the GAR became a strong supporter of the tariff policy complex. Cynics commonly referred to the organization's initials as meaning "Generally All Republicans."

An Interlocking Relationship Between Developmental Policies

Although the tariff massively redistributed wealth from farmers in the South and West to industry in the northeastern and midwestern manufacturing belt, the primary impact on American industrialization was political. Simply put, tariff protection was easily the most popular developmental policy among American voters and, for that reason, members of Congress. The tariff policy complex thus became the policy backbone of most national and state Republican election campaigns, making all three developmental policies interlocking features of a Republican-led industrial program in which tariff protection politically subsidized both the gold standard and the national market. Congress became the most important site where the Republican party worked out this program, tinkering at the margins with tariff schedules, buying off opposition to the gold standard with purchases of silver bullion, and enacting federal regulatory policies that turned out to be dead letters. The "Senate Four" — Nelson Aldrich, William Allison, Orville Platt, and John Spooner — even centralized decisions in the otherwise individualistic Senate to push this program.

However, Congress was much more than a site where representatives and senators gathered to deliberate federal policy. As one of the three branches of the national government, it possessed an identity and repertoire of powers that channeled its choices in particular directions. In some ways, the Republican industrial program propelled Congress to center stage in the federal troika of the period.

With respect to the tariff, Congress almost completely dominated the policy process. When proposed revisions of the tariff were considered, congressional committees would entertain the opinions of interest groups, trade associations, labor organizations, and individual companies.

During congressional hearings in 1888–1889, for example, the American Window-Glass Manufacturing Association and the Collar and Shirt Manufacturers' Association presented briefs pleading for protection from the "pauper labor" of Europe. Receiving these petitions and other testimony, members of the House and Senate constructed the tariff from the bottom up, schedule by schedule, maximizing through log-rolled bargains the political benefits to be harvested from their decisions. From the Republican party's perspective, only a few central features of the tariff had to be placed beyond this otherwise decentralized process. Protected by party leaders, such as William McKinley and Nelson Dingley, both of them chairmen of the House Ways and Means Committee, the schedules placing duties on iron and steel, raw wool, and sugar were the pivots around which the rank and file, including significant numbers of Democrats, constructed the remainder of the tariff. With rare exceptions, presidents never intervened in these congressional deliberations; when they did, it was only to urge higher (McKinley in 1897) or lower (Cleveland in 1893–1894) duties. The Supreme Court was almost completely irrelevant to tariff policy.

The nation's major parties bitterly fought over the tariff throughout this period, with the Republicans supporting protection and the Democrats generally backing a modified form of free trade in which the tariff would be maintained solely for the purposes of raising revenue. However, the Republican tariff policy complex, by extending support for protection to sheep-raising farmers and Union veterans, was extremely popular throughout most of the North and West. In fact, the tariff was so popular there that many Democratic members of Congress, particularly from the Northeast, were almost as protectionist as Republicans. What kept the Democratic party as a whole from endorsing protection in elections was the overwhelming opposition of the South. The South had few Union veterans, fewer sheep, and, with a regional economy based on cotton and tobacco, was on the losing end of this redistribution of wealth. Since representatives and senators from the South usually made up most of the Democrats in Congress, the region could usually commit the party to lower duties in theory.

In practice, however, northern Democrats with protectionist proclivities tended to defect whenever the tariff was up for revision. The most important renegade was Samuel Randall of Pennsylvania, who served as Speaker of the House from 1876 to 1881. Because tariff protection was overwhelmingly popular in his industrial Philadelphia district, he was able to lead a band of similarly minded northeastern Democrats, who, out of all proportion to their number, were able to stymie legislative attempts to lower duties. Their defection halted tariff reform on several occasions when the Democrats controlled the House of Representatives and were thus in a position to initiate a revision of duties (e.g., 1878, 1884, and 1886). On the one occasion when the Democrats were able to enact a new set of schedules (the Wilson Tariff, in 1894), the revision was almost as protectionist as the Republican tariff that preceded it. When the Republicans dominated the national government, tariff revision usually went more smoothly (as in 1883, 1890, and 1897).

Deliberations on the tariff were both episodic and centered in the committee system, with the floor assuming an active amending role. Although the House of Representatives sometimes debated and passed bills (e.g., "popcorn bills" lowering or raising duties on one commodity) that everyone knew would not become law (e.g., in the waning days of the Fifty-fourth Congress, when the Republicans controlled both chambers but Cleveland was certain to veto higher duties), most deliberations were oriented toward an instrumental revision of the tariff schedules.

In terms of sheer energy and time devoted to legislative deliberations, the gold standard may have garnered almost as much attention from Congress as did the tariff. However, Congress deliberated very differently on monetary policy because the gold standard was politically unpopular with most voters. For most of this period, one or both chambers contained majorities hostile to the gold standard. Although the Treasury pegged the dollar to gold, Congress refused to confirm that practice as official policy. Instead, it asserted that the federal government was formally committed to bimetallism, a policy that would have pegged the dollar to both silver and gold simultaneously. Because the value of silver in terms of gold fluctuated (and vice versa), bimetallism was viewed by most observers as unworkable. In practice, if the United States had attempted to adopt a bimetallic monetary standard, the price of silver would have been pegged too high and, as a result, driven gold out of Treasury vaults. The result would have been to push the United States off gold and onto a silver standard.

When manifested in legislation such as the 1890 Sherman Silver Purchase Act, congressional bimetallism usually took the form of mandatory purchases of silver bullion by the Treasury. When the budget was running a sizable surplus, these purchases helped to return gold to the domestic economy and, in addition, operated as a commodity price stabilization program for silver. However, when the budget ran a deficit, these purchases of silver bullion threatened to force the United States to redeem paper money in silver instead of gold, effectively turning the silver accumulating in the Treasury into the nation's monetary medium. At that point, the United States would have been placed on a silver standard, thus destroying the basis for the fixed exchange rate between the American dollar and the British pound.

Whenever investors and financiers feared that budget deficits and silver purchases would compel the Treasury to abandon gold, American securities (stocks, corporate debt, and federal bonds) would be sold on the New York exchanges, the proceeds converted into gold, and the gold shipped abroad for safekeeping. This liquidation of American holdings dried up both foreign and domestic investment in the United States, throwing the nation into a deep recession. The most serious crisis occurred during 1893 when budget deficits induced by the Sherman Silver Purchase Act dramatically lowered the Treasury's gold reserve. President Cleveland then stepped in, replenishing the gold reserve by issuing federal bonds (syndicated by J. P. Morgan and August Belmont, the American agent for the Rothschild family). Because Congress had many years earlier provided legislative authority for these Treasury issues, Cleveland could sell these bonds without seeking new approval from Congress. Otherwise, there was little doubt that one or both chambers would have defeated legislation authorizing new bonds in order to maintain the gold reserve. However, these bond issues did not solve the chronic budget deficits, which were steadily undermining the credibility of the nation's commitment to the gold standard. Here Cleveland was compelled to seek congressional repeal of the Silver Purchase Act. Wielding presidential patronage as both carrot and stick, Cleveland was able to persuade just enough Democrats to support repeal, and the act was removed from the statute books in the autumn of 1893 after one of the most striking displays of presidential influence in American history. Left to its own devices, Congress would certainly have scuttled the gold standard by letting silver purchases absorb the Treasury's gold reserve.

Aside from these struggles over the purchase of silver bullion, Congress engaged in symbolic demonstrations against the gold standard. Many votes, for example, occurred on proposals to coin all the silver at the nation's mints into silver dollars. One of the more serious challenges arose in 1886 when Richard Bland, the chairman of the Committee on Coinage, Weights, and Measures, attempted to place a free silver coinage bill before the House of Representatives. His procedural motion easily drew the necessary two-thirds majority, but when the chamber voted on passage, his bill was narrowly defeated. Because presidents were uniformly committed to the gold standard during the late nineteenth century and consequently prepared to veto hostile legislation, most congressional votes during this period were symbolic since silver, however popular, rarely enjoyed a two-thirds majority in either chamber. Members of Congress from soft-money districts could thus vote for silver in full confidence that their positions would not bring down the gold standard.

Hard-money policy was unpopular in most of the nation because the gold standard caused the American dollar to increase steadily in value through deflation. Because the world's stock of gold was decreasing compared to the expanding economies of nations belonging to the gold community, the stock of money in each of the member nations was declining compared to the number of transactions in their respective markets. The result was a worldwide deflation, which was slightly worse in the United States than in the remainder of the gold community. As a result, the interest on long-term debts, such as mortgages and government bonds, became more onerous. Because the agrarian South and West were debtor regions, dependent on the importation of capital from the Northeast and foreign countries, the deflationary impact of the gold standard fell heavily on these areas, and Populists consequently blamed that impact for their economic distress.

Drawing most of its members from the more prosperous and developed regions of the Northeast and industrial Midwest, the vast majority of all Republicans supported the gold standard, opposed by an equally vast majority of Democrats from the South and West. In their effort to maintain gold payments, many of the Republicans used the popularity of the party's tariff policy to compensate for the unpopularity of "hard money."

Congress thus played three different roles in American industrialization. On the subject of tariff protection, Congress was the institution in which the Republicans designed the policy complex that gave them a significant electoral advantage over the Democrats. With its sizable commitments to specific agrarian sectors and military veterans, tariff protection was, in economic terms, a very inefficient way of subsidizing industrial expansion. However, because it forged the electoral backbone of the Republican party, it was even more valuable politically. Concerning the gold standard, Congress played the role of spoiler. Outnumbered in most sessions by soft-money Democrats and monetary renegades from the nation's agrarian periphery, gold Republicans fought to prevent the passage of legislation that would have irrevocably put the nation on silver. But this was a rearguard action in which congressional Republicans could only partially deflect attacks on the much more effective actions and policies of the executive branch. If Congress alone had been responsible for monetary policy, the United States would have abandoned gold long before the great crisis in 1893.

In terms of the national market, Congress played a different but equally important role. By refusing to challenge Supreme Court rulings that circumscribed state and local regulatory authority, Congress in effect legitimated a favorable judicial construction of the interstate commerce clause of the Constitution and a substantive due process reading of the Fourteenth Amendment (the latter prohibited any regulation that prevented a person or corporation from earning a reasonable return on capital). As one result of these rulings, Congress became the sole branch of government with regulatory authority over interstate commerce. However, it rarely exercised this power; even when it did, Congress passed vague legislation that managed to assuage an enraged popular opinion without imposing an effective regulatory framework. Whether this legislation was intended to be ineffective is not clear; however, when the courts emasculated these laws, Congress rarely complained. In all these ways, it was the developmental program of the Republican party that both shaped American industrial development and determined the most salient policy relationships between the great federal branches during the late nineteenth century. These relationships placed Congress in a clearly dominant role with respect to the tariff, a coequal position on the construction of the national market, and a clamorous but ultimately subordinate relation to the executive branch in monetary policy. Using Congress as a policymaking arena and coalition-building site in all three cases, the Republican party constructed a national political economy in which both rampant democracy and robust industrial power could coexist.

— RICHARD BENSEL

BIBLIOGRAPHICAL NOTES

Most of the scholarly literature on the rise of American industry can be divided into political or economic histories of the period. For a review of politics, see Paul Kleppner, *The Third Electoral System, 1853–1892: Parties, Voters, and Political Cultures* (Chapel Hill, N.C., 1979), and *Continuity and Change in Electoral Politics, 1893–1928* (Westport, Conn., 1987). On economics, the most important work is probably Alfred D. Chandler Jr., *The Visible Hand: The Managerial Revolution in American Business* (Cambridge, Mass., 1977). For monetary policy, the most thorough treatment is Milton Friedman and Anna Jacobson Schwartz, *A Monetary History of the United States, 1867–1960* (Princeton, N.J., 1971). For work on the political economy of the American state and party system, see Daniel P. Carpenter, *The Forging of Bureaucratic Autonomy: Reputations, Networks, and Policy Innovation in Executive Agencies, 1862–1928* (Princeton, N.J., 2001), and Elizabeth Sanders, *Roots of Reform: Farmers, Workers, and the American State, 1877–1917* (Chicago, 1999). For an elaboration on some of the themes of this essay, see Richard Bensel, *Yankee Leviathan: The Origins of Central State Authority in America, 1859–1877* (New York, 1990), and *The Political Economy of American Industrialization, 1877–1900* (New York, 2000).

Part III

THE COMMITTEE ERA

1910s–1960s

The United States Capitol, ca. 1905, with added wings and the Statue of Freedom atop the new dome.

IF THERE WAS EVER a period when Congress gained an unfavorable reputation, it was during the committee era. For many observers, this era showed why Congress was an inferior branch of the federal government. In the modern age of centralization and bureaucratic efficiency, Congress seemed to be a relic from an earlier century, a decentralized body in which authority was scattered among committee chairs and where policymaking took a long time. One scholar called it an "oxcart in the age of the atom."[1] These characteristics seemed especially noticeable when viewed against the aura of the modern presidency: Theodore Roosevelt, Woodrow Wilson, Franklin Roosevelt, Dwight Eisenhower, John Kennedy, and Lyndon Johnson captivated public attention as citizens came to think of presidents as the embodiment of government. This was not the case with Congress; there, elderly legislators representing sparsely populated rural areas held inordinate power in a century that many Americans felt was characterized by youth, industry, and cities. Congress favored complex, jerry-built compromises that frustrated ideologues on both the left and right.

The committee era involved more than the power of committee chairmen. It was defined by a complex procedural framework that dictated the character of representative government. There were several pillars to the committee process. At the electoral level, states preserved outdated district lines that favored rural constituencies and failed to reflect the growth of urban and suburban populations. Senators were elected directly by voters and were thus far less beholden to the organized party machines that ran the state legislatures. To finance campaigns, representatives and senators depended on a handful of prominent families, corporations, and unions to make large contributions. Legislators depended increasingly on these sources as the cost of elections rose steadily due to the cost of radio and television advertising. As parties with strong ties to the electorate weakened, moreover, politicians turned to interest groups to deliver blocks of voters.

The system worked effectively for those who gained office. During the committee era, the length of incumbency in the House and Senate reached historically high levels. In this context, elected officials started to perceive their positions as careers. Promotions within each chamber were granted on the basis of seniority. Rules and norms strongly discouraged younger members from challenging their elders.

Party caucuses rarely purged members from a committee for party disloyalty or incompetence. The weak Democratic and Republican caucuses barely met, avoided taking strong policy positions, and shied away from imposing demands on members. The most influential party leaders in these decades, such as Speaker of the House Sam Rayburn (D-Texas) and Senate Majority Leader Lyndon Baines Johnson (D-Texas), were successful because they worked closely with their committee chairs, not around them.

It was a highly secretive time. Access to information was restricted to committee chairs and a few select senior members. The public rarely had a chance to see Congress in action, with the exception of a few high-profile hearings, and even trained experts had trouble finding information about Capitol Hill. When the campaign finance expert Herbert Alexander went to the Clerk of the House to collect information about campaign contributions in the 1950s, he was ushered into a small dark room littered with incomplete records; he was not allowed to bring a typewriter with him to record information. Legislative negotiations were dominated by policy communities that were composed of committee chairs, representatives from the executive branch and agencies, powerful interest groups and their lobbyists, and policy experts. When new actors wanted to enter this stage, they usually did so through interest groups rather than the parties.

In this relatively insular world, committee chairs did not have much to fear from the national media. Only a few reporters, such as Drew Pearson, continued the muckraking tradition. By and large, however, the mainstream media (still dominated by newspapers) were respectful of Congress as an institution, even when calling for reform. Often reporters were openly favorable when discussing the House and Senate or, on some occasions, actually assisted legislators. Reporters usually kept quiet about legislators' private lives. They did not write about congressmen who appeared drunk on the floor or who were known for making sexual advances to female reporters.

The emergence of the committee process was woven into numerous political movements at the turn of the century that sought to reconstruct America's government institutions: voting process reform, the expansion of the executive branch's bureaucracies and commissions, and the direct election of senators, among others. They all attempted to wrestle power away from entrenched elites and promote a new policy agenda as the role of strong parties in Congress waned.

The committee process did not instantly fall into place but took time to establish itself. Even after the historic revolt against Speaker of the House Joseph Cannon (R-Illinois) in 1909 and 1910, a climactic moment in the establishment of the committee process, party caucuses remained extremely influential. President Woodrow Wilson worked closely with congressional Democrats to push through bold expansions of the federal government, including the creation of the Federal Trade Commission and the Federal Reserve. Yet by the time of the New Deal, the committee process defined Congress.

Southern Democrats and the committee process came to be seen as inseparable toward the end of the New Deal. To be sure, there were Northerners, such as New York's Emanuel Celler, who thrived on committee politics. But they were few and far between. Southerners claimed the greatest rewards from the committee process since they tended to remain in office for longer periods of time due to the lack of competition in their elections. Southerners also constituted a disproportionate percentage of the Democratic party. After the Democrats regained control of Congress in 1933 (and held it for most of the next sixty years), Southerners ascended to the most important chairmanships.

Starting around 1937, the committee process became a significant source of political tension for liberals. President Franklin D. Roosevelt took the unusual step of campaigning against five conservative Democrats in the 1938 election. He even went so far as to attack Senator Walter George (D-Georgia) directly during a speech in his district. Roosevelt's efforts failed, however. He was able to unseat only one Democratic conservative from New York, Representative John O'Connor. Moreover, the Republicans made large gains in the 1938 elections. Conservative Democrats replaced liberals and moderates in several southern districts. After the elections, tensions flared between the southern chairs and northern Democrats. Southerners were not opposed to the expansion of the federal government. Indeed, they had strong incentives to do so throughout the twentieth century because rural and agricultural areas were the major beneficiaries of programs in the 1930s and 1940s. Southerners also benefited from the expansion of the Cold War military-industrial complex when large amounts of defense spending poured into their region.

While southern Democrats were a diverse lot, however, they generally agreed on two pivotal issues: opposition to both unionization and federal civil rights policies for African Americans. As northern Democrats began to champion these matters in the 1940s, liberals discovered that the committee process could be a major obstacle. Besides the procedural power of conservative chairmen, a conservative coalition of southern Democrats and Republicans formed a potent voting block. Southern senators also relied on filibusters to kill legislation that escaped from the committees.

The pressures that Congress faced during this era were tremendous, for America was changing rapidly. In the first part of the century, national corporations came to dominate an economy that had been characterized by decentralized small businesses. The corporate structure produced enormous tensions on the shop floor, causing workers to organize through unions. The nation's social fabric underwent further changes with the influx of southern and eastern European immigrants. Most of the newcomers flocked to the booming cities. For the first time, the U.S. census of 1920 showed that more Americans were living in urban areas than in the countryside. Even electoral politics were transformed. The initiative and referendum and other reform measures diminished the electoral influence of parties. Women mobilized to expand the reach of the federal government into areas concerning families and the right to vote, which they obtained in 1919. Meanwhile, white Southerners, assisted by their senators and representatives, continued to deny African Americans their right to vote. The rest of the committee era was filled with equally dramatic social, cultural, and economic developments: the advent of television, the movement of African Americans to northern cities, the reconstruction of gender roles, and unprecedented economic growth, to name a few.

Although the committee process was slow, Congress passed some of the most expansive federal programs in American history between the 1910s and 1960s. The growth of the federal government started in the progressive era, when multiple interests concluded that a larger federal role was needed to regulate the national economy and to mediate social tensions. World War I pushed the government to embrace new challenges, such as creating the War Industries Board to coordinate wartime production. Amid the economic crisis of the New Deal in the 1930s, the government tackled a host of problems, from the failures of the banking system to the financial crisis of farmers.

The growth of the federal government did not abate in World War II. In many respects, the crisis of war allowed it to grow in ways that would have been impossible in peacetime. During the war, the government initiated a mass income tax through which the Treasury Department withheld money directly from the paychecks of wage earners and regulated the prices and distribution of consumer goods. A decade later, Congress poured funds into scientific research, highway construction, and civil defense — all in the name of the Cold War. The 1960s offered another burst of government activity. Almost ninety years after the end of Reconstruction, Congress passed the Civil Rights and Voting Rights Acts of 1964 and 1965. Under the banner of President Lyndon Johnson's Great Society, Congress even attempted to alleviate long-intractable problems such as poverty, environmental desecration, health care, and urban decay.

The government also expanded its international role in this period. Progressive Era activism, imperialism, corporate economic interests, and white racism converged when officials extended the nation's reach into Latin America and parts of Asia. During World War I, elected officials hesitantly shed their isolationist traditions to participate in a brutal war between the world's major nation-states. During World War II and the Cold War, the American government mobilized vast resources and manpower to combat fascism and communism. The Cold War simultaneously brought the nation into covert warfare and overt Third World conflicts when the United States, the Soviet Union, and China fought through their proxies. The most notorious example is Vietnam.

As the federal government grew in size and strength, so too did the executive branch. Some observers believe that this period was dominated by "the Imperial Presidency." Many presidents boasted about this power. Theodore Roosevelt recalled how he had fostered a revolution in Panama so that it would allow the United States to build and control the Panama Canal, proclaiming: "I took the Canal Zone and let Congress debate!" In many ways, Congress delegated authority to the executive branch, especially in the area of warfare. Yet Congress did not lay down its arms. In the creation of domestic and international programs, committee chairs retained a tight grip over the evolution of the modern state. The appropriations committees, for example, never relinquished their authority over military spending. Legislators such as Senator J. William Fulbright (D-Arkansas), moreover, influenced the agenda through congressional hearings, investigations into the military and executive branch, and conversations with the media.

Just as the growth of presidential power had its limits, so too did the expansion of the federal government. Legislators adhered to the principles of federalism, usually granting state and local governments a large role in the implementation and funding of programs. Since most politicians were highly sensitive to how Americans hated taxation, Congress allocated meager financial resources for most programs (with the exception of those that used special taxes to overcome this dilemma). Certain programs never received sufficient political support to pass Congress. From the time of the New Deal, national health insurance became a contentious item. Although Congress never passed health insurance for all Americans, it did pass a comprehensive program for the elderly and the nation's poor.

The move toward internationalism in foreign policy was also uneven. Even at the height of the Cold War, legislators such as Senator Robert Taft (R-Ohio) used the power of the purse to constrain the size of the military and to impose barriers on the nation's international obligations.

Americans' hostility toward Congress greatly intensified in the 1960s, as did their frustration with all government institutions. Liberals denounced Congress for being too timid in its support for the Great Society and for allowing Presidents Kennedy, Johnson, and Nixon to prosecute the Vietnam War. At the same time, conservatives attacked Congress for being inefficient, spendthrift, and corrupt. Middle-class public interest reformers lambasted Congress for failing to represent the average American citizen and for stifling authentic democracy. Although the Watergate scandal centered on the presidency, there was a strong belief among reformers that Congress could only regain its stature by dismantling the committee process.

There are two perspectives through which observers understand the relationship between Congress and the expansion of the federal government in the twentieth century. One argues that the government grew in spite of Congress. In this view, Congress was a conservative force that blocked progressive ideas. Liberal presidents and social movements had to circumvent legislators who, depending on one's perspective, either favored conservative elite interests or represented a broader conservatism among Americans. The second perspective posits that Congress helped to expand government in a nation that was historically uneasy with federal power. America was created through a revolution against central authority; consequently the political culture harbored a deep tradition of antistatism and isolationism. This second perspective depicts the committee process as an intricate mechanism that made difficult compromises possible. The New Deal was the most dramatic example of legislative initiative and productivity. With all the frustrations that the committee process generated, these scholars say, its incremental nature enabled legislators to craft politically viable programs.

Regardless of their point of view, most agree that by the early 1970s a new congressional era was on the horizon. During the first four years of the decade, Congress adopted procedures that the parties could use against committee chairs. After the 1974 elections, the "Watergate babies" deposed four powerful committee chairmen, weakened the procedural autonomy of committee chairs, and reformed the filibuster process to make it easier to end debate. Congress also passed reforms that promised to strengthen the legislative branch, in terms of budget and warmaking power, in relation to the president. For many people who worked in Washington, D.C., this moment constituted a sea change in the House and Senate. While congressional committees did not vanish, the committee process was no longer dominant.

NOTE

1. George Galloway to Senator Robert La Follette and Representative Mike Monroney, 14 November 1945, Records of the Joint Committee on the Reorganization of Congress, National Archives, RG 128, Box 321, File: 37.

19

The Transformation of the Congressional Experience

IN THE DECADES following Reconstruction the U.S. Congress, led by the Republican party, turned from the South and toward the West to consider the political and economic development of the land between the Mississippi and the Pacific coast republics. Making these territories into states and binding them to the East with railroads allowed the creation of national industries. These mighty combines prospered by extracting the wealth of the earth that the farms of the western prairies and the forests and mines of the mountains produced in such plenty. Under the Republicans, Congress adopted tariffs and other subsidies favoring the extractive, manufacturing, and transportation industries that profited from the new continental national economy. The resulting concentration of riches in the hands of a few efficient entrepreneurs created a new class of men whose influence over electoral politics concerned other Americans.

At the same time, the creation of those western states brought into Congress a new class of legislators whose constituencies — farmers annoyed by falling commodity prices in the new, efficient economy, migrants displaced by an industrial and urban society — did not care for the Republican policies supporting the interests of concentrated capital. By bringing the West into the Union, the Republicans supported a national economy that soon became the envy of the globe; they also bought themselves several decades' worth of political trouble.

The uncooperative politics of those new states provoked Republican congressional leaders into tightening their grip on the legislature. House Speakers Thomas Brackett Reed (R-Maine) and Joseph Cannon (R-Illinois) both wore the epithet "czar" in their time. The Senate leader Nelson Aldrich (R-Rhode Island) ran a "gang" of pro-business Republicans who rigorously controlled the legislative agenda. Their regimes proved hard but brittle under pressure, broken by innovations designed to destroy their partisan power — and that shaped the congressional experience for decades to follow. The Congress that emerged from the rubble of its czars featured professional and systematic organization: hierarchical committees favoring seniority rather than personality and elections run by rules meant to keep money away from campaigns. These structural reforms allowed the legislature to contain the sectional turmoil that emerged in the late nineteenth century.

Lawmakers arriving on Capitol Hill for the Forty-seventh Congress in 1881 came to a more nearly normal legislature than their predecessors had known for two decades because the North and South had at long last reached a truce. The Civil War triumphalism that so favored Republican representation and diminished Democratic power had worn away as the memory of Democratic secession faded. White Democrats pursuing policies of black disfranchisement made the South a solid Democratic bloc. Competitive government returned: in the Forty-sixth Congress the Democrats ran the Senate and the House, and in the Forty-seventh the Republicans had both; afterward divided government prevailed, with Republican Senates and Democratic Houses. The black faces that represented Reconstruction's electoral effects largely vanished along with the brief commitment to enforce voting rights. The coming legislative agenda would not feature Reconstruction legislation to keep Ku Kluxers and other southern terrorists in check. Even the monetary controversy that flourished during the war-begotten inflation fell idle for a time: legislation in the 1870s that fixed the greenback supply and resumed specie payments combined with a business boom to keep the currency issue, hardy perennial though it was, momentarily dormant. So ordinary did the political circumstances appear that the Forty-seventh Congress turned, with some degree of seriousness for the first time since the Civil War, to the tariff schedule.

But these ordinary conditions would not last. Though the Reconstruction-era chance to build a strong Republican party in the South on the disfranchisement of traitors and the enfranchisement of freedmen dimmed every day, the possibility of assembling a new base of Republican loyalty in the West looked altogether brighter and begot a new sectional controversy. Homesteaders following the railroad boom, employers and employees alike in extractive industry, stood to benefit from the Republican-sponsored subsidies. And during boom times they did. But with economic hardship, the Westerners proved less amenable to Republican wrangling than expected, and the consequent unruliness of later Congresses spawned the iron rules of Reed and Cannon — reigns of personal shrewdness that foundered on their own rigidity and yielded a more professional Congress almost by accident.

The Congress that emerged from these battles proved in the long term less susceptible to personal domination and more rule-abiding in its hierarchy and membership. Committees blandly ruled in chambers where czars had once walked. But in the short term the waging of partisan warfare with truly blunt instruments — the adding and subtracting of constituencies, the thwarting and rewriting of electoral law — characterized the legislature, and the danger of these double-edged swords made itself felt in both chambers and on both sides of the aisle.

The Politics of Admission and the Politics of Development

While the continent remained undeveloped, the admission of new states presented a sore temptation to leaders seeking to affect the congressional balance swiftly. In 1881 a swath of prairie territories separated the eastern states from the western. California, Oregon, and Nevada occupied a distant eminence — and among them Nevada stood out as the peculiar result of a wartime adventure, an invention urgently assembled in 1864 to provide a margin of safety in passing the Thirteenth Amendment and reelecting Abraham Lincoln, and whose official population dwindled rapidly after statehood. The Dakota and Indian Territories, Montana, Washington, Idaho, Wyoming, Utah, New Mexico, and Arizona retained territorial status and remained under the control of national politicians. By admitting these territories as states, the Republicans traded a useful training ground and lucrative patronage network for a herd of unruly congressmen whose tendency to rebel against the pro-business GOP policy would require a firmer hand in the leadership.

From the point of view of the party masters, the admission of a new state — and with it the addition of a couple of Senate votes, a House seat, and three electoral college votes — had to outweigh the temptation of preserving territorial status, and with it, the network of patronage that had served the parties so well as a proving ground. Even if a new state stayed loyal to the party that created it — scarcely a certainty, as it turned out — its local politics would inevitably affect patronage and reduce its reliability to the national party. To borrow Howard Lamar's terms of analysis, the politics of admission vied with the politics of development in the partisan interest.

The politics of territorial development served the Republicans particularly well in bringing loyal partisans up through the ranks so long as the GOP held the reins of the patronage system, and the new federal legislators in the late nineteenth century had often cut their teeth in territorial office. The territorial councils, post offices, judicial benches, and governors' offices provided temporary homes for politicians who often would not even serve out their terms before moving on to other employment. For new states like Colorado and Wyoming, between half and three-quarters of the first congressmen had served in federally appointed or approved territorial offices.

Not until the 1884 elections put a Democrat in the White House to supplement a Democratic majority in the House did the Republicans feel real pressure to admit some of the territories as states to improve their electoral chances. After the 1888 elections returned Republicans to power, an omnibus bill to admit two Dakotas, Washington, and Montana as states passed the lame-duck Congress, followed in the next year by bills for Idaho and Wyoming.

But just as in the era of slavery — when the admission of midwestern states destroyed the carefully brokered sectional compromise — playing politics with statehood backfired. Rather than line up loyally in the Republican column, the new western states hosted third-party insurrections — silver revolts and People's parties — disturbing the congressional balance yet further. It turned out that when the national party withdrew the hand of patronage from the reins of government, local interests — particularly those of farmers chafing at the power of eastern mortgage holders and railroad owners — took hold. So unsettling did this lesson prove that the admission of New Mexico and Arizona was postponed because Republican leaders suspected those western states might likewise support one faction or another. (Senator Albert Beveridge [R-Indiana], a progressive, worried that New Mexico would support the conservative Republicans; other Republicans feared it might support the Democrats. Some politicians also worried that the territories were too Hispanic. In the end New Mexico and Arizona often went Democratic once admitted, and New Mexico sometimes sent Latino legislators to Washington.)

Yet the movement westward continued, partly under the pressure of entrepreneurs who sought clear title and secure holdings to their valuable properties in the new West. As the Republicans supported this westward progress of business, it too begot unintended consequences.

"Boodle Is Become an Indispensable Factor"

Congressmen from the new western states had often spent time in the mining or timber business or the banks that backed them. This business background naturally affected their opinions on the tariff and currency policies then in place; it also gave evidence of the ever-closer connection between corporations of national scope and national politics. Through this conduit flowed opinions and a vast quantity of money.

Money had long lubricated the congressional candidate's passage to Washington, and as partisan competition tightened in the 1880s, its judicious expenditure grew more important. At first it was an ordinary business expense and did not cost a great deal; one vote-buyer was known only as "Two-Dollar" Dudley. In southern districts, money had an indirect effect on voting (the direct effect was achieved through violence and intimidation), and there the price of a Democratic victory might amount merely to the cost of shotguns. Although historians have disagreed over the extent of the corruption, Mark Wahlgren Summers notes that both parties deployed it as they believed necessary. "Satan must be fought with his own weapons sometimes," one Republican newspaper piously remarked.[1]

The revolt of the new western states in the 1890s raised the stakes and also the prices of buying elections. Fixers like Mark Hanna sensed the concern of steel-, oil-, coal-, and timbermen and lined them up behind corporation-friendly candidates like William McKinley. No quid pro quo could be proven, though it was widely known that Congressman McKinley (R-Ohio), as chair of the Ways and Means Committee, had lent his name to the most protectionist tariff legislation in history. Indignant investigations early in the twentieth century showed corporations and their chief officers had given somewhere between one- and three-quarters of the war chests of Republican and Democratic National Committees since 1896. More corporate money went to Republicans, whose national policies tended to favor industry, but often for local or strategic reasons it was useful for businessmen to favor Democrats.

Support for campaign finance reform grew in reaction to this corruption. Though both parties took contributions from wealthy men, the Republicans had won more elections thereby, so campaign finance reform did not enjoy substantial GOP backing. One of its earliest supporters, Senator William E. Chandler (R-New Hampshire), had long opposed the influence of railroad corporations on the politics of his state. But his career proved the danger of taking such a position in a Republican state: the railroad used its free passes and retainers to run him out of office in 1900. Private citizen Chandler then crossed party lines and enlisted Senator Benjamin R. "Pitchfork Ben" Tillman (D-South Carolina) to sponsor a law banning corporate campaign contributions in the Fifty-ninth Congress. The *Washington Post* reported that "it is impossible to make a case against the . . . bill on any other grounds than that boodle is become an indispensable factor in our elections." The Republican Congress adjourned without bothering to make such a case explicit, though after the elections the Tillman Act passed in 1907.[2]

The Democratic House and Republican Senate of the Sixty-second Congress responded to further sentiment against financial corruption by producing campaign finance legislation in 1911 that was designed to hamper both parties. The Democrats had to allow disclosure laws for primary as well as general elections — in the solidly Democratic South, the primary was the decisive election — and the Republicans had to concede ceilings on spending and individual contributions.

Whatever the intent of the reforms, they did not halt the change in campaign style that had begun with the influx of new money. In the 1880s and 1890s, the parties began to use the new media and means of communication to centralize political campaigns, to focus them on the particular candidate rather than the party ticket, and to induce the voter to make a private decision based on available information. As Michael McGerr writes, "[E]ducation replaced marching"[3] as the means of electioneering. Borrowing from national advertising campaigns, politicians used publicity stunts, with demonstrations and slogans, to fuel the use of cameras and press coverage. And although old-time day marchers might have wanted two dollars or a flask of rum apiece, campaigns of education cost even more. Advertisements had to be placed in the press. Wax cylinders of speeches needed recording and distribution. Paid operatives in celluloid collars writing copy in national bureaus had to gin up and place publicity.

The packaging and marketing of candidates not only cost money, it changed the character of politics. The parties no longer enlisted the citizen as a soldier in a partisan army; instead they wooed the voter in private, offering blandishments as they would to a discriminating consumer, seeking to persuade him — or, increasingly, her. As McGerr notes, the shift in style occurred simultaneously with the greater involvement of women in partisan politics, as they gained the franchise in those same new states of the West that continued to provide surprises for the political establishment.

Full woman suffrage crept slowly from one state to the next, beginning with Wyoming in 1890 and spreading to its neighbors Colorado, Utah, and Idaho by 1896. Western states, as pioneer polities with proportionally few women residents, had much to gain and little to lose by extending the suffrage. Enfranchised women could help native-born Americans outvote the heavily male immigrant populations. Politically active women, who might identify themselves as consumers, were also supposed to support reforms limiting the power of corporations.

Though fourteen years would pass before more states offered the full franchise to female citizens, women's voting nevertheless became common throughout the nation, especially west of the Mississippi. At the turn of the century, women had a partial franchise and could vote on school, municipal, taxation, or bond issues in twenty-eight states and territories.[4] Congress quietly filled with men — some of them heads of important committees, like Senator George Shoup (R-Idaho), chairman of Education and Labor; Senator Weldon Heyburn (R-Idaho), chairman of Manufactures; Representative James Belford (R-Colorado), chairman of Expenditures; and Senator Clarence Don Clark (R-Wyoming), chairman of Railroads — responsible to constituencies that included enfranchised women. On the eve of the Nineteenth Amendment's passage, only eight of the forty-eight states had no woman suffrage of any kind. As Robert Max Jackson writes, men came slowly and steadily to support woman suffrage over time, mainly because "experiments with woman suffrage showed ordinary men that women voting had little impact on people's personal lives, just as they showed politicians that they need not fear practical political costs."[5]

Maybe not immediately; but over time, McGerr suggests, the shift toward a money-driven, educational method of campaigning for office, correlated with the development of politics-as-consumerism, weakened the ordinary citizen's link to his or her congressman. Bringing the western states into the union begot all these unforeseen consequences, generating reactive changes in national politics. The parties scrambled to control increasingly varied and far-flung constituencies, becoming remote, national entities that directed policy struggles from commanding heights. The organization of Congress reflected this change.

The Emergence of Rational Rules

When the Forty-seventh Congress took up the tariff schedule, it did something new: it authorized the appointment of an expert commission to give advice on revision. The experts turned out to be just as partisan as the congressmen — they were staunch protectionists to a man — but this example of accumulating outside expertise marked a new era in legislation. Along with the contemporaneous establishment of the standing Rules Committee, the appointing of commissions indicated an increasing professionalism in congressional behavior.

As Morton Keller notes, the Congresses of the 1880s and 1890s undertook "a gradual but steady regularizing of congressional procedure."[6] The committee system inaugurated in the early nineteenth century underwent a modern overhaul. All bills and reports now went through the clerk of the House to the floor. The new standing Committee on Rules, established in 1880, became the hub of the House, determining how bills could reach the floor and who would be heard and when. The Senate adopted a similar, though informal, centralization of leadership in the post of party caucus chairman. To a degree, these innovations simply continued the ongoing trend of what Nelson Polsby calls "institutionalization."[7] Yet though this process of professionalization can be shown to have been a long time coming, it reached a crisis in the early twentieth century with the revolt against the office of the Speaker as it had evolved to that time. And both the increasing power of the Speaker and the insurgency against him resulted from the effort to wrangle the West into line.

Through the nineteenth and early twentieth centuries, the proportion of new legislators in each Congress diminished, reaching a gradual rate of decline in the 1910s and 1920s, when the ratio sank slowly from 20 toward 10 percent. Seniority eventually displaced favoritism in determining stature, setting a rule for appointing the heads of committees. Speakers of the House tended more and more to be career congressmen who had served for decades. Whereas Henry Clay (W-Kentucky) had become Speaker in 1811 after eight months in the House and went in and out of the Congress at the lure of appointive office, Joseph Cannon (R-Illinois) served as a congressman almost continuously from 1873 to 1903 before becoming Speaker — and when his Speakership ended in 1911, he returned as a congressman till the end of his political career in 1923. The office of representative, once envisioned as a republican duty for the Cincinnati of the commonwealth, was becoming a profession.

The Senate lagged the House in this process of becoming professional, but by 1900 it too had begun to acquire a streamlined polish. Increasingly under the control of the career senators Nelson Aldrich (R-Rhode Island) and his allies William Allison (R-Iowa), Orville Platt (R-Connecticut), and John Coit Spooner (R-Wisconsin), the Republican Senate directed fiscal and monetary policy through the floor leadership. In both chambers, the men who implemented these changes had their eyes on the untrustworthy West.

Congressman Thomas Reed (R-Maine), the frank cynic who was the first to define a statesman as "a successful politician who is dead" and whose friend Senator Henry Cabot Lodge (R-Massachusetts) eulogized him as "a good hater [who] detested shams, humbugs, and pretence above everything else," looked an unlikely man to lead a pious party and nation.[8] In the new era of consumer politics, he ultimately proved too honest and original to be properly packaged for national sale, and his presidential ambitions fell before the blandly smiling and dutifully platitudinous William McKinley. Yet it was Reed's brusque insistence that politics was a contest for power, and a contest he intended his party to win, that made him a successful Speaker in the 1890s.

Reed first became Speaker at the start of the Fifty-first Congress, in 1889, succeeding John G. Carlisle (D-Kentucky), who had held the chair since 1883. Reed knew all the ways even a small number of congressmen could stop a bill in its tracks, and he proposed now to wield House rules to abolish them. Chief among the offending techniques was the "disappearing quorum." Congressmen physically present in the chamber might refuse to answer a roll call and would thus not be counted in determining whether a quorum existed. A sufficient minority could thus block the passage of legislation. Reed simply counted everyone present, whether they answered the call or not. Aghast Democrats fulminated, spewing expostulations like that of Richard Bland (D-Missouri): "I denounce you as the worst tyrant that ever ruled over a deliberative body." The new rule stood, and soon other measures shoring up the power of the majority followed. The spirit of the Reed rules was summed up in a single sentence: "No dilatory motion shall be entertained by the Speaker."[9]

In time, Democrats would accept these rules, and the new system would give the House an efficient air that the Senate could only strive to match: the Senate rules continued to allow endless debate until the adoption of a cloture rule in 1917 — and even that measure proved largely ineffective. But in the short run the Reed rules made trouble for the Republicans who hoped to benefit by them. Historians of organizational processes emphasize that Reed's Speakership came in an era when the sheer scale and scope of American life demanded some centralization. But in Reed's mind — as the political scientist Eric Schickler has recently reemphasized — the particular conditions of 1889 were more pressing than long-term trends. The Republicans held only twenty-seven more seats than the Democrats. And, with the tariff and the currency looming as important issues once more, William Robinson notes, "sectional differences were likely to assume serious proportions." Reed wanted to prevent the possibility of obstructionism.[10]

The proximate issue for Reed was less one of rationalization than one of power, as he would cheerfully have admitted. When the Republicans gained control of the House in 1888 and took back the presidency from Grover Cleveland, it was by the slimmest of margins — Benjamin Harrison had in fact lost the popular vote, though he won the electoral college. The Republicans had mortgaged themselves to the hilt for this whisker-thin win, promising currency reform to Westerners complaining of deflation and protectionist positions to every conceivable constituency. Reed's party needed all the advantages it could get.

The rules provided enough of an edge for that session, but only just — and their cost proved dear indeed. Operating under Reed's rules in 1890, Republicans drafted the protectionist McKinley Tariff while keeping inflationist measures favored by western farmers and silver miners off the House floor. But the representation of the western states in the Senate was such that the McKinley Tariff could only pass in exchange for some measure that would devalue the currency and relieve Westerners beset by low commodity prices. As a result, Reed had to put through the Sherman

Silver Purchase Act. The combined effect was economically disastrous and suggested a downside to rigidly efficient legislative rule. Under the new tariff, imports fell, and so did federal income. The Silver Act forced the Treasury to use gold to buy silver. When the nation descended into the economic doldrums, gold leached from the Treasury at an alarming rate, creating a panic by 1893.

Western settlers, aided and comforted by eastern investment during boom times, keenly felt the sudden withdrawal of capital. The ire of Westerners at the corporate East sent the new states, which were supposed to have helped the Republicans, into revolt in the depression of the early 1890s. Four new states — Idaho, Nevada, Colorado, and North Dakota — cast electoral votes for the Populist party in 1892. Thirteen Populists came into the next Congress. The presidency, the House, and the Senate all went to the Democrats, along with much of the traditionally Republican Midwest. With the states west of the Appalachians holding the balance of power in Congress, their concerns — rapid urban development, the consolidation and industrial changes in agriculture, the effects of immigration and global trade — came to the fore.

The Worries of the West

The farmers of the West and South "had the incentive and provided the muscle" for the reformist agenda in Congress at the turn of the century, Elizabeth Sanders argues.[11] The strongest support for regulatory reform came from those regions where the farmers keenly felt the political and economic pressure from the increasing importance of the cities. If, as the economic historians Susan Previant Lee and Peter Passell write, "farmers are always unhappy," they are surely especially unhappy when their federal legislature appears increasingly controlled by a party leadership in league with the banks, railroads, manufacturers, and other urban interests that farmers regard as their natural enemies.[12] As scholars have long emphasized, these particularly unhappy farmers sought partners to support them in seeking to overthrow the reign of pro-business, conservative Republicans. Progressive reform depended on some amalgam of farmers and laborers, farmers and urban immigrants, or farmers and self-identified consumers. In the end, various combinations of these groups stood behind the reforms that sapped the strength of congressional leaders.

The most profound structural reform in Congress at this time came in 1913 with the ratification of the Seventeenth Amendment, providing for the direct election of senators instead of the original constitutional method of appointment by state legislatures. Like woman suffrage and a number of other reform measures, the new procedures for naming senators had been a long time coming and in the end happened because state governments — principally in the West — adopted it before Congress did.

First proposed in 1826, an amendment providing for the direct election of senators passed the House in 1893, 1894, 1898, 1900, and 1902. The reasoning was simple: with more money in politics, Senate seats were too easily bought by big corporations, so farmers obsessed with the undue power of railroads and banks supported it. Opponents of direct election, like George Frisbie Hoar (R-Massachusetts), snarled that it would give control of the Senate seats to the "great cities and masses of population" — and so it would too, at least in those states that had such cities, which was why urban, immigrant, and ethnic-fueled machines tended also to support it.[13]

The Senate remained unmoved. Aldrich, Allison, Platt, and Spooner responded to the disruptions of the 1890s (when six Republican senators adopted the party label of "Silver Republicans") by tightening their control on the leadership, creating what Schickler calls an "interlocking directorate" of caucus, party, and committee leaders. It was reinforced by Aldrich's cozy relations with the interlocking directorates of the private sector: Aldrich "made his position as a powerful influence on the campaign-contribution habits of corporations clear to his fellow Republican senators."[14] Under such leadership, senators would scarcely consider changing the rules of their election.

Denied recourse at the federal level, reformers sought change through the states. And by 1912 twenty-nine states had adopted some measure — such as a referendum deemed binding on the state legislature — to effect the popular election of senators. In 1912 the new Congress approved the measure that would become the Seventeenth Amendment. The anti-business farmers and urban dwellers had combined their incentive and muscle on a major democratizing reform.

But it was a fragile alliance. For much of the first decade of the century, only the personality of Theodore Roosevelt — a Manhattanite as well as a Dakota rancher — held together urban and western interests within the Republican party. Roosevelt could simultaneously accept enormous campaign contributions from J. P. Morgan and major corporations while advocating reforms that would regulate those corporations. Morgan told Congress, "[G]ratitude [for these contributions] has been rather scarce in my experience."[15] Roosevelt swept to election in 1904 trailing clouds of glory, winning a solid band of northeastern, midwestern, and western states. Accompanying him was a Congress more solidly Republican than any since Reconstruction, whose majority of 114 seats almost quadrupled that of the previous term. But the triumph was largely illusory: the Republicans in Congress, like the Republican in the White House, were sectionally divided themselves.

Straddling the party's divisions was Reed's successor as Speaker and rules-maker, Joseph Cannon of Illinois. Like Reed, he had a talent for the memorable phrase and for controlling the House — both lay behind his aphorism that "this House could pass an elephant if it chose." Cannon had served like Reed on the Rules Committee, and he followed in the same tradition of running the House in his party's interest. Like Reed, Cannon manipulated committee appointments to ensure that Republicans who were orthodox fiscal conservatives controlled tariff and appropriations legislation. And again like Reed, Cannon's rule created the appearance of Republican cohesion. As Cannon said in wounded retrospect, there was not much new in his approach to the Speakership: "I have tried, but failed, to find the difference between Cannonism and Carlisleism, or Reedism, or Crispism, or Hendersonism, or the 'ism' of any other Speaker who has presided during the long years I have been a member."[16] And he was right: he was simply another in a line of Speakers whose efforts to wield power contributed to the modernization of Congress. But he had the misfortune to serve at the particular moment when progressive Republicans, led by western insurgents, were preparing to split from their party.

The crisis came in mid-March 1910, when the western Republicans — who supported corporate regulation and electoral reform far more vigorously than their eastern peers — were prepared to vote with the Democratic minority to upset the parliamentary rigidity of the prevailing Speakership. Encouraged by a skirmish in which the Speaker allowed that a resolution privileged by the Constitution could come to the floor without vetting by the appropriate committees, George Norris (R-Nebraska) put a resolution to change the composition of the Committee on Rules so that "the speaker should not be a member of the committee on rules."[17]

Thereupon began two days of argument that started with the question of whether Norris's resolution could be heard and moved into the question of why Norris — a Republican — would seek to unhorse the Speaker — also a Republican — and why, as it increasingly appeared, so many of the party would ally themselves with Norris and against their leader. As the parade of speakers traipsed into and out of the well of the Congress, it became increasingly clear that none of them could quite say what an American political party really stood for — or whether it stood for anything at all.

Jacob Fassett (R–New York) took the floor in a flush of party loyalty to claim the soul of Norris and every other Republican contemplating disloyalty: "Every man who is a man, and not a jellyfish, is a partisan. We were all elected by partisans because we were partisans. A man ought to have opinions and convictions. He ought not to be a political chocolate éclair." Fassett warmed to his theme: there were great Republican principles that bound the party together and transcended petty squabbles over what resolutions could be heard and when. He rounded on the Democrats to declare that even Norris and his friends "are not for what your platform declares for. They do not believe in your follies of cheap money, of fiat money, or free trade. They believe in Republican principles; they are here after being nominated on a Republican platform, and they see the light in accordance with the intelligence God has given them to see the light."[18]

In the end Fassett proved first wrong, then right. Forty-two insurgents voted to adopt Norris's resolution — but only nine of them afterward voted to declare the Speakership vacant. Cannon thus retained the Speakership, though stripped of his power to determine rules. Cannon sourly remarked that "if anything else was accomplished by the revolution I do not remember."[19]

Yet the insurgency proved important. Not only did it portend the Republican vulnerability to splitting, which Roosevelt (running as a Progressive for president against his Republican successor, William Howard Taft) and the Democrats exploited at the polls in 1912, it changed congressional practice. As Polsby, Gallaher, and Rundquist note, the weakening of Cannon marked the beginning of a shift from a congressional system in which "seniority figured as a criterion" in the Speaker's discretionary organization of committees to "a full-blown seniority *system*."[20] The overthrow of the iron speakers devolved decision-making to the committees. As the leaders' interests and whims diminished in influence, the role of procedure and custom increased in importance.

The Senate changed its habits, too, though without the theatrics of the House. When the Democrats took over the upper chamber after the election of 1912, their conference chairman, John Worth Kern (D-Indiana), adopted a system meant to serve the legislative program of the Democratic president, Woodrow Wilson. A flurry of measures dear to western populists and progressives passed under the Democratic regime: the lower tariff and the income tax, the Federal Reserve Act, and regulatory legislation including the Clayton Antitrust Act and the Federal Trade Commission Act. These laws largely placated the Westerners, who were already benefiting from two decades of inflation and thus had decreasing reason to protest in the 1910s.

The Democratic Senate of the early Wilson years acted equally and opposite to the Republican Senate under the Aldrich gang, ignoring the custom of seniority and pushing through legislation favored by the party leadership. Benefiting from wartime controversies, however, the Republicans recaptured the Senate in 1918 and the presidency in 1920, whereupon the new Senate majority conference chairman, Henry Cabot Lodge (R-Massachusetts), reorganized the chamber's committee structure so that it strengthened procedure at the expense of personal leadership.

Thus by the 1920s both houses of Congress had moved away from the centralized leadership whose rigidity had generated turbulence at the turn of the century. A committee system coupled with a seniority system dominated the legislative branch, inaugurating an era of stable but slow and uninspiring lawmaking. The giants who once bestrode Capitol Hill had been felled, their places yielded to crowds of committee chairmen, each supreme in his own fief.

The decades after Reconstruction saw a scramble for partisan advantage based on the need to control an electorally satisfactory sectional spread. The admission of western states meant to augment the Republican majority created a chaos of corruption, rebellion, and reaction that produced centralized party regimes and revolts against them. But once Congress had assimilated the riches and tamed the rebels of the West, there were no more dangerous territorial weapons to wield in political battle, and the matter of congressional disputes turned technical once more, as befitted a more professional body of lawmakers, now intent on attaining power through correct procedure.

— Eric Rauchway

BIBLIOGRAPHICAL NOTES

On sectional tensions and shifting congressional coalitions, see Richard Franklin Bensel, *Sectionalism and American Political Development, 1880–1980* (Madison, Wisc., 1984); Elizabeth Sanders, *Roots of Reform: Farmers, Workers, and the American State, 1877–1917* (Chicago, 1999); Eric Schickler, *Disjointed Pluralism: Institutional Innovation and the Development of the U.S. Congress* (Princeton, N.J., 2001). On the territorial system, Howard R. Lamar, *The Far Southwest, 1846–1912: A Territorial History* (New Haven, Conn., 1966); Jack Ericson Eblen, *The First and Second United States Empires: Governors and Territorial Government, 1784–1912* (Pittsburgh, 1968). On the control of Congress, Sarah A. Binder, *Minority Rights, Majority Rule: Partisanship and the Development of Congress* (Cambridge, U.K., 1997). On House leaders, L. White Busbey and Katherine Graves Busbey, *Uncle Joe Cannon: The Story of a Pioneer American* (New York, 1927); William A. Robinson, *Thomas B. Reed, Parliamentarian* (New York, 1930); Roger H. Davidson, Susan Webb Hammond, and Raymond W. Smock, eds., *Masters of the House* (Boulder, Colo., 1998). On the organization of Congress, Nelson W. Polsby, "The Institutionalization of the House of Representatives," *American Political Science Review* 62 (March 1968): 144–68; Nelson W. Polsby, Miriam

Gallaher, and Barry Spencer Rundquist, "The Growth of the Seniority System in the U.S. House of Representatives," *American Political Science Review* 63 (September 1969): 787–807; Morton Keller, *Affairs of State: Public Life in Late Nineteenth Century America* (Cambridge, Mass., 1977). On corruption, Mark Wahlgren Summers, *The Era of Good Stealings* (New York, 1993); also Peter H. Argersinger, "New Perspectives on Election Fraud in the Gilded Age," *Political Science Quarterly* 100 (Winter 1985–86): 669–87. On political style, Michael E. McGerr, *The Decline of Popular Politics: The American North, 1865–1928* (New York, 1986). On the franchise, Alexander Keyssar, *The Right to Vote: The Contested History of Democracy in the United States* (New York, 2000).

NOTES

1. Mark Wahlgren Summers, "Party Games: The Art of Stealing Elections in the Late-Nineteenth-Century United States," *Journal of American History* 88 (September 2001): 433.
2. Robert E. Mutch, *Campaigns, Congress, and Courts: The Making of Federal Campaign Finance Law* (New York, 1988), 6.
3. Michael McGerr, "Political Style and Women's Power, 1830–1930," *Journal of American History* 77 (December 1990): 869.
4. Alexander Keyssar, *The Right to Vote: The Contested History of Democracy in the United States* (New York, 2000), tables A17–20, pp. 387–89.
5. Robert Max Jackson, *Destined for Equality: The Inevitable Rise of Women's Status* (Cambridge, Mass., 1998), 40.
6. Morton Keller, *Affairs of State: Public Life in Late Nineteenth Century America* (Cambridge, Mass., 1977), 300–302.
7. Nelson W. Polsby, "The Institutionalization of the House of Representatives," *American Political Science Review* 62 (March 1968): 144–68; Nelson W. Polsby, Miriam Gallaher, and Barry Spencer Rundquist, "The Growth of the Seniority System in the U.S. House of Representatives," *American Political Science Review* 63 (September 1969): 787–807.
8. Henry Cabot Lodge, *The Democracy of the Constitution and Other Addresses and Essays* (New York, 1966), 191, 200.
9. William A. Robinson, *Thomas B. Reed, Parliamentarian* (New York, 1930), 224.
10. Ibid., 220.
11. Elizabeth Sanders, *Roots of Reform: Farmers, Workers, and the American State, 1877–1917* (Chicago, 1999), 164.
12. Susan Previant Lee and Peter Passell, *A New Economic View of American History* (New York, 1979), 301.
13. Charles Austin Beard, *Contemporary American History, 1877–1913* (New York, 1914), 291–92.
14. Eric Schickler, *Disjointed Pluralism: Institutional Innovation and the Development of the U.S. Congress* (Princeton, N.J., 2001), 56–57.
15. Jean Strouse, *Morgan: American Financier* (New York, 1999), 536.

16. L. White Busbey and Katherine Graves Busbey, *Uncle Joe Cannon: The Story of a Pioneer American* (New York, 1927), 247.

17. George W. Norris, *Fighting Liberal: The Autobiography of George W. Norris* (New York, 1945), 115.

18. *Congressional Record,* 62nd Cong., 45:3, p. 3302.

19. Busbey and Busbey, *Uncle Joe Cannon,* 268–69.

20. Polsby, Gallaher, and Rundquist, "Growth of Seniority," 791, 807.

Nelson Aldrich

November 6, 1841–April 16, 1915

Nelson Aldrich

Nelson Wilmarth Aldrich was the archetype of a successful self-made man in the Gilded Age. From a meteoric rise through the business world of Providence, Rhode Island, and in thirty years of service in the Senate, Aldrich and his powerful Republican bloc championed business interests through several presidential administrations. So effective was Aldrich in forwarding the conservative agenda that, even after his retirement, Democratic reformers sought to distance their Federal Reserve Act (1913) from the senator, although much of its groundbreaking legislation was derived from a plan he had presented in 1911.

Born in Foster, Rhode Island, a descendant of the Puritan clergyman Roger Williams, the young Aldrich came of age during the difficult period when the farming and seafaring culture of New England gave way to the mechanical and mercantile ways of the industrial revolution. Educated in the local schools, by the age of seventeen Aldrich was hard at work as a clerk in a Providence grocery firm. After serving briefly in the 10th Rhode Island Volunteers in 1862, he became a junior partner of the firm in 1866. That same year he married Abby Chapman, who had inherited family money, but Aldrich was determined to make it on his own. The couple had eleven children together; their daughter Abby would, years later, marry John D. Rockefeller, making Aldrich the grandfather of Nelson, David, and Winthrop Rockefeller.

Aldrich's achievements compounded like interest. He became a city councilman in 1869, a partner of the wholesale grocery firm in 1872, a member of the state's General Assembly in 1875, the legislature's speaker the following year, president of the First National Bank in Providence in 1877, and a congressman in 1878. Aldrich was elected to two terms in the House before being appointed to the Senate to fill the seat of General Ambrose Burnside, who died in September 1881.

In his five Senate terms, Aldrich was a zealous advocate of industry, especially the interests of East Coast manufacturers. Suspicious of most federal attempts to regulate business, he opposed the Interstate Commerce Act (1887) and, throughout the following decade, was a champion of protective tariffs. When those tariffs did not serve business interests, however, he reversed course and worked, for example, to lower import duties on the raw materials needed for manufacturing or to spur international trade. These tariff manipulations, as well as his close relationships with corporate leaders, drew some criticism. Today, charges of impropriety would hound any senator who borrowed investment capital from an industry magnate whose interests had been served by recent legislation. But in the business-driven culture of the 1890s, with both houses under the thumb of the Republicans, Aldrich did just that in order to acquire a Rhode Island railway. He also profited handsomely from investments in other utilities and commodities like oil, sugar, and rubber.

Even the fiery Theodore Roosevelt, whose presidential administration (1901–1909) aggressively pursued policies to regulate business and curb trusts, was wary of Aldrich's power. "I'm just a president, and he has seen a lot of presidents," said Roosevelt. But changes in the Senate membership, along with Aldrich's dismissive treatment of the progressive politicians in his own party, cracked the Republicans' power hold. Aldrich remained a capable legislator, but because the millionaire financier embodied the conservative Old Guard, his effectiveness diminished. Almost seventy years old, he declined to run for reelection in 1910. He spent his last few years in politics, trying to pass legislation that would create a National Reserve Association, banks that would allow the currency supply to grow or shrink according to economic needs. With the Democrats in control of Congress and the White House, any "Aldrich Plan" would probably have been blackballed. The Federal Reserve Act, although it could be considered his stepchild, may actually have benefited from his public criticism. The following year, a few days after a reconciliatory meeting with Roosevelt arranged by Cornelius Vanderbilt, Aldrich died in New York.

References

Steffens, J. L. 1931. *The Autobiography of Lincoln Steffens.* P. 506.

Williams, P. G. 2000, February. "Aldrich, Nelson Wilmarth." *American National Biography Online.* Retrieved June 30, 2003, from http://www.anb.org/articles/05/05-00008.html.

20

Economic Regulation in the Progressive Era

CONGRESS IN THE PROGRESSIVE ERA created the foundations of the modern regulatory state. To expose corporate wrongdoing and prepare the way for legislation at a time when bureaucracy was still rudimentary, the legislature conducted thorough investigations of modern industrial and financial structures and conditions. Legislatively, it provided for the effective public control of corporate competitive practices, transportation and marketing networks, food and drug safety, labor-management relations, banking, currency, farm credit, warehouses, and commodity exchanges. It also established, if only temporarily, a trade policy based on the principle of minimal tariffs rather than industrial protection and created the income tax as a fairer way to finance government than taxing consumption through the tariff.

In the late nineteenth century, Congress had laid the cornerstones of a framework for the regulation of the modern industrial economy. At that time, it was the center of national policymaking. By the first decade of the twentieth century, however, the president, who had scarcely been visible in congressional debates on the Interstate Commerce Act of 1887 and the Sherman Act of 1890, began to play a major role. Still, most of the details of railroad, shipping, antitrust, labor, futures trading, warehouse, and banking regulation laws were fought out in Congress, party caucuses, committees, and on the floor; and most of the new pSrogressive-era legislation had clear roots in the agrarian radicalism of the late nineteenth century.

The Progressive era was, then, both the end of the era of congressional dominance of national government and a transitional period. The agrarian animus against corporations still inspired regulatory politics. But the expanding role of the president — as the unifier of a sectionally diverse national party coalition and the spokesman for a national reform impulse that now reached beyond farmers into the urban middle classes and the intelligentsia — brought a significant and permanent change to the legislative process. Henceforth, important legislative proposals would increasingly originate with the president and the bureaucracy, and those origins would bring new statutory forms. Rather than embody precise lists of prohibited actions and penalties that could be invoked in court by the victims of corporate abuse, regulatory laws would increasingly rely on vague mandates (like "promotion of fair competition") that left major discretion to presidentially appointed bureaucrats who would determine the meaning, targets, and enforcement methods of the law. The more the bureaucracy grew, the more executive branch officials participated in the design and implementation of laws; and the more active the president became, the more likely regulation was to take an ambiguous bureaucratic form. In the first two decades of the twentieth century, then, one sees the beginning of developments that would come to full flower in the New Deal.

The Congressional Origins of Progressive Reform: The Tariff and the Cannon Revolt

Scholars usually date the progressive era from presidential events — for example, Theodore Roosevelt's revival of the Sherman Act (blocking the Northern Securities railroad merger) in 1902 or his consumer-pleasing mediation of a coal strike in the same year. The Pure Food and Drugs Act of 1906, conceived and promoted by an official in one of the largest and oldest federal agencies, the Department of Agriculture, is another candidate for harbinger. So, too, is the first significant railroad rate reform law of the twentieth century, the 1906 Hepburn Act, which Roosevelt initiated and got passed with a bipartisan, agrarian-led coalition in Congress. These actions did signal a budding sensitivity of elected officials to the popular anxiety about business behavior. But the events that would split the Republican party and unleash the surge of legislative creativity that we know as the national progressive reform era began in Congress in 1908–1909. The victory of the bipartisan reform legions in the famous "Cannon Revolt" gave progressive reform a powerful new momentum, enabling its advocates to surmount the formidable institutional obstacles maintained by the conservative "stand-patters" to whom Roosevelt had, of necessity, shown great deference.

The major economic regulatory function of the federal government, after the maintenance of the gold standard, was the tariff. Positions on protection constituted the major axis dividing the two parties, and the construction of the tariff, with its hundreds of product schedules, was preeminently a congressional function. The Democratic party, centered in the agricultural South, had always advocated a minimal "tariff for revenue only" (not, that is, for protection from import competition). But in the first decade of the twentieth century, opposition to high protective tariffs grew significantly in other regions as well.

As if taking its cue from William McKinley's presidential victory in 1896 and the historically high rates of the Republicans' 1897 Dingley Tariff Act, an unprecedented six-year merger wave created the giant "trusts" that became household names: American Tobacco, Quaker Oats, International Harvester, Eastman Kodak, U.S. Steel, to name a few. Soon, over a hundred industrial fields were dominated by a single company. Whether coincidental or not, the rising cost of living between 1900 and 1910 was attributed by many to the elephantine trusts and the high tariff walls that protected these corporate giants from foreign competition. Northern workers, traditionally so easily seduced by the Republican promise of industrial prosperity through the tariff, began to have second thoughts when the trusts set out to crush the labor movement. By this point, another key advantage of the tariff for Northerners — its funding of the generous Civil War pension system — was also waning as veterans died off; the growing ranks of immigrant workers were, of course, ineligible for those pensions, as were former Confederates.

The stage was set, then, for a revolt against high tariffs. Outside the South, the proponents of tariff reduction were most numerous in the Midwest. Agricultural producers there drew little or no benefit from the tariff, and workers were quite aware both of the corporate assault on unions and the rising prices of consumer goods. In Wisconsin, Iowa, and Minnesota, new reform governors — Robert M. La Follette, Albert B. Cummins, and John A. Johnson — took office early in the decade, after campaigns condemning monopoly and high tariffs. These states would later send pioneering insurgent Republicans to the Senate. Meanwhile, representatives from midwestern farm districts — men like George W. Norris, Edmund H. Madison, and Victor Murdock — carried the fight against northeastern railroads, banks, and industrialists to the House of Representatives, where they enlarged the ranks of Democratic agrarians with similar goals. The Republican dissidents were particular favorites of "muck-raking" newspapers and the new middle-class-oriented "uplift" magazines that stimulated and publicized the reform movement in the first two decades of the twentieth century.

The rising clamor against the tariff compelled the Republican party to run in 1908 on a platform committed to tariff revision, and President William Howard Taft called a special session of Congress early in 1909 to redeem the pledge. But the first order of business in the House, which under the Constitution must initiate tariff legislation, was to adopt a body of procedural rules. On this question the midwestern and other Republican dissidents were champing at the bit to reform House operations. They had been punished by the autocratic Speaker of the House, Joseph Cannon of Illinois, for their lack of party regularity, and they knew that the reforms they had promised their constituents would not be possible without some restructuring of the ironclad rule of the Speaker and his conservative allies.

Cannon had inherited a body of House rules streamlined for partisan efficiency in 1890 under his Republican predecessor, Thomas Reed. As Speaker, Cannon exploited the "Reed Rules" to maximum effect, using his control over the scheduling and the substance of legislation reaching the floor to forestall reform proposals by the Democratic minority and Republican dissidents. (The Speaker made all committee assignments, chaired the powerful Rules Committee, and recognized people from the floor who wanted to speak or make motions.) Cannon's closest allies included Sereno Payne of New York, who chaired the Ways and Means Committee, John Dalzell of Pennsylvania, and (before he was swept away by the reform tide in his own district) James Tawney of Minnesota.

Cannon and his "stand-pat" organization raised the visibility and power of the House of Representatives. President Roosevelt, who had often ignored the previous Speaker, found it prudent to consult with Cannon several times a week, and the House emerged from the shadow of the Senate when Cannon established a routine collaboration with the powerful Senate leader, Nelson Aldrich of Rhode Island, and his controlling faction. As equal obstructors, the two conservatives worked to defeat or weaken many important reform bills.

At the end of the Sixtieth Congress, the reformers had been able to extract one modest decentralizing rule for House procedure: the designation of one day a week ("Calendar Wednesday") on which committees would be called in alphabetical order to bring their proposals to the floor without having to go through the Speaker and Rules Committee for scheduling. The new (Sixty-first) Congress, convened in March 1909 to deal with the tariff, contained a larger House Democratic minority and a more rambunctious crop of about two dozen Republican dissidents, many of whom had made opposition to "Cannonism" part of their election campaigns. The Speaker was thus compelled to yield a few additional modifications in the House's procedure: a provision strengthening Calendar Wednesday, the creation of a "consent calendar" for minor, noncontroversial bills (which could also be brought to the floor without going through the Speaker), and permission for the minority party to offer a recommittal motion encapsulating its objections or alternatives before the vote on final passage of a bill. Cannon was able to thwart further decentralizing rules changes by making bargains with a group of Tammany (New York City) and southern Democrats. However, the degeneration of tariff "revision" into another round of protectionist increases in the 1909 Payne-Aldrich Act brought forth another burst of outraged reform once the tariff was signed into law.

Under the guidance of Sereno Payne, the House acknowledged the popular clamor by passing a tariff bill containing some modest downward revisions. In the Senate, however, tariff revision was fatally sabotaged, as House conservatives no doubt expected. Nelson Aldrich, a millionaire son-in-law of John D. Rockefeller and a brilliant elite tactician, presided over the Finance Committee in the upper chamber. The committee proposed over eight hundred revisions to the House (Payne) bill; the vast majority were increases in the product rates. With President Taft's collusion, Aldrich and the stand-pat Republican conservatives also headed off an attempt by dissident Republicans and southern Democrats to add a personal income tax proposal to the bill.

Reminding their colleagues that in 1895 the Supreme Court had struck down an income tax law on individuals as unconstitutional, the Senate conservatives offered to substitute a tax on corporate income. Intended as a temporary stratagem to block the personal income tax, the corporate tax would, in effect, be paid by consumers nationwide rather than wealthy individuals, as with the personal income tax. Such was the sentiment for a personal income tax, however, that the conservatives were compelled to agree to the separate passage of a constitutional amendment legitimating the tax in order to avoid a filibuster of the tariff bill. They no doubt hoped that the amendment would not survive the state ratification process. (To their great disappointment, it did.)

The Senate oligarchs met an energetic opposition from the midwestern Republican reformers. This group was led by Robert La Follette of Wisconsin, the very epitome of the angry young insurgent, together with the older, highly respected Jonathan Dolliver of Iowa, a recent convert to his region's reform movement. La Follette and Dolliver were joined in the tariff fight by the intense and determined Joseph Bristow of Kansas, Albert Cummins of Iowa (like La Follette, a reform governor before being elected to the Senate), Moses Clapp and Knute Nelson of Minnesota, Coe Crawford of South Dakota, and Albert Beveridge of Indiana. William Borah of Idaho, though locked into Republican protectionism by his state's desire for substantial tariffs on its mining and cattle products, nevertheless played a leading role (with Cummins) in pressing for an income tax. The Democratic cosponsor was Joseph Bailey of Texas. Respected for his legal brilliance, Bailey was on the conservative side of his state's political spectrum, but he usually sided with reformers in the national legislature.

When neither tariff reduction nor an income tax was included in the

Senate's tariff bill, outraged reformers and a critical press turned to the president and conference committee for remediation. But Cannon stacked the House conference contingent with protectionists who backed most Senate revisions, and President Taft was too late and light-handed with his pressure on the conservatives to salvage any significant reduction. To wide public condemnation, the protectionist Payne-Aldrich tariff was signed into law in early August 1909. A few days later, the Speaker announced his committee assignments; not surprisingly, the insurgents had lost their chairmanships and their preferred assignments.

The following January, the president and Speaker let it be known that the insurgents would receive no financial help in their 1910 campaigns (in fact, conservatives were urging their defeat in Republican party primaries), and only party "regulars" could expect to share in administration patronage.

A Republican leadership less averse to reform might have avoided or at least mitigated the two momentous events that followed. In the spring of 1910, a coalition of insurgent Republicans (most from the Midwest) and Democrats (most from the South) succeeded in overthrowing the Cannon rules in the House, and an electoral rebellion produced big Republican losses in November.

The rules fight that punctuated the Cannon revolt took place in March. The insurgent Republicans were ably led by Representative George Norris of Nebraska, whose motto was, "I'd rather be right than regular." The Nebraskan would shortly go on to the Senate and serve for thirty years as a respected Progressive reformer. Norris's principal comrades-in-arms in the rules fight were Victor Murdock and Edmund Madison of Kansas, John M. Nelson and Irvine Lenroot of Wisconsin, Charles Lindbergh of Minnesota, and Miles Poindexter of eastern Washington. All but Nelson represented agricultural districts. The Democratic collaboration was organized by Champ Clark of Missouri and Oscar Underwood of Alabama. On the critical votes, around 30–40 Republicans joined a highly unified bloc of 145–60 Democrats in support of the decentralizing revolution in House rules.

The reformers stripped the Speaker of his seat on the Rules Committee, which was expanded from five to ten members and made elective. A few months later a discharge rule was adopted, allowing individual members to file a motion to discharge a committee of a bill in its purview. A particular day of the week was designated for the consideration of such motions, which would succeed in bringing a bill to the floor if a majority of the membership so voted. After the Republicans used the new rule to invoke frequent time-consuming roll calls in order to delay other business, the discharge motion was hedged with some restrictions in the

Sixty-second Congress. The reformers' goal in creating the procedure was, and remained, to allow popular legislation to reach the floor over the opposition of committee or party leaders.

When they took over the House in 1911, the Democrats continued to disperse power. They removed another major prerogative that the Speaker had held since the early 1790s: the ability to appoint members of standing committees. This power was now handed to a party collective, the Democratic contingent on the Ways and Means Committee. These members were themselves elected by the Democratic caucus (with consideration given to their progressive tendencies). The chair of the Ways and Means Committee was elected by the caucus to serve as the party's floor leader, a post previously appointed by the Speaker.

Though supporters of progressive reform in and outside Congress celebrated the overthrow of centralized party government under an autocratic Speaker, the Cannon revolt neither ended party dominance of the legislative process nor, in the long run, furthered democratic reform. Parties were strong, and their caucus decisions shaped policy positions through the remainder of the progressive era (1911–1916). The newly constituted Rules Committee still contained no progressive Republicans (none were selected by the Republican caucus for its contingent on the committee). The new independence of the Rules Committee, the subsequent growth of the powers of standing committees at the expense of the party caucus, and the use of a seniority system guaranteeing continued committee membership and eventual rise to chairmanship for the most electorally successful members eventually produced its own pathologies — granting virtual control over the legislative process to a group of congressmen from uncompetitive districts who might be seriously out of step with their party majorities. But in the progressive era, those developments were still decades away.

Party and Institutional Relations after 1910

As the Republican party splintered, the Democrats grew in numbers and unity. Thanks to public disgust with Republican stand-patters, voters shifted their allegiance to the Democratic party or to progressive Republicans in the 1910 elections. The ranks of Cannon and Aldrich supporters were hit hard; their opponents were highly successful. The Senate's Republican Progressives grew in number with the addition of Asle Gronna of North Dakota, John Works of California, and former representative Miles Poindexter of Washington, along with 9 new Democrats. The Sixty-first House had opened in 1909 with 172 Democrats and 219 Republicans; the Sixty-second in 1911 had 228 Democrats, 161 Republicans, and 1 Socialist.

The victorious House Democrats, back in the majority for the first time since 1894, set out to demonstrate to the country that they represented a united progressive force. Though their leader, the homespun Missouri Progressive Champ Clark, inherited a diminished Speakership, the party caucus held together impressively under the able guidance of Oscar Underwood of Alabama, the new Democratic majority leader.

Meeting behind closed doors to debate and hammer out policy decisions, and then (on a two-thirds vote) binding members to support the measure, the Democrats passed bill after bill in compliance with their Progressive 1908 platform. Many bills died in the Republican Senate, and a few succumbed to Taft vetoes. Still, the Sixty-second Congress created a Department of Labor, passed bills allowing postal workers to join unions and requiring the eight-hour day on government contract work, outlawed phosphorus matches (their manufacture was dangerous to workers' health), and overcame the reservations of some southern Democrats to create a Children's Bureau to investigate the conditions of child labor. It also passed a constitutional amendment for the direct election of senators. Like the income tax amendment passed in the previous Congress, the direct election amendment would achieve the necessary state ratifications by early 1913.

Despite the obstacles of divided government, the Democrats won public favor with their procedural reforms, progressive leadership, unity of purpose, and efforts to pass tariff and labor legislation. Their success in the 1912 elections was also greatly aided by the continued split in Republican ranks. A three-way presidential race (four-way, if one counts the Socialists, now at the peak of their strength) handed Woodrow Wilson a majority in the electoral college. A plethora of Progressive party and Socialist candidates for Congress landed the Democrats in the majority of both House and Senate. The next four years of united Democratic government produced a remarkable outpouring of legislation designed to decentralize wealth and power and address the accumulated economic and social problems of a half century of laissez-faire industrialization.

The first item on the agenda in 1913 was, of course, the tariff. While low tariffs were the defining Democratic issue, there had always been struggles within the party, most recently in the Payne-Aldrich debates. It would be a challenge to herd those representing lumber, hides, sugar, wool, textiles, and other manufacturing districts along the path to tariff reduction; and it was all the more difficult now that the 1910–1912 elections had brought into the party more than eighty new Democrats from the Northeast, urban Midwest, and Pacific coast. But in addition to a strong caucus organization — caucus binding was instituted by Senate Democrats in 1913, following the example of the House Democratic caucus revival in

1911 — the Democrats now had another institution to whip them together: the president.

The President and Congress

While Theodore Roosevelt may be considered the first modern president, his legislative role remained underdeveloped. His contributions to progressivism and to the expansion of presidential influence relied on the exploitation of the prerogative powers in Article II of the Constitution, particularly the executive power and the commander-in-chief power. There was little novelty in Roosevelt's use of legislative powers, and, in fact, not much significant legislation was passed during his two terms. Pressure on Congress to pass the landmark Pure Food and Drugs Act was orchestrated not by the president, but by an entrepreneurial bureaucrat in the Department of Agriculture, Dr. Harvey Wiley.

Though Roosevelt attempted to assuage growing agrarian discontent in 1905 by calling for a law giving the Interstate Commerce Commission the power to set maximum reasonable railroad rates, he merely threw his support to a limited bill constructed by midwestern Republicans in the House. The struggle to get a bill through the Senate was managed by southern Democrats and soon-to-be-insurgent Republicans, with little direct presidential involvement. His successor, Taft, was more active (in a conservative direction), having his attorney general prepare a new railroad bill in consultation with railroad spokesmen. But the insurgent Democratic coalition, feeling their oats in 1910, reconstructed the bill on the floor into a tough regulatory system that was a landmark of progressive legislation. During the Payne-Aldrich tariff process the year before, Taft had plaintively whimpered from the sidelines as his party sacrificed its future to protectionism.

Woodrow Wilson had a much more dynamic view of the presidency. A professor of government before he went into politics, he greatly admired both the British parliamentary system and — despite the personal animosity that would grow between them — the energy Theodore Roosevelt had brought to the presidency. With his determination to be a strong party leader, Wilson might be seen as the first (and last) American prime minister. Still decades away from the "plebiscitary presidency," with its huge bureaucratic power base, independent electoral resources, and foreign policy autonomy, the office Wilson shaped in 1913–1916 was a genuine party government.

Wilson had given some thought to governing with a bipartisan progressive bloc, but this idea was jettisoned. Parties were still strong, federally structured organizations divided by intense, historic loyalties and sharply opposed ideologies. Despite the recent experience of bipartisan congressional reform on House rules, railroad regulation, electoral reform, and a few other policy areas, there were great obstacles to maintaining such a coalition.

Already in the Sixty-second Congress, the Republican insurgents had chafed under Democratic leadership in the House. These Republicans had not abandoned the protectionist religion; they just wanted a more moderate, "scientific" tariff of the sort likely to emerge from an expert commission. The Democrats wanted lower tariffs and were much less enamored of bureaucracy. And while usually more reliable friends of labor and more radical antitrusters and railroad regulators, the Democrats were far more conservative on race, gender, and temperance issues than the Republican progressives.

In addition, the Democrats were starved for patronage, still the mother's milk of politics. Wilson could not be all things to all progressive factions. Predictably, he chose to govern with the Democrats. Progressive Republicans were shut out of both the policy-shaping caucus and presidential appointments. While the 17 Progressive representatives elected in 1912 and other liberal Republicans from the Midwest and West added a modest number of welcome votes to the Democratic side on many regulatory issues, the Democrats in the House now had 291 seats — a 73-seat majority — and thus little need for bipartisan coalitions. Having worked so hard to loosen the shackles of party regularity, progressive Republicans became increasingly alienated by the Democrats' embrace of party government.

Wilson called the new Congress into a special early session in April 1913 to deal with tariff revision, but before it convened, he worked closely with Ways and Means Committee Democrats and the floor leader, Underwood, to ensure that the bill they brought out followed Democratic platform principles and avoided protectionist backsliding. The day after Congress convened, Wilson addressed a joint session to outline the party's tariff program — the first such presidential address to Congress since the administration of John Adams. As the debate on tariff revision progressed, Wilson successfully prodded, cajoled, and lectured his party to overcome the urge to protect their districts' products.

The new president-party collaboration proved very successful on the Underwood Tariff Act as well as subsequent bills. After extensive consultation with party leaders, Wilson would deliver an address to a joint session of Congress, outlining Democratic policy goals for the tariff, trust legislation, banking legislation, and so on. The party in Congress would then prepare and pass the bills. This combination of energetic presidential shepherding and caucus discipline in Congress kept the Democrats impressively cohesive on the floor during the controversy-laden construction of a new regulatory state.

Because this collaboration was so novel, there was considerable criticism (especially from Republicans) of Wilson's "dictatorship" and his party's "blind obedience." But in truth it was a relationship of mutual and common interest, and the economic policy initiatives were typically rooted in past Democratic platform pledges and party bills. As Wilson himself described the president-party relationship, "They are using me; I am not driving them."

Presidential influence was most visible in reining in stragglers on the Underwood Tariff, imposing a Federal Trade Commission to enforce the new antitrust laws in 1914, and appending a presidentially appointed board at the top of the new Federal Reserve System erected in 1913 (though in the last case, it is unclear whether the innovation represented an attempt to expand presidential power or capitulation to the party's radical Bryanites, who insisted on a publicly controlled banking system).

But the president's influence could also be negative for some of his copartisans. Wilson was, at least before 1916, less supportive of labor than the Democrats in Congress were, and he resisted attempts to deliver to the trade unions the relief from judicial interference that the 1908 and 1912 platforms had promised. He opposed a 1913 appropriations rider (which his party insisted on passing anyway) that forbade the Justice Department to initiate prosecutions of labor practices under the Sherman Antitrust Act. His obstinacy also prevented a clear exemption of labor unions from prosecution in the 1914 Clayton Antitrust Act. The resulting ambiguity inserted a fatal weakness into the law's attempt to rescue labor unions from devastating court injunctions, leaving the Supreme Court enough latitude to eviscerate the act's intended labor protection.

The Child Labor and Workmen's Compensation laws of 1916 were finally rushed through in time to win northern labor votes in the upcoming elections. However, both bills had been languishing in committee and could have been passed earlier had it not been for Wilson's indifference or opposition. The 1915 seamen's rights law could also probably have passed in 1914 if the president had not opposed it.

Wilson's legislative energies appeared to flag in late 1914. Once the tariff, banking, and antitrust bills were passed, he considered the party program essentially complete. Congressional Democrats, on the other hand, saw an unfinished agenda. They wanted farm credit and labor legislation, a new federal road construction program, federal aid for vocational education, and government help with the shipping crisis that emerged in the wake of the European war. It would take persistent congressional pressure and heightened presidential concern about reelection to complete the progressive program in 1916.

But before 1915, the relationship between the president and congressional Democrats was strongly cooperative. The congressional party needed the president's support, and he, theirs. His preference for measures less antagonistic to business and for bureaucratic discretion (where the congressional Democrats preferred specific and sanction-laden statutes) and his conservative appointments to the ICC and Federal Reserve Board were tolerated, in part because they could be justified as necessary appeasement of bitter opponents in the business community and in part because Wilson's public standing and patronage were important to his party's success. The Democrats knew they were living on borrowed time; they had been elected in flukey, four-party elections with the help of dissident Progressives, many of whom would return to the Republican party in a few years. The passage of ambitious reform legislation required unity and dispatch — and thus the president's cooperation.

War and Peace

This harmonious party government ruptured with the outbreak of the world war. By mid-1915 the president's attention had become fixated on the need for an American military buildup, for "preparedness." This meant a large increase in spending for the army and navy and — in the minds of Wilson, his secretary of war, and northeastern Republican and business leaders — a thorough restructuring of the country's antiquated, state militia–based army in the direction of a permanent, national, professional military establishment.

Most rural Democrats (and midwestern progressive Republicans) were strongly opposed to these innovations. They saw the "preparedness" campaign and the administration's insistence on Americans' right to travel on armed ships bearing munitions and other supplies for the Allies as dangerous violations of neutrality. These sentiments reflected the adamant opposition of farm and labor groups, urban social reformers, women's peace groups, and most of the public outside the Northeast to getting involved in the European war. The former secretary of state William Jennings Bryan (who had resigned in protest in 1915) began to tour the country on behalf of American neutrality and peace and was met by wildly enthusiastic crowds.

In the House, about two dozen Republicans and three dozen Democrats, most from rural districts in the South and West, formed the core of the contingent against preparedness. Their passionate leader was none other than the new Democratic majority leader, Claude Kitchin of North Carolina. Kitchin inveighed against the "sudden, radical, and stupendous move for war preparations" and the danger that, under Wilson's leadership, the Democratic party might "fall victim to the wiles of the patriots for profit" advocating the defense buildup.

The Speaker of the House, Champ Clark, was also clearly sympathetic to the pacifists. The Democratic members of the House Military Affairs Committee and its chair, James Hay of Virginia, were also opposed to the administration's ambitious preparedness plans and were on bad terms with the secretary of war, Lindley Garrison. The secretary resigned upon the loss of his "Continental Army" restructuring proposals.

This peace sentiment in Congress clearly influenced Wilson's diplomacy and his efforts to force concessions from the Germans in their submarine warfare against merchant ships en route to the Allies. The apparent success of his gentler diplomatic approach in mid-1916 was met by a great public sigh of relief and a closing of party ranks. Bitterness within the party subsided, and the Democrats were able to get on with their domestic policy agenda and outreach to northern Progressives.

In 1916, faced with the prospect of a crippling transportation strike and finally recognizing the need for labor votes, Wilson embraced a landmark bill guaranteeing the eight-hour day to railroad workers. That summer also saw the passage of bills outlawing child labor (by prohibiting the movement of their products in interstate commerce), providing a generous system of workmen's compensation for injuries to government workers, regulating crop storage warehouses, and creating a system of government-aided farm loan banks. The Democratic convention celebrated its legislative accomplishments and urged the president's reelection under the slogan "He kept us out of war." But for Wilson, the slogan was not a heart-felt commitment. Neither, one suspects, was the broad domestic policy agenda of late progressivism.

The three major social movements of the Progressive era — farmers, workers, and women — generally found a more sympathetic audience in Congress than in the executive branch or the courts. As is usually the case with social movements, they sought specific legislative goals: outlawing monopolistic practices, expanding the supply of money, legalizing union activities, banning child labor or interstate liquor shipments, and so on. Their significance as constituents gave them access, and the specificity of their goals conformed to the value Congress placed on the legislative control of policy through specific statutes. Of course, the three groups securing new benefits from the progressive-era legislation shared another characteristic as well: they were white. Any benefit won by black Americans in this era was almost pure coincidence, a spillover from the benefits gained by white farmers, workers, and women.

Nevertheless, the progressive-era Congresses created an impressive surge of democratic responsiveness to pent-up popular demands. Without the spur of an economic crisis like the Great Depression, and with growing anxiety about the European war, it is remarkable that so much controversial legislation could issue from Congresses chosen by a shrinking electorate, with the popular election of senators still not completely phased in, an old guard of "plutocrat" sympathizers far from vanquished, and presidents often weakly committed to reform.

— ELIZABETH SANDERS

BIBLIOGRAPHICAL NOTES

The classic accounts of progressive-era politics in the first twelve years of the twentieth century are George E. Mowry, *Theodore Roosevelt and the Progressive Movement* (New York, 1946), and *The Era of Theodore Roosevelt* (New York, 1958); Kenneth W. Hechler, *Insurgency: Personalities and Politics of the Taft Era* (New York, 1964); and J. Lawrence Holt, *Congressional Insurgents and the Party System* (Cambridge, U.K., 1967). For the Wilson years, the standards are Arthur S. Link, *Woodrow Wilson and the Progressive Era 1910–1917* (New York, 1954), and Link's masterful five-volume sequence: *The Road to the White House, The New Freedom, The Struggle for Neutrality, Confusions and Crises,* and *Campaigns for Progressivism and Peace* (Princeton, N.J., 1946–65). Taking up where Link leaves off is Seward W. Livermore, *Politics Is Adjourned: Woodrow Wilson and the War Congress, 1916–1918* (Middletown, Conn., 1966).

The congressional Democrats are the focus of David Sarasohn's *The Party of Reform* (Jackson, Miss., 1989); Anne Firor Scott's "A Progressive Wind from the South," *Journal of Southern History* 29 (February 1963): 53–70; James S. Fleming, "Reestablishing Leadership in the House of Representatives: The Case of Oscar W. Underwood," *Mid-America* 54 (October 1972): 234–50; and Virginia Haughton, "John W. Kern, Senate Majority Leader and Labor Legislation, 1913–1917," *Mid-America* 57 (July 1975): 184–94. For legislative accounts of the Roosevelt and Taft Congresses, see also Claude E. Barfield, "The Democratic Party in Congress, 1909–1913" (unpublished Ph.D. dissertation, Northwestern University, 1965), and Jerome M. Clubb, "Congressional Opponents of Reform, 1901–1913" (unpublished Ph.D. dissertation, University of Washington, 1963). My own *Roots of Reform: Farmers, Workers, and the State, 1877–1917* (Chicago, 1999), also contains a number of progressive-era legislative histories.

Good accounts of the congressional rules fights of the era can be found in Sarah A. Binder, *Minority Rights, Majority Rule* (Cambridge, U.K., 1997), and Eric Schickler, *Disjointed Pluralism* (Princeton, N.J., 2001).

Joseph Gurney Cannon

May 7, 1836–November 12, 1926

Joseph Gurney Cannon

Joseph Gurney Cannon ruled the House of Representatives with colloquialisms, partisan loyalty, sheer stubbornness, and an iron fist. Becoming both Speaker of the House and chair of the Rules Committee in 1903, he controlled committee assignments, determined which members could speak on the floor, made arbitrary rulings, and fought battles with two administrations. By raising the power of the Speaker to authoritarian levels, however, he almost surely inspired his own downfall.

Born in Guilford County, North Carolina, Cannon was the son of a country schoolteacher and self-taught doctor. His parents, as Quakers, abhorred slavery, and in 1840 they moved north to Bloomington, Indiana. Cannon studied law at Cincinnati Law School, was admitted to the bar in 1858, then moved to Illinois, where he worked as a state's attorney for seven years. During that time, he married and started a family. In 1869 the family moved to Danville, Illinois, which remained their home; fifty years later, Cannon spent his retirement there. He was first elected to Congress in 1872 and slowly moved into positions of increasing power, from the chair of the Committee on Expenditures in the Post Office Department to chair of the Committee on Appropriations.

As Speaker, Cannon clashed with two presidents. His disagreements with Theodore Roosevelt dated from Roosevelt's work as a civil service commissioner. Although Cannon was not sympathetic to the president's reform agenda, he either secured the enactment of Roosevelt's programs or modified them to suit his needs. Cannon broke with the president on tariffs and his conservation program: he would not consider lowering protective tariffs and announced that the government would spend "not one cent for scenery." His relationship with President William Howard Taft started off badly and did not improve before Cannon's ouster.

Turning seventy in 1906, Cannon seemed to grow even more arbitrary and arrogant. In 1910, led by the increasingly insurgent Republican George Norris of Nebraska, a coalition of Democrats and reformist Republicans outmaneuvered the reigning parliamentarian and succeeded in removing him from the Rules Committee.

Although defeated for reelection in 1912, Cannon returned to office in 1914 and served until his retirement, at eighty-seven. In his last stint of public service, Cannon was no longer as powerful a figure on Capitol Hill. When he retired, his was the longest tenure in office of any member, spanning five decades — from Reconstruction through World War I, through the administrations of twelve presidents. In 1962 Congress voted to rename the oldest congressional office building after Cannon. Completed in 1908, during his term as Speaker, the House Office Building became known as the Cannon House Office Building.

Despite his increasing influence and longevity in the House, no remarkable piece of legislation bears his name. Cannon was a resourceful and often ruthless politician, with a tendency for making pithy, if sometimes coarse, remarks. He liked to play the part of an uneducated "Hayseed Member from Illinois," although the ploy may have served him less well in Washington than it had in Illinois politics. Nevertheless, he was generally liked for his sprightly manner and respected by his party for his steadfast conservative views.

References

"Cannon, Joseph Gurney." *Encyclopedia of World Biography,* 2nd ed. 17 vols. Gale Research, 1998. Reproduced in Biography Resource Center. Farmington Hills, Mich.: Gale Group. 2003. Retrieved June 30, 2003, from http://www.galenet.com/servlet/BioRC.

Lowitt, R. 2000, February. "Cannon, Joseph Gurney." *American National Biography Online.* Retrieved June 30, 2003, from http://www.anb.org/articles/05/05-00123.html.

Robert Marion La Follette

June 14, 1855–June 18, 1925

and

Robert Marion La Follette, Jr.

February 6, 1895–February 24, 1953

Robert Marion La Follette

Robert Marion La Follette, Jr.

Robert Marion La Follette started out as a successful attorney in Wisconsin and became a popular lawmaker in the House of Representatives for six years, when public reaction to the McKinley Tariff of 1890 turned him and many other Republicans out of office. La Follette happily went home to Madison, where he was an ambitious but scrupulous lawyer with a devoted wife and four children. When a wealthy client wanted him to intervene in a case being judged by La Follette's brother-in-law, the former congressman became irate at the apparent bribe. The incident changed La Follette's life, for he began to question the aims of the Republican party.

During the 1890s, a period of economic turmoil when many people doubted the benefits of industry, "Fighting Bob" La Follette forged a coalition of farmers, laborers, small businessmen, and municipal reformers. On his third attempt, in 1900, he captured the governor's office. When the Republican legislature defeated his reform bills, La Follette traveled throughout the state, reading his opponents' voting records to constituents, spurring a grassroots movement that helped him gain control of the legislature. The effort allowed him to make unprecedented reforms, many of which were adopted by other states. His "laboratory for democracy" included trust-busting, tax reform and consumer protection laws, and the hiring of nonpartisan policy experts to help shape legislation.

In 1905 the legislature elected La Follette to the Senate, although he stubbornly postponed taking his seat until the legislature established his railroad regulatory commission. Once in Washington, La Follette immediately spoke out on reform issues, chastising absent lawmakers and skirmishing with President Theodore Roosevelt. Both men favored reforms, but La Follette, ever suspicious of big corporations, hated to compromise. He remained a thorn in the side of successive presidents Taft, Wilson, Harding, and Coolidge, helping to defeat Wilson's Treaty of Versailles and uncovering the Teapot Dome Scandal of Harding's administration. But La Follette's hard-handed dealings with the Republican party served only to undermine his presidential bids in 1912 and, as a third-party candidate, in 1924. La Follette died the following year.

His son, Robert Marion La Follette, Jr., had served as his father's chief aide since 1916, and he won the special election to fill his father's unexpired term. He continued much of his father's progressive legacy and became, at the onset of the Great Depression, the chief congressional advocate for a broad government response to the economic crash. He found an ally in Franklin D. Roosevelt, whose New Deal legislation was no doubt influenced by La Follette's ongoing crusade for the common laborer. Like his father, La Follette opposed the entry of the United States into war, but he threw his support to the president after the Japanese attack on Pearl Harbor. Like his father, he was known for being sincere, honest, and intelligent. Having studied politics virtually since the age of six, he was also respected as a skilled parliamentarian. In one of his last achievements in the Senate, he shepherded through the Legislative Reorganization Act of 1946, which streamlined the committee system and modernized many congressional procedures.

Ironically, La Follette had never really wanted to fill his father's shoes despite being groomed for the position. Before his father's death, he had considered careers in business and journalism but remained by his father's side. His brother, Philip, a three-time governor of Wisconsin, had always been more ambitious. The senator grew increasingly unhappy with public life, ignored his constituents, and almost completely stopped campaigning for office. When he lost the Republican primary to Joseph R. McCarthy in 1946, La Follette became a consultant to the Truman administration. He lived a private life in Washington with his wife, who had worked as a secretary for both him and his father, and their two children. He had suffered from periodic bouts of depression and his health was in decline, but few appreciated how unhappy he really was. One afternoon in 1953, the fifty-eight-year-old La Follette left his office, went home, and shot himself to death.

• • •

Having senators in the family is no longer the rarity it once was. Fathers and sons who have occupied seats in the Senate have included the Tennessee Democrats Al Gore Sr. (1953–1971) and Al Gore Jr. (1985–1993) and the Indiana Democrats Birch Bayh (1963–1981) and Evan Bayh (1999–present). In 2002 the Republican Frank Murkowski (1981–2002) resigned from his fourth Senate term to be Alaska's governor and appointed his daughter, Lisa Murkowski, to serve out the remaining two years of his term.

References

Maney, P. J. 2000, February. "La Follette, Robert Marion, Jr." *American National Biography Online.* Retrieved June 30, 2003, from http://www.anb.org/articles/06/06-00355.html.

Ritchie, D. A. "La Follette, Robert Marion." *American National Biography Online.* Retrieved June 30, 2003, from http://www.anb.org/articles/06/06-00351.html.

21

Redesigning Congress: The Seventeenth and Twentieth Amendments to the Constitution

IF THE ORIGINAL INTENT of the Founders of the United States still held, Congress would not be chosen nor would it operate in the manner that prevails today. No senator would have to face a state's voters. Every Congress, following the election of its successor, would meet for a session in which defeated or retiring members would exercise power under circumstances encouraging them to pursue personal advantage. These "lame-duck" congressmen would be beyond the voters' reach but would still possess the authority to make decisions on legislation, Supreme Court nominations, declarations of war, or presidential impeachment. By design or inadvertence, the Founders created a Congress far less bound by the democratic will than became the case after the constitutional reforms of the early twentieth century.

At the Philadelphia convention of 1787 the inventive American Founders devised a two-house Congress to resolve a fundamental power struggle between the most populous states and their smaller counterparts. The biennial election of representatives by the voting public and the selection of senators for a six-year term by their state legislators struck a balance between the contending political philosophies of democracy and republicanism, that is, between popular rule and the delegation of decision-making to well-suited and responsible persons insulated from momentary passions. The distribution of authority between the Senate and the House of Representatives gave each body independent power while encouraging their cooperation in order to enact legislation, adopt budgets, and check the authority of the executive and the judiciary. The elegance of Congress's basic architecture overshadowed the imperfections in the original structure, which could be corrected only by formally altering the Constitution itself.

The original 1787 design of Congress rarely faced fundamental reexamination, but twice in the early twentieth century aspects of the Founders' work underwent meaningful reform. The first significant change remains somewhat visible; the second seems scarcely noticed, much less appreciated for its importance. Nevertheless, these two measures, embodied in the Seventeenth and Twentieth Amendments to the Constitution, altered the character of Congress. One reformed the means of senatorial selection; the other ended the legislative abuses inherent in biennial lame-duck congressional sessions. Widespread and long-standing public discontent with some characteristics of Congress coupled with rising optimism about the possibility of constitutional amendment propelled these reforms. No less vital were the efforts of knowledgeable legislators at both the federal and state levels, for they were able to surmount the formidable challenges of constitutional alteration.

Throughout its long history, Congress has been profoundly influenced by the accepted practice for choosing who would sit in its chambers as well as by the pressures upon its members for action and delay. Its first century produced certain practices of senatorial selection and legislative maneuver that generated demands for reform. However, because these practices rested on specific constitutional directives, change could only be accomplished by means of another of the Founders' notable creations: the Article V process of constitutional amendment. Desiring governmental stability but aware of the need to provide an avenue for reform, the Founders allowed for constitutional amendments whenever two-thirds of Congress agreed on a measure or called a convention to do so in response to petitions from two-thirds of the states. Thereafter, three-fourths of the states had to ratify the proposed amendment. Except in the early days of the republic and the extraordinary aftermath of the Civil War, the supermajority requirements of Article V had frustrated any efforts to alter the Founders' design. The Progressive era's faith in the possibilities of constitutional reform, a confidence embodied in a series of amendments including these two, deserves to be recognized, in context, as quite noteworthy.

The Seventeenth Amendment

The Founders' stipulation that state legislators choose United States senators soon became a target of those who desired greater popular control of government. Members of the House of Representatives began offering direct election constitutional amendments in the 1820s, but no antebellum House consensus for reform, much less its Senate counterpart, ever emerged. Andrew Johnson of Tennessee, a consistent populist, advocated the reform, first as a congressman in 1851, later as a senator in 1860, and finally as president in 1868. From the 1870s onward, the number of amendment resolutions on the subject grew steadily in each congressional session.

By the 1890s the Senate had gained a reputation in the press and among social and economic reformers as an unrepresentative, unresponsive "millionaires club," high in partisanship but low in integrity. Senators were often perceived to have gained their seats as the result of financial influences in the state political parties and legislatures that selected them; they were thought to keep their positions by heeding the wishes of party leaders and corporate sponsors rather than constituents. In all, the Senate seemed to embody the most self-serving and undemocratic aspects of American politics. A few revelations of bribes paid to state legislators to influence senatorial choices stirred suspicion that the practice was widespread.

Frequent state legislative deadlocks over the choice of a senator furthered the image of a defective electoral system. In no fewer than forty-five instances in twenty states between 1891 and 1905, legislatures, unable to reach agreement on candidates, delayed filling seats. Fourteen seats remained empty for at least one entire congressional session. In the worst case, Delaware had only one senator in place during three Congresses and none at all from 1901 until 1903. "The Senate ranks lower in popular estimation today than it has at any time in the history of the country," declared the *Seattle Post Intelligencer* in January 1897. Two months later the *Louisville Courier Journal* lamented, "To be a Senator is to be a suspect."

Appeals deluged Congress for the direct popular election of senators as a remedy for the upper house's perceived flaws. Beginning in 1892, the People's party platform regularly demanded direct election; the Democratic platform did likewise, starting in 1900. On January 16, 1893, the House of Representatives, the most sensitive national barometer of mass political opinion, first approved by a two-thirds voice vote a constitutional amendment resolution providing for the direct election of senators. On July 21, 1894, a similar measure passed, 141–50. Fifteen state legislatures joined the amendment call by 1897. Three subsequent Houses endorsed similar resolutions, on January 12, 1898, 185–11; on April 13, 1900, 242–15; and on January 21, 1902, without a recorded vote.

These actions went for naught because Senate incumbents were comfortable with their own selection by state legislatures and happy that they did not have to undertake statewide campaigns for popular votes. Senators steadfastly refused to countenance direct election. House resolutions were referred to the Senate's Committee on Privileges and Elections, from which they never emerged except once in 1896. Even then, the measure was not brought to a vote. The Senate allowed all amendment resolutions to expire despite the rising clamor for reform outside the chamber.

Stymied by the congressional roadblock, reformers turned to other solutions through the states. In 1893 the Nebraska legislature, which eighteen years earlier had established the first senatorial primary election, tried again to set an example. Propelled by the Populist spirit that would soon lift its favorite son, William Jennings Bryan, to national prominence, Nebraska legislators sought to employ for the first time Article V's alternate process for initiating amendments. If two-thirds of the states filed petitions, Article V required Congress to call a constitutional convention that could in turn submit a direct election amendment to the states for ratification.

States had never before allied to demand a convention, but in 1900 a committee of the Pennsylvania legislature suggested just such a coordinated effort. The Senate would not act, the committee believed, unless compelled to do so. Pennsylvania sent every other state a copy of its convention petition, encouraging them to follow suit. Soon a dozen states did. Others, nervous about what might occur at a constitutional convention, followed the examples of Georgia and Arkansas in "most respectfully" requesting Congress to propose a direct election amendment. By 1912 thirty-one state legislatures, only one less than the required two-thirds, had taken one action or the other. Because some states sought a convention while others asked Congress to act on its own, there was room to argue that the point at which Article V required the amending process to be set in motion was not even close to being reached. But the possibility of a constitutional convention, one that might follow the 1787 example of turning from limited to wholesale governmental reform, began to concern some members of Congress.

Meanwhile, reformers were exploring other options. Oregon, a pioneer in progressive initiative and referendum laws, improvised a system for the de facto direct election of senators. In 1904 Oregon required petitions of candidacy for the state legislature to include a statement as to whether the candidate felt bound to support the senatorial candidate receiving the highest popular vote in a state primary election. Most candidates pledged to respect the popular preference. Bribery and deadlocks quickly became mere memories in Oregon. In 1907 a local news report exulted, "On the first ballot, in twenty minutes, we elected two Senators, without boodle, or booze, or even a cigar!" Two years later, Oregon's Republican legislature demonstrated the system's effectiveness by electing a Democratic senator who had won the popular contest. By 1911 over half of all the states had adopted the Oregon system or a similar method approximating direct election. The number of senators popularly chosen and ready to insist that their colleagues be similarly selected was increasing rapidly.

The Oregon approach reduced but did not altogether eliminate the electoral problem. Some states chose not to adopt faux direct election. Legislative contests in Wisconsin and Rhode Island in 1907 and Kentucky in 1908 produced more taint and deadlock. A 1909 Illinois scandal highlighted the continuing difficulty. The legislature deadlocked for five months before finally, amid charges of bribery and corruption, settling on six-term Republican congressman William Lorimer of Chicago. A yearlong investigation left four legislators accused of accepting large payments from a $100,000 corporate "slush fund" to vote for him. After further probing, the Senate declared his election invalid in 1912.

The unfolding Lorimer scandal led Kansas senator Joseph Bristow in 1909 to propose that a provision for direct election of senators be added to the income tax amendment resolution then being debated. New to the Senate, the insurgent Republican Bristow had won Kansas's first senatorial primary the previous year, partly on his pledge to support direct election nationally. The Senate's Republican majority leader, Nelson Aldrich, objected to Bristow's motion as not pertinent to the original resolution. A Senate majority agreed. Once again, defenders of the senatorial status quo had dodged a bullet.

Bristow did not abandon the fight. At the start of the next session, he submitted a direct election amendment resolution, asking that it be considered by the Judiciary Committee, of which his ally Idaho's Senator William Borah was a member, rather than the Committee on Privileges and Elections, which had repeatedly buried similar proposals. Following a year's delay, the Judiciary Committee finally issued a favorable report on the measure as revised by Borah. Growing Progressive demands for a Senate more attuned to popular concerns than the special interests of the wealthy were manifested throughout the nation in the November 1910 elections, and no doubt had more to do with the committee's decision than the impatient Bristow's repeated calls for action. Eighteen years after the initial House vote on a direct election amendment, the Senate took its first roll call on the issue on February 28, 1911. The vote, 54–33, fell five votes short of the two-thirds required for passage. Few observers thought that a reform victory was close at hand.

From the outset, the issue of race complicated the struggle over the direct election of senators. Southerners had found ways around the Fourteenth and Fifteenth Amendments' race-neutral suffrage requirements by using literacy tests and poll taxes to disenfranchise black voters. Southern senators successfully filibustered an 1890 federal elections bill to standardize voting rights, but they remained nervous about the federal control of elections. Whenever a direct election amendment was put forth, southern Democrats indicated that the price of their support would be a provision to ensure state regulation of elections.

When a three-member Senate Judiciary subcommittee took up the issue in 1910, the swing member, Maryland's Democrat Isidore Rayner, insisted upon removing the federal power to regulate elections. Subcommittee chairman Borah agreed to gain Democratic support. When Borah's resolution came before the full Senate, however, some Republicans objected. Henry Cabot Lodge of Massachusetts spoke against surrendering national power to the states, and his colleague Chauncey Depew of New York bluntly opposed "deliberately voting to undo the results of the Civil War." Northern supporters of direct election who could not abide the prospect of unrestrained southern states faced a dilemma. Meanwhile, those northern senators who thought direct election too populist and preferred the status quo found a convenient excuse to oppose reform. A majority of the Senate supported a motion to retain federal authority over elections, but thereafter the direct election amendment itself fell short of passage.

Ten senators who had voted against direct election met defeat in the 1910 elections. Their replacements, mainly a cohort of progressives, encouraged the measure's advocates to press forward in the next Congress. Joseph Bristow believed that the uncompromised amendment could now pass by three or four votes. The House acted first, however, adopting an amendment on April 13, 1911, that eliminated federal control of elections. When the Senate took up this version, Bristow led a fight to preserve a measure of federal control by retaining the Constitution's requirement that federal voting qualifications be the same as for the largest branch of each state's legislature. The Bristow revision won by the narrowest of margins on Vice President James Sherman's tie-breaking vote. The Senate then adopted Bristow's version of the amendment, 64–24, well above the required two-thirds.

The Senate's action on June 12, 1911, did not end the matter because its version of the amendment differed from that passed by the House. A conference committee met sixteen times without resolving the racially charged issue of state or federal control of elections. Finally, in April 1912 the frustrated Senate voted to insist that the House accept its version, and House Democratic leaders grudgingly agreed that doing so was better than sacrificing the entire measure. On May 12, 1912, the House voted, 238–39, to concur with the Senate resolution and send the amendment to the states. Every Republican and more than three-quarters of the Democrats gave their approval; all remaining opposition came from the ranks of southern Democrats.

Ratification of the direct election amendment required the assent of only five states more than the thirty-one that had already demanded it. The ratification process got under way quickly: Massachusetts, Arizona, and Minnesota acted within four weeks. Other state legislatures were either not in session or preferred to await the outcome of the fall elections. Once new legislatures began to convene, however, ratification came with remarkable speed. Nine states ratified in January 1913, seventeen in February, four in March, and three during the first eight days of April. Only Utah rejected the amendment. When Connecticut became the thirty-sixth state to ratify on April 8, 1913, less than eleven months had elapsed since the dam of congressional resistance had been breached.

The Senate was not fully a popularly chosen body until the terms of the last senators chosen by state legislatures expired after the 1918 elections. Thereafter, the body's stature appeared to increase. One sign was the increased frequency with which former senators were nominated for the presidency or vice presidency during the next half century. Previously, the most common steppingstones to executive office had been cabinet duty, military service, a governorship, or House membership. The visibility associated with service in the smaller congressional body and the experience of thinking in terms of larger, broader constituencies may help explain this trend. But those conditions all prevailed before the Seventeenth Amendment. What the direct election amendment introduced was the need for senators to campaign for office in the largest constituencies other than the nation as a whole. Their aspirations to executive office were legitimated by statewide electoral success.

After the Seventeenth Amendment recast the Senate, only a few of the hundreds of individuals who served there ever moved to the other end of Pennsylvania Avenue. However, senators selected by tens of thousands of voters brought a different sensibility to Washington than that of their predecessors chosen by a state legislature, every member of which they might know. Before the passage of the Seventeenth Amendment, some senators may have always considered their constituents' needs and preferences, but others clearly felt unconstrained by the public interest. After the amendment passed, however, senators became much more sensitive to public opinion in their state. Interests that once curried favor with state legislatures continued to wield influence by financing senatorial campaigns. For the senators themselves, however, accountability to a broad electorate assumed far greater importance.

The Twentieth Amendment

The reshaped Senate steadfastly championed the second effort in twenty years to make Congress more responsive to the democratic will. While senators had resisted their own direct election, they repeatedly embraced the so-called lame-duck amendment. The measure bore most heavily on the House of Representatives because the requirement that all of its members face voters every two years strictly limited its mandate. The Senate, in contrast, had a continuous character because only one-third of its members stood for election each biennium. The lame-duck amendment involved only subtle alterations in the calendar of government rather than dramatic electoral change, but it nevertheless had important consequences for the legislative process. It was another significant reform that could only be accomplished by using Article V.

The lame-duck amendment was necessitated, its proponents believed, by circumstances that the Founders had failed to anticipate. Having experience only with the Articles of Confederation, the Philadelphia convention found it impossible to predict when the Constitution might be ratified and therefore could not establish a schedule for putting it into effect. The Founders did, however, set the first Monday in December as the annual meeting date of Congress. Soon after remarkably swift ratification was achieved in the summer of 1788, the last Confederation Congress determined that the new government would begin to function as soon as possible after the necessary electoral process, which states would conduct that autumn. The new government, it was agreed, would be set in motion on the first Wednesday in March of the following year. Thus the terms of representatives, presidents, and senators began on March 4, 1789, and by constitutional stipulation ran for two, four, and six years, respectively. The constitutionally mandated regular sessions of the First Congress would commence in December 1789, thirteen months after its election, and December 1790, after the election of its successor. The combination of starting dates and term length stipulations locked in a calendar that was constitutionally binding on every Congress thereafter.

The calendar at first proved workable if not ideal. The greatest problem seemed inadvertent — the long lag between a Congress's election, its empowerment, and its first required meeting. President George Washington made it seem minor, as he quickly called the First Congress into an extremely productive special session. From the outset, a March starting date after November federal elections provided ample time for presidential electors and state legislatures that were selecting senators to make their choice as well as for the new government to assemble. As communication and transportation improved, as the electoral college became little more than a quaint device for acknowledging a popular choice, and as the Seventeenth Amendment took effect, the various justifications for the lengthy transition of government evaporated. By the 1910s, attention had shifted to the negative features of the constitutional calendar.

Presidents from Washington to Lincoln to Franklin Roosevelt called special sessions to advance the initial meeting date of a Congress. Expiring Congresses occasionally arranged for their successors to convene early, as had been done during Reconstruction to prevent Andrew Johnson from acting without congressional supervision. Setting an earlier annual date for Congress to meet — March 4, for instance — could have been accomplished fairly easily. As early as 1795 members of Congress, uncomfortable with the long delay between elections and the next required meeting date, began offering amendments to revise the calendar. Others pointed out that a change in the routine starting date of congressional sessions could be achieved legislatively.

A much more serious problem was the continuation of a congressional session beyond the subsequent national election. Indeed, the second constitutionally mandated session of each Congress did not even begin until after its successor had been elected. Such a session became known as the "short session" because it began on the first Monday in December and was required to end by noon on March 4. In comparison the first, or "long session," could (though it rarely did) continue for twelve months. During the short session, pressure to complete actions before the term expired encouraged hasty, sometimes ill-considered adoption of bills. The short session gave both leaders and minorities powerful tactical weapons that could advance or delay legislation as they desired or at least force compromise. The Republican leadership of the House during the 1920s proved especially resistant to surrendering such legislative tools.

Short sessions acquired the label "lame-duck sessions" because of one of their most notable characteristics. Since the short session was not constitutionally terminated until four months after an election, officials guaranteed their full term of office continued to exercise authority from November to March even after they had been repudiated at the polls. Defeated officeholders could potentially be unusually susceptible to improper inducements, resulting in questionable legislation or worse. If a disputed presidential election were left to Congress to decide, the old Congress, possibly one with a discredited majority, rather than the new one would select the new president and vice president.

The lame-duck session after the 1922 election raised public awareness of this constitutional problem. Many Republicans defeated for reelection and hoping for appointment to an executive or judicial position appeared ready to curry favor with the Harding administration by voting for its merchant marine construction proposal, the "ship subsidy bill," which was highly unpopular with the public and theretofore with a majority of Congress. Outraged, Senator Thaddeus Caraway of Arkansas, a Democrat, quickly introduced a sense of the Senate resolution that members defeated for reelection should abstain from voting on all but routine, nonpolicy matters during the short session. Senators dismissively referred this resolution to the Committee on Agriculture and Forestry since it was a lame-duck bill.

In the Agriculture Committee, however, progressive Nebraska Republican George W. Norris took the matter seriously. Norris had himself served in the House before his move to the Senate in 1913. Within a month, his committee reported that the Caraway resolution would unconstitutionally restrict members of Congress. Instead of dropping the matter, Norris offered a constitutional amendment built on past proposals to eliminate the lame-duck session, advance the commencement of congressional and presidential terms, and provide for the direct election of the president. After he withdrew the last provision, a separate issue that threatened to delay action on the more pressing question, the Senate promptly and with little debate passed his resolution, 63–6, on February 13, 1923. The House, however, declined to consider the measure in the waning days of the session.

Norris's first lame-duck amendment proposal provided that congressional terms would begin on the first Monday in January following a national election. The annual meeting of Congress would convene on the same date. Presidential terms would commence two weeks later, giving the new Congress time to resolve any disputed election. In each of the two subsequent Congresses, the Senate adopted slightly revised versions, but the House again failed to bring the measure to the floor.

Senator Norris told associates in 1924 that there was "no valid argument against the proposal." He believed that, while the public focused its discontent on the "archaic and uncivilized" continuation of defeated legislators in office "contrary to the very fundamental principle of a Republic or a Democracy," the political resistance to change stemmed from other, less obvious reasons. In the short session, it was impossible for either house of Congress to consider all the legislation proposed, allowing the party in power to choose what would be considered. "As the fourth of March approaches," he explained, "this tension increases its strength in a wonderful degree. Members of Congress who are trying to prevent the passage of what they believe to be obnoxious legislation, very often remain silent because they think other legislation in which they are deeply interested may stand some show if they do not take up the time of the Senate or the House in debating what is to have consideration. It therefore often happens that half-baked legislation is enacted." Norris also believed that presidents could improperly influence lame ducks hoping for a federal appointment. "Machine politicians," he concluded, "want to utilize the votes of those who have been defeated to put thru legislation that could not be put thru in any other way, and they do this by means of giving public office to the subservient ones."

An American Bar Association spokesman acknowledged in a 1926 House hearing that as a result of recent amendments, most notably national prohibition, "constitutional amendment is becoming unpopular in the United States." A lame-duck amendment, something the ABA had endorsed for eleven years, possessed a different character, he pointed out. It dealt only with the operation of the federal government without extending its powers. The public did not understand the technical reasons for requiring an amendment to accomplish this reform, but the lawyers who did, he assured the House, considered it vital.

After the Senate approved a lame-duck amendment for the fourth time in January 1928, House leaders began to demonstrate the truth of Norris's assessment of the self-serving nature of their objections. A bill emerged from the House Elections Committee providing that, while annual sessions of Congress should all begin on January 4, in election years they should end on May 4, ostensibly to provide time for campaigning. In this way the short session, with its fixed terminal date, would be preserved. House leaders were willing to abandon the lame-duck session but wanted to retain the tactical opportunities inherent in the short legislative session.

When the full House debated the lame-duck amendment for the first time in March 1928, every one of its complicated features was considered at length. When the roll was called, the amendment obtained only 209 aye votes to 157 nays and died well short of the needed two-thirds. A House Republican confided to Norris that the leadership had not even allowed the amendment to be discussed until they obtained enough pledged votes to assure its defeat. Norris, frustrated, thought the House "silly to make the argument that we ought not make any change because the Constitution is sacred and we cannot improve upon the work of our fathers."

In the next Congress, House Speaker Nicholas Longworth, a master at the use of the short session and a politician loath to surrender useful tools, delayed referring Norris's proposal to committee for nearly a year after the Senate provided its usual strong endorsement. He then used the very short-session tactics that were a target of the reform to try to broker a compromise. His party's loss of its House majority in the November 1930 election and his own impending loss of the Speakership gave his efforts extra urgency. On February 24, 1931, the about-to-adjourn Republican-dominated House finally adopted a lame-duck amendment, a Longworth substitute almost identical to his previous measure. The Cincinnati congressman clearly calculated that he could use the end-of-session tendency to compromise that had worked so often in the past. "By such a provision the biennial threat of a filibuster which now occurs just before March 4 would merely be shifted to the beginning of May," observed the *Cleve-*

land Plain Dealer. "Better postpone the Norris resolution again — after its many postponements — than pass it with the Longworth amendment." When a conference committee was unable to resolve the differences between the Norris and Longworth versions, the measure died for the fifth time.

The congressional tide turned when, for the first time since 1916, the Democrats obtained a majority in the House. Norris hoped in vain that the 1930 Republican defeat might cause Longworth to have a change of heart. Thereafter, the constitutional provision that allowed President Hoover to avoid confronting the new Congress until December 1931 came in for rising criticism.

When the Seventy-second Congress finally did convene, the lame-duck amendment moved forward quickly. As usual, the Senate acted first, adopting the measure, 63–7, on January 6, 1932, after its opponents could only muster 18 votes to substitute the Longworth version. The new Speaker, John Nance Garner of Texas, favored Norris's amendment and promptly brought it before the House. The opposition, never able to mount principled objections, found itself reduced to complaining about wasting time on such matters in the midst of a serious depression. A New York congressman grumbled that the amendment had been "conceived by crackaloos, propagated by crackpots, and supported by thoughtless demagogues." Nevertheless, the House embraced the Norris amendment, 336–56, on March 2.

As finally approved by Congress in 1932, the Twentieth Amendment provided that congressional terms would begin on January 3 following an election and presidential terms on January 20. This schedule was thought necessary and adequate to accommodate recounts and settle election disputes. Congress would meet annually on January 3 unless it appointed a different day. (Qualms about being occasionally compelled to convene on Sunday led Congress to add the device to alter the meeting date.) Complicated provisions were made for presidential succession in the event of a president-elect's death before inauguration.

Senator Norris made no effort to prepare the way for the amendment's state ratification by communicating with governors or state legislators. Nevertheless, nine states ratified within thirty days. Eight more did so before the year ended. When new legislatures, believing that they carried a mandate from the electorate, convened in 1933, they promptly completed action. Seventeen states approved within the first three weeks of January. On January 23, four more added their sanction to conclude the Article V process. Six more states concurred before January came to an end, and when Florida ratified on April 26, every state had endorsed the lame-duck amendment. Never before had an amendment been unanimously approved on its initial consideration, even in the days of a much smaller union. To say that state legislators were eager to remove power from the hands of lame-duck congressmen may understate the case.

Ratification of the Twentieth Amendment was completed in the midst of one of the most memorable lame-duck sessions of Congress ever held. In the depression election of November 1932, eighty-one congressmen, mainly Republicans, together with President Herbert Hoover, had been turned out of office. Because Franklin Roosevelt, the new president, would not be sworn in until March 4 and the new Congress with its large Democratic majority could not be convened until then, a discredited government remained in office, incapable of action during the bleakest winter of the Great Depression. Lame-duck votes in the House and a Huey Long filibuster in the Senate brought Congress to a standstill. The hostile and long-drawn-out transfer of power rendered the federal government almost completely powerless at a moment of national crisis. (The only comparable situation had occurred between the election and inauguration of Abraham Lincoln on the eve of the Civil War.) The Twentieth Amendment was completed too late to avoid the long interregnum of 1932–1933, but that experience underscored the value of this constitutional reform.

Even the more rapid congressional transition mandated by the Twentieth Amendment did not entirely eliminate the possibility of a lame-duck session. In 1998 the Congress voted to return for a session after the November elections. Then the House Republican majority, with lame-duck members providing crucial votes, impeached President Bill Clinton. Complaints about the illegitimacy of the action fell on deaf ears since it was clearly within the bounds of the Twentieth Amendment. With that notable exception, however, the lame-duck amendment produced a fundamental change in the functioning of Congress, enabling it to meet nearly continuously, reducing the pressure for hasty legislative compromise, and ending the biennial empowerment of lame ducks.

The Seventeenth and Twentieth Amendments produced significant changes in Congress. The legislative branch of the government emerged fundamentally altered by the new process of senatorial selection as well as the redrawn congressional calendar. In both instances, the original intent of the Founders had been perceived by later generations as flawed. Desiring to restructure constitutional arrangements, reformers were able to make effective use of one of the Founders' most important if seldom used inventions, the Article V amending process. Overturning the Constitution's original intent in order to strengthen democracy represented a notable achievement for early-twentieth-century federal and state legislators. The 1913 and 1933 amendments proved to be far more than a needless diversion by "crackaloos, crackpots, and thoughtless demagogues."

— David E. Kyvig

BIBLIOGRAPHICAL NOTES

Neither the Seventeenth nor the Twentieth Amendment has received the scholarly attention it deserves. The fullest treatments appear in broad studies of constitutional amending, most notably Alan P. Grimes, *Democracy and the Amendments to the Constitution* (Lexington, Mass., 1978), Richard B. Bernstein with Jerome Agel, *Amending America: If We Love the Constitution So Much Why Do We Keep Trying to Change It?* (New York, 1993), and David E. Kyvig, *Explicit and Authentic Acts: Amending the U.S. Constitution, 1776–1995* (Lawrence, Kans., 1996). For the Senate "millionaires club" prior to reform, see David J. Rothman, *Politics and Power: The United States Senate, 1869–1901* (Cambridge, Mass., 1966). For the struggle for the Senate's reform, see John D. Buenker, "The Urban Political Machine and the Seventeenth Amendment," *Journal of American History* 56 (1969): 305–22, and Larry J. Easterling, "Sen. Joseph L. Bristow and the Seventeenth Amendment," *Kansas Historical Quarterly* 41 (1975): 488–513. On the Twentieth Amendment, there is useful information in Richard Lowitt, *George W. Norris: The Persistence of a Progressive, 1913–1933* (Urbana, Ill., 1971).

22

Women's Activism

WOMEN LOBBYISTS on Capitol Hill from the 1880s to the 1920s faced a unique set of challenges as they tried to press their legislative agenda. The male representatives and senators were highly conscious of gender differences and wanted to maintain their sense of superiority. When lobbyists for the National American Woman Suffrage Association (NAWSA) succeeded in convincing Congress to support the creation of a separate Woman Suffrage Committee to bring a federal amendment to the floor of the House in 1917, for example, they found this victory to be problematic and incomplete. Their celebration was cut short when they heard that North Carolina's Democratic representative, Edwin Yates Webb, chair of the Judiciary Committee, was insisting that the new committee would not bring a constitutional amendment to the floor. When two prominent NAWSA lobbyists, Helen Gardner and Maud Wood Park, confronted one of their (unnamed) powerful friends in the House, he defensively responded that he had only agreed to help them get to the committee but had not said it could handle a constitutional amendment. An indignant Park was about to protest that the suffragists had been deceived when Gardner gave her a "covert pinch." Once they left his office, Gardner explained that the representative simply had not known about this rule and would rather have the women think that he had double-crossed them rather than admit that he had been confused about House procedure. Determined to maintain his support, Gardner refrained from criticizing or humiliating him. When Park looked into the matter and found that other amendments had been adopted through other committees, she wanted to take her information directly to their friend in the House. Gardner again restrained her, suggesting, "We mustn't let him think we know more than he does."[1] Instead, she secretly arranged to have his secretary give him the information so that he could claim ownership of the idea and sustain his "superiority" in the face of women lobbyists. When women lobbied congressmen and senators they had to walk a thin line, pushing for what they wanted without seeming to be too forceful or more knowledgeable than the male politicians. Gardner's "womanly" discretion won the day: the Rules Committee subsequently allowed the Woman Suffrage Committee to handle the amendment.

Sometimes major legislative action has come about because of pressure from outside Congress, not within it. In the history of women's attempts to pass critical pieces of legislation, Congress only reluctantly gave way to the massive pressure brought to bear by women's rights advocates, who teamed up with pivotal legislative allies. Women reformers helped to push for the expansion of the role of the state and to set the legislative agenda of the federal government.

From the 1890s through the 1920s, women's political activism increased at all levels as they tried to set up homes for single working girls in the cities, to demand new protective labor legislation for women and children — and its subsequent enforcement — at the state level, and to gain federal legislation. There are many examples of women organizing at the turn of the century to fight for federal legislation, such as the prohibition of alcohol, woman suffrage, censorship laws, and the creation of a Children's Bureau.

This chapter will focus on two successful campaigns — for a Children's Bureau and for woman suffrage — that were led by women who achieved their goals at the height of the Progressive reform movement, in the 1910s. The campaign for a federal Children's Bureau was more limited; reformers did not need to work for a constitutional amendment, nor did they therefore need to build up majority support in so many states. They could focus on lobbying the members of Congress and could achieve their goal with a simple majority vote. So, too, the issue of child welfare, even of child labor, was comparatively less controversial than national voting rights for women, which still seemed like a real threat to conventional gender roles and male political dominance early in the twentieth century.

Women achieved many of their legislative goals at the turn of the century in part by highlighting their role as mothers (and future mothers) who had a right to intervene in politics to demand protection for children. The Children's Bureau could clearly be framed as a maternalist concern, but so was the right to vote. Although some women insisted on their full equality with men and denied that there were any crucial differences between the sexes, other suffragists emphasized their difference from the current electorate, insisting that they would vote as mothers. Their vote, they argued, would be informed by higher moral considerations. The Woman's Christian Temperance Union (WCTU) was a major organization that by 1881 supported woman suffrage as the "Home Protection Ballot."

Similarly, Progressive reformers like the settlement house founder Jane Addams advocated for woman suffrage as a form of "civic housekeeping" by suggesting that women, as experienced mothers and housekeepers, would be better than men at cleaning up corrupt urban politics, the disease-ridden and poverty-stricken tenements, and the dangerous factories. The rhetoric of maternalism was central to women's legislative success.

Women's attempts to move legislation through Congress were coordinated by large, well-organized groups such as the National Federation of Women's Clubs and the WCTU. Operating at a grass-roots level with local efforts coordinated by state officers and a national body with prominent leaders, the many-layered structure of most women's groups allowed them to mobilize a rapid national response to their issues. Because women's reform groups were organized at the local, state, and federal levels, they were particularly adept at influencing Congress. In the case of the Children's Bureau and woman suffrage, although individual members of Congress sponsored legislation at the behest of women, the initiative for these reforms did not come from Congress. Yet, in the end, the legislative branch played a central role in shaping social change. A coalition of reform Republicans and urban machine Democrats, for example, would pass the woman suffrage amendment.

The Creation of the Children's Bureau

Before obtaining the right to vote, women gained considerable legislative experience in their organized efforts to expand the protective role of the federal government. One prime example was the fight for the creation of a federal Children's Bureau between 1906 and 1912. The women's message to their national legislators was that all women — as mothers and potential mothers — had a vested interest in seeing the creation of a department that could chart the health and welfare of children in the United States. Convinced of this need, Progressive leaders of the settlement house movement, the National Congress of Mothers (later, the Parent-Teacher Association), the General Federation of Women's Clubs, and the National Consumers' League coordinated their lobbying efforts. These organizations were all formed to promote the welfare — broadly defined to include labor conditions and education — of women and children. Together, they solicited the assistance of the National Child Labor Committee (NCLC), a group of mostly men but led by Florence Kelley, which fought for protective child labor laws; the women hoped that it could help garner support on Capitol Hill. Its members approached sympathetic congressmen and wrote the legislation sponsored by two prominent Republicans, Senator Winthrop Crane of Massachusetts and Representative John Gardner from

New Jersey. Revealingly, the special status obtained by the women's lobby is evident in Senator Crane's sponsorship of this bill. Crane, who came from the Bay State's paper manufacturing family, was a prominent "old guard" Republican and President Taft's top legislative contact after Rhode Island's Nelson Aldrich retired in 1911. Crane, who had attacked many Progressive reforms, such as the Hepburn Act in 1906, endorsed this measure. Crane and Gardner brought this bill to a vote every year from 1906 until it passed in 1912. The women's groups, especially the large umbrella organization the General Federation of Women's Clubs, which had been founded in 1890, put pressure on Congress by writing to their representatives and senators and by visiting their home district offices. Women's groups generated the necessary votes on Capitol Hill by bringing leaders from state affiliates to speak before committees such as the Senate's Committee on Education and Labor. The opposition in Congress was greatest from those who opposed government interference in families and from factory owners who wanted to maintain a plentiful supply of cheap child labor.

High on the agenda of organized women's groups was the elimination of child labor exploitation, as well as efforts to decrease infant and maternal mortality rates. The outgoing Republican president, Theodore Roosevelt, was convinced by the settlement house founder Lillian Wald to sponsor, in early 1909, a White House Conference on the Care of Dependent Children. This conference brought national attention to the issue, provided a platform where women social workers and progressive activists could speak and be received as authorities on child welfare, and led to new congressional hearings on the creation of a Children's Bureau. In 1912 Congress and President William Taft, also a Republican, were under pressure from a new third party — the Progressive party and its presidential candidate, Theodore Roosevelt. Although Woodrow Wilson and the Democrats won the 1912 election, the creation of the Progressive party made the other two parties take the Progressive platform seriously. Politicians from both major parties co-opted its issues in an attempt to weaken the new party. In this context, Congress approved the Children's Bureau in 1912 on a vote in the House, 177–17 (many representatives simply did not vote, perhaps because they did not want to be on record as having opposed the Children's Bureau).[2] Taft appointed a Progressive reformer and settlement house worker, Julia Lathrop, as the first female head of a federal bureau.

Once established, the Children's Bureau regularly had to fight in Congress for its political survival. Lathrop's sense of the real battles that lay ahead came in 1913 when she asked Congress for a substantial increase in her annual operating budget and staff for the fiscal year 1914–1915. The

House Appropriations Committee denied her request. Determined to increase the size and power of the bureau, Lathrop enlisted the help of women settlement house workers to spread the word about the bureau's plight.

The rapidity and breadth of the campaign were impressive. Members of the National Child Labor Committee lobbied Congress and requested the help of the American Federation of Labor in order to protect the wages and working conditions of adult workers from child labor. The General Federation of Women's Clubs and the National Federation of Settlements notified all their members and called on other organizations that were part of their local networks to contact their senators and congressmen. The historian Robyn Muncy observes that their next step lay in a media campaign designed to enlist the help of average Americans who may not have been connected to a particular club movement. Settlement house leaders like Jane Addams wrote editorials in many of the major newspapers and popular magazines across the country. With many thousands of letters of support pouring in to Congress, the House reversed the decision of the Appropriations Committee and increased the funding for the Children's Bureau to Lathrop's original request on a lopsided 276–47 bipartisan vote in April 1914. Clearly, the extensive grass-roots campaign had turned the tide for Lathrop and the bureau, but the lack of deeper congressional support proved to be a persistent problem for the advocates of a strong agency. Because women did not yet have the vote, they could not rely on the consistent support of either political party. Just as the creation of the bureau showed how effective this women's network could be as a legislative force, these subsequent difficulties reaffirmed to women reformers that they needed to gain the right to vote in order to increase their political clout on Capitol Hill.

Work for Suffrage in the Nineteenth Century

Whereas the fight for a Children's Bureau begins and ends in the first two decades of the twentieth century, the fight for woman suffrage began before the Civil War. Both the white and black women who had worked so hard for the abolition of slavery before the war expected that women would be given the right to vote after the war. They were sorely disappointed. Their abolitionist and Republican party allies betrayed them, saying that this was the "Negro's hour" and that women would have to wait. When Congress drafted the Fourteenth and Fifteenth Amendments to the Constitution, it added the word "male" for the first time — a huge setback to plans for "universal" suffrage. Some white and most black women accepted this compromise, understanding the importance of giving the recently freed black men full political citizenship. Others resented being left out. In their subsequent struggle for the vote, white women were sometimes willing to leave black women behind if necessary.

In 1871 the suffrage advocate and freethinker Victoria Woodhull became the first woman to speak before a congressional committee when Representative Benjamin Butler of Massachusetts, a reform-oriented Republican (and later a Democratic governor of Massachusetts), arranged for her appearance before the House Judiciary Committee. Woodhull argued that women had already gained the right to vote through their inclusion as citizens in the Fourteenth and Fifteenth Amendments to the Constitution. Although the committee rejected her arguments in its majority report on woman suffrage, for the first time a favorable minority report was issued by the Republicans Benjamin Butler and William Loughridge of Iowa and distributed to twenty-one thousand prominent individuals. Yet narrow and unsupportive Supreme Court decisions forced advocates for woman suffrage to conclude that they could not pursue Woodhull's argument.

Thus, in 1877 the National Woman Suffrage Association (NWSA), led by Susan B. Anthony and Elizabeth Cady Stanton, began a petition drive demanding a constitutional amendment for woman suffrage and collected ten thousand signatures to present to the Senate. The woman suffrage amendment was introduced in Congress in 1878 by the Republican senator Aaron Sargent of California, who had met Stanton and Anthony when they campaigned in his state (he had also spoken at a NWSA convention in 1874). A state constitutional convention of 1878–1879 made it an important time for the issue in California; backers like Sargent, who pointed to its success in Wyoming, almost won a heated attempt to gain woman suffrage but lost by 10 votes. Women did not win the right to vote in California until 1911.

Although the issue was being actively considered by the western states, NWSA's petitions and proposed amendment were not taken seriously by the great majority of Sargent's colleagues in 1878. One newspaper recounted that "the entire Senate presented the appearance of a laughing school practicing sidesplitting."[3] When Sargent then arranged for Stanton to testify before the Senate Committee on Privileges and Elections, the senators were rude and inattentive, clearly not afraid of any negative consequences. Later, in 1887, the Republican Henry Blair of New Hampshire, sponsored a bill on woman suffrage in the Senate. His support was consistent with his sponsorship of other reform legislation, such as prohibition laws and an unsuccessful (but popular with reformers) national education bill that promised equal funding for black schools and students. The Senate defeated the proposed amendment, 34–16, with 26 abstentions. Every southern senator voted against it, suggesting the difficulties the suffragists faced.[4]

Elizabeth Cady Stanton appeared before the House Judiciary Committee in 1890 as the president of the newly united National American Woman Suffrage Association. She argued against the notion that women should be confined to the private sphere, suggesting that both men and women could function effectively in the domestic and public realms. Whether moved by her arguments or by the growing unity of the movement, the committee reported favorably on the proposed woman suffrage amendment only to see it die before the full House.

The Woman Suffrage Campaign, 1900–1919

After 1900, reform Republicans became reliable supporters of a constitutional amendment in favor of woman suffrage. While the urban machine and southern factions of the Democrats led most in the party to oppose woman suffrage, there were influential exceptions such as Champ Clark of Missouri, the Speaker of the House, who took over from "Uncle Joe" Cannon of Illinois in 1911. Although most congressmen in both parties were not strong supporters of woman suffrage — and many were active opponents — the exceptions seemed to be those who represented states that had already passed woman suffrage or those who had family or political ties to prominent suffragists. The strongest opponents came from the South, a haven for states' rights and opponents of any suffrage extension, as well as from old guard Republicans who opposed any new extension of the right to vote.

By the mid-1910s, the suffragists were gaining influence on Capitol Hill. A combination of lobbying, state suffrage victories, petitioning, media campaigns, and the use of more militant tactics such as picketing and hunger strikes gained the attention of the generally reluctant, indifferent, and sometimes hostile members of Congress. Reform-oriented Republicans supported by Progressive and independent voters were more willing to identify themselves publicly with woman suffrage. In a rare tribute to a woman in the Capitol's Statuary Hall, for instance, suffragists held a memorial service in 1916 for Inez Milholland Boissevian, featuring speeches by members of Congress. Milholland Boissevian had led the first suffrage parade in Washington, D.C., on the day before Woodrow Wilson's inauguration in 1913. When she later collapsed from exhaustion at a suffrage rally and then died, she became a martyr for the cause. The main speakers at her service were George Sutherland, a Republican senator from the woman suffrage state of Utah, who later became a Supreme Court justice; a former Republican representative from New York, Rowland Mahany, a family friend; and the suffragist wife of William Kent, a Republican representative from California.

Whereas the Progressive party endorsed a constitutional amendment for woman suffrage in its national platform in 1912, the Republicans did so only in 1916, while the Democrats endorsed state-by-state suffrage as more consistent with states' rights. This delaying tactic enabled a majority of Democrats to insist that their opposition to a federal amendment did not mean that they were opposed to voting rights for women.

Organizations for Woman Suffrage

Two organizations emerged by the mid-1910s as rival leaders of the movement for woman suffrage. The older, more established National American Woman Suffrage Association (NAWSA) worked to gain support from both Democrats and Republicans at the state level. The National Woman's Party (which began as the Congressional Union in 1912) focused on gaining a constitutional amendment immediately. Although both groups hoped ultimately for a constitutional amendment, they disagreed on whether to focus on a more moderate wooing of Congress, whether to use public militant activism, and whether to focus on a state-by-state or federal approach.

The Congressional Union (CU) had been created in 1912 as a special lobbying branch of NAWSA. However, it rejected NAWSA's careful attempts to lobby members of Congress by catering to their prejudices and carefully cultivating relations with them and their staff and instead was more openly confrontational. In 1914, for instance, Alice Paul and Lucy Burns of the CU decided to punish the Democrats for their lack of support by imploring women in suffrage states to vote for politicians from other parties. The CU observed that the Democrats had a majority control in both houses of Congress and that President Wilson was a Democrat. Clearly, the Democrats' votes were crucial in passing a constitutional amendment. Therefore, since the party was resisting a federal amendment, it should be held responsible and defeated in the 1914 (and the 1916) elections. In particular, the CU suggested to women who had already won the right to vote — in several western states such as Wyoming, Colorado, Idaho, Utah, Washington, and California — that they should vote against all Democratic candidates until the party endorsed national woman suffrage. Suffrage proponents had suffered setbacks in 1914 and 1915 when Congress rejected a federal amendment. Clearly, new strategies were necessary. Paul's CU decided to pursue more militant methods and broke completely from NAWSA, becoming the National Woman's Party (NWP) in 1916.

Paul's more confrontational style conflicted with that of NAWSA's new president, Carrie Chapman Catt. Catt's "winning plan," launched in 1916, was based on the premise that state gains increased the number of legislators at the national level who would be compelled to vote yes. These national congressmen could become cooperative partners in an alliance supporting suffrage if they were carefully cultivated and not alienated by the aggressive tactics of the NWP. Catt's plan included getting the legislatures in states where women could vote to pass resolutions to be sent to Congress that favored a federal amendment. The NAWSA activist Maud Wood Park later credited the "winning plan" with changing the political climate. She explained that "our state organizations did their work so well that before the Nineteenth amendment was adopted twenty-six legislatures sent resolutions to the Congress asking for the amendment . . . In less than three years the number of presidential electors for whom women could vote jumped from 91 to 339."[5] Catt focused on gaining votes for women in New York State, in particular, since it had largest number of representatives in Congress. She had organized that state's woman suffrage movement before becoming NAWSA's president in 1916 and was largely responsible for the suffrage victory there in 1917. It, in turn, ensured suffragists of the support of many of New York's Democratic legislators, thereby shifting the Democratic party away from its opposition to a federal amendment. NAWSA attributed the ultimate success of the woman suffrage amendment to its "winning plan," which focused on gaining the vote for women in each state.

Also in 1916, the National Women's Party renewed its pledge to hold the party in power responsible for the continued failure of the woman suffrage amendment, forcing the Democrats to recognize their vulnerability in the upcoming elections. The Democrat James Cantrill, of Kentucky, explained that he voted for the constitutional amendment in the House because he was afraid of losing the support of women voters in his state in the next election.

While the Democrats bitterly resented being targeted by the NWP, some Republicans used it to advantage. For example, Representative Franklin Mondell of Wyoming — a strong supporter of states' rights and a champion of western interests — tried to underscore the fact that if woman suffrage was defeated, it would be the Democrats' fault. He claimed, "It is up to our friends on the Democratic side to see that the amendment is not defeated through hostility or indifference on their side."[6] Representative Irvine Lenroot of Wisconsin, a leader of the progressive wing of the GOP, suggested, "From a Republican standpoint — from a partisan standpoint, it would be an advantage to Republicans to go before the people in the next election and say that this resolution was defeated by southern Democrats."[7]

When intensive lobbying failed to change the minds of some reluctant Republican congressmen, the women relied on the influence of a political insider and ally, the former president Theodore Roosevelt. Using his political network and fame to try to secure more minority party votes for woman suffrage, Roosevelt wrote personally to recalcitrant Republicans; if that did not work, he issued weekend invitations to his estate on Long Island.

Pressure Tactics in Washington, D.C.

Whenever an important vote was pending on the floor of the House or the Senate after 1916, the two main suffrage groups took daily polls to see if they had gained or lost any votes in their campaign for the necessary two-thirds majority. The NWP and its political department lobbied regularly and intensively on Capitol Hill at the same time that it engaged in more visible and dramatic picketing, parades, and hunger strikes. Even as it ran state campaigns, NAWSA gained fame for its intensive lobbying at the national level.

As part of its "winning plan," NAWSA created a congressional committee in 1916 to promote and coordinate its efforts. It consisted of fifteen full-time lobbyists in Washington, D.C., whose work with members of Congress was supported by other women who rotated in and out of the Capitol as necessary. The committee issued an instruction sheet, "Directions for Lobbyists," which instructed the women to read biographical information about each member and then try to set up an interview through his secretary. Once an interview was secured, the lobbyist was reminded: "If the member is known to be in favor show that you realize that fact and ask him for advice and help with the rest of the delegation," thereby forcing him to take more direct action and responsibility for the success of woman suffrage. Just as important, the lobbyist must be "sure to keep his *party* constant in mind while talking to him."[8] Arguments that might work for a member of the Republican minority would not necessarily work for a member of the Democratic majority. Once the interview was over, the lobbyist was instructed to find a "'ladies' dressing room" where she could take notes for an official report, highlighting the "member's argument in detail" along with any new information about his family or friends. The report was to be given to the Washington committee the following day in order to keep accurate polls of the votes.[9] Although these women lobbyists were volunteers, they were in fact well-trained professionals.

To counter any negative stereotypes among the legislators and the Washington elite about "unwomanly" female lobbyists, NAWSA emphasized its members' respectability and womanly virtues by sponsoring formal tea parties for the wives and daughters of influential politicians, clerks, secretaries of congressmen, and others who might have influence on Capitol Hill. NAWSA's headquarters in Washington was a large, elegant mansion where the tea parties as well as planning sessions were held. Its account of the fight for suffrage, *Victory: How Women Won It*, explained that

> Mabel Willard, our chairman of social activities, was successful in getting as guests of honor at a series of teas many of the most prominent women in Washington. The wives of some of the opposed senators were frequent callers and their daughters often handed about our tea and cakes. Though we gained no votes that way, we removed many prejudices against women lobbyists.[10]

The women sometimes used other gendered strategies. Frances Perkins, a leader of the National Consumers' League who later became secretary of labor — and the first female cabinet member — under President Franklin D. Roosevelt, observed that women reformers and lobbyists succeeded when they managed to remind politicians "subconsciously of their mothers."[11] By appealing to more conventional values and appearing as nonthreatening and maternal as possible, the women lobbyists built goodwill and support for their cause even among the legislators who were otherwise hostile to women in politics.

Creating a political structure resembling a strong and intricate web, NAWSA had workers at the national, state, and local levels who were all in constant communication with one another. In addition to the efforts in Washington, lobbyists in the members' home districts also kept tallies, which were checked against those in the Capitol. Ninety-five women designated as "congressional aides" were "chosen for their political influence . . . [W]hen we needed 'backfires' in the district of a wobbly congressman, we called on our aides in his state to stir up publicity and see that he heard from important constituents."[12] When members of Congress voted for suffrage, they were personally congratulated and encouraged to do even more.

Although it did engage in lobbying, the NWP gained notoriety as the first group in American history to picket the White House. It initiated this new form of protest when President Wilson refused to influence his party to adopt a plank supporting a federal amendment. Thus, in January of 1917, just as the United States prepared to enter World War I, the NWP placed "sentinels of liberty and self-government" with protest banners in front of the White House. Once the United States formally entered the war, in April, the picketers highlighted the contradictions between Wilson's wartime ideals, such as democracy and self-determination, and the United States' undemocratic denial of the vote to American women. This approach was condemned as unpatriotic by angry congressmen and President Wilson. It also enraged Catt and NAWSA as being highly impolitic and counterproductive in a wartime environment that demanded conformity. The NWP rejected this argument, instead arranging for rotating groups of picketers featuring, for instance, women munitions plant workers on one day and Women's Reserve Corps members on another.

Many members of Congress, but especially Democrats, were openly hostile to these innovative and seemingly unwomanly tactics. Democrats condemned the picketers as disloyal to the wartime president. They were equally displeased to find a line of picketers at the Capitol when the Sixty-fifth Congress convened its "War Session" in April. Since picketing was not illegal, the suffragists were arrested beginning in June on relatively minor charges, such as blocking sidewalks, and were sentenced to the district jail and its workhouse, usually for refusing to pay fines. The women's banners boldly condemned the president as "Kaiser Wilson" and asked, "Mr. President, How long must women be denied a voice in a government which is conscripting their sons?" The Democratic senators Charles Culberson of Texas, the chair of the Judiciary Committee, and Henry Myers of Montana responded by trying to cast the women's actions as even more disgraceful by making it illegal to picket in front of the White House. Although they were unsuccessful, some Democrats clearly wanted to silence those who were calling attention to the inaction of their president and their party. Furthermore, the Democratic caucus decided that only "war measures" would be considered for legislative action. While they denied that woman suffrage was a proper wartime measure, the NWP and some Republican supporters insisted that it was.

The jailing of suffragists in 1917, especially in the harsh conditions of the Occoquan Workhouse in Virginia (usually reserved for hardened criminals and prostitutes), created sympathy for these respectable women among some members of Congress. Often, personal observations swayed them. The Democratic whip in the Senate, J. Hamilton Lewis of Illinois, for instance, was forced to take an interest in the conditions at the workhouse, where the women were compelled to sew, scrub floors, do laundry in silence, and were fed inedible fare. Among them was a prominent constituent of his, Lucy Ewing — the daughter of a judge, a niece of the former vice president Adlai Stevenson, and a niece of the former minister to Belgium. Senator Lewis visited the workhouse and then proclaimed: "In all my years of criminal practice . . . I have never seen prisoners so badly treated, either before or after conviction."[13] He was particularly shocked that real "ladies" would be subjected to cruel and unnecessary indignities such as coarse clothes, bad food, filthy conditions, and strip searches. The protests of the New York Democratic representative Charles Bennet Smith about the treatment of Mrs. Frederick Kendall, who was being held in solitary confinement on a diet of bread and water, led to improved conditions for her. The Speaker, "Champ" Clark of Missouri, arranged for his daughter to visit her friend, the same Mrs. Kendall, who then fainted from weakness as she walked out of her cell. Finally, the recalcitrant Democratic senator Andrieus A. Jones of New Mexico, chairman of the Suffrage Committee — who for six months had refused to let the suffrage bill out of committee to face a vote on the floor — decided to release it with a recommendation for a favorable vote the day after his visit to the workhouse in September. Shortly after these visits and on hearing other reports of workhouse conditions, Jeannette Rankin, a suffragist Republican representative from Montana, introduced Resolution 171 in October to authorize an investigation into the district's workhouse.

When the administration persisted in arresting the picketers and sending them to the jail and workhouse, the prisoners protested more forcefully that they should be recognized as political prisoners, not common criminals. To highlight their conditions and their claim to be political prisoners, they began the radical act of conducting hunger strikes. As they got weaker and weaker, the prison wardens resorted to force-feeding them to avoid having any of them die in prison and in hopes of deterring new suffragist prisoners from joining the hunger strike. When this ploy did not deter the severely weakened women, the administration unconditionally released them at the end of November.

Black Women's Fight for Suffrage and Inclusion

Unable to win universal suffrage just after the Civil War, women suffragists had tried to benefit from Reconstruction's Fourteenth and Fifteenth Amendments by claiming to see women's voting rights as those of full citizens. Showing the fissures and limits of the woman suffrage movement, white women later made a hypocritical move, deciding to accommodate segregationists in Congress and beyond. NAWSA thus allowed its local affiliates to define their own positions on women's voting rights, thereby enabling the southern states and other areas where racism dominated to support votes for white women at the expense of black women. Similarly, the NWP forced black women to march at the end of the line in its national suffrage parade in 1913. When the northeastern affiliates of the National Association of Colored Women formally applied for membership in NAWSA in 1918, their request was rejected (they were asked to withdraw the request and complied) as a possible offense to the southern supporters of women's suffrage. Highlighting the raw politics of the suffrage campaign, white women calculated that they needed all the Democratic votes they could get and pushed African American women back in order to reassure southern Democrats who were displeased of the idea of equality in a broader sense. Black women were particularly concerned as the amendment neared passage in Congress because southern senators tried to revise it to explicitly disenfranchise black women and men. For instance, John Williams of Mississippi proposed that the woman suffrage amendment read: "The right of white citizens to vote shall not be denied."[14] In 1919 Louisiana's Edward Gay tried to shift enforcement from the federal government to the states, and another Mississippi senator, Byron "Pat" Harrison, again tried to add the word "white." Although these attempts were not successful, black women recognized their vulnerability since support from the main woman suffrage organizations was so tenuous.

Congressional Insider: Jeannette Rankin

Even as the debates about black women's voting rights continued and as the pressure on Congress increased from both the NWP and NAWSA, the successful passage of the woman suffrage amendment depended on critical members of Congress to push from the inside. One of its primary supporters was Representative Jeannette Rankin of Montana, who was, in 1916, the first woman elected to Congress. Rankin had made a name for herself through her successful leadership of the drive to enfranchise women voters in Montana in 1913. Although her pacifist stand against the war concerned many suffragists, Rankin turned out to be an important member of the House and continued to make suffrage her defining issue.

To get along with her male colleagues, she adopted a variety of strategies. First, when she heard a rumor that "the men, the Republicans, were thinking of asking the Democrats to give me the chairmanship of the women's suffrage committee," she went to the meeting and announced that she did not want to be chairman because "it may cost us a vote or two from the Democrats." Her personal ambitions were less important, in this instance, than whether the appointment of a woman suffragist to the chairmanship would alienate some of her colleagues. She was thinking, in particular, of one member of the committee, the Republican representative Joseph Walsh of Massachusetts, who was "violently opposed to woman's suffrage." She purposefully sat behind him on the floor of the House so that her presence would not be a constant irritant to him. When her manager scheduled a speech for her in Walsh's district, she generously praised him to his constituents before saying: "He has one fault, and that's *your* fault. It's because you haven't converted him. He's against woman's suffrage!" When Walsh learned of her speech and heard her turn down the committee chairmanship, he was disarmed. As Rankin put it, when she declined the chairmanship, "he could not talk against what I was saying. And so he was all mixed up . . . He and I had agreed."[15] The next day he apologized to a bemused Rankin for his earlier hostility and thanked her. As she described it, "[H]e came around to me, and it was the funniest thing I ever heard. He's trying to apologize for being nasty, when I hadn't accused him." Rankin defused the tension surrounding his apology: "I was just pleasant and bashful and pretended I didn't know what he was talking about."[16] Playing the "bashful" and naive young woman, she managed to play on Walsh's paternalism. From that point on, Rankin recounted, they chatted and joked whenever they saw each other, but they never spoke about woman suffrage. He knew her position but, as she explained, "I hadn't beat him over the head every time he came in the office."

When the crucial vote came up in the House in 1918, however, she felt she could ask him for an important favor: "'If you are against woman's suffrage, I'm not going to ask you to vote for it. But I *am* going to ask you *not* to make a speech against it.' I said, 'Your speeches will convert them, and you're such a good speaker.'"[17] Flattered, he agreed to abide by her request and even encouraged other representatives not to change their votes from woman suffrage during the critical recount. Rankin believed that using stereotypically feminine behavior, such as being cheerful, respectful, and deferential, made her appear less threatening and helped her be more successful with male colleagues like Walsh. It was through such strategies that Rankin strengthened support for woman suffrage in the House and Senate.

A Federal Amendment for Woman Suffrage

In January 1918 the House debated the woman suffrage amendment in a new climate: women were claiming the right to vote as patriotic citizens who had been serving their country as volunteers and war workers, New York State had approved woman suffrage, thereby adding to the Democratic support for the amendment, and the imprisoned suffragists had dramatically increased public awareness of their cause. During the intense debate on the floor of the House, both sides restated their positions.

The Democrat William Gordon of Ohio voiced his strong disapproval of woman suffrage and, especially, of the militant activism of the NWP:

> We are threatened by these militant suffragettes with a direct and lawless invasion by the Congress of the United States of the rights of those States which have refused to confer upon their women the privilege of voting. This attitude on the part of some of the suffrage Members of this House is on an exact equality with the acts of these women militants who have spent the last summer and fall, while they were not in the district jail or workhouse, in coaxing, teasing, and nagging the President of the United States for the purpose of inducing him, by coercion, to club Congress into adopting this joint resolution.[18]

Emphasizing states' rights and belittling the suffragists' protests, Gordon used gender-stereotypical language to delegitimize women's political activities. He condemned pro-suffrage lawmakers for weakly succumbing to the women's ostensibly illegitimate demands.

Even those legislators who voted for woman suffrage denied that they were helping to challenge conventional gender roles. Scott Feris, an Oklahoma Democrat, for instance, admitted that he would (reluctantly) vote for woman suffrage but denied that his vote should be interpreted as support for NWP feminists:

> I do not approve of wild militancy, hunger strikes . . . I do not approve of the course of those women that . . . become agitators, lay off their womanly qualities in their efforts to secure votes. I do not approve of anything unwomanly anywhere, any time, and my course today in supporting this suffrage amendment is not guided by such conduct . . .[19]

Feris's fear of "unwomanly" behavior suggests his anxiety about the New Woman — represented by the suffragists in the NWP — who rejected a demure, self-effacing role in favor of independent assertion. The Democrat Frank Clark of Florida raised other fears of women's independence, suggesting that the suffragists' seemingly modest claims that women needed the ballot "for protection" were in fact more ominous. He recounted with horror that a suffragist had explained during a congressional hearing that women wanted protection *from men.* Clark feared the larger impact of woman suffrage on conventional gender roles, wherein women ostensibly were protected *by men.* Some members of Congress used their opposition to the picketing as an excuse to reject the arguments of suffrage lobbyists. The Republican William Greene of Massachusetts had a litmus test, as he explained:

> I have met with several women suffragists from the State of Massachusetts. I have immediately propounded to them this one question: "Do you approve or disapprove of the suffrage banners in front of the White House . . . ?" The answer in nearly every case to my question was "I glory in that demonstration" . . . the response to my question was very offensive, and I immediately ordered these suffrage advocates from my office.[20]

Andrew Volstead of Minnesota made a strong defense not only of woman suffrage but of the picketers. A ranking Republican on the Judiciary Committee, he already had the loyalty of women's groups such as the WCTU for his support of a broad range of moral reforms, including the prohibition of alcohol. With Frances Willard at its head, the WCTU had worked for temperance and woman suffrage since 1881. Since Volstead's career was tied to the support of issues identified as important to women, such as wife abuse, drunken husbands, legal regulation of alcohol, and voting rights, he had much to gain from his prominent endorsement of suffrage. He proclaimed:

> In this discussion some very unfair comments have been made upon the women who picketed the White House. While I do not approve of picketing, I disapprove more strongly of the hoodlum methods pursued in suppressing the practice. I gather from the press that this is what took place. Some women did in a peaceable, and perfectly lawful manner, display suffrage banners on the public street near the White House. To stop this the police allowed the women to be mobbed, and then because the mob obstructed the street, the women were arrested and fined, while the mob went scot-free.[21]

Even one of suffragism's strongest supporters felt compelled to claim that he did not approve of the picketing but then condoned it as a legal peaceful protest.

Some heroic efforts were made to secure a suffrage victory in the House. For instance, James R. Mann, a Republican from Illinois and a close colleague and ally of Jeannette Rankin's, fulfilled his promise to vote for woman suffrage. As Rankin remembered, "[B]efore the vote came, James R. Mann had said to me, 'We'll put this over,' and he asked about the suffragists and what they were doing, and I told him and he said, 'Well you and I will put this over.'"[22] To do so, he had to leave his hospital bed and have assistance as he voted for the amendment while suffrage supporters in the chamber cheered.

Only a day after President Wilson called it a wartime measure in January 1918, the House passed a federal suffrage amendment in a historic vote. A large majority (more than 80 percent) of Republicans supported the amendment, with about half of the Democrats in agreement. The final vote was 274 in favor, 136 opposed — one vote more than the two-thirds majority needed for passage. Analyzing the successful vote, Maud Wood Park of NAWSA explained that the amendment received "100 more [positive votes] than when the amendment had its previous vote. Of this number 56 were due to changes in the votes from the states where there had been recent suffrage victories — 30 of them from men who had voted 'no' in 1915. Clearly it was state gains that carried us over the top."[23] When North Dakota gave women the right to vote, for example, the Republican senator Porter McCumber changed his vote to favor a constitutional amendment: "My own judgement is against this resolution . . . but the legislature of the state of North Dakota passed an act which extended the right of suffrage to women . . . and I feel as a representative of the State I should vote their views rather than my own upon this subject."[24]

NAWSA and the NWP now turned their attention to gaining the amendment in the Senate and applied pressure on the senatorial candidates in the 1918 elections. The NWP made an exception to its policy of punishing the party in power for suffrage defeats in 1918, when the Senate was only two votes away from passage. The NWP then announced it would support the Democratic candidates in two races because they explicitly pledged to vote for the amendment. That year the two organizations flexed their increasing political muscle by running parallel and sometimes successful campaigns to defeat important Senate candidates of both parties who did not support suffrage.

As debate continued in the Senate later that year, NWP activists were arrested while trying to give speeches in Lafayette Park, across from the White House. No charges were filed against them at the time, provoking an outraged response from Senator Charles Curtis of Kansas, a Republican, who pointed out that "the forty-eight suffragists are arrested upon absolutely no charges, and that these women, among them munitions workers and Red Cross workers, are held . . . while the United States attorney for the District of Columbia decides for what offense, 'if any,' they were arrested."[25] The presence of war workers among those arrested lent weight to their demands for full citizenship, to include both rights and responsibilities. Furthermore, the women were placed in a prison that had been deemed uninhabitable and had been closed since 1909. After several senators visited their constituents, the authorities were forced to release all of them. Once free, some of the women traveled around the country in a car called "the prison special." Wearing their prison uniforms and giving rousing speeches, they raised people's awareness of the sacrifices women were making in their attempts to win the vote. The prison special generated a great deal of media attention and drew huge, sympathetic crowds that condemned the women's cruel treatment.

Intense pressure from the suffragists ultimately forced President Wilson to produce the last two votes needed in the Senate, where it had been more difficult to overcome the power of the southern Democrats. Although reluctant to use political capital on this issue when he was in the midst of negotiating the Versailles peace treaty in Paris, Wilson found that he could not ignore the negative publicity that women's protests about a lack of democracy in America were having on his attempts to guarantee democracy abroad. With one vote needed, he telegraphed the new Democratic senator William Harris of Georgia to come to Paris, where he personally gained his vote.

Victory

The Susan B. Anthony amendment finally passed in a Republican Congress in May 1919, 304–89. Whereas nearly all the Republican senators voted for it, only just over half of the Democrats voted for it (the vote was 66–30). It then took fourteen months to gain the thirty-six states needed to approve the amendment by a two-thirds majority. Tennessee, the thirty-sixth state, was barely won by the suffragists. All women were finally allowed to vote in the national election of November 1920.

Subsequent Gains and Losses

Once women achieved the vote, expectations were raised even higher about what organized voting women could accomplish legislatively. Women found they had gained — at least temporarily — increased clout in debates about congressional legislation. Before the amendment was passed, there was a strong belief among the senators and representatives (as well as the women themselves) that women would vote in blocs on issues that were ostensibly of particular importance to women. In particular, any legislation affecting infants, children, and mothers was expected to be embraced by the great majority of voting women. As women came close to securing the vote, legislation was introduced in Congress to provide federal support for prenatal and infant care as well as for the training and health of pregnant women and new mothers; it passed in 1921 as the Sheppard-Towner Act. Yet in the 1924 elections, politicians saw that women — just like men — split their votes among parties and followed the class and ethnic ties that claimed their loyalty just as much or more than their gender. Women's voting patterns showed no "gender gap," ironically suggesting to politicians that it would be easier than it had been in the past two decades to resist or ignore women reformers' calls for changes in federal laws. Once their fear of women as a unified bloc of millions of voters had diminished, congressional opponents of social welfare legislation went on the offensive against women's claims to a legitimate place in public policy debates and government agencies. They attacked social welfare legislation, for example, as an expensive and even communistic attempt to subvert states' rights and parental rights.

Overall, women's influence in Congress grew in the early twentieth century. Organized women's groups brought a variety of important issues before Congress, ranging from suffrage, temperance, the Children's Bureau, censorship legislation, legislation against lynching, and the Sheppard-Towner Act. The women pressed their demands through petitions, lobbying, letters and telegrams to their representatives, picketing, hunger strikes, parades, holding the party in power responsible, making changes in laws at the state level, and strong grass-roots networking. Many members of Congress, especially Republicans reformers and later urban Democrats, felt they could not ignore the organized women. Thus, a coalition of women's organizations and legislative insiders pushed Congress to act, helping to shore up the coalition of both Republicans and Democrats that approved the creation of a federal Children's Bureau and passed the woman suffrage amendment.

— Alison M. Parker

BIBLIOGRAPHICAL NOTES

For an overview of the gradual move toward universal suffrage, see Alexander Keyssar, *The Right to Vote: The Contested History of Democracy in the United States* (New York, 2000). The history of the U.S. Congress and constitutional amendments is explored in David E. Kyvig, *Explicit and Authentic Acts: Amending the U.S. Constitution, 1776–1995* (Lawrence, Kans., 1996). A history of the Children's Bureau is Robyn Muncy, *Creating a Female Dominion in American Reform, 1890–1935* (New York, 1991). Efforts to attain mothers' pensions and the Children's Bureau are explored in Theda Skocpol, *Protecting Soldiers and Mothers: The Political Origins of Social Policy in the United States* (Cambridge, Mass., 1992); Linda Gordon, *Pitied but Not Entitled: Single Mothers and the History of Welfare, 1890–1935* (New York, 1994); and Alisa Klaus, *Every Child a Lion: The Origins of Maternal and Infant Health Policy in the United States and France, 1890–1920* (Ithaca, N.Y., 1993). For discussions of women's progressive activism, see Noralee Frankel and Nancy S. Dye, eds., *Gender, Class, Race, and Reform in the Progressive Era* (Lexington, Ky., 1991). Fascinating explorations of maternalist activism are Seth Koven and Sonya Michel, eds., *Mothers of a New World: Maternalist Politics and the Origins of Welfare States* (New York, 1993), and Molly Ladd-

Taylor, *Mother-Work: Women, Child Welfare, and the State, 1890–1930* (Urbana, Ill., 1994).

For useful discussions of the fight for woman suffrage, see Jean H. Baker, ed., *Votes for Women: The Struggle for Suffrage Revisited* (New York, 2002); Edith Mayo, "Introduction," in *Jailed for Freedom: American Women Win the Vote,* by Doris Stevens, ed. Carol O'Hare (New York, 1920; reprint 1995); and Marjorie Spruill Wheeler, ed., *One Woman, One Vote: Rediscovering the Woman Suffrage Movement* (Troutdale, Ore., 1995).

NOTES

1. The National American Woman Suffrage Association, *Victory: How Women Won It, A Centennial Symposium, 1840–1940* (New York, 1940), 129–31.
2. Theda Skocpol, *Protecting Soldiers and Mothers: The Political Origins of Social Policy in the United States* (Cambridge, Mass., 1992), 484.
3. As quoted in Elisabeth Griffith, *In Her Own Right: The Life of Elizabeth Cady Stanton* (New York, 1984), 168.
4. Alexander Keyssar, *The Right to Vote: The Contested History of Democracy in the United States* (New York, 2000), 185–87.
5. *Victory,* 124.
6. Doris Stevens, *Jailed for Freedom* (New York, 1920), 249.
7. Ibid., 251.
8. *Victory,* 170–71.
9. Ibid., 171.
10. Ibid., 134.
11. Eileen Borris, "The Power of Motherhood: Black and White Activist Women Redefine the 'Political,'" in *Mothers of a New World,* 230–31.
12. *Victory,* 126–27.
13. Stevens, *Jailed for Freedom,* 142.
14. As quoted in Rosalyn Terborg-Penn, "African American Women and the Woman Suffrage Movement," in *One Woman, One Vote,* 149.
15. *Suffragists Oral History Project: Jeannette Rankin: Activist for World Peace, Women's Rights, and Democratic Government* (Berkeley, Calif., 1974), 18.
16. Ibid., 254.
17. Ibid., 18–19.
18. Stevens, *Jailed for Freedom,* 253.
19. Ibid., 135.
20. Ibid., 258.
21. Ibid., 174.
22. *Jeannette Rankin,* 20.
23. *Victory,* 133.
24. Ibid., 127.
25. Stevens: *Jailed for Freedom,* 272–73.

Hattie Caraway

February 1, 1878–December 21, 1950

Hattie Caraway

Few of Hattie Wyatt Caraway's contemporaries may have expected her to become the first woman elected to the Senate. Appointed to fill out the remaining months of her deceased husband's term in 1931 and dubbed "Silent Hattie" for her pensive manner, Caraway proceeded to be twice elected to the Senate, becoming the first woman to preside over a Senate session and the first woman to chair a Senate committee.

Born in 1878 near Bakersville, Tennessee, Hattie Wyatt earned a bachelor's degree in 1896 at Dickson (Tennessee) Normal College, where she met a fellow student named Thaddeus Horatius Caraway. They were married in 1902, had three sons, and settled in Jonesboro, Arkansas, where Thaddeus practiced law and Hattie managed the couple's farm.

Thaddeus entered local, then state politics. He was elected to the House of Representatives in 1912 and to the Senate in 1920. Reelected in 1926, he died unexpectedly in 1931, and the governor of Arkansas appointed Hattie to fill his seat in November. In January 1932 she won a special election to complete the remaining months of her husband's term. Visitors to the Senate chamber noticed the woman sitting quietly at her desk, knitting or working on crossword puzzles. When asked why she never spoke on the Senate floor, Caraway remarked, "The men have left nothing unsaid."

To the surprise of many, she decided to run in the general election that fall and received the strong support of Huey Long (who was allegedly motivated by his dislike for Joseph T. Robinson, the powerful senator from Arkansas who served as majority leader). Long drove up from Louisiana to join Caraway on a whirlwind campaign tour, driving two thousand miles and making forty speeches in one week. Caraway won the 1932 election with twice as many votes as her nearest competitor.

Some may attribute this victory to Long's support, but Caraway ran on her own political record and her advocacy of New Deal programs when she was reelected to the Senate in 1938. In the years leading up to the war, she opposed isolationism and supported the rights of veterans and organized labor. In 1943 Caraway marked two milestones. She was the first woman in Congress to cosponsor the Equal Rights Amendment. And on October 19 she formally took up the gavel as the Senate's first woman acting president pro tempore.

But in 1944 Caraway lost the Democratic primary nomination to Representative J. William Fulbright; after thirteen years in the Senate, she retired. She then remained in Washington, working in civil service positions until her death in 1950.

Caraway's achievements in the Senate, like those of other politicians, were perhaps eclipsed by the monumental issues of the period — the Depression, the New Deal, and World War II. On her final day in office, however, her Senate colleagues honored Caraway with a standing ovation. More than half a century later, in 2001, the postal service issued a 76-cent Hattie Caraway stamp as part of its Distinguished American series.

References

"Caraway, Hattie." *Biographical Directory of the United States Congress.* Retrieved on June 11, 2003, from http://bioguide.congress.gov/scripts/biodisplay.pl?index=C000138.

"Caraway, Hattie Wyatt." Retreived June 11, 2003, from U.S. Senator Blanche Lincoln's Web site, http://www.senate.gov/~lincoln/html/hattaway.html.

Malone, D. 1989. *Hattie and Huey: An Arkansas Tour.* Fayetteville: University of Arkansas Press.

Jeannette Pickering Rankin

June 11, 1880–May 18, 1973

Jeannette Pickering Rankin emerged from Montana to become one of the most powerful suffragists in the United States and, possibly, the country's most enduring antiwar activist. She was the first woman to speak before the Montana legislature, the first woman elected to the U.S. Congress, and the only legislator — man or woman — to vote against the United States entering World War II after the Japanese attack on Pearl Harbor. "As a woman," she argued, "I can't go to war, and I refuse to send anyone else." In or out of political office, Rankin advocated peace over the course of five decades. She was the only legislator to vote against U.S. involvement in both world wars, each vote sabotaging any hope of her reelection. In the following years, Rankin spoke out against the Korean War and the military buildup of the Cold War, and in 1968, at the age of eighty-eight, she led a group of approximately five thousand women in a march on Capitol Hill to deliver a petition calling for the withdrawal of all U.S. forces from Vietnam.

Gender aside, Rankin was something of a rarity in Congress when she arrived in 1917. As one of Montana's two at-large representatives, she was an idealistic and dedicated crusader for social, political, and economic reform. She had no trouble taking stands that alienated many of her colleagues, as well as her constituents. She was one of only 49 House members to vote against the declaration of war on Germany, which put her at odds with suffragists who felt a pacifist position would hurt their movement. Nonetheless, her efforts contributed to the passage of the Nineteenth Amendment, guaranteeing women the right to vote. Rankin also fought to ensure equal employment for women in wartime work and exposed illegal working conditions at the U.S. Bureau of Printing and Engraving, which were soon halted. She introduced legislation to allow women to retain their U.S. citizenship after they married men from other nations, and she sponsored a bill to establish a government program to instruct women about maternity, child care, and, controversially, birth control. Both bills were passed after her congressional term had ended. Less than a year into her first term, however, Rankin spoke out for Montana's miners in a dispute with the Anaconda Copper Company, which did not sit well with the industry-influenced Montana legislature. By the time she was up for reelection in 1918, lawmakers had split the state into two congressional districts, with Rankin's gerrymandered to be overwhelmingly Democratic. Unwilling to concede defeat, Rankin campaigned unsuccessfully for a Senate seat, first as a Republican, then as a third-party candidate. After leaving office, she attended a prestigious women's congress abroad and returned to Capitol Hill to lobby for various pacifist organizations.

When Rankin again arrived in Congress, in 1941, there were seven other women in Congress, but Rankin remained an outsider. Her vote against the declaration of war on Japan met with universal condemnation. Her political career was obliterated after her term expired, and she almost disappeared from the public eye, although she continued campaigning for peace. In 1967, the Women's Strike for Peace sought her out to lead its march on Washington, which was dubbed the Jeannette Rankin Brigade. Until her death six years later, she took part in many peace demonstrations.

Rankin was born on a ranch near Missoula, the oldest of seven children. Her parents supported her education, and she received a bachelor's degree in biology from the University of Montana in 1902. After graduation, she traveled to Boston to visit her brother, then enrolled at Harvard University and was deeply affected by the scale of urban poverty she witnessed. The experience ignited her passion for reform, and she proceeded to do social work and to study at the New York School of Philanthropy and the University of Washington. Through her work and her studies, Rankin was introduced to many national figures in the suffragist movement, and she returned to Montana to organize the Equal Franchise Society, which led to her historic speech before the Montana legislature in 1911. In her later years, Rankin said, "If I had my life to live over, I would do it all again, but this time I would be nastier."

References

"Jeannette Pickering Rankin." *Encyclopedia of World Biography,* 2nd ed. 17 vols. Gale Research, 1998. Retrieved December 10, 2003, from http://galenet.galegroup.com/servlet/BioRC.

"Jeannette Rankin." *Contemporary Heroes and Heroines,* Book III. Edited by Terrie M. Rooney. Gale Research, 1998. Retrieved December 10, 2003, from http://galenet.galegroup.com/servlet/BioRC.

"Jeannette Pickering Rankin." *Dictionary of American Biography,* Supplement 9: 1971–75. Charles Scribner's Sons, 1994. Retrieved December 10, 2003, from http://galenet.galegroup.com/servlet/BioRC.

23

The Transformation of American Immigration Policy

Congress has dominated American immigration policy for more than a century. Modern presidents have shown uneven interest in the subject; the courts and bureaucratic agencies have tended to defer to congressional plenary power in this area; and state governments have lacked the authority to make their own policies. Congress, however, has actively governed immigration, its committees regularly crafting immigration reform laws great and small. But the story is far from simple because congressional activism on immigration is the legacy of the pivotal transitional period of the late nineteenth and early twentieth centuries, when American society, the legislative process, and national immigration policy were all transformed.

The unprecedented variety and sheer volume of immigration between the 1880s and 1920s set the tone for this season of change. During the heyday of German, Irish, and Scandinavian immigration, from 1841 to 1880, roughly 8.3 million newcomers arrived in the United States. Between 1881 and 1920, the immigrant tide soared to over 20 million. These massive numbers dramatically extended the ethnic and religious diversity of American society. Most newcomers before the 1890s could trace their origin to northern and western Europe; the leading source countries in the 1880s, for instance, were Germany, England, Ireland, and Sweden. From the 1890s on, however, the large majority of immigrants came from southern and eastern European countries like Italy, Russia, Hungary, Poland, and Greece. And by the turn of the century, immigration was increasingly Jewish and Eastern Orthodox in faith, unsettling Protestant America as much as the heavily Catholic inflows had done since the 1840s.

As in the past, these new waves of immigration inspired broad opposition. Northeastern academics, upper-class professionals, and political leaders formed the Immigration Restriction League as the last line of defense for Anglo-Saxon traditions. Their efforts were applauded throughout the country by social scientists and eugenicists, whose studies emphasized the hereditary inferiority of the southern and eastern European arrivals. The nativist coalition also attracted Asian exclusionists on the West Coast as well as southern politicians, Grangers, and Farmers' Alliances that saw immigration as a menacing racial and urban force. Numerous patriotic societies like the Junior Order of United American Mechanics and the Daughters of the American Revolution lent support to the cause. Finally, the nation's preeminent labor organization, the American Federation of Labor, embraced stringent immigration restriction as a means of guarding native-born workers.

At the same time, an equally broad coalition emerged to defend the new immigration. Associations of older ethnic groups, such as the German-American Alliance and the Ancient Order of Hibernians, set out to oppose the restrictionist initiatives. Newer organizations followed suit, forming a Liberal Immigration League to counterpoise the Immigration Restriction League. Jewish organizations like the American Jewish Committee and the Hebrew Immigrant Aid Society were especially active. These associations found common cause with a variety of business groups with an interest in sustaining large-scale immigration. In particular, the National Association of Manufacturers, railroad and steamship companies, and large industrial employers championed unfettered access to the immigrant labor market. Prominent social reformers like Jane Addams and Frances Kellor as well as cosmopolitan intellectuals such as Horace Kallen and Charles Eliot also defended a largely tolerant, laissez-faire approach to new immigration. In Congress, only northern Democrats representing urban districts or states with large immigrant populations consistently opposed restrictionist designs.

Despite these formidable coalitions on both sides of the issue, the cause of immigration restriction ultimately triumphed decisively in the early twentieth century. It was not so in the beginning. For decades after the short-lived Alien and Sedition Acts of 1798, Congress was largely content to leave the task of immigration control to a handful of states whose port cities received the bulk of the nineteenth-century tide of new arrivals from Europe. Several immigration laws that Congress did enact before the Gilded Age were largely designed to encourage sustained European inflows by establishing easy terms of naturalization, promoting safe overseas passage, and making white male aliens eligible for free western lands under the Homestead Act. Despite the best efforts of nativist political movements like the Order of United Americans and the Know-Nothings, the cause of immigration restriction languished in Congress until late in the century. When the 1880s began, virtually no federal legislative framework or regulatory apparatus concerning immigration existed. Less than half a century later, however, national lawmakers constructed an elaborate system of draconian restrictions, including eugenics-inspired national origins quotas, racial exclusions, and literacy tests. Congress also gave administrative teeth to these formidable legal barriers by establishing a rigorous process of overseas consular inspection for prospective immigrants by new and efficient State Department agencies.

Why did Congress come to impose such sweeping restrictions on immigration after its benign neglect for most of the century? The answer lies in both structural innovations within Congress and powerful new pressures outside it. As we shall see, this reinvention of American immigration policy would reflect the profound social and political changes ushered in by the Progressive era and the First World War, including unprecedented southern and eastern European immigration, the elevation of social scientific expertise, new forms of interest group activism, greater international engagement, and the rise of the national security state. It also would be propelled by important shifts in the legislative process itself, as the power of party leadership and discipline in Congress gave way to increased committee government and legislative professionalism.

Partisan Politics and Immigration Restriction: A Tale of Two Policies

Large-scale immigration was fueled throughout the nineteenth century by the nation's insatiable appetite for Europeans to meet its enormous labor needs and to settle its vast, undeveloped western lands. In turn, new waves of immigration inspired popular and organized opposition, from the anti-Masons of the 1830s and the Know-Nothings of the 1850s to the American Protective Association of the 1890s. Yet neither congressional leaders nor a majority of the rank-and-file members were eager to abandon the federal government's essentially tolerant, laissez-faire policy toward the newcomers. Once large-scale immigration began, easy naturalization and voting laws for white male newcomers created important voting blocs with whom party politicians, especially Democrats, curried favor by defending robust alien admissions and rights. At the very start of the century, Jeffersonians made much of the xenophobia of their opponents during elections. Democratic Republicans enacted easy terms of admission and naturalization, and they promised immigrant voters that the United States would be a New Canaan where they would "be received as brothers." Decades later, during the election of 1884, the Democratic platform touted "the liberal principles embodied by Jefferson . . . which makes ours the land of liberty and the asylum of the oppressed of every nation" as "cardinal principles in the Democratic faith."

On the few occasions when the Whig and Republican presidential campaigns openly embraced xenophobic positions, they usually paid dearly for it in crucial electoral states such as New York. Immigrant and kindred ethnic voting blocs overshadowed the benefits of restrictionist appeals. Moreover, Republican politicians tended to view European immigration as consistent with broader ambitions for national economic development by providing workers to fuel industrial growth and western territorial development. The Homestead Act of 1862, for instance, offered 160 acres of free land to citizens and newcomers alike who worked it for at least five years. As warfare took its toll on the American labor force, Abraham Lincoln praised immigration "as one of the principal replenishing streams, which are appointed by Providence to repair the ravages of internal war, and its wastes of national strength and health." Overall, national labor needs and the vibrant partisan and electoral politics of nineteenth-century America — sufficiently democratic to extend broad political rights to white male newcomers — routinely frustrated nativist policy designs in Congress until late in the century.

Chinese immigration caused Congress in the 1880s to take the first tentative steps toward regulating and restricting immigration.

Roughly 250,000 Chinese entered the United States between 1850 and 1882 to fill the labor demands of western railroad construction, mining, and agriculture. Although the number of arrivals was rather modest compared to the European inflows, the Chinese quickly became a target of popular hostility and official discrimination on the Pacific coast. Federal naturalization laws deprived them of citizenship and the ballot box. When jobs became scarce for white workers in California and other western states in the 1870s, labor unions and civic associations organized a large, grass-roots Sinophobic movement that blamed the immigrants for a host of social and economic ills. After a powerful new Chinese Exclusion League demonstrated its ability to command a broad and passionate following among West Coast voters, California's political leaders rushed to enact stringent restrictions on Chinese immigration and civil rights.

Judicial activism was the next crucial catalyst. Without judicial intervention, Congress may have remained on the sidelines as agitation against the Chinese played out in regional politics. In 1874, however, the state's efforts to restrict Chinese admissions were challenged in California's federal circuit court. In his ruling, Justice Stephen Field expressed sympathy with the "general feeling" of Californians that "the dissimilarity in physical characteristics, in language, in manners, religion and habits, will always prevent any possible assimilation of them with our people." He nevertheless invalidated the state's efforts to curb Chinese entry on the grounds that they encroached on exclusive congressional authority to regulate foreign commerce. The death knell for state regulation of *all* immigrant admissions — Chinese and European — came one year later when the Supreme Court determined that officials in coastal states lacked the constitutional authority to exercise even modest control over the vast immigrant traffic through their urban ports. The landmark *Henderson v. Mayor of New York* (1875) decision urged Congress to provide for national uniformity in its alien admissions policy. "The laws which govern the right to land passengers in the United States from other countries ought to be the same in New York, Boston, New Orleans, and San Francisco," the Court averred.

Judicial activism in immigration law dramatically altered the strategy of the Sinophobes. Immediately after the Civil War, activists against the Chinese directed most of their energies to shaping state and local policies. Judicial limitations on state police powers created new imperatives; Chinese exclusion could be achieved only if Congress established new federal controls. "Our only hope," Senator Aaron Sargent of California told his Sinophobic constituents, "is in the National Government."

In the fiercely competitive party system of the time — characterized by rock-hard sectional partisanship both north and south of the Mason-Dixon Line — many national party leaders saw the protean electorate of the far western states as crucial to future electoral mastery. With overwhelming bipartisan support, Congress in 1875 addressed two perceived evils associated with Chinese immigration by barring the admission of alien prostitutes and Asian contract workers whose presence was perceived as hurting native-born laborers. A year later, the leaders of the Democratic House and Republican Senate raced to create a Joint Special Committee to Investigate Chinese Immigration. Senator Sargent, a prominent figure on the Special Committee, was once an enthusiastic supporter of the 1868 Burlingame Treaty which encouraged Chinese immigration, believing that it would yield lucrative trade relations with the Far East. As Sinophobic politics swept over California in the 1870s, however, he became one of the most vociferous advocates of Chinese exclusion. When the Joint Special Committee was established, Sargent was a vice president of the San Francisco Anti Coolie Union.

The committee's final report, written by Sargent, was all but a foregone conclusion concerning the undesirability of Chinese arrivals. It asserted that they were incapable of self-government and harmful to native white workers. Soon thereafter, lawmakers from both parties began crafting Chinese exclusion bills, like the Fifteen Passenger Bill of 1875, which hoped to bar vessels from transporting more than fifteen Chinese passengers in order to discourage large inflows. President Rutherford B. Hayes vetoed the bill on the grounds that only the executive could abrogate the Burlingame Treaty. The maelstrom of criticism that followed shook the president, who expressed dismay that his veto was "bitterly denounced in the west" and had led to his being burned in effigy in violent protests. Hayes soon threw his support behind Chinese exclusion efforts.

Against this backdrop, the former abolitionist William Lloyd Garrison publicly assailed the "demagogical, partisan rivalry between Republican and Democrat as to who should most strongly cater to the brutal, persecuting spirit which is so rampant in California." According to the editors of the *New York Times*, the political stakes were obvious: "Which great political party is foolish enough to risk losing the votes of the Pacific States by undertaking to do justice to the Chinese?" Congress in 1882 overwhelmingly passed the ignominious Chinese Exclusion Act, which suspended the immigration of Chinese laborers for ten years, provided for new means of deporting Chinese from U.S. territory, and clarified that no state government or federal court could grant citizenship to resident Chinese. In subsequent years (usually on the eve of national elections), large bipartisan majorities in both houses of Congress enacted increasingly draconian exclusion legislation that barred Chinese immigration for longer periods of time, eliminated exceptions, and imposed harsh restrictions on the liberties of resident Chinese. Under the Geary Act of 1892, for example, Chinese newcomers were required to prove that their residence was legal by producing a white witness to testify that they resided in the country before 1882. In addition, the act denied bail to Chinese defendants in habeas corpus proceedings and required all Chinese to register for and carry a certificate of residence. The law also renewed the immigration ban of the original Chinese Exclusion Act of 1882.

If the judicial nullification of state immigration controls fueled Chinese exclusion, it elicited a markedly different response from Congress on European immigration. For six years after the Court's *Henderson* ruling, Congress turned a deaf ear to demands from the legislatures and immigration boards of New York, Massachusetts, Maryland, and other "front line" states that the federal government assume responsibility for the economic and social burdens of European immigration. In contrast to the demands of the Pacific coast states for Chinese exclusion, in which precious western votes were at stake, the fiscal complaints of northeastern states were anything but compelling for national lawmakers. Moreover, each of these major states had strong immigrant voting blocs — thanks to generous naturalization laws for white men — that promoted only a modest regulation of European inflows.

Frustrated by delays, in 1881 New York's Board of Emigration Commissioners threatened to shut down the nation's largest immigrant-receiving station, Castle Garden, and to cease all forms of state-level immigrant assistance. Congress reluctantly responded by adopting legislation that essentially nationalized the state policies on European immigration that had been struck down by the Court. The Immigration Act of 1882 borrowed language from state statutes to restrict the admission of "any convict, lunatic, idiot, or any person unable to take care of himself or herself without becoming a public charge." It also established a system of funding immigrant inspections and providing for the welfare of new arrivals by assessing head taxes on each entrant. However, the federal government lacked the administrative capacities to enforce these modest new regulatory policies. Congress resolved this dilemma by authorizing state immigration boards and commissioners to enforce federal legislation as directed by U.S. Treasury officials. The 1882 law essentially placed the national government's imprimatur on well-established state regulations and restored the power of state and local officials to implement these policies under Treasury Department guidance.

Amid immigration surges and economic depression in the early 1880s, American labor unions clamored for federal legislation to prohibit industrial employers from importing immigrant workers to break strikes or to hold down wages. The Democratic leaders who controlled the House responded to this mounting pressure with great care. While the Democratic party positioned itself as the traditional defender of European immigrants, it also nurtured close ties with labor unions, including the first mass movement of U.S. workers, the Knights of Labor. To avoid offending either of these vital constituencies, the House Democrats assailed only that European immigration which resulted from "greedy capitalists" establishing contractual agreements with unskilled alien workers. The House party leaders proposed an Anti-Contract Labor Bill in 1884 that would make it unlawful for any person or corporation to pay for the passage or assist in the importation of aliens in exchange for labor in the United States. Lest foreign-born voters misinterpret the law's intent, the Democrats explained that it "in no way seeks to restrict or prohibit voluntary or free immigration." During the 1884 campaign season, congressional Republicans also endorsed a ban on contract labor. Within a year, a federal contract labor ban became law.

Although Congress finally assumed responsibility for regulating immigration in the 1880s, it is significant that its early legislation was neither intended to nor had the effect of disturbing the nation's long-standing tolerance of expansive European immigration. Labor needs and foreign-born votes continued to reinforce established policy patterns of encouraging new waves of European arrivals. In the decade Congress assumed regulatory control, European immigration to the United States reached 5 million (nearly twice that of the previous decade) and represented close to 40 percent of the country's total population growth.

An Era of Transition: Immigration and Progressivism

In 1890 standing immigration committees were established in the House and Senate illustrating the expanding scale and complexity of legislative work at the turn of the century as Congress undertook significant new policy responsibilities. Woodrow Wilson astutely described the standing congressional committees of this period as "little legislatures" that often served as "the most essential machinery of our governmental system." The House and Senate immigration committees were no exception. They were dominated early on by New England patricians like Senators William Chandler (R-New Hampshire) and Henry Cabot Lodge (R-Massachusetts) and Representative Samuel McCall (R-Massachusetts). Lodge became enamored of immigration restriction while studying at Harvard University, where he received its first doctorate in political science by writing a thesis on Anglo-Saxon law and heritage. By 1891 Lodge noted with alarm that European immigration was "making its greatest relative increase from races most alien to the body of the American people and from the lowest and most illiterate classes of those races" — namely, that of southern and eastern Europeans.

The new standing committees welcomed independent expertise, favored policy activism, and specifically backed new restrictions on European immigration. In the process, they came to institutionalize formal input from immigration experts and interest group activists and regularized the drafting and proposal of reform legislation. A national immigration policy network of restrictionist and pro-immigration lobbies centered in the nation's capital soon grew around them. In coming years, however, the innovative designs of the new committees would face tough scrutiny — and sometimes decisive opposition — from congressional party leaders with very different goals.

The initial proposals of the committees were not controversial. They called for a new federal bureaucracy, the Immigration Bureau, within the Treasury Department to screen and assist immigrants. Passed easily in both houses, the Immigration Act of 1891 replaced state agencies and private associations with a corps of U.S. immigration inspectors at new federal immigration stations like Ellis Island in New York City. In addition, the law made it possible to exclude persons suffering from contagious diseases and polygamists. However, the work of the congressional committees soon focused on the more volatile question of whether new southern and eastern European immigrants — Italians, Hungarians, Slavs, Greeks, and Jews fleeing persecution in Russia, Poland, and Romania — were less desirable than newcomers from Germany, England, Ireland, France, and Scandinavia. The committees embraced the view of social scientists and interest groups associated with a new immigration restriction movement that southern and eastern Europeans "are beaten men from beaten races," whose entry must be discouraged. Early in 1896, the House and Senate immigration committees endorsed a literacy test that would screen out potential immigrants who were naturally inferior and thereby could not be assimilated. On the Senate floor, Henry Cabot Lodge explained that the genius of the literacy test was its capacity to filter out racial and ethnic undesirables. He assured his colleagues that the test "will bear most heavily" upon southern and eastern Europeans "and very lightly, or not at all, upon English-speaking emigrants or Germans, Scandinavians, and French." Highlighting social Darwinian and eugenicist ideas, Lodge warned that "it involves nothing less than the possibility of a great and perilous change in the fabric of our race."

On the heels of economic depression and widespread public concern about the sheer volume of immigration (9 million immigrants entered the United States in the last two decades of the nineteenth century), Samuel McCall and other reform-minded members of the House immigration committee won approval of a literacy test bill by emphasizing expert findings that the test would not slow traditional northern and western European immigration. On the eve of the 1896 election, however, Republican leaders in the Senate balked at acting on the measure during the campaign. Their reluctance was heightened by Democratic charges that the "real purpose" of the bill was "hostility to the Catholic Church" and sweeping immigration restriction. The Senate GOP leaders eventually compromised with Lodge, promising to consider his bill after the election. When the Senate opened its new session, Lodge's literacy test bill was passed with broad Republican support. Its success owed much to the endorsement of the immigration committee, prominent support from social scientists, and the relative absence of opposition from interest groups. But as the House and Senate conferees met, business and ethnic groups favoring immigration mobilized to defeat the measure. German-American groups sent petitions and telegrams of protest to every member of Congress. The conference report later passed the Senate by only two votes, a reflection of the growing organized opposition. After being lobbied heavily by various ethnic leaders, President Grover Cleveland, a Democrat, ultimately vetoed the bill. "It is said that the quality of recent immigration is undesirable," his blistering veto noted. "The time is quite within recent memory when the same thing was said of immigrants, who, with their descendants, are now numbered among our best citizens."

Immigration committee sponsors of the test were initially optimistic about their chances of obtaining reform legislation after the 1896 election. The Republicans gained seats in both houses, and Cleveland's successor, William McKinley, supported the test. But Republican congressional leaders and party managers grew cautious as organized resistance mounted from the National Association of Manufacturers, steamship and railroad companies, and other business groups. Huge national rallies were organized by German, Italian, Irish, Jewish, and Catholic leaders to denounce Lodge's proposal. On a platform adorned with a colorful array of national flags, ethnic leaders warned the Republican leaders that "the votes of foreign-born men elected William McKinley President" and that continued support for the literacy test would cost the party dearly. The Republican leaders chose not to try to override Cleveland's veto and delayed action on literacy test bills in later years. As Representative McCall explained to the Immigration Restriction League in 1898, business and ethnic group pressure "frightened a good many of the members" and left the House Speaker Thomas Reed with little room to maneuver. Faced with an impasse, Congress decided to establish the Industrial Commission to collect and study information on immigration and to offer legislative recommendations. The new body offered party managers a brief reprieve from divisive immigration debate.

The Industrial Commission conducted extensive research and hearings that culminated in a nineteen-volume report in 1901. Congress codified most of its recommendations in 1903 legislation, including the exclusion of anarchists, epileptics, and the mentally insane, the creation of a new system for guarding U.S. borders, and the improvement of Chinese exclusion and contract labor laws. With President Theodore Roosevelt's endorsement, Senator Lodge reintroduced and won broad support for a literacy test of all immigrants older than sixteen in 1906. In the House, this proposal elicited a clash between old and new legislative norms. The bill was most prominently championed by reform-minded members of the House Committee on Immigration and Naturalization, like Augustus Gardner (R-Massachusetts), who took pains to link their restrictive proposals to expert research and the ideals of social control and racial purity. Gardner was in fact Lodge's own son-in-law and an equally fervent restrictionist who believed that southern and eastern European immigration would taint the nation's older Anglo-Saxon stock.

Nativist lawmakers like Gardner in the House ultimately faced withering opposition from Speaker Joseph "Uncle Joe" Cannon, whose "stand-pat" principles contrasted with the Progressive reform spirit. Cannon and other House "organization" Republicans had special reasons to oppose the immigration bill. Lobbied intensely by ethnic groups and the Liberal Immigration League, they worried that the measure might provoke electoral retaliation from foreign-born voters; Cannon also worried about his own Illinois constituents, who included a cross section of European immigrants and kindred ethnics. House party managers also joined business groups in claiming that sweeping immigration restrictions would deprive employers of a critical labor supply. In contrast to the nativist Progressives, who called for legal mechanisms to deter southern and eastern European inflows, Cannon and his loyalists saw the country as "a hell of a success," requiring little change, and he was prepared to use the ample powers of the partisan Speakership to block immigration reform.

When Augustus Gardner's literacy test bill was reported out by the House Immigration Committee in 1906, for months Cannon flatly refused to permit it to reach the House floor. He relented only after Gardner and his allies threatened to appeal to the entire House Republican caucus. However, his subservient Rules Committee stipulated that no yea or nay vote could be taken on the bill's literacy test provision, limited the debate to three hours, and permitted only one amendment for each section of the bill. During the final minutes of the floor debate, the goals of the Rules Committee became apparent when Charles Grosvenor (R-Ohio), a critical member of Cannon's leadership team, stunned the restrictionists by proposing an amendment substituting a new investigatory committee for the literacy test. An enraged Gardner insisted that Grosvenor's amendment was not germane to the literacy test section. "Why here is the report of the Senate, and here is the report of the House, and here is the report of the Industrial Commission," Gardner fumed. "Yet you are talking this nonsense about another commission." The presiding chair, a Cannon lieutenant, overruled Gardner's objection. When a simple division (entailing those for and against a measure to stand until counted by the chair) was held on Grosvenor's amendment, it failed, 136–123. In a brazen exercise of power, Cannon successfully ordered a recount on the grounds that a simple division was inadequate. The members now were required to register their votes by passing between official tellers stationed in the well of the House. As the rank-and-file members milled down to the tellers, they were confronted personally by Cannon and his lieutenants. Newspapers reported the next morning that Cannon grabbed wavering members by their coat lapels, convincing a handful to switch their votes and others to retreat to the cloakrooms without voting. Grosvenor's amendment prevailed, 128–116, in the recount, thereby defeating Gardner's provision.

The next day, the *New York Times* reported that Cannon "overrode the Committee on Immigration" in "one of the most extraordinary spectacles ever seen on the floor of the House."

For months, Cannon loyalists squared off in conference committee against the Senate conferees led by Lodge and William Dillingham (R-Vermont), who pressed for the literacy test. Eventually the Roosevelt administration persuaded the senators to end the stalemate by conceding the literacy test in favor of the Immigration Act of 1907, which established a new investigatory commission, restrictions on those with tuberculosis, and an increased immigrant head tax. Cannon called for an investigatory commission in order to delay action on restrictionist immigration reform proposals, but the new Dillingham Commission had a profound effect on legislation in an era that increasingly celebrated expertise and scientific government. Its exhaustive forty-two-volume study of immigration matters seemed to legitimize the claims that southern and eastern Europeans were less able to assimilate than older immigrant groups, and its lengthy recommendations were unequivocally restrictionist initiatives, including the literacy test and a national origins quota scheme for reducing unwanted immigration.

Reverently invoking the commission findings, the congressional immigration committees endorsed a so-called Dillingham bill in 1913 that most prominently featured a literacy test provision. The bill passed both houses with ease, quietly aided by institutional reforms associated with the 1910 revolt against Cannon that enervated his powers to obstruct reform initiatives and elevated the significance of restriction-minded committees. Once again, however, the literacy test legislation was vetoed by the White House, for William Howard Taft, influenced largely by employer groups, opposed it. Another comprehensive literacy test bill sailed through a Democratic Congress in 1915, supported by bipartisan coalitions of conservative southern Democrats and northern and western Republicans. Because of discrepancies between President Woodrow Wilson's restrictionist scholarly writings and his 1912 campaign appeals to new European immigrants, the activists were uncertain how he would respond to the legislation. When quizzed by southern lawmakers, Wilson confessed that "I find myself in a very embarrassing situation about that bill. I myself made the most explicit statements at the time of the Presidential election about this subject to our fellow citizens of foreign extraction. I do not see how it will be possible for me to give assent to this bill." However ambivalent Wilson may have been privately, his 1915 veto was infused with characteristic morality. He blasted Congress for passing legislation that violated "the humane ardors of our politics" and "the natural and inalienable rights of men." It was not until 1917 that the conservative coalition of southern

Democrats and northern and western Republicans succeeded in enacting literacy test legislation over another Wilson veto. Fortified by expert findings, popular sentiment against immigrants, and effective lobbying by nativist interest groups, the Immigration Act of 1917 established a literacy test for all aliens over sixteen and the exclusion of Asian persons from a zone known as the Asia-Pacific triangle. Senator "Cotton Ed" Smith of South Carolina, a Democrat, explained at the time that many of his colleagues endorsed these limitations for the same reason they embraced Jim Crow institutions that excluded native-born African Americans: each barrier was necessary to guard the nation's racial purity.

The First World War unquestionably enervated the efforts of ethnic and business groups to guard the nation's favorable immigration traditions. Well before the United States entered the war, rallies by the German-American Alliance dismayed the non-German-American public in 1915–1916 and accentuated native fears about the loyalties of its large foreign-born population. As urgent questions arose during and after the war about the nation's assimilative capacities and the impact of ethnocultural diversity on American security, ethnic groups were increasingly constrained in their efforts to promote generous immigration policies. Whereas patriotic societies, labor unions, and the Immigration Restriction League could link their cause to enhanced national security and "citizenship absolutely undivided," ethnic groups lobbying against new restrictions seemed to confirm the nativist charges that "hyphenated Americanism" placed special interests above the national well-being. In the war's aftermath, the first Red Scare enlivened public fears that the nation's large immigrant population made it vulnerable to Bolshevik revolution, anarchy, and other forms of menacing foreign radicalism. The Red Scare gave Americanization programs a harder edge, and in 1920 Wilson's attorney general, A. Mitchell Palmer, launched a campaign to seize and expel hundreds of alien radicals in what his assistant secretary, Louis Post, called a "deportations delirium." Business groups began to question their devotion to immigrant labor. America's engagement in an unsettling international environment strengthened the popular and congressional sentiment against immigrants.

When the Republicans took control of Congress in 1919, the new House Immigration Committee chair, Albert Johnson (R-Washington), hired an "expert eugenics agent" to structure its investigations and to link policy recommendations to eugenics research. Johnson, a former member of the Asiatic Exclusion League, owed his political ascendance to demagogic campaign appeals on the immigration question. Having served on the Dillingham Commission as a young House member, he embraced pseudoscientific notions of racial hierarchy and was eventually elected president of the Eugenics Research Association. Fueled by fears of foreign radicalism and war-inspired patriotism, Congress in 1920 enacted a Johnson bill that eased the deportation of aliens who advised, advocated, taught, or published any views promoting the overthrow of government or were somehow associated with organizations that did so. Johnson also won House approval for "emergency" legislation suspending all immigration for one year (as immigration soared to 800,000 in 1920), but the Senate balked at this plan. Instead, its Immigration Committee set about devising a national-origins formula for restricting immigration since the literacy test had failed to slow the southern and eastern European inflows. Although nativists offered conspiratorial theories of foreign nations helping their emigrants pass the test, the truth is that southern and eastern European men proved more literate than the restrictionist lawmakers had anticipated. Total immigration during the first two decades of the twentieth century soared to 14.5 million and accounted for more than 45 percent of the nation's population growth.

The Senate ultimately settled on legislation that set annual quotas for each nationality group at 3 percent of foreign-born people of a given European nationality, using figures from the 1910 census. It also set a new ceiling on immigrant admissions, 355,000 per year. Both houses of Congress passed this Quota Act of 1921 by overwhelming margins. Working closely with restrictionist groups, Johnson and Senator David Reed (D-Pennsylvania) crafted legislation in 1924 that revised the 1921 quota system in order to place more draconian restrictions on southern and eastern European immigration. Behind the scenes, prominent eugenicists like Madison Grant, the renowned author of *Passing of the Great Race,* assured Johnson that the new quotas would effectively close the gates for racially inferior immigrants. The Immigration Act of 1924 assigned a quota to each nationality based on 2 percent of the number of foreign-born from that country who lived in the United States at the time of the 1890 census (when the older stock of European immigration predominated) for the next three years. Thereafter, quotas would be based on the national origins of the American population as a whole. The legislation also widened the so-called Asiatic barred zone and shifted the immigrant screening process overseas by requiring all European immigrants to obtain an entry visa and pass inspection at American consular offices overseas before they embarked on their journey to the United States. "The day of unalloyed welcome to all peoples, the day of indiscriminate acceptance of all races, has definitely ended," a triumphant Albert Johnson proclaimed.

This new system helped secure what the literacy test had not: a dramatic reduction in annual admissions and in Italian, Greek, Russian, Polish, Hungarian, Slavic, and Jewish immigration in particular. By 1925, annual immigration fell below 300,000 and southern and eastern European inflows dropped by 85 percent. The restrictionist policy regime built by Congress proved chillingly effective in subsequent years, reducing annual immigration to a trickle and denying entry to nearly all persons deemed racially inferior — including Jews desperately seeking to escape the Holocaust. This dramatic transformation of American immigration policy, which had looked so strikingly tolerant and receptive to newcomers only a few decades before, was fueled by the extraordinary evolution of Congress's internal power structure, a formidable new restrictionist movement, the elevation of eugenicist ideas, and powerful national security anxieties in the late nineteenth and early twentieth centuries.

— Daniel J. Tichenor

BIBLIOGRAPHICAL NOTES

Numerous scholars have chronicled the development of American immigration laws during the late nineteenth and early twentieth centuries. The definitive treatment remains John Higham's classic *Strangers in the Land: Patterns of American Nativism, 1860–1925* (New York, 1966). The most sweeping legislative history of U.S. immigration law is Edward P. Hutchinson's *Legislative History of American Immigration Policy, 1789–1965* (Philadelphia, 1981).

Several works examine nineteenth-century nativist movements and parties, including Ray Billington, *The Protestant Crusade, 1800–1860: A Study of the Origins of American Nativism* (New York, 1939); Thomas Curran, *Xenophobia and Immigration, 1820–1930* (Boston, 1975); and David Bennett, *Party of Fear* (New York, 1995). Kitty Calavita's *U.S. Immigration Law and the Control of Labor, 1820–1924* (New York, 1984), offers an interpretive overview of labor market influences on nineteenth-century immigration policy. The role of organized labor in the immigration politics of this period is explored in Gwendolyn Mink, *Old Labor and New Immigrants in American Political Development: Union, Party, and State, 1875–1920* (New York, 1986).

On Chinese exclusion, see Roger Daniels, *Asian America: Chinese and Japanese in the United States since 1850* (Seattle, Wash., 1988); Lucy Salyer, *Laws as Harsh as Tigers* (Chapel Hill, N.C., 1995); Elmer Sandmeyer, *The Anti-Chinese Movement in California* (Urbana, Ill., 1973); Alexander Saxton, *The Indispensable Enemy: Labor and the Anti-Chinese Movement in California* (Berkeley, Calif., 1971); and Charles McClain, *In Search of Equality: The Chinese Struggle against Discrimination in Nineteenth Century America* (Berkeley, Calif., 1994).

Fresh research and interpretations of American politics and policies during the early twentieth century are provided by Desmond King, *Making Americans: Immigration, Race, and the Origins of Diverse Democracy* (Cambridge, Mass., 2000); Gary Gerstle, *American Crucible: Race and Nation in the Twentieth Century* (Princeton, N.J., 2001); Keith Fitzgerald, *The Face of the Nation: Immigration, the*

State, and the National Identity (Stanford, Calif., 1996); Morton Keller, *Regulating a New Society: Public Policy and Social Change in America, 1900–1933* (Cambridge, Mass., 1998); and my own *Dividing Lines: The Politics of Immigration Control in America* (Princeton, N.J., 2002).

On immigration policymaking in subsequent periods, see Robert Divine, *American Immigration Policy, 1924–1950* (New York, 1972); David Reimers, *Still the Golden Door: The Third World Comes to America* (New York, 1992); Lawrence Fuchs, *The American Kaleidoscope* (Middletown, Conn., 1990); and Michael LeMay, *From Open Door to Dutch Door* (New York, 1987).

24

Prohibition

On December 17, 1917, the House of Representatives conducted its final debate on the proposed Eighteenth Amendment to the Constitution, intended to ban the manufacture, sale, exportation, importation, and internal transportation of beverage alcohol throughout the United States. Meeting in the fevered atmosphere of wartime, the House proceedings nevertheless took on a detached, almost fatalistic quality. Beneath the characteristic hyperbole and special pleading of congressional oratory, the positions seemed rehearsed, drummed into familiarity by a generation of prohibitionist lobbying and wet counterargument. No one appeared to doubt the outcome, and, after a single afternoon of debate, the House voted, 282–128, to send the Eighteenth Amendment on to the states. The following day, without debate, the Senate agreed to the House version of the bill. With a swiftness that surprised even the zealous agents of the Anti-Saloon League (ASL), the most prominent antiliquor association, three-quarters of the state legislatures ratified the amendment by January 16, 1919. One year later, national prohibition commenced. Dry activists had worked with a singleness of purpose to enshrine national prohibition in the Constitution. Congress, on the other hand, had hoped to hide it there.

For most members of Congress in 1917, the demand for national prohibition had become a millstone weighing down congressional business, party unity, and the reelection plans of individual members. The dry lobby, led by the skillful, hectoring representatives of the ASL, had since 1913 applied unrelenting pressure to build a prohibitionist majority in Congress. The ASL's focus unnerved and frustrated those in Congress, even many drys. Senator George W. Norris of Nebraska, a leading Republican insurgent and a moderate prohibitionist, complained that the fight against liquor was "not the only pebble on the beach" and should make way for other important legislative matters. Moreover, the nonpartisan strategy of the dry advocates cut dangerously across party lines. The

House vote on the Eighteenth Amendment recorded 140 Democrats and 138 Republicans in favor of the measure and 64 Democrats and 62 Republicans opposed, with a smattering of independents on either side. Press reports observed that "party lines were entirely disregarded" in the August 1917 Senate vote, with 29 Republicans and 36 Democrats favoring the submission of the amendment to the states and 8 Republicans and 12 Democrats opposed. Instead, the voting reflected geographical, ideological, ethnic, and religious differences. The opposition votes clustered in urban areas, especially in the immigrant-heavy Northeast and Midwest, among opponents of interventionist government, and among Catholics and non-evangelical Protestants. Prohibition sentiment was strong in the rural Midwest and West where native Protestants clustered, was especially robust among southern evangelicals, and attracted some reform enthusiasts. Such divisions, if allowed to harden, could fracture coalitions within both major parties. Finally, since 1905, when it engineered the defeat of Ohio's Governor Myron Herrick, the ASL had shown a terrifying ability to unseat uncooperative officeholders.

By voting to submit the prohibition amendment to the states, some congressmen followed their consciences, but many more acted to take the liquor issue "out of politics" and place it on someone else's desk. As the House hurried to pass the amendment, the Alabama Democrat J. Thomas Heflin, an outspoken and bigoted demagogue uncharacteristically advocating restraint, vainly argued that "no member of this House can dispose of this question simply by saying that he was tired of being bothered with it." The hard-drinking, genial senator from Ohio, Warren G. Harding, was one of many, however, who sought respite from the lobbyists. Although Harding had crafted a critical compromise in the Senate that helped pass the amendment and had voted for the bill himself, he was not a dry and declared it "unwise, imprudent and inconsiderate to force the issue" during wartime, when safeguarding national unity was vital. For the future president, however, it was even more critical "to see this question settled . . . to take it out of the halls of Congress and refer it to the people." In private, California senator Hiram Johnson, an influential progressive Senate Republican who voted for prohibition, was more succinct than the fumbling Harding. "Damn the liquor question, anyway," he muttered.

The vote on the Eighteenth Amendment, marked by self-interest as much as principle, political calculation as well as constitutional scruple, revealed the awkward confluence of politics and governance that beset Congress as it weighed the enormous expansion of federal power inherent in the adoption of national prohibition. The popular memory of prohibition is of an anomalous misstep outside the mainstream of sensible American governance, a sour, repressive attempt to curb the cosmopolitan habits of an ethnically diverse, modern culture to fit the plainer virtues of small-town Anglo-Saxon Methodists who equated national values with their own provincial outlook. The prohibition movement was part of the cultural wars that thundered across American communities in the late nineteenth century and intensified between 1900 and 1920 as the country experienced record immigration levels, anxiety over its national identity, and the patriotic display associated with its participation in World War I. Undeniably, national prohibition was coercive and overreached the limits of popular support for alcohol regulation, especially in the Northeast and urban Midwest.

Yet its popular image neglects its enormous appeal during an era of rapid and bewildering change. As cities grew and industry expanded, many Americans feared that their social institutions would crumble and political freedoms wither. Business consolidation and monopoly power alarmed the public. Many protested political corruption. Newly aware of environmental factors and health concerns, doctors and social workers warned of the physical and social costs of disease, overcrowding, and various urban pathologies. Advocates worked for children, women, and the family. The battle against saloons and the liquor industry unified these concerns. Americans had begun drinking more at the turn of the century; alcohol consumption rates in 1910 were the highest since 1840. Most of the drinking was done by working-class men in saloons serving highly perishable draft beer. Saloons were usually "tied houses," owned by breweries. Urban political machines, labor unions, and men's clubs often operated out of such saloons. A minority of saloons permitted gambling and prostitution. Men therefore drank and socialized outside the family sphere in establishments linked, in middle-class minds, to political corruption, crime, and immorality. Excessive drinking harmed families through lost wages from binges or alcohol-induced industrial accidents, domestic violence, birth defects, and shattered affections. The reformers portrayed saloons as evidence of the political power and irresponsibility of the liquor industry. Even in the rural South, where racial tension was taut, saloons were magnets for disorder. "In any Southern community with a bar-room a race war is a perilously possible occurrence," warned a Georgia clergyman in 1908. For many prohibitionists, the liquor traffic embodied all the problems that beset America. It was, in the apocalyptic vision of a northern minister, "the acme of evil, the climax of iniquity, the mother of abominations, and the sum of villainies." In contrast, prohibition offered a compact solution to this catalogue of difficulties, a panacea for modern, industrial America.

The prevailing image of prohibition also obscures the political modernity of the enterprise. The adoption of national prohibition paralleled the emergence of an active, regulatory state committed to the health and welfare of its citizens and the efficient order of society. Its advocates were disciplined professionals, expert in the practice of nonpartisan political pressure. Prohibition, in short, was a progressive reform. Americans during the Progressive era of the early twentieth century increasingly sought legislative solutions to social, economic, and even moral problems. They organized and entered politics to advance their particular visions of reform, first at the local and state levels. Then, at about the time prohibition enthusiasts began to bombard Congress with model bills and election day threats, a broad array of activists turned to Washington for comprehensive national policies on issues ranging from child labor regulation to farm loans. The prohibitionist wave that flooded through Congress in 1917 was thus part of the general drive toward government activism that would characterize Congress, and American government, in the twentieth century. Yet its ultimate failure, concluded by the constitutional amendment in 1933 that repealed national prohibition, became a reminder of the perils of moral regulation that has chastened Congress ever since.

Congress and the Drys

Basic to the rise of prohibition was the new, more politically supple temperance lobby developed in the 1890s by the ASL. Temperance reform reached back to the 1820s. Some states passed short-lived prohibition laws in the 1850s. The Prohibition party was formed in 1869, and between the 1870s and 1890s, clusters of dry Republicans or Democrats occasionally took control of local or state party organizations and forced statewide prohibition. Yet dry campaigns conducted by third parties or splinter groups within the dominant parties faced insuperable barriers in the rigidly partisan atmosphere of late-nineteenth-century America. The Prohibition party never won more than 2.2 percent of the national vote, and the dominant parties learned, through a series of devastating political backlashes that followed prohibitionist victories, that the liquor issue fractured party unity.

By the 1890s, the major parties adopted a code of silence on prohibition and rebuffed dry activists. "Your kind of people are all right at a prayer meeting, but they're no good at a caucus," barked Ohio's Republican boss, Senator Mark Hanna, to Wayne Wheeler, the young representative of the ASL in Ohio. But Hanna, controlling state GOP operations from his Senate seat, learned to respect Wheeler's organization. Formed in 1893 as a loose federation of Protestant churches directed by salaried professionals, Ohio's ASL became the model for a national association, which by 1900 had developed into a powerful network of temperance activists connected to the influential voices and votes of American Protestants.

The ASL revived dry influence with a new legislative strategy and made headway by stressing three points. First, it attacked the liquor industry rather than individual drinkers. Dismantling the drink monopolies — and the politically corrupt, socially disruptive saloon culture that the industry reputedly subsidized — aligned prohibition reform with the Progressive impulse to regulate arrogant corporations and diverted attention from coercive restrictions on individual freedom. Second, as a nonpartisan organization, the ASL avoided the traps of third-party politics and party factionalism and sought assurances from individual officeholders or candidates that they would support specific dry measures. Basing its decisions on careful attention to its legislative scorecards, the league supported its friends whether or not they were personally dry, reformers, Democrats, or Republicans. Third, the ASL worked incrementally and settled for realistic gains. Until 1907 it built prohibition territory through local option elections — referenda that banned alcohol sales at the precinct, municipal, or county level. Then, starting with several southern states, the league and its ally the Woman's Christian Temperance Union (WCTU) began to achieve statewide prohibition by statute or constitutional amendment.

During this period, Congress maintained its customary aloofness from prohibitionist agitation. Some individual members held strong dry convictions, but few endorsed national prohibition laws. The first Congressional Temperance Society in 1834 acted "more by the hope of its moral influence upon the public mind, than by the expectation of any direct agency" in promoting sober habits. More than sixty years later, Nebraska's Representative William Jennings Bryan, a teetotaler and champion of moral reform in Congress in the 1890s and a three-time Democratic presidential nominee between 1896 and 1908, still balked at legislative solutions to intemperance. Bryan, who was invited onto the House floor to celebrate the passage of the prohibition amendment in 1917, did not endorse local liquor regulation until 1910 and withheld his support of national prohibition until after the 1916 presidential election.

Still, the dry lobby worked its influence on Congress. The ASL had established a national legislative office in Washington in 1899. The men who served as the national legislative superintendent until the adoption of national prohibition were masters of political pressure: Edwin Dinwiddie, a former Prohibition party official who chipped away at areas of federal responsibility for liquor regulation; William H. Anderson, a tall, slender propagandist who reveled in the rough-and-tumble of political infighting; the Virginian James Cannon, a curt, unflappable Methodist bishop who was the league's chief lobbyist when Congress had a Democratic majority;

and Wheeler, the small, intense lawyer who stage-managed national prohibition, delighted in his reputation as the nation's "biggest legislative bully," and became a force in the Republican party until his death in 1927. The WCTU had also maintained a legislative department in Washington since 1895. Its representative, Margaret Dye Ellis, visited with congressional wives and confided to one of them that "the *Congressional Record* is in my hands constantly, I am studying it more than I am my Bible." The two organizations applied pressure in different ways. The ASL cultivated relationships with legislators and relied on its relentless publicity during elections to enforce cooperation. The WCTU used mass petitions — its signature method — and coordinated letter and telegram campaigns to support specific legislation. Representative Charles E. Littlefield, the son of a minister and a Republican lawyer from the dry state of Maine, sat on the influential Judiciary Committee and acted as the chief congressional spokesman for the ASL and WCTU from 1899 to 1908. An ardent dry, he was otherwise a party regular, notable even among Republicans for his rigid opposition to organized labor.

At first, the dry forces targeted clear areas of federal jurisdiction for legislation against liquor. Congress preferred to restrict prohibition as a matter for the states to contend with, and even many prohibitionists, especially Southerners, were skittish about states' rights and intrusive national authority. Josiah W. Bailey, an ASL official in North Carolina, declared in 1907 that prohibition "would require a centralization of authority contrary to all the American precedents and really subversive of the spirit of American institutions." Despite his convictions, Bailey insisted that "self-government does not proceed from the national head downward; it proceeds from the local community upward." Bailey resigned from the ASL and, as a U.S. senator in 1933, supported prohibition repeal. During the 1917 debate, Alabama's Heflin warned that "the federalistic theories" embedded in constitutional prohibition represented an advance onto "dangerous ground."

But no one disputed congressional responsibility for military bases, Indian affairs, American territorial possessions, and the District of Columbia. In December 1900, with the evidence of outrages committed in the Philippines by undisciplined American troops fresh in congressional minds, Littlefield added to an army reorganization bill a WCTU amendment barring alcohol sales at military canteens. To the loud applause of WCTU women in the galleries, the amendment carried, 150–51, was retained by the Senate, 34–15, and was included in the bill enacted in January 1901. With assistance from the House Committee on Territories, the ASL's Dinwiddie wrote a clause into the 1906 Oklahoma statehood bill that preserved prohibition in Indian Territory. Dry lobbyists also launched a campaign, unsuccessful until 1917 (1918, in the case of Hawaii), to impose prohibition in the District of Columbia and overseas territories. None of these initiatives represented a substantial break with past dry demands, but the ASL demonstrated a fresh and opportunistic outlook in its policy toward the federal liquor excise tax, which the Internal Revenue office required of all liquor producers and vendors, even unlicensed ones. The Prohibition party argued that the tax legitimized the drink trade, even to the point of conferring what looked like a federal license to illegal dealers, and demanded that the symbolic linkage between government and whiskey be dissolved. ASL lobbyists, on the other hand, recognized the tax as a potential tool in the enforcement of state and local prohibition laws. After a 1906 law proposed by Mississippi's Representative Benjamin Humphreys gave state and local authorities access to the list of federal liquor excise taxpayers, the league used the list to identify and prosecute illicit dealers in dry territory.

By applying federal power to close the gaps in the network of state prohibition, the dry lobby's innovative use of the liquor tax increased the demands for congressional action against the traffic in alcoholic drinks and anticipated the logic of concurrent state and national action that underlay national prohibition. It also embroiled the prohibitionists in congressional politics. The immediate issue was the regulation of interstate commerce. The drys complained that interstate shipments of liquor to prohibition states undercut state efforts to abolish the trade in intoxicants. In 1908 Littlefield sponsored a House bill to prevent the resale of liquor shipped into dry territory. The proposal raised important constitutional questions concerning congressional versus state control of interstate commerce, but more obvious to the dry lobby was the imperious swiftness with which the Republican Joseph G. Cannon, Speaker of the House from 1903 until 1911, crushed all such legislative efforts. The crusty "Uncle Joe," a reactionary opponent of activist government who resolved to "stand by the status," used his control of the House Rules Committee and dictatorial appointment powers to throttle most attempts at legislative innovation, including that of the drys, for which, as a wet and a constitutional conservative, he reserved special contempt. Cannon so effectively bottled up dry legislation in hostile committees that most of the prohibitionist proposals passed during his tenure, like Littlefield's canteen measure and Oklahoma's prohibition, had to be attached as amendments to other bills. Cannon buried the Littlefield bill in the Judiciary Committee, which he had made reliably wet by removing the dry Maryland Republican George A. Pearre. The ASL tried to prevent Cannon's reelection in 1908, but it failed and at the same time alienated many dry Republicans, including Littlefield, from the league. In 1906, with Cannon's aid, Littlefield had weathered a determined effort by the American Federation of Labor to defeat him; now he repaid the Speaker by helping confine his own bill in committee and urging Cannon's reelection. By approving a milder measure that barred COD liquor shipments into dry states, Cannon also won the support of Dinwiddie, then temporarily estranged from the league. Stricken, the ASL replaced Littlefield, who resigned from Congress, as its House leader with the Kansas Republican James M. Miller and belatedly approved the COD law. Only after congressional insurgents curbed Cannon's power over the House rules by 1911 and Democrats won control of Congress in 1912 did the national dry forces rediscover their unity and strength.

Toward National Prohibition

The turning point for significant national action to dry up the liquor trade was reached in 1913. By then, a new generation of skillful dry legislators — most notably E. Yates Webb, William Kenyon, and Morris Sheppard — had begun to replace colorful but ineffective figures such as Richmond Hobson, an Alabama Democrat. From 1907 until he lost a Senate bid in 1914 the most visible prohibitionist in the House, Hobson was a naval hero from the Spanish-American War and a popular Chatauqua lecturer; his trademark address, "Alcohol the Destroyer," reflected a theatrical and uncompromising style that won headlines but few legislative victories. Throughout his stormy congressional tenure, Hobson quarreled with wets and expended little effort in building coalitions. In contrast, the dry North Carolina Democrat E. Yates Webb, a coauthor of the landmark Webb-Kenyon Act and House manager for the Eighteenth Amendment, maintained cordial relationships with wets and demonstrated a cool reliability in drafting legislation and guiding bills. The son of a Baptist minister, he played football and baseball at Wake Forest College and practiced law before entering Congress in 1903. Active in the North Carolina ASL, Webb consulted regularly with ASL officials but also proved his worth to President Woodrow Wilson by framing a compromise that helped enact the Clayton antitrust bill in 1914. In 1919 Wilson appointed him a federal judge. Between those dates, Webb chaired the House Judiciary Committee, a position he used to revise and promote the spate of dry laws passed in 1917 and 1918.

The Republican William Kenyon of Iowa provided fresh leadership in the Senate. The son of a minister, like Webb, Kenyon advocated progressive legislation ranging from the income tax to the direct election of senators. He was also part of the emerging farm bloc that pushed for federal agricultural programs. Although he was only forty-one years old when elected in 1911, Kenyon proved adept at working through the legislative process. Senator Morris Sheppard of Texas, a Democrat, was the third important new dry leader. A Yale-trained lawyer who abstained from tea, coffee, and tobacco as well as liquor, he entered the Senate in 1913 after several years in the House. He was one of the most progressive Democrats in Washington and soon earned the enmity of southwestern conservatives. Explaining his support for prohibition, Sheppard described liquor as "a source of danger to posterity because the alcoholic taint foredooms the unborn millions to degeneracy and disease. I shall oppose this scourge from Hell until my arm can strike no longer and my tongue can speak no more." Since Sheppard introduced the prohibition amendment in December 1913 he was celebrated by the dry faithful as "the father" of national prohibition.

A revitalized ASL lobby, talented dry congressional leaders, and the influence in Congress of southern Democrats representing the driest section of the nation in 1913 aided prohibition. But just as significant was the disorganization in the wet camp. The drink trade allowed the ASL to frame the prohibition debate around images of the unruly saloon and the liquor trust. Rather than uniting against the dry threat, industry groups such as the United States Brewers' Association and National Liquor Dealers' Association blamed one another for intemperance and disorder. Brewers defended their product as a temperance beverage but conceded that "all people hate drunkards and whiskey makes them." Distillers, in turn, charged the brewery-owned saloons for misdeeds that fueled prohibition sentiment. As a tarnished industry, liquor interests attracted few strong independent defenders in Congress. Instead, meaningful opposition to dry thrusts came from strict constitutional constructionists, such as the 1914 Senate newcomers Oscar W. Underwood, the Alabama Democrat who ousted Hobson, and New York's Republican James Wadsworth, or representatives of wet working-class or ethnic districts, such as Adolph Sabath, the congressman from a Czech section of Chicago who pilloried the Webb-Kenyon Act as the handiwork of "narrow-minded and prejudiced persons."

The Webb-Kenyon Act of 1913 illustrated the dry energy and wet confusion that marked the path to national prohibition. At a convention organized by the ASL in December 1911, a team of temperance activists and legislators, including Webb and two senators from strong prohibition states, the Republicans Charles Curtis of Kansas and Porter J. McCumber of North Dakota, drafted an interstate commerce bill that barred liquor shipments into a state if the alcohol was intended for use "in violation of any law of such state." This proposal went further than any previous legislation in using federal authority to support state prohibition laws. The dry forces were careful and resourceful in their planning. To avoid logjams, they introduced identical versions of the bill in the House and the Senate in 1912. They familiarized themselves with successful precedents, such as the Lacey Act of 1900, which barred interstate shipments of illegally killed game birds. Webb and his friends assured the guardians of localism that congressional authority in this case reinforced a state's right to rid itself of alcohol and was thereby not intrusive. Dry lobbyists orchestrated a publicity campaign to support the proposal, burying congressmen in letters and filling the congressional galleries with enthusiastic prohibitionists.

Dry precision was met with wet ineptitude. Liquor lobbyists testifying against the bill were unfamiliar with its contents. The West Virginian John W. Davis, a brilliant lawyer and future Democratic presidential nominee, spoke eloquently against Webb's House version of the bill and then voted for it on February 8, 1913, stating that his constituents supported it. Two more of the sixteen House speakers against the bill did likewise as the measure passed, 239–64, with about two-thirds support from both Democrats and Republicans. The Senate dropped Kenyon's bill in favor of the House version and passed it on February 10 without a roll call. Dramatic confirmation of the new dry strength in Congress came when William Howard Taft, in one of his final presidential actions, vetoed the Webb-Kenyon Act on February 28, 1913, and Congress resoundingly overrode the veto, 63–21, in the Senate that same day and 246–95 in the House on March 1. Fewer than a third of the Senate and House Republicans voted with Taft. Public affirmation of the dry lobby's power increased further after Wayne Wheeler successfully defended the constitutionality of the law, in *Clark Distilling Co. v. Western Maryland Railroad,* before the Supreme Court in 1917.

The Webb-Kenyon victory persuaded the ASL and its allies to push for a constitutional amendment establishing national prohibition. Cautious voices advised that a political and educational campaign of perhaps twenty years might be necessary. The major parties still sidestepped the issue; indeed, the ASL did not ask for platform statements endorsing prohibition until 1916. Millions of Americans, especially those tied to European cultural traditions, enjoyed alcoholic beverages and deeply resented any attempts to criminalize their social customs. Virtually the entire northeastern seaboard and the industrial pockets in the Midwest and on the Pacific coast held out against the prohibition movement; fourteen of these states rejected state prohibition. Deep wet resistance from German communities in Wisconsin to the streets of Manhattan complicated any nationwide prohibition strategy.

For other drys, the intractability of wet strongholds like Chicago, New

York, San Francisco, and New Orleans justified the need for constitutional prohibition and made it imperative to accelerate the campaign. Only national prohibition could destroy the liquor industry and safeguard dry communities from wet infection. After 1920, congressional reapportionment, incorporating nearly 6 million new immigrants, would strengthen the wet representation in Congress by an estimated forty seats. In the Senate, the new system of direct election of senators introduced by the Seventeenth Amendment would eventually give weight to these wet votes, but the ASL believed its superior electoral organization would defeat the liquor lobby in the 1918 elections, the first in which all senators would be popularly elected. By striking quickly to enact a prohibition amendment, the drys hoped to outflank the large wet population by confining the ratification vote to a tally of states, where prohibitionists had the advantage. Cementing prohibition into the Constitution would also safeguard it from future congressional tampering.

Launching their effort in December 1913 with a parade to the Capitol, the ASL and WCTU presented draft prohibition resolutions to Hobson, still the symbolic dry champion in the House, and Sheppard. Hobson was soon a lame duck (and replaced as dry leader by the steadier Webb), but his resolution won a 197–190 majority in December 1914, short of the two-thirds approval necessary for a constitutional amendment but a good measuring point for the dry lobby. During the 1914 election campaign, the ASL spent $2.5 million, and its presses printed up to ten tons of material a day, increasing its efforts in 1916. In two elections the dry forces added 85 House votes to the Hobson resolution majority of 1914. "We knew that the prohibition amendment would be submitted to the States by the Congress just elected," Wheeler later boasted.

Yet the push for national prohibition was risky. Most dry advocates denied any intention of interfering with the personal consumption of alcohol. Many prohibition states allowed personal-use exemptions by which drinkers could order shipments of liquor from outside the state for their own consumption. The ASL even struck personal-use bans from the prohibition resolutions before Congress. Yet national prohibition, by outlawing the manufacture and sale of intoxicants, would effectively curtail the personal use of liquor. In February 1917 James A. Reed, a product of the Kansas City Pendergast machine and the Senate's most audacious wet, tried to catch drys in this contradiction by adding a bone dry amendment, which barred all interstate shipments of alcohol for beverage use into prohibition territory, to a Senate bill banning the advertising of liquor in dry states. Even though the bill forced bone dry standards onto prohibition states with more liberal regulations and the ASL refrained from either endorsing or opposing the amendment, excited House members, amid shouts of "bone dry" and to Reed's great distress, passed the bill into law, 321–72.

America's entry into World War I produced a cluster of prohibition measures faster than drys had anticipated. The crisis atmosphere and enhanced congressional war powers in 1917 and 1918 provided a "short cut" to prohibition, explained the ASL's William Anderson, "that is one of the compensations of such a catastrophe of war." Pouncing on news that brewers had funded the German-American Alliance, Wheeler charged that "the liquor traffic aids those forces in our country whose loyalty is called into question at this hour." Acting through Senator Thomas Martin of Virginia, the conservative Democratic floor leader and an associate of the Virginian James Cannon of the ASL, the dry lobby agreed to speed passage of the Lever Food Control bill, a wartime conservation measure urged by President Wilson. In return the bill, which passed overwhelmingly in August 1917, shut down the wartime distilling industry to save grain. Wilson later used powers granted in the Lever act to cut the alcohol content of beer to 2.75 percent and reduce grain allotments to brewers.

Wartime themes of patriotism and sacrifice also framed the argument for the prohibition amendment. As the Senate's debate on the amendment opened in late July, Kenyon asked, "If liquor is a bad thing for the boys in the trenches, why is it a good thing for those at home?" Seizing the moment, Wheeler consented to "trade jack-knives" with fence-sitting wets to put the amendment over. Senator Warren Harding, an Ohio acquaintance, told Wheeler that three colleagues (California's Republican Hiram Johnson and the Democrats John H. Bankhead of Alabama and Key Pittman of Nevada) would vote for prohibition if a six-year time limit (later amended to seven years) on ratification were imposed. Harding, for one, hoped that time would run out before ratification. Wheeler agreed to the deal and to a one-year grace period after ratification for liquor businesses to arrange their affairs. Lobbyists persuaded other doubters, such as Senator Robert La Follette of Wisconsin, to support the amendment in the name of democracy. The fiery Republican Progressive voted to let the people decide the issue in the states but added a speech opposing prohibition. These last-minute tactics persuaded four additional wet senators (Joseph S. Frelinghuysen of New Jersey, Philander Knox of Pennsylvania, LeBaron B. Colt of Rhode Island, and Marcus A. Smith of Arizona) to switch their votes. By December 1917, still in the flush of wartime zeal, the Eighteenth Amendment was submitted to the states. To the delight of the drys and the shock of the wets, the state legislatures, besieged by dry lobbyists, ratified prohibition in thirteen months. Even before that, on November 21, 1918, energized drys attached a wartime prohibition measure to a vital agriculture appropriations bill, despite the opposition of Wilson and the end of the war. This final wartime thrust banned the sale of intoxicants after June 30, 1919. "The average member of Congress is more afraid of the Anti-Saloon League than he is even of the President of the United States," concluded a wet observer.

Complications

Planned for years but passed hastily by a Congress anxious to remove the issue, the prohibition amendment banned the manufacture, sale, and transportation of intoxicating liquors and gave concurrent enforcement responsibilities to the states and the federal government. But it did not define "intoxicating liquors" or prescribe enforcement details. The Volstead Act, quickly drafted by the senior Republican on the House Judiciary Committee, Andrew Volstead of Minnesota, after the ratification of the Eighteenth Amendment and passed by Congress on October 27, 1919, over Wilson's veto (he objected to its extension of wartime prohibition), filled in those details in a surprising and confusing way. Although Volstead, an unknown in temperance matters, claimed principal authorship of the law, Wheeler's firm hand was clearly evident.

The law defined intoxicating drinks as those with an alcohol content of at least 0.5 percent, thus crushing the hopes for a return of wartime 2.75 percent beer. The Internal Revenue commissioner was charged with enforcement, and agents were given the authority to seize, shutter, or sell property used to move, store, or sell illegal alcohol. Industrial alcohol was tightly regulated, and permits were required for medical or sacramental use. But the law featured unusual loopholes. Private enjoyment with "bona fide guests" of pre-Volstead liquor was permitted, as was the home production of "nonintoxicating" ciders and fruit juices, which fermented into hard cider and wine. Private dwellings were exempt from searches unless illegal sales were apparent. The law was effectively neither wet nor dry, complained one critic, but rather "amphibious," adaptable to either environment. So, it turned out, was the Congress that enacted it.

Although national prohibition eliminated the objectionable "old-time" saloon and substantially cut alcohol consumption, from the outset poor funding, corruption, and inept enforcement crippled the Volstead Act. State governments, Congress, and the dry lobby shared the blame. The drys had draped prohibition with the promise of concurrent enforcement by state and national authorities. But twenty-eight states with enforcement laws allocated no money for them in 1927. Without effective state enforcement, the federal Prohibition Unit (later Bureau) was overwhelmed. Eager to control the appointments, Wheeler had prevented federal prohibition agents from coming under civil service protection. Anxious as well to make prohibition appear to be achievable, he claimed that a cut-rate budget of $5 million would be sufficient for enforcement. In both cases, Congress was happy to comply. The Prohibition Unit became a source for congressional patronage, and congressional appropriations for enforcement between 1921 and 1926 were a skimpy $6 million to $10 million. Underpaid, politically placed agents proved unreliable and vulnerable to corruption. One of them accidentally shot and seriously wounded Senator Frank L. Greene of Vermont in 1924 after the curious lawmaker investigated sounds of gunfire coming from an alley off Pennsylvania Avenue in Washington and blundered into a shootout between prohibition agents and bootleggers.

Throughout this dreary period, Congress remained reliably dry. Bumbling as policy administrators, the organized drys maintained legislative discipline by means of the ASL's still formidable electoral machine. In 1924, for instance, Wayne Wheeler targeted Kentucky's A. Owsley Stanley for defeat after the Bluegrass Democrat denounced the ASL on the floor of the Senate. Wheeler dispatched an aide to Kentucky to organize the campaign against Stanley, fought past the damaging revelation that Stanley's dry opponent, the Republican Frederic M. Sackett, maintained a personal stock of pre-Volstead wines and liquors, and openly took credit for defeating the wet incumbent. Overall, eleven of the thirteen new senators elected in 1924 backed prohibition, and 219 of the 262 House candidates publicly opposed by wet organizations were elected to Congress. According to Wheeler, the congressional dry majority rose that year to a 72–24 cushion in the Senate and a 319–105 bulge in the House. Conspicuous among senatorial drys was the Republican William E. Borah of Idaho, a fixture in the chamber from 1907 until he died in office in 1940. Renowned as a leader of the western bloc of isolationist Progressives who supported domestic reform measures and opposed American intervention abroad, Borah considered prohibition enforcement the crucial issue of the 1920s. Ohio's Frank B. Willis, a former college professor who owed his election to the ASL, was another vigilant Republican dry. Sheppard and Tennessee's Kenneth D. McKellar, who served in the Senate from 1917 until 1953, were the upper chamber's leading Democratic prohibitionists. The arid hosts in the House were legion; only the most flamboyant attracted attention. Chief among them was the Democrat William D. Upshaw of Georgia, who was noticed for his crutches (the result of a disabling farm accident as a youth), his popularity as a writer (under the name Earnest Willie) of devotional and patriotic reflections, his defense of the Ku Klux Klan and the rights of labor, in whose interests he sometimes wore overalls in Congress, and, most consistently, as a one-time ASL orator who was widely identified as the league's spokesman during his tenure from 1919 to 1927. But Upshaw was too much of a maverick for Wheeler to trust as a legislative steward. ASL officials altered a bill introduced by Upshaw that would have punished purchasers of illegal alcohol rather than, as the league preferred, the bootleggers who produced it. The Georgian further embarrassed the league in 1926 when his persistent demands to be paid for ASL-sponsored speeches were made public. Failing renomination that year, Upshaw ran for president in 1932 on the Prohibition ticket, then, at the age of seventy-two, became a Baptist minister in California and, shortly before his death in 1952, claimed that his paralysis had been healed at a Los Angeles revival. Louis C. Cramton of Michigan, who advocated deporting alien violators of prohibition laws and suggested that the Treasury Department monitor the alcoholic stock of foreign embassies in Washington, was the most excitable dry on the Republican side of the aisle.

Most wets glumly agreed with Clarence Darrow that the repeal of prohibition was "well-nigh inconceivable." Fighting a guerrilla action, congressional wets sniped at prohibition and suggested modifications of the Volstead Act allowing beer and light wines, but these efforts stagnated. In 1926 Senator Underwood, a respected wet, retired, and Senator Wadsworth of New York, a dignified critic of prohibition, lost his seat, a fate shared by Baltimore's Democratic representative John Philip Hill, a tireless mocker of the noble experiment. Brooklyn's Emanuel Celler, a Democrat, read George Washington's recipe for small beer into the *Congressional Record,* the Massachusetts Democrat George Tinkham denounced prohibition as an expression of religious bigotry, and other wet northeastern congressmen kept up a harassing fire against the drys, but the most determined efforts came from the Senate. The Democrats Edwin S. Broussard of Louisiana, William Cabell Bruce of Maryland, New Jersey's Edward I. Edwards, and James Reed joined New Jersey's Republican Walter E. Edge to publicize enforcement outrages and demand loosening the act's strict ban on beverage alcohol. Wheeler sarcastically labeled the collection of wet senators the BEER group, after the initials of Bruce, Edwards, Edge, and the unquenchable Missourian, Reed. Urged on by Bruce and Edge, Reed used his Senate Judiciary Committee seat to dominate the hearings on prohibition reforms in 1926, but the committee endorsed prohibition as "morally right and economically sound." Next, Reed investigated primary campaign expenditures, admonishing Wheeler not to "monkey with" the political process. Reed demanded the financial records of the ASL and leaked them to the press, but little resulted from this embarrassment.

Prohibition ended, not because of congressional leadership, but because of outside forces that prompted Congress to support a sudden movement for repeal. Reform and new resolve characterized the prohibition effort after 1927. The Prohibition Bureau was reorganized, civil service was introduced, and, with the election of Herbert Hoover in 1928, an administration committed to enforcement took office. But these initiatives were vitiated by Wheeler's death, scandals in the dry ranks that besmirched Anderson and James Cannon, violence by bootlegging criminal gangs, and, most of all, the Great Depression. Politicians outside Congress, led by New York's governor and 1928 Democratic presidential candidate Al Smith and the Association Against the Prohibition Amendment (AAPA), a repeal lobby headed by conservative industrialists, took the lead in reversing prohibition. Once unthinkable, prohibition repeal became a real possibility after a blue ribbon commission appointed by Hoover described the many failures of national prohibition in 1931. After the election of Franklin Roosevelt, who included a repeal plank in the overall Democratic rejection of Hoover's policies, a repeal amendment swept through Congress in 1933 like a mirror image of the prohibition amendment in 1917. Goaded by Senator Joseph Robinson of Arkansas, the formerly dry 1928 Democratic vice-presidential candidate, the lame-duck Congress hastened to enact the repeal plank of the triumphant Democrats. The final version of the bill stipulated that special state conventions, rather than sitting legislatures, would meet to ratify the amendment. This provision, long favored by the AAPA, sidestepped rural dry influence in state legislatures and approximated a national referendum on repeal. Just before the final congressional vote, the Voluntary Committee of Lawyers, a repeal group allied with the AAPA, produced a model bill to help the states organize conventions and speed up ratification. In the Senate, 29 Republicans joined 33 Democrats (and one Farmer-Laborite) to pass the repeal amendment over the opposition of 14 Republicans and 9 Democrats. The 289 repeal votes in the House (179 Democratic, 109 Republican, and 1 Farmer-Laborite) reversed the 282 cast in favor of prohibition in 1917. A disgruntled minority of 89 Republicans and 32 Democrats held out for the continuation of the dry reform. Congress legalized beer after Roosevelt took office, and in December the Eighteenth Amendment was officially repealed. Lightning had struck twice.

Despite its defensive posture during the making and dismantling of prohibition, Congress still acted assertively. It overrode two presidential vetoes, passed two amendments to the Constitution, and enacted a reform that closed a major industry, attempted to regulate the behavior of 100 million Americans, and created an enforcement apparatus that, however flawed, expanded the authority of the national government. Yet the legacy of prohibition has been to promote government caution, especially on the part of Congress. Congress avoided constitutional remedies to social problems after prohibition and has looked to the courts for leadership on sensitive social and cultural issues. Most clearly, prohibition's failure introduced a new orthodoxy in Congress that moral questions, especially those that divide public opinion, cannot be solved legislatively. Yet the intersection of politics and governance in Congress that allowed the dry lobby to force prohibition onto the national stage persists. As the prohibitionists discovered, interest groups cannot govern, but, as Congress is reminded daily, neither can they be excluded.

— THOMAS R. PEGRAM

BIBLIOGRAPHICAL NOTES

The most comprehensive study of national prohibition is Andrew Sinclair, *Prohibition: The Era of Excess* (London, 1962). Charles Merz, *The Dry Decade* (New York, 1930), is an excellent contemporary analysis. A more recent political history of temperance reform is Thomas R. Pegram, *Battling Demon Rum: The Struggle for a Dry America, 1800–1933* (Chicago, 1998). Jack S. Blocker Jr., *American Temperance Movements: Cycles of Reform* (Boston, 1989), provides critical social and cultural context. Essential for understanding the dry lobby in Congress are K. Austin Kerr, *Organized for Prohibition: A New History of the Anti-Saloon League* (New Haven, Conn., 1985), and Richard F. Hamm, *Shaping the Eighteenth Amendment: Temperance Reform, Legal Culture, and the Polity, 1880–1920* (Chapel Hill, N.C., 1995). Christopher N. May, *In the Name of the War: Judicial Review and the War Powers since 1918* (Cambridge, Mass., 1989), is good on the interaction among Congress, the drys, and World War I. For a portrait of the wartime Congress, see Seward W. Livermore, *Politics Is Adjourned: Woodrow Wilson and the War Congress, 1916–1918* (Middletown, Conn., 1966). Imogen B. Oakley, "The Prohibition Law and the Political Machine," *Annals of the American Academy of Political and Social Sciences* 109 (September 1923): 165–74, attacks congressional enforcement of the dry law. David E. Kyvig, *Repealing National Prohibition,* 2nd ed. (Kent, Ohio, 2000), remains the best analysis of prohibition's decline and of the repeal movement. The most thorough documentary compilation on the workings of the law is the National Commission on Law Observance and Enforcement, *Enforcement of the Prohibition Laws,* 5 vols. (Washington, D.C., 1931).

25

The First World War

ON MARCH 10, 1917, following the rupture in U.S.-German relations prompted by the German government's resumption of unrestricted warfare in the Atlantic, President Woodrow Wilson summoned the recently elected Sixty-fifth Congress to a special session, which was to convene on April 2. As the members of Congress arrived in Washington, they faced a momentous decision that would have profound implications for the federal government and the role of Congress within it. The mood around the Capitol on that fateful day was tense and uncertain. Scores of peace activists milled outside the offices of senators and representatives, one of them even getting into a hallway tussle with the hawkish Senate minority leader, Senator Henry Cabot Lodge of Massachusetts. On the House side, the members had yet to determine how their chamber would be organized and who would lead it, since the voters had elected 216 Democrats, 210 Republicans, and 6 Independents. Not until the morning of the second, when a Progressive Republican from Minnesota renominated the Democrat Champ Clark of Missouri to another term as Speaker of the House, was it completely clear that the Democrats would organize the body. Thus, when Wilson strode into the House chamber at 8:32 P.M., announcing that he "called the Congress into extraordinary session, because there are . . . very serious choices of policy to be made," he addressed an understandably agitated group of lawmakers. Four days later, after an occasionally bitter debate, these legislators voted to send the people of the United States into their first war in Europe, a decision destined to alter the nation's history in ways that none of them could imagine.

In the weeks and months that followed, Congress took up a multitude of the "serious choices of policy" that Wilson had foreseen. The results of its wartime action were profound. By the time an armistice was declared on November 11, 1918, debates over war policy had sown damaging divisions among the Democrats, broken their fragile hold on power, and catapulted the Republican party to large majorities in both houses of Congress, dealt a crushing blow to the vision of the prime ministerial presidency that Wilson had done so much to advance before the war, and undermined the Progressive reform politics that had set the national political agenda between 1910 and 1916.

None of this could have been foreseen when Europe plunged headlong into war in August 1914. At that time, the Democrats securely controlled both houses of Congress, with a 73-vote majority in the House. They were ably led by Wilson, a president who admired the British parliamentary system and who intervened in the drafting of laws to an unprecedented degree, successfully steering New Freedom legislation through Congress as if he were himself a prime minister. The Democratic party, successfully exploiting the divisions between the forces of Theodore Roosevelt and William H. Taft in the Republican party to appeal to independent voters in the Midwest and West, was on its way to shedding its image as the creature of the agrarian South and credibly refashioning itself into *the* national reform party.

Yet each of these trends — the Democratic control of Congress, the transferral of legislative initiative from Congress to the presidency, and the Democrats' efforts to build a durable national political coalition — had set off a backlash that would be exacerbated by the U.S. entry into World War I. Together these dynamics would disrupt much of the legacy that the progressives had imparted to Congress.

Congress and the Politics of Preparedness

The war's potentially disruptive impact was evident even before Congress decided to enter the conflict. The Sixty-fourth Congress, elected as Europe's guns blazed in the fall of 1914, was the first to be drawn into the political maelstrom of the Great War. Most Americans who had elected that Congress had little desire for war, despite the pleadings of pugnacious interventionists such as Theodore Roosevelt. Sensitive to the dominant neutrality sentiment, Congress was reluctant to be perceived as inching closer to U.S. intervention. By the fall of 1916, however, German submarine warfare and the approach of an election campaign in which Republicans were attacking Democrats for their failure to prepare for the possibility of war set the stage for the passage of the first significant preparedness measures. "There seems to be a preparedness germ or an epidemic that has swept the country," lamented the antiwar progressive Republican senator George Norris of Nebraska, who resisted the shift in congressional sentiment. "Nearly everyone has it," he mourned.

But the extent of the "preparedness epidemic" was not yet clear in 1916, when President Wilson asked for an appropriation of $300 million to fund a military buildup. Congressional Democrats, against the army's spending plans, were not willing to go that far for their president. Instead, they sought to use the politics of preparedness to advance a progressive agenda. Claude Kitchin of North Carolina, a leading Democratic progressive who was opposed to U.S. intervention in Europe, chaired the Ways and Means Committee when it took up the president's request. Kitchin was determined to divert the growing clamor for defense spending toward the passage of reform legislation. He simultaneously opposed the size of Wilson's request and advocated a tax on high incomes to fund military expenditures (making use for the first time of the Sixteenth Amendment, which had been ratified in 1913). The twofold aim of Kitchin and his progressive allies was to slow the nation's drift toward war and reform its methods of revenue collection. The result was a tax bill in 1916 that established the principle of the progressive national income tax for the first time in the nation's history. Under its provisions, more than 95 percent of the federal tax revenue was raised from those whose annual incomes exceeded $20,000. According to a leading journal of reform, the *New Republic,* the bill represented "a powerful equalitarian attack on the swollen income."

Yet tensions between the congressional Democrats and the president persisted and grew as war pressures rose. A large group of the Democrats were sympathetic to the views of Secretary of State William Jennings Bryan, who had resigned in protest of Wilson's foreign policies in 1915, criticizing the president for holding the German government solely responsible for the submarine warfare in the Atlantic. In 1916 Representative James McLemore of Texas, a maverick Democratic legislator who opposed his president's handling of the growing crisis, proposed a resolution to forbid U.S. citizens from traveling on the ships of belligerent nations. His initiative enjoyed significant support among progressive Republicans as well Democrats opposed to intervention. Wilson himself was forced to prevail on members of Congress in order to derail the McLemore resolution.

McLemore's defeat, however, scarcely put an end to the growing tensions between the president and Congress over the crisis. Indeed, during the winter of 1916–1917 the president found himself dealing with a delicate set of congressional dynamics. On the one hand, he was pressured toward opposing Germany by interventionist Republicans such as Henry Cabot Lodge. On the other hand, he faced strong opposition to his preparedness measures from both powerful Bryanite Democrats such as Kitchin and influential Progressive Republicans such as Senator Robert M. La Follette of Wisconsin. Whichever way Wilson turned on the question of war preparedness, he was bound to be assailed by one powerful faction or the other. If crafting a stable congressional majority in favor of his foreign policies proved extremely difficult in the Sixty-fourth Congress, Wilson was destined to find the task even more difficult following the election of the nearly evenly split Sixty-fifth Congress and his own very narrow reelection over the Republican Charles Evans Hughes in 1916.

Evidence of trouble ahead was already clear in the waning days of the Sixty-fourth Congress in February 1917. With German submarine warfare escalating, Wilson asked Congress for a bill that would provide for the arming of U.S. merchant ships. In the Senate, La Follette and Norris led a group of anti-interventionists who filibustered the bill. As the Sixty-fourth Congress ended its days locked in this bitter squabble, Wilson condemned these midwestern Republican senators and their Progressive supporters, who had once been his allies in passing important reform legislation. They were nothing but a "group of willful men," Wilson insisted, whose stubborn opposition to preparedness legislation put the nation at risk.

This bitter conflict left its mark on the Senate. Filibusters had been a feature of Senate life since early in its history, yet it was not until the aftermath of the 1917 deadlock over the arming of merchant ships that the Senate adopted a method for cutting off a filibustering debate. In response to a plea from President Wilson to the new Sixty-fifth Congress, which took office in April 1917, the Senate adopted Rule XXII, which allowed a two-thirds majority to invoke cloture, ending a filibuster; it remained substantially unchanged until 1975, when the cloture threshold was lowered to three-fifths of those members present and voting. Filibusters did not again trouble the Senate during World War I, but as he learned during the war, Rule XXII by no means eliminated Wilson's problems with "willful men."

Congress Goes to War

Speaking before the special joint session of Congress that he had summoned on April 2, 1917, Wilson noted that it "is a fearful thing to lead this great people into war." But now that he was ready to summon the nation to battle, Wilson made it clear that he should take the initiative in formulating war policies. The war, he argued, could best be conducted by the nation's chief executive and his cabinet, "upon which the responsibility of conducting the war and safeguarding the nation will most directly fall."

The president's words reached a Congress and a nation in which a significant minority expressed either deep suspicion of the war or outright opposition. Abroad in the nation, the Socialist party and the Emergency Peace Federation hastily organized opposition to the war declaration.

Within Congress itself, voices were also raised against war. Two senators, the Democrat James K. Vardaman of Mississippi and the Republican La Follette, refused to join their colleagues in wearing American flags in their lapels during the president's April 2 war address, reflecting the sentiments of two groups that would complicate the president's enactment of war policies for different reasons. Many southern agrarian Democrats were wary of the changes that war mobilization might thrust on their region and worried that the rise of a powerful wartime government would encroach on southern regional interests; many midwestern progressives believed that the nation was "going into war at the command of gold," as Senator Norris memorably put it.

Such opposition made itself felt during the debate that followed. In the House, Claude Kitchin announced that "[e]very feeling of humanity, every sentiment of loyalty, every obligation of duty within me combine in forbidding my consent" to war. On the Senate floor, Norris warned his colleagues that "belligerency would benefit only the class of people who will be made prosperous should we become entangled in the present war." "I feel that we are about to put the dollar sign on the American flag," he lamented. "Treason! Treason!" shouted several colleagues. When La Follette seconded Norris's view, he prompted a bitter retort from the Democrat John Sharp Williams of Mississippi, an administration loyalist and friend of the president's. La Follette's speech against war was "worthy of [the German chancellor] Bethmann Hollweg in the Reichstag," exclaimed Williams. La Follette was not only "pro-German" and "pro-Vandal," he declared, but "anti-American President and anti-American Congress, and anti-American people."

Ultimately, Wilson's side prevailed, for on April 6, 1918, the U.S. Congress formally declared war. The vote in the Senate was 82–6, in the House, 373–50. In the end, the vast majority of Democrats, especially those in the South, supported the president. Kitchin was among only four Southerners to oppose the war measure in the House. Yet persuading Congress to declare war at a moment of such high drama was Wilson's easiest task. The lopsided approval of the war resolution in fact hid a good deal of congressional concern, which would soon emerge. And it would be far more difficult, Wilson learned, to keep a stable coalition that would accept his leadership on the formation of war mobilization policies than it was to persuade Congress to go to war.

In fact, the war complicated congressional politics in ways that were not immediately visible to observers. Publicly, the members paid fervent lip service to the principle of bipartisanship. "Both Democrats and Republicans must forget party in the presence of common danger," Henry Cabot Lodge told the Senate on April 4. As the months went on, however,

Lodge and his Republican colleagues lost few chances to score partisan points. Controlling Congress as well as the chief executive, it fell to the Democrats to organize the nation's war machinery. But with a razor-thin majority in the House and deep sectional divisions within the party over how to organize the war machinery, the Democrats soon fell to squabbling among themselves and wrestling with the president for the policymaking initiative. The Republican leaders were happy to exploit the divisions among the Democrats, in the process consolidating the ranks of the long-divided GOP.

Controversy, Factionalism, and the Reassertion of Congressional Initiative

The hottest issue Congress took up in the weeks following the declaration of war was the effort to raise an army. President Wilson asked for a conscription bill in April 1917. Both Speaker of the House Clark and majority leader Kitchin opposed this request, and they found support among agrarian Democrats, who feared granting power to the federal government to dragoon men into the armed forces against their will. As Champ Clark put it, his constituents "saw precious little difference between a conscript and a convict." When the Democratic chair of the House Military Affairs Committee refused to support the bill, the administration had to rely on the committee's ranking Republican to move it to the floor. Intense partisan politicking followed. Theodore Roosevelt's public campaign for a volunteer force under his command complicated the debate. In the end it probably helped Wilson get the bill he wanted with comfortable margins in both houses, since few Democrats wanted to give Roosevelt another chance to become a popular war hero. Yet the passage of the Selective Service Act scarcely ended the debate. The Democratic senator from Missouri, James A. Reed, predicted that the draft would trigger rioting similar to that which had greeted the Civil War draft. That this prophesy did not come to pass scarcely silenced Reed and other disgruntled Democrats in the months afterward.

The Senate Republicans gladly exploited the growing tensions between the president and his congressional partisans and sought to join forces with such recalcitrants to wrest the power to shape the war effort from the White House. Thus Senator John W. Weeks of Massachusetts, a conservative Republican party loyalist with presidential ambitions, offered a resolution for the creation of a "joint committee on the conduct of the war" to oversee the war effort. The bill was inspired by Congress's Wade-Chandler Committee, which, as Wilson knew, had continually challenged Abraham

Lincoln's leadership during the Civil War. Wilson had no intention of ceding such power to Congress, and he tenaciously fought off the Weeks proposal despite significant Democratic support for it. Only by appealing directly to the Democrats on the Rules Committee was Wilson able to prevent Weeks's initiative from reaching the floor.

Still, partisan controversy dogged almost every effort to place the nation on a war footing. When the president created the Committee on Public Information to handle wartime censorship and propaganda, funding it out of a special $100 million appropriation for which no specific accounting was required, Republicans assailed the committee for its failure to submit to tight congressional oversight. An espionage bill introduced in 1917 also encountered strong opposition among Republican senators such as Warren G. Harding of Ohio, who attacked its provisions concerning newspaper censorship, causing them to be struck from the bill. The location of sixteen cantonment sites for training the American Expeditionary Force also caused partisan rifts in Congress. Northern Republicans alleged that southern Democrats established too many training camps in their region; its intensely hot climate, they claimed, was ill suited to preparing soldiers for war in France.

But it was not only partisanship that bedeviled Wilson's war program in Congress. The administration also endured the repeated attacks of a group of Democratic senators who frequently broke with their president, especially Thomas W. Hardwick of Georgia, James K. Vardaman of Mississippi, Thomas P. Gore of Oklahoma, and James Reed of Missouri. These legislators, suspicious of federal and executive power, looked askance at the growing war bureaucracy in Washington and the loss of congressional prerogatives it implied, and they seized every opportunity to harass the administration when they disagreed with its direction. Such roiling political tensions inevitably affected the efficiency with which Congress responded to the war mobilization. Whereas Lincoln's first war Congress had accomplished its major legislative work in only one month in 1861, the Sixty-fifth Congress argued well into October 1917. After the question of the draft was settled, food and fuel price controls and war financing proved the most difficult and divisive questions.

The nation faced a significant food problem, to which Congress was forced to respond. Poor wheat crops in 1916 and 1917, Europe's demand for additional grain, and the farmers' tendency to hold crops back to push up prices during the early months of the war led to shortages and skyrocketing prices. Wilson tried to stem that crisis by establishing the Food Administration on May 20, 1917, without congressional authorization. The leaders of Congress distrusted the new administration and its director, Herbert Hoover, fearing that his effort to control food production from

Washington would alienate their agricultural constituents. Midwestern Democrats were especially worried about the administration's support for wheat price controls, which promised to eliminate the anticipated windfall profits of their region's struggling farmers. Significantly, the administration could get congressional support for measures against war inflation like the wheat price cap only by placating the powerful bloc of southern Democrats by agreeing not to install cotton price controls. This decision, in which the administration seemed to favor southern interests over those of other regions, in time drove a wedge through the Democratic coalition and turned much of the Midwest against the ruling party. Even after paying such a heavy political price for his food program, however, Wilson still could not get the legislation to his desk without dodging another attempt by Senator Weeks to create a committee on the conduct of the war. With the help of the Democratic dissidents Gore, Reed, and Vardaman, Weeks attached his pet rider to the food bill. Wilson was forced to rely on the Conference Committee that reconciled the House and Senate food bills to delete the Weeks rider. In that instance, Wilson required the aid of Senator Francis E. Warren of Wyoming, a Republican. Perhaps Wilson's naming of Warren's son-in-law, John J. Pershing, commander of the American Expeditionary Force explains Warren's insistence in the conference committee that the Weeks rider be scratched. In any event, both Wilson and Warren were satisfied with the results.

Wrangling over war financing was no less charged. The United States faced perhaps greater initial obstacles to achieving efficient war financing than any other belligerent nation during the Great War. The federal government had comparatively slight taxing power at this time, and the need for funds was enormous, given that Americans would fight overseas and that they would have to help finance the war effort of their allies. Debate naturally roiled around the question of the proper way to pay for the war: conservative Republicans generally favored having the government borrow money through interest-bearing bonds and loans; agrarian Democrats favored using a steeply graduated income tax and charged that the use of war bonds would allow the wealthy to finance the war at a profit. The rhetoric grew heated. Kitchin, who chaired the crucial House Ways and Means Committee, declared: "I want the man who comes home with an empty sleeve to feel that the Congress which sent him away has not favored the profit-taker who stayed at home." The investment banker J. P. Morgan countered that any attempt to raise more than 20 percent of war revenue from taxation would ruin the economy. The ensuing debate exposed how deeply the financing question resonated with class and sectional politics. What ultimately emerged from the House on May 24 was a $1.8 billion tax bill, which split the difference between Kitchin's vision and

Morgan's. It provided for income taxes, surtaxes, and war profits taxes that together accounted for approximately 31 percent of the war's estimated cost.

Getting such a bill through the Senate, however, proved difficult. Lodge, who served on the Senate Finance Committee, vowed his opposition. Sensing a bruising battle ahead, the Democratic leaders put off the issue until the food bill was passed. By the time the Senate took up the financing question in late August, however, war expenditures had outstripped the limits of the House legislation, giving Senate conservatives leverage to demand more loans. Ultimately, the progressives achieved a less favorable financing plan than they had hoped for. Five Liberty Loan drives and forty-eight series of short-term notes were issued by the Treasury Department. Some $23 billion was eventually borrowed, more than twice the sum raised through taxation. This heavy borrowing contributed considerably to inflation, creating political problems for Wilson and the Democrats in the years immediately following.

The Deepening Crisis in the War Effort and Relations Between Congress and President

By January 1918 the war effort was entering a crisis to which Congress was forced to respond. Mobilization was bogged down amid one of the worst winters on record in the early twentieth century: a massive blizzard struck the East Coast on December 28, 1917, followed by extended periods of subzero temperatures. Fuel shortages emerged, railroad traffic snarled, and inflation continued to spiral. Headlines announced that the army's training schedule was months behind and that the nation's airplane building program was a failure. Meanwhile, the U.S. troops' battlefield victories did not begin to divert attention from these failures on the home front until May 1918, when Americans helped repulse a German offensive along the River Marne and at Belleau Wood. It was mid-July before the U.S. troops finally went on the offensive in the Aisne-Marne campaign. In the meantime, Congress had plenty of time to express its concerns with the war effort and, not coincidentally, with the president's war bureaucracy, which, it believed, was sapping congressional powers of governance.

Thus, by January five major investigations of the war effort were under way on Capitol Hill. The Senate Committee on Manufactures, under the prickly leadership of Senator Reed, investigated the Food Administration. The examination became a forum in which Reed could vent his animus against the administration. He lashed the Food Administration for its policies and then refused to let Hoover testify or enter a statement into the record in defense of his agency. The Fuel Administration fell under similarly withering scrutiny. On January 16, as the fuel crisis deepened, its administrator, Harry Garfield, ordered all industrial plants east of Mississippi to close for four days to conserve fuel. This order set off a tidal wave of protest in Congress. Senator Gilbert Hitchcock of Nebraska, one of Wilson's most reliable Democratic antagonists, wrote a resolution to postpone the implementation of Garfield's order until it could be investigated. Though the crisis was soon averted, an aroused Congress now probed the administration's war agency with increasing vigor, and Democrats took the lead in demanding corrective action.

The War and Navy Departments were natural targets for increased scrutiny. Congress demanded that Secretary of War Newton D. Baker and the chief of the department's Ordnance Bureau, General William Crozier, answer reports that military cantonments were unable to feed and house recruits properly, that trainees had been forced to drill with broomsticks rather than rifles, and that 7.5 men per thousand were dying in the training camps due to inadequate sanitation and medical facilities. Calls for the resignation of Secretary Baker and Secretary of the Navy Josephus Daniels abounded. Even more ominous for the administration, Senator George Chamberlain of Oregon, a Democrat, called for the creation of a civilian war cabinet that would take over the control of the mobilization from the president. Conflict over the War Department's problems came to a head on January 10–12, when Baker testified before the Senate. He acquitted himself well enough to preserve his job. Yet Chamberlain pressed for a thorough reorganization of his department. Ultimately, Wilson fended off Chamberlain's war cabinet initiative by again pleading directly with the senators. Having put out that fire, the president was continually beset by new flare-ups.

The approaching congressional elections of November 1918 naturally added urgency to the tussles over war policy. Republican leaders hedged their attacks on Wilson in order not to appear too opportunistic and incur the wrath of uncommitted voters. They named Will Hays chairman of their party in 1918, and under his leadership the divisions between the Old Guard and the Insurgents that had weakened the party since 1910 began to abate. On May 26, Taft and Roosevelt ended their long feud at a meeting in a Chicago hotel. Thereafter, the increasingly unified Republicans attacked the Democrats by focusing attention on the predominant influence of Southerners in Congress and alleging that sectional favoritism had led the Democrats to shift the burden for the war to regions outside the South: the prominent example of cotton prices unencumbered by government price ceilings made the Republicans' task of persuasion fairly easy.

President Wilson also had his mind on the elections. Thus, on May 27 he lectured a joint session of Congress on the subject of partisanship. In a speech that called for new taxes on excess profits, he urged Congress to put the nation's interests ahead of those of party. For the duration of the war, he said, "politics is adjourned." Wilson assured the lawmakers that the voters would reward those politicians who put patriotism above party. Unhappily for Wilson, these words came back to haunt him. Whenever he criticized Republican obstructionism in the months after this speech, he found himself assailed as a hypocrite.

The Sixty-sixth Congress and the Postwar Settlement

The congressional election of 1918 was unusual in many respects. Wrangling over a multitude of war issues had kept the incumbent members of Congress in Washington through September, far deeper into the campaign season than they liked, contributing to the ferocity of the politicking that fall. And by the time the voters went to the polls, rumors of an imminent end to the hostilities in Europe were circulating wildly across the country, and the epidemic of the deadly Spanish influenza, which ultimately took the lives of half a million Americans, had led to the banning of public meetings in many communities. Amid these extraordinary conditions, the Republicans clearly held an advantage — and not only because midterm elections usually favor the party out of power. The flush Republican party spent twice as much on the 1918 campaign as it had in 1916, while the Democrats were still in debt from their 1916 effort. And unlike the increasingly united Republicans, the Democrats were more embroiled than ever in conflict. Most damaging for them were the politics of wheat and cotton. As the Republicans endlessly pointed out, Wilson had approved a price cap on wheat of $2.20 a bushel during the war, keeping the value of wheat crops well below their market level, even while raw cotton prices were allowed to soar 400 percent. Such facts made the agrarian districts of the Midwest an electoral gold mine for Republicans.

With the direction of the postwar world at stake, Wilson had strong reasons to want to counter the Republican electoral offensive, and he tried to do so. But in the end his efforts backfired. Without consulting his cabinet, Wilson drafted a blistering message to voters on October 24, calling for the defeat of those Republicans who "sought to take the choice of policy out of my hands and to put it under the control of instrumentalities of their own choosing." This was "no time for divided leadership," Wilson asserted. The appeal was nothing less than a huge political blunder. The Republicans immediately accused the president of using the war for partisan political advantage, a charge made all the more effective in light of Wilson's own plea for bipartisanship during his May appeal for the "adjournment" of politics.

Given the circumstances, it is hardly surprising that the Democrats faced disaster at the polls on November 5. The Republicans took control of both houses in Congress. A total of 51 seats changed hands in the House, giving Republicans a 237–193 margin, with 5 seats held by other parties. Democratic losses were greatest in the farm belt, where wheat price controls undermined the Democratic candidates. Both Democrats and Republicans pulled fewer voters to the polls than they had in the previous two elections, but the Democratic erosion was sharper and more devastating. The electoral defeat constituted a blow not only to Democratic control but to the progressive reform movement that had been so influential in Congress over the previous decade. As one member of Wilson's war bureaucracy saw it, the Sixty-sixth was "the least enlightened, most reactionary Congress that this generation has known."

The armistice that ended the fighting in Europe on November 11, 1918, only days after the election of the new Congress, strengthened the hands of the legislators. Now that the fighting had ceased, President Wilson lost some of the leverage he had accrued as commander in chief during wartime. He was left to face a Congress dominated by his political opponents and determined to take from him the initiative to shape the postwar settlement at home and in Europe. In domestic affairs, the Sixty-sixth Congress capitalized on the revival of traditional American anti-statism, triggered by the expansion of government during the war to hastily demolish the powerful wartime agencies Wilson had created. Among the first to go were those that had shaped the nation's labor policies in wartime, such as the National War Labor Board, an agency that had routinely supported the workers' efforts to organize unions. In abolishing such agencies, the Republicans frequently had the support of many southern Democrats who had never been enthusiastic about Washington's meddling in the labor affairs of their region.

Congress also asserted its will in foreign affairs when the Senate effectively blocked the ratification of the Versailles treaty, negotiated by the president. Its most controversial elements had to do with the League of Nations and the obligations of collective security embodied in Article 10. When Wilson formally presented the pact to the Senate on July 10, 1919, he urged its quick ratification and cautioned that to reject the treaty would "break the heart of the world." Yet it held little appeal for Senator Lodge, who chaired the Foreign Relations Committee, and he was not alone. Ultimately, three groups in the Senate opposed the treaty: irreconcilables opposed it in any form; strong reservationists advocated significant reservations; and mild reservationists posed objections that could be met relatively easily. It was the strong reservationists, led by Lodge himself, who held the fate of the treaty in their hands. This scarcely boded well for the president. No friend of Wilson's, Lodge once confided to Theodore Roosevelt that he "never expected to hate any one in politics with the hatred I feel towards Wilson." With Lodge at their front, the strong reservationists argued that the collective security provisions of the treaty violated congressional prerogatives when it came to committing U.S. forces to war. Fatefully, Wilson refused to concede to any of their objections, which only strengthened Lodge's hand.

Rather, as he had done in seeking his breakthrough 1913 tariff legislation, Wilson attempted to speak over the heads of the senators to gain the support of the American people for ratification. He embarked on an ambitious speaking tour in the West in early September 1919 and was greeted enthusiastically enough to lead some observers to argue that he might have been able to force ratification had he been able to complete this tour — although it would have required support from as many as 20 Republican senators. Yet Wilson fell ill on September 25 in Pueblo, Colorado, aborted the tour, and returned to Washington. There he suffered a nearly fatal stroke on October 2 that incapacitated him for months.

With Wilson removed from the field of battle, Lodge had little trouble in prevailing in the Senate. He supported a series of fourteen reservations to the treaty, then called for a vote with these reservations. Wilson's allies joined the Irreconcilables to prevent the ratification under Lodge's terms. But when Wilson's allies themselves proposed ratification without reservations, they too could not come up with the necessary two-thirds majority. A stalemate of several months ensued, and efforts to achieve a compromise were launched. When they came to naught, the treaty was again put to a vote on March 19, 1920. In this vote, 21 Democrats broke with their president to accept Lodge's terms, but Lodge still could not gain a two-thirds majority. Having failed to adopt the treaty, Congress decided simply to rescind its declaration of war. Strangely, the president vetoed this measure in order to keep the treaty issue alive in the 1920 elections, which he hoped would provide a "great and solemn referendum" on the League of Nations. His strategy failed; the Republicans not only retained their control of the House and Senate but regained the presidency behind Senator Harding. Harding's theme of a "return to normalcy" was fitting for the Sixty-seventh Congress, which itself was concerned with restoring previous patterns of stability.

World War I came at a moment of turmoil and change in Congress, and the war that so shaped the modern world also changed Congress. As World War I erupted in 1914, a healthy, multiregion Democratic coalition was busy passing a flurry of progressive measures under the unprecedented legislative intervention of President Wilson. But the war helped reverse all of this. It contributed to destructive divisions among the Democrats, helped to catapult the Republicans back into the control of Congress, and triggered an aggressive reassertion of congressional power against the encroachments of the executive branch. The war also thwarted hopes that the Wilsonian Democratic party could build a durable, national, reform-oriented legislative coalition. Although congressional reformers managed to influence wartime policymaking in a progressive direction in several important instances — including the creation of a relatively egalitarian military conscription bill, a progressive income tax, and a moderately progressive war financing program — ultimately the war was politically disastrous for progressivism. It would take nearly two decades for both the Democrats and progressives to reconsolidate the level of power that they had held in 1914.

— JOSEPH A. MCCARTIN

BIBLIOGRAPHICAL NOTES

The best treatment of the Congress during World War I remains Seward W. Livermore's *Politics Is Adjourned: Woodrow Wilson and the War Congress* (Middletown, Conn., 1966), a paperback edition of which appeared under the title *Woodrow Wilson and the War Congress, 1916–1918* (Seattle, Wash., 1968). The best analyses of the Democratic party's congressional politics during this period can be found in David Sarasohn, *The Party of Reform: Democrats in the Progressive Era* (Jackson, Miss., 1989), and David Burner, *The Politics of Provincialism: The Democratic Party in Transition, 1918–32* (Westport, Conn., 1967).

Congressional leaders of this era have also been the subject of useful biographical treatments. See Alex Mathews Arnett, *Claude Kitchin and the Wilson War Policies* (Boston, 1937); Evans C. Johnson, *Oscar W. Underwood: A Political Biography* (Baton Rouge, La., 1980); David P. Thelen, *Robert M. La Follette and the Insurgent Spirit* (Boston, 1976); Richard Lowitt, *George W. Norris: The Persistence of a Progressive, 1913–1933* (Urbana, Ill., 1971); and Ruth Warner Towne, *Senator William J. Stone and the Politics of Compromise* (Port Washington, N.Y., 1979).

Some studies of the Wilson presidency illuminate the politics of Congress in this period. Foremost among them are the works of Arthur S. Link. See especially *The Higher Realism of Woodrow Wilson and Other Essays* (Nashville, Tenn., 1971); *Woodrow Wilson: Revolution, War, and Peace* (Arlington Heights, Ill., 1979); and *Woodrow Wilson and the Progressive Era, 1910–1917* (London, 1954). Other works with useful insights are John Morton Blum, *Woodrow Wilson and the Politics of Morality* (Boston, 1956), and Kendrick A. Clements, *The Presidency of Woodrow Wilson* (Lawrence, Kans., 1992).

Larger studies of America's wartime experience shed considerable light on the war's impact on Congress and the context in which congressional actions played out. Among them are David Kennedy's *Over Here: The First World War and American Society* (New York, 1980); Robert H. Zieger's *America's Great War: World War I and the American Experience* (Lanham, Md., 2000); and Ellis W. Hawley's *The Great War and the Search for a Modern Order: A History of the American People and Their Institutions, 1917–1933* (New York, 1979).

Studies of the war mobilization bureaucracy reveal some of the political controversies that embroiled Congress. See Daniel R Beaver, *Newton D. Baker and the American War Effort, 1917–1919* (Lincoln, Neb., 1966); Ronald Schaffer, *America in the Great War: The Rise of the War Welfare State* (New York, 1991); Steven Vaughn, *Holding Fast the Inner Lines: Democracy, Nationalism, and the Committee on Public Information* (Chapel Hill, N.C., 1980); and Joseph A. McCartin, *Labor's Great War: The Struggle for Industrial Democracy and the Origins of Modern American Labor Relations* (Chapel Hill, N.C., 1997).

The best recent treatment of Wilson's failed effort to have the Versailles treaty ratified by the Senate appears in Thomas J. Knock, *To End All Wars: Woodrow Wilson and the Quest for a New World Order* (New York, 1992).

Henry Cabot Lodge

May 12, 1850–November 9, 1924

Henry Cabot Lodge

Henry Cabot Lodge is most often remembered for blocking, as Senate Foreign Relations Committee chairman, membership in the fledgling League of Nations at the close of World War I. During more than a year of contention and committee maneuvering, Lodge fought against President Woodrow Wilson, who, although recovering from a stroke, was equally determined that the treaty should pass. The drama did not cease until 1921, when Congress passed a joint resolution to end the war and ratified peace agreements with several European powers. It is perhaps difficult to separate Lodge's opposition to the treaty, which he and others argued would compromise America's sovereignty, from his fierce partisanship and his immense dislike of Wilson.

Lodge did not like being crossed. He could be a loyal friend, but to his opponents he was ruthlessly vindictive and allowed personal grudges to warp his political perspective. Although a respected scholar and historian, Lodge was not above deception if it was a means to an end. On the other hand, he was known as a patriotic and devoted public servant who worked diligently in committee assignments and took care of his constituents. The wealthy senator avoided even the appearance of a conflict of interest by selling investments that might be affected by legislation under consideration. Whether respected or disliked by his contemporaries, Lodge was widely understood to be combative and temperamental.

Lodge was born into a reputable Boston family. His great-grandfather George Cabot was an influential New England shipowner and former senator; Lodge's grandson, who was named after him, would become a senator and diplomat. Lodge studied at Harvard College, graduating in 1871, earning a law degree there in 1874 and, two years later, a Ph.D., one of the first doctoral degrees in history granted in the United States. His mentor at Harvard was Henry Adams, the distinguished historian descended from two presidents. After graduation, Lodge lectured at Harvard and appeared to have a promising academic career before him. He married, took a year-long honeymoon in Europe, and started a family. He and his wife had three children, one of whom became a fairly respected (if under-appreciated) American poet. Lodge himself was a successful writer, publishing more than twenty books, including *Life and Letters of George Cabot, A Short History of the English Colonies in America,* biographies of Alexander Hamilton, Daniel Webster, and George Washington, and *The Senate and the League of Nations,* which was issued after his death.

Lodge's entry into politics was spurred by his Harvard mentor, Adams, who like many intellectuals was appalled by the corruption and partisanship of President Ulysses S. Grant's administration. Elected to the Massachusetts house of representatives as a Republican in 1878, Lodge quickly excelled in politics. He managed a successful gubernatorial campaign, participated in Republican national conventions, and was elected to the House in 1886. His loyalty to the Republican party cemented his political career but alienated independents and his intellectual friends in Boston. Responding to their opposition, Lodge displayed some of the resentment and aloofness that characterized much of his career.

Elected to the Senate in 1893, Lodge adopted the conservative party line on domestic issues but worked aggressively in foreign policy legislation, favoring the annexation of Hawaii, Puerto Rico, the Philippines, and Cuba. Although a close friend of Theodore Roosevelt's and despite his own disdain for unprincipled "robber barons," Lodge was reluctant to enable the government to regulate business interests, and he opposed progressive bills that sought to change the nature of government. He had a low opinion of President Woodrow Wilson, who, like Lodge, had an academic background in history and opposed much of the administration's "New Freedom" domestic policies, including three successful constitutional amendments (the 17th, providing for the direct popular election of senators; the 18th, establishing prohibition; and the 19th, extending suffrage to women).

Lodge's dislike of Wilson dated to his election as president. He felt Wilson's initial response to World War I was weak and his call for war in 1917 long overdue. More than a decade earlier, Lodge had been advocating a strong national defense. As Foreign Relations Committee chairman, he supported the war effort but was no doubt incensed when Wilson ignored the Republicans during the negotiations with European leaders at Versailles. Lodge's determined opposition to the Treaty of Versailles and the League of Nations brought the senator his greatest notoriety.

References

Garraty, J. A. 2000, February. "Lodge, Henry Cabot." *American National Biography Online.* Retrieved June 30, 2003, from http://www.anb.org/articles/05/05-00442.html.

Petillo, Carol Morris. 2000, February. "Lodge, Henry Cabot." *American National Biography Online.* Retrieved June 30, 2003, from http://www.anb.org/articles/07/07-00526.html.

26

The Forgotten New Deal Congress

OVERSHADOWED from the start by Franklin D. Roosevelt, Congress has never received the star billing it deserves for its role in the New Deal. The image still persists of Roosevelt as legislative mastermind, bending a docile Congress to his will, especially during the dramatic first months of his administration. One distinguished student of the modern presidency, Clinton Rossiter, put it this way: "In the first Hundred Days he gave Congress a kind of leadership it had not known before and still does not care to have repeated. In the golden days of the New Deal, he initiated a dozen programs designed to save a society from the defects of its virtues." Or, as one of FDR's biographers described the same period: "Bills originating in the White House were passed almost daily. This was presidential power without precedent — FDR could dream up an idea, something that had never been tried, and set the huge machinery of government in motion to implement it." In yet a third account, the president "proposed, and proposed, and proposed again," while Congress "scampered in panic to approve those proposals as fast as it could."

That's simply not the way it happened. Far from being the brainchild of one person, the enduring accomplishments of the Depression decade were the products of a richly collaborative process in which FDR, presidential advisers, government bureaucrats, well-organized interest groups, grass-roots activists, and legislators all played parts. But of the participants in the New Deal, it was Congress, not the president, that took the lead in initiating and shaping most of the legislation not only during the first hundred days but throughout Roosevelt's first term. Even after 1936, when Roosevelt assumed more of the legislative initiative, Congress remained a critical force.

i

Franklin Roosevelt's first inaugural address is remembered today almost exclusively for its reassurance that "the only thing we have to fear is fear itself." But those who heard it at the time, either in person or on the radio, found another passage even more stirring. If Congress failed to act immediately to confront the Depression, the new president said, he would ask Congress for the power to act himself: "for the one remaining instrument to meet the emergency — broad Executive power to wage a war against the emergency, as great as the power that would be given to me if we were in fact invaded by a foreign foe." Eleanor Roosevelt, sitting behind her husband on the inaugural platform, momentarily shuddered at the crowd's thunderous response. It was "a little terrifying," she recalled. "You felt that they would do anything — if only someone would tell them what to do."

On assuming office, Roosevelt summoned Congress into special session. Then ensued the famous Hundred Days, from March 9 to June 16, 1933, when Congress passed and the president signed some fifteen major pieces of legislation. This unprecedented productivity offered something to almost everyone: the Agricultural Adjustment Act (AAA) provided hard-pressed farmers with the promise of higher prices; the National Industrial Recovery Act (NIRA) authorized industries to form cartels in order to eliminate inefficiency and wasteful competition; that same measure recognized labor's right to organize and bargain collectively; the Federal Emergency Relief Act (FERA) gave the unemployed money to buy food, shelter, and clothing; the Public Works Administration (PWA) and the Civilian Conservation Corps (CCC) promised to put the jobless back to work. Other measures protected homeowners, bank customers, and stock market investors.

Although Roosevelt dominated the public spotlight during this whirlwind stretch, only two of the fifteen measures actually originated with him. One was the Economy Act, which honored his campaign pledge to slash government spending, even if it meant cutting the pensions of veterans and the salaries of government employees. The other was the justly celebrated CCC, which employed a half-million young men on a variety of conservation projects. To this short list should probably be added bank reorganization; while not FDR's brainchild, it was largely driven by executive branch members, including holdovers from former president Herbert Hoover's Treasury Department. Most of the remaining measures of the first hundred days originated in Congress or devolved out of its attempt to respond to the president's bold inaugural challenge to act.

Indeed, when measured by their accomplishments and the overall quality of their members, the Seventy-third Congress and its successors during the New Deal equaled, if they did not surpass, any Congress in history. True, no legislators of the stature of Daniel Webster, Henry Clay, or John C. Calhoun served during the Roosevelt years. And there were a few buffoons and small-time demagogues. But the New Deal Congresses had an unusually large number of legislators of uncommon intelligence, high-mindedness, and creativity — senators such as Hugo Black of Alabama, Robert M. La Follette Jr. of Wisconsin, George W. Norris of Nebraska, Robert F. Wagner of New York, and Edward P. Costigan of Colorado; and representatives such as Fiorello La Guardia of New York, David J. Lewis of Maryland, and Maury Maverick and Sam Rayburn of Texas.

ii

For the first time since early 1919, when Woodrow Wilson was president, the Democrats controlled both houses of Congress. In 1932 they had carried not only the South, as they had in every election since Reconstruction, but every other region except New England. For the first time in nearly a century, Democrats could claim membership in a truly national party. Despite their electoral dominance, they lacked ideological cohesion. The Democratic ranks included states' rights Southerners, northeastern liberals, and western progressives. There were budget cutters and spenders; friends of organized labor and foes of unions. But somehow, out of this diverse mixture came programs — lots of them.

The Roosevelt administration projected an image of dynamic change — of idealistic young men and women flocking to Washington to throw out the old guard. That influx helped fuel the Roosevelt myth. "And with the New Deal came the New Dealers," wrote the historian Arthur M. Schlesinger Jr. "The old capital did not know what to make of the invasion." In actuality, the congressional architects of the New Deal, almost to a man, were long-time veterans of Capitol Hill. The Senate Democratic leadership comprised four Southerners with 105 years of congressional service among them. Best known was the sixty-five-year-old president of the Senate, John Nance Garner of Texas, who had resigned his post as House Speaker to become Roosevelt's running mate. The cigar-chomping, whiskey-drinking Garner, who reputedly said that the vice presidency wasn't "worth a warm bucket of spit" (disagreement persists over the spelling of the last word), was a caricaturist's delight. But he was also a congressional insider, highly respected by his former colleagues, as well as a national figure who had come close to wresting the presidential nomination from Roosevelt at the Democratic convention. The second member of the Democratic high command, the sixty-one-year-old majority leader, Joseph T. Robinson of Arkansas, was something of a hothead. At least twice in his career he came close to exchanging blows with a colleague. But he was efficient and loyal, and he had a reputation for getting things done. Byron "Pat" Harrison of Mississippi, a one-time semipro baseball player, owed his leadership position to both his tight control over the powerful Finance Committee and his popularity with Senate insiders of both parties. The fourth member, James F. Byrnes, although almost unknown outside his home state of South Carolina or Capitol Hill, was a shrewd tactician — "the smartest politician I knew in Washington," recalled the *New York Times* correspondent Turner Catledge, whose career spanned the decades from the 1930s to the 1960s. These Senate leaders were more conservative than many of their fellow Democrats, including the president. But they supported Roosevelt because of party loyalty and because their states desperately needed federal help.

The principal Democratic leaders in the House were also old-timers, including the seventy-four-year-old Speaker, Henry T. Rainey of Illinois, who was elected to his position when Garner became vice president, and the sixty-four-year-old majority leader, Joseph W. Byrns of Tennessee. Despite thirty years of service in the House, Rainey was something of an outsider. An outspoken liberal with a strong independent streak, he had never penetrated the House's southern-dominated inner circle. Indeed, he owed his Speakership to the support he had received from incoming members of the House, most of whom hailed from outside the South.

In both houses the Democratic leaders were facilitators, not innovators. The legislative craftsmanship they left to more issue-oriented colleagues like Robert Wagner and "Young Bob" La Follette in the Senate and David Lewis and Sam Rayburn in the House. Though the leaders did not write the bills, they did almost everything else. They scheduled the debates, engineered the compromises, and mustered the votes for passage. Without them, the New Deal would not have stood a chance. Rainey and Byrns played a particularly important role by eliminating a potential roadblock. They saw to it that the House Rules Committee — the most powerful committee in either house of Congress — and its accommodating chairman, Edward W. Pou of North Carolina, adopted rules limiting the members' ability to amend bills reaching the floor from committee. Consequently, the bills surviving committee consideration had relatively smooth passage. Fast-track rules enhanced the power of already powerful committees like Ways and Means, Appropriations, and Interstate and Foreign Commerce, where the real work of the House was done.

The congressional Republicans, for their part, lacked the manpower and the will to present a united front against the new administration. In addition to depleting the GOP's ranks, the 1932 election had shifted the party's center of gravity slightly to the left, especially in the Senate, where several of the party's most conservative and experienced members had gone down to defeat. Four progressive Republican senators had even campaigned for Roosevelt: La Follette, Hiram Johnson of California, Bronson Cutting of New Mexico, and George Norris of Nebraska. The Republican minority leader in the Senate, Charles L. McNary of Oregon, a veteran of the farm relief battles of the 1920s, had no interest in opposing the Democrats just for the sake of opposing. He privately conceded to his brother that he enjoyed working with Roosevelt more than he had with his fellow Republican Herbert Hoover. The House Republicans, under the leadership of Bertrand Snell of New York, were not as accommodating as their Senate counterparts, but even they were of no mind to offer wholesale resistance to the early New Deal.

In addition to the Democrats and the Republicans, two congressional subgroups, the southern Democrats and the progressives, played important roles in the New Deal. The southern Democrats formed the most closely knit group on Capitol Hill. They socialized with one another and could often be found having a drink together at the end of the day (or earlier). They revered Congress as an institution and steeped themselves in its rules and traditions. Many of them were single, so their lives revolved around Congress. Because most of them came from "safe" districts or states, they had accumulated more seniority than their colleagues from other regions and therefore occupied a disproportionate number of committee chairs and leadership positions. As a group, they were more conservative than the northern Democrats. But with the exception of civil rights, to which they marched lockstep in opposition, they did not form a voting bloc. The southern Democrats produced some of the earliest and most strident critics of the New Deal, such as Virginia's Senators Carter Glass and Harry F. Byrd, but also some of its most effective supporters, including Robinson, Harrison, and Byrnes in the Senate and Sam Rayburn in the House.

The congressional progressives, dubbed "the Sons of the Wild Jackass" by a conservative foe, had organized themselves into a loose coalition in the 1920s to combat the conservative Republican administrations of that decade. Better organized in the Senate than in the House, the progressives came primarily from the Middle West and the West. Most prominent among them were the Republicans George Norris of Nebraska, William E. Borah of Idaho, Johnson of California, Gerald P. Nye of North Dakota,

Cutting of New Mexico, and La Follette of Wisconsin, and the Democrats Burton K. Wheeler of Montana and Edward P. Costigan of Colorado. The progressives decried the exploitation of "the people" by "the special interests," favored using the antitrust laws to break up big corporations, called for a downward redistribution of the nation's wealth, and championed the interests of farmers. In foreign affairs, most of them opposed extensive involvement of the United States in Europe. As a group, they applied pressure to Congress and the administration from the left, especially on federal spending and regulatory issues. Of them, Norris and La Follette, who sponsored a number of enduring measures, made the largest contributions to the New Deal.

iii

There's no better example of legislative initiative than the Federal Emergency Relief Act of 1933 (FERA), which helped millions of jobless Americans stave off hunger and homelessness and probably touched more lives than any other early New Deal program. The battle for federal unemployment relief began not with Roosevelt's inauguration but two years earlier, when Hoover was president and Roosevelt, then governor of New York, was still on record as opposing federal relief. In 1931 several prominent social workers went door-to-door on Capitol Hill, pleading with legislators to sponsor relief legislation. The first to respond was La Follette, the youngest member of the Senate and the heir to Wisconsin's famous political dynasty (and later the model for the tragic main character of Allen Drury's classic political novel, *Advise and Consent*). Earlier in the year, Young Bob had sponsored Senate hearings that demonstrated beyond a doubt that the Depression had exhausted the capacity of private charities and state and local governments to cope with the needs of millions of unemployed Americans. In the fall of 1931, he introduced a bill to provide federal relief to the unemployed. Signing on as cosponsors were Senator Costigan, the quietly effective Democrat from Colorado, and Representative David J. Lewis of Maryland, surely one of the most underrated and interesting members of Congress. A self-made man, Lewis had gone to work in a Pennsylvania coal mine at the age of nine; at sixteen, he had taught himself to read and write not only in English but also in French and German. The La Follette–Costigan-Lewis bill assumed various forms and passed through several stages of consideration, gathering more and more supporters at each stage. In the summer of 1932, during the waning months of the Hoover administration, Congress passed, and Hoover signed, a scaled-down version of the bill, the Emergency Relief and Construction Act, which authorized loans to the states for relief purposes. The measure represented the crossing of an ideological Rubicon: for the first time the federal government had formally, if grudgingly, accepted responsibility for the plight of the unemployed.

A month before the inauguration, La Follette, in the company of Cutting, the progressive Republican from New Mexico, met with Roosevelt at his home in Warm Springs, Georgia. La Follette laid out the case for a new unemployment relief bill, this one appropriating $500 million in outright grants, not loans, to the states. Roosevelt endorsed the concept and so notified his Senate leaders. On March 21, three weeks after the inauguration, Roosevelt sent Congress a formal message, urging it to enact a relief measure. La Follette, now joined by several colleagues in both houses, introduced the bill he had been working on and to which Roosevelt had already agreed. A Senate debate ensued; the Democratic leaders Garner, Robinson, Harrison, and Byrnes helped line up support; a vote was taken; and a bill was passed, 55–17. Three weeks later the House concurred by an even larger margin. The president signed the bill, and the act became law. Except for a larger appropriation and a more elaborate administrative structure, the FERA was almost identical to the bill that La Follette, Costigan, and Lewis had introduced in Congress a year and a half earlier. Other New Deal measures followed the same trajectory: they began in Congress; moved to the administration for alterations and editing; and came back to Congress for debate, amendment, and final consideration.

The speed with which the lawmakers acted on the FERA and other bills reinforced the impression of Congress as a rubber stamp. "Congress doesn't pass legislation any more," quipped the humorist Will Rogers. "They just wave at the bills as they go by." But in the case of unemployment relief, appearances were deceiving. Because Congress had been debating the issue in one form or another for almost two years, by 1933 even the most loquacious members had little more to say.

A second landmark measure of the Hundred Days, the bill creating the Tennessee Valley Authority (TVA), had an even longer legislative history. In 1916, the year before the United States entered the First World War, the Wilson administration hoped to generate electricity for national defense by building a huge dam on the Tennessee River at Muscle Shoals, Alabama. But when the war ended, the project seemed less urgent, and Wilson's Republican successors in the White House — Warren Harding, Calvin Coolidge, and Herbert Hoover — all favored selling the dam to private utilities. At that point, the progressives in Congress, led by George Norris, rose up in opposition. Rather than privatize the dam at Muscle Shoals, they argued, the federal government should use it both to produce affordable electricity for the hundreds of thousands of residents of the Tennessee Valley and to control flooding along the Tennessee River. Muscle Shoals was one of the most contentious issues of the 1920s. Six times Norris and his supporters proposed legislation to develop Muscle Shoals, and six times they met defeat, twice by presidential veto. Finally, in 1933 Norris found an ally in the White House, and the TVA became a reality.

Few New Deal agencies are as well known or more closely identified with Roosevelt than the Federal Deposit Insurance Corporation (FDIC). But when Senator Arthur Vandenberg, a conservative Republican from Michigan, and Representative Henry Steagall, a Democrat from Alabama, first proposed creating a federal agency to insure bank deposits, Roosevelt thought it a bad idea. To guarantee the savings of all depositors, no matter how good or bad their banks might be, the president argued, would encourage sloppy and dishonest banking practices. Roosevelt eventually reversed himself, but only when it became clear that Congress would pass an insurance measure with or without his approval.

When Congress wasn't initiating legislation, it was prodding the administration to do so. Thus, for example, Roosevelt put forth the national industrial recovery bill in part to head off a movement led by Senator Hugo Black of Alabama to create new jobs by limiting the hours of factory workers to thirty per week. The president also required prodding to support public works projects that would create jobs. One day he would tell legislators he favored public works; the next he would express doubts that they would do much for the economy. Finally, in May, Senators La Follette, Costigan, and Cutting decided to force his hand by introducing a bill to spend an unprecedented $6 billion on public works. If passed, the expenditure would have been the largest single appropriation in American history to date. Doubtless sensing that he would have to offer some alternative to have any say in the matter, Roosevelt agreed to support a more modest appropriation of $3.3 billion.

Congress also used its investigatorial powers both to nudge the administration and to build public support for its initiatives. The most important investigation during the Hundred Days was an ongoing probe by the Senate Banking and Currency Committee into malfeasance on Wall Street. Under the relentless questioning of committee counsel Ferdinand Pecora, some of the nation's wealthiest and most influential financiers admitted to an array of shady practices, from insider trading to tax evasion. J. P. Morgan Jr. filled the headlines for days when he reluctantly disclosed that he and his moneyed partners had paid no income tax for three years in a row. The Pecora hearings created a groundswell of support for New Deal measures separating commercial from investment banking and regulating the stock exchange.

iv

When the Hundred Days ended in June, Roosevelt believed that he and the Congress had put together a program that, with a little tinkering here and there, would lift the country out of the Depression. Hence, when Congress reconvened in 1934, he did not seem as receptive to legislative initiatives as he had been the previous year. He did support important measures creating the Securities and Exchange Commission (SEC) to regulate Wall Street, insuring home loans by private lenders, devaluing the dollar in the hopes of raising prices, and empowering the president to negotiate reciprocal trade agreements with foreign nations.

Beyond them, however, he refused to go, as he demonstrated in reaction to a pair of initiatives designed to boost the well-being of wage-earners. In each case Roosevelt found himself at odds with his fellow Democrat from New York, Senator Robert Wagner. Born in Germany and raised in a working-class neighborhood on New York City's Upper East Side, Wagner had ascended through the ranks of the city's famous political machine, Tammany Hall, serving first in the state legislature, then on the state supreme court, and finally in the Senate, where, as the author of a half-dozen or so enduring pieces of legislation, he achieved great distinction. Years before, during their joint service in the state senate, the two New Yorkers had frequently crossed swords. Since then they had become political allies, but they still remained slightly wary of each other.

The first of Wagner's legislative initiatives in 1934 sought to address an increasingly urgent labor problem. Following the passage in 1933 of the NIRA, which had contained a clause recognizing the right of workers to organize and bargain collectively, labor had made some impressive advances, even managing to gain a foothold in such bastions of anti-unionism as the automobile and steel industries. By 1934, however, many industries had launched an all-out push to block any further labor gains. Labor-management disputes increasingly flared into violence, and in 1934 alone, forty-six workers died in clashes with local authorities and company guards.

With evidence mounting that the pro-labor provisions of the NIRA did not sufficiently protect workers who wanted to organize, Wagner introduced a labor relations bill that he believed not only would bring harmony to the workplace but also boost the economy, leading to higher wages and increased mass purchasing power. Roosevelt remained unmoved by his arguments. Viewing the bill as class legislation and preferring moral suasion to coercion, he convinced the disappointed senator to defer action until a future session of Congress.

Roosevelt similarly rebuffed legislative efforts to create a federal-state system of unemployment compensation. Proponents argued that just as people needed health insurance as a hedge against illness, so too did they need unemployment insurance as a hedge against another of modern life's uncertainties. Congress had been debating the issue since the Hoover administration, and by 1934 a majority of its members favored unemployment compensation in some form. Although its proponents disagreed among themselves over funding mechanisms, they united in support of a bill introduced by Wagner and Representative David Lewis of Maryland that would encourage the states to experiment with compensation systems of their own. Wagner and Lewis had every reason to believe that the president's endorsement would be forthcoming, for he had supported the principle of unemployment insurance since his governorship, and he already had approved an earlier version of the bill. As time went on, however, Roosevelt had second thoughts, and in the summer he withdrew his support from the bill, saying that the entire issue needed further study. Even though he promised to support an even more comprehensive measure the following year, proponents of unemployment compensation threw up their hands in frustration. "One cannot be too optimistic about the future promises of persons who are instrumental in blocking present progress," complained one of the framers of the Wagner-Lewis Bill.

v

By the time Congress convened in 1935, Roosevelt had all he could do to prevent a full-scale rebellion. Although the lawmakers approved his request for $5 billion for public works, congressional insurgents almost succeeded in attaching to the measure a provision that would require the administration to pay workers on federal projects the prevailing wage in various sections of the country, thus placing the government in direct competition with private industry for labor services. Only an all-out effort by Roosevelt's allies prevented the provision from becoming law. The administration proved unable to head off a movement to restore the cuts in veterans' pensions that Roosevelt had made two years earlier; Congress passed the measure over his veto. Finally, the Senate dealt the president the single biggest defeat of his first term when it refused his request for American membership on the World Court, part of the League of Nations.

Finally, during the summer of 1935, a combination of factors prompted the president to act. Roosevelt remained overwhelmingly popular, to be sure. But increasingly, as the excitement of the first hundred days wore off, the public was becoming restless with the slow pace of economic recovery and beginning to listen to other leaders who offered quick remedies for the nation's ills. The Louisiana firebrand, Senator Huey P. Long, was attracting millions of poor Southerners to his Share Our Wealth movement, with its promise of a guaranteed annual income for every American family. Francis Townsend, a sixty-seven-year-old doctor from California, was organizing millions of elderly Americans in his crusade for old-age pensions. And each week 40 million listeners were tuning in to hear a charismatic radio priest, Charles E. Coughlin, castigate Wall Street. Roosevelt worried that Long, Townsend, and Coughlin might unite around a third-party candidate to challenge him in the next election. Meanwhile, critical business and financial leaders were becoming increasingly strident in their denunciations of Roosevelt and the New Deal — so strident that there seemed nothing Roosevelt could do to appease them. With events starting to spin out of control, some of Roosevelt's key supporters pleaded with him to seize control while he still could. Roosevelt responded. In June, just as the legislators were preparing to leave the capital for the summer, he suddenly insisted that they postpone adjournment until they had passed four central measures: a bill curbing the spread of inherently unstable corporate entities known as holding companies, a banking reform measure, a labor proposal by Robert Wagner, and a social security bill. A week later he added tax reform to his "must" list. There soon ensued a period of legislative activity comparable to that of the Hundred Days.

Although Roosevelt provided the impetus for their final passage, most of the enactments of this period, as earlier, developed independently of the president. Thus, for example, Roosevelt had relatively little to do with the Wealth Tax Act or the reforms in the Federal Reserve System. The National Labor Relations Act (NLRA), which guaranteed labor the right to form unions, was the very same measure that Roosevelt had persuaded Wagner to shelve the year before. But in 1935 the New York senator reintroduced the bill, and Roosevelt put it on his "must" list, but only after the Senate had already acted favorably on the measure and the House seemed certain to do likewise. The president, his labor secretary Frances Perkins later recalled, "never lifted a finger" for the measure. "All the credit for it belongs to Wagner."

The passage of the NLRA thrust its author into the national spotlight. At first glance, Robert Wagner was easy to underestimate. Short and thick-set, friendly but unassuming, he could walk into a room without anyone's taking notice. Although obviously intelligent, he did not possess an original or incisive mind, and he was an average speaker at best. Yet, lacking any apparent attributes of the first order, he was one of the most effective legislators of his or any other time. In some ways, the very lack of an outsized persona probably worked to his advantage. His disarming lack of pretension and an affecting self-consciousness (he blushed when he mispronounced a word or mangled his syntax) made him many friends. And, as his biographer J. Joseph Huthmacher pointed out, Wagner may not have been brilliant, but he didn't hesitate to seek advice from those who were. With Congress providing meager resources for staff support, he was one of the few lawmakers (La Follette and Rayburn were others) who brought experts in from outside to help research and write legislation. As a result, the typical Wagner proposal was simply better thought out and more amply documented than the alternatives. But the real key to his success was his ability to speak to the needs of the urban working class, many of whom were first- or second-generation immigrants. He could speak to their needs because he was one of them. "I lived among the people of the tenements," he once said. "Unless you have . . . you cannot know the haunting sense of insecurity which hangs over the home of the worker."

Wagner's two noblest efforts were expended in losing causes. During the 1930s, he and Colorado senator Edward Costigan sponsored a bill to make lynching a federal offense. Although the lynching of blacks by white mobs, mostly in the South, had long been a national scandal, the Depression seemed to exacerbate racial tensions. In 1933 alone, twenty-eight such incidents occurred. For decades, the National Association for the Advancement of Colored People (NAACP) had been seeking legislation to make lynching a federal offense, and during the Depression decade its leaders decided to try again. But the Wagner-Costigan bill twice fell victim to threatened filibusters by southern Democrats. Both times Roosevelt, who had publicly condemned lynching, declined to press the issue for fear of jeopardizing other legislation.

Years later, as the Second World War approached, Wagner joined Representative Edith N. Rogers of Massachusetts to introduce legislation to loosen the immigration laws so that German Jews and other victims of Nazism could more freely enter the United States. With public opinion running overwhelmingly against any relaxation of the laws, the Wagner-Rogers bill never even came to a vote.

Wagner was also a critical player in the formulation and passage of the most enduring product of the second hundred days, the Social Security Act, which established systems for old-age and survivors' insurance and unemployment compensation. It was the one measure during this period on which Roosevelt also left his mark. By the mid-1930s, 125 foreign countries and 18 states provided some form of assistance to the elderly. By that time, too, legislators, including Wagner, had introduced bills to establish systems for old-age insurance and unemployment compensation.

To coordinate these ongoing activities, Roosevelt had created a cabinet committee to develop an economic security program, and in 1935 he urged Congress to enact its recommendations.

Roosevelt was no latecomer to the cause of social security. For many years he had been arguing, often eloquently, that society had an obligation to protect its citizens from the vicissitudes of modern life, and in doing so he had helped create public support for a government-sponsored social security system. Privately, he told aides that he favored a comprehensive, cradle-to-grave program, including, presumably, national health insurance. Given Roosevelt's enthusiastic support for the cause, some proponents of social security expressed surprise and deep disappointment when, in the final accounting, he helped limit its scope. For one thing, fearful that too broad a program would lessen the likelihood of passage, he successfully opposed including a national health insurance provision in the bill. He also insisted that a special tax on the earnings of currently employed workers rather than the income tax should provide the principal source of funding for the old-age insurance system. Critics opposed this funding plan because they believed that a payroll tax not only would impose the heaviest burden on those persons least able to pay but also would remove from the masses billions of dollars of purchasing power, thereby retarding economic recovery. Roosevelt held firm. A payroll tax, he argued, would protect the social security system from future political assault. "We put those payroll contributions there so as to give the contributors a legal, moral, and political right to collect their pensions and their unemployment benefits," he explained, adding, "With those taxes in there, no damn politician can ever scrap my social security program." In truth, Roosevelt's controversial financing scheme probably did help shield the system from conservative assault.

In August 1935 Roosevelt's call for a "breathing spell" from any new initiatives signified the end of one of the most productive periods in American legislative history. Although Congress and the administration would expand existing programs and create new ones in the succeeding years, by 1935 they had completed the basic structure of the New Deal.

vi

To say Congress played a much greater role in the New Deal than commonly supposed is not to suggest that all congressional influence was positive. The devil lay in the details, and the details of some New Deal measures denied aid to those who needed it most. Congressional insistence on maximum state participation in federal programs led to many abuses. In the South, lax federal control of the AAA allowed white landowners to cheat black sharecroppers and tenant farmers out of their fair share of agricultural subsidies. Many black Southerners also found themselves systematically excluded from Aid to Dependent Children — a program in the social security system — the benefits from which were arbitrarily low in the region to start with. The abuses reached as far north as Maine, where a field investigator for FERA found that "the relief administration in some places is awful," largely because the local officials in charge of dispensing aid were often "inexperienced and unsympathetic." "Weekly food orders," the investigator noted, "are written out by men who apparently haven't the slightest idea of the food needs of a family. Nor its other needs." In one case, a large family with small children received a food order that included lots of coffee and molasses but hardly any milk or meat. Conservative Democrats and Republicans may have taken the lead in limiting federal control, but they were not alone. No legislator was more committed to federal action to combat the Depression than Wisconsin's La Follette. But even he wanted to ensure that his state, with its pioneering reform tradition, had ample leeway to implement federal programs without federal strings attached.

Nor is an emphasis on the role of Congress meant to relegate Roosevelt to the wings. With the possible exception of Woodrow Wilson, Roosevelt involved himself more directly in lawmaking than any of his predecessors. He helped coordinate legislative activity, backing some measures and opposing or modifying others. In his speeches and fireside chats, he mobilized public support for the New Deal and articulated its rationale. He dispensed patronage and public works to build support for the programs he wanted, and he made liberal use of his veto powers. But if Roosevelt played a more active part in legislative affairs than had his predecessors, he was less active than most of his successors, several of whom, including Lyndon Johnson and Bill Clinton, carved out for themselves legislative roles larger than FDR ever dreamed of.

What Roosevelt didn't do may have been more important than what he did. In his inaugural address he issued a dramatic call to action, then he allowed Congress to assume the initiative. He was a kind of Wizard of Oz, infusing Congress and the public with the confidence to do what it had been in their power to do all along. His real genius was his ability to inspire creative action in others.

No one would have been more surprised at Roosevelt's posthumous reputation for legislative mastery than Roosevelt himself. For he believed that moral leadership and public education, not lawmaking, were the primary functions of the president. The presidency, he told a reporter, is "preeminently a place of moral leadership," adding, "I want to be a preaching president like my Cousin Teddy."

vii

But whatever the legislative division of labor, the voters approved the results, and in 1936 they gave Roosevelt and the New Deal's supporters in Congress one of the greatest victories in American history. Roosevelt swept every state except Maine and Vermont and received 61 percent of the popular vote. The Democrats picked up enough seats in Congress to have the largest majorities in history, outnumbering Republicans and independents by a 76–16 margin in the Senate and 331–89 in the House. The election was significant not only because of the magnitude of the Democratic sweep but also because it heralded the arrival of a new electoral coalition — the New Deal coalition — that would shape American politics for decades. The Democratic party achieved enduring majority status by expanding its traditional base among white Southerners to include large numbers of low-income urban dwellers, most of them of recent immigrant stock. The typical party recruit was a blue-collar worker, of southern or eastern European ancestry, Catholic or Jewish in religious affiliation, living in one of the big cities of the Northeast or the Great Lakes region, and probably voting for the first time. African Americans, where they could vote, also joined the new coalition, although they were more likely to vote for Roosevelt than for congressional Democrats because of the party's identification with white supremacy. The New Deal coalition did not emerge fully formed in 1936. It had been evolving since the 1920s and would continue to develop in subsequent elections.

The 1936 election marked a dramatic turning point in the relations between Roosevelt and Congress. As Roosevelt began his second term, he suddenly seized the legislative initiative by proposing a bold agenda of his own. His most controversial requests were for the enlargement of the Supreme Court and the reorganization of the executive branch of government. But when lawmakers, including members of his own party, balked at these requests, he added a third item: the purge of errant Democrats from Congress.

Roosevelt's first order of business was the Supreme Court. In 1935 and 1936, the Court had invalidated a host of New Deal measures, including the NIRA and the AAA. It had also struck down several important measures at the state level, creating, in Roosevelt's words, a "no-man's land," where neither federal nor state governments had the jurisdiction to act. If the Court maintained its present course, as seemed likely at the time, the Social Security Act, the National Labor Relations Act, and just about anything else Congress might come up with would be the next to fall.

Shortly after his second inauguration, Roosevelt asked Congress for a law empowering him to appoint up to six additional justices to the Supreme Court. That Roosevelt would address the Court crisis should have come as no surprise. Given the gravity of the situation, he had little choice. But his plan for resolving the crisis, quickly dubbed Court-packing by critics, and the manner of its presentation surprised and shocked the members of Congress. At the very beginning, Roosevelt made two critical mistakes. First, he disingenuously said that his proposal was not aimed at securing a liberal majority on the Court but at improving the performance of the judicial system. The pretense fooled no one, and Roosevelt quickly dropped it. But the damage was done. He looked not only devious but unsure of the merits of his plan. Else why resort to a ruse? "Too clever — too damned clever," wrote one normally friendly newspaper editor.

Even worse, Roosevelt sprang the proposal without having consulted a single legislator, including his floor leaders, who would have to muster the votes for passage. Why he abandoned the collaborative approach that had served him so well during his first term was puzzling. Perhaps he believed the element of surprise would give him the advantage over Court defenders. He may also have wanted to preempt any consideration of alternative proposals then making the rounds in Congress. He was particularly skeptical of a proposal to amend the Constitution to give Congress the power to overturn Supreme Court decisions in much the same way it could overrule presidential vetoes. Constitutional amendments, he believed, simply took too long to pass and were too easy to defeat. But Roosevelt badly miscalculated. Many legislators felt hurt and angry. Despite their contributions to the New Deal, Roosevelt apparently didn't value their advice on the most important initiative of his presidency. William Bankhead of Alabama, who had recently become Speaker of the House, expressed the sentiments of many Roosevelt loyalists when he said to a friend, "Wouldn't you have thought that the President would have told his own party leaders what he was going to do? He didn't because he knew that hell would break loose."

A storm of protest, unexpected in its intensity, greeted the president's proposal. Some of the opposition came from entirely predictable sources. Judges, state bar associations, professors at elite law schools, conservative foes of the New Deal — all shrilly denounced the president as a would-be dictator bent on undermining the Constitution. Roosevelt expected, perhaps even welcomed, opposition of this sort, and because much of it seemed so transparently self-serving, it probably did little harm to his cause. Such was not the case with the unexpected opposition of many Democrats and liberals. In the Senate, where Court-packing would receive its first test, administration stalwarts, such as Joseph C. O'Mahoney of Wyoming and Burton Wheeler of Montana, came out against the president's proposal, while Robert Wagner, whose name was practically synonymous with the New Deal, conspicuously absented himself from the looming battle. Wheeler's opposition was particularly damaging, for he had been the first senator to endorse Roosevelt for the presidency and he had impeccable liberal credentials. No one could accuse him of personal or ideological animus. Nor could Roosevelt credibly claim that his opponents were simply reactionary foes of the New Deal.

Wheeler raised the obvious question: If a liberal president could pack the Court with liberals, what was to stop a conservative president from doing the same with right-leaning appointees? Other critics argued that Roosevelt's proposal would do nothing to alter the fact that the Supreme Court, even though not elected and therefore not accountable for its actions, had the power to thwart the public will. Only a constitutional amendment, they argued, no matter how long it took to pass, could protect the people from judicial usurpations of power.

Roosevelt compounded his problems with heavy-handed efforts to win legislative support. To oversee the Court fight, he dispatched to Capitol Hill his brilliant young adviser Thomas G. Corcoran. "Tommy the Cork," as Roosevelt called him, had helped write some of Roosevelt's best speeches and draft some of the major legislation of the first term. Yet for one entrusted with the delicate task of handling the Court-packing issue, Corcoran possessed severe handicaps. Chief among them was, in the words of two reporters, his "faint contempt for the legislative process, which he regarded as a messy business, to be got over as quickly as possible, like an attack of the mumps." Working from the premise that every legislator had a price, Corcoran offered patronage, federal projects, and threats of political reprisal to induce congressmen to support Roosevelt's proposal. When he offered Wheeler a role in the selection of Supreme Court justices in exchange for his vote, the indignant Montana senator redoubled his efforts to defeat the measure.

In mid-June the Senate Judiciary Committee, under the chairmanship of Henry F. Ashurst, a loyal Democrat from Arizona, delivered the death blow to Court-packing. In a carefully prepared report to the full Senate, the committee described the bill as "a needless, futile and utterly dangerous abandonment of constitutional principle," the ultimate effect of which would be "to make this government one of men rather than of law." Underscoring the breach that had developed between Roosevelt and Congress, the report concluded that Court-packing "should be so emphatically rejected that its parallel will never again be presented to the free representatives of the free people of America."

Soon after the committee filed its report, an angry and unrepentant Roosevelt authorized the majority leader, Joseph Robinson, to salvage what he could from the original bill. Robinson harbored deep reservations about Court-packing but soldiered on in the hope — a hope probably encouraged by Roosevelt — that he would be nominated for one of the new seats on the High Court. But even the fates seemed to have conspired against Roosevelt. In mid-July Robinson collapsed and died of a heart attack before he could negotiate a compromise. An open copy of the *Congressional Record* was found near his side. His death not only destroyed whatever chance remained for a compromise, but it also exacerbated the hard feelings between the president and many of Robinson's colleagues, who believed that the strain of the Court fight had contributed to the majority leader's demise. These same legislators also faulted Roosevelt for failing to attend Robinson's funeral in Arkansas and, additionally, for meddling in the contest to select a new majority leader — a contest that pitted Alben W. Barkley of Kentucky, who had supported Court-packing, against the Finance Committee chairman, Pat Harrison, who had remained noncommittal. Roosevelt lobbied heavily behind the scene on behalf of Barkley, who won by a single vote.

Subsequent developments allowed Roosevelt's supporters to claim that he had lost the Court-packing battle but won the war. In an apparent about-face, the Supreme Court began upholding New Deal legislation, including the NLRA and Social Security. Then, too, retirements and deaths among the incumbent justices eventually allowed Roosevelt to appoint an unprecedented eight members to the High Court and to raise a ninth member to the chief justiceship. But if Roosevelt had won the war, victory had come at a great cost, for the Court fight tarnished his reputation, emboldened his foes, and destroyed Democratic unity. The fight also spurred the growth of a congressional coalition of conservative Democrats and Republicans. With roughly 35 members in the Senate and 180 in the House, the conservatives lacked the numbers to roll back the New Deal legislation. But they did have the power to rebuff new initiatives, which they did for the remainder of Roosevelt's presidency and for decades to follow. Given the direction of the administration, conservative opposition was inevitable. But Roosevelt's clumsy handling of Court-packing hastened its development.

Soon Congress dealt Roosevelt a second blow. During the first term, the proliferation of new federal agencies, combined with existing government departments, had created a cumbersome federal apparatus comprised of bureaus with different, even contradictory, administrative philosophies. To suggest how he might bring order to and establish control over this jerry-built system, Roosevelt in 1936 created a panel of distinguished political scientists and public administration experts. Drawing on its recommendations, the president proposed restructuring the executive branch to modernize its procedures, centralize its operations, increase the president's control over budgetary, personnel, and administrative matters, and give the federal government a greater role in national economic planning and in the allocation and use of natural resources.

This reorganization encountered unexpectedly fierce resistance in Congress. Coinciding with the Court fight at home and the rise of Adolf Hitler in Germany and Benito Mussolini in Italy, executive reorganization struck some critics as a step toward dictatorship. The president's proposal, said one senator, would plunge "a dagger into the very heart of democracy." In 1937 Congress shelved executive reorganization. Two years later it did approve a truncated version of Roosevelt's proposal, which, although significantly modernizing the executive branch, fell far short of his original goals.

In 1938, reeling from the defeat of Court-packing and legislative reorganization, Roosevelt tried to regain the initiative with one bold stroke. As the 1938 elections approached, he attempted to oust the conservative Democrats from Congress by campaigning against them in the primaries. From the beginning everything seemed to go wrong. Even if he had performed flawlessly, Roosevelt would have encountered formidable obstacles. As it turned out, most primary contests turned on state and local issues, and try as he might, he could not focus attention on broader issues of national concern. Despite his popularity with the voters, he could not counter the image of himself as an interloper in local matters, dictating how citizens should vote. But Roosevelt also hurt his own cause. Because he left himself too little time to recruit strong candidates, some of the primaries became monumental mismatches between liberal nonentities and powerful conservative incumbents. Nor did Roosevelt clearly define his criteria for opposing some candidates and supporting others. He described as a "dyed-in-the-wool conservative" one of his chief targets, Senator Walter F. George of Georgia, even though George had supported a half-dozen or so critical New Deal measures, including the NIRA, the AAA, the Social Security Act, and the Wagner Act. Yet in other states, Roosevelt supported, or at least did not oppose, candidates with records comparable to George's. In some states, heavy-handed electioneering practices imparted an unsavory odor to the president's realignment campaign. In Kentucky and Florida, workers on the payroll of the WPA actively campaigned for Roosevelt's candidates. In other states federal bureaucrats suddenly released funds for long-delayed federal highway and bridge projects.

By the end of the primary season, Roosevelt had suffered an embarrassing series of defeats. Of the ten conservative Democrats he had opposed, all but one won renomination. Worse still, those legislators who had survived the purge now had all the more reason to battle the president. A conversation between two prominent senators who returned to Washington despite Roosevelt's opposition summed up his predicament. One of the senators said, "Roosevelt is his own worst enemy." The other responded, "Not so long as I am alive."

The November elections brought more bad news. Just two years before, in the aftermath of Roosevelt's great reelection victory, some political experts had sounded the death knell for the Republican party. In 1938 the GOP demonstrated that it was alive and, if not completely well, at least much recovered as it picked up 82 seats in the House and 7 seats in the Senate. Among the new Republican faces in Congress was Senator Robert A. Taft of Ohio, who not only would become a major force in the GOP but one of Roosevelt's most effective critics. The congressional Republicans did not pick up enough seats to set the legislative agenda. But now, working with the conservative Democrats, they had the power to block Roosevelt's domestic initiatives.

In a sure sign that the Roosevelt spell had broken, at least in Congress, some ardent New Dealers began to distance themselves from the president. "There was a time when I would have bled and died for him," said Montana's Senator James Murray, "but in view of the way he has been acting I don't want to have any more dealings with him and I just intend to stay away from him and he can do as he pleases."

To be sure, Roosevelt's second term was not completely devoid of accomplishment. In 1937 and 1938 Congress extended relief and public works programs, passed a major farm bill, created a public housing program, expanded the social security system, enacted a landmark child labor measure, and established a national system of minimum wages and maximum hours. Significantly, these measures, which may have been important enough to constitute a third New Deal, were hardly lone triumphs for the president. Like the famous legislation of the first term, each had been in the works for a long time and each was the product of a richly collaborative effort.

Roosevelt's second term also coincided with two notable congressional investigations, one in each house. From 1936 to 1940 a special committee of the Senate, known as the La Follette Civil Liberties Committee, held the most extensive hearings in American history to that date into employer violations of the rights of workers to organize and bargain collectively. Conducted by Young Bob La Follette, they exposed the heavy-handed, often brutal tactics used by many of the nation's leading corporations to prevent workers from forming unions. By turning the spotlight on these oppressive labor practices, the hearings put corporations on the defensive and helped spur the growth of organized labor.

A committee in the House, meanwhile, was conducting hearings of a different sort. Beginning in 1938, the House Un-American Activities Committee (HUAC), chaired by the Texas Democrat Martin Dies, offered a platform for congressional critics of the administration, who accused it of harboring communists and radicals. Although HUAC did not achieve fame (or infamy) until after Roosevelt's death, it served as a symbol of conservative resurgence.

viii

With the outbreak of war in Europe in September 1939, the New Deal Congress entered its final act. Once again Roosevelt assumed charge of the legislative agenda, this time with more success. Between 1939 and December 1941, when the United States entered the war, he pressed Congress to aid the allies — Great Britain, France, and later the Soviet Union — in their fight against Germany. His efforts divided Congress into rival camps. On the one side were the so-called isolationists, who opposed aid to the allies for fear of being dragged into the war. On the other side were the interventionist backers of such aid. The foreign policy debate reconfigured the alignments in Congress. Roosevelt now found himself opposing former friends like La Follette, a leader of the isolationists, and courting former foes, including the very same conservative Democrats he had tried to purge from Congress. Indeed, Roosevelt abandoned any plans he may have had to liberalize the Democratic party as he reached out to conservative lawmakers, especially from the South. As a result, the southern Democrats became more entrenched in Congress than ever.

In mobilizing support for lend-lease and other measures to send aid to the allies, Roosevelt demonstrated that he had learned much from the Court-packing debacle. Instead of springing such proposals on Congress at the last minute, he involved important lawmakers in the drafting process. Then, during the ensuing floor debates, he allowed his legislative leaders to carry the burden of the fight so that he himself would not become the issue. Just as Roosevelt's first term had been the high point of Congress's legislative leadership, so the years between 1939 and 1941 represented the high point of Roosevelt's legislative leadership. For the first time, his legislative leadership actually matched the brilliance of his historical reputation.

In pushing his proposals, Roosevelt did not always play by the rules of fair play. He and his supporters called the isolationists appeasers and implied that they were wittingly or unwittingly aiding the enemy. The isolationists sometimes responded in kind, accusing Roosevelt of being a dictator and warmonger. Ultimately Roosevelt rendered the isolationists, many of whom were progressives on domestic matters, largely ineffective. Unlike the southern Democrats, who survived the war with their influence intact, congressional progressives entered peacetime vastly diminished.

ix

Following America's entry into the war in December 1941, Congress suffered a severe loss of prestige. Although it may not have gotten all of the credit it deserved for the New Deal, as late as 1939 it enjoyed a favorable public approval rating almost identical to Roosevelt's. After Pearl Harbor, however, Congress became the whipping boy for the accumulating frustrations of wartime. In 1942, for example, a routine measure — bringing legislators into the government's retirement system — provoked a storm of protest. Another angry outburst greeted the news that the legislators had allotted themselves extra gasoline rations to visit their home states. They were demanding sacrifices from everyone else, people complained, while lining their own pockets.

Influential commentators even began to question Congress's legitimacy as a coequal branch of government. "The ignorance and provincialism of Congress," wrote the distinguished journalist Raymond Clapper, "render it incapable of meeting the needs of modern government." The historian Henry Steele Commager defended presidential ascendancy over Congress by claiming that "democracy apparently flourishes when the Executive is strong, languishes when it is weak." The presidential scholar Clinton Rossiter even exempted the presidency, though not the Congress, from Lord Acton's famous dictum that power corrupts and absolute power corrupts absolutely. "The Presidency," he wrote, "is a standing reproach to those petty doctrinaires who insist that executive power is inherently undemocratic" and "no less a reproach to those easy generalizers who think that Lord Acton had the very last word on the corrupting influence of power."

Meanwhile, Roosevelt's relationship with Congress grew increasingly tense. On most war-related matters, Congress had proved exceedingly accommodating, granting Roosevelt broad authority to manage the war and the economy as he and his agents in the executive branch saw fit. Other matters proved different, however, and since Pearl Harbor, Congress had defeated most of Roosevelt's recommendations. "The Congress is in a state of revolt against the President," one Senate veteran wrote. "In all the years I have been in and around Washington I have never seen a Congress so bitter toward the president." The journalist Allen Drury, who reported on the Senate, later recalled that "there was an ugly hostility, a bitter jockeying for political advantage and power, a mutual mistrust and dislike that constantly clouded his relations with Congress." It was no exaggeration to say, Drury concluded, that the president and Congress "despised each other."

Roosevelt was not solely to blame. The Republican legislators, confined to what increasingly appeared to be a permanent minority status, lashed out at the president in frustration. The southern Democrats, worried that administration policies would undermine white supremacy in the South, fought the president even on trivial matters. Other legislators were concerned about the precipitous decline in the power and prestige of Congress during the war, and they fought desperately to prevent a further erosion of legislative prerogative. In all of this, Roosevelt became a scapegoat for the accumulated frustrations of them all.

But Roosevelt had made a bad situation worse by neglecting his Democratic base of support and by ineptly handling legislative matters. To the dismay of the Democratic party leaders, he assumed a wartime stance of nonpartisanship, refusing to campaign on behalf of or even endorse most of his party's congressional candidates. The memory of Woodrow Wilson's ill-fated attempt to influence the outcome of the 1918 election doubtless contributed to Roosevelt's approach to electoral politics. But just as Wilson had paid a heavy price for involving himself in legislative races, so Roosevelt paid a heavy price for remaining aloof. In the midterm elections of 1942, many Democrats, including several loyal New Dealers, had gone down to defeat, and the party officials blamed the reversals on Roosevelt's failure to intervene. Actually, Roosevelt behaved no differently in 1942 than he had throughout most of his presidency. Except for his abortive purge attempt in 1938, he had never made a concerted effort to build ideological majorities conducive to reform; nor, besides allowing Democratic candidates to hold on to his long coattails, had he ever done much to support his fellow party members during campaigns. By 1944 he was paying the price for past neglect.

Roosevelt further hurt his cause by needlessly offending his legislative leaders. Periodically over the years he had subjected them to embarrassment. His failure to inform them of his Court-packing plan and his intervention in the Senate leadership fight, both in 1937, were only the most egregious examples. Another incident occurred in February 1944. Both houses had passed a tax bill that in Roosevelt's view raised insufficient revenue and contained gaping loopholes that favored well-to-do interest groups. In fact, Roosevelt stood on solid ground in criticizing the bill. But the way that he expressed his displeasure — a stinging veto message that called into question the integrity of the Democratic congressional leadership — prompted his Senate majority leader, the usually loyal and pliable Alben Barkley, to resign his post in protest. In truth Barkley, who had already acquired the dubious reputation of being Roosevelt's errand boy in the Senate, probably was looking for an opportunity to assert his independence. In any event, Congress issued a double rebuke to the president. It promptly overrode his veto of the tax bill, and Barkley's Democratic colleagues reelected the Kentuckian to the majority leader's post.

The Barkley episode exemplified the troubled relationship between the executive and legislative branches of government and underscored one of the paradoxes of Roosevelt's presidency. Despite his unquestioned skill as a politician, Roosevelt frequently displayed striking weaknesses as a legislative leader. Only in the years immediately before Pearl Harbor, when he had steered measures to aid the allies through Congress, had his legislative performance matched the brilliance of his performance in certain other aspects of the presidency. Roosevelt's standing on Capitol Hill was so low that in the months before his death in April 1945, some insiders were predicting that his plan for the United Nations would meet the same fate as Woodrow Wilson's plan for the League of Nations.

x

Memories of the troubled relationship between the president and Congress gradually faded after Roosevelt's death. The hostility to Congress that had developed during the war carried into the postwar years. The presidency was in favor; the Congress was out of favor. In the succeeding decades, the history of the New Deal was rewritten to accord with the new preference. College students in the fifties and sixties learned of FDR's legislative prowess but little about Congress's role. The *New York Times* reporter R. W. "Johnny" Apple, who studied history at Princeton and Columbia, recalls being taught that "Roosevelt and the Brains Trust and not the young legislators . . . had most of the responsibility" for the New Deal. It's not surprising that Washington reporters in the post-Roosevelt era, including Apple, made FDR the standard by which they measured his successors, even going so far as to use Roosevelt's first hundred days as a benchmark to assess the performance of new presidents. This practice even spread to other countries. South Africa's Nelson Mandela and Britain's Tony Blair each received their hundred-days report cards from the press. The irony is that not even Roosevelt performed the feats by which commentators measured other leaders.

From time to time historians might note, as Arthur M. Schlesinger Jr. did, that Congress "played a vital and consistently underestimated role in shaping the New Deal," or, in William E. Leuchtenburg's words, that "despite the growth of the Presidency, this was a period in which Congress had great influence." But such insights never made their way into the nation's historical consciousness or into the minds of Roosevelt's successors. "Ever since Roosevelt's day," President John F. Kennedy remarked to a friend, "all the laws have been pretty much written downtown," meaning in the executive departments. And in truth, most Roosevelt scholars, including Schlesinger and Leuchtenburg, didn't have the heart to call attention to Congress's contributions to the New Deal. Their sympathies lay with Roosevelt, and they were mainly interested in telling the story of his towering leadership, including his masterful legislative leadership. Congress was an afterthought.

Because we still look to the Roosevelt presidency as a model, bringing Congress back into the story may also affect the way the federal government conducts its business. One wonders, for instance, if President Bill Clinton, who steeped himself in Rooseveltian lore while running for office, might have handled health care reform differently had he realized that his top-down approach was inadvertently emulating the FDR of Court-packing and not the FDR of the early New Deal. So restoring Congress to its rightful place at or near the center of the unfolding drama of the New Deal years is not just a matter of academic interest.

— Patrick Maney

BIBLIOGRAPHICAL NOTES

This chapter is adapted from my "The Rise and Fall of the New Deal Congress, 1933–1945," *OAH Magazine of History* 12 (Summer 1998): 13–19; *Young Bob: A Biography of Robert M. La Follette, Jr.* (Madison, Wisc., 2003 [1978]); and *The Roosevelt Presence: The Life and Legacy of FDR* (Berkeley, Calif., 1998 [1993]).

My basic perspective on the legislative history of the New Deal, with its emphasis on the critical role of Congress, derives in large part from research done in the preparation of earlier studies of Robert M. La Follette Jr. and FDR. Because La Follette had a hand in most of the legislation of the New Deal, his papers at the Library of Congress — and the related collections, at the Library of Congress and elsewhere, of other core legislators such as George Norris, Bronson Cutting, and Robert Wagner — contain a wealth of information on the origins and development of nearly all of the legislative enactments of the 1930s.

The absence of a general study on Congress during the Roosevelt administration is one of the conspicuous gaps in the literature. James T. Patterson, *Congressional Conservatism and the New Deal: The Growth of the Conservative Coalition in Congress, 1933–1939* (Lexington, Ky., 1967), is the closest we have to such a study and provides much useful information and many insights. Otherwise the story must be pieced together from studies of individual lawmakers. The standard works on some of the important members of Congress include J. Joseph Huthmacher, *Senator Robert F. Wagner and the Rise of Urban Liberalism* (New York, 1968); Patrick J. Maney, *Young Bob: A Biography of Robert M. La Follette, Jr.* (Madison, Wisc., 2003 [1978]); Richard Lowitt, *George W. Norris: The Persistence of a Progressive, 1913–1933* (Urbana, Ill., 1971), and *George W. Norris: The Triumph of a Progressive, 1933–1944* (Urbana, Ill., 1978); Richard Lowitt, *Bronson M. Cutting: Progressive Politician* (Albuquerque, N.Mex., 1992); Fred Greenbaum, *Fighting Progressive: A Biography of Edward P. Costigan* (Washington, D.C., 1971); Arthur Mann, *La Guardia*, 2 vols. (Philadelphia, 1959–65); Howard Zinn, *La Guardia in Congress* (Ithaca, N.Y., 1959); Alfred Steinberg, *Sam Rayburn: A Biography* (New York, 1975); David Robertson, *Sly and Able: A Political Biography of James F. Byrnes* (New York, 1994); James T. Patterson, *Mr. Republican: A Biography of Robert A. Taft* (Boston, 1972); Donald C. Bacon, "Joseph Taylor Robinson: The Good Soldier," in *First Among Equals: Outstanding Senate Leaders of the Twentieth Century*, ed. Richard A. Baker and Roger H. Davidson (Washington, D.C., 1991); Roger T. Johnson, "Charles L. McNary and the Republican Party During Prosperity and Depression" (Ph.D. diss., University of Wisconsin, Madison, 1967); Ronald M. Peters Jr., *The American Speakership: The Office in Historical Perspective* (Baltimore, 1990); and Roger H. Davidson, Susan Webb Hammond, and Raymond W. Smock, eds., *Masters of the House* (Boulder, Colo., 1998).

Standard accounts of the Roosevelt administration include David M. Kennedy, *Freedom from Fear: The American People in Depression and War, 1929–1945* (New York, 1999); Frank Freidel, *Launching the New Deal* (Boston, 1973), and *Franklin D. Roosevelt: A Rendezvous with Destiny* (Boston, 1990); William E. Leuchtenburg, *Franklin D. Roosevelt and the New Deal, 1933–1940* (New York, 1963); Basil Rauch, *The History of the New Deal* (New York, 1963 [1944]; Arthur M. Schlesinger Jr., *The Age of Roosevelt: The Crisis of the Old Order; The Coming of the New Deal;* and *The Politics of Upheaval* (Boston, 1957–60); James MacGregor Burns, *Roosevelt: The Lion and the Fox*, and *Roosevelt: The Soldier of Freedom* (New York, 1956, 1970); and James F. Sargent, *Roosevelt and the Hundred Days: Struggle for the Early New Deal* (New York, 1981). See also E. Pendleton Herring, "First Session of the Seventy-third Congress, March 9, 1933, to June 16, 1933," *American Political Science Review* 28 (February 1934): 65–83, an influential and much-cited article on FDR's legislative leadership. Written shortly after the completion of the Hundred Days and without the manuscript sources available to later scholars, Herring is now more useful as an indication of how contemporaries viewed the unfolding New Deal than as an accurate account of the legislative history of the period. None of these works accords Congress the prominence that I do, but a careful reading of them, along with works on individual legislators, allows one to weigh the relative contributions of FDR and the Congress.

Huey Pierce Long

August 30, 1893–September 10, 1935

Huey Pierce Long

Born in the hill country of Louisiana into a somewhat prosperous farming family, Huey Pierce Long carved a state political empire unparalleled in modern times. For seven years he dominated politics and virtually every state institution in Louisiana, including the legislature, the bureaucracy, and the courts. While undermining democratic state functions and creating intense political factions, Long fostered many positive changes for his state, most notably public improvements to the infrastructure, social services, health care, and education. However, as a ruthless demagogue, he made many personal and political enemies, one of whom gunned him down in the state capitol in 1935.

Ambition drove Long from an early age. As a high school student, he worked as a traveling salesman. He did not attend college but studied law at the University of Oklahoma and Tulane University. Although he never earned a degree, Long passed the Louisiana bar and was practicing law in his hometown by 1915. However, politics was his primary interest. His successful defense in a well-publicized court case helped him get elected to the Louisiana Railroad Commission, soon renamed the Public Service Commission. Drawing on populist themes, Long quickly distinguished himself as a champion of the common people against the powerful political elite who, bankrolled by the state's oil industry and private utilities, had controlled state government. After an unsuccessful run for governor in 1924, he staged an aggressive campaign again in 1928 and won.

Compared to his predecessors, Long was a progressive politician, making modest changes in the tax codes to increase revenue from corporations and wealthy individuals. While championing a populist ideology, Long ruthlessly consolidated power almost like a dictator. He campaigned heavily to get his loyal supporters elected to the legislature, filled the bureaucracy with his people, fought off an impeachment attempt in 1929, and pushed through legislation that increased even further the power of his office. Procuring an appointment to the Senate in 1930, he remained in Louisiana as governor for almost two years to ensure the election of a docile ally.

Long's control of Louisiana politics continued from his Washington office, where he became an energetic and influential supporter of Franklin D. Roosevelt's presidential campaign. But Long felt underappreciated by Roosevelt's administration and argued that the New Deal programs were not going far enough to redistribute wealth. Splitting with Roosevelt in 1933, Long concentrated little effort on his Senate obligations and began publicizing his New Deal alternative, called the Share Our Wealth Plan, publishing a national newspaper, the *American Progress,* and writing his autobiography, *Every Man a King* (1935) — all of which supported his independent presidential bid in 1936. Although the Share Our Wealth Plan was an insolvent approach, Long's charisma and populist appeal gave him an air of celebrity and a following that worried even the popular Roosevelt.

By 1935 polls commissioned by the Democratic National Committee showed that Long might garner 10 percent of the national vote, which could throw a close election to the Republican candidate. Roosevelt responded by withholding patronage to Louisiana and having the Internal Revenue Service investigate Long's colleagues. At the same time, Long was working to consolidate his power base even further, pushing through laws that required all the state employees to contribute a portion of their pay to the Long machine's campaign fund. The growing storm came to an abrupt end when Long was killed in a statehouse corridor by the son-in-law of one of his political rivals. Robert Penn Warren based his Pulitzer Prize–winning novel, *All the King's Men* (1946), on the rise and fall of Huey Long, known as the Kingfish, whose political legacy dominated Louisiana politics for decades. His son, Russell Billiu Long (1918–2003), served in the Senate for four decades.

Reference

Brinkley, A. (2000, February). "Long, Huey Pierce." *American National Biography Online.* Retrieved July 3, 2003, from http://www.anb.org/articles/06/06-00378.html.

27

World War II: Conservatism and Constituency Politics

WAR, RANDOLPH BOURNE observed in 1918, is the health of the state. To be more precise, it is the health of the executive branch. The prosecution of wars demands unified action, relatively quick decision-making, often-secretive processes — characteristics seldom associated with the routines of a bicameral congress. The imperative of patriotic support generally reduces legislative bodies to the role of enablers; they pass huge appropriations bills and authorize vast administrative power without participating meaningfully in the management of the conflict itself. Although largely unavoidable, wartime imperatives generate dissatisfaction among legislators accustomed to power and deference from the other branches of government. Moreover, in a democratic society with a constitution mandating regular elections, politics can never be adjourned. Even popular wars generate irritations and dissatisfactions, sometimes among ethnoreligious groups, often among well-defined economic interest groups.

Such issues can touch the most reflexive nerves of legislators who come to Washington as the beneficiaries of group politics with mandates to represent the interests of those who elected them. And they provide an outlet for a more general frustration. Unable to control the movement toward war, do much to affect its management once the battle is joined, or be the guiding force in its settlement, the World War II Congresses could at least express the resentments and needs (not necessarily irrational) of their constituents. They did so with particular force because their rough ideological center of gravity was a conservatism bitterly hostile toward the domestic New Deal liberalism of the executive branch. They at least had something of a braking effect on the domestic regimentation that accompanied the war, and they set a political tone for the return to peacetime. The unifying theme of congressional politics in World War II, then, was a consistent and unusually intense hostility toward the executive branch, reflecting both partisan rivalry and strong ideological divisions.

The Parties and Their Leaders

World War II, as conventionally dated, began during the Seventy-sixth Congress (elected in 1938) and ended in the early months of the Seventy-ninth (elected in 1944). The numerical party strength on Capitol Hill fluctuated a bit from Congress to Congress, but the fundamental structure of the power and weight of the ideological attitude was constant. The election of 1938, fought out in a mood of reaction against a badly stumbling New Deal, had laid bare deep divisions within the Democratic party and established in many respects the basic profile of American legislative politics for the next quarter of a century.

The Democrats, a majority in both houses of each World War II Congress, were deeply divided on many domestic issues. A majority, the New Dealers, largely based in northern and western cities and heavily laced with ethnocultural minorities, was fervently attached to President Franklin D. Roosevelt, supportive of the regulatory-social welfare state he had established during his first six years in office, and behind every effort to expand it. A very strong and durable Democratic minority was based in the South, composed mostly of old stock Americans, more small town and rural in location, hostile to the urban minorities at the core of Roosevelt's support, especially concerned with preserving a white supremacy that was coming under attack from black civil rights organizations, increasingly cool toward Roosevelt himself, and even cooler (if selectively so) toward the expansion of the state that he had engineered. The Republican party on Capitol Hill was not without divisions of opinion itself, but the presence of a relatively small number of "progressives" notwithstanding, its prevailing demographics (old stock), ideological attitudes (antistatist), and antipathy to the president meshed pretty well with that of the minority Democrats.

It is a bit of a stretch to say that this convergence laid the basis for a "conservative coalition." The minority Democrats, a few principled economizers aside (most notably Senator Harry Flood Byrd of Virginia), loved agricultural subsidies for cotton, rice, and tobacco; they could not get enough rural electrification. The Republicans, who were more consistently critical of the New Deal state, usually did not possess the southern Democratic visceral ethnoreligious and racial bigotry but did share a common distrust of big government. Not a formal structure superimposed on the party organizations, the conservative coalition was mostly a convergence of voting patterns facilitated by some informal cooperation. On many issues, however, it did maintain a common front against the works of the New Deal and its liberal president.

Foreign policy issues complicated the picture. Most New Deal Democrats were foreign policy "interventionists" and "internationalists." So were most Democratic conservatives. Most Republican conservatives (especially those from the West and the Midwest) viewed Roosevelt's interventionist bent with the same hostility they reserved for the New Deal, and many of their progressive colleagues joined them. Despite generally predictable differences, congressional fault lines shifted not only between domestic and foreign policy but were also determined by individual constituencies' interests and attitudes. Party leaders on both sides had to pull their ranks together one issue at a time, rarely achieving unanimity.

In the House of Representatives, the Democrats were led for most of the wartime period by Sam Rayburn of Texas (Democratic leader, 1936–1940; Speaker, 1940–1947, 1949–1953, 1955–1961) and John McCormack of Massachusetts (leader, 1940–1961, Speaker, 1961–1971). In his twenty-eighth year as a congressman when elected Speaker, Rayburn typified in many respects the provincial character of so many House members. A native of the East Texas hill country, mildly populist in his political preferences, plainspoken and straightforward in his dealings, he was typical of numerous influential Capitol Hill Democrats in his willingness to reach out to both wings of his party. Cognizant of the limitations of his power, he relied on personal persuasion and counseled his fellow Democrats to "get along and go along" with one another; he derived much of his considerable authority from the widespread respect, trust, and affection of both sides of the House. McCormack, a gentlemanly Boston political pro with close ties to organized labor and urban Democratic machine leaders, was the mandatory northeastern urban counterpoint to Rayburn and in most respects shared his nonideological approach to congressional politics.

Joseph Martin of Massachusetts (Republican leader, 1939–1947, 1949–1953, 1955–1959; Speaker, 1947–1949, 1953–1955) headed the opposition. A poor boy made good, the owner of two small newspapers and an insurance agency, he was an archetypical small enterpriser representing a district dominated by small business Republicanism. His public face was that of a militantly conservative partisan struggling to rally his much more cohesive delegation against Democratic New Dealism. Privately, he took much the same approach to party leadership as did Rayburn and McCormack. All three, in a fashion that typified the Congresses of those days, softened sometimes intense political disputes with cordial personal relationships, lubricated by generous late-afternoon cocktail hours.

The Senate Democratic leader, Alben Barkley of Kentucky (leader, 1937–1949; vice president, 1949–1953), was in much the same mold as Rayburn, a liberal-leaning representative from the periphery of the South who enjoyed genial relations with almost all of his colleagues and massaged intraparty ideological conflicts by counseling compromise. Like Rayburn, Barkley had first been elected to Congress in 1912. He also was much liked by his colleagues, albeit more valued as a source of good conversation and bonded bourbon than respected as an effective leader. It did not help that he had succeeded one of the strongest of Democratic leaders before him, Joseph Robinson of Arkansas. Until 1941 he was ably seconded by James F. Byrnes, a "sly and able" South Carolinian who served as the primary broker between the White House and the southern Democrats. After Byrnes was named to the Supreme Court in mid-1941, nobody filled his role, although Harry Truman of Missouri seemed poised to do so by 1944. Tom Connally of Texas, a big, swaggering figure with an imposing mane of white hair, was the major Democratic foreign policy spokesman. Generally underestimated because of his propensity for bombastic speechmaking and a tendency to dress like a cliché southern senator, he employed his chairmanship of the Foreign Relations Committee shrewdly and effectively to advance the cause of international involvement.

On the Republican side, Charles McNary of Oregon (leader, 1933–1944) was a mild progressive, much liked by his colleagues but more a unifier than a policy force. After his death in 1944, he was succeeded by Wallace White of Maine, his assistant leader, who was chosen primarily for his inoffensiveness and his willingness to steer a careful course between the party's two Senate heavyweights, Robert A. Taft of Ohio and Arthur H. Vandenberg of Michigan. The real tone of the Republican opposition came from Taft. The political and ideological heir of his father, William Howard Taft, he bluntly observed that the duty of the opposition was to oppose. Possessing the charm of a bank vice president in charge of foreclosures, he was respected for his hard work and formidable intellect ("the best mind in the Senate until he made it up," some detractors said). He was especially credible to other Republicans as a critic of the New Deal, less so as an advocate of foreign policy isolationism. On the latter issue Vandenberg, converted to American international involvement after Pearl Harbor, seized the leadership from Taft. In some respects, he was almost as much a caricature of a senator as the Democrat Connally — tall, vain, cigar-chewing, equally prone to old-time oratory. An isolationist in the 1930s, he was also a realist who understood that the clock could not be turned back. A newspaper editorial writer in his former life, he was capable and persuasive, and he brought half the Senate Republicans into foreign policy cooperation with the Democrats.

Prelude to Pearl Harbor: Toward Total War

Until the outbreak of war in Europe on September 1, 1939, most congressional sentiment was strongly at odds with the president's propensity toward U.S. involvement in European affairs. Existing legislation even forbade loans and the sale of munitions to belligerent countries, although such provisions could only harm friendly and democratic nations. The fact of war gave the initiative to Roosevelt and led, step by step, to the dismantling of the congressional veto on foreign policy. Under presidential prodding, Congress quickly agreed to the sale of munitions on a cash-and-carry basis (1939), authorized a peacetime draft (1940), effectively revoked the ban on loans with the Lend-Lease Act (1941), and authorized the use of U.S. shipping in deliveries to Britain (1941). Nor did Congress fight back when Roosevelt used his authority shrewdly and sometimes deviously to bypass the treaty process in the destroyers-for-bases deal with Britain (1940), to deploy American naval vessels on "patrol" as escorts for convoys to Britain (1941), and to establish what amounted to an informal alliance with Britain at his Argentia, Newfoundland, meeting with Winston Churchill (1941).

The isolationists, led by Taft and Vandenberg among the Republicans, Burton K. Wheeler and Bennett Champ Clark among the Democrats, and Robert La Follette Jr. among the independent progressives, undertook a futile resistance characterized most memorably by Wheeler's declaration that Lend-Lease would be the military equivalent of the New Deal's agricultural program — it would plow under every third American boy. The passage of Lend-Lease by 2–1 margins, however, revealed a new pattern in American politics that would later in the decade be confirmed by strikingly similar votes on the Truman Doctrine, the Marshall Plan, and NATO. A substantial majority of Americans, persuaded that Nazi totalitarianism had to be stopped, would in the immediate postwar years apply the same conclusion to Stalinist communism. In periods of perceived danger, presidents led and Congress followed. The pattern was already established before December 7, 1941, but the isolationists remained a fervent, noisy minority convinced of the righteousness of their cause.

Pearl Harbor ended any semblance of a debate. Within the Democratic party, isolationists became a vanishing breed — Clark and Wheeler were both defeated the next time they faced the voters. Other isolationists recanted fully; foremost among them was Vandenberg, who increasingly gave his support to the administration's moves toward continued involvement in the postwar world. In January 1945, with the 1944 elections out of the way and the end of the war in sight, he delivered a major Senate speech in favor of a permanent American role in organizing the postwar world. In April he became the major Republican in the American delegation to the founding conference of the United Nations in San Francisco. Recalcitrants for the most part confined themselves to criticizing details of the war effort — consumer shortages, defense production shortfalls, specifics of diplomacy. The one great issue on which they attempted to rally — the rebirth of the League of Nations as the United Nations — only displayed their irrelevance. On July 28, 1945, the Senate ratified the UN Charter, 89–2.

Wartime Melee: Interest Groups and the Struggle Against the New Deal State

For six years before the outbreak of World War II in Europe, Congress had been overshadowed and largely dominated by the president and his domestic New Deal. Early signs that the act was wearing thin had come in 1937 when the legislative branch had successfully blocked the president's effort to pack the Supreme Court. A steep economic recession further emboldened New Deal opponents. The 1938 election results cut into the New Deal's strength on Capitol Hill and began the era of the so-called conservative coalition. Roosevelt meanwhile concentrated on executive reorganization in the hope of developing a quasi-independent "administrative state" capable of carrying on the New Deal legacy at one remove from the conservative influence in Congress. Although foiled in his attempt to enlarge the Court, he effectively recentered both it and the entire federal judiciary one appointment at a time. The cumulative result of these developments was a complex politics characterized by frequently bitter legislative-executive tensions fueled in the beginning by domestic issues, then further irritated by foreign policy.

Elected to an unprecedented third term in 1940, FDR remained popular with the people but faced a Congress that increasingly resented his sometimes imperious leadership, was not responsive to the urban, working-class, religious minority groups that constituted his core support, and above all hated the administrative bureaucracy he had erected. After Pearl Harbor, the character of that state was transformed in a fundamental way. No longer primarily a dispenser of various forms of largesse to a Depression-wracked population, it became an administrator of controls that denied to an increasingly affluent American people the fruits of an expanding, productive economy. No longer a reassuring security blanket, it was a creator of discontent. One new powerful administrative agency after another collectively became the face of a government that was the creature of the executive, garbed in the cloak of a national emergency, and dictating to its citizens as never before. The wartime New Deal state was the perfect target for an insurgent Congress.

Throughout American history, save in times of extreme stress, the formula for political dominance has been the search for the middle, in practice a quest for the pulse of a vast middle class. For much of World War II, the Republican-conservative Democratic opposition seemed to have its finger on that pulse more surely than the Roosevelt administration and its dwindling band of Democratic loyalists in Congress. Britain, a nation under intense attack from the enemy, was far more prone to accept the annoyances of wartime as the price of survival and regard the intrusive authority of government as the force that protected people against a foe bent on destroying them. Americans, immune to direct attack, felt the irritations far more keenly; this was especially true of the rapidly expanding group with middle-class incomes but deprived of the luxuries of middle-class life. The war brought high taxes, the rationing of consumer goods, interference with one's business in the form of price controls and multitudinous regulations, wage freezes, inflation, labor shortages, equipment shortages, housing crunches — something for everyone to complain about. It brought bureaucracy into the life of almost every American. Congress responded to these complaints by expressing the dominant skepticism about the New Deal that had prevailed on Capitol Hill since 1939.

Farmers, traditionally the most volatile American voters, were among the most disaffected. Having suffered through hard times during the past two decades, they welcomed the high prices brought by the war and bitterly fought any efforts to hold them down. The farm representatives in Congress, often supported by business-oriented Republicans who understood that farmers were essentially individual businessmen, struggled to raise price ceilings throughout the war. In 1941 they briefly secured government price supports at 110 percent of parity. In late 1942 Roosevelt asserted that farm prices had to be controlled as a prerequisite to wage and price ceilings throughout the rest of the economy. If Congress would not act, he declared, he would, by executive order, presumably under his powers as commander in chief. The president's constitutionally tenuous threat worked. Congress rolled agricultural prices back to 100 percent of parity.

Far from suffering during the war, farmers enjoyed their greatest prosperity in twenty years. Still, they toiled in the knowledge that a free market would have rewarded them more handsomely, and they ran their operations despite widespread shortages of equipment and the high cost of seasonal labor — when available. A revived congressional farm bloc, two decades earlier connected with progressive causes, had moved staunchly into the anti–New Deal camp. Few if any, of its members, incurred damage at the polls for their stand. Roosevelt, on the other hand, lost the major midwestern farm states in 1944.[1]

As the farmers felt, so did most businessmen — not prime defense contractors who were making tons of money with cost-plus contracts from the government, but those who produced or sold civilian goods. Among them, the small enterprisers tended to be the hardest hit. Almost all civilian goods were rationed and price-controlled; both activities required detailed specifications of all sorts of goods. The wholesale beef code, for example, ran to 40,000 words, with minute definitions of all allowable cuts of beef. The garment trades faced similar restrictions in the production of clothing. Retailers had to toe the line on long lists of maximum prices, account for their inventories, and, when necessary, collect ration coupons, all the while worrying about harassment from government inspectors or self-appointed vigilantes. However, the most emblematic assertion of the government's authority over business came in 1944 when the government seized one of America's biggest corporations, Montgomery Ward, for failing to obey a War Labor Board order. Front pages all across the country displayed a picture of Ward's chief executive, Sewell Avery, being carried out of his office, seated in his desk chair, by uniformed soldiers.

Avery's support ranged far beyond the Fortune 500; the incident resonated powerfully with Main Street businessmen and small factory owners across the country. Such people were perhaps the most natural constituency for an antistatist congressional majority. They met and talked regularly at Rotary Club and other civic meetings. Already overwhelmingly hostile toward the New Deal state, they expressed themselves freely to their congressmen. Their views counted on Capitol Hill more than those of the barons of American business. It followed naturally that Senator Pat McCarran of Nevada, chair of the Judiciary Committee, quickly scheduled hearings on the episode. A Democratic maverick who had long been out of sorts with the New Deal, McCarran appointed himself to head a special three-person subcommittee that produced a report scathingly attacking the takeover. The McCarran report was released in mid-1944, the same time that House Republicans were demanding an investigation of Office of Price Administration (OPA) hearings that denied legal counsel to accused business violators. Southern Democrats, meanwhile, were waging an all-out fight against a piddling $500,000 appropriation for the Fair Employment Practices Committee (FEPC).

Americans in their roles as consumers might not be horrified by Avery's eviction or the practices of the OPA, but neither were they pleased by the control apparatus. The claims of war on the economy meant that civilian goods would be in short supply. Efforts to distribute the shortages equitably through rationing to some extent spelled disappointment for every American. Attempts, also in the interest of equity, to control prices inevitably led to "black markets," in which items were diverted from normal commerce and sold off the books above the controlled prices; less visibly, price controls also distorted markets and made the production of some goods unprofitable. None of the major wartime agencies was more associated with the New Deal ethos than the OPA, in many respects the last refuge of the technocratic liberals who had staked their career on their faith in a managed economy.

The OPA gave consumers affordable prices when what they wanted was available. But in much of America almost everything was in short supply at one time or another: coffee, shoes, red meat, tires, razor blades — the list was nearly endless. Few people stopped to consider that the United States was a cornucopia of consumer goods compared to Britain or any of the other major belligerents. Few were opposed to price controls in principle, but most resented the inconvenience and irritation they generated. These resentments were transmitted to Congress, which in turn exerted most of the effective pressure on the agency, not in the form of efforts to abolish it but in constant general complaints, demands for changes in specific rulings, and threats to trim appropriations.

This opposition from Capitol Hill forced Roosevelt to dismiss the OPA's first administrator, Leon Henderson, a blunt New Deal economist with little patience for fools or members of Congress. His successor, Prentiss Brown, had just been defeated for reelection as a Democratic senator from Michigan. Clearly, the administration hoped to mollify Congress by appointing one of its own to run the control mechanism. Although empowered with a strong "hold the line" command from the president, Brown proved an all-too-willing mollifier and lasted only a few months. He was replaced by Chester Bowles, an advertising executive with a businessman's experience, a New Dealer's viewpoint, a gift for public relations, and the good fortune to take over the agency just as most of the kinks had been worked out of the economy. Bowles acknowledged its past mistakes to Congress, mounted an advertising campaign that identified controls with patriotism, and managed to keep prices steady — at least in those transactions that were on the books. Here, as in so many other of the contests between the president and Congress, the result was an effective draw. Congress could harass, obtain concessions, and occasionally spring the trap door on a hated liberal administrator. It could not eliminate an administrative apparatus created by a popular chief executive empowered by the reality of total war.

Roosevelt's attempt to appease Congress by naming Brown to head the

OPA failed, but similar ploys were more effective. In October 1942 the president already had established the Office of Economic Stabilization (OES) and in a master stroke persuaded James F. Byrnes to resign from the Supreme Court and head it. As the Senate's most influential power broker until he had gone on the Court hardly more than a year earlier, Byrnes had enjoyed unrivaled prestige on the Hill. As economic stabilizer, he had loose jurisdiction over all the wartime agency decisions affecting prices and wages. With an office in the White House, he also had easy access to the president. He quickly got a grip on agricultural prices for the administration by persuading the president to dump Chester Davis as food administrator and replace him in early 1943 with the federal judge Marvin Jones, formerly an influential Texas congressman. Jones's willingness to enforce the main outlines of the administration's agricultural policy while negotiating on specifics with his many friends and associates in Congress served the needs of both the legislative and the executive branches.

In mid-1943 Byrnes, tired of the minutiae of setting prices and the tedium of labor disputes, persuaded Roosevelt to create a new Office of War Mobilization (OWM), with himself as its director. The new position carried wide authority (if not the large staff necessary to maximize it) over about every aspect of the civilian side of the war effort. To replace Byrnes at OES, Roosevelt went again to a former congressman of great stature, Judge Fred M. Vinson. A Kentuckian in the tradition of Alben Barkley, Vinson enjoyed enduring respect for his work as a critical legislator in the House. A man of the upper South who leaned toward New Dealism, he related well to both the liberals and conservatives in the Democratic party while giving neither all they would have wished. An administrator of considerable ability, he was both an excellent choice to succeed Byrnes and seldom a target for the sort of congressional rhetoric that would have greeted and constantly harried an ideological New Dealer without roots on Capitol Hill.

Congress and the president thus reached an uneasy accommodation on the war's administrative bureaucracy by putting the major agencies under the control of respected former congressmen who had a sure sense of when to hold and when to fold in dealing with their one-time colleagues. All but the most critical senators or representatives had to admit that the war demanded an emergency bureaucracy, however distasteful it might be; they could grudgingly accept it if run by practical men like themselves. Other matters were not so easily finessed. They involved a reaction to New Deal constituencies at odds with the congressional conservatism and to a set of issues regarding the future of the New Deal itself.

Congress and the Politics of the Wartime New Deal

No group in American politics was more hated by Capitol Hill conservatives than organized labor, especially the Congress of Industrial Organizations (CIO), which had been a major beneficiary of the New Deal. The southern Democrats saw cheap labor as their region's answer to economic development and had little use for the ethnic minorities so visible in the CIO. Most Republicans saw unions as predatory attempts to gain control of an indifferent labor force and interfere with the prerogatives of business management. Much of the American middle class, moreover, detested the CIO's first president, John L. Lewis, for the repeated strikes of his United Mine Workers (UMW) union during the war; in addition, they long had been agitated by the charges (mostly accurate) that many CIO activists and organizers were communists. The administration's War Labor Board strove with tact and difficulty to contain union militance in the face of its own hold-the-line-on-wages policy. Congressional conservatives deployed a blunt instrument.

In early 1943 a wave of strikes sparked by repeated job actions of the UMW led a dozen state legislatures to pass laws restricting union activity. Congress was not far behind. A few months later it passed the War Labor Disputes Act, decisively overriding a presidential veto. Popularly known by the names of its conservative Democratic sponsors, Representative Howard W. Smith of Virginia and Senator Tom Connally of Texas, the Smith-Connally Act authorized the president to seize and operate vital defense facilities threatened by strikes, compelled all workers to stay on the job during government operation, made unions liable for damages if they struck without giving thirty days' notice, and prohibited labor organizations from contributing to political campaigns. The law was less a blow to labor than an expression of vehement congressional opinion, which in this case substantially replicated the attitude of much of the public. Roosevelt's first use of the law was to have Sewell Avery carried out of Montgomery Ward. The ban on contributions to campaigns was quickly circumvented by the establishment of political action committees nominally separate from the Democratic party. The political tone verified by Smith-Connally was, however, important. Congress, not the president, had accurately gauged public hostility toward a vital New Deal constituency.

Another vulnerable constituency was the black population. During World War II, the United States entered an early phase of what would eventually become the civil rights revolution of the 1960s. American blacks still lived in a segregated world as second-class citizens, formally repressed by a large body of state and local law in the South and treated only marginally better by whites in the North. Nonetheless, black civil rights consciousness and political activity had developed in many ways during the 1930s. Northern blacks themselves moved heavily into the Democratic party and were among the most devoted constituents of the president and his wife, Eleanor. In the late 1930s the NAACP had lobbied assiduously, if futilely, for a law against lynching. The main lesson from that effort — that the southern Democrats would filibuster to death anything resembling civil rights legislation in the Senate — remained the rule throughout the war. Inevitably, it led to efforts to obtain court decisions and executive actions. In 1941 A. Philip Randolph, the president of the Brotherhood of Sleeping Car Porters, threatened a mass march on Washington to protest job discrimination in defense industries. Roosevelt prevented the demonstration by establishing a Fair Employment Practices Committee (FEPC).

Never authorized by Congress nor voted a dime of legislative funds, the FEPC drew its uncertain powers only from a presidential executive order and its money only from discretionary executive accounts. The southern Democrats, motivated by the race issue, loathed it; the northern Republicans, motivated by resentment against federal bureaucratic interference in management hiring practices, detested it almost as much. Outside the black community and the world of New Deal liberals, it had little support. Much of the white core New Deal working-class constituency resented it. In 1944 Congress approved legislation that required all war agencies to operate only on direct appropriations from the legislative branch. Here also the congressional conservative leadership had accurately sensed an administration vulnerability and acted on it. With no money forthcoming from Capitol Hill, the FEPC would be terminated in late 1945.

Other targets were even easier. In 1943 Congress had quickly eliminated three New Deal relief agencies — the Works Progress Administration (WPA), the National Youth Administration (NYA), and the Farm Security Administration (FSA) — notwithstanding liberal protests that all could be useful in the war effort. The liberal argument was a bit of a stretch, but more important in the minds of the congressional establishment was the conviction that all three agencies were wasteful, encouraged sloth, and (especially in the case of the FSA, which financed the purchase of small farms by tenants and sharecroppers) were engaged in programs that subverted the existing social order.

The most revealing ideological triumph, however, was the elimination of the National Resources Planning Board (NRPB). A small, relatively insignificant agency from early in the New Deal, the NRPB became a haven for liberal visionaries who saw the war as an opportunity to do just what the conservatives accused them of wanting to do — subvert the existing order and reshape American society. In 1943 it issued an annual report calling for an Economic Bill of Rights, thereby demonstrating the impact on America of Keynesian economics and the British Beveridge plan for a comprehensive postwar welfare state. Calling for large public works to undergird postwar prosperity and a vast enlargement of social security, the document assumed more New Dealism after the war than ever before. Congress terminated the agency forthwith, placing what turned out to be a well-founded bet on the belief that the postwar economy would resurge without government stimulus or guidance.

The administration from the beginning hoped to pay for the war to the greatest extent possible through high, progressive income taxes. The congressional conservatives, then as later, had never met a tax hike they liked. Nonetheless, the war left no alternatives. The tax-writing committees were both chaired by men who had no affinity with the New Deal — Representative Robert "Muley" Doughton of North Carolina and Senator Walter George of Georgia. (George still bitterly resented FDR's attempt to "purge" him in his state's 1938 Democratic primary. There is at least a modicum of poetic truth to the story that when someone remarked to him that Roosevelt was his own worst enemy, George responded, "Not as long as I'm alive!") Both nonetheless felt that fiscal responsibility required drastic measures.

In 1942 Congress passed legislation that established the basic World War II revenue policy: increasing income taxes substantially, raising rates, and sharply lowering the threshold at which they took effect. Before the war, the federal income tax had hit only the upper half of the middle class; now it became a part of the experience of almost every working American. A dispassionate observer looking back sixty years might correctly remark that, given this event, subsequent wartime tax arguments occurred mostly at the margins of policy. Debate at the time, all the same, was loud and impassioned, especially after the Republican gains in the 1942 congressional elections substantially increased the anti–New Deal sentiment on Capitol Hill. Most members of Congress in any event felt a very real resentment against any executive efforts to dictate the deeply valued taxing prerogative of the legislative branch.

The first dispute involved the institution of withholding taxes from paychecks, proposed by the Treasury for tax year 1943 in the recognition that millions of new taxpayers would find it difficult to make a one-time, lump-sum tax payment each March 15. These same taxpayers, however, facing the need to make a lump-sum payment for 1942 while simultaneously having money withheld for their 1943 taxes, revolted. Congress heard them and, the administration's opposition notwithstanding, passed legislation that effectively forgave the 1942 obligation. The administration argued, correctly enough, that the move disproportionately benefited the upper crust. Most congressmen knew that constituents with modest incomes cared less about that than about their own situations.

The administration was convinced that even higher taxes were the price of victory. Secretary of the Treasury Henry Morgenthau and his advisers, concerned with the problems of managing huge bond drives and servicing ever-greater mountains of debt, pressed hard for increased taxes, arguing that they would mostly soak the wealthy. As with earlier such urgings, the argument spoke to the sensibility of neither Congress nor many of its distinctly unwealthy constituents. When in mid-1943 Morgenthau asked for $12 billion in new taxes, a wary Roosevelt shaved the request to $10.5 billion. Congress, jealous of its power of the purse and resentful of administration "meddling," responded in early 1944 with a bill that raised scarcely $2 billion. Roosevelt issued a stinging veto, characterizing the legislation as "not a tax bill but a tax relief bill providing relief not for the needy but for the greedy." It was the first presidential rejection of a tax bill in fifty years, and the backlash was stunning. Congressmen grumbled that Roosevelt was trying to discredit them as part of a fourth-term reelection strategy. Senator George and Representative Doughton denounced the president's message. Alben Barkley resigned as Democratic leader in the Senate and made public an angry rebuke to the president. Realizing that he had a full-scale rebellion on his hands, Roosevelt hastily wrote a "Dear Alben" letter, expressing regret and asking Barkley to reassume the Senate leadership. He was unanimously reelected to the post by his colleagues; both houses swiftly overrode the veto.

The incident was not simply one more demonstration that the conservatives could usually swing a majority. It equally displayed that many congressmen — conservative and liberal — were more in touch with the grass roots than was the administration; it is likely that no one who opposed high taxes was damaged by this stand. Finally, it demonstrated that on crucial points, Congress had an institutional impulse to fight back against a president who displayed a lack of respect for its most cherished powers. A liberal Democratic senator told the journalist Allen Drury that many of those who would have voted to sustain the president could not do so. "It has become an issue of the Executive versus the Congress, to determine once again which has the final say-so. Of course in the long run we do, and we shall vote in a way which will leave no doubt of it."[2] It was emblematic of how much institutional rivalry and personal resentment had eclipsed substance that the vote made no discernible difference to the country's fiscal stability; the national debt remained stable through the remainder of the war.

The Seventy-eighth Congress (1943–1945) was the most conservative of the war, intensely adversarial toward the Roosevelt administration and determined to hold spending down. Yet with little debate in 1944 it passed one of the largest and most generous welfare programs in American history — the G.I. Bill of Rights. The conventional explanation for this apparent contradiction — that the necessities of an impending election overrode ideological conviction — is best characterized as neither wrong nor wholly sufficient. Every member of Congress was old enough to remember the founding and subsequent influence of powerful veterans groups after World War I. All the same, the cornucopia of benefits, subsidies, and preferments that Congress threw at the returning soldiers could be justified even by the hardest right-wingers as just pay for dangerous, ill-compensated work. Many of the same congressmen who shouted the G.I. Bill through to passage opposed Roosevelt's suggestions for a general "economic bill of rights," a proposal that had no ready-made mass constituency with an intense interest in it. The economic bill of rights, as opposed to the targeted G.I. bill of rights, went nowhere.

At the same time, Republicans and southern Democrats had been willing to wage a determined and, on the whole, successful fight against a special federal ballot to be distributed to soldiers overseas in 1944. (Servicemen properly registered to vote in their states could request absentee ballots, but their timely delivery to and return from overseas war zones would be problematic.) The Southerners, in addition to a general concern for states' rights, feared any precedent by which the federal government might claim the right to establish voting qualifications and thereby challenge black disenfranchisement. The Republicans shared the constitutional reservations and worried strongly about the possibility that the troops would be all but forced to vote for Roosevelt. As was so often the case with congressional-presidential disputes during the war, the result was a compromise. It made a federal ballot available under tightly limited conditions, the most important of which was state approval; in the end, fewer than 112,000 of these were voted. But an additional 4.4 million service personnel, using regular absentee request procedures, managed to cast ballots. In all, about 48 percent of those servicemen and -women of voting age appear to have actually voted. The rate was not terribly less than that of a civilian population that had moved around a lot during the war. It is unlikely, simply because of logistical difficulties, that many of the military absentee ballots were cast from distant combat zones. And the

Southerners, of course, prevailed in preventing a significant Negro absentee vote in their states.

The 1944 Elections: Gridlock Continues

As World War II and the Roosevelt presidency moved toward their end in early 1945, the new Seventy-ninth Congress, its modest Democratic gains notwithstanding, exhibited much the same tone as its predecessor. Roosevelt's need to reestablish lines of communication with the legislative branch had prompted a number of his wartime appointments. It continued to be an imperative in 1944, leading to the most important decision of all. The president had dropped Henry A. Wallace as his vice president and acquiesced in his replacement by Senator Harry S. Truman, nationally acclaimed for his investigations of the domestic war effort. Truman's popularity with his former colleagues remained high, but his brief vice presidency demonstrated that personality could not transcend hard differences of opinion. With the greatest of difficulty, Truman brokered a deal that allowed the New Dealish Wallace to become secretary of commerce over the emotional opposition of the conservatives, but he encountered a stone wall in his efforts to guide the equally New Dealish Aubrey Williams to confirmation as rural electrification administrator. When Roosevelt suddenly died on April 12, 1945, he had already seen the face of a Congress as unyielding as the preceding one. Truman would fare little better.

World War II had demonstrated that once a national emergency was widely perceived, the legislative branch had to yield to an energetic executive in matters of military strategy and diplomacy. But on issues that might be called primarily domestic, war could bring only trouble for a government compelled to exact large sacrifices from a people unused to deprivation in good economic times and no longer needing the kinds of government assistance that the New Deal had bountifully distributed. The result was to confirm and harden a pattern that had first appeared toward the end of the 1930s — the rise of a congressional conservative coalition that on domestic issues would largely dominate American politics until the presidency of Lyndon Johnson.

— Alonzo L. Hamby

BIBLIOGRAPHICAL NOTES

Roland Young, *Congressional Politics in the Second World War* (New York, 1956), is a relatively complete but less than satisfactory account of its topic. Among more general works, John Morton Blum, *V Was for Victory: Politics and American Culture During World War II* (New York, 1976), and Richard Polenberg, *War and Society: The United States, 1941–1945* (Philadelphia, 1972), stand out. Among numerous useful biographies are James T. Patterson, *Mr. Republican: A Biography of Robert A. Taft* (Boston, 1972), and David Robertson, *Sly and Able: A Political Biography of James F. Byrnes* (New York, 1994). Arthur H. Vandenberg Jr., ed., with the collaboration of Joe Alex Morris, *The Private Papers of Senator Vandenberg* (Boston, 1952), remains the best volume on its subject. Allen Drury, *A Senate Journal, 1943–1945* (New York, 1963), is absorbing and evocative.

NOTES

1. Roosevelt lost Kansas, Nebraska, South Dakota, North Dakota, and Iowa while winning only Minnesota among the predominantly agricultural states just west of the Mississippi. East of the Mississippi, he lost Wisconsin. Among the "rust belt states" that balanced strong manufacturing economies with a substantial agriculture sector, he lost Ohio and Indiana while winning Illinois.
2. Allen Drury, *A Senate Journal, 1943–45* (New York, 1963), 91.

Sam Rayburn

January 6, 1883–November 16, 1961

Sam Rayburn

Samuel Taliaferro Rayburn, a Texas Democrat, first entered the House of Representatives in 1913, serving for forty-eight years through the administrations of eight presidents from Woodrow Wilson to John F. Kennedy. Responsible for the passage of much of President Franklin D. Roosevelt's New Deal program, Rayburn served as Speaker (1940–1946, 1949–1953, 1955–1961) longer than anyone in the nation's history. Four years after his death, construction was completed on the last of three office buildings near the Capitol to house the offices of members of Congress. In fitting tribute, it was named the Rayburn House Office Building.

Sam Rayburn was born in Roane County, Tennessee, the eighth of eleven children. His family moved to northern Texas in 1888, and the young Rayburn attended Mayo Normal School (now East Texas State University), graduating in 1903. He taught for several years before becoming a candidate for the Texas legislature. His political success relied not on his public speaking skills but on the connections of his large family, his close ties to the farming community, and his reputation for integrity. While serving in the legislature, Rayburn studied law at the University of Texas Law School and was admitted to the bar in 1908.

As Speaker of the Texas house, Rayburn was able to influence the boundaries of congressional districts, which helped him win election to the House of Representatives in 1912. He was befriended by the charismatic Texas congressman John Nance Garner, who became his mentor. During most of his early career, the Democrats operated as the minority party. That completely changed in 1931. The Democrats regained control of the House, and Garner became a candidate for president. Rayburn managed his campaign and was instrumental in getting Garner selected as Franklin D. Roosevelt's running mate. During Roosevelt's New Deal, Rayburn served as chairman of the Interstate and Foreign Commerce Committee, which mustered through much of the landmark New Deal legislation, including the Federal Securities Act (1933), the Securities Exchange Act (1934), the Public Utility Holding Company Act (1935), and the Rural Electrification Act (1936).

When Speaker William Bankhead died in 1940, Rayburn was quickly elected to take his place. He became a strong supporter of the war effort, using his parliamentary skills to ensure the passage of a draft extension in 1941, just months before Japan attacked Pearl Harbor. During Harry Truman's administration, Rayburn eventually moderated his views on racial segregation and, despite the consternation of many of his constituents, endorsed the Civil Rights Act of 1957.

Rayburn was a short, stocky man who was completely bald by the time he was middle-aged. He had a legendary temper, and colleagues observed that his entire head turned purple with rage when someone aroused his anger. Conversely, he was known for his gentle support of the powerless and as a fastidious caretaker of his constituents. He married once — the union lasted less than six months — and remained a bachelor the rest of his life. He was considered a lonely man who sought solace by working on weekends. His eyesight diminished during the 1950s, but Rayburn was able to conceal his handicap by having associates whisper the names of members in his ear to help him recognize colleagues on the House floor.

At that time Rayburn was increasingly interested in the political career of his protégé, Lyndon B. Johnson, whom he had helped along since the 1930s, and he was a strong supporter of Johnson's bid for the presidential nomination in 1960. Perhaps because he understood Garner's disappointment as vice president under Roosevelt thirty years earlier, Rayburn was initially opposed to Johnson's accepting the nomination for vice president. But, ever the loyal Democrat, Rayburn supported Johnson's place on the ticket and, not long before he died, used his political weight to ensure the passage of progressive legislation sponsored by the Kennedy administration.

Reference

Champagne, A. (2000, February). "Rayburn, Sam." *American National Biography Online.* Retrieved July 3, 2003, from http://www.anb.org/articles/07/07-00245.html.

"Samuel Taliaferro Rayburn." *Encyclopedia of World Biography,* 2nd ed. 17 vols. Gale Research, 1998. Reproduced in *Biography Resource Center.* Farmington Hills, Mich.: Gale Group. 2003. Retrieved July 3, 2003, from http://www.galenet.com/servlet/BioRC (Document Number: K1631005472).

28

The Cold War

At the end of World War II, both diplomats and politicians struggled to devise a strategy for confronting and containing the forces of international communism that fit traditional foreign policy philosophies and approaches. Given that the three basic themes of twentieth-century diplomacy — isolationism, unilateralism, and internationalism — seemed mutually exclusive and that American foreign policy was traditionally as much or more a function of domestic politics and culture as events in the international arena, the task was daunting. Indeed, if America was to present the communist monolith with a noncommunist monolith of sufficient strength and unity, isolationism, unilateralism, and internationalism would have to be modified and harnessed in support of the Cold War. That is precisely what happened; appropriately enough for a nation with a republican form of government, the articulation and reconciliation of cold war imperatives with traditional approaches to foreign affairs took place in the Congress of the United States.

Not surprisingly, foreign affairs was much on the minds of Congress, particularly the Senate, as World War II drew to a close. Franklin Roosevelt had paid almost as little attention to that body as he had to the State Department in the war years, bypassing the Senate and relying on executive agreements rather than treaties in the conduct of wartime diplomacy. The president bullied and cajoled Congress into creating dozens of new bureaucracies — the War Production Board, for example — which in effect usurped congressional prerogatives. Although it had made significant gains in the midterm elections of 1942, the Republican party had been out of power for twelve years, and its leaders were determined not to let the Democrats monopolize the peacemaking. That determination was reinforced by the defeat of Thomas Dewey's "me-too" presidential candidacy in 1944. Though the southern Democrats were as offended by the growth of the federal bureaucracy and presidential power as the GOP, the Democratic leadership in Congress had little problem arousing partisan sentiment among the rank and file and persuading them to support first Roosevelt's and then Truman's diplomatic initiatives. In the wake of the Yalta Conference in February 1945, then, the halls of Congress rang with the debate over America's proper role in the postwar international community. There existed in 1945 three clearly identifiable foreign policy impulses or alternatives around which the legislators coalesced: traditional isolationism, or "noninterventionism," as its defenders referred to it; conservative internationalism; and liberal internationalism. A fourth option, which the historian Justus Doenecke has labeled liberal isolationism, existed but was given very little credence in 1945. It is worth noting, however, that that approach provided the foundation for the New Left–revisionist critique of U.S. diplomacy that played such an important role in American intellectual and political life during the 1960s.

There were those in Congress who refused to acknowledge that World War II had forever changed the world and the role that America would play in it. The hard-core isolationists had come to terms with the fact that German, Italian, and Japanese fascism constituted an authentic threat to American interests and that war had been necessary. But as they looked to the future in 1945, they continued to see Britain rather than the Soviet Union as the primary threat to U.S. independence and sovereignty. The isolationists were staunchly anticommunist, but they believed that Europe was a European problem. They feared that the Europeans, particularly the British, would once again attempt to use the United States as a cat's paw, expending American blood and treasure to maintain a continental balance of power — "perpetual war for perpetual peace," to use Harry Elmer Barnes's phrase. They insisted that internationalism — and, specifically, the administration's campaign on behalf of a collective security organization — was simply a mask for a policy of realpolitik conducted exclusively by the executive. This new activism would allegedly bankrupt the nation, destroy free enterprise, and lead to the creation of a police state.

The personification of isolationism, or noninterventionism, was Robert A. Taft. Embodying Republican orthodoxy, Taft rose through the ranks to occupy a seat in the Senate and became a regular challenger for the presidency from 1940 through 1952.

The greatest threat facing the United States in the late 1930s, he believed, was not the disintegration of the international order but the growth of executive authority. He opposed an active foreign policy primarily because such a course inevitably augmented the power of the executive. Congress's acquiescence in Rooseveltian "internationalism," which he saw as merely the president's desire for complete freedom of action in foreign policymaking, constituted a threat to the balance of power within the federal system and to the liberties of the people. In 1939 he tried to cut the funding for the Export-Import Bank, a federal agency whose mission was to stimulate foreign trade. The bank, he said, "could finance a European war without Congress knowing anything about it." As early as January 1942 Taft was complaining about the postwar expectations of the "war crowd." He railed against Republicans such as Wendell Willkie, Thomas E. Dewey, and the other members of the eastern establishment who wanted to "out-intervention" the Democratic interventionists. The GOP should no more do this than it should try to "out–New Deal" the New Dealers.

Taft's commitment to congressional independence was rooted not only in his background and education but also in a broader philosophy that encompassed the conservative Republicans' commitment to the nineteenth-century political and economic system. The GOP's attachment to these putative halcyon days dictated its posture on foreign policy. It aligned the Republicans against big government and a strong executive, which they feared would result in dictatorship and destroy political and civil freedom; against large expenditures, which would allow the government to impose "socialist" controls over prices, wages, and the free enterprise system; and against high taxation, which crushed the initiative of the private sector.

Yet, as the political scientist John Spanier and others have pointed out, internationalism in the 1940s, even more than the New Deal, required all of these things — a powerful government capable of negotiating with other powerful governments; a strong president who could act decisively and vigorously; and huge outflows of cash to sustain military establishments and finance foreign aid. In that sense, the orthodox Republican philosophy seemed to make active participation in world affairs incompatible with the preservation of political democracy and free enterprise. Thus did the Taft Republicans oppose the view put forward by the British government and American internationalists — that Europe was vital to American security and that both Great Britain and the nations of the Continent, devastated by the war, had to be nursed back to health and strength by the United States.

These views prompted Taft to become the most articulate and effective opponent in the United States of Anglo-American efforts to create an interdependent world economy — multilateralism. "The Capital is full of plans of all kinds," the Ohioan told a group gathered to celebrate William McKinley's one hundredth birthday in January 1943. "Every economic panacea any long-haired crank ever thought of is being dusted off and incorporated in a magnificent collection of glittering landscapes supposed to lead to Utopia. Nearly every one of them rests on the huge expenditure of Government without telling us where the money is coming from, when we already face a debt of over $200 billion." In the spring of 1944 he attacked specifically the proposed International Monetary Fund and International Bank for Reconstruction and Development, agencies designed to help creditor and debtor nations work together to promote freer world trade. Both institutions were based on the fallacious assumption that underlay all administration foreign policies, namely, "that American money and American charity shall solve every problem."

Committed to the notion that America was and could continue to be economically and strategically self-sufficient, Taft opposed foreign aid in the immediate postwar period and voted against ratifying the charter of the North Atlantic Treaty Organization (NATO). As a staunch anticommunist, he did vote for the Truman Doctrine, but only reluctantly. He was careful to observe at the time that "I do not regard this as a commitment to any similar policy in any other section of the world." America should "withdraw as soon as normal economic conditions are restored."

Taft stood in the wings and cheered on Senator Joseph R. McCarthy of Wisconsin as he conducted his anticommunist witch-hunt in the early 1950s because he saw the campaign against alleged subversives as helpful to the Republican cause. But in supporting McCarthy, Taft acted only partly out of political opportunism. Because McCarthyism represented a variety of isolationism, it buttressed Taft's views on foreign policy. If the real threat to American security came from traitors within, there was no need for alliances, foreign aid, or the United Nations.

Taft also sympathized with the Asia Firsters in his party, men like Senator William Knowland of California and the former president Herbert Hoover, who eschewed engagement in Europe but advocated an aggressive policy in Asia, especially against communism. He supported U.S. participation in the Korean War, thereby acknowledging that America had legitimate economic and strategic interests in the Pacific as well as the Caribbean. But that was as far as he would go.

During his campaign for the Republican presidential nomination in 1952, Taft articulated an approach to foreign affairs that the historian John Spanier has labeled unilateralism. First, Taft proposed that the United States should withdraw from the UN and enter no "entangling alliances" such as NATO. Second, America should stress Asia over Europe, although Taft and his supporters believed that the United States should rely for the defense of its interests in the area on island bases and anticommunist allies. Indeed, the third mainstay of the unilateralist position was that the United States should never become bogged down in a war on the Asian landmass. America's resources were limited, and the world was full of nations willing to use the United States for its own purposes.

Robert Taft, however, spoke for only one sector, perhaps the most orthodox, of the conservative community. World War II converted a number of former isolationists into conservative internationalists. Japan's attack on Pearl Harbor destroyed the myth of impregnability that the America First movement had worked so assiduously to disseminate in the early 1940s. The Atlantic and Pacific were not great barriers protecting "Fortress America" from attack, as the isolationists had argued, but rather were highways across which hostile ships and airplanes could move and assault the Western Hemisphere. Led by the publisher of Time Inc., Henry Luce, old America Firsters decided that if America could not hide from the rest of the world, it must control it. They would support foreign aid, alliances, and a massive military budget, but not out of any Wilsonian desire to improve the lot of other members of the global village. These nationalists sought not to save the world but to safeguard American strategic and economic interests by creating, and dominating, interlocking spheres of influence.

Arthur H. Vandenberg of Michigan, who succeeded to the chair of the Senate Foreign Relations Committee when the Republicans won control of Congress in 1946, was the leader of these conservative internationalists. He shared most of Taft's conservative attitudes toward the Constitution, the role of the federal government in society, the budget, free enterprise, and individual liberty, and he was a thoroughgoing nationalist in foreign affairs. But he became convinced in 1945 and 1946 that the United States could not return to the past and that the best way to preserve the status quo in a dangerous world was to dominate that world.

First elected to Congress in 1928, Vandenberg supported the policies of both Calvin Coolidge and Herbert Hoover. Though showing some of the midwestern Progressives' distrust of Wall Street, he showed himself to be devoted to the conservative domestic agenda. He opposed the New Deal and joined with the members of the conservative American Liberty League in castigating Roosevelt as a would-be dictator and a stalking horse for the forces of collectivization. From 1939 through 1941 he fought against the president's interventionist proposals. War would destroy the free enterprise system; lend-lease, he declared, constituted nothing less than the "suicide of the Republic."

After America entered World War II Vandenberg, like Taft, quickly accommodated himself to the new circumstances. He supported the war effort and paid tribute to the Atlantic Charter. As the war neared its end, however, he turned his gaze not backward to the supposed days of economic self-sufficiency and Fortress America but forward to a postwar world filled with danger and uncertainty. As a thoroughgoing nationalist, Vandenberg believed that the United States had legitimate interests abroad, and he concluded that with the destruction of the balance of power in Europe and Asia, the country would have to don the mantle of world leadership. In January 1945 Vandenberg shocked his colleagues by endorsing the U.S. membership in a collective security organization: "I do not believe that any nation hereafter can immunize itself by its own exclusive action," he told the Senate . . . Our oceans have ceased to be moats which automatically protect our ramparts. Flesh and blood now compete unequally with winged steel. War has become an all-consuming juggernaut . . . I want maximum American cooperation, consistent with legitimate American self-interest, with constitutional process and with collateral events which warrant it, to make the basic idea of Dumbarton Oaks [that is, collective security] succeed.

Vandenberg's journey from isolationist to conservative internationalist culminated with his dramatic speech to the Senate in February 1946. "What is Russia up to now?" he asked. After reviewing Soviet activities in the Balkans, Manchuria, and Poland, he announced that the world had become divided between two rival ideologies: democracy and communism. Peaceful coexistence was possible only if the United States was as vigorous and firm as the Soviet Union in defending its interests. The United States must establish limits beyond which it would not compromise. The Truman administration responded with Secretary of State James F. Byrnes's Overseas Press Club speech — the second Vandenberg concerto, one reporter dubbed it. Byrnes indirectly denounced Soviet activities in Eastern Europe and promised that henceforward the United States could not and would not permit aggression "by coercion or pressure or by subterfuges such as political infiltration."

Vandenberg's views on foreign policy were determined not only by his nationalism but also by his ambition for both himself and his party. He had closely followed the party line under presidencies from Theodore Roosevelt through Franklin Roosevelt. In late 1945 and early 1946 he sensed that President Truman was politically vulnerable, on Yalta specifically and foreign policy in general. Vandenberg and the Republicans came to the conclusion that a hard line toward the Soviets would earn them kudos with the electorate and enable them to recapture the White House in 1948. Yet when Truman and Byrnes took a confrontational stance toward Moscow in 1946 and 1947, Vandenberg proved to be the epitome of bipartisan cooperation. In 1947 the former Michigan isolationist supported the Truman Doctrine and the Marshall Plan, schemes designed to funnel American aid into those areas of Europe directly and indirectly threatened by the forces of international communism. He also supported U.S. membership in NATO in 1949. Vandenburg was forthcoming on these issues not because he wanted to bring the blessings of American civilization to the Greeks and Turks or because he believed that the United States had the duty to promote socioeconomic justice abroad. The purposes of alliances and bases were to establish a Pax Americana that would ensure a stable world and serve America's vested interests. The conservative internationalism that he espoused would remain one of the cornerstones of postwar American foreign policy.

Joining the neo-imperialists in pushing for an active American role in world affairs were Wilsonian internationalists, who believed that if the United States had joined the League of Nations and acted in concert with the Western European democracies after World War I, aggression could have been nipped in the bud. Many of these Wilsonians were veterans of William Allen White's Committee to Defend America by Aiding the Allies, formed in 1941, and supporters of the New Deal who believed that the state had an obligation to help the less fortunate and to intervene in the private sector to ensure equal opportunity. Their efforts on behalf of internationalism culminated in the spring of 1945 when the United States led the way in establishing a new collective security organization whose stated goals were to prevent armed aggression and to promote prosperity and human rights throughout the world. When subsequently the UN proved incapable of guaranteeing the political and economic security of Western Europe, these liberal internationalists supported foreign aid and anticommunist alliance systems as mechanisms that would not only protect America from Soviet aggression but bring social justice and economic security first to Europe and then to the less fortunate peoples of the developing world.

Despite his segregationist voting record and his opposition to organized labor, the first-term senator J. William Fulbright of Arkansas accurately represented the liberal internationalist philosophy. A Rhodes scholar and former president of the University of Arkansas, Fulbright entered politics in 1942, running successfully for the House and then for the Senate in 1944. Steeped in nineteenth-century British liberalism and Wilsonian internationalism and determined to make a name for himself in foreign affairs, in 1943 he coauthored, with Senator Tom Connally of Texas, a resolution placing Congress on record as favoring membership in an international organization dedicated to keeping the peace. Impressed by the subsequent outpouring of public support for the idea of collective security that followed, the Roosevelt administration apparently boarded the internationalist bandwagon. The upshot was America's leadership in the creation of the United Nations. No senator was more active in speaking and lobbying for ratification of the UN Charter than the junior senator from Arkansas.

Time and again Fulbright tried to explain that isolationism was merely a facet of old-fashioned nationalism. Those of his contemporaries who posed as defenders of national sovereignty were in fact advocating a return to the policies of the interwar period, when the United States refused to acknowledge that its fate was linked to that of other democracies. National sovereignty was in fact a trick, an illusion, especially in the world of airplanes, submarines, and atomic weapons. Having equated isolationism with obsessive nationalism, Fulbright observed that both led to a narcissistic attitude toward international affairs. Abnegation, in turn, made possible oppression and poverty, the twin seeds of war. Horrified by pictures of the destruction wrought by the atomic bombs at Hiroshima and Nagasaki, Fulbright called on Congress, the nation, and the world to develop a mechanism capable of restraining blood-and-soil nationalism and channeling modern technology into peaceful uses.

What the freshman senator had in mind was an authentic international federation run on democratic principles. In a speech to the American Bar Association in 1945, Fulbright outlined his vision: "The history of government over the centuries, which is largely the chronicle of man's efforts to achieve freedom from the control of arbitrary force, indicate [sic] that only by the collective action of a dominant group can security be obtained." The hope of the world rested with the establishment of a global organization with a collective security mandate and a police-keeping force sufficient to enforce that mandate. Once the UN Charter was ratified, it should be clearly understood that the president through his delegate would have the authority to commit American troops to military action authorized by the Security Council.

Fulbright was an economic as well as a political internationalist; he fully shared the multilateralist views of his friend Will Clayton, the assistant secretary of state for economic affairs. Unlike Taft, who believed that the United States could remain economically self-sufficient and that economic conditions elsewhere in the world had no bearing on American interests, these intellectual heirs of Adam Smith believed that the line between national and international economics was disappearing and that prosperity was infinitely expandable. They looked forward to the creation of an economically interdependent world free of tariffs, preferences, quotas, and exchange controls. To this end Fulbright helped lead the fight in the Senate in 1945 for the approval of the Bretton Woods Agreements and in 1946 for the passage of the British loan, a $3.5 billion credit designed to rehabilitate Britain's economy and enable it to abandon imperial preference and exchange controls.

Fulbright understood the residual strength of traditional isolationism and the implications of conservative internationalism. As early as the summer of 1945 he began to express doubts about America's commitment to authentic internationalism. He wondered aloud to the Senate why there was unanimous support for the ratification of the UN Charter while, only weeks before, economic nationalists and neo-isolationists had fought vigorously against the Bretton Woods Agreements and the British loan. Could it be, he asked, that they believed that the Charter did not impinge on the nation's sovereignty and that, despite its membership in the United Nations, the United States still retained absolute freedom of action?

In the years that followed, Fulbright continued to preach the internationalist creed, but his globalism, unlike Henry Wallace's, acknowledged the threat posed to the security of Central and Western Europe by Stalinism. He readily admitted that Soviet communism was totalitarian, aggressive, and autarkic. Indeed, like the historian Arthur M. Schlesinger Jr., Senator Hubert Humphrey of Minnesota, and other members of the Americans for Democratic Action (because of his stance on civil rights Fulbright was not a member of this organization, but he was friends and sympathized with most of its founders), Fulbright was an active cold warrior. In the immediate postwar period, he supported the Truman Doctrine, the Marshall Plan, and foreign aid in general. During the 1950s he criticized President Dwight David Eisenhower and Secretary of State John Foster Dulles not only for the rigidity of their thinking but also for their lack of imagination in dealing with the communist threat in the developing world and the general ineffectiveness of their policies. As chair of the Senate Foreign Relations Committee, Fulbright was a vigorous supporter of the presidency of John F. Kennedy. In fact, no figure in Washington was more visible in articulating the liberal, activist philosophy that characterized that administration's foreign policies. Effective resistance against the forces of international communism involved not only military strength, he told the Senate, but a willingness to help developing nations "toward the fulfillment of their own highest purposes."

Though it was considered more of a political philosophy and historical interpretation than a viable foreign policy option, and that only by a handful of legislators in 1945, a fourth approach — liberal isolationism — manifested itself as World War II came to a close. This perspective did not have as conspicuous a spokesperson as the other three; probably its most influential proponent was Robert M. La Follette Jr. "Young Bob," a studious, conscientious public servant authentically dedicated to improving the welfare of his fellow human beings, had succeeded his famous father in the Senate in 1925. A Progressive from Wisconsin, he came from a political tradition that viewed Wall Street — that is, financiers and corporate executives — as avaricious exploiters of the farmers and artisans of the American heartland. The nation's political and economic systems were controlled absolutely by these plutocrats, who set the prices of agricultural commodities and labor at artificially low levels and of manufactured items, especially farm implements, at artificially high levels. The liberal isolationists, which included individuals such as the economist-historian Charles Beard and the Progressive-populist Senator William Langer (R-North Dakota), believed that Wall Street had formed an unholy alliance with British financiers to spread monopoly capitalism abroad and were exploiting the labor and markets of the developing world as well as those of their respective homelands.

La Follette was convinced that wars were caused by imperialism and power politics, that is, the struggle between national corporate elites to dominate various regions of the world. Like his father, who had voted against the Treaty of Versailles, Young Bob opposed any peace settlement that perpetuated an unjust status quo or that denied all peoples of the earth the right of self-determination. He opposed American intervention in Nicaragua during the Hoover administration and was an outspoken champion of disarmament during the 1930s. He supported the Neutrality Acts, pushed for the heavy taxation of war profits, and fought tenaciously to keep the United States out of the European conflict. Though he supported the administration after Pearl Harbor, La Follette expressed grave doubts about the Yalta accords, and he voted against the British loan on the grounds that it would dangerously deplete America's resources.

In essence, La Follette and the other liberal isolationists believed that America's first priority should be social justice and democracy at home, that an activist foreign policy was a diversion from those great objectives, and that as long as the political and economic systems were dominated by Wall Street, an activist foreign policy would result in economic exploitation and political oppression overseas. La Follette was a great defender of the New Deal and even went so far as to advocate the nationalization of the railroads and banking system. His desire, like Charles Beard's, was that America construct a social democracy that would stand as an unobtrusive example to the rest of the world.

After the war, two of the foreign policy approaches articulated in Congress in 1945 — conservative and liberal internationalism — came together to produce an activism that committed the United States to fighting communism on every front, to use the historian Thomas Paterson's phrase. Conservative anticommunists preoccupied with markets and bases backed by a burgeoning military-industrial complex argued that the only way America could be safe in a hostile world was to dominate that world through a network of alliances and overseas bases and through the possession of the largest nuclear arsenal in the world. Joining them were liberal internationalists, many of whom were domestic reformers, who saw America's welfare as tied to that of the other members of the international community. To a degree they supported alliances and military aid, but in addition, they wanted to eliminate the social and economic turmoil that they perceived as a breeding ground for Marxism and an invitation to Soviet imperialism. They wanted to do nothing less than spread the blessings of liberty, democracy, and free enterprise and to guarantee stability and prosperity to peoples threatened by communist imperialism.

Structurally, the stresses and strains of the Cold War, with its bipolarity, ideological fervor, and threat of nuclear annihilation, had two major structural impacts on the formulation of U.S. diplomacy. It accelerated the trend toward the executive domination of foreign policymaking and led to a popular demand for a bipartisanship in foreign affairs. During World War II Americans became willing, as they had not been earlier, to assume their country's burden of responsibility in world affairs, for they felt guilty over their refusal to participate in the League of Nations. If only the most powerful nation in the world had thrown its weight behind a collective security system, the Holocaust and World War II might have been prevented. The war experience had been so painful and after 1945 the prospect of nuclear war was so horrible that Americans were willing to make sacrifices in the form of economic aid for the rebuilding of Europe and to provide funds for defense against the looming threat of Soviet expansion. The realization that positive measures would be needed to prevent a third world war convinced them that their leaders, regardless of party, must cooperate to best serve the nation's interests abroad. In order that the United States have a full and constructive impact on world events, Americans demanded that partisan politics be removed from foreign policy so that the country could speak with a single voice in foreign affairs. Politicians, presidents, senators, and the members of the House of Representatives were to work to develop policies that would receive broadly based support.

Not even the advocates of a foreign policy based on interparty and executive-congressional cooperation were able to agree on a title for this phenomenon. Roosevelt's secretary of state Cordell Hull wanted to classify close executive-congressional cooperation as "nonpartisan" because he refused to share credit with the Republicans. Senator Vandenberg sought acceptance of the term "unpartisan," by which he meant policy developed above partisan purposes and for the national interest. Significantly, only Franklin Roosevelt and John Foster Dulles preferred "bipartisanship," which has become the most widely accepted term.

The succession of Harry S. Truman to the presidency portended well for bipartisanship. Truman knew the senators as friends and colleagues and respected their abilities. He well understood the benefits of working closely with Senate and House committees, and as a new president he needed all the support and advice he could garner. His advisers fashioned a constitutional theory claiming an independent executive power through the commander-in-chief clause. On July 2, 1945, Truman strode down the aisle of the House, basking in the applause of the representatives and senators who had gathered in joint session to hear him ask for their support of the proposed world organization. Do not, Truman appealed to his former colleagues, repeat the mistakes of the past. Collective security would not work without the full and enthusiastic participation of the United States. Opinion polls showed overwhelming support both in and outside the Senate, but such had been the case in 1919. Former isolationists like Taft grumbled but were quickly overwhelmed. In the summer of 1945 the Senate ratified the Charter of the United Nations, 89–2.

Cynics charged that the Truman administration conjured up and wielded the notion of bipartisanship merely to stifle congressional dissent. They had a point. The chair of the Foreign Relations Committee, Tom Connally, a committed cold warrior, equated opposition to bipartisanship with isolationism; Secretary of State Dean Acheson gleefully noted that a bipartisan foreign policy allowed the president to argue that any critic "is a son-of-a-bitch and not a true patriot," and "if people will swallow that, then you're off to the races."

From 1946 to 1949, the Truman administration gradually took a more confrontational stance toward the Soviet expansion into Eastern Europe. On March 7, 1947, the president addressed another dramatic joint session of Congress. He described the political situation in the eastern Mediterranean, where communist guerrillas were threatening the pro-Western monarchy in Greece, and the Soviets were pressuring the Turkish government to allow it to build bases on the Bosporus and other strategic locations. He asked for $400 million in aid to shore up the Greek monarchy in its struggle with the EAS/ELAM insurgents and to enable Turkey to resist Soviet aggression. During the ensuing debate, liberals pointed out that the Greek government was undemocratic, corrupt, and reactionary and that Turkey was not a democracy and had remained neutral during most of World War II. Why not let both pass into the communist orbit? They would simply be changing one form of undemocratic government for another. Administration spokesmen could only answer that under noncommunist regimes there was at least a chance of progress, whereas under Marxist-Leninist governments there was not. Once again, anticommunism carried the day, and the Truman Doctrine passed both houses by overwhelming margins. More important, Congress and the executive, Republicans and Democrats, came together to declare that it would be the policy of the United States "to support free peoples who are resisting attempted subjugation by armed minorities or by outside pressure."

Later that year, the Marshall Plan to fund the reconstruction of Western Europe passed Congress with large majorities on both sides of the aisle. Over the next four years, the United States poured more than $13 billion into areas ravaged by World War II in part out of a belief that communism thrived in areas where economic deprivation and social instability prevailed. In 1949, by a wide bipartisan margin, Congress approved U.S. participation in NATO, the charter of which committed its members to view an attack on one as an attack on all.

By 1950 anticommunism had become perhaps the most important theme in American politics, but it was no longer a rallying point for bipartisanship. The Republicans were deeply frustrated by their inability to win a presidential election. Truman's upset of Thomas E. Dewey in 1948 was particularly galling. The New Deal and the permanence of the emerging welfare state in America had left the Republicans without a compelling domestic issue. After Truman's victory, the party leadership decided that it could no longer afford a me-too position on American foreign policy, that the GOP must out-"hardline" the Democrats. With Wisconsin's Joe McCarthy charging that the administration had permitted Soviet espionage agents to infiltrate the federal government and Senators Robert Taft and Everett Dirksen (R-Illinois) indicting Roosevelt and Truman for selling out Eastern Europe to the Kremlin, the Republicans launched a relentless campaign to portray the Democrats as soft on communism. Its effect was to augment an already strident anticommunism in the United States. In late January 1950 Truman directed the Departments of State and Defense "to make an overall review and reassessment of American foreign and defense policy" in light of the fall of China to the communists and the detonation of an atomic bomb by the Soviet Union (both in 1949). The result was NSC-68, a policy paper committing the United States to combat the forces of international communism wherever and whenever they threatened the status quo. This paper led to a fourfold increase in defense budgets and paved the way for the transformation of the United States into a national security state and the institutionalization of a cold war between the United States and its allies on the one hand and the Soviet Union and its allies on the other that would last until 1989.

The ongoing confrontation with the Soviet Union, and especially the nuclear arms race, gave rise to what President Eisenhower would call the military-industrial complex. In the wake of NSC-68 and the Korean War, federal expenditures for defense mushroomed. By 1969 the total defense budget had reached $79.788 billion, which amounted to 42.9 percent of total federal expenditures, and between 9 and 10 percent of the gross national product. Defense funds went to every state: to 363 of the 435 congressional districts and to more than 5,000 communities. Workers in defense industries and in defense-related production in mining, agriculture, construction, and services made up 10 percent of the total labor force. Thus did the constituents of congressmen and senators and thus the legislators themselves come to have a stake in the Cold War. During the late 1940s and early 1950s many defense industries were established in the South, a trend that proved important in ensuring that the southern wing of the conservative coalition in Congress supported containment. Indeed, after the war the South forged a political alliance with the Pentagon. Led by Senators Richard Russell, John Stennis, and Lyndon Johnson and Congressmen Carl Vinson and L. Mendel Rivers, the South jealously protected the ballooning defense budget while "fortress Dixie" became the home of seven of the nation's ten largest defense contractors. So strongly rooted was the military-industrial complex in the region that William Faulkner was led to observe in 1956, "Our economy is no longer agricultural. Our economy is the Federal Government."

An aggressive stance abroad and massive defense expenditures failed to appease McCarthy and his allies, however. The Republicans continued to hammer the Democrats with the soft-on-communism issue. The Taft wing of the party together with a handful of Democrats quietly but vigorously supported McCarthy's domestic witch-hunt. The right-wing senator Pat McCarran (D-Nevada), a close ally of the FBI's J. Edgar Hoover, pushed through Congress two critical pieces of Cold War legislation — the McCarran Internal Security Act (1950) and the McCarran-Walter Immigration Act (1952). Both were designed to identify communists and their sympathizers and either exclude them from the republic or silence them. Both were symptoms and propellants of a domestic anticommunist witch-hunt.

In 1950, as the so-called Second Red Scare was gaining momentum, U.N. forces, with General of the Army Douglas MacArthur in command, drove invading North Korean troops out of South Korea toward the Yalu River, the boundary between communist North Korea and communist China. In October, 300,000 Chicom troops crossed the river and smashed MacArthur's formations. The U.N. forces retreated below the 38th parallel, which separated the two Koreas, but MacArthur soon halted the advance and mounted a counteroffensive. When the general regained the 38th parallel in March 1951, he asked permission of the Truman administration to once again proceed north. This time the president and his advisers refused. Undaunted, MacArthur wrote to the leading Republican in the House of Representatives, Joseph Martin, asserting that "there is no substitute for victory." When Truman subsequently relieved MacArthur of his command, the Republican leadership decided that they had the perfect presidential candidate for 1952. In May and June, Republican senators ostentatiously held hearings on MacArthur's firing. His demise and the refusal of the administration to reunify Korea under a noncommunist leader was clear proof that the Democrats were either appeasers or softheaded. Senator McCarthy was typically blunt. "The son-of-a-bitch [Truman] ought to be impeached," he commented to a press conference. Europe was a "dying system," MacArthur declared in his congressional testimony, and the "Pacific would determine the course of history in the next ten thousand years." When it subsequently became clear that MacArthur was defying not only Truman but the Joint Chiefs of Staff, who took the position that an all-out war with communist China would make it impossible for the United States to defend Western Europe, MacArthur's popularity faded, and by 1954 so had McCarthy's. The Republicans were forced to look for another war hero to run for president, one more in tune with the Cold War consensus that perceived the greatest threat to the United States to be communism abroad, especially Soviet imperialism.

The key to maintaining the bipartisan consensus on behalf of an activist Cold War foreign policy during this period was a group of Republican internationalists that included Vandenberg, Senator Henry Cabot Lodge (R-Massachusetts), and Senator H. Alexander Smith (R-New Jersey). They supported the Marshall Plan, the Truman Doctrine, the Mutual Security Act, and other Cold War measures while insisting to the more conservative members of the GOP that they were using their influence with the executive to restrain its interventionist, big-spending ways. The opposition party, Lodge insisted, would function as "the voice of conscience though not of power" in international affairs, offering "a calm and deliberate reappraisal" and "constructive suggestions." The Korean War, which ended in a stalemate in 1953 with the country divided at the 38th parallel, left Congress and the American people frustrated and confused. It was in this climate that liberal Republicans urged Truman and Acheson to justify Cold War foreign policy in ideological terms — democracy, human rights, and self-determination — as well as realpolitik. And it was this group that stepped up to challenge the Taft wing of the party for the GOP presidential nomination in 1952. Lodge and his friends succeeded in drafting the World War II hero General Dwight D. Eisenhower.

Eisenhower and his internationalist secretary of state, John Foster Dulles, thoroughly agreed with the containment policies developed by their predecessors. As Republicans, however, they were frightened by the fiscal implications of NSC-68. The threat of communist expansion was always present and had to be met head-on, but at the same time the fiscal integrity of the Republic had to be maintained. Their answer was the New Look defense policy. In the future the United States would rely on its nuclear arsenal and strategic air arm to threaten the communist superpowers with nuclear annihilation whenever and wherever their ambitions seemed to threaten the status quo. Under the protection of this nuclear umbrella, Dulles and Eisenhower more or less successfully managed crises in Central America, the Middle East, East Asia, and Southeast Asia.

During the 1950s many Democrats, particularly Fulbright and his colleagues on the Senate Foreign Relations Committee, suspected that Eisenhower's frequent appeals to bipartisanship were merely attempts to trick the Democratic party into sharing the blame if policies already implemented failed. And by 1956 the liberal internationalists in Congress were convinced that the New Look was fatally flawed. They viewed the concept of massive retaliation as a diplomatic strategy that would lead either to nuclear war or to a communist takeover of the developing world. During a grilling of Dulles in 1954 by the Senate Foreign Relations Committee, Fulbright asked incredulously whether the administration intended to rain atomic bombs on Moscow in response to "a local aggression in Burma, the Middle East or elsewhere." Such a policy was madness and would surely lead to World War III.

Nevertheless, the Democratic majority leader, Senator Lyndon B. Johnson, insisted that congressional Democrats act as partners with Eisenhower and Dulles. He did not intend to stand by and allow the conservatives in Congress to launch a debate on the merits of communism, casting the Democratic party in the role of defender of Marxism-Leninism. The Eisenhower administration actually received more support in Congress from the Democrats than from the conservative wing of its own party. Indeed, led by Robert Taft and the former president Herbert Hoover, conservative Republicans espoused a form of neo-isolationism. They insisted that America's resources were limited and that it ought to concentrate on perfecting its own institutions and guaranteeing its own prosperity. They were particularly adamant about the need to balance the budget. The neo-isolationists opposed stationing American troops in Europe as part of a NATO armed force, and they warned about the perils of being drawn into a land war in Asia. The Eisenhower-Johnson axis prevailed, however, and in December 1954 Congress approved a pact between the United States and Formosa that committed the United States to stationing troops "in and about" the island. In 1957 bipartisan support led to congressional approval of the Eisenhower Doctrine, empowering the president to use military force if any government in the Middle East requested protection against "overt armed aggression from any nation controlled by International Communism." The liberal internationalists grumbled that the Eisenhower Doctrine proposed a military response to what was basically a socioeconomic and historical problem. Fulbright went so far as to introduce a substitute resolution that would commit the United States to a reopening of the Suez Canal and to a long-term political settlement of the Arab-Israeli conflict, but not to the defense of any and every Middle Eastern state. It failed, and the Senate subsequently ratified the Eisenhower Doctrine, 72–19. Rather than making a frontal assault on the administration, Johnson argued, the Democrats in Congress should do everything in their power to help Eisenhower contain communism abroad through alliance building and economic and military aid to the developing world. The real enemy was the clique of neoconservatives in Congress, not Eisenhower and Dulles. The administration and its congressional allies resisted efforts by the conservatives to reduce the American military presence in Europe. In 1953 the Republican senator John Bricker introduced a constitutional amendment that would have effectively given Congress veto power over executive agreements concluded with foreign powers. A former governor of Ohio and Thomas Dewey's running mate in 1944, Bricker was an outspoken champion of private enterprise and states' rights. "Intellectually he is like interstellar space," declared the liberal commentator John Gunther, "a vast vacuum occasionally crossed by homeless, wandering clichés." After nearly a year of debate, Republican internationalists combined with liberal Democrats to defeat the Bricker Amendment.

Structural changes in Congress helped ensure the continued executive dominance of foreign policymaking during the Eisenhower years. Between the end of the Civil War and the outbreak of World War II, the Senate Foreign Relations Committee was the dominant congressional voice on international affairs. Immediately after the war, however, its influence declined as the principal functions over which it had clear jurisdiction, treatymaking and warmaking, fell into disuse. Challenging it for the dominant role in making congressional foreign policy were the Appropriations Committees and particularly the Armed Services Committees of both houses. Both proved markedly unwilling to challenge executive authority. The members of the Armed Services Committees, especially the Southerners that dominated them, were generally in favor of defense — indeed, many, like Richard Russell (D-Georgia) and L. Mendel Rivers (D-South Carolina), were nothing less than representatives of the military-industrial complex. The Senate Armed Services Committee was charged with oversight of the Central Intelligence Agency (CIA). Oversight was the correct term, one critic observed. Senator Russell called for Congress to take CIA statements "on faith," while his committee's ranking Republican, Leverett Saltonstall of Massachusetts, commented that he would prefer not to know the details of CIA activities.

Political considerations threatened and then subverted bipartisanship during Eisenhower's second term, as the Democrats abandoned their position as the loyal opposition and used the emerging subcommittee structure to challenge the foreign policy status quo. Following Adlai Stevenson's second defeat, three Senate subcommittees, each chaired by a Democratic contender for the 1960 presidential nomination, emerged to challenge the diplomatic status quo. The Soviet launch of its Sputnik satellite in 1957 led to charges of a missile gap and to Democratic indictments of the Eisenhower administrations' general passivity. Lyndon Johnson, who in addition to being majority leader chaired the Preparedness Investigations Subcommittee, abandoned his alliance with Dulles and Eisenhower to launch a critical investigation of the nation's "non-existent" space program. "The issue is one which, if properly handled," Johnson's staffer George Reedy informed the senator, "would blast the Republicans out of the water, unify the Democratic Party, and elect you President." In late 1958 Henry "Scoop" Jackson (D-Washington) persuaded the Senate to authorize the Government Operations Committee, on which he served, to investigate the administration's effectiveness in confronting the "problems facing the free world in the contest with world communism." The result was a wide-ranging two-year indictment of the New Look. Finally, Hubert Humphrey spearheaded the creation of the Disarmament Subcommittee of the Foreign Relations Committee to build a case for arms control initiatives.

The emergence of a will to dissent in Congress, expressed substantially through its subcommittees, did not spell a revolt against anticommunism or the policy of containment but rather a willingness to question how the Cold War was being fought. Of particular concern to Fulbright, Johnson, and Humphrey was Eisenhower's perceived overreliance on nuclear arms and the doctrine of massive retaliation and its putative neglect of the educational health of the nation. More important was a lingering uneasiness, expressed first by Senators Claude Pepper and Edwin Johnson during the debates over the Truman Doctrine, that America's willingness to provide economic and military aid to undemocratic regimes in the name of anticommunism was threatening the very ideals on which the Republic was based. The alliance between conservative and liberal internationalists, between realpolitikers and those committed to socioeconomic justice at home and abroad, remained very much intact, however. It would require ten long, bloody years of warfare in Southeast Asia to rend it.

— Randall Bennett Woods

BIBLIOGRAPHICAL NOTES

For background on Congress and American foreign policy, see Wayne S. Cole's comprehensive *Roosevelt and the Isolationists, 1932–1945* (Lincoln, Neb., 1983), and Richard E. Darilek's *A Loyal Opposition in Time of War: The Republican Party and the Politics of Foreign Policy from Pearl Harbor to Yalta* (Westport, Conn., 1986). Justus D. Doenecke's *Not to the Swift: The Old Isolationists in the Cold War Era* (Lewisburg, Pa., 1979) provides an excellent analysis of Taft and his allies, as does James T. Patterson's *Mr. Republican: A Biography of Robert A. Taft* (Boston, 1972). For a solid treatment of the liberal internationalists, see my *Fulbright: A Biography* (New York, 1995). Robert David Johnson's superb *Ernest Gruening and the American Dissenting Tradition* (Cambridge, Mass., 1998) provides useful insights into Western liberalism and Congress's ongoing struggle to play an independent role in the foreign policy–making process. For Congress, the military aid program, and the making of the military-industrial complex, consult Vernon W. Ruttan's *United States Development Assistance Policy: The Domestic Politics of Foreign Economic Aid* (Baltimore, 1996) and Chester Pach Jr.'s *Arming the Free World: The Origins of the United States Military Assistance Program, 1945–1950* (Chapel Hill, N.C., 1991). James Lindsay's *Congress and the Politics of U.S. Defense Policy* (Baltimore, 1994) and Randall Ripley and James Lindsay, eds., *Congress Resurgent: Foreign and Defense Policy on Capitol Hill* (Ann Arbor, Mich., 1993), provide solid information on congressional structure and politics in connection with foreign and defense policy.

Of general interest are Walter McDougal's masterful survey, *Promised Land, Crusader State: The American Encounter with the World Since 1776* (Boston, 1997), and Richard J. Ellis's brilliant *American Political Cultures* (New York, 1993). On politics during the postwar period, there is no better book than Sidney M. Milkis's *The President and the Parties: The Transformation of the American Party System since the New Deal* (New York, 1989). There are a number of excellent works dealing with domestic politics and the Cold War; see especially Alonzo L. Hamby, *Beyond the New Deal: Harry S. Truman and American Liberalism* (New York, 1973), and *Man of the People: A Life of Harry S. Truman* (New York, 1995). Also of use is mine and Howard Jones's *The Dawning of the Cold War: The United States' Quest for Order* (Athens, Ga., 1991). On the Second Red Scare, Richard M. Freedland's *The Truman Doctrine and the Origins of McCarthyism* (New York, 1970) is the standard work. John Spanier's *The Truman-MacArthur Controversy and the Korean War* (Cambridge, Mass., 1959) is still invaluable. For the Korean War and domestic politics, consult William Stueck's *The Korean War: An In-*

ternational History (Princeton, N.J., 1995). On the Republicans' efforts to out-"hardline" the Democrats, read Athan G. Theoharis, *The Yalta Myths: An Issue in U.S. Politics, 1945–1955* (Columbia, Mo., 1970). For the Eisenhower years, there are a number of important works, beginning with Richard H. Immerman's *John Foster Dulles and the Diplomacy of the Cold War* (Princeton, N.J., 1990). See also Saki Dockrill's *Eisenhower's New-Look National Security Policy, 1953–61* (New York, 1996) and Nicol C. Rae's *The Decline and Fall of the Liberal Republicans: From 1952 to the Present* (New York, 1989).

Richard Russell

November 2, 1897–January 21, 1971

Richard Russell

Richard Brevard Russell Jr. was a natural politician. Friendly and outgoing, he identified with popular issues, possessed excellent speaking skills, was well organized and respected for his integrity, and was talented at the art of conciliatory politics. Best known for his strong support of the military, Russell served in the Senate for four decades, making a presidential bid in 1952, and was honored by his colleagues in 1972 when they renamed the oldest Senate office building for him. As a southern politician, however, Russell had a decidedly racist perspective and believed in white supremacy and racial segregation. He denounced liberalizing immigration laws in the 1940s and was a major figure in blocking, for decades, the enactment of civil rights legislation.

Born in Winder, Georgia, the son of a lawyer and judge, Russell attended Gordon Military Institute (now Gordon College) and the University of Georgia, where he earned a law degree in 1918. He served briefly in the navy at the close of World War I and returned to Winder to practice law with his father. Russell never married, and he wasted no time getting into politics. At the age of twenty-three, he was elected to the Georgia legislature, where he served for ten years, two as Speaker of the house. In 1930 he became governor and focused on internal improvements to the state during his two-year tenure. The death of the Democratic senator William J. Harris (1868–1932) opened the way for Russell's advancement to national office. He was elected easily in 1932 and reelected six times. Only once, in 1936, did another Democrat challenge him for the nomination.

During the New Deal, Russell appealed to his agrarian constituents, supporting price supports for crops, appropriations for the Farm Security Administration and the Farmers Home Administration, and limiting social programs such as school lunches. Serving on the Committee on Immigration from 1937 to 1946, Russell favored strict policies. He openly feared that Asian and Latin American immigrants would undermine the Anglo-Saxon culture he represented, sentiments that were not uncommon during this political era.

Adept at behind-the-scenes negotiations, Russell emerged as one of the most powerful senators by 1950. He was appointed to the Armed Services

Committee in 1951 and served on it for fifteen years. Although he favored a strong military and supported the development of high-tech weaponry, Russell was opposed to the role of the United States as the world's police force. Although he initially opposed the American military involvement in Vietnam, he supported President Lyndon B. Johnson once the war began, but remained opposed to the president's Great Society programs.

Reference

Fite, G. C. (2000, February). "Russell, Richard Brevard, Jr." *American National Biography Online.* Retrieved July 3, 2003, from http://www.anb.org/articles/06/06-00783.html.

29

McCarthyism in Congress: Investigating Communism

"I HAVE HERE IN MY HAND a list of 205 who were known to the Secretary of State as being members of the Communist party and who, nevertheless, are still working and shaping policy in the State Department," Senator Joseph R. McCarthy told an audience of Republican women in Wheeling, West Virginia, at a Lincoln's Day dinner in 1950. Congressional investigations into communist subversion and espionage had been under way for years before McCarthy made this sensational accusation, but the senator still managed to shock public opinion and make himself the center of national media attention. McCarthy so heightened the intensity of the postwar anticommunist investigations that "McCarthyism" became the label for a broad range of congressional inquiries, from the House Un-American Activities Committee to the Senate Internal Security Subcommittee and McCarthy's own Permanent Subcommittee on Investigations. The term also became synonymous with smears, character assassination, and the abuse of witnesses, as well as with legislative efforts to restrict civil liberties. Senator McCarthy did not start the investigations, nor was he alone in conducting them, but his recklessness and eventual censure both defined and discredited the congressional anticommunist crusade and led to a series of court rulings that protected the rights of congressional witnesses.

The Formation of HUAC

Congressional investigations of communist activities began gathering steam in 1930, when Representative Hamilton Fish, a conservative Republican from upstate New York, chaired a special committee to examine Soviet propaganda efforts in the United States. The Fish committee reported the existence of some 12,000 registered communists in the United States, with perhaps a half-million communist sympathizers, and warned that communists were actively infiltrating American labor unions. It recommended outlawing the Communist party, censoring mailed communist literature, and deporting all radical aliens. Congress ignored these recommendations, and as the nation slid deeper into economic depression, the Communist party ranks continued to grow as more Americans despaired of capitalism's ability to recover.

In 1934 a Brooklyn Democrat, Samuel Dickstein, sponsored a House resolution authorizing an inquiry into pro-Nazi activities in the United States. Three years later he proposed expanding the special committee's jurisdiction to include all "un-American propaganda" that might incite prejudice and promote the use of force and violence. When his resolution failed, Dickstein endorsed an investigative resolution presented by the Texas Democrat Martin Dies. The result was the creation in 1938 of the Special Committee to Investigate Un-American Activities, with the conservative Dies as its first chairman. Contrary to Dickstein's intentions, Dies devoted more attention to domestic communism than to fascism. The committee, popularly known in the press as HUAC, hired J. B. Matthews as an investigator. A former leftist (although never a communist), Matthews had grown disillusioned with radicalism and shifted politically to the right. He compiled vast indexes of the names of "fellow travelers" like himself who had signed communist petitions or participated in "Communist-front" organizations. Armed with these lists, HUAC began investigating communist influences in such New Deal programs as the Federal Theater Project and the Federal Writers' Project, investigations that contributed to the programs' disbandment. A penchant for grandstanding earned HUAC much contempt from the press. Washington's reporters considered the committee "90 per cent hogwash," said the news columnist Raymond Clapper, but they reported its hearings nonetheless.

Communism in America

While the committee rooted through New Deal agencies for communists, the Communist party of the United States was criticizing Franklin Roosevelt's New Deal as too makeshift and beholden to corporate capitalism. During the Depression, American communists openly joined many progressive noncommunists in a "Popular Front" to promote common goals for racial equality and unionization. Noncommunists signed petitions, attended rallies, and contributed financially to groups that would later be branded communist fronts. But the liberal left became alienated by the Communist party's ideological dependence on the Soviet Union, most clearly demonstrated when the U.S. party endorsed the Nazi-Soviet Friendship Pact of 1939. After Germany invaded Russia, the U.S. party again reversed direction. With the United States and the Soviet Union allied during the war, the American communists disbanded as a political party and promoted Roosevelt's reelection in 1944 — although Roosevelt formally disavowed their support.

Congressional investigators interpreted communism as an international conspiracy rather than a political movement. Citing the party's allegiance to the Soviet Union, anticommunists interpreted party membership as proof of disloyalty and potentially of subversion and espionage, even though it was as legal in the 1930s and '40s to join the Communist party as any other political organization. The Communist party functioned in the open, publishing a newspaper, the *Daily Worker,* holding public meetings, collecting petitions, running candidates for office, and publicly demonstrating for social and economic reforms. Yet at the same time a small wing of the party operated sub rosa. Recruited by Soviet intelligence agents, they provided confidential information from the government agencies in which they worked.

Whittaker Chambers, a bohemian writer and translator (and later an editor at *Time* magazine), operated as a courier to the underground cells in Washington during the 1930s. He later observed that a person could be active in the party for years "without completely understanding the nature of communism or the political methods that follow inevitably from its vision." After Chambers broke with the party, he warned officials in 1939 of a number of communists in the State Department. Preoccupied with other wartime investigations, the FBI did not get around to questioning Chambers until 1942. During the war, the Army Signal Corps intercepted messages between Soviet agents in the United States and Moscow — known as Project Venona — but its cryptographers did not break the Soviet code until 1946. The Venona intercepts confirmed the existence of an extensive Soviet espionage network in the United States, despite the nations' wartime alliance. To avoid alerting the Soviets that they had broken the code, intelligence agencies kept Project Venona secret until the 1990s, after the Cold War had ended.

The Hiss Case

By the end of World War II, the defection of several secret agents in the United States and Canada caused the Soviet Union to abort its espionage operations. Fearing imminent exposure, the Soviets recalled some operatives and sent others into hiding. The press coverage of stunning spy stories goaded President Harry Truman into signing an executive order in 1947 that made membership or "sympathetic association" with communist organizations sufficient cause to deny federal employment. Those accused could appeal their cases to loyalty review boards in the executive departments. Rather than calm public nervousness, however, the executive order only convinced the public of an ominous threat to their national security. The spy stories also provided Republicans with an issue for the upcoming congressional elections.

The House Democratic leadership had planned to let HUAC expire, after Dies's retirement in 1945, but supporters of the investigations surprised them by winning a vote, 208–186, to make HUAC a permanent standing committee. The Republican victory in the 1946 elections (gaining 13 seats in the Senate and 55 in the House to take majorities in both bodies) reinvigorated the committee's investigations. HUAC launched a headline-grabbing investigation of "Hollywood Reds," calling movie stars and studio heads to testify — among them Ronald Reagan, as head of the Screen Actors' Guild. Ten writers and directors were found guilty of contempt of Congress for refusing to answer the committee's questions. In August 1948 HUAC called the former communist couriers Elizabeth Bentley and Whittaker Chambers to reveal what they knew about communist cells operating in the federal government. Among those named by Chambers was a former assistant secretary of state, Alger Hiss, who immediately telegraphed the committee and demanded a hearing to deny the charges — thereby setting up a dramatic confrontation that guaranteed press attention. Hiss refuted Chambers's accusations so adamantly that members of the committee apologized to him. The hearing might have ended then except for the lingering suspicions of the freshman California representative Richard Nixon, a young Republican who had been irritated by Hiss's elitist and "rather insolent" testimony. Nixon was appointed to chair a special subcommittee to continue the probe.

Nixon's investigation took a dramatic turn when Chambers produced reels of microfilm that he had hidden at his Maryland farm in a hollow pumpkin, the "Pumpkin Papers," which contained State Department records he claimed to have gotten from Hiss. When Hiss sued for libel, the American press largely took his side, but after the first trial ended in a hung jury in July 1949, his support began to dwindle. In January 1950 he was convicted of perjury. (Hiss denied the charges to his grave, but the decrypted Venona messages and the opening of some of the Soviet Union's archives provided evidence of his participation in Soviet espionage.) Three weeks later, Senator McCarthy went to Wheeling and made his accusations. With the Hiss case, the communist victory in China in 1949, and the Soviet Union's ability to test thermonuclear weapons, McCarthy's conspiracy theories about communist infiltration in the government helped people make sense of perplexing events and gave them someone to blame. "Senator McCarthy seems to have tapped, quite accidentally, a reservoir of long-hidden malice," wrote Max Ascoli, editor of the liberal *Reporter* magazine.

The Rise of Joe McCarthy

From a hardscrabble youth as a chicken farmer, Joe McCarthy had risen to the position of circuit judge before he joined the Marine Corps during World War II. Returning from the war, he quit the Democratic party and defeated the incumbent senator Robert M. La Follette Jr. in the Wisconsin Republican primary of 1946. McCarthy won his Senate seat in part by exaggerating his combat record in the South Pacific and by accusing his opponents of being soft on communism.

Regarded in Washington as an affable publicity seeker, McCarthy was ecstatic when his Wheeling charges drew national headlines. But he was immediately thrown on the defensive when the State Department demanded that he name all the alleged communists he had cited. The Senate Foreign Relations Committee appointed a special subcommittee, chaired by the veteran Maryland senator Millard Tydings, to investigate these allegations. McCarthy reduced the number of communists he claimed were in the State Department and hastily compiled a list of suspects. Then he diverted attention by naming Professor Owen Lattimore of Johns Hopkins University, a prominent scholar of the Far East and an occasional State Department consultant, as the top Russian spy in America, the "boss of Alger Hiss." Lattimore went before the Tydings Committee to denounce McCarthy's "reign of terror." But McCarthy produced Louis Budenz, the former *Daily Worker* editor turned anticommunist informant, who testified that party officials had identified Lattimore as a communist. Nothing in the Venona decryptions implicated Lattimore and the case against him was thrown out in court, but that occurred long after the furor from the charges had enabled McCarthy to regain the offensive.

Instead of discrediting McCarthy, the Tydings Committee hearings established him as the nation's leading communist hunter. The arrest of Julius and Ethel Rosenberg on espionage charges and communist North Korea's invasion of South Korea in 1950 persuaded a growing number of Americans that McCarthy must have known what he was talking about. McCarthy further stirred the waters by accusing Truman's secretary of defense, General George C. Marshall, of a "conspiracy so immense" to aid and abet international communism. (The Venona transcripts would offer absolutely no evidence of disloyalty against General Marshall or Secretary of State Dean Acheson, another of McCarthy's favorite targets.) McCarthy involved himself in the congressional elections of 1950 in an extraordinary manner and claimed the credit when voters in Maryland defeated

Tydings's reelection bid. Another critic of McCarthy, the Democratic majority leader Scott Lucas of Illinois, also went down to defeat while California sent Richard Nixon to the Senate after a mud-slinging campaign that portrayed his Democratic opponent, Representative Helen Gahagan Douglas, as a "pink lady."

In his crusade, McCarthy could count on the support of a loose coalition of right-wing anticommunist activists in the press and the business community. Reporters from the *Chicago Tribune* and the Hearst newspaper chain not only gave him favorable publicity but drafted his speeches and conducted much of the research to bolster his accusations. Conservative businessmen provided financial assistance, suggested areas of investigation, and fed the senator theories about conspiracy at the highest levels of government.

In a ringing speech in 1950, Maine's Republican senator Margaret Chase Smith declared that she did not want to see her party ride to victory on "the Four Horsemen of Calumny — Fear, Ignorance, Bigotry and Smear." But only six other liberal Republicans signed her "Declaration of Conscience." By contrast, Ohio's Robert Taft, the de facto Republican leader in the Senate, encouraged McCarthy to attack the Truman administration, and willingly overlooked his roughshod tactics. That attitude changed when the Republican Dwight Eisenhower won the presidency in 1952, and his coattails restored Republican majorities in the Senate and the House. As they returned to power, the Senate's Republican leaders expected to sideline McCarthy as chairman of the Government Operations Committee, whose oversight responsibilities normally involved issues of graft and corruption. According to Senate rules, investigations of espionage and sedition were under the jurisdiction of the Internal Security Subcommittee of the Judiciary Committee, chaired by William Jenner, a staunchly anticommunist Indiana Republican. But McCarthy exercised his prerogative to chair his committee's Permanent Subcommittee on Investigations, whose mandate he interpreted broadly as enabling him to investigate anything relating to the government, including communist infiltration.

The Permanent Subcommittee on Investigations traced its origin to the Special Senate Committee to Investigate the National Defense Program, which had been created in 1941 to pursue fraud, corruption, and mismanagement in defense contracting. Known as the "Truman Committee" for its first chairman, Missouri's Senator Truman, it continued its probes even after the Second World War had ended and Truman was in the White House. When the Legislative Reorganization Act of 1946 streamlined the congressional committee system and eliminated the plethora of special committees, the Senate turned the Truman Committee into a subcommittee of the Committee on Government Operations. McCarthy, who had served on the Truman Committee, stayed on after the reorganization and rose by seniority to chairman.

McCarthy Investigates

As chief counsel to conduct his investigations, Chairman McCarthy hired Roy Cohn, a brash, young New York attorney who had prosecuted subversives for Truman's Justice Department. The Hearst columnist George Sokolsky had recommended that Cohn, as a Jewish Democrat, could defuse the suspicions of anti-Semitism that might arise from calling many Jewish witnesses. Aggressive and ambitious, Cohn exercised no moderating influence on McCarthy's freewheeling style. Together they launched one inquiry after another — they claimed a total of 157 investigations in 1953 alone. That schedule stretched the subcommittee's small staff perilously thin and resulted in uneven research and preparation. At public hearings, the chairman basked in the television lights, which sometimes blinded observers to the inconclusiveness of his inquiries. Nathaniel Weyl, a former communist who turned cooperative witness, pointed to the unfairness of these investigations. Even those who could disprove the accusations made against them suffered irreparable damage. "The public had neither the time nor the inclination to study the labyrinth of charges and countercharges," Weyl pointed out. "All that it was likely to remember about a man was that he had been accused."

Convinced that they were on the trail of subversion and espionage, McCarthy and Cohn held hearings into State Department practices, particularly the Voice of America and the U.S. Information Libraries, which had been merged into the State Department after the war. McCarthy caused the dismissal of the Information Agency's deputy administrator Reed Harris because, as a Columbia University student twenty years earlier, he had written a book, *King Football,* some of which had been reprinted in the *Daily Worker,* and he had belonged to the League of American Writers, later cited as a subversive organization. Harris, who denied any communist leanings, was later rehired by the U.S. Information Agency, and nothing in the Venona transcripts impugned his loyalty.

Secretary of State John Foster Dulles felt dubious about mixing foreign policy and propaganda, and he viewed the Voice of America as an unwanted appendage to his department. He was not unsympathetic to the demands for some housecleaning and attempted to accommodate the congressional inquiries. Before long, however, the Eisenhower administration began to worry that McCarthy's effort to clean out the "left-wing debris" would undermine morale in the executive branch and disrupt its own efforts to reorganize the government.

The investigation of alleged communist books stocked by the U.S. Information Libraries overseas permitted McCarthy to call the famous authors of those books to testify, a list that included Howard Fast, Dashiell Hammett, and Langston Hughes. Among those interrogated was James Wechsler, editor of the *New York Post* and one of Senator McCarthy's most outspoken opponents. Although a member of the Young Communist League in the 1930s, Wechsler had broken with the party and pursued a strongly anticommunist editorial line in the *Post,* for which he was regularly criticized in the *Daily Worker.* With this record, Wechsler felt he had little to fear from McCarthy, but the senator questioned whether he had actually inspired the *Daily Worker's* attacks on himself as a form of cover. "That way madness lies," wrote the conservative analyst James Burnham of McCarthy's logic. "By this kind of reasoning, no one could ever prove his loyalty. If you support communist objectives, you are obviously a Communist; if you attack them, this is a deception maneuver, and you are still a Communist." The U.S. Information Library investigation ended in the spring of 1953, when Roy Cohn and his close friend G. David Schine, an unpaid consultant to the subcommittee, traveled to Europe to examine the library shelves. The international press roundly assailed them as junketing "book burners." Realizing that their trip had been a public relations disaster, the subcommittee retreated from the issue and turned instead to charges of subversion in the Government Printing Office and the U.S. Army.

Cohn's lack of administrative skills resulted in considerable disorganization in the day-to-day operations of the subcommittee. To restore order, McCarthy appointed J. B. Matthews as staff director in June 1953. But Matthews's article, "Reds in Our Churches," had just appeared in the *American Mercury.* His accusation of widespread communist sympathy among the nation's Protestant clergy caused a public uproar and forced him to resign immediately. The three Democratic senators on the subcommittee, John McClellan of Arkansas, Henry "Scoop" Jackson of Washington, and Stuart Symington of Missouri, also resigned in protest over the chairman's unilateral hiring and firing of staff. Without a minority to keep him in line, McCarthy held more subcommittee meetings outside Washington, often at short notice, which ensured that the other Republican senators would be absent and enabled him to conduct hearings entirely on his own. McCarthy's "one-man rule" gave witnesses the impression, wrote the dean of Harvard Law School, Erwin Griswold, that they were facing a "judge, jury, prosecutor, castigator, and press agent, all in one."

All congressional investigative committees made it a practice to hear witnesses first in closed executive sessions before taking their testimony at open public hearings. That way the committees could avoid cases of misidentification and determine how forthcoming witnesses were likely to be. While the closed hearings ostensibly protected the witnesses, they also permitted the chairman and his staff to offer their own version of events to the press. John G. Adams, who served as counsel to the U.S. Army, attended many of McCarthy's closed hearings and observed that at their conclusion the chairman would step outside to tell waiting reporters "whatever he pleased." In this manner, McCarthy shaped the story as well as public opinion before the witnesses had a chance to testify publicly. Since the senator tended to exaggerate the evidence against the witnesses, his remarks generated banner headlines before the public hearings — where the findings rarely justified his hyperbole.

Witnesses before either closed or public hearings had the right to decline to answer if they felt an answer might incriminate them, but McCarthy interpreted a refusal to answer as an admission of guilt. Some witnesses were willing to discuss their own past relations with the Communist party but not to "name names" of others with whom they had associated. Some stood firm on the principle that the subcommittee had no right to inquire about their political beliefs or activities. In 1953 and 1954, the annual reports of the Permanent Subcommittee on Investigation cited 106 witnesses who invoked the Fifth Amendment in public testimony, 9 who used the First Amendment to justify their refusal, 2 who claimed marital privileges, and 1 who declined to invoke any constitutional grounds for not responding. For those teachers or government employees or anyone who worked for defense contractors, exerting the right not to testify against themselves automatically cost them their jobs and branded them, in McCarthy's words, as "Fifth Amendment Communists."

McCarthy could cite both statutes and court rulings to support his contentions that recognized an almost unlimited authority of congressional investigation. After the Teapot Dome investigations, the Supreme Court had ruled in *McGrain v. Daugherty* (1927) that anyone, even a private citizen who was neither a government official nor an employee, could be compelled to testify under subpoena to a congressional committee. In *Sinclair v. U.S.* (1929), the Court further recognized the right of Congress to investigate anything remotely related to its legislative and oversight functions. In 1940 Congress passed the Alien Registration Act (known as the Smith Act for its principal author, Virginia's Representative Howard

Smith), which made it illegal to advocate overthrowing the government by force or violence. During the early Cold War years, the Justice Department used the Smith Act to initiate legal proceedings against the leaders of the Community party of the United States. The government indicted twelve of them in 1948 for having conspired to organize "as a society, group and assembly of persons who teach and advocate the overthrow and destruction of the Government of the United States by force and violence." In *Dennis v. U.S.* (1951), the Supreme Court upheld these convictions on the grounds that the government's power to prevent an armed rebellion enabled it to subordinate free speech. During the next six years, the government indicted 126 individuals solely for being members of the Communist party. Congress also passed the Mundt-Nixon Act in 1950, which barred Communist party members from employment in defense facilities, denied them passports, and required them to register with the Subversive Activities Control Board. In *Rogers v. U.S.* (1951), the Supreme Court ruled that a witness who admitted having been treasurer of a local Communist party could not claim privilege under the Fifth Amendment when asked to whom she had given her records. Her initial admission had waived her privilege, and she was guilty of contempt for failing to answer.

These rulings reinforced McCarthy's operating assumption that those who belonged to the Communist party were committed to overthrowing the government by force and violence, and that those who claimed the Fifth Amendment must be guilty of the accusations made against them. He believed that the subcommittee gave him license to interrogate anyone about any possible links to communism and that nothing could be too private or personal to escape notice. The need to uncover disloyalty, in his mind, justified all the means available, including the verbal abuse and intimidation of witnesses and the firing of suspected subversives without due process.

McCarthy's expansive charges guaranteed broad newspaper and television coverage of his public hearings, which helped build his national constituency. He adroitly manipulated reporters, providing his own summaries of the executive sessions that they could not attend and making harsh charges close to their deadlines, leaving no time for checking the facts. Most reporters also felt constrained by the rules of objective journalism, which prevented them from refuting him. Those reporters and commentators who dared to take McCarthy on could expect him to retaliate. Drew Pearson, who regularly assailed him in his newspaper columns and broadcasts, lost his radio sponsor, Adam hats, after McCarthy declared that anyone buying one of their hats was "keeping that communist spokesman on the air." Unintimidated, in 1953 and 1954 the CBS news broadcaster Edward R. Murrow devoted several episodes of his popular TV show, *See*

It Now, to McCarthy's accusations. Murrow focused most tellingly on Annie Lee Moss, an African American suspended from her job as a communications clerk at the Pentagon on the testimony of a government informer who had never met her. At a televised hearing before McCarthy's subcommittee, Moss had denied having been a communist or having attended any party meetings, although during the war she had paid dues to a cafeteria workers' union that was later accused of having communists in its leadership. The frail woman appeared perplexed over a reference to Karl Marx and seemed an unlikely espionage agent even to McCarthy, who excused himself and left midway through her testimony. The hearing, as replayed on *See It Now,* proved another public relations disaster for the subcommittee. The army reinstated Moss, shifting her to a "nonsensitive" post in its finance and accounts office.

The Army-McCarthy Hearings

In the fall of 1953, McCarthy launched an investigation of suspected espionage in the Army Signal Corps at Fort Monmouth, New Jersey. Having promised stunning revelations of a spy ring masterminded by Julius Rosenberg, the inquiry got nowhere until it stumbled on an army dentist, Irving Peress, who had been promoted and given an honorable discharge despite his failure to answer questions about his purported membership in the Communist party. "Who promoted Peress?" became McCarthy's rallying cry. At a closed hearing, the senator lost his temper with Peress's commanding officer, General Ralph Zwicker, and declared him "not fit to wear that uniform." When this attack was published, it shocked even McCarthy's friends. The usually supportive *Chicago Tribune* suggested that the senator learn to "distinguish the role of investigator from the role of avenging angel."

McCarthy's assault on the army prompted his critics to question why neither Roy Cohn nor David Schine, still in their twenties, had served in the military. In November 1953, Schine was drafted into the army as a private, and Cohn started pestering officials in the Pentagon for special privileges for his friend. Anxious to terminate the Fort Monmouth hearings before they further damaged morale, army officials made Cohn's requests public in a lengthy chronology. The charges and countercharges between the chairman and the military led to a nationally televised confrontation from March until June of 1954 known as the Army-McCarthy hearings. As a principal subject of the investigation, McCarthy had to step aside as chairman in favor of another Republican, Senator Karl Mundt. Despite having relinquished the gavel, McCarthy continued to dominate the hearings by interrupting with repeated points of order. But he met his match in the army's wily counsel, Robert Welsh, a Boston attorney who used humor, logic, and moral outrage to combat McCarthy's tactics. The hearings reached their climax when McCarthy gratuitously questioned the loyalty of one of Welsh's associates, who had not participated in the hearings because of his past membership in the National Lawyers Guild. "Have you no sense of decency, sir, at long last?" demanded Welsh. The public agreed with Welsh, and McCarthy's slide in the polls invigorated his opponents in the Senate.

After the hearings, the Vermont Republican Ralph Flanders introduced a resolution in the Senate to censure McCarthy, and the Utah Republican Arthur Watkins chaired a select committee to hear the charges. It was McCarthy's contemptuous response to his accusers — not his abusive treatment of witnesses — that enabled his colleagues to coalesce against him. In December 1954 half of the Senate's Republicans joined all but one Democrat in a vote, 67–22, to censure McCarthy for conduct unbecoming a senator. (The lone Democrat was John F. Kennedy of Massachusetts, who was hospitalized for back surgery.) McCarthy also lost his chairmanship when the Democrats regained the majority in the 1954 elections. Without an investigative vehicle, he faded from the headlines and into obscurity until his premature death in 1957.

After McCarthy

Not until McCarthy's investigations had ended did the Supreme Court intervene to restrict the government's ability to prosecute under the Smith Act and to broaden the rights of witnesses. On June 17, 1957, the liberal majority, led by Chief Justice Earl Warren, handed down a series of sweeping decisions that rebuked the investigators' presumptions. In *Yates v. U.S.* (1957), it reversed the convictions of fourteen Communist party members under the Smith Act. The Court found that joining the Communist party was not synonymous with advocating the overthrow of the government by force and violence, a ruling that convinced the Justice Department to cease further indictments under the Smith Act. In *Watkins v. U.S.* (1957), the Court bolstered the rights of witnesses by insisting that an investigating committee had to demonstrate a legislative purpose to justify probing into private affairs, that public "education" was insufficient reason to force witnesses to answer questions under the penalty of being held in contempt, and that the Bill of Rights applied to anyone subpoenaed by a congressional committee. Despite McCarthy's routine threats of imprisonment for perjury or contempt, not a single witness went to jail for testimony given to the subcommittee during his chairmanship. Although several were tried for contempt, all of their convictions were overturned on appeal.

After McCarthy, the Permanent Subcommittee on Investigations returned to its traditional focus on corruption rather than communism. Both the House Un-American Activities Committee and the Senate Internal Security Subcommittee declined in stature until they were abolished in 1975 and 1977, respectively. Congress also repealed the most restrictive anticommunist laws. Congressional investigations continued to bear the stigma of "McCarthyism" until the Watergate investigation of 1973–1974 rehabilitated their public image. Ironically, the Watergate inquiry ended the presidency of Richard Nixon, whose own national political life had begun as a congressional investigator.

The opening of American and Soviet intelligence agency archives since the Cold War have provided more evidence about the scope of Soviet espionage in the United States. The Venona transcripts verified Whittaker Chambers's testimony about underground communist cells in the federal government during the 1930s. Venona also contained the names of a handful of witnesses who appeared before McCarthy's subcommittee but included none of his principal targets. Although McCarthy's supporters justified his excesses on the grounds that he had made the public more vividly aware of the threat of international communism, the weight of evidence indicates that he seriously misled the public with his unsubstantiated charges, character assassinations, and reckless sensationalism.

— DONALD A. RITCHIE

BIBLIOGRAPHICAL NOTES

The burgeoning literature on anticommunist investigations includes David Caute, *The Great Fear: The Anticommunist Purge Under Truman and Eisenhower* (New York, 1978); Walter Goodman, *The Committee: The Extraordinary Career of the House Committee on Un-American Activities* (New York, 1968); Ted Morgan, *Reds: McCarthyism in America from Woodrow Wilson to George W. Bush* (New York, 2003); Robert P. Newman, *Owen Lattimore and the "Loss" of China* (Berkeley, Calif., 1992); Ellen Schrecker, *Many Are the Crimes: McCarthyism in America* (Boston, 1998); and Allen Weinstein, *Perjury: The Hiss-Chamber Case* (New York, 1978).

Useful essays on the Dies and McCarthy hearings are included in Arthur M. Schlesinger Jr. and Roger Bruns, eds., *Congress Investigates, 1792–1974: A Documented History* (New York, 1975). Also of value are Telford Taylor, *Grand Inquest: The Story of Congressional Investigations* (New York, 1955); Robert Griffith, *The Politics of Fear: Joseph R. McCarthy and the Senate* (Lexington, Ky., 1970); Victor

S. Navasky, *Naming Names* (New York, 1980); and the many volumes of congressional hearings and reports.

McCarthy's leading biographers are David Oshinsky, *A Conspiracy So Immense: The World of Joe McCarthy* (New York, 1983), and Thomas C. Reeves, *The Life and Times of Joe McCarthy* (New York, 1982), while Edwin R. Bayley, *Joe McCarthy and the Press* (New York, 1981), and William Bragg Ewald Jr., *Who Killed Joe McCarthy?* (New York, 1984), add important dimensions to the story. McCarthy's defenders include William F. Buckley Jr. and L. Brent Bozell, *McCarthy and His Enemies: The Record and Its Meaning* (Chicago, 1954); Roy Cohn, *McCarthy* (New York, 1968); Arthur Herman, *Joseph McCarthy: Reexamining the Life and Legacy of America's Most Hated Senator* (New York, 2000); and Ann H. Coulter, *Treason: Liberal Treachery from the Cold War to the War on Terrorism* (New York, 2003).

New revelations on Soviet spying are discussed in John Earl Haynes and Harvey Klehr, *Venona: Decoding Soviet Espionage in America* (New Haven, Conn., 1999), and Allen Weinstein and Alexander Vassiliev, *The Haunted Wood: Soviet Espionage in America — The Stalin Era* (New York, 1999).

30

The Second Reconstruction

On April 11, 1968, three hundred people gathered in the White House to witness President Lyndon Johnson sign a civil rights bill prohibiting discrimination in the sale or rental of housing. It was a bittersweet moment, for the nation was still reeling from the assassination of Martin Luther King Jr. a week earlier. Since King's death, violence had erupted in hundreds of cities; indeed, as Johnson signed the legislation, federal troops remained on patrol in the District of Columbia. Well aware of the turmoil, the president invoked the memory of the slain leader's commitment to nonviolent change. "I think we can all take some heart that democracy's work is being done," Johnson observed. "In the Civil Rights Act of 1968 America moves forward and the bell of freedom rings out a little louder." The new civil rights statute, the third since 1964, brought to a close an extraordinary period known as the Second Reconstruction.

Years of Failure, 1945–1956

As the historian Harvard Sitkoff has argued, the roots of the civil rights reforms of the 1960s lay in the 1940s. World War II helped nationalize racial issues as hundreds of thousands of African Americans moved from the rural South to the urban North, where many found work in defense-related industries. Because African Americans in the North could vote, some politicians in each major party paid at least cursory attention to their concerns. African Americans were also leaving farms in the South for its growing industrial cities, where their expectation of what was possible underwent a dramatic change. The war deepened public awareness of the nation's hypocrisy on race as many civil rights advocates pointed to the incongruity of championing ideals of freedom and democracy against Hitler's theories of white supremacy while the nation consigned African Americans to legal and social second-class status. Foreign policy boosted the civil rights cause later in the decade when proponents noted how the Soviet Union turned America's racism into propaganda. (On the other hand, opponents of civil rights used the Cold War to their advantage by denouncing racial reforms as communist inspired.) Most important, black protests took on a heightened assertiveness in this era through efforts such as the "Double V" campaign, which stressed victory over racism at home as well as triumph on the battlefield abroad. Many black soldiers returned from Asia and Europe determined to resist racial injustice. Membership in the NAACP soared by nearly four hundred thousand people during the war. In 1941 a threat by the labor activist A. Philip Randolph to stage a massive march on the nation's capital helped prompt President Franklin D. Roosevelt to issue an executive order creating a wartime federal Fair Employment Practices Committee (FEPC), to ensure equal job opportunities for minorities in firms with government contracts. A year later, the Congress of Racial Equality (CORE), a group that sought nonviolent change through direct action protests, was formed to combat injustices in the North.

Federal lawmakers remained largely immune to these trends during the 1940s and 1950s, however. Congress was firmly in control of a bipartisan coalition of southern Democrats and northern Republicans. This alliance, which had formed in the late 1930s in opposition to many of Roosevelt's economic programs and plans to reform the Supreme Court, routinely crushed any effort to address the nation's racial problems.

The Democrat Richard Russell of Georgia led the coalition. A descendant of Old South aristocracy who had entered the Senate at the age of thirty-five, Russell fiercely defended his region's racial customs. Many southern politicians, such as Senator Theodore Bilbo of Mississippi, had openly proclaimed black inferiority in opposing antilynching and other civil rights measures in the 1930s, but Russell instead emphasized abstract constitutional principles about the virtues of limited government. Such rhetoric drew numerous Republican allies who were put off by Bilbo's blunt rhetoric but were nonetheless concerned about the increased federal power that many civil rights plans would bring about. A hard-working bachelor, Russell was also a master parliamentary strategist who possessed an encyclopedic knowledge of Senate rules. The chief weapon in his arsenal was the filibuster, a practice whereby a senator, or a group of senators, would attempt to kill legislation by holding the floor, thus preventing other business from being addressed until the rest of the Senate dropped the bill under discussion. The Senate had long prized unlimited debate, and Southerners had regularly used the filibuster, or the threat of one, to block antilynching and anti–poll tax bills in the 1920s and 1930s. Senators favoring civil rights had few options. They could hope the Southerners would wear down, an unlikely event because Russell had organized a solid team of eighteen members who only had to speak every few days. They could try to invoke Rule XXII, the cloture rule, to break a filibuster, but it was nearly impossible because cloture required the approval of two-thirds of those present and voting. The near unanimity among non-Southerners needed to achieve cloture demanded a sense of commitment, organization, and discipline that did not exist.

Civil rights opponents also benefited from the seniority system, which placed the leadership of powerful congressional committees and subcommittees in the hands of the southern Democrats. Committee chairs could kill civil rights legislation by keeping it off the agenda, stretching out hearings on civil rights bills, or by not having the committee meet at all. James Eastland of Mississippi once publicly revealed how, as chair of the Senate Subcommittee on Civil Rights, he blocked civil rights proposals. "You know the law says the committee has got to meet once a week," he stated. "Why, for three years I was chairman, that committee didn't hold a meeting. I had special pockets put in my pants, and for years I carried those bills around in my pockets everywhere I went and every one of them was defeated." Much to the dismay of civil rights proponents, Eastland became head of the influential Judiciary Committee in 1956. Between 1953 and 1965, only 1 of 122 civil rights bills sent to the committee was reported back to the Senate, and that only due to specific instructions from the larger body.

A similar situation existed in the House, where the staunch segregationist Howard Smith of Virginia chaired the powerful Rules Committee. The committee guided bills to the House floor for debate by granting each a "rule." It could kill a measure simply by refusing to do so. Throughout the 1950s and early 1960s the committee was a graveyard for civil rights and other progressive legislation thanks to Smith, who often went to his farm to avoid hearings on such matters. On one occasion, he delayed a civil rights bill by claiming that the committee could not meet because he had to inspect a barn that had burned down. Speaker Sam Rayburn of Texas commented, "I knew Howard Smith would do most anything to block a civil rights bill, but I never suspected he would resort to arson."

Arrayed against these formidable obstacles stood a small, bipartisan coalition of legislators who supported civil rights. In the Senate, this group included the Democrats Hubert Humphrey of Minnesota, Paul Douglas of Illinois, and Herbert Lehman of New York, as well as the Republicans Irving Ives of New York and Wayne Morse of Oregon. (Morse became a Democrat in 1955.) In the House, strong civil rights advocates included the Democrat Emanuel Celler of New York and Republicans such as Jacob Javits of New York and Clifford Case of New Jersey. (Both

Javits and Case would carry on their fight for civil rights on their election to the Senate in 1956 and 1954, respectively.) Motivated by personal beliefs in racial equality, concern over how racial injustice damaged American foreign policy, and a desire for black votes, the members of this coalition sponsored numerous civil rights bills that routinely went down to defeat. Pro–civil rights Democrats, moreover, saw racial equality as an essential next step in New Deal reforms to ensure a more just nation. Republican advocates, meanwhile, believed that their party had to uphold the tradition of Abraham Lincoln and saw segregation and disenfranchisement as unjust, artificial barriers to individual advancement. Lacking seniority, most in the civil rights camp were on the margins of the power structure of Congress. They found few allies, as most of their non-southern colleagues, especially those from areas with few black voters, did not regard civil rights as a high priority.

These civil rights proponents appeared to receive a much-needed boost in 1948 when Harry Truman became the first president to ask Congress to enact civil rights legislation. Though Truman privately held racist views, he was genuinely appalled at the wave of violence inflicted on black veterans returning from the war, and he promptly appointed the President's Committee on Civil Rights to study racial problems. The committee endorsed a range of legislation in its October 1947 report, *To Secure These Rights,* including FEPC, an end to the poll tax, creation of a Civil Rights Division in the Justice Department, the establishment of a Civil Rights Commission, making lynching a federal crime, protecting voting rights, ensuring nondiscrimination in the use of federal funds, and the desegregation of interstate transportation. These proposals formed the basis of the civil rights legislative agenda for the next fifteen years. On February 2, 1948, Truman sent a message to Congress calling for ten civil rights reforms as outlined by the committee. Politics played a role in his decision, for he hoped to rally African Americans in the November presidential election and fend off challenges from the Republican Thomas Dewey and the Progressive Henry Wallace, both civil rights supporters.

The president's program was dead on arrival on Capitol Hill. Believing that he had sold out the loyal Democratic South to win black votes in the North, Russell and other Southerners launched a vehement attack on the president. "The orders of Joe Stalin have trickled down through his stooges right into our White House," one southern senator complained. Some Southerners talked openly of fielding a third-party candidate for president. Indeed, that July an angry group of white Southerners formed the States' Rights party, or "Dixiecrats," and nominated South Carolina's governor, Strom Thurmond, for president. Worried about losing support among Dixie voters in November and among southern legislators for his foreign policy toward the Soviet Union, Truman refused to push for his civil rights plans.

Truman won the election and Congress reverted back to Democratic control, but neither of these developments changed the civil rights situation in 1949. In January a small, bipartisan group of senators decided that the only hope of getting a civil rights bill passed was to reform Rule XXII. They pressed for cloture by a simple majority. The southern Democrats promptly launched a filibuster when the majority leader, Scott Lucas of Illinois, brought the cloture issue before the Senate. Russell eventually forced Lucas to agree to provisions that strengthened the South's hand in return for ending the filibuster. Under the final agreement, which was strongly backed by Republicans and southern Democrats, cloture could be invoked only by two-thirds of the entire Senate (64 members) instead of two-thirds of those present and voting. Cloture was also henceforth prohibited on filibusters against future attempts to reform Rule XXII. The new rules, therefore, appeared permanent. Civil rights advocates won a token victory in that the agreement allowed for cloture on motions to take up legislation (whether cloture could be invoked on a motion or only on a bill itself had been subject to dispute), but this provision still meant that two filibusters would likely have to be broken before a civil rights measure could pass the Senate.

The House did pass a bill against the poll tax in July 1949, as it had in 1945 and 1947, when Republicans joined with northern Democrats to overcome the southern opposition. The poll tax was the least controversial civil rights proposal; several southern states had repealed their poll tax laws in the 1920s and 1930s. For many Republicans, protecting the right to vote was an appropriate function of the federal government, whereas federal involvement in employment matters through FEPC was a dangerous extension of federal control over business. Once again, however, the poll tax proposal died in the Senate.

The strength of the southern Democrat–Republican coalition was evident again a year later. Worried over mounting job losses among African Americans, the NAACP and other civil rights groups lobbied their allies in Congress to press for FEPC legislation. The House approved one measure in February, but the conservative alliance ensured that its enforcement provisions had been stripped. Under the House plan, the FEPC could simply hold hearings, investigate, and make recommendations. In the Senate, meanwhile, two cloture votes failed as Southerners filibustered FEPC legislation to death that spring. Even milder bills, to make lynching a federal crime and create a Civil Rights Commission, went nowhere in each house of Congress over the next two years.

The reformers again set their sights on Rule XXII as a new Senate convened in 1953. Trying to get around the provision that forbade cloture on any motion to change the rules, they contended that Senate rules did not carry over from one Congress to another. A simple majority had formally to adopt the rules and could thus write a new Rule XXII. Conversely, the southern Democrat–Republican coalition insisted that because only one-third of all the senators were up for reelection every two years, the Senate was a continuing body, and therefore old rules carried over from one Congress to the next. The Senate flatly rejected the reform proposal, which was tabled by a 70–21 vote.

Though civil rights advocates in both the House and Senate continued to offer bills based on the Truman program, the legislation remained frozen for the next four years. There was no help from the White House, where the Republican Dwight Eisenhower remained convinced that education, not laws, would bring greater progress for African Americans. Eisenhower also did not regard civil rights as a high priority, was wary of strengthening federal power, and personally sympathized with white Southerners on many issues related to race and segregation.

The Tide Turns, 1957–1960

By 1957 several developments had coalesced to shake up the status quo. The Eisenhower administration had begun to rethink its approach to legislation late in 1955, when Attorney General Herbert Brownell drafted a civil rights bill that would create a Civil Rights Commission, establish a Civil Rights Division in the Justice Department, and enable the department to seek injunctions against civil rights violations, including voting. Brownell and others in the administration were especially troubled over the continued denial of voting rights. Violence, including the shocking murder of fourteen-year-old Emmett Till in Mississippi, was escalating across the South in the wake of courageous efforts by African Americans to register to vote and force compliance with the Supreme Court's landmark 1954 school desegregation decision, *Brown v. Board of Education.* The southern Democrats appeared to grow even more intransigent in 1956 when they issued the Southern Manifesto, which called *Brown* "a clear abuse of judicial power" and pledged to resist its implementation. Internationally, continued civil rights violations meant that the United States was suffering a public relations nightmare in its propaganda war with the Soviet Union. Racial tensions had reached new heights.

Domestic politics also played a critical role. After Eisenhower suffered a heart attack in 1955, Brownell worried that should the popular president not seek a second term, another GOP candidate would need increased black support. Eisenhower recovered and coasted to victory in 1956, but many Republicans deepened their interest in civil rights after the president increased his vote total among African Americans to 39 percent from 21 percent in 1952. Eisenhower could rightly boast of some civil rights accomplishments that included desegregation in Washington, D.C., and the armed forces as well as an effort to promote equal employment opportunity in firms with government contracts. African Americans, moreover, supported Eisenhower in part out of their anger over the continued power of the Southerners in the Democratic party. Democratic civil rights advocates viewed the election results with alarm and pressed the majority leader, Lyndon Johnson of Texas, for action. Johnson had opposed civil rights legislation since joining the Senate in 1949, but now he decided that the way to further his goal of reaching the White House was to engineer the passage of a civil rights bill. Such a move, he hoped, would boost his standing among northern liberals and remove the roadblock that had prevented a Southerner from winning the Democratic presidential nomination. Russell, who wanted Johnson to be president, understood this as well.

Signs that the momentum was shifting were evident in January 1957 when civil rights proponents in the Senate once again attempted to modify Rule XXII. They suffered defeat, but this time the vote to table the majority cloture proposal was 55–38. Five Democrats and twelve Republicans had now joined the ranks of the reformers since 1953. Three absent senators went on record in favor of majority cloture. Furthermore, Vice President Richard Nixon had helped the reformers' cause with a parliamentary ruling that a majority of the Senate could devise its rules at the start of a new Congress.

Knowing that a filibuster could derail his presidential ambitions, Johnson set out to craft a bill acceptable to both civil rights advocates and southern Democrats. Achieving such a delicate balance would require all the parliamentary skills he could muster. Russell opened the southern attack in June when he charged that the administration's measure, which Eisenhower and others had portrayed as a voting rights bill, was instead a clever trick to enforce school integration. Technically, his point was legitimate, for the bill's Title III would enable the attorney general to go to court to obtain injunctions in school cases. Eisenhower, who probably was unaware of this feature, quickly backed off, claiming that all he wanted was a voting bill. Well aware that the Republican support for Title III was eroding, Johnson then arranged for the passage of a bipartisan amendment to delete it.

The South was not appeased, however. The southern Democrats next focused on the failure of Title IV, which dealt with voting rights, to guarantee jury trials. They knew that no white jury was going to convict a white election official for keeping blacks from voting. Johnson persuaded two Democrats to sponsor a jury trial amendment, but the majority leader was in a more difficult position than he had been on Title III because there was stronger support in the Senate for voting rights than for school integration. The administration, moreover, was firmly opposed to the amendment. The South needed allies, and Johnson found some among the western Democrats, for whom civil rights was not a pressing matter. The Westerners had agreed to cooperate with the South on civil rights in exchange for southern votes on a public power measure important to their constituents. In fact, the Westerners gained little, for public power eventually died in the House. Johnson then deftly maneuvered behind the scenes to rally additional opposition, and as a result the jury amendment passed without a filibuster. Strom Thurmond of South Carolina, however, established a Senate record when, against the wishes of his fellow Southerners, he talked for twenty-four hours and eighteen minutes against the measure.

President Eisenhower signed the bill in September 1957. The first civil rights act in eighty-two years, it created a Civil Rights Commission (for two years), established a Civil Rights Division in the Justice Department, and aimed to boost black voting rights. The southern Democrats could rightly tell their constituents that they had stripped the legislation of its strongest provision and significantly weakened another. Though clearly disappointed by their defeats, civil rights advocates could also justly claim that the measure represented progress. The commission would prove to be a valuable source for documenting civil rights abuses in future years. The bill was also a tremendous symbolic breakthrough. Hubert Humphrey correctly predicted, "This is not the end of civil rights legislation. It is only the beginning."

Additional victories were not forthcoming as the racial situation in the South deteriorated during the late 1950s. Progress in school desegregation occurred only in a handful of communities in the upper South and the border states. Just days after Eisenhower signed the 1957 Civil Rights Act, he sent troops to Little Rock, Arkansas, to enforce school integration. Violence intensified across the Deep South as African Americans were murdered, beaten, or had their churches, schools, and homes burned or bombed. Civil rights proponents in both houses of Congress submitted the old Title III and legislation to offer financial and technical assistance to districts that desegregated, but these proposals stalled in committee. The southern Democrat–Republican coalition, which had temporarily crumbled in 1957, had reformed, as few in Congress were eager to revisit racial matters. The administration weakly enforced the already cumbersome voting provisions of the 1957 law, which required case-by-case adjudication, by bringing just three suits in two years. Declaring that the Civil Rights Act had failed, the Civil Rights Commission released a report in 1959 that offered a wealth of specific examples of southern chicanery on voting matters. Civil rights proponents in Congress, bolstered by the election of many supportive Democrats in the 1958 congressional elections, quickly moved that year to introduce legislation to implement the commission's proposal that voting registrars be sent to troubled areas to monitor polling places, administer election laws, and register voters. The House Rules Committee blocked the legislation. In the Senate all the civil rights forces could win was a promise from Lyndon Johnson that Congress would revisit the issue the following spring.

The ongoing turmoil in the South, as well as the upcoming presidential election, stirred interest in civil rights in both parties in 1960. But as it had three years earlier, the conservative coalition ensured that a weak measure was adopted. In 1959 the House had removed from an administration civil rights plan sections that would have created a permanent commission to ensure equal job opportunities in firms with government contracts and offered federal assistance to desegregating school districts. Attempts to add these provisions, as well as Title III, failed in the House and the Senate in 1960. The debate would thus center on voting rights.

Johnson sneaked civil rights onto the Senate agenda in February by having the Republican Everett Dirksen of Illinois offer an administration proposal based on voting referees as an amendment to an unrelated bill up for debate. The administration's plan was far weaker than the registrar proposal, for referees would be empowered only to observe polling places and report violations of voting laws; enforcement would come only on a case-by-case basis through a lengthy judicial process.

Johnson, who coveted his party's presidential nomination that year, again had to walk a fine line between northern liberals and southern segregationists. His skillful maneuver meant that the bill would not have to go to Eastland's Judiciary Committee, and irate southern Democrats immediately launched a filibuster. Johnson tried to break the filibuster by ordering round-the-clock sessions, but the Southerners held strong. They frequently made quorum calls at all hours of the day, thus giving themselves a chance to rest and deepening interest in concessions among their colleagues, some of whom had resorted to sleeping in their offices. The weary Senate rejected a cloture motion in March, 42–53, far short of the 64 votes needed. A month later both the House and Senate agreed to a bill that provided for voting referees, increased penalties for violating voting rights, and made it a federal crime to engage in interstate transportation of explosives to blow up buildings. Once again, the South had won. A voting rights bill that again featured case-by-case enforcement mechanisms posed no great threat to the racial status quo. Even some civil rights advocates publicly admitted defeat. "The bill sets up an elaborate obstacle course which the disenfranchised . . . must successfully run before he will be permitted to register at all," a dejected Paul Douglas commented.

Civil rights advocates on Capitol Hill received little help from John F. Kennedy after he became president in 1961. He too generally did not regard racial issues as a high priority. Furthermore, the Democrats had lost seats in both houses of Congress in the 1960 election, leaving the president heavily dependent on southern support for his domestic and foreign policies. Kennedy preferred to aid African Americans through executive action and broad economic programs such as increasing the minimum wage rather than waste precious political capital on a legislative fight for civil rights that he seemed certain to lose. He did join Speaker Sam Rayburn in a successful effort to reform the Rules Committee by adding three members who the president and others hoped would thwart conservative opposition to progressive legislation, but Kennedy sat on the sidelines for much of 1961 and 1962, as unsuccessful bipartisan efforts were made in Congress to reform Rule XXII, adopt Title III, and pass other long-standing civil rights proposals.

As criticism from civil rights groups mounted, Kennedy tepidly entered the legislative fray in 1962, sponsoring a constitutional amendment to outlaw the poll tax in federal elections. Whether it would meaningfully address the suffrage problem was in grave doubt, for only a few states still had poll taxes; many southern states used more devious means, such as literacy tests, to deny African Americans the franchise. The poll tax plan, which even several southern lawmakers supported, cleared Congress and in 1964 became the Twenty-fourth Amendment. Kennedy also backed a proposal to establish the completion of the sixth grade as proof of literacy in places that had a vague literacy requirement rather than detailed exams. Civil rights activists were not impressed, and the administration did not mount much of an effort to get the bill through Congress. In the Senate, the Southerners filibustered when the plan was added as an amendment to an unrelated measure. Two weeks later, a move for cloture failed badly, with just 43 senators in favor and 53 against.

The Legislative Triumphs of 1964 and 1965

The moribund legislature received a dramatic jolt in the spring of 1963. Martin Luther King Jr. and his Southern Christian Leadership Conference had targeted Birmingham, Alabama, widely regarded as the most segregated city in the nation, for a series of direct action protests in hopes of precipitating a crisis that would force federal leaders to take dramatic steps to aid blacks in the South. Since the early 1960s, direct action protests had spread quickly across Dixie. Some of the demonstrations had drawn federal attention, but as far as King and thousands of others were concerned, too little had changed. He thus began protests in Birmingham in April 1963 to end segregation in public places and promote equal employment opportunities for African Americans. The city's police chief, Eugene "Bull" Connor, responded with violence. What made Birmingham's different from other demonstrations, however, was the presence of the media. Television and newspaper cameras captured horrifying images of water cannons and police dogs being turned on demonstrators, some of them young children.

With the racial situation spinning out of control (in the ten weeks following Birmingham, there were 758 demonstrations in 75 cities in the South), pressure mounted on the national lawmakers. Republican civil rights advocates in Congress, led by Senators Jacob Javits of New York and John Sherman Cooper of Kentucky, met in early June and decided to press for broad measures to address the crisis. The president concluded that he, too, needed to act boldly. Kennedy had offered a civil rights package to Congress in February, but now he concluded that those measures were too timid. He reworked his proposals into a new plan with several components, the most important of which outlawed segregation in public accommodations (Title II) and forbade discrimination in federally assisted programs (Title VI).

The debate in Congress began that summer. Kennedy hoped that if his legislation passed the House first, the civil rights forces would gain strength for a certain fight against a Senate filibuster. Lobbyists from the NAACP and other civil rights groups brought pressure on House members to strengthen some parts of the bill and, more important, add a section forbidding employment discrimination and creating an Equal Employment Opportunity Commission (EEOC) for enforcement. Thanks in large part to the Republicans, led by William McCulloch of Ohio, such a provision was added in the Judiciary Committee. The Republicans played another important role by moving the bill along in the Rules Committee instead of taking their more customary stand of siding with the southern Democrats. As the House took up the measure in late January 1964, McCulloch worked closely with the Democrat Emanuel Celler to engineer the defeat of nearly every crippling southern amendment. One important amendment, offered by Howard Smith, did pass. The Virginian tried to sink the bill by proposing that its equal employment provisions apply to women as well as men, but his plan backfired. Just nine days into debate, the House approved the measure, 290–130. The key to success had been the shift in loyalties among the Republicans: 138 Republicans backed the legislation, with just 34 opposed.

The battle now moved to the Senate. The NAACP and other civil rights groups feared a repeat of previous civil rights debates, in which the Southerners were able to force significant concessions in return for halting their filibuster. All eleven cloture attempts that had been made on previous civil rights measures had failed. Russell's forces began a filibuster when the legislation came before the Senate in March. The bill, they claimed, was an unwarranted — and unconstitutional — increase in federal power. They concentrated their fire on Title II, which prohibited segregation in public accommodations, and Title VII, which forbade employment discrimination. Both provisions, the Southerners insisted, violated private property rights. Title VII, they also contended, would promote hiring quotas and lead to reverse discrimination against whites.

Civil rights advocates were determined not to retreat, however. Following the assassination of Kennedy in November 1963, President Lyndon Johnson publicly called on Congress to pass the civil rights measure as a memorial to the slain leader. Johnson knew that a strong civil rights bill would cement his legitimacy as president. His administration had also promised McCulloch that it would not weaken the House legislation. Moreover, the forces for civil rights in Congress were far better organized than they had been. Johnson had given Hubert Humphrey the task of getting the bill through the Senate. Humphrey, with the assistance of the Republican Thomas Kuchel of California, assigned several senators from each party to produce several colleagues for quorum calls, a favorite delaying tactic employed by the Southerners. Two senators, one from each party, were assigned to take responsibility for each section of the legislation and rebut southern arguments in Congress and the media. Humphrey and Kuchel also developed a daily newsletter for each senator. It helped the senators keep abreast of developments related to the bill and to counter opposing points. Humphrey attempted to shape public opinion by urging celebrities, such as the actor Marlon Brando, to talk favorably about the measure and by meeting with several religious leaders. To Humphrey, religious groups were vital to swaying midwestern Republicans and western Democrats, both of whom had sided with the Southerners in the past. Humphrey and Kuchel convened daily strategy meetings attended by several senators, Justice Department officials, and representatives from the Leadership Conference on Civil Rights (LCCR), an umbrella organization comprising seventy-four groups.

Achieving cloture, Humphrey and Johnson knew, meant gaining the support of the minority leader, Everett Dirksen. The Illinois senator had been elected as a midwestern isolationist committed to smaller government, but since then he had moved in a more moderate direction. Though he had voted for the 1957 and 1960 Civil Rights Acts, Dirksen had not been a member of the small bipartisan group that most strongly supported civil rights. If he favored cloture, however, other midwestern Republicans would presumably follow. Getting Dirksen would not be easy, for he had expressed doubts about the increased federal powers in Titles II and VII. As the filibuster dragged on into May, Humphrey and Justice Department officials met with Dirksen to hammer out a compromise. On Title II, Dirksen favored allowing the Justice Department to file suits only when a widespread "pattern or practice" of discrimination in public accommodations occurred. This ensured that the title was aimed at the South. Dirksen also demanded that the EEOC not be allowed to file suits on behalf of individuals claiming discrimination. Instead, it would only sue where a widespread "pattern or practice" of discrimination existed. Dirksen also wanted the EEOC to defer to state or local fair employment agencies to see if a dispute could initially be settled there. Viewing these as relatively harmless modifications, Humphrey and the Justice Department officials agreed to them, rejecting several other Dirksen proposals.

As summer approached, the civil rights debate reached its culmination. With the galleries packed to capacity, the Senate voted on June 10 to apply cloture, 71–29. Forty-four Democrats and 27 Republicans favored the move, while 23 Democrats and 6 Republicans opposed. In an especially poignant moment, the Democrat Clair Engle of California, who was unable to speak due to cancer, was wheeled into the chamber and, when his name was called, pointed to his eye three times. "I guess that means aye," the clerk stated. The seventy-five-day filibuster, the longest in Senate history, was over. It was only the sixth time ever that cloture had been voted, and it was the first success in twelve attempts on a civil rights bill. The near unanimous support of the western Democrats and midwestern Republicans was essential to the victory. Several developments prompted their support. First, public opinion across the nation was firmly behind the bill. Johnson, moreover, had engaged in some last-minute lobbying to bring a few western Democrats, such as Howard Cannon of Nevada, on board. Church groups had also played a vital role. Finally, Dirksen's support was crucial. He was sympathetic to the plight of southern blacks, and he did not want the Republicans to be tagged as a party opposed to civil rights. Nine days later, the galleries erupted in applause as the Senate approved the bill, 73–27. Forty-six Democrats and 27 Republicans backed it, while 21 Democrats and just 6 members of the GOP voted against it. Johnson signed the measure into law on July 2.

The 1964 Civil Rights Act certainly did not solve all of the nation's racial problems, but it stands as one of the most significant acts of Congress in the twentieth century. Title II ended segregation in public accommodations. "White Only" and "Colored Only" signs came down across Dixie in short order. Title VI, which forbade discrimination in programs receiving federal money, gave the federal government a powerful weapon that helped reshape numerous institutions over the next several decades. The outlawing of employment discrimination by race, sex, age, and ethnicity helped ensure greater economic opportunities for millions of people.

Though the law contained a section on voting rights, the southern states, especially those in the Deep South, still effectively blocked African Americans from the ballot. Hoping to create another confrontation that would draw federal attention to this problem, Martin Luther King Jr. targeted Selma, Alabama, for a direct action campaign in the spring of 1965. The pace of black voter registration there, King pointed out, was so slow that it would take 103 years to register the county's eligible African Americans. On March 7 five hundred people began to march from Selma to Montgomery, the state capital, to dramatize the appalling situation. Police officers and state troopers brutally attacked the peaceful marchers with tear gas, nightsticks, and electric cattle prods. The media again captured the dramatic images for the world to see. One Sunday evening, ABC interrupted its Sunday-evening movie, *Judgment at Nuremburg,* for a report on the developments in Selma.

Vowing that "we shall overcome," Johnson sent strong voting rights legislation to Congress ten days later. The president faced a legislature far more favorable to civil rights than ever before, for the triumph of many liberal Democrats in the North and West in the 1964 congressional elections had reduced the power of the South on Capitol Hill. Whereas voting rights customarily had been enforced through the courts, which had resulted in long delays, Johnson's plan relied more on the executive branch. The bill contained an automatic trigger device, which would dispatch federal registrars to counties that used a literacy test and where less than a majority of the eligible voters were registered or had voted in the 1964 presidential election. Literacy tests would be suspended in such areas. This provision applied to several states in the Deep South where the voting rights abuses had been most flagrant. In addition, the federal government had to approve of future changes to the voting laws in affected areas to ensure that they were not discriminatory.

There was solid bipartisan support in Congress for a voting measure; Johnson's bill had 66 cosponsors when it was introduced in the Senate on March 18. The southern Democrats objected on the grounds that the plan was unconstitutional because it stripped the states of their rights to qualify voters. The Southerners did engage in a filibuster, but it lacked the fury of their 1964 effort. Richard Russell was absent because he was recovering from surgery, and several others were also ill or quite elderly. Some Southerners conceded, as a few had in the past, that it was much tougher to oppose a voting bill than other civil rights measures. As a result, the fight centered on how to strengthen the president's proposal. A bipartisan coalition, led by Javits and the Democrat Edward Kennedy of Massachusetts, failed in its effort to include a ban on state and local poll taxes. Even some civil rights advocates, such as Attorney General Nicholas deBelleville Katzenbach, opposed this move, fearing that the courts would find it unconstitutional. Cloture was approved, 70–30, on May 25, just twenty-five days into the debate. Some 47 Democrats joined 23 Republicans for cloture, with 21 Democrats and 9 Republicans against. A day later the Senate passed the bill, 77–19. The House approved a poll tax ban and passed its version of the bill, 333–85, on July 9. A conference committee removed the poll tax provision in favor of a declaration opposing state and local poll taxes and instructions that the attorney general challenge such laws in court. The conference bill included strengthening measures such as enabling a federal court to suspend all literacy tests, not just those found to discriminate, in an area where the attorney general had brought a voting rights suit. The final version, which 43 Southerners approved, easily passed both houses. Johnson signed the Voting Rights Act into law on August 6.

As the historian Steven Lawson has noted, black activism and vigorous enforcement by the federal government over the next several years led to sweeping changes in the South. Black registration in five southern states jumped by 40 percent the first five months the law was in effect. By 1969 approximately three-fifths of all the African Americans in the South were registered. Change was most dramatic in the Deep South. Just 6.7 percent of the eligible African Americans were registered in Mississippi in 1964, but four years later the number rose to 59.4 percent. Blacks in Alabama experienced similar gains.

The Battle over Fair Housing: Civil Rights in the North

Johnson followed up the victories of 1964 and 1965 with a multifaceted civil rights proposal in 1966. To deal with the continuing violence against civil rights activists in the South, the president asked Congress to strengthen criminal statutes, forbid discrimination in jury selection for federal trials, and boost the attorney general's ability to sue to promote school integration. Sensitive to a burgeoning racial crisis in the North, Johnson also urged Congress to outlaw discrimination in the sale or rental of housing. Access to quality housing in integrated neighborhoods, many civil rights lobbyists contended, would lead to better educational and employment opportunities for northern blacks trapped in decaying ghettos.

Whether Congress would approve the president's plan was very much in doubt, however. The lawmakers faced a far different national mood in 1966. Sympathy for the civil rights movement had been high after the brutal attacks on peaceful demonstrators, but now, after the riots in the Watts section of Los Angeles in 1965 and the ongoing violence in the South and elsewhere, the public was far less supportive. Many whites in the North worried that Title VII meant African Americans were going to take their jobs. Housing, as the historian Denton Watson has pointed out, was an especially sensitive issue, for it stirred white fears of integrated neighborhoods and declining home values.

It was no surprise, therefore, that the president's civil rights package ran into stiff resistance on Capitol Hill. Predictably, the southern Democrats opposed the plan, but a clear sign of trouble emerged when Dirksen flatly rejected it due to concerns over the housing and jury provisions. Even some northern Democrats in the House, fearful of angry white constituents, were troubled over the housing issue and voted for a crippling amendment, offered by the Republican Charles Mathias of Maryland, that allowed for broad exemptions to the ban on housing discrimination. The House added an amendment that made it a crime to travel across state lines to incite or support a riot and then passed the weakened measure on August 9. The southern Democrats filibustered when the bill came up in the Senate a month later. Two cloture attempts failed.

Johnson offered his civil rights package a year later, but again he faced strong obstacles. The opposition to civil rights, especially housing, had played a critical role in some of the 1966 elections, which included the defeat of the staunch civil rights advocate Paul Douglas and the triumph of many conservative Republicans in the House. Johnson's plan dropped the provisions for empowering the attorney general to initiate desegregation and added a section adding cease-and-desist powers to the EEOC, but the legislation, which was split into individual pieces to try to ease the passage of its less controversial sections, went nowhere. The House passed a measure to protect civil rights workers in the South as well as an antiriot bill, while the Senate approved legislation eliminating discrimination in jury selection. Neither chamber acted on the housing issue, which was the chief concern of civil rights activists. Clarence Mitchell, the NAACP's top legislative lobbyist, had become so frustrated by the lack of progress that he publicly said that Dirksen had replaced Eastland as "the greatest single roadblock to civil rights legislation."

As a new legislative session opened in 1968, few political observers expected Congress to move on civil rights. The white backlash had intensified in the wake of the enormously destructive riots in Newark and Detroit during the previous summer, and the lawmakers seemed reluctant to take up such a controversial measure as housing during an election year. Many legislators from both parties viewed new civil rights laws as unwarranted rewards for rioters.

The pundits were proved wrong. Thanks to intense lobbying by Mitchell and the LCCR, a bipartisan group of senators, led by the Democrat Walter Mondale of Minnesota and the Republican Edward Brooke of Massachusetts, decided to attach an open housing amendment to the bill passed in the House protecting civil rights workers. The southern Democrats began a filibuster. Two cloture votes failed, but the close nature of the outcomes, coupled with the fact that a majority of Republicans supported cloture in opposition to their leader Dirksen, convinced the civil rights proponents to press ahead. Bowing to pressure from his fellow Republicans, Dirksen hammered out a housing compromise with Mondale. When a third cloture attempt on March 1 came up short by just 4 votes, the Johnson administration intensified its lobbying efforts. Three days later cloture was achieved with precisely two-thirds of the Senate, 65 members, favoring ending the filibuster and 32 opposing. The Senate adopted the bill, 71–20, a week later.

Attention now shifted to the House. The Republicans were divided. The minority leader Gerald Ford of Michigan favored sending the bill to a conference committee, where it would likely be weakened. On the other hand, a coalition of northern Republicans, led by Charles Goodell of New York and Albert Quie of Minnesota, wanted simply to adopt the Senate version. The latter prevailed. Across the aisle, Speaker John McCormack of Massachusetts called for the quick approval of the measure to blunt the effects of an intense lobbying campaign from the real estate industry, which strongly opposed the Senate bill. This effort failed, as on April 10 the House passed the Senate measure intact, 250–172. The tragic murder of Martin Luther King Jr. just a few days earlier may also have helped push some representatives into the affirmative column. Lobbyists for the real estate industry had been convinced they had enough votes before King's assassination to send the bill to a conference committee, where it would likely have been weakened. The Civil Rights Act of 1968 outlawed discrimination in the sale or rental of 80 percent of the nation's housing by 1970, provided criminal penalties for those who interfered with individuals exercising their civil rights, created federal penalties for those engaged in interstate activities to start or promote riots, and guaranteed constitutional rights to Native Americans.

Congress and Civil Rights

Compared to the other two branches of the federal government, Congress had been slow to address racial matters. Its efforts, moreover, left unsolved many of the nation's racial problems. Nevertheless, in a span of four years it had accomplished much that would reshape the nation. In the South, legal segregation finally died. African Americans were at last able to exercise their right to vote, thus setting the stage for the election of thousands of black officials across the region in the decades ahead. The Democratic party, which had led the fight against civil rights, now appealed for black ballots, while many whites, angry over the civil rights laws, became Republicans.

The impact of Congress's action extended far beyond Dixie. The federal government now had an agency, the EEOC, to combat employment discrimination across the nation. Title VI of the 1964 Civil Rights Act reshaped education and many other programs receiving federal funds to open doors of opportunity for minorities. The housing provisions of the 1968 law helped integrate neighborhoods.

Even Congress itself felt the effects of the civil rights revolution. The election of more African Americans to Congress, many from the South, boosted the membership of the Congressional Black Caucus. Rule XXII was finally modified in 1975 to allow for cloture by three-fifths of the Senate. Civil rights, moreover, helped weaken the seniority system in the 1950s; Lyndon Johnson, in an effort to boost his presidential ambitions, went against Senate tradition by naming younger northern liberals to important committees.

The civil rights victories of the 1960s were far from inevitable. Broad structural forces and heroic direct action protests by African Americans set the stage, but Congress, too, helped bring about the Second Reconstruction and gave it its particular characteristics. The small civil rights coalition during the 1940s and 1950s shaped proposals that eventually became law. Rather than rubber-stamp what Presidents Kennedy and Johnson had favored, the legislative branch strengthened the 1964, 1965, and 1968 statutes in important ways. Skillful leadership prevented the opponents of civil rights from watering down those measures significantly, as they had done in 1957 and 1960. As a result, the nation made long overdue but important strides toward fulfilling its democratic promise.

— Timothy N. Thurber

BIBLIOGRAPHICAL NOTES

Several works examine the legislative history of civil rights laws. The 1957 and 1960 Civil Rights Acts are explored in J. W. Anderson, *Eisenhower, Brownell, and the Congress: The Tangled Origins of the Civil Rights Bill of 1956–1957* (Tuscaloosa, Ala., 1964), and Daniel Berman, *A Bill Becomes a Law: The Civil Rights Act of 1960* (New York, 1962). On the 1964 Act, see Charles and Barbara Whalen, *The Longest Debate: A Legislative History of the 1964 Civil Rights Act* (Washington, D.C., 1985); Robert Loevy, *To End All Segregation: The Politics of the Passage of the 1964 Civil Rights Act* (Lanham, Md., 1990); and Robert Mann, *The Walls of Jericho: Lyndon Johnson, Hubert Humphrey, Richard Russell, and the Struggle for Civil Rights* (New York, 1996). No book looks solely at the legislative history of the Voting Rights Act, but the law itself and earlier efforts to win the franchise are covered in Steven Lawson's *Black Ballots: Voting Rights in the South, 1944–1969* (New York, 1976). Lawson's *Running for Freedom* (Philadelphia, 1991) offers a broad overview of black politics since World War II. David Garrow's *Protest at Selma* (New Haven, Conn., 1978) looks at the Selma crisis, the efforts to pass the Voting Rights Act, and early implementation of the law. Likewise, there is no single book on the 1968 Civil Rights Act, but Denton Watson's *Lion in the Lobby: Clarence Mitchell Jr.'s Struggle for the Passage of Civil Rights Laws* (Lanham, Md., 2002) chronicles the efforts of the NAACP lobbyist on behalf of that and other civil rights bills.

Historians have also examined the careers of several legislators who were closely tied to the battle over civil rights. Timothy Thurber's *The Politics of Equality* (New York, 1999) traces Hubert Humphrey's involvement with racial issues from the 1940s through the 1970s, while Gilbert Fite's biography *Richard B. Russell, Jr.: Senator from Georgia* centers on the leader of the southern opposition. Byron Hulsey's *Everett Dirksen and His Presidents* (Lawrence, Kans., 2000) touches on the efforts of the Illinois Republican.

Congress plays a significant role in several works on presidents and civil rights. On the 1940s, see William Berman, *The Politics of Civil Rights During the Truman Administration* (Columbus, Ohio, 1970), and Donald McCoy and David Ruetten, *Quest and Response: Minority Right and the Truman Administration* (Lawrence, Kans., 1973). Robert Burk, *The Eisenhower Administration and Black Civil Rights* (Knoxville, Tenn., 1984), is the most thorough treatment of the Eisenhower years. Carl Brauer, *John F. Kennedy and the Second Reconstruction* (New York, 1977), explores civil rights during the New Frontier. Mark Stern, *Calculating Visions: Kennedy, Johnson, and Civil Rights* (New Brunswick, N.J., 1992), looks at both Kennedy and Lyndon Johnson. Robert Dallek's two-volume biography of LBJ, *Lone Star Rising* (New York, 1992) and *Flawed Giant* (New York, 1998), offers important insights into Johnson as both Senate leader and president. Similarly, Robert Caro's *Master of the Senate* (New York, 2002) covers Johnson as majority leader and includes a detailed account of the enactment of the 1957 Civil Rights Act.

31

The Warren Court and the Political Process

IN JUNE 1964, the United States Supreme Court handed down major cases dealing with legislative districting. Sitting in the courtroom, the *New York Times* reporter Anthony Lewis passed Solicitor General Archibald Cox a note asking him how it felt "to be present at the second American Constitutional Convention." Cox, who had argued for the plaintiffs and won, nevertheless understood the revolutionary nature of the decisions and responded "awful." Many politicians joined Cox in feeling that the Court had overstepped its bounds by inserting itself into what had previously been a legislative prerogative.

For more than 170 years under the Constitution, state legislatures drew both their own district lines and congressional district lines without any interference. Furthermore, after the ballots were cast and the votes counted, the legislatures then determined who was the rightful winner in contested elections. These were entirely matters of legislative prerogative, and any outside body that was part of the process acted only because the legislature itself authorized the participation. The legislatures jealously guarded these basic prerogatives, and neither the executive nor judicial branch of government interfered.

Under Chief Justice Earl Warren, the Supreme Court transformed the relationship between the legislative and judicial branches. The Court claimed the right to interfere in the creation of congressional districts as well as those of state legislatures. This unsettled incumbents, who were far more enamored than the Court with the status quo because it preserved their grip on power. They were chilled by the hopes of reformers that "one person, one vote," as the Court found the Constitution mandated, would help prevent partisan gerrymandering and therefore would create competitive districts with greater legislative turnover. Ironically, since most congressional districts had stood for decades, the Court's decisions virtually invited gerrymandering, and this in turn accelerated the trend of creating "safe" congressional districts. An unanticipated consequence, however, was that the decisions, when combined with the effects of the Voting Rights Act, would end the dominance of the Democratic party in the South and therefore make the Democrats more liberal and the Republicans more conservative.

The "Political Questions Doctrine"

Before the Warren Court, the Court had explained its belief in avoiding these legislative questions through its so-called political questions doctrine. It believed that some types of disputes were simply not appropriate for judges to resolve. In the 1840s, for instance, because of the Dorr Rebellion, there were two governments in Rhode Island claiming to be the legitimate one; the Court refused to choose. In the twentieth century the Court ducked issues relating to whether a declaration of war was required for the commitment of troops in the wars in Korea and Vietnam. Similarly, it consistently refused to determine what an appropriate legislative district would be.

This political questions doctrine protected both politicians and courts. It protected the politicians by recognizing their historic prerogatives and allowing them to continue without judicial interference. It simultaneously protected the courts by keeping them away from issues that were thought so politically charged that political retaliation against the judiciary might occur. Such retaliation could threaten the independence of the judiciary and therefore the rule of law.

By 1960 the conclusion that the political questions doctrine barred courts from deciding issues of legislative districting was colliding with the stark realities of the population imbalance between rural and urban districts and the resulting inability of state legislatures or Congress to deal with pressing urban issues. The dominance of rural districts resulted in the election of state legislative officials who favored these voters. Many conservative state machines, moreover, tended to protect the districts of their representatives. The result was an entrenched status quo. Despite state constitutions requiring redistricting every ten years, most congressional districts had not been redrawn since 1930, and a number of state legislatures had not been touched since the turn of the century. Voters in states without the ballot initiative were helpless to change the districts that had become obsolete because of the population's movement to cities and their suburbs. These districts existed everywhere — Alabama, California, Connecticut, Illinois, Tennessee, to name some of the worst.

Under the leadership of Chief Justice Warren, a former three-time California governor and the 1948 Republican vice-presidential candidate, the Supreme Court took a first step toward changing the situation in *Baker v.*

Carr (1962). This case, involving Tennessee (one of the states that had not touched its legislative districts since 1901), concluded that the political questions doctrine properly understood did not bar the courts from hearing cases involving legislative districts. Although earlier cases had concluded that there was just no way to tell a properly drawn district from an unconstitutional one, *Baker v. Carr* asserted that such a standard existed and, indeed, was well known (although the Court did not say what it was); therefore, the courts could safely act. Implicit in the decision was the idea that a democracy includes the right to fair representation in one's government. President John F. Kennedy made it explicit when he praised the Court's decision: "The right to fair representation and to have each vote count equally is, it seems to me, basic to the successful operation of a democracy."

The Reaction to Baker v. Carr

Everyone understood that *Baker v. Carr* meant that overrepresented rural districts would be forced to cede some political power to more populous areas. Most political observers, including the justices themselves, assumed that ending rural dominance would necessarily mean that a more liberal, urban-oriented legislative body would emerge. Thus it was no wonder that northern Democrats like Kennedy were so supportive of the Court. What many observers had not taken fully into account, however, was the explosive growth of suburbs after World War II. The suburbs, too, were shortchanged by the existing apportionment, and their voters were Republicans. Thus Kennedy's likely 1964 Republican opponent, Senator Barry Goldwater of Arizona, also praised *Baker v. Carr* and its promise to equalize voters in legislative districts.

Southern politicians were exceptions to those celebrating *Baker v. Carr.* They were from states that largely prevented African Americans from voting. Furthermore, these states had long political memories and associated Republicans with the Reconstruction era after the Civil War and the folly of African American legislatures. As a result, in the first half of the twentieth century the Republicans had never been competitive, and the South was controlled exclusively by the Democrats. This led to legislators from the South who had seniority that dwarfed that of their northern colleagues, who had to face opposition at the polls.

Anything that challenged the way states ran elections threatened southern politicians in three ways. First, it might put their own seats at risk by changing the conservative rural districts and the political machines that protected them. Second, it could imply that the federal government could do something about the systematic disenfranchisement of

African Americans. Third, *Baker v. Carr* looked like one more attack by a liberal Supreme Court intent on undermining the integrity of the South (which southern politicians understood to mean white supremacy).

For southern politicians, *Baker v. Carr* was a second instance of the Supreme Court's interfering with white supremacy. The first was *Brown v. Board of Education* (1954), in which the Court held "separate but equal" schools unconstitutional. *Brown* stood for much more, however, as everyone understood that it also held white supremacy unconstitutional. In 1956 Senators Richard Russell of Georgia, Harry F. Byrd of Virginia, and Strom Thurmond of South Carolina wrote the "Southern Manifesto," whereby most of the elected representatives from the South called for defying the Court's ruling in *Brown*. Speaking again for the South, Russell blasted *Baker v. Carr* as yet "another major assault on our constitutional system. If the people truly value their freedom they will demand that the Congress curtail and limit the jurisdiction being exercised by the Court." Russell was prescient. *Baker v. Carr* and its aftermath, when coupled with the enfranchisement of African Americans under the Voting Rights Act of 1965, transformed southern politics.

"One Person, One Vote"

Immediately after *Baker v. Carr* was decided, President Kennedy had an opportunity to replace two of the more conservative members of the Court, and he selected Byron R. White and Arthur J. Goldberg to fill the vacancies. Goldberg, by far the more liberal of the two, created a five-justice liberal majority on the Court. With Warren, Hugo L. Black, William O. Douglas, and William J. Brennan, Goldberg turned a modestly liberal body into the most liberal Supreme Court in American history, one that had no affection for "federalism" when local elites were thwarting national values. It did not bode well for rural America, for this liberal majority came together just in time to decide seven cases that fleshed out the full implications of *Baker v. Carr*. These implications dealt with "vote dilution." The Court defined this problem as the inequality existing when one citizen's vote is not as important as another's just because of where they live. In the simplest terms, a voter in a district with 100 people has twice the opportunity to influence the outcome of an election as a voter in a district with 200 people. A perfect districting, without vote dilution, would be two districts of 150 each.

The most important case after *Baker v. Carr* was *Reynolds v. Sims* (1964) from Alabama, which, like Tennessee, had not touched its legislative districts since the turn of the century. *Reynolds* begins with a homage to the right to vote: "Since the right to exercise the franchise in a free and unimpaired manner is preservative of the basic civil and political rights, any alleged infringement of the right of citizens must be carefully and meticulously scrutinized." With an emphasis on *meticulous,* the Court held that the Equal Protection Clause of the Fourteenth Amendment required "one person, one vote" in equal population districts.

With the exception of racial cases, the equal protection doctrine had previously accorded legislatures reasonable flexibility in reaching solutions, and most observers thought *Baker v. Carr* would too. A consensus existed that the Court would hold excessive imbalances unconstitutional but allow some population disparities when the legislature had a reason for their existence. That, however, misjudged how seriously the now highly liberal Court took "one person, one vote." "Legislators represent people, not trees or acres. Legislators are elected by voters, not farms or cities or economic interests." *Reynolds* held that to be constitutional, districts should approach precisely equal population. "Since the achieving of fair and effective representation for all citizens is concededly the aim of legislative apportionment, we conclude that the Equal Protection Clause guarantees the opportunity for equal participation by all voters in the election of state legislators."

Reynolds then proceeded to drop a bombshell that surprised virtually everyone. *Both* houses of a state legislature must be apportioned on the "one person, one vote" basis. States were constitutionally forbidden — by the Equal Protection Clause — from adopting the example of the United States Senate and having one chamber that represented economic or geographic interests or existing jurisdictional boundaries. The unstated reason for this conclusion was that if urban problems were to be addressed by state legislatures, a rural veto in any chamber had to be eliminated.

Forbidding a state from copying the national government, with an upper chamber apportioned with no concern for population numbers, was both an attack on former state prerogatives and a verbal slap at the Senate. The Court had already directed a real blow at the House in *Wesberry v. Sanders* earlier in 1964. *Wesberry* invalidated Georgia's unequal congressional districts where Atlanta's district was more than twice as populous as the next largest one. Relying on the theretofore uninterpreted language of Article I, section 2, of the Constitution — that members of the House were to be chosen "by the People of the several States" — the Court concluded that "by the People" meant that the congressional districts in each state must have equal population. About 400 of the 435 districts in the nation failed to meet this standard: 37 states had population disparities of more than 100,000 people between districts.

The other cases were not as explosive but nevertheless maintained the authoritative tone of *Reynolds* and *Wesberry*. The Court held (1) that states could not elect a governor by a mechanism that was roughly parallel to the electoral college used to elect the American president (*Gray v. Sanders,* 1963); (2) that voters, even by solid majorities, were not free to change any of the outcomes of *Reynolds, Wesberry,* or *Gray* (*Lucas v. 44th Colorado General Assembly,* 1964); and (3) that federal courts were not to countenance delay in redistricting as they had "with all deliberate speed" in school desegregation (*Reynolds*). While it was impossible to draw new lines for the 1964 elections (to be held in a little more than four months), redistricting should be in place by 1966.

The Reaction in the House of Representatives

Both the House and the Senate immediately began their efforts to restrict the Court's decisions, thereby revealing the great threat presented to many members of the Congress. The House, pushed by Representative William Tuck, a former governor of Virginia, considered using the textually explicit grant to Congress of the power to define the jurisdiction of the federal courts to preclude them from hearing any cases dealing with reapportionment. Jurisdiction stripping, as it was known, was a draconian remedy and rarely attempted. If the federal courts had no jurisdiction over reapportionment, then they could not order the dismantling of state senates or, more important, congressional districts.

Brooklyn's Emanuel Celler led the opposition to jurisdiction stripping. Celler represented a middle-class Jewish district and was already a twenty-term congressman (on his way to a fifty-year career). Therefore he was that rare Northerner with a committee chairmanship, in this case that of the House Judiciary Committee. Celler, like other northern liberals, was highly supportive of the Warren Court because it had proven to be the most liberal branch of the federal government. Celler called the jurisdiction-stripping proposal the product of "deliberations of angry men, irate men," as well as "a rather vicious attack upon the Supreme Court." Tuck, for his part, defended the bill as necessary to "preserve the Constitution of the United States, already bleeding from assaults made upon it by the Supreme Court."

Many legislators liked Tuck's proposal because it would protect them. Under *Wesberry,* a number of heretofore safe congressional seats were likely to be contested with the result that some members of the House could expect to be unemployed in the near future. Few things focus the political mind so well as a prospective loss of power, and Tuck's jurisdiction-stripping bill passed the House, 218–175, in mid-August.

The Reaction in the Senate

The passage of the Tuck Bill in the House shifted action to the Senate, where the critical person was the conservative Republican minority leader, Everett McKinley Dirksen. He was colorful and witty – coining the now well-known statement that "a billion here, a billion there, and pretty soon you're talking about real money" – with curly silver locks and a honey-coated voice. In 1964 Dirksen was at the height of his power and prestige because he had guided the Senate Republicans to join with northern Democrats in the first successful cloture vote against a southern civil rights filibuster. With Lyndon Johnson and Hubert H. Humphrey, Dirksen was one of the three most important players in the enactment of the Civil Rights Act of 1964.

Dirksen proposed a two-year moratorium on the implementation of *Reynolds,* hoping that during the delay, the Constitution could be amended to authorize one legislative chamber to be based on a nonpopulation basis should a state so choose. Compared to the House bill, his moratorium proposal was quite mild, and it was substantive, not purely a job protection bill like Tuck's. Dirksen's moratorium had no chance of getting through the Judiciary Committee in the little time remaining in the session, so he attached it as a rider to a foreign aid bill. But liberals wanted neither Dirksen's moratorium nor Tuck's end of federal intervention. Despite a long-standing opposition to the filibuster as a legislative tactic (because Southerners had always used it against civil rights), liberals adopted it and prevailed. Eventually the Senate compromised on a "sense of Congress" resolution, 44–38, that federal courts should give legislatures one legislative session plus thirty days to comply with future court orders. The House found the tepid Senate response so unsatisfactory that it chose to do nothing rather than accede to the Senate's position.

Dirksen, as his colleague Birch Bayh of Indiana noted, "was deadly serious" about giving states the opportunity to have one house apportioned on a nonpopulation basis. In no small part, his reasons flowed from his being from central Illinois, and *Reynolds* meant a substantial transfer of power to Chicago. Given the corrupt Democratic machine that ran Chicago, Dirksen simply could not fathom granting it additional power in Illinois politics. Furthermore, he believed that the analogy to the Senate was not only good for his home state but for the nation as well. Dirksen's Illinois counterpart, the Democratic senator Paul Douglas, a former economics professor at the University of Chicago, disagreed. Like Celler in the House, Douglas was an enthusiastic supporter of the Warren Court, and he led the senators opposing any actions to undo the reapportionment decisions (although he, too, disliked the corrupt Chicago machine).

In the new Congress, Dirksen sought to undo *Reynolds* by constitutional amendment. By January 1965 he had thirty-seven cosponsors. Those opposing the amendment did so for one or more of three reasons: first, they respected the Warren Court too much to challenge it; second, they claimed that *Reynolds* was a proper interpretation of the Constitution; and third, even if *Reynolds* went too far, malapportioned legislatures ought not be allowed to draw up plans to perpetuate themselves. After the bill had languished for six months in the Judiciary Committee, Dirksen attached his proposal to a measure already on the floor, a bill to proclaim National American Legion Baseball Week. Although Dirksen had softened his proposal to mandate that all ratifications had to come from legislatures already apportioned on a population basis, he still could not get the necessary two-thirds vote in the Senate. Southerners and rural senators provided the bulk of his 57 votes, but 39 were opposed, and he was 7 short of the necessary two-thirds majority.

Dirksen refused to give in, tying up Senate business until he was promised that the Judiciary Committee would allow another vote the following spring. That vote was a virtually identical 55–38, and time was now truly running out as legislatures or courts created new districts to comply with *Reynolds* and *Wesberry*. In the last gasp of the old order, a number of states attempted to implement, for the first time in American history, the part of Article V that provides that two-thirds of the states could "call" for a constitutional convention. There were numerous legal difficulties with it, not the least of which was whether any convention could be limited to topics in the "call," but the number of states involved peaked at thirty-two in 1967, and not all were "calling" for the same amendment — indeed, several dated to 1963. Some were proposals to overturn *Baker*, and the most extreme one hoped to make the fifty state chief justices a final court of review to rule on Supreme Court cases dealing with state powers.

The Effects of the Reapportionment Decisions

The problem for those hoping to reverse *Reynolds* was that the federal analogy had never caught on, and as states came rapidly into compliance with *Reynolds*, there was neither a public outcry to return to the past nor a desire of the newly elected to return to private life. *Wesberry* and *Reynolds* had created self-fulfilling prophesies. Once their mandates were complied with, the objections to the decisions largely vanished because, on the one hand, those objecting most were redistricted out of office and, on the other hand, in the conclusion of the historian David Kyvig, the principles of *Reynolds* "rapidly became embedded in the national sense of democratic values." *Reynolds* thus went from debatable in 1964 to unquestionable in 1968. The reapportionment expert Robert McKay stated then that "the mood, even among politicians, is that the decisions are acceptable; the accommodations have largely been made."

In the short run the Democrats gained from *Wesberry* and *Reynolds*. The state legislatures had no time to respond until 1965, and then, because of Lyndon Johnson's landslide Democratic victory, the Democrats controlled the redistricting process. Thus, despite Richard Nixon's twin presidential victories, the Democrats broke even in 1968 and had only three fewer seats in the House after Nixon's landslide in 1972. Had redistricting been delayed, the Republicans in suburbia would have profited far more.

In the long run, Russell's fears about reapportionment undoing the South were correct, although not for his reasons. Redistricting when combined with the Voting Rights Act of 1965 recreated the solid South, but the South went from solidly Democratic in 1960 to solidly Republican by the end of the century (a switch delayed by the albatross of Watergate for the Republicans).

Throughout the process, the accommodations required of politicians were nowhere near as great as the reformers had hoped and the incumbents had feared. First, as long as legislative districts were of equal population, the courts did not interfere (at least before the Voting Rights Act of 1982). As an initial matter, a legislature always had the first opportunity to decide what districts would look like. Second, the Court did not prohibit incumbent-protecting districts. Thus the threat that *Baker, Wesberry,* and *Reynolds* initially posed passed quickly. In fact, legislatures did protect incumbents, especially those with seniority, and turnover occurred largely when seats became vacant.

To the extent that the Court had the implicit goal of greater numbers of competitive districts (those where no candidate was likely to win by a greater margin than 55–45), it failed because the requirement to redistrict every ten years allowed politicians to keep their gerrymanders up-to-date. Instead of becoming more competitive, districts became safer for incumbents. After World War II, 60 percent of incumbents were in "safe" districts. This jumped to 75 percent in the 1960s, and in the 1968 election a then-record 396 incumbents were returned to the House. Safe districts became even more common — fewer than 10 percent are competitive — after computers allowed legislators to pick their voters rather than vice versa. Thus, even in the dramatic 1994 Republican takeover of the House, over 90 percent of the incumbents were reelected.

If safe rather than competitive districts were an unanticipated outcome of redistricting, so was the increased polarization of the two political parties. Safe districts meant that only the dominant party's primary mattered, which gave party activists added influence. Since Democratic activists are more to the left and Republicans more to the right, those elected to Congress were more ideologically split than before; party-line voting increased significantly and with it a new tone of incivility validated by party leaders like the Republican Newt Gingrich of Georgia and the Democrat David Bonior of Michigan.

The Legislative Control of Membership

If the gains and losses were not quite as expected, one loss was lasting. The state legislatures had lost the ultimate control of redistricting. Judicial supervision over these legislative matters had gone from unthinkable to debatable to unquestionable in less than a decade. The change became clear at the end of the 1960s, when the Warren Court proceeded to strip Congress of yet another legislative prerogative — the power of each house to control its own membership. The Constitution is explicit on the point: "each House shall be the Judge of the . . . Qualifications of its own Members." This Court decision, rooted in the new legal outlook surrounding redistricting, culminated in the rise of judicial power in this area.

The case, *Powell v. McCormack* (1969), involved Harlem's flamboyant representative Adam Clayton Powell Jr., who became the chairman of the House Committee on Education and Labor in 1961. First elected in 1944, Powell quickly began offering the "Powell Amendment" — barring federal funds to any project that supported segregation — to all spending bills. It never passed, but Powell became known as "Mr. Civil Rights" and was decidedly unpopular in the South.

As he gained power and seniority, Powell became, in a phrase even he liked, "arrogant but with style." He would miss important votes in Congress and happily spent federal dollars on his own vacations. In 1960 he referred to a Harlem widow as a "bag woman," collecting money from the corrupt police. She sued for defamation and prevailed. Powell not only refused to pay the judgment against him, he refused to appear in court to explain his failure to pay. Powell had become a public problem to the Democrats in the House, and a standing subcommittee of the Eighty-ninth Congress was directed to investigate his flouting of the courts and his alleged misuse of public funds. He responded by treating the matter as if it were a racist attempt to silence an important civil rights advocate. The subcommittee issued findings that were adverse to him, but Congress took no action.

When the Ninetieth Congress convened, however, Powell was asked to step aside while the other new members took their oath. Then a select committee was appointed to determine Powell's eligibility. It recommended censure and loss of seniority. The full House went farther and voted, 307–116, to exclude him from Congress and declare his seat vacant. Powell both sued and stood for his vacated seat. In the special election held to fill the vacancy, he trounced his opponents but chose not to present himself to the House or ask to be given the oath of office. Instead, he partied in the Bahamas. In the November 1968 elections he prevailed again, and the House seated him in the Ninety-first Congress.

By that time, the federal court of appeals for the District of Columbia, in an opinion by Warren E. Burger, affirmed that the issue between Powell and the House was a "political question" and hence the federal courts could not interfere. On Powell's appeal, Chief Justice Earl Warren rejected his now-known successor's views and instead concluded that the voters, not Congress, determine membership in the House.

Warren's opinion treated the political questions doctrine just as the Court had in *Baker v. Carr*. It was the responsibility of the Court to interpret the Constitution, and that is inconsistent with ducking cases based on an amorphous concept like political questions. Furthermore, while each House was the judge of its members' qualifications, at least the Constitution was explicit on what those qualifications were: twenty-five years old, seven years a citizen, and residence in the state to be represented. Powell met them; the House therefore could not exclude him by adding other qualifications like good behavior.

But what about the other prerogative of either house to "punish its Members for disorderly Behavior, and, with the Concurrence of two thirds, expel a Member"? The vote on Powell, after all, had been close to 3–1. The Court's answer was that the House had not voted to expel Powell; it had voted to exclude him. This, the Court concluded, was a distinction with a constitutional difference.

Powell marked the first time the Court had asserted jurisdiction to settle constitutional questions involving internal congressional matters. Yet it fit perfectly with the Court's voting rights cases, and there was no outcry that the Court had transgressed an impermissible barrier. Under the Court's egalitarianism, all adults got to vote, and their votes were to be weighted equally. Unstated but obvious was the proposition that the candidate of the majority of voters got to represent them. (Powell, however, no longer would represent Harlem; ailing and dying, he was defeated in the next Democratic primary by Charles Rangel.)

It is well known that for fifty years from Franklin Roosevelt onward, war, both hot and cold, witnessed an accretion of power to the executive branch at the expense of Congress. It is less appreciated that during the 1960s the Supreme Court likewise gained powers once deemed exclusively the province of the legislature. The Court probably could not have done it alone. But by the mid-1960s, liberalism encompassed the tenet that a Great Society needs a Great Court and that the nation had one. Accordingly, Democratic liberals would do nothing that might weaken the authority of the Warren Court, for they revered it so much.

The end of the Cold War saw a reassertive Congress vis-à-vis the executive (although since 2001 the War on Terror has caused a reversion). We have yet to see Congress regain the powers taken by the Warren Court. Indeed, the cases from *Baker v. Carr* to *Reynolds v. Sims* to *Powell v. McCormack* laid the predicate for the Supreme Court in 2000 to believe that it had the right to decide which Florida votes counted and eliminated the Congress's necessity of determining which candidate won Florida and therefore the presidency.

Bush v. Gore (2000) involved the question of hand-counting so-called undervotes, ballots that the voting machines had registered as not voting for the presidency. Under Florida law, if a voter's intent can be ascertained, then the ballot must be counted accordingly. But Florida law does not specify how to determine intent, and the Florida Supreme Court allowed each county canvassing board to set its own standards to determine the undervoters' intent (although the Florida legislature stood by, ready to award the state's electoral votes to Bush regardless). Five Supreme Court justices ruled that allowing different standards for determining voter intent meant that voters in some Florida counties would be treated differently than voters in other counties. Relying exclusively on the Warren Court's decisions, the five-justice majority held that this was an example of vote dilution and thus violated the Equal Protection clause. The irony of the Rehnquist Court's conservatives relying on the liberal Warren Court's decisions to reach the result that comported with their politics did not pass unnoticed.

— L. A. Powe Jr.

BIBLIOGRAPHICAL NOTES

Good, reasonably contemporaneous accounts of the reapportionment cases, their causes, and the legislative and judicial responses to them can be found in Robert B. McKay, *Reapportionment: The Law and Politics of Equal Representation* (New York, 1965); Robert G. Dixon Jr., *Democratic Representation: Reapportionment in Law and Politics* (New York, 1968); and Ward Elliot, "Prometheus, Proteus, Pandora, and Procrustes Unbound: The Political Consequences of Reapportionment," *University of Chicago Law Review* 37 (Spring 1970). Recent longer-range and more questioning looks at the effects of reapportionment can be found in Garry W. Cox and Jonathan N. Katz, "The Reapportionment Revolution and Bias in U.S.

Congressional Elections," *American Journal of Political Science* 43 (July 1999): 812–41, and Nathaniel Persily, Thad Kousser, and Patrick Egan, "The Political Impact of One Person, One Vote: Intended Consequences, Perverse Effects, and Unrealistic Expectations," *University of North Carolina Law Review* 80 (September 2002). This latter piece is part of a symposium volume commemorating the fortieth anniversary of *Baker v. Carr.* The best single source for the law, statutory and judicial, of the electoral process is Samuel Issacaroff, Pamela S. Karlan, and Richard H. Pildes, *The Law of Democracy: Legal Structure of the Political Process,* 2nd ed. (Mineola, N.Y., 2001). The Warren Court is discussed in detail and context in Lucas A. Powe Jr., *The Warren Court and American Politics* (Cambridge, Mass., 2000).

Everett Dirksen

January 4, 1896–September 7, 1969

Everett Dirksen

Everett McKinley Dirksen was a consummate politician. An impressive orator in the Senate, he became a national television personality in the 1960s. Respected by his peers for his collegial manner and parliamentary skills, he was a loyal Republican who valued a conciliatory legislative process over fruitless partisan rancor, and he even mediated between the factions of his own party. His congressional service spanned the Great Depression and the Vietnam War, overlapping presidents from Franklin D. Roosevelt to Richard M. Nixon.

Born in Pekin, Illinois, near Peoria, Dirksen was one of four boys raised in near-poverty by his widowed mother. He was the only child to finish high school and attend college. A finalist in a national oratorical contest, he enrolled at the University of Minnesota, planning to become a lawyer, but in order to prove his patriotism in World War I, Dirksen (like many other young men of German descent) enlisted in the army. He served for two years in Europe and rose to the rank of second lieutenant. Returning home in 1919, Dirksen worked in several businesses, including a wholesale bakery in partnership with one of his brothers and as the general manager of a dredging company on the Illinois River. He was active in local theater and politics, and through the civic theater, met the woman he would marry, Louella Carver. In 1927 they had a daughter, Joy, their only child, who twenty-three years later married Howard Baker, who became an influential Republican senator from Tennessee.

Dirksen's success in his first political office, as Pekin's commissioner of finance (1927–1931), led to greater aspirations. Motivated by the Depression, he ran unsuccessfully against the local Republican congressman William Hull in 1930. Two years later he won the nomination and the election, a surprising achievement given the Democratic landslide that brought the Roosevelt administration to office. In the House of Representatives, Dirksen established himself as a good speaker and a hard-working, pragmatic politician. He supported many New Deal programs, including the banking acts of 1933 and 1935, federal emergency relief, the Agricultural Adjustment Act, the National Industrial Recovery Act, Social Security, the Soil Conservation and Domestic Allotment Act, and the Civilian Conservation Corps. During this busy legislative period, he also studied law at night and was admitted to the bar in 1936.

Until the eve of World War II, Dirksen was an avowed isolationist and opposed all legislation that might lead to war. In September 1941, however, recognizing the threat of Nazi Germany, he led many Republican colleagues to support Roosevelt's foreign policy. After flirting with a presidential bid in 1943, Dirksen continued to support both Roosevelt's, then Truman's, foreign policies, even as he opposed their domestic agendas. His political career was oddly interrupted by an eye ailment in 1948, which led to his brief retirement from the House. After recuperating, he ran for the Senate in 1950 and narrowly beat an old friend, the Democratic majority leader, Scott Lucas, after a closely contested election.

In the Senate, Dirksen became a close associate of both Robert Taft of Ohio and Joseph McCarthy of Wisconsin, but his reputation survived McCarthy's red-baiting and eventual disgrace and Taft's unsuccessful bid for the 1952 GOP presidential nod. The Eisenhower administration catered to Dirksen to earn his loyalty, and he in turn became an important ally of Eisenhower's in Congress. His equanimity also earned the respect of Presidents John F. Kennedy and Lyndon B. Johnson. As minority leader, Dirksen's oratory upstaged the modest style of the majority leader, Mike Mansfield of Montana, and he became the most powerful and respected Republican in Washington, delivering critical Republican votes on major issues, such as the Nuclear Test Ban Treaty of 1963, the 1964 tax cut, and the Civil Rights Acts of 1964, 1965, and 1968. With weekly television appearances and his fame as a recording artist — Dirken's recitation of fourteen stories of American adventure sold half a million LPs and earned an Emmy award in 1967 — the senator was as visible a public figure as the president. That changed, however, with the ascendancy of the Nixon administration, which steered its own course and made high-level appointments over the still-powerful senator's objections. When Dirksen died after an operation for lung cancer, his body lay in state in the Capitol Rotunda. He was the fifth senator to be so honored.

References

"Dirksen, Everett McKinley." *Encyclopedia of World Biography,* 2nd ed. 17 vols. Gale Research, 1998. Reproduced in *Biography Resource Center.* Farmington Hills, Mich.: Gale Group. 2003. Retrieved July 3, 2003, from http://www.galenet.com/servlet/BioRC.

Schapsmeier, E. L. 2000, February. "Dirksen, Everett McKinley." *American National Biography Online.* Retrieved July 3, 2003, from http://www.anb.org/articles/07/07-00077.html.

Adam Clayton Powell, Jr.

November 29, 1908–April 4, 1972

Adam Clayton Powell, Jr.

The legacy of the charismatic clergyman and civil rights activist Adam Clayton Powell, Jr., is difficult to measure. From his success organizing the politics of Harlem to his rise and fall in the U.S. House of Representatives, Powell owed much of his success — and failure — to his flamboyant persona, his defiance of the establishment, his stubbornness, and his incessant challenges to the legislative process. The congressman did not care whom he alienated, which, given his longevity in office, is testament to his political power. However, his personal foibles — his mismanagement of government funds, his income tax trouble, his reputation as a playboy, his poor handling of an important libel suit, and his egotism — eventually led to his downfall.

Born in New Haven, Connecticut, Powell was the son of the Reverend Adam Clayton Powell, who became the pastor of New York City's Abyssinian Baptist Church. The oldest African American congregation in the North, it was also one of the largest Protestant churches in the United States. The pastor sent his son to City College of New York, then packed the underachieving teenager off to Colgate University. The young Powell graduated in 1930 and briefly studied for the ministry at Union Theological Seminary before transferring to the Teachers College of Columbia University, earning a master's degree in 1932. Powell's political activities began in earnest during the 1930s, when he led demonstrations against racially discriminatory hiring practices in the city's bus company, local utilities, and Harlem stores. He took over the pulpit of the Abyssinian Baptist Church in 1937, when his father retired. In 1939 he chaired the Coordinating Committee on Employment, which picketed outside the offices of the World's Fair in New York City until jobs for black workers were guaranteed. Building on his political power base, Powell was elected to the New York City Council in 1941, the first African American in that position. He served for four years and continued his attacks on the white power structure.

When a New York congressional district was redrawn in 1943 to ensure the election of a black candidate from Harlem, Powell rose above the field of aspiring politicians, winning endorsements from Democrats, Republicans, the American Labor party, even the local Communist party. From his first days in the House, Powell earned a reputation as a maverick Democrat. For several years he attached a provision to bills funding education, health, and housing. Known as the Powell Amendment, the rider denied federal funds to any agency or district that practiced racial segregation or discrimination. The amendment caused conservatives to scuttle many pieces of legislation, but Powell would not negotiate with liberal politicians who begged him to stop.

Powell reached his high point in the House during the 1960s as chairman of the Committee on Education and Labor. This committee handled almost half of the domestic legislation in the Kennedy administration's New Frontier and the Johnson administration's Great Society programs, and Powell earned accolades as an able leader. It was also the beginning of his end, however. Powell's multiple personal and professional transgressions, coupled with his combative style, made him a target of congressional inquiry.

Reacting to charges of corruption, in February 1967 Powell's congressional colleagues voted, 307–116, to exclude him from membership. Although he won a special election in April, he did not take his seat in Congress; rather, from 1967 to 1969 he took his fight to the courts until a Supreme Court decision ruled the exclusion unconstitutional. Meanwhile, his Harlem constituents went unrepresented. At the same time, Powell's activities were overshadowed by the assassinations of the civil rights leader Martin Luther King, Jr., and Senator Robert F. Kennedy of New York. Returned to office, Powell was no longer considered an effective legislator.

Powell's congressional career ended after he was defeated in the 1970 primary election by Charles Rangel. His district had been redrawn again, and he may have lost because of the addition of Manhattan's West Side voters, many of whom considered him a reckless demagogue. Although Powell called the election results a fraud and threatened to challenge them in court, his power was gone. He resigned as minister of his church in 1971 and retired to the Bahamas. When he died in 1972 from complications of prostate surgery, thousands lined the streets of Harlem, and his funeral was attended by his two sons, two of his three former wives, and his female companion. He left behind a mixed but formidable reputation — dauntless agitation against racial discrimination tempered by personal and political mistakes.

References

"Adam Clayton Powell, Jr." *Dictionary of American Biography,* Supplement 9: 1971–1975. Charles Scribner's Sons, 1994. Reproduced in *Biography Resource Center.* Farmington Hills, Mich.: The Gale Group. 2003. Retrieved December 10, 2003, from http://galenet.galegroup.com/servlet/BioRC.

"Adam Clayton Powell, Jr." *Contemporary Authors Online,* Gale, 2003. Reproduced in *Biography Resource Center.* Farmington Hills, Mich.: The Gale Group. 2003. Retrieved December 10, 2003, from http://galenet.galegroup.com/servlet/BioRC.

"Adam Clayton Powell, Jr." *American Decades CD-ROM.* Gale Research, 1998. Reproduced in *Biography Resource Center.* Farmington Hills, Mich.: The Gale Group. 2003. Retrieved December 10, 2003, from http://galenet.galegroup.com/servlet/BioRC.

32

The Great Society

JOHN MCCORMACK, the veteran congressman from South Boston who replaced Sam Rayburn as Speaker of the House in 1961, described the Eighty-ninth Congress as one of "accomplished hopes" and "realized dreams." He was referring to the fact that in 1965 and 1966 Congress had passed a landmark voting rights bill, started a program of national health insurance for the elderly, and initiated an enduring program of federal aid to education. In addition, Congress tackled persistent and troubling problems such as the deterioration of the nation's cities and the degradation of the environment, even as the country embarked on an escalation of the war in Vietnam that demonstrated its continuing commitment to the Cold War. All of this activity followed a period in which Congress appeared unwilling to pass social legislation that offered any significant challenge to prevalent racial segregation in the South. In 1963 the political scientist and Democratic partisan James McGregor Burns had written that the nation was "mired in governmental deadlock, as Congress blocks or kills not only most of Mr. Kennedy's bold proposals of 1960 but many planks of the Republican platform as well."

Hence, the Great Society marked a period of unanticipated and concerted congressional activity that took the federal government into new areas of American life and started a debate over the effectiveness of federal social engineering that culminated in the Reagan years.

The death of President Kennedy in November 1963 helped to set the Great Society in motion. The new president, Lyndon Johnson, worked with and battled against an assertive Congress to pass liberal legislation that, in the case of health insurance for the elderly and money for school construction, had been stalled since 1953. Johnson put a high priority on the passage of this legislation and worked as hard and as effectively as any president in history to assure its passage. Having entered Congress in 1937 and risen to the rank of Senate majority leader in 1955, Johnson courted his former colleagues. Using techniques he had developed as majority leader, he bullied, encouraged, and cajoled the members of Congress. He told his aide Jack Valenti, "The most important people you will talk to are senators and congressmen." Speaking with characteristic hyperbole, he asked that each congressman be treated as if he were the president of the United States. That meant their calls should be answered immediately and their concerns dealt with as promptly as possible. "I am not for denouncing Congress all the time. I am not like you writers who think of congressmen as archaic buffoons with tobacco drool running down their shirts," he told the presidential historian William E. Leuchtenburg. Carl Albert, the Democratic congressman from the "little Dixie" region of Oklahoma who became majority leader in 1962 and Speaker of the House in 1971, noted that Johnson "had his staff, himself personally, working with not only the leadership, but with committees — everybody that had something to do with them. I am sure that in all the history of Congress there never has been so much Presidential activity in passing legislation." It was normal for Johnson to speak to up to thirty different legislators on any given day.

The results were clear. Congress passed 69 percent of Johnson's proposals in 1965 in contrast to those of his predecessor, John F. Kennedy, who managed to pass only 27 percent in 1963. One of the reasons for this success had to do with congressional relations. The Johnson White House featured a competent congressional liaison staff, headed by Lawrence O'Brien, whom Johnson had inherited from Kennedy. Perhaps more important was that many members of Congress responded to the change in public opinion after Kennedy's death. Johnson seized the moment and convinced Congress that to give meaning to the life of the martyred president, it was necessary to pass the legislation that he had left behind. Because Kennedy died so close to the end of his term, Johnson had little time to build up negative public opinion.

The circumstances of Kennedy's death helped propel Johnson to what at the time was the greatest victory ever in a presidential election. In 1964 the voters also elected 28 Democratic senators, gaining 2 seats that increased the Democratic majority to 68, and 295 Democratic representatives, for a net gain of 38 seats. Also reelected were nearly all of the northern liberal Democrats elected to the Senate in 1958, such as Edmund Muskie of Maine and Harrison Williams of New Jersey. Along with incumbents, such as John Pastore of Rhode Island, and newcomers, such as Robert Kennedy of New York, they constituted a formidable liberal block in the Senate. After 1964, therefore, LBJ encountered a Congress with strong liberal majorities eager to expand the power of the federal government. In both the House and the Senate there were twice as many Democrats as Republicans. Democratic legislators, such as Richard Bolling (D-

Missouri) and Paul Douglas (D-Illinois), who had been fighting for new domestic initiatives for more than a decade and had been stifled by the party leadership, now saw an opportunity to move their agenda forward, ironically under the presidency of an individual who had once been sympathetic to their southern opponents.

Such large margins meant little in an institution in which committee chairmen, many of whom were Southerners who held conservative views on such questions as civil rights legislation and aid to education, could effectively block legislation from coming to the floor. The problem was particularly acute in the House, where certain committees, such as Ways and Means, effectively legislated for the House and where the Rules Committee could prevent legislation from reaching the floor. After the 1964 election, therefore, the Democrats reformed the House to weaken the power of committee chairs. For example, the House increased the ratio of Democrats to Republicans on the Ways and Means and Appropriations Committees. Further, they took steps to temper the power of the Rules Committee by allowing the Speaker to force a bill from the committee to the House floor.

The Eighty-ninth Congress met at a favorable time for the passage of costly legislation that expanded the powers of the federal government. It was a time of prosperity, before Vietnam emerged as a divisive issue and as a competitor for federal funds that would otherwise go to social programs. To be sure, controversial matters, such as school integration, remained to be faced, yet even civil rights proved more tractable than previously. The reason was the 1964 passage of the Civil Rights Act, which, among other things, made it illegal to discriminate against African Americans in employment and public accommodations. Thanks to both these political and economic factors, a Congress with a determined liberal majority met a president with a firm agenda. The result was congressional passage of the Great Society.

The Great Society

The president formally unveiled his Great Society programs in May 1964 in a commencement address in Ann Arbor, Michigan. He emphasized that the Great Society rested on abundance. Although, as the historian Paul Conkin has noted, the Great Society was not particularly ideological in its orientation, it could be thought of as a series of federal initiatives aimed at giving people the opportunity to participate in America's abundance. As more people gained the skills necessary to overcome poverty and as the nation's stock of human capital increased with the added investment in education and health and the lessening of racial barriers in the labor market, the country would become even more affluent and the quality of life would improve. A more prosperous society would be able to afford more time to enjoy the arts and visit the nation's parks and forests; a Great Society would have the necessary resources to rebuild its cities, clean the air, and improve its transportation system. Between 1964 and 1967, Johnson pushed for legislation to accomplish each of these objectives and more.

The members of Congress tended to see the problems facing the nation in practical rather than theoretical terms. A shortage of human capital manifested itself in Congress as too few elementary and secondary classrooms to accommodate the large baby-boom generation. The quality of education might be improved by increasing teachers' salaries, and the capacity of colleges could be increased through grants to construct more buildings. Each measure had its congressional champion, and legislation had been introduced on each of these subjects during the 1950s. Health insurance for the elderly had, for example, first received serious congressional consideration in 1957. The advocates of these liberal measures tended to be from the Northeast or West rather than the South. Between 1957 and 1960, Senators Hubert Humphrey of Minnesota and Joseph S. Clark of Pennsylvania cosponsored nearly every liberal education and health care bill. In contrast, no senator from Virginia, Mississippi, or North Carolina agreed to cosponsor any of the bills. The 1958 and 1964 elections increased the number of northeastern and western Democrats in Congress, so the climate for the passage of such liberal measures became more favorable. President Johnson did not have to build either the contents of or the political support for these measures from scratch. Instead, he could draw on ideas from previously drafted legislation and on issue coalitions that had already been established and awaited only the push of the 1964 elections for success.

The War on Poverty

One of Johnson's principal Great Society measures did, however, come from the executive branch. Formulated by the staff of Kennedy's Council of Economic Advisors and by officials in the Departments of Justice, Labor, and Health, Education and Welfare, the Economic Opportunity Act began as a demonstration program to test various approaches to combating poverty; it emerged in 1964 as a focal point of Johnson's declared war on poverty. Congress contributed little to its contents, which included a variety of programs designed to increase the skills of people in poverty, such as the Jobs Corps. Intended as a successor to Roosevelt's Civilian Conservation Corps, it would allow underprivileged young people to learn job-related skills in special camps dedicated to that purpose. Disappointed by how the executive agencies pushed their existing legislative programs (such as the Department of Health, Education and Welfare's advocacy of medical care) for inclusion in the war on poverty rather than finding new ways to fight poverty, the Council of Economic Advisors recommended a "coordinated community action program." As written in the final legislation, community action agencies were supposed to coordinate and concentrate the responses to poverty in a particular area.

Introduced in April 1964, the bill became the responsibility of the House Education and Labor Committee, which was headed by a congressman from the Northeast rather than the South. Adam Clayton Powell, Jr., the Democrat committee chairman from New York, once described himself as "the first bad Negro they had in Congress." He had replaced a staunch southern conservative Democrat, Graham Barden of North Carolina, who had used his power to derail anything smacking of civil rights. The son of the pastor of New York's Abyssinian Baptist Church, Powell had enjoyed a privileged position in the black community that enabled him to attend Colgate University, Union Theological Seminary, and Columbia University Teacher's College. Elected to Congress in 1944, he became one of two black congressmen in the House in 1945. His Harlem constituency reelected him nearly two dozen times, enabling him to gain seniority and in 1961 to become the chair of the Education and Labor Committee. A controversial figure accused of tax fraud, accepting kickbacks, and going on unnecessary junkets with female staff members, Powell was expelled from Congress but pursued his case through the courts and eventually won his seat back. He remained in Congress until 1971. During the Kennedy and Johnson years he often acted erratically, failing, for example, to show up for important committee sessions. Nonetheless, he remained committed to legislation that he believed would benefit African Americans, such as the Economic Opportunity Act.

Not content to leave this important bill in Powell's hands, Johnson conferred with Speaker McCormack about finding a conservative Southerner to lead the fight in the House. As Lawrence O'Brien put it, "We realized that if by any chance Phil Landrum [a conservative Georgia Democrat with an antilabor reputation] would take the lead on this, it could be just a tremendous plus for us." To O'Brien's surprise, Landrum accepted the assignment, for he believed that the antipoverty program, which had little connection to organized labor, would be popular among the poor whites in his district. His support cut far enough into the southern conservatives that the measure could pass, and it meant, according to one close observer, that "since the most powerful southern congressman on the committee was for it and managing it, there was not going to be any

Democratic opposition to it." That fact alone assured its passage in the House, and the Senate, even more liberal than the House, never gave the measure close scrutiny. The Senate even dispensed with formal hearings on the bill — a good example of how the legislative climate had changed between the fall of 1963 and the summer of 1964. Like other pieces of legislation during this period, with President Johnson's imprimatur, the Economic Opportunity Act was passed as a memorial to President Kennedy.

However, its passage marked more than congressional deference to the president. Within the broad framework that Johnson crafted, Congress worked to shape the particulars of the bill. Sensitive to issues about the separation of church and state and patronage, Congress made sure, for example, that grants to religious organizations should only be made for secular activities and that governors had the authority to veto Job Corps and community action projects within thirty days. Edith Green, an Oregon Democrat elected to Congress in 1954, was a schoolteacher who had entered politics as the legislative chairman of the Oregon Congress of Teachers and Parents. From the very beginning of her tenure, which lasted until the end of 1974, she served on the Education and Labor Committee and took particular interest on issues related to primary and secondary education. Conservative in her belief that education and other social welfare projects should be controlled at the local rather than the federal level, Green nonetheless supported the Economic Opportunity Act. She made sure, however, that the Job Corps accepted women for training, as well as men, thereby leaving her mark on the legislation. John Bell Williams, a conservative congressman from Mississippi, insisted that those enrolled in the War on Poverty programs take a loyalty oath to the U.S. government. He could thus view the program as consistent with the nation's objectives in the Cold War, paving the way for his favorable vote.

Beyond influencing the language of the legislation, Congress also played a major role in implementing the War on Poverty. Conservatives, such as Representative Mendel Rivers of South Carolina, forced the president to agree that Adam Yarmolinsky, a Jewish civil rights advocate and the son of a communist, would not serve as a deputy in the Office of Economic Opportunity. Hence, even at its most deferential, Congress made adjustments to the president's most visible legislation.

Federal Aid to Education

After his election in 1964, President Johnson used his leverage with Congress to pass the two main items that had been debated since the mid-1950s but never passed: the Elementary and Secondary Education Act of

1965 and the Social Security Amendments of 1965 (which contained a hospital insurance program for the elderly called Medicare). In both instances, Congress built on legislative deliberations from the previous decade and shaped the laws in ways that differed from Johnson's original proposals.

Federal aid to education marked a response to the baby-boom generation's entering school at a time when opinion leaders considered a good education important to individual success and the nation's triumph in the Cold War. America's schools needed to produce more scientists and other technical personnel if the country expected to match the technological feats of the Russians in launching satellites and developing nuclear weapons. Although imbued with a national purpose, schools depended on local revenues that were often inadequate to build enough classrooms to meet the new demand, and salaries were not high enough to attract enough teachers. Education experts called for direct federal revenues to local schools, but the proposal was fraught with political complications. White Southerners, who ran in districts where few African Americans voted, objected to the leverage that school financing would give the federal government to enforce other social goals, such as school integration or the imposition of modern science curricula. Urban Northerners hoped that aid might be obtained for Catholic schools, which angered those who defended the strict separation of church and state. With the core constituencies of the Democratic party at odds, it was difficult to obtain a consensus in Congress.

Previous efforts to deal with this issue kept getting stifled in Congress. President Kennedy had made aid to education a priority and lost badly. In 1961 three separate education measures died in the Virginian Howard Smith's notorious House Rules Committee because the northern Democrats and southern Democrats could not agree on which measure to send to the floor first. Each faction made strategic alliances with the Republicans. In 1962 the administration concentrated on aid to higher education, but even after versions of the legislation had passed both houses of Congress, it could not get the measure out of a deadlocked conference committee. Both Edith Green and Senator Pat McNamara (D-Michigan) thought that the conference committee was "hopeless" because of disagreements over whether private colleges should receive grants, as the House favored, or loans, as the Senate preferred, from the federal government. In 1963 the administration opted for an omnibus strategy in which it submitted one large education bill in place of several small ones. Although the Senate, led by the Democrats Wayne Morse (D-Oregon), Joseph Clark, Lister Hill (D-Alabama), and McNamara maintained a sense of discipline in considering this bill, a debilitating turf war broke out among the subcommittee chairs in the House. Carl Perkins (D-Kentucky), in charge of vocational and adult education, worried that Edith Green, in charge of higher education, was trying to get her part of the bill to the full Education and Labor Committee before his part. Perkins felt that Chairman Powell was not paying sufficient attention to the various parts of the omnibus bill and thus creating "a complete vacuum of leadership." In the end, Congress passed a vocational education law and a higher education law but not one that covered general aid to education.

Hence, Johnson hoped to make aid to elementary and secondary education a priority in the Eighty-ninth Congress. Behind the scenes, the administration negotiated with Representative John Dent (D-Pennsylvania) and Senator Wayne Morse, two liberals who were influential on education policy, to substitute a new formula for federal aid to education. Instead of basing aid on the number of public school students in a particular district, the new formula was devised according to the number of poor children in a district. In this manner urban locations, with many poor children attending Catholic schools, would not be at a disadvantage with those places where nearly all of the students attended public schools. In addition, the congressional leadership and lobbyists impressed upon the southern Congressmen that they had nothing to fear from the new legislation since civil rights was already law. As one administration official put it, "Well, the Civil Rights Act of 1964 is passed anyway. If you now vote to deny federal aid to education, you are not helping yourself, you are just making it worse, because you might comply in some places and might as well pick up the money."

The South's interest in federal funds influenced Congress's behavior toward the Great Society. Almost all of the Great Society legislation offered federal grants to states and localities for problems of perceived national importance. By voting for a Great Society program, whether it involved child safety, urban mass transit, or vocational rehabilitation, legislators were bringing federal money into their districts and creating opportunities for their constituents to spend it. During the period between 1960 and 1967, the number of programs with federal grants increased from 132 to 379. Before the Great Society, federal grants had been given for such basic government functions as highways and public assistance; they were now used for a bewildering number of purposes, from family planning to school breakfasts. The cost of these grants grew from $8.6 billion in 1963 to $20.3 billion in 1969.

Southerners had always been enthusiastic supporters of grant programs, such as the Hill-Burton Hospital Construction Program of 1946, which allowed communities to maintain segregated facilities. Indeed, Southerners such as Lister Hill, a congressional leader on all matters concerning health care and medical research, had worked with the executive branch to tilt the distribution of funds toward the states with the lowest per capita income. Hence, southern states received a disproportionate share of the funds for such things as vocational rehabilitation and hospital construction. Even as they supported these sorts of small-scale social welfare programs, the southern congressmen remained wary of highly visible programs such as aid to education and federal health insurance for fear that they would lead to the racial integration of schools and hospitals. Hence, Wilbur Mills, an influential Democrat and head of the Ways and Means Committee who represented a conservative district in Arkansas, supported federal grants to his district for mental retardation facilities but opposed Medicare. Once the civil rights debates settled down, however, even legislators from the most conservative regions gained significant electoral incentives to accept new federal programs.

In this context, the House put aside its long history of contentiousness over federal aid to education and passed the legislation by 263–153, with 41 of 95 southern Democrats voting in favor of the bill. President Johnson signed the Elementary and Secondary Education Act of 1965 in April. Congress had adjusted the bill that it received from the administration but did not derail it. The Northerners in the House made sure that the receipt of welfare would not disqualify a family from being counted as poor. Those congressmen concerned over the issue of the separation of church and state, such as Jewish congressmen from the New York delegation, tightened the provisions related to the purchase of textbooks so that they became the property of a public school district and only lent to private schools. Howard Smith and Representative William Colmer of Mississippi, the chair and highest-ranking Democrat on the Rules Committee, were critical of the bill for the way it inserted the federal government into what they considered local affairs. They lacked the votes needed to keep the bill bottled up, however. With Wayne Morse, a former dean of the Oregon Law School with a deep interest in education policy, taking the lead, the Senate passed the House bill, thereby negating the need for a possibly contentious conference committee. For example, Morse, described by one historian as "the Senate maverick, its hair shirt," detested his fellow Oregonian Edith Green, and both could have been expected to serve on the conference committee.

Because of these actions, Congress authorized $1 billion for federal aid to the nation's elementary and secondary schools. As White House staff members noted, Congress had broken "through the roadblock that stymied federal aid to elementary and secondary schools." Liberal legislative proposals from the 1950s, tempered by compromises brokered between the White House and legislative leaders over the terms of the federal aid formula and conditioned by changes in the nation's civil rights laws, became law in 1965. In turn, ESEA, as the Washington insiders called it, became a cornerstone of the Great Society.

Medicare

In the frenzied atmosphere of the Eighty-ninth Congress, the members hardly stopped to catch their breaths and plunged into the controversial matter of health insurance for the elderly. Although this law, like the others, promised to confer benefits on every congressional district in the nation through payments to local hospitals, it represented an area of policy that Congress had always approached with extreme caution. The issue of national health insurance was an old one. In 1938 Senator Robert Wagner, a liberal New York Democrat with close ties to organized labor, had introduced a bill that would have provided federal grants to the states to establish health insurance programs. The idea failed to get the attention of the Senate Finance Committee and never came close to passage. When President Truman tried to reinvigorate the idea in the late 1940s, he too could not gain the interest of Congress. A core group of liberals, such as Senator James Murray of Montana and Wagner's successor in New York, Herbert Lehman, supported the measure. A far larger group opposed it. The main reason was that the medical profession, as represented by the American Medical Association (AMA), a grass-roots organization of doctors with members throughout the nation, objected to the proposal as a form of "socialized medicine." They saw in national health insurance the possibility of federal regulation of their activities, which in their minds outweighed any financial benefits that increased access to health care would bring them, and they believed that it threatened the autonomy of the doctor-patient relationship. In an era of perceived improvement in the quality of health care, doctors, the purveyors of the "miracles" that saved people's lives, enjoyed considerable respect and prestige that translated into political power for the AMA.

The proponents of national health insurance, who worked in the national headquarters of the American Federation of Labor and in the offices of the Social Security Administration, realized they needed a new strategy to sell national health insurance. At the very end of the Truman administration, they hit on the idea of limiting national health insurance to elderly individuals, most of whom were Social Security beneficiaries. In this way, they hoped to capitalize on a weakness in the private health insurance market, which covered few retirees, and to link the cause of national health insurance with the increasing popularity of Social Security. Both strategies were aimed not at making the legislation better in a policy sense but rather at making it more acceptable to the public and to Congress in a political sense.

Even this limited measure faced significant opposition in 1957. Along with the American Hospital Association, the AMA continued to exercise considerable influence over the conservative Democratic senators who controlled the Finance Committee in the 1950s and early 1960s, such as Harry Byrd (D-Virginia) and Robert Kerr (D-Oklahoma). Social Security measures originated in the House, where they fell under the purview of the Ways and Means Committee. There, proponents could interest neither the chairman, Jere Cooper (D-Tennessee), nor the ranking Democrat, Wilbur Mills, in introducing the legislation. They were forced to turn to Aime Forand, a liberal Rhode Island Democrat, who lacked sufficient standing to get the committee's approval of the measure. There the matter died.

Mills, who became head of the Ways and Means Committee in 1957 after Cooper's death, considered himself an expert on tax policy. He took particular pride in his careful stewardship of Social Security and insisted that it be kept in what Social Security insiders called "long-range actuarial balance." That meant that the revenues the program received through payroll taxes should be enough to pay out benefits over a long period of time. Mills feared that Medicare, as health insurance for the elderly came to be called in the Kennedy era, would turn out to be an expensive and unpredictable program and would undermine Social Security's financial stability, so he approached the measure with particular caution.

The Kennedy administration had tried to overcome Mills's objections and pass Medicare. In 1962 the matter came up for a vote in the Senate. Senator Kerr worked out a complex vote trade with Jennings Randolph (D-West Virginia) to defeat the measure by one vote. Randolph, a liberal senator and normally a reliable supporter of Social Security expansion, voted against Medicare because he feared that Kerr would use his influence in the Finance Committee to penalize West Virginia for the way it managed its welfare program. Even with Kerr's death in 1962 and the infirmity of Harry Byrd, the measure could not make it past the Senate Finance Committee. In September 1964 the Senate bypassed the committee and passed a version of Medicare. Although Mills had indicated in the House that he would support a compromise, he refused to take up the measure in conference. Once again the measure died.

Before the start of the Eighty-ninth Congress, Social Security experts in the executive branch prepared what they hoped would be the final draft of Medicare. They worked in complete cooperation with Mills, who read the election results to mean that Medicare could now be released from his committee. In the Senate, the administration chose Clinton Anderson

(D-New Mexico), a member of the Senate Finance Committee with liberal credentials who had served in the Truman cabinet, to be the lead sponsor. The American Federation of Labor–Congress of Industrial Organizations, working through its Washington representative, Nelson Cruikshank, was also influential in this stage of the drafting process.

In a political climate that favored the measure, the Republicans on the Ways and Means Committee, led by John Byrnes of Wisconsin, realized they needed a realistic alternative to Medicare. Byrnes therefore introduced a proposal, dubbed by some as "bettercare," that contained protection against the costs of both hospital stays and doctors' bills for the elderly (the administration's bill covered only the cost of the hospital). The Republican plan, modeled in part on a policy available to federal employees through the Aetna Insurance Company, would be voluntary, and the elderly would pay for it themselves. Even the American Medical Association came up with an alternative to Medicare in the form of state-run insurance available to low-income individuals who could not afford the cost of medical care. After completing an initial review of the administration's bill in his committee on March 2, 1965, Mills shocked most of his colleagues when he raised the possibility of combining all three approaches in one bill. He proposed that doctors' services be covered through a voluntary program. While hospital insurance would be paid through Social Security taxes, the voluntary program, similar to the Byrnes proposal, would be funded in part through general revenues. This scheme would limit the financial burden on Social Security and allow Mills and other conservative proponents to say that doctors would not be part of a mandatory federal program. Mills also suggested the creation of another program, which became known as Medicaid, to help the states finance medical care for those on welfare or those near the poverty line, who would find health insurance premiums an undue financial burden.

Mills's proposal met with the immediate approval of the president and his advisers on Social Security policy. The Republicans found it difficult to oppose the measure since Mills had incorporated their proposal into the bill. According to one administration official and a Social Security expert, Wilbur Cohen, "The doctors couldn't complain, because they had been carping about Medicare's shortcomings and about it being compulsory. And the Republicans couldn't complain, because it was their own idea. In effect, Mills had taken the AMA's ammunition, put it in the Republicans' gun, and blown both of them off the map." Hence, with Mills now an active sponsor of the legislation, it moved out of his committee to the floor of the House. Congress passed the law on July 28, 1965, pretty much as Mills had written it. Wilbur Mills, every bit as much as officials in the executive branch and their allies in the labor unions, was the author of Medicare.

Another legislative log jam had been broken because of the election of 1964, the changed composition of the Ways and Means Committee, the resulting conversion of Mills to the program, and the fact that the robust economy enabled him to save face by advocating the simultaneous adoption of previously competing alternatives.

Developments in 1966

As the election of 1966 approached, the Vietnam War was heating up and more Great Society measures were meeting with controversy. Some of it centered on congressional wariness: Was the president trying to do too much at the national level and creating hastily designed programs that overlapped with one another?

The domestic situation also became more volatile, resulting in more divisions inside Congress. Particularly after the race riots of August 1965, legislation that aided urban areas came in for close congressional scrutiny. When President Johnson sent his Demonstration Cities Program before Congress in January 1966, he discovered that the congressmen reacted extremely cautiously to a law that promised to create integrated housing. Neither John Sparkman, the Southerner from Alabama, nor Paul Douglas, the liberal Northerner from Illinois who had made a name for himself in the 1950s as a bomb-throwing liberal who attacked southern conservatives and their filibuster, would agree to fight for the legislation. That assignment went to the unlikely choice of Edmund Muskie of Maine, a state with little vested interest in such a program. Liberals such as Robert Kennedy (D-New York) believed that the president was not doing enough for the cities; conservatives thought he was doing too much. A balance between the two could no longer so easily be struck.

The changed atmosphere affected the outcome of the 1966 elections, which reduced the operating margins for Great Society legislation. The Republicans gained 47 seats in the House, well above the average increase for the party out of power over the course of sixty years. The number of northern Democrats, crucial to the chances of Great Society legislation, fell from 191 to 156. In the Senate the Republicans picked up 4 seats, including that of Senator Douglas, who was replaced by Charles Percy. The situation thus changed with the resurgence of the congressional conservatives.

The Ninetieth Congress

After the election, many Great Society programs began to experience problems in Congress. They came not only from the committees that created and maintained social programs but also from the committees that allocated money to federal agencies. For example, the Johnson administration had hoped to spend $5 billion on the Elementary and Secondary Education Act by 1969. As the date approached, however, it became clear that education programs would receive nowhere near that amount of money. In the end, Lister Hill and Representative John Fogarty (R-Rhode Island) — and after Fogarty's death in 1967 Dan Flood (D-Pennsylvania) — who headed the authorization committees for health, education, and welfare in their respective houses, could only convince their colleagues to spend $2 billion on these programs in 1969. The administration officials, under pressure to finance the war and maintain social programs without producing runaway inflation, concurred in this decision. Indeed, White House and Department of Health, Education and Welfare staff members met personally with Jennings Randolph, Joseph Clark, Robert Kennedy, Jacob Javits (R-New York), and Winston Prouty (R-Vermont) to convince them to hold down increases in the education programs.

This fight over education expenditures was just one component of a debate that journalists characterized as "guns versus butter." In the president's 1967 State of the Union message, he argued that the society was "healthy enough, its people are strong enough to pursue our goals in the rest of the world while still building a Great Society here at home." He did request a temporary surcharge on corporate and individual income taxes to help finance the war and to tamp down the effects of inflation. Congressional leaders, such as Wilbur Mills and the minority leader, Gerald Ford (R-Michigan), insisted that more than a tax cut was required. Mills wanted a firm commitment from the White House that there be no new domestic programs in 1969. Johnson balked and could not come to an agreement with Mills. As the matter stretched into 1968, Mills, Senator Russell Long, the Louisiana Democrat and son of Huey Long who had succeeded Byrd as chair of the Finance Committee, and John J. Williams, a conservative Republican from Delaware on the Finance Committee, pressed for a spending cut as the price of a tax increase. In the end Mills forced the administration to accept over $6 billion in expenditure reductions. As an authority on Mills has noted, the "Revenue and Expenditure Control Act of 1968 reestablished the principle of expenditure control temporarily by gutting the Great Society and by slashing spending increases that had been built into existing appropriations laws."

The congressional conservatives now felt more secure about directly attacking Great Society programs. The War on Poverty programs, in particular, came in for strong congressional criticism. One of the president's legislative aides told him at the beginning of 1967 that "I think I should alert you to an increasing amount of talk our office is picking up on the Hill to the effect that the Ninetieth Congress will dismember" the Office of Economic Opportunity (OEO). He meant that the office would be eliminated, along with many of the programs that made up the War on Poverty. Those that Congress wished to keep, such as Head Start, the preschool enrichment program for underprivileged children, would be taken away from the OEO and put in more traditional federal agencies, such as the Office of Education. Only the fact that southern congressmen, such as Joseph Waggonner of Louisiana, disliked the Office of Education as much as the Office of Economic Opportunity prevented the move. When an official from the OEO went to see James Eastland, an extremely conservative senator from Mississippi and an important supporter of the Vietnam War, to tell him that the OEO programs were going to the Office of Education, run by its commissioner Harold Howe, Eastland was apoplectic. He detested Howe, who was responsible for the government's desegregation efforts in education. "I wouldn't vote a red turd to Doc Howe," Eastman said. "When is that amendment coming up?"

Another sign that many congressmen held different priorities than the president came in the renewed congressional interest in legislation to crack down on crime and welfare recipients in 1967 and 1968. The Republicans and southern Democratic members of the conservative coalition succeeded in adding language to Johnson's Safe Streets and Crime Control Act, proposed in 1967 and passed in 1968, that emphasized such police missions as combating riots and civil disorders and downplayed gun control. The Great Society's efforts to provide welfare recipients with skills that would enable them to leave the welfare rolls were derailed after riots occurred in Newark and Detroit during the summer of 1967. Congressmen in the Ways and Means Committee and the Senate Finance Committee, particularly Russell Long, retaliated by freezing the level of welfare recipients. After the National Welfare Rights Organization staged a sit-in at the hearing room of the Finance Committee to protest the freeze, Long suggested that its members might be better occupied by picking up the litter in front of their houses: "If they can find time to march in the streets, picket, and sit all day in committee hearing rooms, they can find time to do some useful work."

Even Medicare, perhaps the most acclaimed of the Great Society programs, ran into difficulties after 1965. When it went into operation in July 1966, the actual costs soon exceeded the costs that had been forecast, inhibiting efforts to make it more liberal by extending protection to new groups, such as those with disabilities or pregnant women. In addition, institutional rivalry between the Senate and the House complicated the program's implementation. In April 1966, only three months before it was scheduled to begin, the Finance Committee held closed hearings in which staff members attacked how the Social Security Administration proposed to reimburse hospitals for their costs. They argued that the cost-plus method of reimbursement would inflate costs and make the program difficult to control. Although the Social Security Administration got the General Accounting Office to intercede on its behalf and endorse its policies, the hearings nearly forced the agency to change its method of cost accounting, which would have delayed the start of Medicare. Long agreed to the disruptive hearings because he and his committee felt frozen out of the policy negotiations. He believed that in writing the law, Congress had shown too much deference to Mills and the Committee on Ways and Means. "I think that the Senate Finance Committee wanted a real role after passage and since they hadn't had too much to do in the shaping of the legislation, they could take a very aggressive stand in critiquing what went on," the Social Security commissioner Robert Ball said. When it came time to issue regulations implementing Medicare, therefore, Long's committee decided to exercise its muscle and show that the Social Security Administration had exceeded its authority.

Congressional disapproval of executive agencies was a common theme after 1966. Whether the program sought to improve the quality of education, eradicate poverty, or pay for the medical care of the elderly, Congress subjected it to considerable scrutiny and often failed to appropriate as much money for the program as the congressional liberals had hoped.

The End of the Great Society?

In 1968 the Republicans captured the White House at a time of deep societal division over Vietnam and other social issues, such as the rising welfare rates and the apparent alienation of the baby-boom generation from the larger society. Although the Democrats maintained firm control of Congress, their margins slipped to their lowest levels of the decade, 243–192 in the House and 58–42 in the Senate. Richard Nixon realized, however, that he would have to deal with the Democratic leaders if he expected to pass his own social programs, such as the Family Assistance Plan to reform the welfare system and a mandated system of national health insurance. In the House, the southern Democrats such as Sonny Montgomery of Mississippi continued to exercise considerable power, and Nixon sought to make alliances with them. Despite the gain in Republican seats and the election of Robert Dole from Kansas, the Senate retained its liberal character. Indeed, one congressional authority noted that "it was more liberal than ever." Part of that had to do with the waning power among the southern Democratic conservatives, such as Richard Russell (D-Georgia), who was in ill health, and Strom Thurmond of South Carolina, who had become a Republican. As if to symbolize the liberal resurgence, Edward "Ted" Kennedy (D-Massachusetts) replaced Long as Democratic whip in 1969. Not surprisingly, the Nixon administration failed to get its version of welfare reform or national health insurance through the Senate.

Ironically Congress, which had put the brakes on the Great Society during the Ninetieth Congress, became its defender in the Ninety-first. The congressmen defended what they had created and protected such programs as Medicare and federal grants to local school districts for elementary and secondary education. The administration did win some victories, as in its successful effort to index Social Security benefits to the rate of inflation. Even in this instance, however, the president needed to accommodate the liberal interests in Congress. Hence, Congress accompanied the indexing of Social Security benefits in 1972 by a 20 percent increase in benefit levels. Shortly afterward, Congress voted to extend Medicare protection to people with disabilities. The only new health insurance initiatives that made it through Congress were those favored by Senator Kennedy, such as the federal encouragement of health maintenance organizations.

In this way Congress helped both to create and institutionalize the programs of the Great Society. Between 1964 and 1967, President Johnson proposed and Congress passed a record number of social policy initiatives and collaborated in such legislation as the Economic Opportunity Act, Medicare, and the Elementary and Secondary Education Act. These pieces of legislation, and many more besides, left a permanent imprint on American life by bringing the federal government into the lives of millions of Americans by helping them obtain education, receive adequate health care, and move out of poverty. The programs became so ingrained in the pattern of American life that in subsequent decades, many people were not even aware that they were the beneficiaries of public policies created during the Great Society.

Although many of the programs endured, they remained contentious and occasioned debate in Washington and the states for the rest of the century. Policymakers made many attempts to reform Medicare, for example, by trying to cut the rate of growth in reimbursements to doctors and hospitals. Yet the politicians would fight over how to reform Medicare rather than try to eliminate it. More than anything else, the acceptance of the programs as a starting point of discussion reveals the success of Congress at institutionalizing the Great Society. Four subsequent decades of conservative government have not erased its legacy.

— EDWARD D. BERKOWITZ

BIBLIOGRAPHICAL NOTES

Good biographies and reminiscences of President Johnson that comment on his skill at congressional relations include Paul Conkin, *Big Daddy of the Pedernales* (New York, 1987); Robert Dallek, *Flawed Giant: Lyndon Johnson and his Times 1961–1973* (New York, 1998); Bruce J. Schulman, *Lyndon B. Johnson and American Liberalism* (Boston, 1995); and Joseph A. Califano Jr., *The Triumph and Tragedy of Lyndon Johnson: The White House Years* (New York, 1991).

On the domestic legislation of the Great Society, see Michael Barone, *Our Country* (New York, 1990); Irving Bernstein, *Guns or Butter: The Presidency of Lyndon Johnson* (New York, 1996); Edward D. Berkowitz, *Mr. Social Security: The Life of Wilbur J. Cohen* (Lawrence, Kans., 1995); Michael L. Gillette, *Launching the War on Poverty: An Oral History* (New York, 1996); Julian E. Zelizer, *Taxing America: Wilbur D. Mills, Congress, and the State, 1945–1975* (New York, 1998); and James L. Sundquist, *Politics and Policy: The Eisenhower, Kennedy and Johnson Years* (Washington, D.C., 1968).

33

The Vietnam War

In 1973 a new phrase entered the American political lexicon with the publication of Arthur M. Schlesinger Jr.'s *The Imperial Presidency*. The book described the appropriation by the American presidency, and especially the twentieth-century presidency, of powers given to Congress by the Constitution and by the nation's early practice, and it placed special importance on foreign policy. "By the early 1970s," Schlesinger wrote, "the American President had become on issues of war and peace the most absolute monarch (with the possible exception of Mao Tse-tung of China) among the great powers of the world."

Schlesinger maintained that the assumption of this imperial power by the presidency had been gradual and usually under the pretext or demand of an emergency, and he left little doubt that it was as much a matter of congressional abdication as of presidential usurpation. The Vietnam War hangs heavy over the text — the book appeared mere months after the signing of the 1973 Paris Peace Accords that effectively ended America's military intervention in Indochina. It was in Vietnam, Schlesinger believed, that the presidency overwhelmed most fully the traditional separation of powers in foreign affairs. "The Presidency Rampant," he called the chapter on Lyndon B. Johnson's escalation of the U.S. involvement.

It was a powerful argument, perhaps too powerful. There can be no denying that for much of the quarter century of significant U.S. involvement in Vietnam — from 1950 to 1975 — Congress accorded the executive branch wide latitude in decision-making. Particularly during the major escalation of the early and middle 1960s, the presidents and their principal aides generally determined the broad contours as well as the narrow specifics of policy. Nor can it be disputed that the lawmakers were by and large content with this situation. With rare exceptions, they were only too happy to disclaim responsibility for decisions pertaining to a murky struggle thousands of miles from America's shores, often pointing out that they lacked clear signals from their constituents and, in any case, did not have the facts. That one party had firm control of two branches of government during Johnson's Americanization of the war surely mattered as well: the Democrats in Congress were loath to challenge a Democratic president on the subject of war and peace, particularly one with so demanding and unrelenting a personality as LBJ. In this way Vietnam in the 1960s conformed to the pattern laid down by Thomas Jefferson at the beginning of the 1800s: the president's authority over foreign affairs tends to be enhanced when his party is in control of Congress.

At the same time, though, Congress significantly shaped the decision-making on Vietnam in both direct and indirect ways. For example, its skepticism regarding the wisdom and viability of a large U.S. military commitment to South Vietnam appeared earlier and ran deeper than used to be believed, a reality that renders problematic the common view that the war had broad support on Capitol Hill until well after the major fighting began. (The 1965 escalation in Vietnam did not cause the cracks in the Cold War consensus; it merely deepened them.) We also know that presidents and their advisers were aware of this skepticism and worried about it; and that the perceived need to forestall overt opposition from leading Senate Democratic doves — notably the majority leader, Mike Mansfield of Montana, the Foreign Relations Committee chairman J. William Fulbright of Arkansas, and the Armed Services Committee chairman Richard Russell of Georgia — helped convince the Johnson administration to opt for a gradual escalation. Although influential Senate doves were not willing to work hard and in concert to prevent and then end the war, the task of keeping them nominally onboard helped determine the spectrum of acceptable escalation and to strengthen the position of those in the administration arguing for pauses in the bombing aimed at getting negotiations started. In the Nixon and Ford years, the doves played a significant role in further limiting the range of policy options and, later, in winding down the U.S. involvement.

Of course, the war always had many supporters on Capitol Hill, and the Johnson and Nixon administrations courted these hawks no less assiduously than they wooed the doves and the fence-sitters. Johnson, in particular, depended enormously on the vociferous backing he received from prowar senators such as the Democrats John Stennis of Mississippi and Gale McGee of Wyoming and Republicans such as Karl E. Mundt of South Dakota, John Tower of Texas, and the minority leader, Everett Dirksen of Illinois. Dirksen was especially important for his ability to keep the Republicans — always the more hawkish party on Vietnam after the start of 1964 — more or less in line with Johnson's policy. "I'm getting kicked around by my own party in the Senate, and getting my support from your side of the aisle," Johnson told Dirksen on the phone in February 1965, just as the critical Americanization decisions were being implemented. He would make that observation many times in the years that followed, and with good reason — the GOP was indeed "the loyal opposition" in the Johnson years, at least as far as Vietnam was concerned (notwithstanding the presence of dissenters in the party such as John Sherman Cooper of Kentucky, Jacob Javits of New York, George D. Aiken of Vermont, and Margaret Chase Smith of Maine). From time to time leading Republican voices, including the future White House occupants Gerald Ford and Richard Nixon, would express frustration with LBJ's handling of the war and call for stepped-up military action, but Dirksen's close working relationship with Johnson kept these efforts from gaining much momentum. With some justification, Johnson always claimed that his war policy had bipartisan support.

The Early Years

In the years immediately after World War II, as the Truman and then the Eisenhower administrations decided to back France in its effort to preserve a colonial empire in Indochina, Congress played a small role. Even then, however, policymakers in the executive branch would on occasion acknowledge the limits on acceptable policy options set by Congress. In 1954 Dwight Eisenhower consulted its leaders on the question of whether the United States should intervene militarily to assist the beleaguered French forces at Dien Bien Phu. From a broad cross section of lawmakers in both parties, he received the clear message that there should be no unilateral American military intervention to save the French and no dispatch of ground troops. The idea of a ground war so soon after Korea had little appeal among the general public, the legislators knew. Lyndon Johnson of Texas, then minority leader in the Senate, declared that "we want no more Koreas with the United States furnishing 90 percent of the manpower." Richard Russell, a southern conservative who was considered the leader of the Senate, worried that even if the U.S. action was initially limited to air strikes, a quagmire loomed. "Once you commit the flag," he asserted in a high-level meeting on April 3, in words that would take on a haunting prescience a decade later, "you've committed the country. There's no turning back. If you involve the American air force, why, you've involved the nation." And if you involved the nation, ground forces would soon follow. Russell said he was "weary" of "seeing American soldiers being used as gladiators to be thrown into every arena around the world." The congressional leaders made it clear that they would support U.S. intervention only if allies (that is, the British) were found to participate in joint military action. The British ruled out any such step, and no intervention occurred.

Just how important these congressional assertions were to the outcome of the policy discussion that spring is a matter of debate. Some writers maintain that Eisenhower and his secretary of state, John Foster Dulles, gave serious thought at least to an air campaign to support the French and that the warnings of Johnson, Russell, and others were instrumental in causing them reluctantly to abandon the idea. Others say that Eisenhower actually had little intention of resorting to military force in 1954 and that he engaged in a charade with lawmakers to give himself an excuse to explain his lack of action to the French; the president, according to this view, indeed wanted his options limited. Whichever interpretation is correct — and the two can to some extent be reconciled — it's fair to say that the leaders on Capitol Hill played a significant role in forestalling direct U.S. involvement in the First Indochina War.

When the Eisenhower team, in the wake of the Geneva Conference that summer, moved energetically to create and sustain an independent, noncommunist South Vietnam, few in Congress objected. As that effort expanded in the second half of the 1950s, the administration could count on broad support from both Democrats and Republicans. Indeed, certain individual lawmakers were instrumental in boosting the fortunes of the South Vietnamese leader, Ngo Dinh Diem. One was Senator John F. Kennedy, a young Democrat from Massachusetts who had met Diem and been impressed by him and who shared Diem's Catholic faith. Another was Mike Mansfield, who over the course of a decade and a half devoted more attention to the Vietnam issue than any other member of Congress. In the 1960s Mansfield would be a persistent critic of the war, but in the mid-1950s he saw the conflict as an important theater in the struggle against global communism. In the months and years after Geneva, he would be such an ardent supporter of the Saigon leader that he would be known, with some justification, as "the godfather" of Ngo Dinh Diem. He trumpeted Diem's qualifications at every turn and became an important element in the Eisenhower administration's campaign to sell skeptics on the notion that this aloof, aristocratic Catholic from central Vietnam was the best person to lead a South Vietnam in which 90 percent of the population practiced some form of Buddhism.

For a long time, though, Mansfield was an exception: a congressman paying close and continuing attention to the Vietnam issue. Not until 1963, when the politico-military crisis in South Vietnam escalated sharply, did there emerge a consistent level of congressional comment. That spring the number of U.S. military advisers to the Diem regime totaled more than 16,000, yet victory over the Vietcong seemed further away than ever. The Saigon government, run by Diem and his increasingly influential brother Ngo Dinh Nhu, seemed intent on alienating as many of its constituents as possible, and it was increasingly resistant to exhortations from Washington. On Capitol Hill in late summer and early fall, Kennedy administration representatives were subjected to tough questions not merely about the conduct of the war but also about its viability and importance. Several centrist and liberal Senate Democrats — Albert Gore of Tennessee, Ernest Gruening of Alaska, Wayne Morse of Oregon, Frank Church of Idaho, and George McGovern of South Dakota, for example — cast considerable doubt on the long-term prospects of the war and wondered whether the United States might use the Diem regime's repressive policies as an excuse to get out of Vietnam. The Foreign Relations Committee chairman, J. William Fulbright, worried about the prospect of an open-ended commitment, as did Mike Mansfield, whose doubts had increased dramatically following a trip to Vietnam the previous year.

When that fall the administration made public a plan to withdraw a thousand advisers from Vietnam by the end of the year, an important rationale was the growing cognizance on the part of JFK and his aides that they would have to make a strong case to Congress for continuing U.S. involvement. A partial withdrawal, so the argument went, would suggest to the lawmakers that the current course was the correct one and that the administration did not plan for Americans to take over the main burden of fighting the war.

Johnson's War

What never emerged, however, either in the fall of 1963 or in the critical eighteen-month period that followed, was a sustained legislative effort on Vietnam policy. In the spring of 1964, growing numbers of lawmakers in the Senate came to the conclusion that Vietnam was not worth the loss of American lives, that the outlook of the war effort was bleak, and that avenues of withdrawal should be actively sought. The group included the powerful trio of Mansfield, Fulbright, and Russell — the foreign policy leadership in the Senate — as well as several other Democrats and moderate Republicans. Publicly, however, these and other skeptics kept largely silent. The Democrats among them were anxious to avoid a party rift on Vietnam, given LBJ's frequent assertions that he saw no option but to stay the course, and especially with Johnson new to the presidency and about to enter an election campaign. Fulbright spoke for many when he said, in response to a reporter who asked him why he kept his reservations quiet, "I don't think Senators spouting off help the situation." Intensely loyal to

Johnson and hoping someday to be appointed secretary of state, Fulbright accepted the administration's assurances in mid-1964 that it sought no escalation of the fighting. On the rare occasion when he spoke out publicly on the war, he tended indeed to support the U.S. policy.

Fulbright's loyalty faced a tougher test in early August, after alleged North Vietnamese attacks on American ships in the Gulf of Tonkin and a massive U.S. retaliatory air attack on targets in North Vietnam. It was the first direct military confrontation between the United States and North Vietnam, and it brought the war to the forefront of Congress's agenda for the first time since 1954. The reason: with the bombings came a request from the administration for a congressional resolution granting Johnson the authority to take whatever steps necessary to defend the U.S. interest in Indochina.

Johnson charged Fulbright with the task of securing the quick passage of this resolution with the largest possible vote. He believed that the liberal Democrats in the Senate, many of whom had already expressed misgivings about the enterprise in Southeast Asia, respected Fulbright and would listen to him. He was correct. Fulbright performed a potentially decisive role, for the resolution initially provoked a significant amount of grumbling and reticence among the lawmakers — much more so than is generally recalled. In the Senate debate, in particular, expressions of skepticism were frequent, as even a cursory examination of the *Congressional Record* makes clear. The Republican John Sherman Cooper spoke for many when he cautioned on the Senate floor against a deepened U.S. involvement in the war. In an often-cited exchange with Fulbright, he asked prescient questions about the powers it granted the president to make war:

> COOPER: Are we now giving the President advance authority to take whatever action he may deem necessary respecting South Vietnam and its defense, or with respect to the defense of any other country included in the [Southeast Asian Treaty Organization] treaty?
>
> FULBRIGHT: I think that is correct.
>
> COOPER: Then, looking ahead, if the President decided that it was necessary to use such force as could lead into war, we will give that authority by this resolution?
>
> FULBRIGHT: That is the way I would interpret it.

Cooper expected to get these answers, and he worried about them, yet he was not prepared to vote against the resolution. Like most everyone else on Capitol Hill, he understood that Johnson's position was hard to attack. The president had asked Congress to approve an action he had already taken, and the members felt compelled to go along. The country's flag was involved. The administration had skillfully cultivated a crisis atmosphere that seemed to leave little time for debate. And, of course, an election loomed right over the horizon, perhaps the most important consideration of all. Every House member and a third of the senators would be up for reelection and were loath to be charged with helping to put the flag in danger. With mere days until the Democratic convention, most in the majority party would have considered it unthinkable to deny Johnson his request, especially since his Republican opponent, Barry Goldwater, stood to benefit.

Still, as the Cooper-Fulbright exchange indicated, some members were nervous about the scope of the resolution. Here is where Fulbright's role was critical. Though in their exchange the Arkansan affirmed Cooper's sense that the measure gave Johnson the authority to take the nation into war, he worked hard to convince skeptics such as Mansfield, McGovern, and Church that LBJ would consult fully with Congress before embarking on any escalation of the conflict. When Gaylord Nelson declared his intention to introduce an amendment calling for efforts to avoid "a direct military involvement" in the region, Fulbright successfully moved to prevent the amendment on the grounds that it was unnecessary. After all, he told Nelson, "the last thing we want to do is become involved in a land war in Asia." That was the pattern: almost every time a senator expressed reservations (and a significant number, from both parties, did so), Fulbright would rise and say that he shared their concern, that he opposed a wider war, and that as far as he knew the administration did not plan a wider war. In the end, only Wayne Morse and Ernest Gruening voted against the resolution in the Senate (Gruening called it a "predated declaration of war"); in the House the vote was unanimous.

Morse predicted that his colleagues would come to regret their votes, and many of them did. Most would explain their vote by pointing to the administration's deception and withholding of crucial information, and that is no doubt part of it. Nor should it be forgotten that Congress had passed similar resolutions in the recent past — under Eisenhower and Kennedy — that had not led to massive U.S. troop commitments; hence Fulbright's assurances seemed quite plausible in the context of the time. But if scores of legislators were unenthusiastic about voting yes, it is true that, with a few notable exceptions, they did not ask the hard questions, despite opportunities to do so and despite the capacious language of the resolution. It is no doubt true that most never expected the resolution to become the functional declaration of war that it did, but everyone knew that its language could allow the landing of large American armies in Vietnam. Fulbright had admitted as much to Cooper.

This tendency continued in the crucial months that followed, even after South Vietnam descended into politico-military chaos and a Vietcong victory appeared imminent. In December 1964 and January 1965, as South Vietnam seemed to teeter on the brink of collapse, many liberal and moderate lawmakers, including the entire Senate Democratic leadership, privately warned against any Americanization of the conflict and publicly predicted that a full-fledged congressional debate on Vietnam was imminent. But no such debate took place, even though a prime reason for the Democrats' reticence in earlier months — the need to avoid doing anything that might help the hawkish Goldwater win the presidency — no longer pertained now that LBJ had won a crushing victory. On Johnson's orders, senior administration officials worked hard behind the scenes in January to head off or at least delay a Senate debate, with evident success — when the debate at last took place in mid-February it was a limited affair.

In late March, after the pivotal decisions to commence the sustained bombing of North Vietnam and to dispatch the first ground forces to the South, the doves stepped up their efforts to bring about a political solution to the war — but only slightly. At no point in the spring and summer months did anyone in the Senate leadership seem willing to fully confront the administration over Vietnam. Mansfield, Fulbright, and Russell were prescient in foreseeing the problems in any attempt to Americanize the war and felt certain that Washington should adopt a more flexible negotiating position, but they weakened their case by at the same time praising Johnson as a man of peace and affirming the need to continue to help the Saigon regime. Virtually all the congressional skeptics were unwilling to say what they really believed: that Vietnam was not worth the price of a major war, that even the "loss" of South Vietnam would not have serious implications for American security, that a face-saving negotiated settlement was the best that could be hoped for. White House officials, all too aware of these widespread concerns, were relieved when no genuine debate on the war occurred in the first half of 1965. They had been particularly worried about the Senate, generally the more independent of the two houses on foreign policy matters and in this case possessing leaders dubious about the commitment.

Why this congressional reticence? Partly it resulted from the administration's assurances to legislators that it was considering all the options, that it genuinely sought a peaceful solution, that it saw real reasons for optimism in the Saigon government's prospects; these claims caused many in Congress — whether hawk, dove, or somewhere in between — to remain steadfast in support of the war. Partly, too, it resulted from the certainty among the majority Democrats that Johnson would not look kindly on public opposition to the policy — the president left little doubt that he expected party members to fall in line. At the same time, though, there was among the legislators a certain willingness to be deceived about the war plans, a willingness to be strong-armed by the president. Many were quite content to escape responsibility from a policy that seemed to be getting steadily more complicated and for which few of them had a clear prescription. Perhaps no military solution existed, but how could they come up with a viable framework for a political settlement? It proved a very difficult question to answer, and most in Congress chose to swallow their concerns and trust that the president — who after all presumably had more information at his disposal — knew what he was doing.

Nevertheless, an important point remains: the opposition to an American war in Vietnam by the senior members of Congress was fully formed well in advance of the major decisions of early 1965. Exact numbers are hard to come by, but it seems clear that in the Senate a majority was either downright opposed to Americanization or ambivalent; perhaps more important, the number of committed hawks that spring was astonishingly small. (Congressional support would rise dramatically in the summer, after Americanization had begun in earnest, in a textbook example of the rally-around-the-flag effect.) It is misleading to suggest, as countless historians do, that the war enjoyed broad support on Capitol Hill in the early years of large-scale war. In the significant months of decision, the support was lukewarm at best.

(Quiet) Rumblings of Discontent

As the U.S. military involvement increased in late 1965 and into 1966, many lawmakers continued to hope for the best and to back the administration's policy. Some who had been doves before the escalation, such as Richard Russell, became hawks on the theory that the decision had been made and there was no longer an option but to support the troops and hence the policy. At a meeting between congressional leaders and LBJ on January 25, 1966, Russell called Vietnam the most frustrating experience of his life. "I didn't want to get in there," he said, "but we are there." He pleaded with the president to end the bombing halt then under way — and indeed step up the attack. "For God's sake, don't start the bombing halfway. Let them know they are in a war. We killed civilians in World War II and nobody opposed it. I'd rather kill them than have American boys die. Please, Mr. President, don't get one foot back in it. Go all the way."

Of the seventeen members of Congress who attended this meeting, only two — Mansfield and Fulbright — raised objections to a resumption of the bombing. Both believed it essential to get to the negotiating table as quickly as possible and that the way to do so was through a cease-fire, not renewed military escalation. Though they were the lone voices at the meeting, others shared their views. Two days later, on January 27, fifteen liberal Democrats signed a letter to Johnson urging him not to renew the bombing. Johnson, outraged, privately called the letter's lead author, Indiana's Vance Hartke, a "prick." As a warning to others who might step out of line, LBJ made it clear that there would be a price to pay for dissenting: he refused to appoint Hartke's nominees to the agricultural stabilization committee in Indiana.

It was more worrisome to the administration when, in late January and February, Fulbright convened televised hearings on the U.S. policy in Vietnam. In 1964 he had smoothed the passage of the Gulf of Tonkin Resolution through Congress, and at important points in the winter and spring of 1965 he had voiced public support for Johnson's policy. The subsequent Americanization stunned him, and in the autumn he had grown steadily more outraged by the escalating violence. He had been deceived, he now believed, into believing that the administration sought a peaceful resolution to the conflict and would avoid major military escalation. He hoped to use the hearings to ask tough questions of top administration officials and to invite testimony from distinguished skeptics with impeccable foreign policy credentials — men such as George F. Kennan, one of the architects of America's Cold War containment strategy, and the retired general James M. Gavin, the former commander of the 101st Airborne Division. Both testified that the United States had committed too many resources to Vietnam and that, in Kennan's words, America's "preoccupation" with Vietnam was undermining its global obligations.

Administration officials, meanwhile, including Secretary of State Dean Rusk, endured tough questioning from Fulbright and other senators about how long the war would last and what America's objectives were. Some exchanges got testy, as when Wayne Morse confronted the former ambassador to Saigon General Maxwell Taylor. "I happen to hold to the point of view that it isn't going to be long before the American people, as a people, will repudiate our war in Southeast Asia," Morse said. "That, of course, is good news to Hanoi, Senator," Taylor countered, but Morse shot right back: "I know that that is the smear that you militarists give to those of us who have honest differences of opinion with you, but I don't intend to get down in the gutter with you and engage in that kind of debate, General."

Judging the impact of the hearings on congressional and public opinion is not easy. On the one hand, they appear to have caused no radical shift in thinking. When Morse in February introduced a bill to repeal the

Gulf of Tonkin Resolution, it was voted down, 92–5. Not long thereafter, the Senate approved another $12 billion for the war. Public opinion polls in early 1966 did not show a major change as a result of the hearings. Nevertheless, the hearings were in some respects the first serious national discussion of the U.S. commitment in Vietnam, and they forced Americans to think about the conflict and the nation's role in it. To an important degree, they made it legitimate to dissent publicly on the war. And no longer could anyone doubt that there were deep divisions on Vietnam among public officials or that two of them, Lyndon Johnson and William Fulbright, had broken completely over the war.

In the months that followed, Johnson privately derided the Arkansan as "Senator Halfbright" and labeled him and other foes of the war as a bunch of "nervous Nellies" who lacked the courage to drive on to victory. At the same time, the president took evident satisfaction that most lawmakers remained onboard in support of the war. The congressional hawks, led by Stennis, Tower, and Dirksen, were never as visible or articulate as their dovish counterparts — and thus they have never been given as much attention by students of the war — but they mattered a great deal. They kept the congressional profile on Vietnam low throughout the period of major escalation in the Johnson years (by 1968, there were more than half a million ground troops in South Vietnam), and, in the case of the Republican leaders, they subtly pressured Johnson to pursue a military solution and resist the calls for disengagement.

The GOP leadership, keenly aware that Goldwater's attempt to make militancy on Vietnam a winning campaign issue in 1964 had been a dismal failure, was careful in the year that followed to adhere to a policy of backing the administration (a task made easier because Johnson ended up adopting, broadly speaking, the kind of aggressive military actions that Goldwater had championed in the campaign). In mid-May 1965 the Republican Policy Committee pledged to support the president's "firm actions to halt communist aggression" in Vietnam and elsewhere. At the same time, the party leaders avoided as much as possible publicly associating themselves with the Americanization policy — they knew it was smarter politically to let the Democrats take the responsibility for dramatically expanding the U.S. involvement, thereby giving themselves more room to maneuver in the future.

Privately, the Senate's minority leader, Everett Dirksen, urged Johnson in 1965 and 1966 to maintain the course and pursue a military victory. "If we are not winning now," he said at the White House in January 1966, "let's do what is necessary to win. I don't believe you have any other choice. I believe the country will support you." Johnson heard the same refrain that year and the next from many other Republicans as well as conservative Democrats, and he came increasingly to depend on that support as public frustration with the war mounted. From time to time Republican hawks such as Senator John Tower of Texas and Representative Ross Adair of Indiana criticized the president as overly timid, as not being aggressive enough in fighting the war, but they gained little traction on Capitol Hill — to suggest that round-the-clock bombing and a steadily expanding troop commitment to a weak regime 10,000 miles away represented timidity on the president's part was not an easy sell. In their own way, however, these hawks, though comparatively few and lacking in influence, helped shape administration policy, if only indirectly. Johnson, telling anyone who would listen that he was getting pressure from both sides, the peaceniks and the warmongers, pointed to the congressional hawks' carping to say that he was adhering to the only sensible path: the middle of the road. It was a disingenuous claim — he always traveled much closer to the escalation side of the street than to the withdrawal side — but for a long time it worked.

All of which helps to explain why the Johnson years witnessed no major effort on the part of Congress to insert itself forcefully into Vietnam policy. The opposition articulated in 1966 and 1967 by Mansfield and Fulbright no doubt helped turn public as well as congressional opinion against the war, but neither man was by temperament or training the type to lobby colleagues to the cause, especially with a fellow Democrat in the White House. Both also understood that with growing numbers of Americans fighting and dying in the war, the pressure would be great on lawmakers seeking reelection to support the troops and justify the deaths through a continued push for victory. General confusion about what was really going on in South Vietnam further inclined the legislators toward inaction and deepened the divisions about the U.S. commitment in both parties. The administration insisted through 1967 that William Westmoreland's strategy was working and that the war was being won; many in Congress swallowed their reservations and chose to accept the claim — or at least to keep their mouths shut.

The Hanoi government's bold Tet Offensive in early 1968 gave the lie to the public optimism (even if its results were inconclusive) and generated increased congressional calls for a fundamental reevaluation of foreign policy and a more active attempt at gaining a negotiated settlement. Even then, however, a combination of factors — election-year strategizing and the desire of many legislators to avoid taking positions that could hurt them at the polls; Johnson's announcement in March that he would not seek reelection; and the start of negotiations in Paris in April — kept Congress at the margins of policymaking. Many liberals and centrists on Capitol Hill pinned their hopes on the possibility that, at long last, a deal might be struck that would end to the bloodshed.

Nixon Versus Congress

It did not happen, of course. The negotiations in Paris failed to yield meaningful results, and the fighting continued to rage as the year drew to a close. The new president, Richard Nixon, had said during the campaign that he had a "secret plan" to end the war, but on taking office he unveiled no major policy initiative. Continuity was the watchword in the early months. Yet Nixon encountered a more assertive Congress on the subject of Vietnam than his predecessor had. Already in late 1968, shortly after the election, a group of Senate doves met in Mike Mansfield's office, among them John Sherman Cooper, Jacob Javits, and George Aiken, as well as the Democrats Frank Church, Stuart Symington of Missouri, Phil Hart of Michigan, and a few others. According to Cooper's aide William Miller, the lawmakers avoided specifics but agreed on a critical proposition: if the war in Southeast Asia could not be stopped, at least they could work for the next best thing — to keep it contained. Subsequently, by carefully choosing issues and by highlighting the Senate's constitutional obligations toward foreign policy, the doves could hope to start squeezing the war, working at its margins in order to compress it. With hard work and a little luck, it might be possible to increase the antiwar sentiment on Capitol Hill and thereby shrink the war.

The result was a series of amendments, introduced from 1969 to 1972, aimed at curbing any further U.S. military involvement in Southeast Asia. Two important players during much of this campaign were the Republican Cooper and the Democrat Church. At first glance they were an unlikely pair, representing different parties and different regions of the country, even different generations — Church was not yet born when Cooper graduated from Yale in 1923. But they were united in their conviction that American foreign policy had gone astray, as shown most dramatically by Vietnam, that the nation was on the wrong side of history, that successive administrations had lost sight of the principles on which the United States was founded. At the same time, both were not prepared to advocate an immediate U.S. withdrawal, and both believed that whatever Congress might do, Nixon should be left with sufficient flexibility to protect the American soldiers already in Indochina.

The Cooper-Church team won its first victory in mid-December 1969, when the Senate approved their amendment (to a Defense appropriations act) prohibiting the use of funds for sending American ground forces into

Laos or Thailand. The vote was 78–11. Cooper and Church were openly skeptical of Nixon's Vietnamization policy (in which American troops would be gradually withdrawn, to be replaced by stepped-up South Vietnamese forces) and concerned about the air war in Cambodia and Laos. Here was a way to, at the very least, reassert congressional prerogatives on foreign policy and perhaps also limit the scope of the war. Cooper had produced the original draft with Mansfield and had wanted to include Cambodia on the list, but Mansfield resisted on the grounds that the neutral Prince Norodom Sihanouk might be offended.

Mansfield had reason to regret that decision, for in the coming months Cambodia moved to the center of the debate over the war. In March 1970 a coup d'état against Sihanouk brought General Lon Nol to power, and disorder engulfed Cambodia. Rival gangs clashed in the streets, and vigilantes massacred local Vietnamese. Though Nixon and his national security adviser, Henry Kissinger, insisted that the coup surprised them, they moved quickly to bolster the new regime. When Lon Nol pleaded for assistance in mid-April and the administration pledged to provide it, the Senate doves registered their alarm. Spurred on by the GOP's Aiken and Majority Leader Mansfield, Cooper and Church decided to expand their amendment to include a prohibition against U.S. ground troops entering Cambodia. On April 30 Church discussed the amendment with reporters and warned Nixon not to open "a new front" and jeopardize "his declared policy of de-escalation."

Unbeknownst to Cooper and Church, four days earlier Nixon had decided to send U.S. troops into Cambodia. "We would go for broke," Nixon wrote in his memoirs. Intent on sending a forceful message to Hanoi, he also wanted to show his domestic critics, including those in the Senate, that he would not be pushed around. The battle lines were drawn — the White House and Senate would again square off over the powers of the presidency and Congress. In the next three months, as America shook with renewed protest and violence, the Nixon administration pulled out all the stops to try to defeat the amendment, tapping congressional allies, cabinet members, and even organized labor to work against it. Cooper and Church refused to withdraw the amendment, but under pressure from administration defenders they agreed to alter it to target only funds spent after July 1, thus giving Nixon ample time to get the troops out of Cambodia. They also agreed to add a disclaimer denying any intention to question the president's constitutional powers to protect the lives of U.S. soldiers. When the revised amendment passed, 58–37, on June 30, 1970, various voices in the antiwar movement criticized Cooper and Church for allowing their amendment to be watered down. The journalist I. F. Stone, for example, faulted them for being too busy splitting "constitutional hairs" and for leaving untouched the air war over Cambodia except to say that the bombing could not be in "direct" support of the Phnom Penh government.

Stone had a point. There were holes in the amendment, holes that left Nixon a good deal more maneuverability than the two senators had originally vowed. But the antiwar critics would also have to ask themselves whether tougher wording would have had any chance of passage. Stone declared his preference for an amendment sponsored by the Democrat George McGovern and the Republican Mark Hatfield, which would have required the administration to withdraw all U.S. forces from Vietnam by the end of 1971. The McGovern-Hatfield motion failed on September 1, 55–39. Cooper and Church and their supporters felt confident that they had achieved about as much as was politically feasible in the summer of 1970 and that they had taken an important step toward ending the U.S. involvement. The Senate had taken aim at the economic lifeblood of the war — its funding. The final version of the amendment failed to address the air war — the votes were not there, Church said — but the *Washington Post* still called it "one of the most significant aspects of the Ninety-first Congress. It is the first time in our history that Congress has attempted to limit the deployment of American troops in the course of an ongoing war." William P. Bundy, in his history of Nixon's foreign policy, writes of Cooper-Church that the administration "did not dare challenge its dictates" regarding policy in Cambodia. Many who had voted against the amendment privately were nevertheless sympathetic to it, the White House knew. Testing their loyalty to the president would not be wise.

That autumn Church exulted in speeches and on television that "the doves have won." After all, he said, their two principal aims — a withdrawal of U.S. forces and a negotiated settlement — were now the Nixon administration's policy. But questions remained regarding when these objectives would be met. Church and his colleagues knew that significant though the Cooper-Church amendment may have been in reducing Nixon's military options, it was not a true end-the-war amendment. Accordingly, in 1971 several attempts were made to go one step further, beyond merely limiting the war to actually ending it. None of these efforts went very far — the votes simply weren't there — and by the end of the year the idea was dead. Nixon's authority to wage war, it was clear, remained considerable. He retained strong backing in the House of Representatives, where Speaker John W. McCormack and his successor in 1971, Carl B. Albert, maintained support for the administration; in the Senate the president commanded enough votes to sustain any veto of antiwar legislation he found particularly objectionable.

Even so, Congress remained very much on Nixon's mind as 1972 began. His awareness of the growing antiwar sentiment in the Senate added to his sense of urgency about the negotiations in Paris — the majority Democrats would not keep funding the war much longer, he knew. Henry Kissinger and his North Vietnamese counterpart, Le Duc Tho, reached agreement on a deal in October 1972, but the South Vietnamese leader, Nguyen Van Thieu, thwarted the deal before it could take effect. In December, after winning reelection, Nixon launched the so-called Christmas Bombing, a massive eleven-day aerial attack of Hanoi and Haiphong designed to get the North Vietnamese back to the negotiating table. One of Nixon's motives in choosing this form of heavy bombardment: he desperately wanted a deal in place before Congress returned in early January.

Nixon did not quite make his deadline, but he came close: the Paris Peace Accords were signed in late January 1973. America's longest war, including eight years of large-scale fighting, was effectively over. No more end-the-war amendments would be needed. For most legislators on Capitol Hill, as in the country at large, the end came as a relief, but it also brought with it a need for the lawmakers to reflect on their role in Vietnam policymaking over the previous two-plus decades. The wartime divisions proved difficult to heal even after the fighting stopped — they were indeed evident a quarter of century later, as the century drew to a close. Antiwar critics blamed the war partly on what they saw as pusillanimous Congresses that had been too quick to compromise and had ceded too much power to the executive branch. Defenders of the war, meanwhile, accused Congress of "meddling" in an area of presidential authority in the Nixon years and of helping to bring on the end of South Vietnam in 1975 (by refusing to authorize enough assistance to the Saigon regime after the U.S. withdrawal in 1973). Not for the first time in their nation's history and not for the last, Americans were in fundamental disagreement over how to strike the proper balance between Congress and the White House in making war and peace.

This schism would carry less historical importance were it not for what recent research has demonstrated: that the foreign policy leadership in the Senate had deep doubts about the Vietnam commitment early on and was opposed to the 1965 Americanization before it happened. They foresaw disaster should Lyndon Johnson choose to make Vietnam an American war. Yet they stayed largely silent until after the major decisions had been made and policies implemented. Just what would have happened had these influential, well-respected legislators worked hard to thwart escalation in the winter and spring of 1965 can never be known, but certainly they would have been a powerful voice in any national debate. And whatever one's position on the morality and strategic wisdom of America's long and tragic involvement in Indochina, there can be no denying that such a debate would have served the nation well.

— FREDRIK LOGEVALL

BIBLIOGRAPHICAL NOTES

An abundant literature deals with Congress and the Vietnam War, though few works center on the subject. The most thorough treatments are Robert Mann, *A Grand Delusion: America's Descent Into Vietnam* (New York, 2001), and William C. Gibbons, *The U.S Government and the Vietnam War: Executive and Legislative Relationships*, vols. I–IV (Princeton, N.J., 1986–1995).

The executive-legislative interaction during the escalation of the war in 1963–1965 is examined in Fredrik Logevall, *Choosing War: The Lost Chance for Peace and the Escalation of War in Vietnam* (Berkeley, Calif., 1999). Important insights into Johnson's handling of Congress in the same period can be gained from Michael R. Beschloss, ed., *Taking Charge: The Johnson White House Tapes, 1963–1964* (New York, 1997), and *Reaching for Glory: The Johnson White House Tapes, 1964–65* (New York, 2001). The congressional role during the Nixon years is well handled in William P. Bundy, *A Tangled Web: The Making of Foreign Policy in the Nixon Administration* (New York, 1998).

Broader studies of Congress's role in foreign policymaking after 1945 include James Lindsay, *Congress and the Politics of U.S. Defense Policy* (Baltimore, 1994); Louis Fisher, *Presidential War Power* (Lawrence, Kans., 1995); and Arthur M. Schlesinger Jr, *The Imperial Presidency* (New York, 1973).

Among the more notable memoirs about the domestic politics of the war are George McGovern, *Grassroots: The Autobiography of George McGovern* (New York, 1977); Hubert H. Humphrey, *The Education of a Public Man: My Life in Politics* (Garden City, N.Y., 1976); Lyndon Baines Johnson, *The Vantage Point: Perspectives of the Presidency, 1963–1969* (New York, 1971); and Richard Nixon, *RN: The Memoirs of Richard Nixon* (New York, 1978). Important biographies include LeRoy Ashby and Rod Gramer, *Fighting the Odds: The Life of Senator Frank Church* (Pullman, Wash., 1994); Randall Bennett Woods, *Fulbright: A Biography* (New York, 1995); Robert David Johnson, *Ernest Gruening and the American Dissenting Tradition* (Cambridge, Mass., 1996); and Gilbert C. Fite, *Richard B. Russell, Jr.: Senator from Georgia* (Chapel Hill, N.C., 1991). On Mansfield's role, see Don Oberdorfer, *Senator Mansfield: The Extraordinary Life of a Great American Statesman and Diplomat* (Washington, D.C., 2003); Gregory Allan Olson, *Mansfield and Vietnam: A Study in Rhetorical Adaptation* (East Lansing, Mich., 1995); and Francis R. Valeo, *Mike Mansfield, Majority Leader: A Different Kind of Senate, 1961–1976* (Armonk, N.Y., 1999). The attitudes among Republicans during the Kennedy-Johnson years are examined in Terry Dietz, *Republicans and Vietnam, 1961–1968* (New York, 1986).

Unless otherwise indicated, all quotations in the text are drawn from the volumes by Mann, Gibbons, and Logevall.

34

The Environment

THE YEAR IS 1963, and the United States Senate, that most venerable of government institutions, has just gone Hollywood. Unfortunately, the Capitol does not come equipped with a marquee; otherwise, the Committee on Public Works might have announced the release of *Troubled Waters*, the first congressionally produced motion picture, with suitable fanfare.

The thirty-minute documentary, sponsored by the committee's new Subcommittee on Air and Water Pollution, surely poses no threat to Tinsel Town. The film cost about $200,000, just enough to hire a scriptwriter, borrow a camera crew from the Public Health Service's Communicable Disease Center, and rent an air force plane for location shoots. The renowned actor Henry Fonda endowed the project with star power by serving as the narrator, but he refused to appear onscreen, much to the disappointment of committee staff members.

In fact, the real star of the show is sewage. *Troubled Waters* introduces viewers to the growing problem of water pollution in the United States, broadly defined to include industrial and municipal waste, thermal discharges, agricultural runoff, acid mine drainage, radioactive materials, and oil slicks. "If America's waters are troubled," Fonda intones, "it is because they are overworked." To support this assertion, the film presents pollutants in all their vivid hues: from the reds of a meatpacking plant in Kansas City and the blacks of a Maine textile factory to steel mill browns, white detergent suds, and green algae. Water users appear in uncomfortable proximity to questionable effluents: children splash near a factory outflow pipe, and a water-skier glides beneath a plane's pesticide trail. To hammer the message home, Fonda evokes the image of a fallen ancient civilization:

> To live, man must use and pollute the water. But if he abuses it and fails to do his best to restore its natural purity, then water will no longer be

> able to serve him. And factories will close, farms will dry up, people will disappear, and the lessons of Babylon will not have been learned.

At the film's end, a tall, rather wooden figure stands uncomfortably before the camera. Edmund S. Muskie, a first-term Democrat from Maine and chairman of the Subcommittee on Air and Water Pollution, proposes various legislative solutions for these problems. He is no Henry Fonda. The wide distribution of *Troubled Waters* to schools and civic groups across the country, however, ensures that many more citizens will know who he is and what his subcommittee is doing.

There is much in this brief sketch that seems counterintuitive. Why begin an account of Congress and post–World War II environmental policy in 1963? Why not 1970 — the year another senator, Gaylord Nelson (D-Wisconsin), helped organize Earth Day, a nationwide eco-celebration that heralded a sea change in cultural and political values? Why would the Public Works Committee, whose members never met a dam, channel, or highway they didn't like, feel compelled to produce a movie about pollution? And how did Edmund Muskie — who as governor of Maine in the fifties spent much of his time trying to attract industry to his decidedly rural state — become the spokesman for a distinctively urban problem?

The answers to such questions reveal the history of postwar "environmentalism" to be a story about Congress as well as one of social and cultural change. They demonstrate that Congress is *the* point of departure for comprehending a critical transformation in American public life between 1945 and 1975. As a representative body, the legislative branch was uniquely attuned to shifting perspectives and proved most responsive to citizens' concerns about the deteriorating quality of the natural world.

This level of responsiveness to new interests and voting blocs grew out of Congress's own postwar evolution. Indeed, congressional pioneers frequently ran ahead of the curve in the fifties and sixties, laboring to manufacture receptive constituencies for environmental policies before a discernible mass movement actually existed. Even when the public embraced the cause in the late sixties and early seventies, demanding stronger federal laws to protect the environment, the legislative process (and the legislation it produced) was not simply reactive. Though receptive to external pressure, it also reflected internal priorities, individual personalities, and pragmatic agendas. What followed was not just a set of new laws, but rather an entirely new regulatory regime that redefined the federal government's scope and relationship to its citizens.

Congress's approach to environmental policy is emblematic of the postwar political landscape in one further respect. Like every other modern institution, it turned to experts to help define problems and determine solutions. The legislators took their cues from scientists and government technocrats as well as from grass-roots activists and public interest groups. Institutionally, then, Congress has embodied the tensions between expertise and democratic participation that characterized much of the twentieth century. The legislative branch mediated among different ideologies — old and new, popular and professional — that informed environmental regulation in often surprising ways.

Of course, Congress did not invent environmental consciousness, nor did such a consciousness spring forth suddenly in the late sixties. Its social and cultural roots can be traced to the shifting demographics of a dynamic postwar society. The most notable trend was the growth of an affluent, educated, middle-class population, concentrated in urban or suburban centers, who tended to define "quality of life" with increasing references to leisure, health, and community. The natural world was integral to this new standard of living.

As the "consumption" of environmental amenities increased, so did the public demand to preserve them. Organized citizen participation registered its greatest success in the effort to set aside woodland areas. Congress responded to interest groups in Washington like the Wilderness Society, whose growing membership reflected the popularity of outdoor activities and undeveloped landscapes, with legislation that included the Wilderness Act of 1964.

Conservation groups also had occasional success in defeating proposals to develop pristine areas. In the most celebrated case during the fifties, the Sierra Club and Wilderness Society halted the construction of a proposed Bureau of Reclamation dam at Echo Park (Dinosaur National Monument), near the Utah-Colorado border. To do so, they boldly challenged the hydrological data presented by the bureau's engineers during House and Senate hearings and countered local economic interests by skillfully appealing to a national audience. The predominantly western legislators on the Irrigation and Reclamation subcommittees were used to operating in an insulated forum, catering exclusively to client interest groups and administrative agencies. Faced with a well-publicized dispute featuring opposing expertise and an aroused public, however, they begrudgingly acquiesced.

By contrast, no comparable mass support existed for federal pollution laws. Although growing dissatisfaction with local problems had inspired citizen activism since the fifties, air and water quality control remained a prerogative jealously exercised by the individual states. Federal officials had little incentive to encroach on their autonomy, and state officials had little incentive to impose strict regulations on dischargers in urban and industrial areas. Simply put, the political influence of conservation organizations paled in comparison to that of corporate interests. The federal government's foray into pollution control, then, owed less to the grass roots than the legislative branch.

The Making of a Policy Entrepreneur

The year is 1959, and Lyndon B. Johnson (D-Texas), the most powerful and influential majority leader the Senate has ever known, has just gone ballistic. The object of his ire is Edmund Muskie, the new senator from Maine. Muskie's mistake was politely resisting the "treatment," a skillful combination of charm and intimidation that usually helped wayward senators see things Johnson's way — in this case, on an upcoming vote regarding parliamentary procedure. Johnson may have sensed smugness in the newcomer's demurral; whatever the reason, Muskie would soon pay.

At Johnson's urging, the Democratic Steering Committee ignored the freshman's top committee preferences — Foreign Relations and Commerce — and placed him instead on the decidedly less sexy Government Operations and Public Works committees. Under the watchful eye of the conservative Democratic oil baron Robert Kerr of Oklahoma (arguably the most powerful man on the Hill after Johnson), the latter committee served as a sort of purgatory for liberals and other troublemakers in the Senate. Muskie was off to a rough start.

This cautionary tale reveals the centrality of committees in determining congressional career paths. But this system also helped structure postwar policy formation, particularly with respect to new agendas like the environment. Ultimately, neither the sublime memory of Maine's pristine wilderness nor the hue and cry of the electorate drove Muskie to make a career of pollution control. Rather, he mastered a relatively arcane field in order to maximize his power and influence in the postwar Senate.

To understand the roots of environmental policy, it is thus important to understand how Congress worked. Unlike most institutions in the twentieth century, Congress became more modern as it became less hierarchical. In the years leading up to the Second World War, a combination of institutional and partisan reforms diminished the traditional sources of authority (like the Speaker of the House and the Democratic Caucus), solidified the seniority system, and effectively dispersed power to the committees. Part of the stability of the committee system until the 1970s derived from a lack of turnover in the House and Senate — more than 80 percent tended to be reelected from one term to another. Since seniority replaced leadership discretion as the mechanism for distributing institutional resources, electoral longevity enabled the members to secure committee chairs and build independent bases of power. Largely free from external interference or sanction, chairmen exercised nearly total control over their committees' agenda and staff, and they enjoyed great autonomy in proposing, considering, or blocking legislation.

Knowledge itself proved to be among the most vital institutional resources. Committee members secured access to experts from government, academia, and the private sector; their information allowed chairmen to become recognized authorities in their given jurisdictions. Generalists in Congress usually deferred to an individual committee's expertise, particularly as policy grew more complex. The proliferation of specialized subcommittees attested to the burgeoning workload and explosion of technical data.

But subcommittees served another important institutional function as well. In the Senate especially, a substantial underrepresentation of liberals among the committee chairmen generated considerable resentment. Between the Eighty-sixth and Ninety-first Congresses, conservatives held over half of these prized slots, despite the influx of northern Democrats that began in 1958. Given the limited upward mobility in committees dominated by southern conservatives, the expansion of subcommittees helped to alleviate the regional disparity in the Senate's distribution of power. Between 1957 and 1968, the number of Senate subcommittees grew from 86 to 103, while the percentage of southern subcommittee chairmen declined from 45 to 31.

Ed Muskie was among the beneficiaries of subcommittee politics, becoming chairman of the new Subcommittee on Air and Water Pollution in 1963. Ironically, he wanted no part of it at first. Following Robert Kerr's sudden, fatal heart attack in 1962, Muskie angled for the vacated chair of the Rivers and Harbors Subcommittee. He had observed how Kerr skillfully converted channels and dams into political currency, consolidating his influence in the Senate by controlling the distribution of pork barrel projects. Even as specialized knowledge became more important, the mastery of "distributive politics" still represented a time-honored path to power in Congress, especially as the postwar federal expenditures on public works soared into the billions.

Distributive politics also embodied the traditional, developmental approach to natural resources. Kerr's 1960 book, *Land, Wood, and Water,* reflected his enthusiasm for the government's comprehensive river basin development in the Southwest (and specifically Oklahoma). But Kerr was hardly unique in his utilitarian approach to nature. Wayne Aspinall (D-Colorado), chairman of the House Interior Committee (1959–1973), shared a similar passion for economic development. As the primary overseer of public lands in the expansive, underdeveloped West, he too accumulated considerable power and influence and used it to promote the interests of the region's ranchers, miners, and industrialists. Not surprisingly, Kerr and Aspinall had little stomach for environmental initiatives that interfered with their vision of development.

Rivers and Harbors boded well for Muskie's career and Maine's economy; sewage and smog, on the other hand, held no such promise. Indeed, the idea behind an air and water pollution subcommittee originated with Abraham Ribicoff (R-Connecticut), who at the time did not even belong to the Public Works Committee. Ribicoff, a former secretary of the Department of Health, Education and Welfare, was searching for a platform from which to introduce air quality legislation, and he lobbied Chairman Patrick McNamara (D-Michigan) to establish a new subcommittee for that purpose. Ribicoff was assigned to the Government Operations Committee, however, where he launched a nationally renowned investigation of agricultural pesticides. But McNamara acted on his original suggestion, assigning Muskie to the new position rather than to the one he wanted. Muskie's response hardly resembled a battle cry for environmentalists: "Air? What the hell do I know about air coming from Maine?"

Despite this inauspicious beginning, within eighteen months Muskie had transformed himself into the leading Senate expert on both air and water pollution. As such, he made the most of the hand Johnson and McNamara had dealt him, embracing specialized knowledge as his path to power. He realized that his modest subcommittee provided an institutional base from which to publicize a new social problem, develop legislation, and cultivate constituencies to lobby for continuous implementation. In short, he became a legislative entrepreneur.

Like any good entrepreneur, Muskie understood the importance of publicity. Pollution control stood to benefit a broad, diffuse public, but its costs would be concentrated among discrete and powerful interests (i.e., polluters). As a consequence, the latter would be motivated to organize and oppose the policy, while the majority of the beneficiaries lacked the cohesion and incentive to support it. As late as 1965, a Gallup poll reported that only 17 percent of its respondents viewed air and water pollution as problems worthy of government attention. So the senator turned to innovative solutions, like the motion picture *Troubled Waters,* to raise people's awareness of the issue. A rigorous speaking schedule and frequent appearances on television and radio also kept the issue in the public eye. Likewise, his subcommittee frequently went on the road during the sixties, conducting a series of hearings around the country designed to document regional pollution problems and drum up support for legislative solutions.

But Muskie's ultimate effectiveness stemmed directly from the credibility he garnered as an articulate expert. He immersed himself in the arcane details of economics, chemistry, and engineering, analyzing programmatic options for pollution control with a Socratic rigor and a pragmatic eye. In the Senate, where specialization and dedication to legislative work stood out as valued norms of conduct, Muskie's labors earned him a great deal of respect. In turn, he used his professional authority to build a broad policy consensus among legislators, the executive branch, local officials, technicians, businessmen, and conservationists.

The 1965 Water Quality Act and the 1967 Air Quality Act, the decade's signature pollution control statutes, emerged as the products of that consensus. In actuality, Muskie's entrepreneurial legislation reflected a number of traditional political agendas and professional discourses. Both laws, for example, were grounded in what Muskie called "creative federalism": state officials would take the lead in setting and enforcing regionally specific ambient air or stream standards, while the federal government would provide technical assistance and the threat of intervention if loose deadlines and expectations were not met. Of course, local bureaucrats and business interests vigorously opposed across-the-board national standards or a stronger federal presence. But Muskie had real faith in this cooperative approach. It accommodated existing organizational arrangements and local prerogatives and allowed for a flexible response to environmental conditions that varied with geography. He also believed that a uniform process for setting standards, backed by an enumerated policy of "quality enhancement," would overcome local recalcitrance, ratchet up expectations, and bring about incremental but steady improvements.

The administrative process that Muskie's subcommittee created and oversaw relied on experts to regulate pollution. But the legislation itself made no effort to dictate the proper control technologies or the precise scientific criteria that defined clean air or water. State sanitary engineers, economists, wildlife biologists, and natural resource planners made most of those decisions, often in consultation with business and community leaders. Newer sciences, particularly ecosystems ecology, had little direct impact on pollution policy, despite the inroads that popular authors like Rachel Carson (*Silent Spring*) had made on the public. Although the Johnson administration itself came to adopt a more aesthetic, holistic approach to the environment in the mid-sixties, traditional developmental priorities still prevailed.

For example, the specter of water shortages constituted a far greater concern than disease or ecological imbalance among postwar policymakers. As such, concerns about water quality were never far removed from issues of quantity. The experts Muskie consulted saw pollution mainly as an obstacle to economic growth, rendering limited water supplies unfit for multiple use. Such an outlook naturally resonated with the Public Works

Committee, which saw dams and pollution control as solutions in kind. Although Muskie hoped to raise the quality standards to allow streams to support higher-end uses like recreation and sport fishing, economic development remained the dominant rhetoric.

Indeed, a similar developmental rationale had provided the impetus for the first permanent Federal Water Pollution Control Act back in 1956. The story of its sponsor, Representative John Blatnik (D-Minnesota), and his exploits as the chairman of the House Subcommittee on Rivers and Harbors demonstrate that environmental legislation and distributive politics were not mutually exclusive.

Blatnik was a New Dealer at heart; he detested the avarice of large corporate polluters but also championed the federal development of natural resources. He characterized pollution as a waste of water and pitched abatement as a conservation tool to ensure a continually expanding economy. More important, Blatnik realized that a bill with even the most minimally coercive abatement requirements stood little chance of approval without support from constituencies more numerous and influential than the Audubon or Wilderness Society. So he built support by bringing municipal governments and organized labor onboard with a new grant-in-aid program for the construction of sewage treatment plants. The combined backing of these interests helped counter industrial opposition and create a reliable new constituency for pollution control. Along with the promise of federal money and jobs, Blatnik made pollution controllers out of reluctant congressmen who had channels to dig or harbors to deepen.

Blatnik's deft distribution of pork helped earn him the title "the father of water pollution control," yet it was Muskie who ultimately was recognized as Congress's "Mr. Clean." In the end, the power of pork alone could not match Muskie's own institutional advantages. As time went on, Blatnik found it increasingly difficult to build support for tougher environmental legislation in the House Public Works Committee. Its membership was three times as large as the Senate's and included many southern conservatives and representatives from industrial districts who vigorously resisted federal regulation (members of the House, elected biannually, always took more direct heat from disgruntled interests than senators did). Muskie, on the other hand, enjoyed a collegial relationship with his colleagues, for scrupulous bipartisanship was a hallmark of his leadership style. His alliances with important Republicans, particularly Caleb Boggs of Delaware and later Howard Baker of Tennessee, ensured strong, unified committee support for pollution control legislation, despite pressure from the congressional GOP leadership or the Nixon White House.

Moreover, Muskie could count on the help of a skilled and energetic staff, an absolutely indispensable resource as the amount and complexity of the work increased. Blatnik could not, nor did he boast quite the grasp of complex detail that the senator did. Perhaps more than anything else, staff support allowed legislative entrepreneurs to exploit the authority of expertise. By the mid-sixties, then, all of these institutional factors had helped shape Muskie's career — and the substance of much of the nation's environmental policy.

The Transformation of the Policy Landscape

The year is 1970, and Ed "Mr. Clean" Muskie, widely regarded as the Senate's foremost environmental authority, has just gone on the defensive. Consider the following:

• A report on air pollution, sponsored by Ralph Nader's Center for the Study of Responsive Law, condemns the federal air quality program as a cumbersome and ineffective disaster. Its authors cite Muskie's ill-advised faith in federalism, his fetish for consensus, and his unwillingness to take on corporate polluters as evidence that it is time for him to resign his chairmanship. Meanwhile, the Nixon administration also criticizes the current system and introduces its own legislation, calling for national ambient air quality and emissions standards. For good measure, the upstart representative Paul Rogers (D-Florida) uses the House Commerce Committee's Subcommittee on Public Health and Welfare as a forum to introduce his own ambitious air quality legislation. Rogers, a novice outsider, educates himself just enough to raise fundamental questions about Muskie's handiwork.

• An obscure nineteenth-century statute threatens to circumvent the enforcement provisions of the 1965 Water Quality Act. The 1899 Rivers and Harbors Act long ago declared it unlawful to "throw, discharge or deposit . . . any refuse matter of any kind . . . into any navigable water of the United States" without a permit from the Corps of Engineers. Since then, the Corps and virtually everyone else had dutifully ignored that clause, known as the Refuse Act. In March 1970, however, Representative Henry Reuss (D-Wisconsin), chairman of the House Government Operations Committee's Subcommittee on Natural Resources and the Environment, releases a report urging the Corps to enforce the Refuse Act more vigorously. Long frustrated with the inability of the federal water pollution laws to halt the despoliation of the Great Lakes, Reuss also encourages the Justice Department to prosecute violators. Under the Refuse Act, court-ordered injunctions can halt illegal discharges immediately; the Water Quality Act's cumbersome state-federal enforcement procedures cannot. In the wake of Reuss's activism, the Nixon administration announces a

Federal Refuse Act Permit Program in December 1970, a parallel system of water pollution regulation conceived independently of Muskie's legislative authority.

• Henry "Scoop" Jackson (D-Washington), chairman of the Senate Interior Committee, shepherds the National Environmental Policy Act (NEPA) through Congress. Its sponsor promises it will rationalize and coordinate the federal management of the "total environment." Jackson had played an active role supporting individual conservation initiatives like the Wilderness Act during the sixties. But his staff, working with prominent scholars of public administration, urged him to embrace a more comprehensive strategy. NEPA's primary innovation is the Environmental Impact Statement (EIS), which will require all federal agencies to scrutinize their own activities (building dams, licensing nuclear power plants), incorporate diverse sources of information into their decisions, and consider alternatives less harmful to the environment. The EIS creates a new level of administrative accountability; external government offices, organizations, or citizens can comment directly on agency determinations or even challenge them on environmental grounds in court (presumably, an EIS would have exposed the flaws in the Echo Park dam project long before Congress had a chance to consider it). Jackson's open-ended, information-based strategy and his holistic emphasis on "the total environment" pose a regulatory alternative to the specialized pollution control system under Muskie's jurisdiction.

At the turn of the decade, then, Muskie found himself surrounded by a new generation of legislative entrepreneurs seeking to carve out their own environmental policy niches. But these legislators knew they no longer had to *create* receptive constituencies for their initiatives; by 1970 public concern about the environment had become nearly universal (more than 50 percent of Gallup's respondents now listed pollution as a critical government concern).

Environmental degradation had not radically accelerated in less than ten years; what had changed was the public's perception and sense of urgency. Disturbing, well-publicized incidents like the Santa Barbara oil spill created an atmosphere of crisis in 1969 that cast business interests and government — already targets of growing public distrust — in a decidedly negative light. The intensified media coverage of persistent local problems also exposed a credibility gap between the promise of federal pollution control programs and their actual performance. Moreover, by 1970 a new ecological discourse had attained broad cultural resonance, providing a vocabulary to challenge traditional developmental assumptions about nature.

The success of Earth Day in April 1970 confirmed that a mass movement had coalesced around ecological values. An estimated twenty million people participated in Senator Gaylord Nelson's "National Teach-In on the Crisis of the Environment," including students of all ages, housewives, blue-collar workers, and businessmen. Earth Day had obvious countercultural overtones; likewise, its decentralized organization and participatory spirit reflected the legacy of other grass-roots movements — civil rights, antiwar — championed by university activists.

But Nelson consciously sought to build the broadest environmental constituency possible, attracting the silent majority as well as the New Left. Earth Day targeted the middle-class mainstream, combining social critique with an atmosphere of education, celebration, and optimism. As such, the senator adhered to a centrist brand of environmentalism that had worked so effectively in Wisconsin, where his sponsorship of outdoor recreation, natural resource planning, wild rivers legislation, a ban on DDT, and increased federal regulatory powers won broad bipartisan support among the electorate. Given the increase in urban representation brought about by court-ordered redistricting in the sixties, health and quality-of-life issues like those Nelson highlighted now demanded greater congressional and executive attention. By 1970 Richard Nixon himself acknowledged the national consensus. Seeking in part to neutralize the presidential ambitions of Democratic frontrunners like Muskie and Jackson, he recommended an accelerated federal response to environmental degradation and signed off on a major executive branch reorganization that created the Environmental Protection Agency (EPA) in December 1970.

The interactions between this broad grass-roots movement, an active Congress, and a responsive administrative bureaucracy brought about a revolution in American government that scholars call the "new social regulation." Traditional modes of regulation involved the oversight of specific economic markets or interests (railroads, trucking, the communications industry); federal commissions exercised quasi-judicial authority over discrete matters such as rate-setting or trade practices that affected most Americans only indirectly, if at all. By contrast, the new social regulation applied to millions of people nationwide — users of environmental amenities, consumers, minorities, and so on. Congress created or empowered new agencies to protect citizens from present and future harm. The policies they implemented to do so were often complex.

In this context, the legislative process underwent two notable changes. The first involved a proliferation of public interest organizations in the late sixties and early seventies. These groups lobbied on behalf of millions of citizens who stood to benefit from the new social regulation, giving voice to a diffuse, mass constituency that had eluded legislative entrepreneurs like Muskie in the sixties. Wielding considerable electoral clout, this new professional class of lobbyists offered a permanent political counterweight to corporate interests, largely replacing organized labor in this role.

Associations like Friends of the Earth, the League of Conservation Voters, Environmental Action, and "Nader's Raiders" were run by young, middle-class, college graduates. They were more dedicated to urban ecological issues, more suspicious of growth-oriented policies, and more confrontational than traditional conservation organizations like the Sierra Club or the National Wildlife Federation. They also had access to legal and scientific expertise that allowed them to vet pollution control laws and administrative practices, publicize their deficiencies, and pressure the lawmakers to correct them. Nader's widely read investigative reports, *Vanishing Air* and *Water Wasteland*, vocally challenged Muskie's incremental approach and, by extension, his authority. But environmental advocates also used their expertise to shape the substance of environmental legislation, both in committee hearings and behind closed doors.

The substance of that legislation represented the second important change. In the fifties and sixties, statutes deferred to the autonomy of states in the federalist system; granted state and federal administrators considerable discretion; refrained from pushing the technological envelope for pollution control or demanding hard deadlines for the improvement of air or water quality; placed the burden of proof on the government during the enforcement process; provided multiple opportunities for polluters to appeal administrative decisions; and gave citizens little or no opportunity to participate.

By the seventies, however, a transformed political and cultural climate enabled — indeed, practically compelled — the legislators to support tough new laws that would have been unthinkable only a few years earlier. Ed Muskie's groundbreaking 1970 Clean Air Act and 1972 Clean Water Act represented two cases in point. Their regulatory scope and ambition far outstripped his subcommittee's most recent efforts and outflanked rival bills that already promised significant innovations (the Nixon administration's legislation proposed more rigorous federal enforcement than any comparable Great Society initiative). Although the White House and industrial lobbyists condemned the anticipated expense and bureaucratic intrusiveness of Muskie's handiwork, Congress approved both bills by wide margins: the Clean Water Act passed, 74–0 in the Senate, 366–11 in the House, and easily weathered a presidential veto, while the vote on the Clean Air Act proved even more lopsided.

Muskie's environmental laws authorized considerable sums of money

— $1.1 billion for air pollution research and state grants, an astounding $18 billion for sewage treatment plants — but largesse alone did not make them revolutionary. What set them apart from their sixties' predecessors was an "action-forcing" (nonincremental) approach to regulation. Both statutes were long, complex documents that concentrated enforcement at the federal level and spelled out how administrators had to act in explicit detail. They required the EPA to promulgate ambitious uniform national standards for effluent discharges, determined almost exclusively by technology or considerations of public health — external economic factors were largely excluded from such formulas. Strict timetables governed the implementation of controls, virtually compelling technological innovation in order to meet unprecedented policy goals. The Clean Air Act mandated 90 percent reductions in current carbon monoxide and hydrocarbon levels for 1975 model cars; the Clean Water Act required industrial plants to install the "Best Practicable Technology" (BPT) by 1977, "Best Available Technology" (BAT) by 1982, and actually declared a goal of *zero-discharge* by 1985. Polluters were granted only limited opportunities to contest most agency standards, either administratively or before a federal Court of Appeals. Meanwhile, citizen-suit provisions enabled environmentalists to sue the EPA administrator if implementation fell short of Congress's intent. Ironically, even as the environmental legislation of the seventies institutionalized a suspicion of experts and government bureaucrats, the complex, technology-driven regulatory system it created looked to them more than ever.

Ed Muskie may have begun the decade on the defensive, but the knowledge and institutional resources he enjoyed as subcommittee chairman allowed him to reassert his advantage. He regained the initiative on air pollution legislation by presenting tough automotive standards and deadlines that the Nixon administration opposed and less experienced legislators could not articulate. Moreover, Muskie did not simply respond reflexively to the demands of public interest advocates.

Although environmentalists did work closely with the members and staff of the Senate Public Works Committee during the drafting of the Clean Water Act, for example, its substance can be traced to many different sources. Its stated objective — "to restore the physical, chemical, and biological integrity of the nation's waters" — derived from the work of professional ecologists (not simply popularizers like Barry Commoner), who advised the subcommittee and convinced its members to rethink the basic tenets of sanitary engineering. Their decision to abandon ambient standards entirely in favor of technology-based effluent standards and a zero-discharge goal actually caught environmental groups off-guard and can be attributed to a number of surprising influences, from the Corps of

Engineers to California's aerospace industry. But it also grew out of prolonged, detailed discussions between Muskie and his colleagues about what the legislation's goals should be and the best way to achieve them in light of past failures. Finally, certain issues, such as how to incorporate the Refuse Act Permit Program into the bill, were hammered out in conference with members of the House Public Works Committee. In short, exclusive focus on an amorphous movement, or the political pressures exerted by its most prominent interests and actors, is not sufficient to explain how and why the actual substance of environmental legislation changed in the early seventies.

Of course, Congress could not always control the scope or direction of the new social regulation — environmental policy proved no exception. Public interest litigants frequently solicited federal courts to redefine the government's regulatory priorities in ways Congress had never anticipated. Judges chose to interpret NEPA's environmental impact language quite broadly, siding with environmentalists who sued to halt the construction of dams, channels, power plants, and highways nationwide. NEPA proved to be a blunter instrument against development than even Henry Jackson — a champion of western water projects — had intended. Likewise, when a virtually unanimous Congress approved the groundbreaking Endangered Species Act of 1973, it understood the law to protect "charismatic megafauna" like blue whales and bald eagles. Those same legislators expressed considerable vexation in 1978 when the Supreme Court, prompted by environmentalists, upheld a lower court's injunction against the Tennessee Valley Authority's multimillion-dollar Tellico Dam on behalf of a tiny, little-known fish called the snail darter.

Nor could members of Congress ever be certain that executive agencies would implement environmental legislation exactly as they intended, despite the specificity of the statutory language. The president himself still had the authority to impound appropriated funds, as Nixon did with the Clean Water Act. On the other hand, the dispersal of oversight authority among multiple committees also threatened to undermine environmental goals. For example, because no parallel congressional reorganization followed the creation of the EPA in 1970, the House and Senate Agricultural Committees retained jurisdiction over its pesticides programs (formerly the domain of the Department of Agriculture). Representative Jamie L. Whitten (D-Mississippi), the longtime chairman of the House Agricultural Appropriations Subcommittee and Congress's most vocal champion of farmers and pesticides manufacturers, actually controlled all appropriations for environmental and consumer protection until 1974. Congressional reforms after Watergate addressed some of these anomalies, but the decentralized structure of the committee system continued to militate against streamlined oversight. By 1993 thirteen congressional committees and twenty-six subcommittees claimed oversight responsibility for the EPA.

Critics on both the left and the right may legitimately question many aspects of Congress's environmental policy over the last four decades. This narrative was not intended to praise that record, but neither was it meant to bury it. The point worth reiterating in the end is that Congress did reflect, more than any other institution, the diversity of ideas and interests that informed one of the most important social policies of the twentieth century. No other body proved as capable of balancing the knowledge of experts with the will of the people for the sake of nature.

— Paul C. Milazzo

BIBLIOGRAPHICAL NOTES

The following books provide a useful introduction to Congress's role in the broad field of environmental policy: Christopher J. Bosso, *Pesticides and Politics: The Life Cycle of a Public Issue* (Pittsburgh, 1987); Clarence J. Davies, *The Politics of Pollution* (New York, 1970); Mark Harvey, *A Symbol of Wilderness: Echo Park and the American Conservation* Movement (Albuquerque, N.Mex., 1994); J. Brooks Flippen, *Nixon and the Environment* (Albuquerque, N.Mex., 2000); Samuel Hays, *Beauty, Health and Permanence: Environmental Politics in the United States, 1955–85* (New York, 1987); Thomas R. Huffman, *Protectors of the Land and Water: Environmentalism in Wisconsin, 1961–68* (Chapel Hill, N.C., 1994), and "Legislatures and the Environment," in *Encyclopedia of the American Legislative System: Studies of the Principal Structures, Processes, and Policies of Congress and the State Legislatures Since the Colonial Era,* ed. Joel H. Silbey (New York, 1994); Charles O. Jones, *Clean Air: The Policies and Politics of Pollution Control* (Pittsburgh, 1975); Robert Gordon Kaufman, *Henry M. Jackson: A Life in Politics* (Seattle, Wash., 2000); Terence Kehoe, *Cleaning Up the Great Lakes: From Cooperation to Confrontation* (Dekalb, Ill., 1997); Harvey Lieber, *Federalism and Clean Water* (Lexington, Mass., 1975); Richard A. Liroff, *A National Policy for the Environment: NEPA and Its Aftermath* (Bloomington, Ind., 1976); Char Miller, ed., *Water and the Environment Since 1945: A Cross-Cultural Perspective* (New York, 2001); Robert Cameron Mitchell, "From Conservation to Environmental Movement: The Development of the Modern Environmental Lobbies," in *Government and Environmental Politics: Essays on Historical Developments Since World War II,* ed. Michael J. Lacy (Baltimore, 1991); David Nevins, *Muskie of Maine* (New York, 1972); Shannon Petersen, *Acting for Endangered Species: The Statutory Ark* (Lawrence, Kans., 2002); Hal Rothman, *The Greening of a Nation?: Environmentalism in the United States Since 1945* (Fort Worth, Tex., 1998); Steven C. Schulte, *Wayne Aspinall and the Shaping of the American West* (Boulder, Colo., 2002); and James Q. Wilson, *The Politics of Regulation* (New York, 1980).

Part IV

THE CONTEMPORARY ERA

1970s–Today

The United States Capitol today.

AMERICANS HELD high expectations for Congress after President Richard Nixon resigned under fire in 1974. In the aftermath of Watergate and the congressional reforms that had weakened committee chairs and empowered younger members, there were bold predictions of a resurgent legislative branch. At the same time that the young Turks boasted about having internally democratized the institution, they promised that the War Powers Act (1973) and the Budget Control and Impoundment Act (1974) would strengthen Congress in relation to the executive branch. The Imperial Presidency had been tamed, or so it seemed.

Yet it became clear by the latter half of the decade that many of these optimistic predictions might not be fulfilled.[1] In the contemporary era, Congress has fluctuated between extreme fragmentation and strong partisan centralization. In the years that immediately followed the committee era, from the mid-1970s through the mid-1980s, Congress was fractured and chaotic. Individual legislators, caucuses, subcommittees, and the congressional minority pursued their own electoral and ideological interests. Although committee chairs lost their authority, party leaders were unable to step in and impose their will on a rebellious House and Senate floor. Moreover, although the reformers had reduced the number of senators required to stop a filibuster, the use of filibusters *increased* after 1975. Additionally, members were constantly amending committee bills when they reached the floor, thus abandoning the older traditions of deference and tying up business so that little was accomplished. Congress was often thrown off stride by scandal, beginning with several dramatic sex-related incidents in 1974 and 1975 and the notorious FBI sting operation, ABSCAM, in 1980, when several prominent legislators were caught on videotape accepting bribes from undercover agents dressed as Arab sheiks.

In the mid-1980s partisanship took hold of Congress. To some degree, party leaders replaced committee chairs as the center of decision-making in the House and Senate. Party caucuses became influential as two forces converged. First, each party became more homogenous ideologically, thereby creating a greater consensus within each body. As the number of southern conservative Democrats diminished (with the rise of a southern Republican party) and moderates lost their stature in the GOP, Democrats moved to the left and Republicans shifted to the right. Once the members of each party were relatively in agreement on major policy issues, their leaders drew on the procedural tools that had been created by the congressional reforms of the 1970s to strengthen parties; this was the second force expanding their role. Between 1987 and 1989, for example, Speaker James Wright (D-Texas) manhandled the Republican minority and intimidated any Democrat who threatened to stray from the party line. When Ways and Means chairman Dan Rostenkowski (D-Illinois) published a newspaper article criticizing a Democratic tax initiative, Wright threatened to have him removed. Younger Republicans, such as Georgia's Newt Gingrich, rejected the bias of the older GOP moderates who favored compromise with the opposition. Gingrich publicly blasted President George H. W. Bush when he agreed to a tax increase in 1990, breaking his famous 1988 campaign pledge. When Gingrich became Speaker of the House in 1995, he excluded Democrats from the deliberations over most legislation. Although the Senate was known to be an institution of free-floating individuals, party leaders ruthlessly used devices such as the budget reconciliation process to push through their agenda. When the two parties were not battling over policies or elections, they relied on scandal warfare to gain political ground.

This new partisanship differed from that of the nineteenth century because the two major parties no longer had strong connections to most citizens. A majority of Americans did not vote in congressional elections, let alone involve themselves in party activities. Americans seemed to be more interested in whether the two protagonists on the television show *Cheers* would get together romantically than in attending picnics organized by Democrats and Republicans. Those who wanted to support their party tended to do so through financial contributions.

Partisan fighting was fierce in the 1980s and 1990s since neither party was able to maintain solid control over Congress, and the leadership passed back and forth several times. In 1980, for example, the Republicans took control of the Senate only to lose it in 1986. They won both chambers of Congress in 1994, lost the Senate in mid-2001, and regained it two years later. Although control of the House has been more stable, with one seismic shift in 1994, razor-thin margins during much of the 1990s did not foster security among those in power. Nor did the party controlling the House always enjoy a sympathetic Senate. In sum, a single party controlled the presidency and both houses of Congress for only two years and five months (1993–1995 and January–May 2001, respectively) between 1980 and 2002. Therefore, neither party regained the long-term security that the Democrats enjoyed before the 1970s. Strong partisanship fueled bitter interaction among the legislators, including scandal warfare, which diminished trust in the chambers and made bipartisan compromise difficult.

While the 1970s' reforms had promised to make Congress the dominant branch of government, legislators found that they were still working under tremendous constraints. One of the biggest was internal, namely, multiple and competing centers of legislative power, with none achieving absolute dominance and none conducive to legislative compromise. The institutional reforms of the 1970s had exacerbated the fractious tendencies of Congress. Many reformers had hoped to ensure that no part of Congress developed the type of singular strength that committee chairs had done, and with this objective, the reformers were generally successful. The proliferation and empowerment of subcommittees as well as specialized caucuses, for example, produced small fiefdoms that were a formidable obstacle to both party leaders and committee chairs. Even though committee chairs had been stripped of their autonomy, they were still an important component of the legislative process. Furthermore, new rules and norms encouraged mavericks and freshmen to take action when they felt an issue was being ignored by the party leadership. Every legislator, from senior party leaders to the youngest senator and representative, was susceptible to new ethics regulations and norms. Scandals brought down powerful leaders, including Speakers Jim Wright and Newt Gingrich, Senate Finance Committee chairman Robert Packwood (R-Oregon), and Senate majority leader Trent Lott (R-Mississippi). While some legislators, such as the House Republican Tom DeLay, achieved significant influence, they could not afford to ignore the fates of their predecessors.

Public policy has been a second constraint. Since the 1970s, the federal budget has loomed large over every congressional decision. The tremendous increase in committed spending, as well as sizable federal deficits and debt, meant that there was less money for legislators who wanted to construct new types of government programs outside national emergencies. By the 1980s and 1990s, almost half of the federal budget went to entitlement programs, such as Social Security and Medicare, where large and politically powerful constituencies expected generous benefits for long periods of time. For most of these decades, the federal government was spending much more than it took in through tax revenue. This imbalance made deficit reduction a perennial priority for many politicians, who were in turn forced to focus on how much items cost rather than what their benefit might be. In an environment of fiscal constraint, it was hard to create anything new. The nature of the federal budget likewise made it difficult to dismantle programs. When the conservatives took power in the 1980s, culminating in the 1994 congressional elections, they discovered that it was extremely challenging to retrench the largest areas of government outside of federal taxation. Republicans could not touch items like Social Security without severe electoral consequences. This left conservatives with the unattractive option of attacking more modestly priced programs, such as welfare or minority set-aside contracts, that came with the high cost of antagonizing active interest groups or attacking programs important to their own supporters. Even after the 2000 election, with a staunchly conservative president in office, federal spending continued to rise at a historic rate.

The news media constituted a third constraint on legislative power. In contrast to the committee era, the news media now had a hostile relationship with elected officials; any shred of cooperation between these two institutions had evaporated. The rise of adversarial journalism in the 1960s and 1970s had produced a new generation of reporters and editors determined to expose corruption. This outlook would continue to shape the print media as well as television. The technological medium of cable television added to this volatile environment. Producers worked on exposés to attract large television audiences as the number of stations and shows proliferated (including on the networks, which revamped their evening broadcasts and added news magazines to the mix). Cable television created the twenty-four-hour news cycle, which made controlling the flow of news more difficult since stories could go on the airwaves within seconds. Media organizations were always looking for shocking material to fill pages and airtime to generate high ratings. In a period when most Americans distrusted government, sensational scandals emerged as a favorite topic. Since politicians had embraced scandal warfare as a strategy, they were frequently eager to help reporters who knocked on their doors. Legislators also responded by refining their media skills. Party caucuses, for example, elected charismatic leaders who played well on television. They also relied on the cable station C-SPAN, which covered Congress live with no journalistic filter, to speak directly to citizens. Notwithstanding such tactical adjustments, the media posed a significant challenge and political threat to those trying to govern.

It was not just the media that had changed. A fourth challenge confronting Congress turned out to be the fractious world of interest groups, think tanks, and political activists. While all of these organizations had been important throughout the twentieth century, their numbers rapidly proliferated after the 1960s. In a world once dominated by the American

Medical Association, the AFL-CIO, and the Chamber of Commerce, thousands of individual corporations, unions, and specialized trade associations set up permanent offices in Washington. The expansion of federal regulations and domestic policies since the 1950s had increased the incentive for them to lobby national politicians. Moreover, the campaign finance reforms of the early 1970s required small contributions from multiple sources, thus requiring legislators to seek more diverse sources of campaign funding. Public interest advocates formed lobbying organizations such as Common Cause to advocate on behalf of suburban, middle-class interests. The number of think tanks also proliferated. This hyper-competitive and decentralized environment translated into a situation where legislators constantly had to scramble to secure their links with these interest groups. Whereas in the committee era a legislator could form a stable connection with one or two major organizations that lasted for decades, the grounds were now constantly shifting, making it harder to build a solid base. Nor was any single interest group or think tank dominant since there were so many of them on the playing field.

Divided government through much of this period was another factor that made it difficult for legislators who sought dramatic policy change. Certainly, as the political scientist David Mayhew has shown, divided government does not prevent Congress from passing legislation. Indeed, since the 1940s Congress has proven that it could be productive when different parties controlled the White House and Congress. Yet divided government has not offered the most hospitable climate for passing "big ticket" legislation or fostering periods when a burst of major policies transform the infrastructure of government, as occurred with the New Deal and Great Society.

In a period of divided government, Congress also found that the president and Supreme Court remained strong. Although Earl Warren had retired from the bench, the Supreme Court continued to take an active stand on issues such as legislative redistricting and states' rights. This role became evident when the Court stepped in to resolve the controversy over the presidential election in 2000. The presidency also continued to be a dominant institution, as when Ronald Reagan used his office to advance the conservative revolution. In foreign policy, the War Powers Act seemed virtually irrelevant when Reagan authorized military operations in countries such as Nicaragua and El Salvador without congressional approval. Presidents relied on international bodies to legitimate military action. While Congress responded with litigation, investigation, and legislation, the presidency was still extremely powerful. The collapse of the Soviet Union in the 1980s brought credibility to this presidentially led foreign policy, notwithstanding the left-wing critics who had attacked Reagan for using covert (and some said illegal) forms of decision-making. Arthur M. Schlesinger Jr., who popularized the concept of the Imperial Presidency, quipped in 1986 that: "Whatever else may be said about Ronald Reagan, he quickly showed that the reports of the death of the Presidency were greatly exaggerated."[2]

With all the challenges that the legislators faced, high rates of incumbency provided one form of security. The trend toward incumbency that started in the nineteenth century never abated. While the Supreme Court had forced the elimination of congressional districts with unequal populations, it never tackled political gerrymandering. As a result, state legislatures were able to draw district lines to protect incumbents. Campaign finance rules, moreover, favored those who already held office since they could raise large sums of money quickly and receive free media exposure. Citizens also tended to like their representatives and senators even if they did not like Congress as an institution. Although the Senate elections tended to be more competitive during the contemporary era, most legislators could feel secure that they would be returned to office. But once on Capitol Hill, they faced enormous challenges.

Congress has proved that it could still be effective under certain conditions. Although it was nearly impossible to create major new policies or retrench existing ones, Congress succeeded in reforming programs and passing smaller, incremental legislation to address broader problems. During the 1970s and 1980s, it enacted a series of policy reforms that led to major organized interest groups losing important benefits. In 1990, for example, confronted with skyrocketing deficits and debt, Congress further refined the federal budget process and imposed a deficit reduction plan. Following the terrorist attacks on the United States on September 11, 2001, Congress restructured airline security, put money into public health research, and passed one of the most expansive executive reorganization plans in modern American history with the Department of Homeland Security. Congress also created a prescription drug benefit for Medicare.

The full character of today's Congress remains difficult to discern since we are living in the middle of it. With time, scholars will gain sufficient perspective to understand the full limits of the current legislative process. Whether the contemporary Congress has been dysfunctional — as some argue, for it has been difficult for legislators to take bold action and civility has deteriorated — or whether it has been vibrant — with a more open, porous, and accountable process — remains up for debate. What is clear, however, is that legislators today continue to face a bewildering number of constraints; they work in a nation that does not trust their institution, and they have not emerged as the dominant branch of government.

NOTES

1. An extended analysis of the argument in this introduction can be found in Julian E. Zelizer, *The Cloakroom Battlefield* (New York, 2004).

2. Arthur M. Schlesinger Jr., *The Cycles of American History* (Boston, 1986), 293.

35

Congressional Reform

IN THE 1950S, the House and Senate were commonly characterized as rigid feudal systems ruled by a small number of powerful committee barons. By the late 1970s, they were more often depicted as anarchies where members participated on their own terms and without restraint. Here is the story of this vast transformation. Although the major reforms had all been instituted by the late 1970s, the tale does not end there. As they adjusted to the reforms, the two chambers took divergent paths and by the late 1980s, power in the House had centralized under a stronger majority party leadership, whereas the Senate continued as a highly individualistic chamber.

Committee Government

In the House and Senate of the 1950s, the era of "committee government," legislation was produced by a number of autonomous committees headed by powerful chairmen who derived their positions from their seniority on the committee. The chairmen's great organizational and procedural powers — over subcommittee structure and membership, staff, and agenda — enabled them to shape decision-making in their committees. Mutual deference among committees protected most legislation from serious challenge on the floor. Thus two highly influential Southerners largely set congressional defense policy during the 1950s and into the 1960s; Carl Vinson of Georgia chaired the House Armed Services Committee from 1949 through 1952 and from 1955 through 1965; his fellow Georgian Richard Russell chaired the Senate Armed Services Committee in 1951 and 1952 and from 1955 through 1968.

Under this system, the role of the majority party and its leadership was limited. Both the party leaders' meager institutional resources and, especially for the Democrats, party factionalism limited the scope of the party leadership's involvement and influence. The Democrats were in the majority for most of the period after 1930 and continuously from 1955 to 1980, yet for much of this time the party was split into a generally conservative southern wing and a more liberal northern wing.

The congressional Democratic party lacked any mechanism for developing a party agenda or for imposing one on powerful committee chairmen. The president often set the agenda and attempted to shape legislation. But even if he was of the same party as the chamber majority, the committees were not bound to be responsive to his wishes. President Harry Truman, for example, was frustrated when committee chairs blocked many of his domestic policy proposals.

The party leadership's role in the policy process was largely limited to facilitating the passage on the House and Senate floor of legislation written by autonomous committees. The leaders seldom interceded in committees to shape legislation. Lacking any mechanism for holding the committees and their chairs responsible to the party, the leaders coordinated and cajoled but played little policy role. Thus the leadership of Speaker Sam Rayburn (1940–1946, 1949–1952, 1955–1961), the most highly regarded Speaker of the committee government era, was permissive, informal, and highly personal. In his relations with the committee chairs and in building floor coalitions, he relied on personal persuasion and made few demands. Members were seldom pressured to vote a given way; rather, Rayburn, who obtained some leverage from the myriad small favors he performed for members, such as speaking to a committee chair on behalf of a project in a member's district, relied on personal persuasion and the members' sense of obligation.

Even the leadership's role at the floor stage was limited. Although the Speaker of the House had considerable control over the flow of legislation to and on the floor, the independence of the Rules Committee during this period meant that the party leadership had only partial control over the scheduling of legislation for floor consideration. Intercommittee reciprocity meant that most committees could expect to pass most of their legislation on the floor without great difficulty. Consequently, committees and their chairs did not often require help from the leadership. On the other hand, on the highly controversial issues that were fought out on the floor — bills involving race or labor relations, for example — party leaders often confronted a deep North-South split and had great difficulty in successfully building winning coalitions.

Although the actual distribution of influence among committees, the party leadership, and rank-and-file members was similar in the House and Senate in the 1950s, the chambers' formal rules were very different. Since the late nineteenth century, House rules have tightly constrained rank-and-file members' debate time and their right to offer amendments.

In contrast, Senate rules have always given individual legislators enormous power. In most cases, any senator could offer an unlimited number of amendments to a piece of legislation on the floor, and those amendments did not even need to be germane. A senator could hold the floor indefinitely through a filibuster unless cloture was invoked, which required an extraordinary majority of two-thirds. In the 1950s, unwritten norms of behavior limited the use of these formal rules. Senators were expected to serve an apprenticeship, to specialize in the work of their committees, to toil diligently at the unglamorous legislative work, to help out other senators, especially on constituency-related matters, and to use their prerogatives under the rules with great restraint. Therefore, although individuals had more power in the Senate than in the House, senators, in accordance with the norms, restrained their exploitation of the powers the rules gave them.

In the 1950s conservative southern Democrats dominated Congress; they disproportionately held committee chairmanships and positions on the most desirable committees in both chambers. Coming from the one-party South, they accumulated the necessary seniority more easily than their northern colleagues, many of whom represented more competitive constituencies. Thus the system, which allocated desirable positions on the basis of seniority, produced an ideologically biased distribution of influence that benefited the conservative southern Democrats and put the liberal northern Democrats at a disadvantage.

Some conservative Southerners blatantly used their positions of influence to thwart the northern liberals' policy goals. For example, Graham Barden, a very conservative North Carolinian, chaired the Education and Labor Committee, which had jurisdiction over much of the social welfare legislation that liberals advocated during the 1950s. His aim was to prevent the committee from reporting out progressive legislation, and he used all his powers as chair to accomplish that goal. He kept the committee staff small and, reportedly, incompetent; he refused to call committee meetings, and, when committee members attempted to do so, used the chairman's procedural powers to prevent the committee from making decisions; for a time, he refused to set up permanent subcommittees, and later he denied the liberal Adam Clayton Powell of Harlem a subcommittee chairmanship to which he was entitled by seniority.

The Beginnings of Reform, 1958–1961

Throughout the 1950s, liberal Democrats in both houses were unhappy with the distribution of influence. Legislators such as Richard Bolling of Missouri, Stewart Udall of Arizona, and George McGovern of South

Dakota complained that no attempt was ever made to ascertain whether a party position could be reached on policy; instead, policymaking was left solely to the committees. They contended that the senior committee leaders and the memberships of the most important committees were unrepresentatively conservative. They claimed that even when liberal legislation such as aid to depressed areas or the barring of segregation in interstate transportation was reported from a committee in the House, it was likely to be blocked or watered down by the very conservative Rules Committee. Liberals, many of whom were junior, were also unhappy with their limited opportunities to participate meaningfully in the legislative process. A lack of sufficient staff and the distribution of desirable committee positions were sources of dissatisfaction in both chambers. In the House the liberals also complained about autocratic committee chairs; in the Senate they chafed under "folkways" or norms that restricted their full participation and objected to the cloture rule, which made it possible for the Southerners, a minority of the chamber, to filibuster and so kill civil rights legislation.

Until 1959 the liberal Democrats lacked the numbers to do much more than complain. When conservative southern Democrats joined Republicans in committee or on the chamber floor, this conservative coalition was more than large enough to dominate outcomes. The 1958 elections, however, brought in significant reinforcements, most of them liberals from competitive northern states and districts. The 63 new Democrats in the House included John Brademas of Indiana, James O'Hara of Michigan, Robert Kastenmeier of Wisconsin, and Ken Hechler of West Virginia, all strong reform supporters. Among the 15 in the Senate were Eugene McCarthy of Minnesota, Edmund Muskie of Maine, and Philip Hart of Michigan.

In the Senate, the sheer size of the freshman class swept away the apprenticeship norm that dictated limited participation by junior members; when an institution depends on norms to regulate behavior, a widespread refusal to abide by such unwritten rules of behavior can change the system. The senators first elected in 1958 were from competitive states; many had defeated incumbents, and they could not afford to wait to make their mark and so insisted on participating immediately. Understanding these circumstances, their senior party colleagues, led by Majority Leader Lyndon Johnson (D-Texas), gave them unusually good committee assignments for freshmen, and committee chairs became more amenable to requests from junior senators to have new subcommittees established for them to chair. Thus, in response to pressure from the 1958 class, the distribution of influence in the Senate began to change.

In the House, the class of 1958 swelled the ranks of the Democratic

Study Group (DSG), a recently formed organization dedicated to mobilizing votes for liberal legislation and ultimately to reforming the House. It had little other immediate effect, however. The Rules Committee, chaired by the wily veteran "Judge" Howard Smith, a deeply conservative Virginian, continued to block liberal legislation from consideration on the floor. In a particularly notorious instance, Smith and the conservative coalition that controlled the committee refused a rule for a federal aid to education bill that had passed both chambers in 1960. Smith thus stopped the bill from going to a conference committee to work out House-Senate differences. His action killed legislation that liberals had spent years bringing to that point.

The 1960 election of John Kennedy as president confronted the House Democrats with a crisis. Kennedy's program might well be blocked by the Rules Committee in a chamber formally controlled by his own party. The DSG and the administration persuaded Speaker Sam Rayburn that something had to be done. After a tough fight in early 1961, the House agreed, 217–212, to increase the size of the Rules Committee, enabling the majority party to add two usually loyal Democrats, Carl Elliott of Alabama and B. F. Sisk of California. Even so, the Rules Committee was not always responsive to the party leadership or the administration. Aside from a rules change passed in 1965 that made it easier to send bills to conference, no other significant internal reforms were instituted in the House until the late 1960s.

The Transformation of the Senate

The Senate changed significantly before the House did, even though opponents could filibuster proposed changes in Senate rules, whereas in the House a simple majority could pass reforms. During the 1950s and 1960s, Senate liberals had made frequent attempts to change Rule 22, the cloture rule, to make it easier to end filibusters, but they always failed — stymied by the very rule they were trying to alter.

However, in a body dependent on norms to regulate behavior, major change could occur without big changes in the formal rules. When a transformation in the political environment in the 1960s altered the costs and benefits to senators of abiding by committee government–era norms, the senators changed their behavior and, in doing so, changed how their chamber operated. New issues such as environmental protection, women's rights, consumer protection, and Vietnam arose. The number of interest groups active in Washington grew enormously. The media's role in politics became much more prominent. In this new environment, senators were highly sought after as champions of causes and as spokespeople by the media. Successfully playing the role of outward-looking policy entrepreneur brought a senator a reputation in Washington as a player, media attention, and possibly even a shot at the presidency. Thus, an activist style based on a full exploitation of senatorial prerogatives became attractive to more senators; specialization and restraint no longer served their goals. To take full advantage of these opportunities, senators expanded the number of seats on good committees and, by increasing the number of subcommittees, expanded the number of subcommittee chairmanships. They distributed both much more broadly. They also increased the total number of staff aides and made more staff available to junior as well as senior senators.

To be sure, some rules changes facilitated this Senate transformation. The 1970 Legislative Reorganization Act authorized a committee majority to call a meeting if the chair refused to do so. The act limited the number of committee positions and, specifically, the number of positions on the most desirable committees that a single senator could hold. And it assured committee minorities some staff. In the mid-1970s both parties subjected committee chairs and ranking minority members to ratification votes in the party conference. With a change in Senate rules in 1975, committee meetings were opened to the public.

In 1975 the Senate finally succeeded in changing the cloture rule. The threshold for cutting off debate on legislation was reduced from two-thirds of the senators present and voting to three-fifths of the total membership (usually sixty), though stopping debate on a proposal to change Senate rules still required a two-thirds vote.

For the Senate, however, behavioral change was more important than alterations in rules. For example, by the time committee leaders were subjected to a vote of their party colleagues, committee chairs were no longer the "emperors" that William S. White, a journalist who chronicled the Senate of the 1950s, had called them. As another example, junior members' increasing access to the most desirable committee assignments and to subcommittee chairmanships were much more the result of informal pressure on their senior colleagues than of formal limitations in rules.

Senators now had the incentives and the resources to involve themselves in a broader range of issues — which they did. They became much more active on the Senate floor, offering more amendments. Few restricted themselves to proposing amendments to bills from committees on which they served but, rather, offered amendments to a wide range of bills. They exploited extended debate to a much greater extent, and the frequency of filibusters shot up. Filibusters averaged less than 2 per Congress from 1955 through 1964; this figure more than doubled to 5 per Congress in 1965–1970 and more than doubled again to 11.4 per Congress for the 1970s (1971–1980). The media became an increasingly important arena for participation and a significant resource for senators in the pursuit of their policy, power, and reelection goals.

The influential senator in the new Senate, such as Sam Nunn (D-Georgia), Richard Lugar (R-Indiana), or Ed Muskie (D-Maine), could be conservative or liberal, northern or southern, senior or relatively junior. But he was almost always media-savvy and effective at working with advocacy groups to publicize his issues as well as substantively knowledgeable and politically astute.

Thus, in response to the new political environment, the Senate transformed itself from an inward-looking, committee- and seniority-dominated institution in which influence and resources were unequally distributed to an individualist, outward-looking institution with a much more equal distribution of resources. In neither the old nor the new Senate did party play a major role. Policy concerns had motivated liberal reformers, but they did not lead them to strengthening party organs or the powers of the party leadership.

Reforming the House, 1968–1975

Although the enormous policy successes of the Great Society temporarily reduced the liberal pressure for reform, Richard Nixon's election as president in 1968 again strengthened the reform impetus in the House. The liberals feared for the future of the Great Society programs and became increasingly concerned about the Vietnam War. The composition of the Democratic party, in which the reform thrust was centered, had changed greatly in the 1960s and was now much more heavily northern and liberal than it had been in the 1950s. In 1969 the reformers obtained regular meetings of the House Democratic Caucus, which established that body as a forum for further reform efforts. Many of the issues the reformers wanted to address were controlled by party rather than chamber rules and customs.

The first fruit of reform in the House was the 1970 Legislative Reorganization Act, which changed House rules. It was the product of the Joint Committee on the Reorganization of Congress set up in 1965. An informal bipartisan group composed of DSG leaders and junior, reform-minded Republicans (known as "Rumsfeld's Raiders" after their leader Donald Rumsfeld of Illinois) decided to try to strengthen the bill by offering floor amendments aimed at opening up the legislative process to greater public scrutiny. In a brilliant tactical move, the DSG leaders persuaded Tip O'Neill (D-Massachusetts), a well-liked House insider not considered a reformer, to sponsor their most important amendment. Their successful proposal allowed twenty members to demand a recorded vote in the Committee of the Whole, where bills are amended. Previously such votes were not recorded, which worked greatly to the advantage of the committee that had reported the bill and its chairman. If a House member proposed or just voted for an amendment the committee chair opposed, the chair, being on the floor, would know, but constituents and interest groups who supported the amendment would not. So the politically safest course for House members was to support the committee and its chair. Among other significant provisions in the act were several aimed at safeguarding the rights of committee minorities; for example, it made official the minority's right to call witnesses at hearings.

By and large, however, the rules changes included in the 1970 act were the easiest reforms to pass. Reforms that changed the distribution of power in the House more significantly were made over the next five years, and it took a show of might by the reform forces to give them bite.

In 1970 the DSG persuaded the party leadership and then the caucus to set up a committee to study seniority and recommend changes. Dubbed the Hansen Committee after its chair, Julia Hansen (D-Washington), a moderate with close ties to the party leadership, the committee recommended many of the reforms eventually approved by the Democratic Caucus. The DSG, a number of whose leaders served on the Hansen Committee, remained the primary source of reform ideas and their chief internal proponent. Cooperating with outside reform groups such as Common Cause and the National Committee for an Effective Congress, the DSG also worked to arouse media interest and put external pressure on the House to change.

There were competing visions of a reformed House. One was associated with Richard Bolling, a cerebral student of the House as an institution, who had written several well-received books critiquing the House of the committee government era. A protégé of Speaker Sam Rayburn's, who was very familiar with the problems Rayburn had experienced with recalcitrant conservative committee chairs, Bolling advocated a House in which responsible parties governed. Long a loyalist member of the Rules Committee, Bolling saw the problem as one of autonomous committees with powerful chairs that the majority party had no means of holding accountable. His solution was to strengthen the elected party leadership and make the committees and their leaders both responsive and accountable to the party as a whole. Phillip Burton, a hard-charging Californian first elected in 1964, a DSG activist, and a critical member of the Hansen Committee, put more emphasis on a House that gave its members maximum opportunity to participate in the legislative process. To be sure, Burton was a strong programmatic liberal dedicated to policy results, so presumably he did not favor participation at the expense of policy. But whether because he saw no conflict or because of the institutional positions he held (chairman of the DSG and then of the Democratic Caucus but not a member of the core elected party leadership), he usually stressed reforms such as the "Subcommittee Bill of Rights," that, as he expressed it, "spread the action."

From the perspective of the rank-and-file reformer, both policy and participation were important problems that reforms needed to address, and at the heart of both problems were the overly powerful and independent committee chairmen. The rank and file perceived no conflict between increasing the opportunities for all members to participate in the legislative process and making the process better able to produce legislation responsive to the policy preferences of the party majority.

These different perspectives driving reformers account for the seemingly contradictory thrusts of the early 1970s' reforms. While some rules changes displayed a clearly centralizing thrust, others just as clearly tended toward decentralization. Centralizing reforms included granting the Speaker the power to nominate all Democratic members and the chairman of the Rules Committee subject only to ratification by the caucus, a Bolling proposal passed in early 1975. It was intended to give the party leadership true control over the scheduling of legislation for the floor and, in fact, made the committee an arm of the central leadership. Also in 1975, the power to make committee assignments was moved from the Ways and Means Committee's Democrats, a fairly conservative group and one that did not include the Speaker, to a new Steering and Policy Committee. This new committee, which had been created in 1973, was chaired by the Speaker and included the other elected leaders and a number of the Speaker's appointees. Thus the party leadership gained more influence over the composition of the committees as well as resources for influencing its members' behavior. The new party rules that required committee chairmen and the chairmen of the Appropriations subcommittees to win majority approval on a secret ballot in the Democratic Caucus was intended to make them responsive to the party majority and thus also had centralizing implications. The rules on committee chairs were changed in a series of steps in 1971, 1973, and 1975; in 1975 the Appropriations subcommittee chairs, who were considered to have as much policy-making power as many full committee chairs, were made subject to the same procedure.

Another set of reforms implemented at the same time aimed at "spreading the action" and, as such, had decentralizing implications. In 1971 members were limited to chairing only one subcommittee, thus forcing some senior members to relinquish multiple chairmanships and distributing them more broadly among the membership. In addition, each subcommittee chair was authorized to hire one professional staff member. The 1973 "Subcommittee Bill of Rights" took the power to select subcommittee chairs from committee chairs and gave it to the Democratic caucus of the committee. It also guaranteed to subcommittees the automatic referral of legislation and adequate budget and staff. These reforms, which were all strongly advocated by Burton, reduced the control of the full committee chair and of other senior committee leaders over the committee's legislative activities.

There were limits to reform. An attempt to rationalize committee jurisdictions failed. Bolling headed the bipartisan committee that developed a plan that would have reshuffled committee jurisdictions and, in the process, eliminated some committees and taken prized issues away from others. Burton, a member of the Education and Labor Committee, which would have been divided into two by the proposal, led the opposition. With the reform forces split, the plan was defeated in October 1974.

The climax of the reform movement came in early 1975. The 1974 elections, held in the wake of Watergate, brought 75 new Democratic members to the House, most of whom were reform advocates. The more senior reformers cultivated the freshmen and, with these reinforcements, passed the final rules reforms to rein in the committee chairs. Equally important, in January 1975 the Democratic Caucus voted to strip three very senior chairmen — F. Edward Hebert of Louisiana, of Armed Services, W. R. Poage of Texas, of Agriculture, and Wright Patman of Texas, of Banking and Currency — of their chairmanships. Hebert and Poage were very conservative; Hebert, in addition, was known as an autocrat in his committee. Patman, although a liberal of the populist stripe, was considered erratic by many members. Hebert also made the mistake of addressing the class of 1974 as "boys and girls." In a sign of how much the House had changed, the freshmen had asked all the chairs to appear and explain why they should vote for them! The deposing of these chairs put even the least perceptive committee chairmen on notice that they had to be responsive to the party membership if they wished to retain their positions.

During this period, in addition, both committee and personal staffs were expanded and distributed much more broadly among the members. Even junior members thus gained the resources to exploit their new opportunities for participation. Sunshine reforms opened up most committee markups and conference committee meetings to the media and the public, encouraging members to use those forums for grandstanding as well as policy entrepreneurship.

By the mid-1970s the committee government system was dead, and a very different House was emerging. The committee chairmen's powers and control over scarce resources had been severely curtailed; the bases of committee autonomy had been undermined. Committee action shifted from the committee to the subcommittee level, with most hearings and many markups now taking place in subcommittees. The reforms significantly enhanced the powers and resources available to the party leadership for facilitating the passage of legislation. Most notably, the Speaker now controlled the Rules Committee, which sets the ground rules for the debate and amending of legislation on the floor. At the same time, however, rank-and-file members' incentives and capacity for participating in the legislative process had also expanded.

The Consequences of Reform

In the immediate wake of the 1970s reforms, the decentralizing thrust predominated in the House. By the mid-1970s, participation by the rank and file at the committee and the floor stage had increased enormously, and, as a result, the number of significant participants in the legislative process on any particular bill multiplied. The large numbers of inexperienced subcommittee chairmen combined with high participation radically increased the level of uncertainty in the House; predicting who would be involved, what amendments would be offered, and how members would vote became much harder. The Democratic leaders believed — probably correctly — that their members were unwilling to accept significant constraints on their new opportunities to participate and thus made little use of their own new powers.

By the end of the decade, however, many Democrats had become concerned about some unexpected consequences of the reforms. Floor sessions regularly stretched late into the night, legislation crafted by the more representative committees was picked apart on the floor, and the Democrats were repeatedly forced to go on the record on controversial amendments — busing and abortion, for example. Democrats were also having great difficulty passing legislation that they and their supporters badly wanted. For example, despite a Democratic president, Jimmy Carter, and big margins in both chambers in the late 1970s, the Democrats failed to enact labor law reform or to establish a consumer protection agency, both high priorities. The House Democrats began to look to their party leadership for assistance. With the election of the Republican Ronald Reagan as president in 1980, that need became even more acute.

In an attempt to restore some control, the House Democratic leaders began making more aggressive use of the powers and resources the reforms had bestowed on them and, by the mid-1980s, a centralized House closer to Bolling's than to Burton's decentralized vision had taken shape.

Party leaders such as Jim Wright (D-Texas), Speaker of the House from 1987 to 1989, were more involved in policy direction and more assertive in constraining members' floor choices, especially by limiting the amendments that could be offered on the floor; the party caucus or conference was more active and demanded that committee chairs and the party's committee contingents be responsive to its members' sentiment; the rank-and-file members' participation was channeled largely through their party and took forms that benefited rather than endangered the party effort.

The Senate, in contrast, remained a chamber that indulged the individual. To be sure, as the parties became more polarized ideologically, senators chose to work through their parties more frequently. Yet they refused to give their leaders the sort of powers the House leaders had because doing so would have required severely limiting their own prerogatives under Senate rules. Because the political environment continued to reward with visibility and influence those senators who exploited the chamber's permissive rules, senators were unwilling to curb their prerogatives.

The reform era, then, transformed Congress. In both chambers the legislative process became more open to public scrutiny. Both chambers are now more internally democratic, though in different ways. The Senate affords each member enormous influence; the House is controlled by the majority party and its elected leadership, not by a small group of unelected committee chairs. The House can now make legislative decisions expeditiously if the majority party is so inclined. In the Senate, however, minorities can still delay and sometimes block action.

— Barbara Sinclair

BIBLIOGRAPHICAL NOTES

The literature on the postwar Congress is massive and generally excellent, so any selection is perforce somewhat idiosyncratic. A very useful secondary source for the whole period is the *Congressional Quarterly* (both the *Weekly Reports* and the yearly *Almanacs* published since 1946). Also see the citations in the works discussed here.

The classic work on the 1950s' Senate is Donald E. Matthews, *U.S. Senators and Their World* (New York, 1960). For a description and assessment of the House in the 1950s by a member who played an important role in the reform movement, see Richard Bolling, *House Out of Order* (New York, 1965). Two good sources on the House reforms are Lawrence C. Dodd and Bruce I. Oppenheimer, eds., *Congress Reconsidered* (New York, 1977), and Burton Sheppard, *Rethinking Congressional Reform* (Cambridge, Mass., 1985). On the Bolling Committee's efforts to revamp the House committee system, see Roger H. Davidson and Walter J. Oleszek,

Congress Against Itself (Bloomington, Ind., 1977). Barbara Sinclair, *The Transformation of the U.S. Senate* (Baltimore, 1989), is an attempt to describe and explain change in the Senate from the 1950s through the 1980s. David Rohde, *Parties and Leaders in the Postreform House* (Chicago, 1991), and Barbara Sinclair, *Legislators, Leaders and Lawmaking* (Baltimore, 1995), examine how the House changed in the 1970s and 1980s.

36

Restraining the Imperial Presidency: Congress and Watergate

THE WATERGATE SCANDALS, a complex web of illegal activities, drove President Richard M. Nixon from the White House in 1974 and sent many of his senior advisers to prison. Every subsequent episode of political corruption, no matter how petty, has received the suffix "gate." Hence, in the quarter century after Nixon left office in disgrace, Americans have navigated "Contragate," "Koreagate," "Debategate," "Travelgate," "Whitewatergate," "Filegate," even "Fornigate." More important, Watergate substantially reshaped the relationships among Congress, the executive, and the courts. It fueled structural changes in the American government, including the congressional oversight of federal intelligence agencies, the War Powers resolution, campaign finance reform, and independent counsel investigations of malfeasance in the executive branch.

In the process, Watergate focused the national spotlight on Congress as an institution, briefly burnishing its reputation among the American people. The scandal also made prominent key legislators such as Senator Sam J. Ervin (D-North Carolina), the crusty Southerner who chaired the Senate investigating committee. Ervin became a folk hero, revered for his homespun common sense and his passionate dedication to the fundamental liberties of Americans. Watergate also made reluctant celebrities of Representative Peter Rodino (D-New Jersey), chairman of the House Judiciary Committee, who steered the House toward a consensus on impeachment; Howard Baker of Tennessee, the ranking Republican on the Senate Select Committee, who initially stage-managed and ultimately resisted the efforts of the White House to quash the investigation; and Tom Railsback (R-Illinois), the young, photogenic Republican whose agonized vote in favor of impeachment made clear the president's desperate position and pushed him toward resignation. Ironically, the affair also catalyzed a generational shift on Capitol Hill, completing major long-term changes in both the style and substance of American politics.

"What Did the President Know and When Did He Know It?": The Watergate Investigation

The Watergate controversy aroused a Congress already wary of the growth of executive power and determined to reassert its influence in national politics. The Senate had twice rejected Nixon's nominations to the Supreme Court. Refusing to confirm two southern jurists because of their previous support for segregation, Democratic senators suggested a broader, more substantial reading of the upper chamber's responsibility for "advice and consent." Congress had also tangled with the White House over the federal budget and Nixon's impoundments, his refusal to release funds appropriated by Congress. Representative Wright Patman (D-Texas), the seventy-nine-year-old populist maverick who chaired the House Banking and Currency Committee, had long sparred with Nixon over economic policy and particularly resented his impoundments of funds earmarked by Congress for liberal programs. Patman called Nixon's concentration of authority "a grab for power such as we have never seen before."

Most important, Capitol Hill demanded more substantial oversight of the war in Southeast Asia and the conduct of United States foreign policy in general. Nixon's expansion of the war in Indochina, particularly the secret bombing and invasion of Cambodia, convinced many members of Congress that they had granted the executive too much leeway in matters of national defense. On June 24, 1970, by a vote of 81–10, the Senate formally repealed the Gulf of Tonkin Resolution, which had authorized President Lyndon B. Johnson to "take all necessary measures to protect American troops and prevent further aggression in Vietnam." Forty-five supporters of the 1964 resolution voted for repeal.

The Watergate investigation thus began in a climate of profound anxiety and regret. Many observers suggested that congressional leaders pursued the scandal so assiduously to compensate for their earlier failures to monitor and restrain the imperial presidency. In the words of the novelist and social critic Mary McCarthy, Americans used Watergate "to cleanse themselves of guilt for Vietnam."

The congressional investigations of Watergate began in the midst of a presidential campaign. On June 17, 1972, five men broke into the headquarters of the Democratic National Committee in the Watergate apartment and office complex in Washington, D.C. The police apprehended the burglars and two accomplices outside the building, charging them with illegal wiretapping, electronic surveillance, and the theft of documents. At the time of their arrest, the burglars carried large amounts of currency, some of it with consecutive serial numbers. Following the money trail, investigators linked the break-in to Nixon's campaign organization — the Committee for the Re-Election of the President (CREEP). Led by Wright Patman, the House Banking and Currency Committee scrutinized CREEP's fund-raising operations, ostensibly to determine if the president's men had manipulated the banking system to allow money laundering and illegal fund transfers to the burglars.

Exploring the heavy flow of money to Nixon's campaign just before changes in campaign finance law took effect, Patman zeroed in on the activities of Maurice Stans, CREEP's finance chairman. When Stans refused to cooperate, Patman asked the Banking and Currency Committee to grant subpoena power. The committee refused the request, 20–15, with six Democrats joining the Republicans in the majority. In part, the defections reflected the Democrats' impatience with Patman; the maverick Texan had long been a thorn in the side of many members of his own party. It also reflected doubts about the committee's jurisdiction and fears that pursuing so openly partisan an inquiry might backfire during the presidential campaign. Most important, the White House lobbied behind the scenes to derail the inquiry.

Undeterred, Patman and his staff remained on the trail. On October 12, 1972, Patman invited important officials to a public hearing, including Stans, the White House counsel John Dean, and John Mitchell, the CREEP chairman and former U.S. attorney general. Knowing they would not attend, Patman left empty chairs at the meeting to dramatize their lack of cooperation. Two weeks later he released the findings of his staff: the "preliminary report" firmly tied the Watergate burglars to Nixon's campaign committee.

The Patman Committee, while fruitless, nonetheless forced Nixon to broaden and intensify the Watergate cover-up. Led by John Dean, the administration did all it could to stifle Patman's inquiry. These efforts included coordinating legal maneuvers with the defendants in the Watergate burglary to block the investigation, using contacts in Texas to dig up dirt on campaign contributions to Patman from potentially embarrassing sources, and direct attacks on the committee. The White House accused Patman of "a callous abuse of his power as chairman" and dismissed the report as nothing but a "dishonest collection of innuendo and fourth-hand hearsay" designed to revive the "sinking campaign" of George McGovern, Nixon's opponent in the forthcoming election.

When Americans went to the polls in November 1972, Watergate had little impact, and Nixon won reelection in a landslide. The Democrats gained 2 seats in the Senate, claiming a 57–43 advantage, but their majority in the House shrank by 12, to 243–192. Surveys showed little public disapproval for the administration's handling of the scandal. Even after the conviction of the Watergate defendants in January 1973, most Americans regarded the case as run-of-the-mill political shenanigans.

The new Congress moved to clarify the role of the White House in the affair. By a unanimous vote, Senate Resolution 60 established a special Select Committee to investigate the Watergate affair. Unlike Patman's inquiry, the Senate granted its seven members — four Democrats and three Republicans — the power to subpoena witnesses and documents and a substantial budget for staff and expenses. Its chairman, the seventy-six-year-old Sam Ervin, possessed a reputation for integrity and nonpartisanship. A constitutional scholar and a conservative Southerner, he had maintained a relatively low profile on Capitol Hill. Ervin's lack of ambition for higher office and ideological distance from Nixon's liberal opponents enhanced the credibility of the committee.

The Select Committee initially jockeyed with the White House over the scope of the investigation. Claiming executive privilege, Nixon blocked the committee from interviewing top administration officials. Even after the director of the FBI revealed that John Dean had full access to the bureau's Watergate investigation as it unfolded, Nixon asserted, "No president could ever allow the counsel to the president to go down and testify before a committee." The president offered to allow staff members to appear before the committee "informally," but Ervin refused. "They're not royalty," he warned. Nixon agreed to closed-door sessions but asserted lawyer-client privilege to shield Dean from the committee. Behind the scenes, Nixon enlisted Howard Baker, the ranking minority member of the committee, in his effort to derail the investigation. Baker warily maintained his independence, selecting a young Tennesseean, the future U.S. senator Fred Thompson, as minority staff counsel instead of the White House's candidate.

Ervin turned the nuts-and-bolts operation of the investigation over to the committee's talented and dedicated staff, directed by the majority counsel Samuel Dash, a law professor at Georgetown University. Dash outmaneuvered Baker and Thompson, rebuffing the Republican minority's efforts to shape the witness list and narrow the scope of the investigation. Dash concluded secret negotiations known only to Ervin with John Dean, the principal witness against Nixon's top aides.

Ultimately, the public disclosures of the Watergate cover-up forced Nixon to cooperate. On March 23 the presiding judge in the burglary case, Judge John J. "Maximum John" Sirica, released a letter from James McCord, the man convicted of managing the operation at the Watergate complex. McCord revealed that the White House had pressured the defendants to plead guilty, to commit perjury, and to conceal their ties to the administration. McCord also implicated John Dean and John Mitchell. By the time the Select Committee began its public hearings, many important officials in the executive branch, including Mitchell, Dean, the White House chief of staff H. R. Haldeman, and the domestic policy adviser John Ehrlichman, had resigned. At the urging of the Senate, the new attorney general, Elliot Richardson, had appointed a special prosecutor, independent of normal White House executive oversight, and authorized him to investigate not just Watergate but "all offenses arising out of the 1972 presidential election for which the Special Prosecutor deems it necessary and appropriate to assume responsibility, allegations involving the President, members of the White House staff or presidential appointees."

Televised live on all of the major networks, the Select Committee hearings began on May 17, 1973. The broadcasts riveted the nation. Before the 1980s, when cameras broadcast from the Capitol itself, Americans rarely saw Congress in action. The Senate Caucus Room, site of the Army-McCarthy Hearings and the Kefauver Committee investigations of labor racketeering and juvenile delinquency in the 1950s, had been the one public face of the institution. Together with the later deliberations of the House Judiciary Committee, the Ervin Committee hearings brought the institution favorable ratings in the opinion polls.

The star witness, John Dean, admitted his role in the affair and fingered Nixon's closest aides — Haldeman, Ehrlichman, and Mitchell. Dean testified that Nixon himself had participated in the cover-up from an early date and that the two men had discussed clemency and hush money payments for the burglars. But the ambitious young lawyer had received partial immunity in return for his testimony, so his credibility remained suspect. Cross-examining Dean, Baker posed what would become the defining question of the investigation and the ultimate downfall of the Nixon presidency: "What did the president know and when did he know it?"

Two weeks later, during a background interview in private session, a presidential assistant, Alexander Butterfield, let slip the existence of the secret Oval Office tapes. Ervin's staff, along with the special prosecutor's office and other congressional committees, began a year-long struggle over access to the recordings. It ended in July 1974, when the Supreme Court ruled unanimously in *U.S. v. Richard M. Nixon* that the president must turn over the tapes. The recordings demonstrated Nixon's complicity in the Watergate conspiracies from the day after the break-in at the

Washington offices of the Democratic National Committee chairman, Lawrence O'Brien.

By that point, the Ervin Committee had completed its deliberations. The unprecedented public investigation not only documented the president's involvement in the cover-up, it also untangled a complex web of secret operations in the Nixon White House — a veritable rogue government dedicated to criminal activities. The Select Committee exposed among other unsavory operations the illegal activities of the White House "plumbers." Designed to plug leaks to the press, the plumbers ransacked the offices of the psychologist treating Daniel Ellsberg, the former Defense Department employee who had leaked the Pentagon papers to the *New York Times,* in search of damaging material on Ellsberg. The Ervin Committee also questioned Donald Segretti, the leader of the dirty tricks squad assembled by the Nixon campaign committee. His team sabotaged the campaigns of Nixon's Democratic rivals during the 1972 primaries. The president's men also planted a spy in the press detail covering Senator George McGovern, used the Internal Revenue Service and the Justice Department to harass enemies and reward friends, and ordered surveillance on Senator Edward M. "Ted" Kennedy (D-Massachusetts) in an effort to unearth dirt on his personal life.

The mounting evidence led the House Judiciary Committee to debate articles of impeachment against the president. On July 24, 1974, the committee, chaired by Representative Peter Rodino (D-New Jersey), opened six days of nationally televised hearings. A cautious legislator, Rodino assembled a large staff of more than forty lawyers (including the future First Lady and New York senator Hillary Rodham Clinton) to build a detailed, meticulous case. Rodino appointed as chief counsel John Doar, an attorney with a reputation for impeccable fairness who was famous for his role in federal efforts to desegregate the South in the 1960s. By this point, many members of the president's own party, including the House minority leader, John Rhodes, urged the president to resign.

Rodino began the hearings with an opening statement on the solemn oath of office and President Nixon's failure to preserve, protect, and defend the Constitution of the United States. Portraying the proceedings as partisan grandstanding, the administration attempted to discredit the charges against the president. But Representative Thomas Railsback, a betrayed Nixon supporter, spoke out against the president and set off a wave of defections among the GOP congressmen.

On July 27, by a vote of 27–11, the committee adopted its first article of impeachment, charging Nixon with obstruction of justice in the Watergate cover-up. Six Republicans joined the committee's 21 Democrats in the majority. The second article, adopted two days later by a 28–10 margin, cited the president's abuse of power and harassment of domestic opponents. On July 30, a slim 21–17 majority accused the president of defying its subpoenas in violation of the Constitution. The committee failed to pass two other articles — one concerning tax evasion, the other focused on the secret bombing of Cambodia. All in all, the Judiciary Committee hearings produced a bipartisan verdict in the committee, Congress, and the nation that Nixon "warrants impeachment and trial, and removal from office."

To avoid certain impeachment, a disgraced Nixon resigned on August 8, 1974. One month later, President Gerald R. Ford granted him a "full, free, and absolute pardon." The Watergate investigation was over.

Watergate and American Institutions

Watergate forced American policymakers, particularly members of Congress, to rethink the balance of power among the branches of government. At the time, observers like Arthur M. Schlesinger Jr., the historian and former adviser to John F. Kennedy, blamed a "swollen," even "imperial," presidency as the motive behind the scandals. Executive power had steadily mounted since World War II; presidents had acquired too much autonomy and authority. A symptom rather than a cause, Watergate, in Schlesinger's words, "brought to the surface, symbolized and made politically accessible the great question posed by the Nixon administration in every sector — the question of presidential power. The unwarranted and unprecedented expansion of presidential power, because it ran through the whole Nixon system, was bound, if repressed at one point, to break out at another."

Richard Nixon may have possessed unusual psychological and political pathologies, Schlesinger and other contemporary analysts conceded. But the problem lay in the office rather than the man — in its potential for unchecked abuses of power and in the comparative willingness of Congress to cede authority, especially in areas of national security. After all, Presidents Kennedy and Johnson had expanded the Vietnam War without consulting Congress or informing the nation.

Although scholars later faulted Schlesinger's interpretation, members of Congress largely accepted the idea of the imperial presidency. In the immediate aftermath of Watergate, the national legislature established new controls on presidential power. In November 1973 Congress adopted the War Powers Act by joint resolution. In the absence of a declaration of war or other explicit congressional authorization, the president could only commit American troops in defensive operations. In such situations his authority would last for sixty days; the president was obligated to report deployments within forty-eight hours and withdraw the troops before the deadline unless Congress approved the mission. Nixon rejected this explicit restriction on the president's authority as commander in chief of the armed forces, but it passed over his veto. His successor, Gerald Ford, openly denounced the act, but while in office, he duly reported the commitment of troops on four separate occasions.

Congress also established formal procedures for investigating unlawful and unethical activity in the executive branch. After Nixon summarily dismissed Archibald Cox, the Watergate special prosecutor hired by Attorney General Elliot Richardson in what became known as the Saturday Night Massacre (Richardson and his deputy resigned in protest), several congressmen filed bills to define the jurisdiction and powers of independent counsel. Hearings convened in 1974; the independent counsel statute became law as Title VI of the 1978 Ethics in Government Act. At the request of the attorney general, a panel of judges would appoint and supervise the investigators (and potential prosecutors) of high-ranking executive branch officials. Such independent counsel would no longer serve at the pleasure of the president. The Whitewater investigations that led to the impeachment of President Bill Clinton took place under the aegis of this statute. Congress allowed it to lapse in June 1999.

Before Watergate, the White House had enjoyed the unchecked supervision of federal intelligence-gathering agencies. Nixon had abused this power, using the CIA to obstruct the FBI's investigation of the Watergate burglary and interfering with the FBI's operations for political purposes. In response, Congress initiated high-profile hearings concerning illicit activities by the CIA and FBI. The Senate's Select Committee to Study Governmental Operations with Respect to Intelligence Activities — known as the Church Committee after its chairman, Senator Frank Church (D-Idaho) — dazzled the nation with revelations of covert practices including the unauthorized storage of toxic agents, mail opening, illegal searches of U.S. citizens, and assassination plots involving foreign heads of state. Representative Otis Pike (D-New York) led a less celebrated House panel that uncovered systematic abuses by the CIA, FBI, and other intelligence agencies.

In response, Congress established standing intelligence committees with broad oversight powers. The Church Committee had identified what it called "the basic tension — if not incompatibility — of covert operations and the demands of a constitutional system." Secrecy remained necessary for cloak-and-dagger operations like the CIA, but it could also "become a source of power, a barrier to serious policy debate within the government, and a means of circumventing the established checks and procedures of government." The Church Committee concluded that secrecy "contributed to a temptation on the part of the Executive to resort to covert operations in order to avoid bureaucratic, congressional, and public debate." By maintaining permanent intelligence committees with access to classified records, Congress respected the intelligence community's need for secrecy while asserting the people's interest in democratic control and accountability.

In July 1974 the Congressional Budget and Impoundment Control Act also reclaimed power that President Nixon had asserted, subjecting presidential impoundment of federal funds to congressional control. Specifying the president's authority, Title X of the act distinguished between two classes of impoundments with different procedures for legislative supervision. Rescissions (permanent cancellations) required congressional approval in advance; temporary deferrals of expenditures remained in force unless Congress explicitly undid them. The act also broadly reasserted the legislature's control of budgeting by establishing the House and Senate Budget Committees to coordinate the budget-making process and the Congressional Budget Office to provide nonpartisan analysis and information about the budget and the economy.

Watergate had also shed light on corrupt practices in political fundraising prompting campaign finance reform on Capitol Hill. In 1974 Congress enacted amendments to the Federal Election Campaign Act, the most far-reaching campaign finance legislation ever adopted. The new rules strengthened disclosure requirements, imposed strict limits on campaign contributions, capped spending in federal elections, and provided public financing for presidential campaigns. The law also established a new agency, the Federal Election Commission (FEC), to enforce the new rules.

In the end, the reforms enacted after Watergate slowed the growth of the imperial presidency but did not reverse the long-standing accretion of executive power. Neither the War Powers resolution nor intelligence oversight substantially reduced the president's control over military affairs and covert operations. Despite the Budget and Impoundment Control Act, the executive branch largely set the agenda for budget negotiations and new campaign finance rules only intensified the influence of campaign donors.

"Watergate Babies": Congress and American Politics

Watergate reshaped both the process and the content of congressional politics in the United States. It fostered generational change on Capitol Hill and altered the terms of partisan competition in American public life. In the wake of Nixon's resignation and Ford's blanket pardon, the 1974 midterm elections ushered in a huge freshman class of reform-minded members of Congress. Some 75 freshmen Democrats took seats in the House, swelling the party's majority by 43. Many of them represented traditionally Republican districts; nearly all of them embodied a new breed of national legislator. Younger and less experienced in party politics, the class of 1974 possessed strong ideological convictions. Linked more closely to ideas and interests than to party organizations, they displayed little deference toward their party leaders or the seniority system. Many young Democrats, elected in traditionally Republican districts, felt the need to display their independence from the leadership.

The "Watergate babies" included the thirty-five-year-old state's attorney Patrick Leahy, the first Democrat Vermont had sent to the Senate since the 1850s, and thirty-six-year-old Gary Hart (D-Colorado), an avid environmentalist who had cut his political teeth as the manager of George McGovern's upstart 1972 presidential campaign. Across the Capitol, the House swore in new congressmen like Harold Ford, the first black Tennesseean to serve in the chamber, the former navy pilot and legal aid lawyer Tom Harkin (D-Iowa), and Paul Tsongas (D-Massachusetts), a former Peace Corps volunteer. Products of the civil rights movement and the struggles over the war in Vietnam, these freshmen proved more independent, entrepreneurial, and issue-oriented than their senior colleagues, less respectful of party discipline and Capitol Hill traditions. All of them had grown up in the age of television and felt comfortable with the medium.

The class of 1974 hardly originated this new breed, but its sheer numbers gave long-suffering reformers the votes to restructure the committee system, weaken congressional seniority, and diminish the autonomy and authority of committee chairmen. Representative Phillip Burton (D-California), a savvy tactician and passionate liberal first elected in 1964, became the informal leader of the freshman class. Before all the votes had been counted, Burton phoned the new members and solicited their support in his race for chairman of the House Democratic Caucus. Winning the office in January 1975, Burton remade the caucus into a launching pad for congressional reform.

New procedures required the Democratic caucus to approve nominations for committee chairmen; it immediately removed three veteran chairmen who refused to take seriously the Watergate babies' demands for enhanced influence: F. Edward Hebert (D-Louisiana) of Armed Services, W. R. Poage (D-Texas) of Agriculture, and Wright Patman (D-Texas) of Banking and Currency. Patman's removal proved especially ironic. The maverick Texan, first elected to the House in 1928, had pioneered many of the antiestablishment tactics that the Watergate freshmen relied on — the use of alternative media, appeals to targeted constituent and interest groups, and aggressive public advocacy. Patman lost his chairmanship in 1974 when a new generation saw him not as a populist outsider but as an entrenched insider. Despite his lonely stands against rapacious bankers and imperial presidents and a rebellious streak that won him the support of the consumer advocate Ralph Nader, Patman remained a creature of the old Capitol Hill. Devoted to the seniority system and the tradition of autonomous committee chairmen, he was out of step with the Watergate babies.

The new regime also required committees to maintain standing subcommittees with fixed jurisdictions and permanent staffs, further decentralizing power and flattening the traditional hierarchies in both chambers. Increasingly, members of Congress gained influence through their connections to outside interest groups, their appearances in the media, and their membership in regional and ethnic alliances in the Congress. Service to the leadership, party discipline, and seniority meant less and less. "They don't think about party loyalty," lamented Speaker of the House Tip O'Neill in an interview with the *Washington Post* columnist David Broder about the new generation on Capitol Hill. "They were interested in spreading the power. But in spreading the power, we now have 152 subcommittees, each with its own staff, each one trying to make its chairman look good." As Speaker, O'Neill had to confer with "all their caucuses. The freshman caucus. The sophomore caucus. The junior caucus. The black caucus. The Jewish caucus. The Mexican caucus. The Northeast caucus. The Middle American caucus. The steel caucus. The women's caucus."

The arrival of the Watergate freshmen finished off the hierarchy and committee structure that had governed Capitol Hill since the nineteenth century. The aftermath of scandal, investigation, and pardon opened an entirely new chapter in congressional politics.

Congress played a pivotal role in the investigation and resolution of the Watergate controversy. The televised hearings of the Senate Select Committee exposed the existence of Nixon's secret tapes — the pivotal discovery of the affair — and the House Judiciary Committee conducted the impeachment proceedings leading to his resignation. Members of Congress — Sam Ervin, Wright Patman, Howard Baker, Tom Railsback — defined the terms of the controversy and determined its outcome.

But Watergate exerted more than a transitory effect on Capitol Hill. After the turmoil of the Vietnam years and the controversy over the "imperial presidency," Watergate represented a crucial juncture in the history of Congress and the politics of the United States. It marked an attempt, not entirely successful, by the legislative branch to realign the balance of power in American politics through formal legislative initiatives, informal oversight, and a new concern for ethics in American political discourse. Watergate also accelerated a generational shift, replacing an older style of legislator with a new breed ushered in with the class of '74.

— Bruce J. Schulman

REFERENCES

Boylan, Timothy S., "War Powers, Constitutional Balance, and the Imperial Presidency Idea at Century's End," *Presidential Studies Quarterly 29* (June 1999): 232–49.

Eastland, Terry, *Ethics, Politics and the Independent Counsel: Executive Power, Executive Vice, 1789-1989* (Washington, D.C., 1989).

Emery, Fred, *Watergate: The Corruption of American Politics and the Fall of Richard Nixon* (New York, 1994).

Ervin, Sam J., Jr., *The Whole Truth: The Watergate Conspiracy* (New York, 1980).

Felknor, Bruce L., *Political Mischief: Smear, Sabotage, and Reform in U.S. Elections* (New York, 1992).

Kutler, Stanley I., *The Wars of Watergate: The Last Crisis of Richard Nixon* (New York, 1990).

Olmstead, Katherine S., *Challenging the Secret Government: The Post-Watergate Investigation of the CIA and FBI* (Chapel Hill, N.C., 1996).

Schlesinger, Arthur M., Jr., *The Imperial Presidency* (Boston, 1973).

Schudson, Michael, *Watergate in American Memory* (New York, 1992).

Young, Nancy Beck, *Wright Patman: Populism, Liberalism, & the American Dream* (Dallas, 2000).

37

Congress and the Media

THE MEDIA became increasingly important in the work of Congress in the late twentieth century, as they did in other aspects of national political life. Whereas influence in Congress and the work of legislation was "an inside game" before the 1960s, it became increasingly mediated by publicity. Journalists were free to observe nearly all the stages of legislative activity by the end of the century. In a broad cultural transformation in how public policy is made, more actors participated, more actions took place in a public arena, more roads opened up in Congress for individual representatives to influence decisions, and more paths beckoned for citizens as individuals or as members of lobbying organizations to influence Congress. Even with a resurgence of partisanship and a measure of party discipline in Congress in the 1980s and 1990s, there was no turning back to the insular legislative system of the 1950s. The "mediatization" of politics was a vital part of this transformation, affecting the presidency as well as Congress. By the end of the century, it was a factor in the changing political culture of European and other democracies as well as the United States.

In the 1950s the relationship of the press to Congress was characterized both by a compartmentalization of duties and by trusting interaction in a shared social world. Compartmentalization meant simply that much of what happened in Congress happened behind closed doors. This institutional secrecy reflected the widely shared understanding that the work of Congress could and should proceed with relatively little oversight by the general public, either by their reading newspapers or by the proxy oversight of lobbying groups. There was little demand in Congress or in the press that this way be altered; it was standard operating procedure.

For Sam Rayburn, Speaker of the House in 1940–1947, 1949–1953, and 1955–1961, it meant that television had no place in the House. He kept TV cameras from both the House floor and the committees, banning radio and television broadcasts of committee meetings or hearings in 1952. The

House Un-American Activities Committee violated this ruling at a San Francisco hearing in 1957, but this maverick move was never repeated during Rayburn's tenure. Rayburn frequently used the distinction between "showhorses" in Congress, who sought public acclaim, and "workhorses," who diligently acted according to the rules and culture of Congress to gain their ends, and he left no doubt that he approved only of the latter.

At the same time, trust prevailed between members of Congress and reporters. Representatives did not fear that journalists would betray confidences, publicize private behaviors, or risk friendship and access for the sake of a sensational story. Accounts of the relations between Congress and the media in the 1940s and 1950s stress how cozy was the reporter-politician connection, which one analyst described as "overcooperation." Reporters and officials relied on one another in an atmosphere that accepted the basic legitimacy of Congress and its operations. Even Speaker Rayburn, who in most respects kept the press at arm's length, invited an inner circle of trusted reporters to off-the-record sessions of drinking and discussion at the end of the working day. Rayburn's daily five-minute press conferences were almost totally controlled by these insiders, who protected the Speaker from any difficult questions.

Overcooperation could be and sometimes did approach collusion and alliance. Senator Claude Pepper (D-Florida) helped set up a working partnership in 1940 between the nationally syndicated columnist Walter Lippmann and the Roosevelt administration to draft a plan that became the basis for the Lend-Lease bill. In 1945 Lippmann and the *New York Times* Washington reporter James "Scotty" Reston convinced the Republican senator Arthur Vandenberg (R-Michigan) that his isolationism would not serve him well if he ever wanted to be president. Lippmann and Reston wrote a speech for Vandenberg that he delivered in the Senate to great acclaim — then Reston wrote that the speech was "wise" and "statesmanlike," and Lippmann used his column to praise Vandenberg's turnabout. "An older generation of famous journalists," recalled the *Washington Post* editorial page editor Meg Greenfield in 1999, "was much more obliging to its government sources, much more willing to keep its secrets, and much more involved in its actual policymaking than it ever should have been — and than the successor generation in Washington today would dream of being."

Despite the cordial relations between Congress and the media, the public reputation of Congress was not high in the 1940s (and perhaps had never been), although it gradually climbed in the 1950s. Polling data from the 1940s to the 1990s indicate dissatisfaction with Congress (paired with general satisfaction with one's own representative) from start to finish, with less than half of the citizens polled approving of the way Congress handled its job. The public's faith in nearly all leading institutions declined after Vietnam and Watergate. Only the press and organized labor had approval readings under 30 percent in the mid-1960s (of people saying that they had "a great deal" of confidence in the leaders of the institution), with Congress and the executive branch at around 40 percent and the military, education, and medicine at 60 percent or better. By 1975, however, medicine, education, and the military ranged from 30 to 50 percent, the press around 25 percent, while Congress and the executive joined organized labor at 15 to 20 percent.

Toward a More Public Congress

Some developments since the 1960s have made it easier to find out how Congress is legislating for the country; other developments have made it more difficult. What should have made covering Congress easier was the decline of secrecy emerging from the internal congressional reforms of the 1970s. What should have made it harder, by making the legislative process more complex and decentralized, was the weakening of committee chairmen, the proliferation of subcommittees, and the general democratizing of the congressional culture that afforded novice legislators, not just the veterans, a chance to speak and make policy. The growing openness to publicity in Congress included a new House practice of recording how each representative voted on floor amendments; the practice of not recording the votes had allowed representatives to cast votes in secret that they would not publicly acknowledge. It included making committee and subcommittee meetings public. For instance, a 1975 rules change opened all Senate committee meetings to public view. There seems little doubt that it has influenced the legislative process. Citizens' groups like Common Cause (founded in 1970) saw to it that their volunteers attended most committee meetings concerned with taxation and appropriations, for instance, and kept an eye on any efforts to grant political favors to special interests.

Television had influenced Congress as early as 1951, when the coverage of Senator Estes Kefauver's (D-Tennessee) hearings on organized crime made the senator a national figure. The Senate Watergate hearings in 1973 boosted the political ambitions and national visibility of several of the senators on the committee, and the Watergate impeachment hearings of the House Judiciary Committee briefly made its chair, Peter Rodino (D-New Jersey), a household name. Other televised hearings, like the Army-McCarthy hearings, in which Senator Joseph McCarthy (R-Wisconsin) investigated what he believed to be communist infiltration of the armed services (1954), or J. William Fulbright's (D-Arkansas) Vietnam hearings in the Senate Foreign Relations Committee (1966), commanded national public attention. The appearance of politicians on Sunday morning talk shows, beginning with NBC's *Meet the Press* in 1947, sometimes became news events in themselves and were covered in the papers the next day.

This television coverage of Congress notwithstanding, no one since Kefauver has vaulted onto a national president–vice president ticket from media exposure in Congress. Still, television news became the symbolic center of American political communication in the 1960s, with the networks moving from fifteen- to thirty-minute evening news broadcasts and with the battle over civil rights and the controversy over the Vietnam War focusing public attention on Washington more intensely than ever before. Leaders in Congress who had once opposed allowing television into the Congress on a regular basis began to change their views.

The Legislative Reorganization Act of 1970 authorized television coverage of committee proceedings. In 1977 the House conducted a ninety-day test of TV coverage. The following year the House decided to broadcast floor proceedings and committee hearings, insisting that it would maintain control of its own television system, and began to buy equipment. In March 1979 the House began to broadcast live gavel-to-gavel coverage of floor proceedings through the new Cable–Satellite Public Affairs Network (C-SPAN). The cable industry was growing rapidly at that time, and it very much needed both programming and public legitimacy. A group of cable system operators bankrolled C-SPAN, the brainchild of Brian Lamb, the Washington bureau chief for *Cablevision* magazine and a former public information officer for the navy during Vietnam, the manager of a television station, a campaign aide for Richard Nixon in 1968, and the press secretary for the Office of Telecommunications Policy in the Nixon administration. Lamb remains C-SPAN's chief executive.

C-SPAN operated in the House under the rules of the Speaker, and Thomas "Tip" O'Neill agreed to its presence with the qualification that the camera would provide, exclusively, close-ups of the person speaking on the floor. Television coverage, then, was a kind of visual *Congressional Record,* not an arm of the news media under media control. O'Neill altered this policy in 1984 when he allowed the camera to pan the House chamber. He had grown concerned that the Conservative Opportunity Society, a group of conservative Republicans in the House, including Newt Gingrich (R-Georgia), used the "special orders" time each day to make video speeches to a nearly empty House on topics of their choice. These efforts were designed solely to reach the general public, not to contribute to the legislative debate, and O'Neill sought to embarrass them by having the camera pan the empty House chambers. The Republicans were outraged and a "camscam" controversy flared — and quickly passed without the Republicans forcing O'Neill to budge. Camscam did attract considerable notice for C-SPAN. The Senate permitted television coverage in 1986 because the members feared that they were losing public stature to the House.

While publicizing government proceedings is a democratic good in its own right, it is unclear if television has had any large impact on the substance of congressional work, even though it has influenced its style. There is speculation that TV helped improve the quality of floor debate, although a more secure generalization may be that of Senator John Glenn (D-Ohio), who quipped that after C-SPAN "the cost of doing charts for the Senate floor must have gone up 10,000 percent." The members of Congress hoped that greater visibility would result in greater public approval, but the best evidence on this — a 1992 Times Mirror Center for the People and the Press poll — found that regular C-SPAN viewers were more critical of Congress than was the public at large.

The audience most influenced by C-SPAN are the members of Congress themselves and other Washington insiders. The members follow the floor debates from their offices and have come to be more in touch with the operation of Congress as a whole. Members of Congress and people in the executive offices monitor one another's actions through C-SPAN. Public confidence in Congress has continued to sag in the years since television (from 40 percent of people surveyed by Gallup expressing a "great deal" or "quite a lot" of confidence in Congress in 1975 to 30 percent in the early 1980s to around 20 percent in the 1990s). Network television covers Congress more negatively in 1992 than it did in 1972, and the networks draw less on members of Congress and their staffs as sources on congressional stories than in the days before TV. There is no clear indication what difference, if any, television on the floor of Congress has made for the public understanding or public regard of government operations. Brian Lamb remarks, "The impact of C-SPAN has not been a grand rewriting of the American political tradition; rather it is a collection of short stories." He means that C-SPAN has mattered for particular individuals in a variety of ways. One of his short stories concerns Richard Armey (R-Texas), an economics professor when he started viewing C-SPAN who began to feel the people he saw on television "weren't bigger than life and . . . most of them weren't bigger than me." This revelation prompted him to run for Congress. He was elected in 1984 and became an influential House leader.

C-SPAN is not alone in providing sophisticated coverage of Congress to a relatively small but attentive audience. Many of the most widely followed and highly regarded news outlets by the year 2000 emerged in the 1970s era of congressional reform. National Public Radio inaugurated its news coverage in 1971, *The MacNeil/Lehrer Report* premiered as a thirty-minute program in 1976 and expanded into *The MacNeil/Lehrer News-Hour* in 1983. The opinionated PBS talkfest *The McLaughlin Group* was first broadcast in 1982. The Cable News Network (CNN) began broadcasting in 1980, and its round-the-clock news coverage intensified a news-centered public culture — once again, particularly for Washington insiders and the most highly attuned segment of the broader population. Print publications like *Washington Monthly* (founded in 1969), *National Journal* (1969), *Congressional Quarterly* (1945), and insider publications like *Roll Call* (1955) and *The Hill* (1994), as well as the newsletters of a growing number of volunteer organizations with their headquarters in Washington, D.C., have become more prominent and more influential in the past two decades. Despite the demise of several of Washington's daily newspapers (the *Post* absorbed the *Times-Herald* in 1954, and the *Washington Star* folded in 1981), they are probably more than made up for by the significant rise in the quality and quantity of the news coverage at the *Post* since it began an aggressive effort at improvement in the 1960s.

The newly open, media-oriented, even media-friendly operation of Congress is part of a generally more public, participatory, and pluralistic system of decision-making in Washington. It has not made decisions more legitimate than before; it simply rewires how legitimacy is achieved in a world where institutional authority is widely and regularly challenged.

The Culture of the News Media

The greater openness of Congress to the media makes it important to understand how the media themselves operate as businesses and as a cadre of professional interpreters of politics for the general public. Washington journalists, like American journalists generally, believe themselves to be and seek to be objective in their coverage of politics, professionally committed to truth rather than partisanship. This commitment to professional detachment fits smoothly with a paradoxical bias against politics in the U.S. political culture that can be traced back at least to the Progressive movement of the first two decades of the twentieth century. That is, Progressives, supported by muckraking journalists, sought to make politics more scientific, more clean, and more a direct expression of the popular will without the intervention of interest groups or, most of all, parties. Both close observers of today's journalism and journalists themselves acknowledge an affinity with progressive reform in the press.

While there are no systematic, confirming studies, it seems likely that congressional coverage is influenced by journalists' progressivism and has been increasingly so influenced since the remarkable storm of legislative activity from 1964 to the mid-1970s. An unstated assumption among journalists is that action is better than inaction and that measures passed are an index of the effectiveness of a Congress. This means that journalists have in mind a model of a unified, law-producing body, and they tend to value positively new legislation, almost regardless of its content, and to criticize a Congress that blocks more than it promotes.

If a preference for activism is one feature of the Progressive framework that underlies media coverage of Congress, another is a belief that politicians tend to be corrupt or easily corruptible. Thus the press quickly took advantage of the increasing information available through the 1971 and 1974 campaign finance disclosure acts. These acts made covering one aspect of congressional life — the spending of those members (and challengers) who run for Congress — much more accessible than ever before. Unfortunately for Congress, the media have invariably presented these data as an index of corruption, and there seems little doubt that increasing public awareness about campaign financing has contributed to the distrust of Congress. Here the progressivism of campaign finance legislation fused with the progressivism of journalists. One suggestive study by Frank Sorauf found that in the 1980s, even when there was good news about campaign finance, the press minimized it, shading the story toward a view that campaign finance was as much or more a danger to the nation as ever. In 1985, for instance, Federal Election Commission data were released, showing that the amount of money spent on 1984 Senate elections had grown — but at a slower pace than in recent years, and that the amount spent on House elections actually dropped. In news reports, Sorauf observes, the slow pace of the Senate's rise in campaign spending was minimized, and the most surprising development — the decline in House spending — was in some cases not even mentioned.

A changing culture in Congress has been matched and promoted by a changing culture in the news media. Again, the biggest changes can be traced to the late 1960s and 1970s. Spurred by the experience of Vietnam and Watergate and encouraged by obliging younger government officials who were also deeply affected by Vietnam and willing to give reporters inside information, journalists in the 1970s sought many more sources for stories than earlier, when they would have just cited "a high government official." A study by Leon Sigal shows that the *Washington Post* and the *New York Times,* in comparing 1969 to 1949, relied less on "routine channels" of information and more on "enterprise" — in other words, developing stories on their own initiative rather than in response to a government press conference, press release, or other routine, government publicity statement. Lower-level bureaucrats turned up in the news more often than they had before; senior officials were not quite so dominant as they had once been. A new skepticism flourished and received blessings from the print establishment. Newspapers organized special teams for investigative reporting; even the Associated Press in 1967 created a "special assignment team" to report on "the submerged dimension" in government. Investigative Reporters and Editors (IRE) was organized in 1975 and is still a professional association that promotes the cause of investigative journalism.

The cultural shift summarized by "the sixties" was not a change only among the young, but it centered on younger people, who brought with them to every profession, including congressional reporting, a taste of the adversarial culture expanding on college campuses alive with controversy and tolerant of irreverence. That the news grew more skeptical, perhaps even cynical, has been well documented. Presidential candidates have been treated more and more negatively from 1960 through 1992, according to a study of *Newsweek* and *Time* coverage. Newspaper and television coverage of candidates gravitated from reports of candidates' speeches to analyses of the political strategy behind the speeches — implicitly (sometimes explicitly) communicating the message that politicians take the stands they do only in order to get elected.

Skepticism among the Washington correspondents emerged from this general cultural transformation but also from more personal causes. Meg Greenfield, who worked in Washington journalism from 1961 until her death in 1999, looked back to the scandals in and about the government of the 1960s and after and recalled the "chagrin so many of us in my business felt at having been snookered. We were entitled to feel that our affectation of tough-guy, cynical journalists had been rendered ridiculous. We, after all, were the ones who had been disseminating the accepted version of reality now being shattered like plate glass."

Skepticism extended to the politicians' private lives as well as public actions. In the 1970s the women's movement persuaded both elites and the general public that "the personal is political." There does not seem to have been a decisive moment in this change, although the failure of Senator Edward "Ted" Kennedy (D-Massachusetts) to address squarely his role in the car accident and drowning of a campaign worker, Mary Jo Kopechne, at Chappaquiddick, on Martha's Vineyard, in 1969 marks the beginning of a change. So does the episode in 1974 when the powerful House Ways and Means Committee chairman Wilbur Mills (D-Arkansas) was arrested when his car skidded into the Potomac. He was not only drunk but in the company of a young exotic dancer, Fanne Foxe.

Journalists expressed a new critical stance and announced their break from overcooperation by more frequently challenging the politicians they covered, interrupting them in broadcast interviews, and undercutting them in news stories by reporting not only what they said but what political strategy led them to say it. At the same time, the variety of forms of journalism grew. The syndicated opinion column had been important since the 1930s, but the innovation (beginning with the *New York Times* in 1970) of the "op-ed" page, open to politicians, academics, and others outside the journalistic fraternity, expanded and heightened the significance of the opinion piece. Journalists avidly followed the Style section of the *Washington Post,* evolving in the 1970s out of the women's page into broad and often irreverent and opinionated cultural reporting. This encouraged other Washington journalists, including the political reporters who cover Congress, to adopt a more feature-oriented approach to news. The *Boston Globe*'s former Washington bureau chief David Shribman points out that "nearly all congressional correspondents" read the *Post*'s Style section avidly by the 1980s and were bringing its influence to their work with comprehensive portraits of congressmen, lobbyists, and congressional staff, attention to personalities and the culture and folkways of Congress, and increasingly colorful language. He writes, "As 'paper-of-record' coverage declined — most reporters no longer are under instructions not to leave Capitol Hill if either house is in session — feature coverage grew, and it was often written critically."

As Washington news coverage thus grew more negative along one dimension, it became "softer" along another — more human-interest oriented, more attuned to questions of culture, meaning, and recognition rather than economic and political policy narrowly defined. The front page of the *New York Times* focus on government or politics stories, for instance, declined from 84 percent in 1965, to 73 percent in 1975, to 63 percent in 1985, to 55 percent in 1992, according to one study. While some journalists have bemoaned this trend, viewing it as pandering to popular taste or commercial incentives, others believe it was long overdue and enriches public discourse. Clearly, it is related to the efforts of the print media to keep abreast of television-influenced popular taste and to newspaper managements' growing emphasis on the bottom line. But it is also related to a changed public understanding of what counts as publicly important, with the women's movement and gay liberation and other social developments having successfully broadened the horizons of "the political."

In at least one sphere — radio — a partisan media culture developed in the 1980s and early 1990s. Beginning in the 1970s, a number of stations found "all talk" or "all news" formats profitable. Political talk shows, which became especially popular during the Reagan years, have been predominantly run by conservative, often ultraconservative, hosts. The most popular talk show host has been Rush Limbaugh. Limbaugh began his career with a talk show on a Sacramento, California, station in 1984 and went to national syndication in 1988. It very quickly became a big success with devoted adherents, thousands of whom congregated at "Rush rooms" in restaurants and bars where fans would gather to listen. The whole talk radio phenomenon mushroomed. The National Association of Radio Talk Show Hosts was formed in 1989 and had three thousand members by 1995. By that time there were about twenty-five hundred talk or talk and news radio stations around the country.

Operating away from the glare of media publicity, Republicans found new fund-raising success in direct mail, new policy initiatives in independent think tanks, a newly recruitable constituency among evangelical Christians (reached by organized groups like the Christian Coalition through churches and independent Christian schools), and a lively new forum in the old medium of radio. An analysis of the 1994 election, which brought a Republican majority to the House for the first time since 1952, indicates that the big electoral change was greater party loyalty among Republican voters than in the past. Many factors contributed to this change, but surely the energy of the new conservative media outlets was among them.

Although the media have become more prominent in the operation of Congress, Congress has become less visible in the media and in the public eye. Congress still does not often attract a great deal of media attention and receives even less of it today, compared to the president, than in the past. Network news stories focusing on Congress dropped from 124 stories a month in the mid-1970s to 42 stories a month in the late 1980s. Despite the proliferation of power centers in Congress and the increasing capacity of individual legislators to call their own tune apart from the party and congressional leadership, the members of Congress with formal leadership positions receive the lion's share of media attention, with senators invariably more prominent than representatives in the House.

Congressional Media Strategies

Throughout this period, the members of Congress have aimed their publicity efforts at their home districts. To keep their names before their constituents, House members' best chance of news coverage lies with the print media, particularly daily newspapers, because newspapers offer much more attention to Congress than radio or TV and because newspapers are more likely to allow the member of Congress to state his or her own message more fully, often printing press releases from the member's office. Television markets rarely coincide with congressional districts so that, especially in urban markets whose broadcast area may penetrate four or five or more districts, it is very hard to get any television time. Congressmen in such districts rarely use television advertising in campaigns because it is not cost-effective: their constituents may be only a small percentage of the audience reached by television. New York City television stations, for instance, reach more than thirty congressional districts. The Senate is a different story. In the 1978 congressional races, to take one example, Americans polled on their sources of knowledge or contact with congressional candidates reported learning more about both House incumbents and challengers in print than on television; for both Senate incumbents and challengers, television had the edge.

Most congressional incumbents and challengers use a paid staff member to coordinate press relations during election campaigns; they sometimes have private consultants, too, to prepare press releases. Candidates also use paid, rather than free, media, buying ads on television, radio, in newspapers, and using direct mail. Both parties have their own Washington broadcasting facilities, which were used by many candidates in the 1980s and into the 1990s. In 1998, 74 House Democrats and 48 Democratic challengers used these facilities to make or to broadcast political ads, while others used them to appear "live" at fund-raisers in their districts. As technology became better and more widely available in recent years, fewer candidates used these Washington production centers, and their role appears to be growing more advisory than practical.

Senate candidates generally have more money for campaigns, get more press coverage, and produce more intense voter communication than House candidates do. Most House campaigns, the political scientist Paul Herrnson concludes, "do not convey much information about the candidates' ideological orientations or policy positions." Press coverage heavily favors incumbents over challengers, primarily because incumbents have a greater capacity to make news, know better how to attract reporters' interest, and frequently are opposed by candidates without significant experience and so with little political track record to discuss.

A few members, especially in the Senate, have also sought out the national media, but not to please their constituents or to improve their chances of reelection. Instead, they hope to position themselves as authoritative sources on particular issues that could in time bring them a national constituency. In this regard, younger, more northern, more liberal representatives from the 1960s on, and especially from the "Watergate babies" class of 1974, became media savvy and media oriented more quickly than their senior colleagues. But by 1990 representatives who took full advantage of the media could be found as often among Republicans as Democrats, among Southerners as Northerners. The most obvious and powerful example is Newt Gingrich, who pursued a media-oriented strategy in his successful bid to become House Speaker and a national leader of the Republican party. "If you're not in the *Washington Post* every day, you might as well not exist," he told *Vanity Fair* magazine in 1989, even though no one back home in Georgia read it. The showhorse-workhorse distinction no longer had the same force or resonance it had in Speaker Rayburn's day; media-oriented strategies have become legitimate tools of legislative work.

Assessing the Growing Role of the Media

It is hard to disagree with the media analyst Stephen Hess, who believes that the importance of the news media, especially television, in the operation of Congress is regularly exaggerated, especially by the members of Congress and Washington journalists themselves:

> Reality to reporters is what they can see, to politicians what they can touch. And Capitol Hill is always crammed with cameras, lights, sound equipment, tape recorders, news conferences, handouts, stakeouts. This is their reality. This also contributes to the myth of television's power as they react to its presence rather than to its output.

While representatives do pay more attention to publicity than they used to, press secretaries are not at the top of staff hierarchies, and as many as one House member in five finds it perfectly convenient to refrain from seeking publicity almost entirely.

Making laws and making policy in Washington have grown more open and public in the past half century. Very likely, legislating from the 1970s on has been more representative of public opinion; congressional action is more obliged than in the past to consider the views of a broad set of individuals and interests. The policy process is more open because someone — a reporter working for a specialized publication, a lobbying group watching out for its own interest, or a legislator or staff member monitoring bills in committee — can see what is going on. But the competition for public attention was more intense in 2000 than in 1950. Public attention is more often sought, it is more often required, and it is more difficult to capture when the Washington policy agenda is longer than it was, when a potentially attentive public is larger than before, and when the number of claimants for the public eye is greater. In other words, while secrecy or confidentiality is more difficult to sustain, widely shared information may not be any easier to come by. This dizzying visibility creates a different playing field than a process maintained by closely held secrets, and accordingly it requires incorporating an understanding of the news media in the study of Congress. But just how this alters the direction of legislation or the efficiency of Congress or even its democratic quality and the responsiveness of congressional action to the general public is very difficult to know. The mediatization of Washington politics has changed the rules of the game more obviously than it has changed the outcome.

— MICHAEL SCHUDSON

BIBLIOGRAPHICAL NOTES

The most perceptive works on the media and Congress have come from Stephen Hess, a Nixon speechwriter turned astute analyst of the Washington scene. They include *The Washington Reporters* (Washington, D.C., 1981), *The Ultimate Insiders* (Washington, D.C., 1986), and *Live from Capitol Hill!* (Washington, D.C., 1991). See also his "Decline and Fall of Congressional News" in a very useful collection, Thomas E. Mann and Norman J. Ornstein, eds., *Congress, the Press, and the Public* (Washington, D.C., 1994). Leading academic studies are Timothy E. Cook, *Making Laws and Making News* (Washington, D.C., 1989), and Mark J. Rozell's analysis of editorial and op-ed media opinion about Congress through the years, *In Contempt of Congress: Postwar Press Coverage on Capitol Hill* (Westport, Conn., 1996). See also Karen M. Kedrowski, *Media Entrepreneurs and the Media Enterprise in the U.S. Congress* (Cresskill, N.J., 1996), and Joseph Cooper, ed., *Congress and the Decline of Public Trust* (Boulder, Colo., 1999), a valuable set of articles including David M. Shribman's thoughtful "Insiders with a Crisis from Outside." A provocative study of how the press covers campaign finance reform is Frank J. Sorauf, "Campaign Money and the Press: Three Soundings," *Political Science Quarterly 102* (1987): 25–42. Joe S. Foote, "Rayburn, the Workhorse," in Everette E. Dennis and Robert W. Snyder, eds., *Covering Congress* (New Brunswick, N.J., 1998), offers an intimate portrait of Speaker Rayburn's media relations.

A number of general works on Congress offer a chapter or useful material about its relations with the media. They include an earlier work on the Senate, Donald R. Matthews, *U.S. Senators and Their World* (Chapel Hill, N.C., 1960), as well as Burton Loomis, *The New American Politician* (New York, 1988). The best studies of covering scandal are Suzanne Garment, *Scandal* (New York, 1991); Larry J. Sabato, *Feeding Frenzy* (New York, 1991); and for scandals in Congress in particular, Julian E. Zelizer, *On Capitol Hill* (New York, 2004). Leading studies of congressional campaigns, including attention to campaign communications, are Gary C. Jacobson, *The Politics of Congressional Elections,* 5th ed. (New York, 2000), and Paul S. Herrnson, *Congressional Elections,* 3rd ed. (Washington, D.C., 2000).

On the general transformation of the news media over the past half century, two basic works offer a balanced assessment of the simultaneous commercialization of the media and the professionalization of journalists: Daniel Hallin, *We*

Keep America on Top of the World (New York, 1994), and Michael Schudson, *The Power of News* (Cambridge, Mass., 1995). Hallin's earlier work, *"The Uncensored War": The Media and Vietnam* (New York, 1986), is probably the best account of how the Vietnam War affected American journalism. David Halberstam's overwritten *The Powers That Be* (New York, 1979) is still an invaluable account of *Time,* the *New York Times,* the *Washington Post,* and CBS, especially in the 1960s and 1970s. A classic study of the Washington press is Leon Sigal, *Reporters and Officials* (Lexington, Mass., 1973). On C-SPAN, see Stephen Frantzich and John Sullivan, *The C-SPAN Revolution* (Norman, Okla., 1996), and also Brian Lamb, "The American Experience: C-SPAN and the U.S. Congress," in Bob Franklin, ed., *Televising Democracies* (London, 1992). A number of excellent memoirs and studies of the *Washington Post* and the *New York Times* are available, notable among them Katharine Graham, *Personal History* (New York, 1997), and Meg Greenfield, *Washington* (New York, 2001).

Shirley Chisholm

b. November 30, 1924

Shirley Chisholm

Shirley Chisholm is famous as a political trailblazer. She was the second black woman to serve in the New York state legislature, the first black woman elected to Congress, and the first black woman to seek a major party's presidential nomination. While her vanguard status was newsworthy during her career, to fully appreciate Chisholm's legacy one must consider her achievements during her seven congressional terms (1969–1982), her strong political base, and her defiance of state and national Democratic leaders, as well as her contributions to politics and education before and after she left office.

Shirley Anita St. Hill was born in Brooklyn, New York. Her parents, suffering financial difficulties during the Great Depression, sent her and two siblings to live with her grandmother in Barbados, where she attended strict British schools. Returning to New York when she was eleven, she distinguished herself in high school and received several college scholarship offers but enrolled in the more affordable Brooklyn College, which allowed her to live at home. She received an undergraduate degree in education in 1946, worked for seven years as a nursery school teacher, and enrolled at Columbia University, where she earned a master's degree in 1952. At Columbia she met and married Conrad Chisholm, then went on to direct day care centers in Manhattan. Beginning in 1959, Chisholm began consulting for the city's Bureau of Child Welfare and became active in community and civic affairs, including the Brooklyn branch of the National Association for the Advancement of Colored People, the Democratic Women's Workshop, and the League of Women Voters. Her professional and civic connections gave her a solid reputation and a strong political base in the black community. Never a favorite of the local Democratic machine, the articulate and outspoken Chisholm succeeded because of her tireless campaigning and unmatched grass-roots support.

Elected to the New York State Assembly in 1964, Chisholm served for four years and became known as an effective lawmaker and dauntless debater. Her legislative record included support for public day care centers, unemployment insurance for domestic workers, and a program to foster higher education opportunities for black and Puerto Rican students.

Elected to Congress in 1968, Chisholm criticized her liberal white male colleagues who, in her view, paid no more than lip service to equal opportunity for jobs and education. As an urban representative, she was indignant when the Democratic leadership appointed her to the Agriculture Committee's forestry and rural villages subcommittee; instead, she eventually joined the Education and Labor Committee. In her first speech in the House, Chisholm declared she would oppose all defense appropriation bills until the legislature addressed the needs of education and employment. She supported legislation enlarging the powers of the Department of Housing and Urban Development and establishing a cabinet-level Department of Consumer Affairs. Her presidential campaign in 1972 was more symbolic than realistic, but Chisholm used the platform to address many issues that remain relevant today, including gun control, prison reform, drug abuse, and political dissent. She garnered 10 percent of the delegates' votes and did not withdraw her candidacy until the end of the Democratic convention.

Retiring from office in 1982 to care for her ailing second husband, Chisholm criticized the social policies of the Reagan administration and the male-dominated politics of the Congress. She taught political science at Mount Holyoke College in South Hadley, Massachusetts, from 1982 to 1987 and helped found the National Political Congress of Black Women in 1984. In 1993 President Bill Clinton nominated Chisholm as ambassador to Jamaica, but she withdrew her name from consideration, citing health reasons.

References

"Chisholm, Shirley." *Contemporary Black Biography,* vol. 2. Gale Research, 1992. Reproduced in *Biography Resource Center.* Farmington Hills, Mich.: Gale Group. 2003. Retrieved July 3, 2003, from http://www.galenet.com/servlet/BioRC.

"Chisholm, Shirley Anita St. Hill." *Encyclopedia of World Biography,* 2nd ed. 17 vols. Gale Research, 1998. Reproduced in *Biography Resource Center.* Farmington Hills, Mich.: Gale Group. 2003. Retrieved July 3, 2003, from http://www.galenet.com/servlet/BioRC.

Shirley Chisholm 1972 Campaign Brochure Reprint, 4president.org. Retrieved November 26, 2003, from http://www.4president.org/brochures/chisholm72.pdf.

Thomas P. O'Neill

December 9, 1912–January 5, 1994

Thomas P. O'Neill

As Speaker of the House of Representatives, Thomas Philip "Tip" O'Neill, Jr., cut a larger-than-life figure on Capitol Hill — and on television after he enabled C-SPAN to broadcast live coverage of the House proceedings in 1979. Standing six feet two inches tall and weighing close to two hundred and eighty pounds, with a bulbous nose and a mane of white hair, O'Neill became one of the most recognized politicians in the United States. His congressional career bridged the era from postwar liberalism driven by local politics to the slick political landscape dominated by public relations and sound bytes in the more conservative 1990s.

Born into a middle-class Irish Catholic family in Cambridge, Massachusetts, O'Neill became involved in politics as a teenager, working on the 1928 presidential campaign of the Democrat Alfred E. Smith. O'Neill mounted an unsuccessful campaign for the Cambridge City Council in 1935, but the following year, after graduating from Boston College, he was elected to the state legislature. During his sixteen years in the Massachusetts house, O'Neill's political success relied on his parochial approach, party loyalty, leadership skills, and an aggressive political agenda. Appointed minority leader in 1944, he successfully overthrew the Republican control of the house and became its first Democratic Speaker in 140 years. Colloquial and opinionated, O'Neill charmed constituents even as his style underplayed his mastery of the political process.

Elected to the House of Representatives, where he served seventeen terms, O'Neill brought his liberal philosophy to the national stage. He championed the national Democratic party's liberal agenda but never forgot his Massachusetts constituents (he popularized the famous phrase "All politics is local"). A 1958 bill, for example, helped establish the Cape Cod National Seashore, but he fought against the development of the St. Lawrence Seaway because it hurt Boston's status as a major port. An effective behind-the-scenes coalition builder, O'Neill rose through the ranks of the House by allying himself with political heavyweights like Speaker Samuel T. Rayburn (1882–1961) of Texas, who named the Massachusetts congressman to the prominent House Rules Committee in 1955. He became a protégé of John W. McCormack (1891–1980), another Massachusetts Democrat who served as majority whip and Speaker. In the 1960s he supported most of the civil rights, social welfare, housing, and educational reform legislation of the Kennedy and Johnson administrations.

But that was the only time O'Neill had a harmonious relationship with the Oval Office, whether it housed a Democrat or Republican. During the Nixon administration, he quietly urged the House to investigate the Watergate scandal and supported the War Powers Act. Becoming Speaker in 1977, he was especially critical of the Carter administration's naiveté about Washington's political protocol. And he despised the Reagan administration's proposals for tax cuts for the wealthy, increased spending on defense, and the curtailment of social programs.

Ironically, O'Neill's own reform instincts may have hurt him politically. He rose to the Speaker's chair with the support of the younger generation of liberal representatives who, like him, had opposed the Vietnam War. As Speaker, he pressed for reforms that expanded the involvement of the younger representatives in political discourse but diminished some of the Speaker's powers, perhaps weakening party unity. Although O'Neill remained personally popular, his traditional liberalism seemed out of place in the growing conservatism of the 1980s. Citing the need for new leadership in the House, he retired in 1987.

Reference

Kotlowski, D. J. 2000, February. "O'Neill, Thomas Philip 'Tip.'" *American National Biography Online.* Retrieved July 3, 2003, from http://www.anb.org/articles/07/07-00686.html.

38

Congress and the Budget since 1974

BETWEEN December 16, 1995, and January 6, 1996, the U.S. federal government stopped working. The cause of the shutdown was neither terrorist attack nor foreign invasion but an entirely domestic political conflict over the federal budget between the House Speaker Newt Gingrich (R-Georgia) and his party faithful and President Bill Clinton. Energized by their stunning victory in the 1994 midterm elections, the House Republicans in the 104th Congress sought to use the congressional budget process as a vehicle for remaking federal domestic policy in a conservative image. The Senate Republicans were initially cautious but eventually embraced Gingrich's radical fiscal agenda. This budget plan called for the food stamp and Medicaid programs — core features of the federal safety net — to be transformed into block grants and turned over to the states, a move that was anathema to the liberal Democrats in Congress and President Clinton. During the protracted government shutdown, only "essential" federal services, such as national defense and air traffic control, were permitted to operate. Hundreds of thousands of federal workers were furloughed. Citizens were turned away at passport offices. The National Zoo was closed. The effects of the shutdown were felt throughout the nation. High-tech computer firms in Houston, for example, were forced to lay off workers employed under federal contracts.

In the end, the GOP's budget revolution failed. The president stood his ground and the congressional Republicans were forced to back down. The polls showed that most citizens blamed Congress for the crisis and were opposed to major reductions in domestic spending.

What is significant about this showdown is not that the congressional Republicans failed to get their program adopted into law but that they (correctly) saw the arcane budget reconciliation process as an almost ideal vehicle for pursuing a highly ambitious reform agenda with far-reaching implications for the future of activist government. The Republican majority of 1995–1996 was not the first legislative faction to view the budget process this way. In 1981, for example, a coalition of Republicans and conservative Democrats successfully exploited the exact same budget procedures to enact Ronald Reagan's economic recovery program. Like the Gingrich coalition in the 104th Congress, Reagan's legislative supporters were attracted to the budget process because it spanned the jurisdictions over multiple standing committees, streamlined congressional decision-making, and greatly diminished the ability of minorities to block the desires of a simple majority.

This powerful framework for crafting fiscal policy is the institutional legacy of past efforts to safeguard Congress's power of the purse in an age of big government. In most democratic nations, legislators have relatively little influence over the government's major budget decisions. Political executives generally have a monopoly on critical budget information as well as an unchallenged ability to control the policy agenda. American national budgeting is exceptional, for Congress is at the very heart of the process. Article I of the Constitution grants Congress the power to levy taxes and provides that money cannot be withdrawn from the U.S. Treasury except pursuant to appropriations made by law. James Madison, in *Federalist* No. 58, called Congress's power of the purse "the most complete and effectual weapon with which any constitution can arm the immediate representatives of the people."

Formal legal authority is one thing; however, effective political capacity is quite another. While the fiscal primacy of the legislature is constitutionally rooted, Congress's ability to set budget priorities is not guaranteed. Since the early 1970s, it has been challenged by three major developments: political conflict both in Congress and between Congress and the executive over the size and composition of the budget; the rapid growth of spending for long-term "entitlement" programs like Social Security and Medicare; and persistent budget deficits. In response to these challenges, Congress has often sought to avoid hard budget choices in the (usually vain) hope that its difficulties would simply disappear. Its most creative and historically significant response to its ongoing fiscal dilemmas, however, has been to strengthen its budget-making capacity by reforming the process itself.

The most important procedural innovation, the Congressional Budget and Impoundment Act of 1974, established an integrated legislative framework for making tax and spending decisions. With the enactment of this landmark reform, Congress for the first time had a vehicle for deciding on budget totals and relating the whole budget to its component parts. Its consequences have been nothing less than profound. The institutional balance of power between Congress and the presidency, the framing of the policy debate, and the internal workings of Congress — all were radically transformed by the new framework. A formal, central budget-making process today is as much a fixture of the modern Congress as televised hearings, issue polling, and professional staffs.

Budgeting before the Reform Era

To appreciate these sweeping changes, one needs to remember the historical context in which the act was crafted. Before 1974, Congress had no formal, annual process for making tax and spending decisions. Instead, it had one process for mobilizing revenues (directed by the House Ways and Means and Senate Finance Committees) and another process for spending money (led by the House and Senate Appropriations Committees). The Appropriations panels were in turn organized into specialized subcommittees with responsibility for particular agencies and programs. The clear expectation was that the members of each subcommittee wouldn't interfere with the others. "Why, you'd be branded an imposter," said one House subcommittee chairman in a confidential interview with a budget scholar in the mid-1960s, "if you went into those other subcommittee meetings. I'm as much a stranger in another [Appropriations] subcommittee as I would be in [another substantive committee]." Without one single committee responsible for looking at the overall fiscal situation, Congress had no choice but to respond to the president's annual budget proposals in a piecemeal fashion.

Despite its flaws, this informal system worked remarkably well over much of the postwar era. Between 1948 and 1957 the federal government ran annual budget surpluses five times. Between 1958 and 1967 it managed to balance its budget only once, but the deficits it produced were almost always quite small (less than 1½ percent of GDP). While some economists like Arthur Smithies argued that comprehensive reforms were needed to make Congress's budgetary decision-making more rational and integrated, the political scientist Aaron Wildavsky argued in a seminal book, *The Politics of the Budgetary Process* (1964), that Congress's fragmented budgetary system had remarkable virtues. In particular, it simplified complex funding decisions, facilitated workable legislative compromises, and produced outcomes that legislators and constituencies alike considered legitimate. By taking cues from the president and taking advantage of the postwar economic growth, Congress was able to manage the nation's fiscal affairs without creating obvious economic problems or stimulating excessive political conflict.

By the early 1970s, however, this informal, decentralized system had begun to decay. Several factors impelled Congress to establish a new budget process in 1974. First, its ability to control federal outlays through the regular appropriations process was weakened because of the vast expansion of the American welfare state. Although the United States is often considered a welfare "laggard" in comparison with European nations, the New Deal and Great Society witnessed the creation of major new social programs in areas such as pension, health, and income maintenance, and federal spending became a major source of support for millions of American families. The 1968 presidential victory of the Republican Richard M. Nixon did not fundamentally reverse this trend. Not only did his administration leave most Great Society programs intact, it endorsed dramatic increases in domestic spending. In 1972, for example, the administration hiked Social Security benefits 20 percent, signed off on a $30 billion general revenue sharing plan with the states, and approved a $25 billion higher education act that introduced Pell grants for lower-income college students.

This expansion of the U.S. welfare state fundamentally altered the politics of national budgeting. Traditional federal spending is considered "discretionary" because the Appropriations Committees aren't obligated to spend any particular amount in a given year. For example, Congress might pass a law that allows the Appropriation panels to spend up to $10 billion for a defense program. After considering the defense program's needs in light of other priories, the national economic situation, and other factors, the panels might decide to provide, say, only $9 billion. George Mahon (D-Texas), who served as chairman of the House Appropriations Committee from 1964 to 1979, approached his work with the assumption that most bureau chiefs' spending demands needed to be restrained. "They just want to do more than what we think is necessary. And we think they can do what is necessary with less than they do," he stated. The committee was entirely free to exercise such discretion.

But entitlement programs removed this flexibility. The government was *legally obligated* to provide benefits to any person that met the eligibility requirements established by law. If 40 million Americans were determined to be eligible for Social Security, for example, the law required that all 40 million must receive their full allotment of promised benefits, even if other funding needs were not met; congressional budget actors like Mahon had no say over the matter. While annual appropriations were a staple of congressional life, entitlements were institutionally detached from Congress's ordinary legislative routine and rhythm. It was largely as the executive architects of these programs intended. President Franklin Roosevelt, for example, intended for Social Security to be financed out of its own earmarked tax in order to free it from having to compete each year for appropriations. This autonomy greatly benefited the constituents of programs like Social Security, but it weakened Congress's overall budget capacity. By 1974 "mandatory" spending for entitlements had risen to 49 percent of federal spending, up from 32 percent in 1962. In short, almost half the U.S. national budget was going for entitlements — and was thus largely beyond Congress's control.

The second factor behind the congressional budget reform was concern about rising deficits. For more than a century after the nation's founding, federal deficits were regarded not merely as an economic problem but as a political symbol of the nation's moral laxity and corruption. The expectation was that the budget should be balanced except during periods of genuine national crisis. After World War II, the growing influence of Keynesian economics modified the traditional balanced-budget norm among top budget officials. White House economists like Arthur Burns and Walter Heller insisted that the federal government should run budget deficits to stimulate consumer demand when the economy was thought to be performing below its potential. When good economic times returned, the government was expected to run budget surpluses. In sum, the new goal was to produce a balanced budget over the business cycle, not on an annual basis. President Dwight Eisenhower memorably captured the Keynesian stance on deficits when he said there was no need to balance the budget in the particular amount of time it takes the earth to revolve around the sun.

In the Employment Act of 1946, Congress signaled its basic support for Keynesianism by recognizing the government's responsibility to promote a high level of employment. It was understood that this goal might entail running budget deficits during periods of contraction. By the early 1960s, influential legislators were explicitly distancing themselves from traditional budget-balancing concerns. "I have been extremely disturbed by the general public's acceptance of the notion that there is something almost sanctified in a balanced budget," the Democrat Richard Bolling said in 1962. In 1964 Congress passed a major tax cut that President Kennedy's economic advisers had designed before his assassination with the stated aim of stimulating consumer demand. When the economy seemed to improve after the tax cut, the balanced-budget norm further weakened.

The Kennedy-Johnson tax cut was probably the high-water mark for Keynesianism on the Hill. Already by the late 1960s many lawmakers were becoming extremely anxious about the government's inability to maintain any kind of fiscal discipline. The military costs of the Vietnam War combined with the domestic costs of the Great Society led to chronic deficits. Between 1963 and 1973, the federal government managed to run a balanced budget in only one year (fiscal 1969), and only then because the powerful Ways and Means Committee chairman Wilbur Mills (D-

Arkansas) forced President Johnson into approving the tax hikes and spending cuts in the Revenue and Expenditure Control Act of 1968. By 1970, the federal government was back in the red.

The Budget Act of 1974

Were it only a matter of disappointing outcomes, a large bipartisan majority in support of the budget act of 1974 might never have emerged. But when President Nixon challenged Congress's authority to shape budget priorities by withholding — "impounding" — previously appropriated funds for programs opposed by his administration, Congress was compelled to adopt a new framework in order to safeguard its constitutional power of the purse. To be sure, the practice of impounding funds was not invented by Richard Nixon. Almost from the beginning of the Republic, Congress had accepted that if an appropriation item was no longer needed by an agency because its budget needs had changed, the administration could seek, and usually obtain, legislative permission to withdraw it in the interest of sound financial management. In 1803 President Thomas Jefferson impounded $50,000 that Congress had appropriated for the provision of gunboats after a "favorable and peaceful turn of affairs on the Mississippi rendered an immediate execution of that law unnecessary. . . ." Presidents Roosevelt, Truman, Kennedy, and Johnson also issued impoundment orders. Both the size and character of the Nixon impoundments, however, distinguished them from earlier ones. Rather than impounding a modest amount to promote administrative efficiency, Nixon sought to use impoundment as a political weapon, ordering the cancellation of approximately $12 billion of previously authorized spending. One of his most controversial actions was his decision to withhold some $2.5 billion in spending from the Highway Trust Fund. Outraged by his willingness to break faith with the motorists who paid the gasoline taxes from which the fund drew its income, a group of Democratic senators, led by Sam J. Ervin of North Carolina, filed a court suit challenging the action. In a major victory for Congress, the Eighth U.S. Circuit Court of Appeals ruled in 1973 that the administration had violated the law. While pleased with this ruling, the legislators remained convinced that a new congressional budget framework was needed to prevent similar presidential abuses in the future.

Nixon's unmistakable goal in the budget clash was to disempower Congress and strengthen the imperial presidency. Senator Frank Church (D-Idaho) echoed the views of most of the lawmakers when he warned that these impoundments threatened "democratic institutions" by making a mockery of the constitutional separation of powers, saying:

> Once it is widely recognized that a project may be entombed by the executive branch — even when a convincing case has been made before the Congress and after due deliberation monies have been appropriated — the American people will sense the futility of appealing to their elected representatives. They will conclude, if they haven't already done so, that the Executive Branch is the only significant arena for policy making.

With the authority of the legislative branch under threat, Congress was moved to action. A consensus developed that Congress needed to strengthen its independent budget-making capacity, promote internal discipline, and bring the executive's impoundment abuses to an end. In 1972 a Joint Study Committee on Budget Control, cochaired by Jamie L. Whitten (D-Mississippi) of the House Appropriations Committee and Al Ullman (D-Oregon) of the Ways and Means Committee, was established to examine budget reform options. "The question is not whether it must be done, but how," the Federal Reserve Board chairman Arthur F. Burns told the committee at its first hearings. "If you can develop procedures that will enable members of Congress to vote on an overall fiscal policy that adequately reflects congressional priorities, you will revitalize representative government in this country."

The committee issued a report in 1973 that emphasized the need to establish a framework that would allow Congress to coordinate its tax and spending decisions and bargain on an equal footing with the president. The result was the Congressional Budget and Impoundment Act of 1974. Signed by President Nixon less than a month before he resigned from office, it gave Congress important new tools for policy coordination. Many legislators who voted for budget reform were deeply concerned about the rising deficits and the need for fiscal restraint. "The plain facts," said Lee Metcalf (D-Montana) of the Government Operations Committee, "are that regardless of who exercises authority, the budget is in danger of going out of control."

Yet while anxiety about deficit spending was clearly a stimulus for reform, the text of the act did not mandate a balanced budget or the achievement of any other specific fiscal outcome, for that matter. The act was in fact less a substantive reform than a procedural one, and a highly pliable one at that. It permitted Congress to adopt *any* budget position for which a majority coalition could be assembled. If a majority supported a given position, the new framework would prevent the policy from being defeated on the House and Senate floors by minority factions. But if no majority consensus existed in Congress, the act could not magically conjure one up.

The act had three main features. First, it created a system of impoundment control to prevent presidents from simply overriding its spending preferences. Rather than banning impoundments entirely (which would have eliminated the executive's flexibility to withhold budget resources for legitimate managerial reasons), the Budget Act set forth rules governing the conditions under which impoundments could occur. In particular, the president was allowed to delay temporarily the release of appropriated funds — an action known as a "deferral." Deferrals take effect automatically unless either chamber passes a disapproval resolution. If a president wishes to eliminate spending authority permanently (a "recission"), however, he must receive Congress's permission. If Congress does not grant such permission within forty-five days, the president is obligated to release the funds.

Second, a major new organization, the Congressional Budget Office (CBO), was created to give Congress nonpartisan budget advice and technical support. No longer would Congress have to rely on the budget estimates and economic forecasts of the Office of Management and Budget (OMB), whose long-standing reputation for "neutral competence" had been seriously tarnished by the efforts of both the Johnson and Nixon administrations to use the elite agency as a political arm of the White House. Alice Rivlin, a mainstream economist highly respected by the Washington establishment, was subsequently named the first CBO director.

Third, budget committees were created in each chamber to manage Congress's new budget process. Significantly, the new procedures did not eliminate the existing tax-writing and appropriations processes. Rather, it was layered atop them in order to maintain opportunities for broad participation by members in a crucial legislative function. In sum, the new process would feature an important element of centralization, but Congress's traditional institutional character as a democratic body would be preserved. The Senate Budget Committee was originally established with sixteen members who were subject to the same principles of seniority and committee assignment rules as other Senate committees. The House Budget Committee was established with twenty-five members who were picked by a special formula. Five seats were assigned to Ways and Means Committee members and five to Appropriations Committee members. The remaining seats would be occupied by one member from each of the eleven authorizing committees with jurisdiction over substantive policy areas (such as the Agriculture, Interior, and Transportation Committees) and by one member each from the leadership of the Democratic and Republican caucuses.

The two committees were charged with articulating Congress's overall fiscal policy. After reviewing the president's budget proposals, the committees would draw up a concurrent resolution outlining a tentative congressional budget. The initial resolution (to be enacted by May 15) would set target totals for appropriations, spending, taxes, and the size of the budget surplus or deficit. Within these targets, the resolution would break down appropriations and spending among the functional categories (e.g., defense, health, income security) used in the president's budget. To reflect the congressional committee structure, the budget resolutions (which did not require a presidential signature since they were not statutes) would also provide a specific allocation to each committee that considered budget legislation. These allocations were not binding on Congress; they were merely intended to guide the lawmakers as they acted on appropriations bills and other budget measures.

After the enactment of the initial budget resolution, Congress would start processing the thirteen regular appropriations bills for the upcoming fiscal year through its normal appropriations process. The tax-writing committees would also conduct their business. In September, after Congress had finished its action on appropriations, the budget committees would take another overall look at the budget. By September 15, Congress was to have adopted a second budget resolution that could either affirm or revise the targets set by the initial resolution. Unlike the first resolution, the second was supposed to be binding. If the budget committees determined that any actions taken by Congress during the year did not fit the final budget resolution totals, they could direct the committees with jurisdiction over appropriations, entitlements, and revenues to submit recommendations for meeting the final targets in a process known as "reconciliation." The budget committees would then combine the committee recommendations it received into a single package and report them to the floor as a reconciliation bill by September 25, in time for the start of the new fiscal year, October 1.

After Reform

The initial experience with the 1974 reform act was mixed. Debates over budget resolutions instigated sharp partisan conflict in the House. The Republicans in the lower chamber felt that the House Budget Committee chairman, Brock Adams (D-Washington), was too stingy on defense spending and too much of a spendthrift on social programs. The Republicans voted, 128–3, against the first budget resolution in 1975, 111–3 against it in 1976, and 121–7 against it in 1977. In the Senate the budget process enjoyed greater bipartisan support. The Senate Budget Committee chairman, Edmund S. Muskie (D-Maine), and the ranking minority member, Henry L. Bellmon (R-Oklahoma), worked closely together to produce moderate resolutions that could attract votes from both liberals and conservatives.

The act succeeded in halting the presidential abuse of impoundment. In addition, the CBO established itself as a credible budget forecasting institution. Some close observers argued that its existence, together with the new budget procedures, had significantly improved the quality of Congress's deliberation over fiscal issues. "You just can't underestimate how Congress as an institution has advanced in its economic thinking as a result of the Budget Act," the Senate Budget Committee staff director, John McEvoy, said in 1978. "I am convinced the 1960s was the era of the lawyer around here, with civil rights and like legislation being in the forefront. But the 1970s is the era of the economist. Because of the budget process, senators who barely understood tax and spending terms are now talking about things like the 'reflow effects of taxation,'" referring to the way in which a tax cut can stimulate new business.

As far as restructuring budget priorities, however, the act's impact appeared negligible. Those lawmakers who hoped the new process would promote fiscal restraint were sorely disappointed. The budget deficit rose from $6 billion in fiscal 1974 to $74 billion in fiscal 1976. "There is a widespread feeling right now, which I share, that the congressional budget process is in trouble. Congress has followed the new process quite faithfully . . . However, on substantive matters . . . Congress is too willing to negate the restraint implicit in the process whenever it is politically appealing," said the House Budget Committee chairman, Robert Giaimo (D-Connecticut), in 1978.

One problem had to do with the timing of the reconciliation process. Reconciliation was intended to serve as an enforcement mechanism by guaranteeing that the spending cuts that the budget committees had assumed in their initial resolutions would be adopted. By the time reconciliation's bills were taken up at the end of the fiscal year, however, appropriations decisions had already been made. In effect, this schedule required legislators to alter the spending commitments they had made only a few months earlier. Not surprisingly, Congress had a difficult time enacting these cutbacks. Once promises had been made to particular constituencies, it was difficult for lawmakers to renege on them.

In the Carter administration's last year, however, a procedural revolution took place that made the congressional budget process far more potent. The staff of the Senate Budget Committee came up with the idea of moving the reconciliation process from the second budget resolution in September to the first budget resolution in May. This meant the committees could deliver their recommendations for savings to the affected congressional committees *before* that year's funding decisions had been approved. No longer would the appropriations barn door be closed after the spending horses had already galloped away.

Seeking to claim the mantle of fiscal responsibility for the Democratic party, the House Speaker, Thomas P. "Tip" O'Neill (D-Massachusetts), quickly signed off on the new schedule. Some sixteen committee and subcommittee chairmen whose programs would potentially face cutbacks under reconciliation, including Morris Udall (D-Arizona) of the Interior Committee, tried to stop this procedural revolution in its tracks. But Udall's coalition lost badly on the critical floor vote, 127–289. In the Senate the new schedule for reconciliation was approved easily. The process henceforth would begin early in the year. (The requirement for a second budget resolution was scrapped after 1982.)

While the 1980 reconciliation bill constituted a major innovation, its policy impact (about $4 billion in budget savings) was rather modest. The 1981 reconciliation measure — whose passage signaled the arrival of the Reagan Revolution — was another story entirely. Following his landslide victory over Jimmy Carter, Ronald Reagan entered the White House in January 1981 with three ambitious budget priorities: to slash taxes, to strengthen the military, and to curb domestic spending. The reconciliation process gave him the mechanism he needed to win legislative support for his far-reaching agenda. In the Omnibus Reconciliation Act of 1981 (OBRA), Congress passed major reductions in both domestic discretionary items and mandatory entitlements, such as welfare and food stamps. While it is impossible to know for certain, it seems quite unlikely that these cutbacks could have been passed under the fragmented budget process that existed before 1974. Packaging the spending cuts in a single omnibus bill made it much harder for the committees and clienteles targeted by the cutbacks to organize themselves. As David Stockman, Reagan's point man at OMB, later said, "My aim in this tactic was to take the Hill by storm before the interest group opposition to spending cuts congealed."

There was no small irony in an administration using a legislative process designed to strengthen Congress's budget power to serve its executive goals. Stockman, a former House member himself, acknowledged as much when he said, "The constitutional prerogatives of the legislative branch would have to be, in effect, suspended. Enacting the Reagan administration's economic program meant rubber stamp approval, nothing less. The world's so-called greatest deliberative body would have to be reduced to the status of the ministerial arm of the White House." Stockman could pull off this remarkable feat because a majority of the lawmakers accepted the administration's budget agenda as their own. With inflation skyrocketing, federal taxes at a historically high peacetime level (almost 21 percent of GDP), and a growing sense both that the military needed strengthening and that many social programs weren't working, many lawmakers found themselves in fundamental agreement with the president's agenda. Not only did Reagan win overwhelming support from Republicans, he also picked up the votes of more than twenty "boll weevils," conservative southern Democrats who were opposed in principle to many welfare state programs. Some boll weevils in the coalition were also swayed by side deals with the administration. For example, John Breaux of Louisiana was promised that the administration would not oppose the sugar price supports important to his constituents. The reconciliation act signaled a major shift in federal spending policy. Budget estimates at the time projected that outlays would be reduced about $130 billion over three years. Significant cutbacks were imposed on many domestic programs, such as AFDC, food stamps, and unemployment compensation.

Congress also embraced Reagan's proposal for a massive tax cut. The Economic Recovery Tax Act (ERTA), the product of a bidding war between the White House and the Democrats, reduced individual tax rates by almost 25 percent and created many new tax preferences for powerful interests like the oil lobby. "It's terrible that we should be involved in a bidding war," admitted Dan Rostenkowski (D-Illinois) of the House Ways and Means Committee. "But it all depends on whether you want to lose courageously or to win. I like to win." As sweeping as OBRA's expenditure cutbacks were, they were not large enough to offset the huge revenue leakage caused by ERTA. The net result of the Reagan economic program was therefore a dramatic increase in the size of the federal budget deficit. In fiscal year 1982 the deficit stood at $128 billion. In fiscal 1983 it climbed to $208 billion.

The "Fiscalization" of the Policy Debate

Between 1982 and 1996 the budget deficit was the nation's dominant political issue. Washington insiders began speaking of "the fiscalization of the policy debate." By this they meant that policymakers increasingly were debating policy proposals according not to their particular merits but to their potential impact on the government's bottom line. The chief question was no longer whether a given policy idea made sense but what would it do to the deficit.

While the voters generally supported the concept of balancing the budget, opinion surveys at the time revealed that most citizens did not want to see their taxes raised or their favored programs cut. Many citizens erroneously believed that the deficit could be liquidated simply by eliminating "waste, fraud, and abuse." The public also was mistaken in believing that the federal government spent huge amounts of money on welfare and foreign assistance. In reality, the deficit was driven by the rising spending for middle-class entitlement programs that served large, politically active constituencies like the elderly and retired federal workers. Most politicians were extremely reluctant to withdraw promised entitlement benefits.

The single most costly entitlement, Social Security, was essentially declared off-limits to deficit reduction during the 1980s. In 1981 David Stockman called for a sharp, immediate reduction in early retirees' benefits in order to trim the deficit. The proposal immediately generated a political firestorm. Speaker Tip O'Neill said Reagan's proposed Social Security cut was "a rotten thing to do. It is a despicable thing." In the Senate, the Finance Committee chairman, Robert Dole (R-Kansas), sponsored a resolution condemning the plan. It passed, 96–0. The White House quickly abandoned the proposal. The only time Social Security cutbacks were on the political agenda was when the program's own dedicated trust fund was on the brink of insolvency. In 1983 a bipartisan commission, headed by the future Federal Reserve Board chairman Alan Greenspan, won congressional approval for a Social Security "rescue" package that featured substantial payroll tax hikes, a slight reduction in cost-of-living increases, and a gradual increase in the retirement age, to sixty-seven. The clear political lesson from these episodes was that Social Security benefits couldn't be touched unless it was for the express purpose of stabilizing the system's internal finances.

By 1983 a political stalemate had developed. Congressional Democrats claimed the deficit should be eliminated by cutting the Pentagon's budget and raising taxes. President Reagan and his Republican allies in Congress insisted the answer was reducing domestic social programs. In an effort to break the partisan deadlock, Senator Dole offered a plan to raise taxes and cut future cost-of-living increases for benefits such as Medicare and Social Security. Unlike Reagan's earlier Social Security proposal, the spending cutbacks imposed under Dole's plan would mainly affect the distant future. But this compromise failed to gain the support of important leaders. The president announced he would veto any tax increase, and Speaker O'Neill came out strongly against COLA reductions, arguing, "No way are we going to cut senior citizens."

Reform Again

As the budget crisis deepened, some members of Congress came to the conclusion that Congress would never reach a consensus on the budget and that a new procedure was needed to force significant deficit reductions. Two Senate freshmen, Phil Gramm (R-Texas) and Warren B. Rudman (R-New Hampshire), in 1985 joined with their more senior colleague, the former Budget Committee chairman Ernest F. Hollings (D-South Carolina), to introduce what came to be known as the Gramm-Rudman-Hollings (GRH) Act. It required the deficit to be eliminated gradually over six years, with maximum allowable deficits along the way. If the deficit projected for a given year exceeded that year's deficit target, GRH provided for automatic cuts (through a process known as sequestration) in various federal programs. The logic of the reform seemed compelling: either the deficit would be eliminated automatically through across-the-board cuts or else lawmakers, if they couldn't bear the political consequences of "mindless" sequestration, would be motivated into making tough but more orderly cutbacks of their own. Although anxious about the damage it might inflict on his military buildup, President Reagan gave his approval to GRH, arguing that it was "an important step toward putting our fiscal house in order."

But GRH proved both a substantive and political failure. One problem was that it completely exempted from sequestration many big-ticket items (such as Social Security, food stamps, and veterans' pensions), thus requiring disproportionate cuts in the rest of the budget. In addition, the focus on projected deficits invited the lawmakers to use bookkeeping tricks to make the budget forecasts look more rosy. When Congress found itself unable to meet its deficit target for fiscal 1987, for example, it moved a $680 million installment of the federal revenue-sharing program by five days so that it would fall at the end of fiscal 1986 instead of the following year. Countless other gimmicks undermined the integrity of the process and made Congress look foolish. Finally, the deficit targets did not take into account unexpected changes in economic conditions. When the Gramm-Rudman-Hollings deficit-reduction targets started to bite in the mid-1980s, they were postponed and then essentially scrapped.

The Budget Enforcement Act of 1990 (BEA), the groundwork for which was laid at a summit held at Andrews Air Force Base between representatives of President George H. W. Bush and top congressional leaders including the House Speaker, Tom Foley (D-Washington), and the Senate majority leader, George Mitchell (D-Maine), was more successful. Rather than holding Congress hostage to factors (like economic conditions) it couldn't control, BEA made Congress more accountable for its own budget decisions. In this sense, it was a return to the reform spirit of the original 1974 Budget Act. Instead of mandating a balanced budget by a certain date, BEA imposed annual limits on discretionary spending and created a pay-as-you-go framework for entitlements and revenues. The effect of this modest yet more workable reform was to make legislators more responsible for confronting the costs of new budget legislation. If, for example, a new entitlement benefit was to be created, Congress had to identify an offsetting cut in another entitlement program or a specific tax increase to pay for it. In the course of the negotiations, President Bush agreed that tax increases would have to be part of any deficit-reduction package. This abandonment of his famous "no new taxes" pledge would cost him critical votes in his unsuccessful bid to win a second term in 1992.

The most important effect of the new procedural rules in the 1990 package was that it strongly discouraged Congress from making expensive new budget promises. This ensured that deficits would eventually recede as economic growth caught up with the growth rate of existing policy commitments. At the start of the 1990s, however, the deficit picture momentarily worsened due to an economic slowdown and an unusually rapid growth in the cost of health care. A sense that the deficit beast would never be slayed by Washington insiders propelled the political maverick Ross Perot to run in the 1992 presidential campaign. Perot's appeal to fiscally conservative Republican voters, in turn, weakened Bush's political base and contributed to Bill Clinton's narrow victory.

Budget Showdowns

Convinced that persistent deficits not only damaged the economy but also stymied liberal government activism, Clinton made deficit reduction an early legislative priority of his administration. His efforts to win legislative backing for his 1993 deficit-reduction package were seriously hampered, however, by the slimness of the Democrats' majorities in both chambers. In the House, Clinton eked out a 6-vote victory for his plan. But in the Senate he met stiff resistance, forcing him to make endless deals to cobble together a winning coalition. To gain the support of Senators David Boren (D-Oklahoma) and Bennett Johnston (D-Louisiana), he agreed to scrap a BTU tax from his plan and substitute a 4.3-cent increase in the gasoline tax. To make up the lost revenue, the Senate Finance Committee removed some tax breaks for the poor that Clinton had proposed. The Senate ultimately passed the deficit-reduction plan, 50–49, with Vice President Gore casting the tiebreaking vote.

The drama then shifted to the conference committee. Some two hundred House and Senate budget negotiators convened to work out a compromise between the two chambers. Before the vote on the conference committee report, the House Speaker, Tom Foley, said it was a "time for courage." As the fifteen-minute deadline for the roll call approached, it became clear that the fate of the measure hung in the balance. The decisive vote was left to Marjorie Margolies-Mezvinsky (D-Pennsylvania), a first-term member who had voted against the Clinton plan the first time around. When she voted yes on the conference bill, the Republicans in the chamber boasted that her constituents wouldn't forgive her for the switch and that her legislative career would soon be over. As it turned out, Margolies-Mezvinsky was a political casualty of the 1994 Republican election landslide.

The action then moved to the Senate, where the vote was almost as close. Bob Kerrey of Nebraska agonized publicly about his decision but finally announced he would vote for the measure. Clinton's deficit-reduction package thus passed in Congress without a single Republican vote in either chamber.

The ideological conflict over the budget continued well into the mid-1990s. In 1994 the Republicans won a majority in both chambers for the first time in more than a quarter century. Led by the House Speaker, Newt Gingrich (R-Georgia), the new majority sought to complete the Reagan Revolution and scale back the scope of domestic government. Speaker Gingrich personally selected Robert Livingston (R-Louisiana), a tough conservative who had long bristled under Democratic majority control, to chair the Appropriations Committee and demanded loyalty from every Republican member of the committee. "You are going to be in the forefront of the revolution," Gingrich told them. "You have the toughest jobs in the House. If you don't want to do it, tell me."

The Republican budget reform strategy hinged on exploiting the reconciliation process, which limited the participation of the Democratic minority. In late 1995 both the House and Senate approved an ambitious Republican deficit-reduction package featuring deep cuts in Medicare, Medicaid, and education programs. But when President Clinton vetoed the measure in early 1996, budget negotiations between the two parties collapsed. And when the Republican congressional leadership declined to pass a temporary spending measure in what turned out to be a mistaken belief that it would force Clinton into agreeing to their terms, the government shut down. Much to Gingrich's chagrin, the polls showed a majority of the public blamed the Republicans for the impasse, not the administration. By January 1996 the Republicans decided to abandon their strategy and bring federal employees back to work. Gingrich announced that he expected the president to leave office without a balanced budget agreement.

Just a year later, however, the Republican congressional leadership and the president negotiated a package, the Balanced Budget and Taxpayer Relief Act of 1997, to eliminate the deficit by 2002. The surprising breakthrough reflected both political and economic factors. President Clinton and the Republican congressional leadership each badly wanted a balanced budget deal, and both sides had strong reasons to avoid another round of legislative brinkmanship. At the same time, the tremendous performance of the American economy over the prior year had greatly improved the budget situation, narrowing the gap between spending and revenues. Forecasts showed that the deficit could be eliminated without wrenching cuts by 2002. As it turned out, continuing rapid economic growth enabled the government to achieve a balanced budget in 1998, four years ahead of schedule.

The disappearance of the deficit did not bring partisan squabbling over fiscal matters to an end, however. In the 2000 presidential race, the Democratic party nominee, Al Gore, argued that the emergence of a budget surplus gave the nation a crucial opportunity to prepare for the coming retirement of the baby boomers. Gore said that the portion of the federal budget surplus generated by surpluses in the Social Security Trust Fund should be put in a "lockbox." By this, he meant that the money should be used to retire the federal debt, with the interest savings credited back to the Social Security system. Gore also called for about $300 billion of the budget surpluses to be deposited in a "rainy day" fund similar to the reserves maintained by many state governments. "This new reserve will guarantee that we will not have to cut education or health care. And unlike the promises made on the other side, we won't be running deficits and endangering America's prosperity," said Gore. George W. Bush, the Republican nominee, insisted that a major portion of the surplus should immediately be returned to the American taxpayer. Bush, of course, was eventually determined to have won the election. Despite the extraordinary circumstances of his triumph, he chose not to modify the ambitious fiscal agenda he had articulated during the campaign, and Congress passed Bush's massive tax reduction bill in early 2001. Most Democrats argued that the nation couldn't afford the tax cut; the Republicans overwhelmingly argued that it could.

By 2002 the budget surplus was gone, at least for a time. The primary cause of the deterioration of the government's short-term budget picture was not the Bush tax cut but rather the economic recession. Over the longer term, however, the Bush tax cut definitely worsened the government's fiscal position. The government's official budget forecasts in 2002 showed that the Bush tax cut was the single most important factor in reducing the size of the ten-year budget surplus that had been projected two years earlier. According to the forecasts, the Bush tax cut would drain the federal coffers of increasing amounts of revenue just as the baby boomers were on the brink of retirement, leading to massive federal deficits. Long-term forecasts are of course subject to a great deal of uncertainty. Most experts agreed, however, that the current path of U.S. fiscal policy was economically unsustainable over the long run.

As the 2004 elections approached, legislators once again found themselves wrestling with the fiscal implications of an activist government. Few lawmakers wished to raise taxes now to address a budget problem that would not become severe for several decades. Fewer still were eager to withdraw promised social benefits. Congress allowed the budget enforcement rules that had provided crucial fiscal discipline during the 1990s to expire in 2002. Many budget experts argued that this was a terrible economic mistake. "The disciplinary mechanisms have disappeared," lamented Alice Rivlin, the former CBO director, in early 2004. But lawmakers disagreed about whether or in what form to reinstate the rules. Some conservative Republicans argued that any new pay-as-you-go rule should not apply to future tax cuts. The Democrats insisted that it should. Congress seemed unlikely to reach a workable, long-term compromise on budget enforcement issues until federal debt reduction became a salient issue with voters, political activists, or the financial markets.

While much of the fiscal discipline of the 1990s had been lost, the institutional framework of the 1974 budget act, which had been established in the wake of an executive attack on Congress's power of the purse in the 1970s, remained in place. The House and Senate budget committees continued to offer lawmakers a forum and a set of producers for considering the federal government's overall financial picture. And the CBO continued to give Congress its own set of budget estimates and long-term economic forecasts. Congress thus retained an independent decision-making process to help it shape the nation's fiscal future. As the new century began, Congress's most difficult budget challenge was developing a majority position on what that future should look like. In a political era characterized by the polarization of policy elites, such a consensus was highly elusive.

When the definitive political history of the postwar America state is written, the congressional budget will likely receive close attention. Indeed, it would be impossible to tell the stories of the rise and fall of such major political figures as Wilbur Mills, Newt Gingrich, and Bill Clinton without attending to the tax and spending choices that Congress has made and rejected over the past three decades. This budget process offers a unique window into the ideological commitments of the two parties; the relationship between the government and the American people, its constituents; and the connection between state and society. On first impression, the congressional budget process seems arcane and even trivial. Its complex rules and byzantine procedures seem purposely designed to mystify. When we peer below its procedural surface, however, we find deep political truths about the struggle over values and scarce resources in a democratic polity.

— Eric Patashnik

BIBLIOGRAPHICAL NOTES

The single best source on postwar congressional budgeting is Joseph White and Aaron Wildavsky, *The Deficit and the Public Interest* (Berkeley, Calif., 1989). Wildavsky's *The Politics of the Budgetary Process* (Boston, 1964) is a modern classic that analyzes budgeting as an incremental bargaining process. John Makin and Norman J. Ornstein, *Debt and Taxes* (Washington, D.C., 1994), places the budget battles of the 1980s in a larger historical context. A compact guide to the major events after 1974 is Lance LeLoup, "Budget Process," in *The Encyclopedia of the United States Congress,* Donald C. Bacon, Roger H. Davidson, and Morton Keller, eds., vol. 1 (New York, 1995). Eric M. Patashnik's *Putting Trust in the U.S. Budget: Federal Trust Funds and the Politics of Commitment* (Cambridge, Mass., 2000) examines the origins and consequences of earmarked funding mechanisms for Social Security, Medicare, and other federal programs. James Savage's *Balanced Budgets and American Politics* (Ithaca, N.Y., 1988) is a careful historical work that argues that the traditional American fear of deficit spending (which dates to the early Republic) reflects political-cultural factors more than objective economic concerns. No student of federal budgeting can afford to miss three books by Allen Schick. *Congress and Money* (Washington, D.C., 1982) describes the 1974 budget act's legislative origins and early impact on congressional behavior. *The Capacity to Budget* (Washington, D.C., 1990) highlights the influence of changing economic conditions and policy commitments on Congress's political capacity to make effective budget choices. *The Federal Budget: Politics, Policy, Process* (Washington, D.C., 1995) is a definitive primer on congressional budget rules and procedures. An essential book on the Reagan administration's fiscal record by a leading insider is David Stockman, *The Triumph of Politics* (New York, 1986). Paul Pierson, "The Deficit and the Politics of Domestic Reform," in *The Social Divide,* ed. Margaret Weir (Washington, D.C., 1998), is an insightful analysis of the budget battles of the Clinton era. A useful secondary source for the whole period is the *Congressional Quarterly* (both the *Weekly Reports* and the yearly *Almanacs* published since 1946).

39

War Power

THE OPEN-ENDED NATURE of presidential power during the Vietnam War prompted Congress to take stock of its institutional and constitutional duties. Out of this debate came the War Powers Resolution of 1973, supposedly designed to reassert congressional power. The statute, clumsily drafted, actually shifted greater power to the president and gave Congress the illusion that its constitutional prerogatives would be protected by statutory procedures. The last three decades have marked a steady increase in unilateral war-making by presidents, with few legislative constraints and no judicial checks. By 2002 the United States had progressed to what the framers feared the most and thought they had put behind them: presidential wars.

Part of the ascendancy of presidential power can be attributed to broad interpretations of executive authority under international and regional organizations, particularly the United Nations and NATO. Instead of presidents coming to Congress for authority, ever since 1950 they have sought "authority" from the U.N. Security Council or the nations of the North Atlantic Treaty Organization (NATO). Harry Truman in 1950, George H. W. Bush in 1990, and Bill Clinton from 1994 to 1999 all used this technique to circumvent the legislative branch and the Constitution.

We debate the constitutionality of war power actions because of a rock-bottom belief held by the framers: it is possible to *structure* government in such a way to protect individual liberties and freedoms. We refer to this concept in different ways: separation of powers, checks and balances, pitting ambition against ambition. To the framers it meant that the clash between institutions is the safest and best way of formulating national policy, whether domestic or foreign. The War Powers Resolution (WPR) relied on this same concept but used different words: "collective judgment." However, the passage of this resolution failed to halt executive dominance over military operations.

The Road to the War Powers Resolution

From 1789 to 1950, lawmakers, the courts, and the executive branch understood that only Congress could initiate offensive actions against other nations. This period is faithful to the intentions of the framers, who rejected the monarchical model of Britain and granted Congress the sole authority to take the country from a state of peace to a state of war. They left the president with certain defensive powers "to repel sudden attacks." Matters changed dramatically in 1950, however, when President Harry Truman took the country to war in Korea without seeking congressional authority. Some commentators have attributed this growth of presidential power to the worldwide responsibilities that moved to the United States in the twentieth century. Yet the two greatest conflagrations — World Wars I and II — were both declared by Congress pursuant to the Constitution.

Of more decisive influence are the treaties adopted after World War II, particularly the United Nations Charter of 1945 and the mutual security pacts entered into a few years later, such as NATO and SEATO. Nothing in the history of the U.N. or the mutual security pacts implied that Congress had given the president unilateral power to wage war. Nevertheless, there has been a pattern of presidents seeking authority not from Congress but from international and regional bodies. Truman in Korea, Bush (Sr.) in Iraq, Clinton in Haiti, Bosnia, and Kosovo — in each instance a president circumvented Congress by relying on either the U.N. or NATO.

The diminished role of Congress dates from the early Cold War. During a Senate debate on the U.N. Charter in 1945, President Truman sent a cable from Potsdam, stating that all agreements involving U.S. troop commitments to the U.N. would first have to be approved by both houses of Congress. For such agreements it would be his purpose "to ask the Congress for appropriate legislation to approve them." This understanding was later incorporated into the U.N. Participation Act of 1945, which stated that the agreements "shall be subject to the approval of the Congress by appropriate act or joint resolution." Yet five years later Truman sent U.S. troops to Korea as part of a U.N. operation without seeking congressional authority. How could he circumvent the clear language of the U.N. Participation Act? — by not entering into a "special agreement." The very procedure enacted to protect legislative prerogatives became a nullity.

In addition to relying on Security Council resolutions to circumvent Congress, presidents regarded mutual security treaties as another source of authority. Both NATO and SEATO stipulated that provisions shall be "carried out by the Parties in accordance with their respective constitutional processes." Nothing in the legislative histories of those treaties suggested that the president had unilateral authority to act in the event of an attack. Richard Heindel and other scholars who examined NATO after its adoption conclude that the language about constitutional processes was "intended to ensure that the Executive Branch of the Government should come back to the Congress when decisions were required in which the Congress has a constitutional responsibility." The NATO treaty, they wrote, "does not transfer to the President the Congressional power to make war."

President Dwight D. Eisenhower thought that Truman's initiative in Korea was a mistake, both constitutionally and politically. It was Eisenhower's policy to seek authority from Congress so that the two branches would act jointly, sending a strong message to both allies and enemies. On covert operations, such as in Iran and Guatemala, Eisenhower acted alone, without seeking legislative authority, but few members of Congress were willing to defend legislative prerogatives during the 1950s. Senator Robert Taft (R-Ohio) stood nearly alone in articulating the constitutional interests of Congress. In 1954 the Senate defeated John Bricker's (R-Ohio) proposed amendment to curtail the power of the president in forming treaties. Unlike Eisenhower, President John F. Kennedy was prepared to act during the Cuban missile crisis solely on what he considered to be his constitutional authority; he claimed "full authority" as commander in chief.

In August 1964 President Lyndon B. Johnson asked Congress to pass the Gulf of Tonkin Resolution to authorize military action against North Vietnam. Because of questions about whether the second attack in the Gulf of Tonkin actually occurred and the subsequent escalation of the war, many members of Congress, including the Arkansas senator J. William Fulbright, came to regret their votes and urged a reassertion of legislative authority. Hearings by the Senate Foreign Relations Committee in 1967 highlighted its concern for the "marked constitutional imbalance" between Congress and the president in determining foreign policy over the previous twenty-five years. Two years later the Senate passed the National Commitments Resolution, which provided that a commitment of military or financial resources to other countries required a treaty, statute, or concurrent resolution supporting the commitment. This resolution had no legal effect, but it represented an important expression of constitutional principles.

The War Powers Resolution (1973)

In 1973 a fierce battle between the Democratic Congress and President Richard Nixon turned to the constitutional issue of presidents making war. Prodded by public opposition to the war in Vietnam, the legislative branch finally stirred itself to challenge a trend that had been under way since 1950. The stated purpose of the War Powers Resolution (WPR) was "to fulfill the intent of the framers of the Constitution" and to "insure that the collective judgment" of Congress and the president will apply to the introduction of U.S. troops to combat. However, both in language and implementation, the resolution actually undermined the intent of the framers and did not ensure collective judgment between the branches.

Much of the ineffectiveness of the WPR can be traced to the incompatibility between the House and Senate versions. As far back as 1970, the members of the House were willing to recognize that the president, in certain extraordinary emergency conditions, had the authority to defend the United States and its citizens without authorization from Congress. Led by Representative Clement J. Zablocki (D-Wisconsin), the House decided it was impractical to define the precise conditions under which presidents may act, so it relied on procedural safeguards. The president would be required, "whenever feasible," to consult with Congress before sending American forces into armed conflict. He was also to report the circumstances necessitating the action; the constitutional, legislative, and treaty provisions authorizing the action, together with his reasons for not seeking prior congressional authorization; and the estimated scope of the activities.

Several senators, including Tom Eagleton (D-Missouri), Jacob Javits (R-New York), and John Stennis (D-Mississippi), refused to give the president such unilateral authority. In 1973 the House agreed to place some time limits on presidential initiatives. Unless Congress declared war within 120 days or specifically authorized the use of force, the president had to terminate the commitment and remove the troops. The House bill allowed Congress, by concurrent resolution, to direct disengagement at any time during the 120-day period. Concurrent resolutions must pass both chambers but are not presented to the president for his signature or veto.

Instead of allowing the president to make war wherever and whenever he liked for whatever reasons, the Senate attempted to spell out the particular conditions under which presidents could act single-handedly. According to the Senate's draft bill in 1973, armed force could be used in three situations: (1) to repel an armed attack on the United States, its territories, and possessions, retaliate in the event of such an attack, and forestall the direct and imminent threat of such an attack; (2) to repel an armed attack against U.S. armed forces outside the United States and its territories and possessions and forestall the direct and imminent threat of such an attack; and (3) to rescue endangered American citizens and nationals in foreign countries or at sea.

The first situation (except for the final clause) conformed to understandings developed by the framers. The other situations reflected changes that had occurred in the concept of defensive war and life-and-property actions. U.S. forces were now stationed around the globe, often because of treaty obligations. Moreover, on dozens of occasions presidents had resorted to the use of military force to rescue Americans abroad.

The Senate bill required the president to cease military action unless Congress within thirty days specifically authorized him to continue. A separate provision allowed him to sustain military operations beyond the thirty-day limit if he determined that "unavoidable military necessity respecting the safety" of the armed forces required continued use for the purposes of bringing about a prompt disengagement.

Pressured to produce a bill, House and Senate conferees fashioned a compromise that ended up widening the president's power. Representative Zablocki and Senators Javits and Edmund Muskie (D-Maine) were among the influential conferees. Sections 4 and 5 allowed the president to act unilaterally with military force for sixty to ninety days. The president could go to war at any time, in any place, for any reason. The resolution merely required him to report to Congress on occasion and to consult with lawmakers "in every possible instance." The breadth of that power cannot be squared with the framers' intent.

When the bill emerged from conference committee in 1973, some members of Congress recognized the extent to which military power had been tilted toward the president. Representative William Green (D-Pennsylvania) initially supported the resolution because he thought it would limit presidential power. Now, examining the product, he objected that it "is actually an expansion of Presidential warmaking power, rather than a limitation." Representative Vernon Thomson (R-Wisconsin) said that the "clear meaning" of the bill pointed to "a diminution rather than an enhancement of the role of Congress in the critical decisions whether the country will or will not go to war." To Representative Robert Eckhardt (D-Texas), the resolution provided "the color of authority to the President to exercise a warmaking power which I find the Constitution has exclusively assigned to the Congress."

Senator Eagleton, a principal sponsor of the resolution when it was introduced, denounced the conference version. Although the media continued to describe the bill as a constraint on presidential war power, Eagleton said that the bill gave the president "unilateral authority to commit American troops anywhere in the world, under any conditions he decides, for 60 to 90 days." He confessed to being "dumbfounded." With memories so fresh about the presidential extension of the war in Southeast Asia, "how can we give unbridled, unlimited total authority to the President to commit us to war?" He charged that the bill, after being nobly conceived, "has been horribly bastardized to the point of being a menace."

Despite these objections, the conference version sailed through Congress with large margins: 75–20 in the Senate and 238–123 in the House. Most of the votes came from Democrats. In the Senate, Republicans supported the measure by a margin of 26 to 14 while Democrats voted overwhelmingly in favor, 49–6. Democratic support in the House was even more striking. Republicans actually voted against the bill, 85–75, while Democrats favored it, 163–38.

President Richard Nixon vetoed the bill on October 24, primarily because he regarded it as impractical and dangerous to fix in a statute the procedure by which the president and Congress should share the war power. He also believed that the legislation encroached on the president's constitutional responsibilities as commander in chief. Both houses mustered a two-thirds majority to override the veto: the House narrowly (284–135), the Senate by a more comfortable margin (75–18). Republicans in the House voted 86–103, while Democrats were strongly in favor, 198–32. Party votes in the Senate: 25–15 for Republicans, 50–3 for Democrats.

Some of the congressional support resulted from partisan calculations. Several legislators decided to score short-term political points at the cost of long-term institutional and constitutional interests. Consider the voting record of fifteen members of the House. Initially they voted against the House bill and the conference version because they considered the legislation too favorable to presidential power. To be consistent, they should have voted to sustain Nixon's veto. Instead, they switched sides and delivered the decisive votes for enactment. Of these fifteen members, eleven were Democrats, including Bella Abzug (New York), Robert Drinan (Massachusetts), Elizabeth Holtzman (New York), and Jamie Whitten (Mississippi).

These members reversed course for a variety of reasons. Some feared that a vote to sustain the veto would lend credence to the high-flying views of presidential power put forth in Nixon's veto message. Others thought that an override might be a step toward impeaching Nixon. Bella Abzug, a liberal antiwar member and strong opponent of Nixon, voted against the House bill and the conference version because they expanded presidential war power, yet she argued for a veto override: "This could be a turning point in the struggle to control an administration that has run amuck. It could accelerate the demand for the impeachment of the President."

The WPR recognized that presidents may use military force for up to ninety days without seeking congressional authority. It also required the president to submit reports to Congress on these military operations and to consult with lawmakers "in every possible instance." The language in the resolution attempted to limit the effect of mutual security treaties. The authority to introduce U.S. forces into hostilities shall not be inferred "from any treaty heretofore or hereafter ratified unless such treaty is implemented by legislation specifically authorizing" the introduction of American troops. In actual operation, as witnessed by President Clinton's military actions in Bosnia and Kosovo, that part of the resolution would have no real impact on the use of NATO's military force.

Implementing the WPR

Both Presidents Gerald Ford and Jimmy Carter understood the need to heal the wounds from the Vietnam War, and they limited the use of military force during their administrations. Ford used the military only for the evacuations from Southeast Asia and during the *Mayaguez* capture, while Carter resorted to military action only in the unsuccessful effort to rescue the hostages in Iran. But those actions were limited and did not threaten the balance of power between Congress and the president. The record from Ronald Reagan to George W. Bush marked the increasing use of presidential war power, with Congress progressively marginalized.

Beyond the problems of statutory language, the implementation of the WPR further expanded presidential power. The bill had a peculiar feature: the sixty- to ninety-day clock began to tick only if the president reported under Section 4(a)(1). Not surprisingly, presidents since 1973 have not reported under 4(a)(1). They report "consistent with" the WPR. The only president to report under 4(a)(1) was Gerald Ford in the 1975 effort to rescue the crew of the *Mayaguez*, which had been seized by Cambodia. But his report had no substantive importance because it was released after the incident was over. In its operation, the WPR allowed presidents to use military force against other countries until Congress adopted some kind of statutory constraint.

The failure of the WPR to restore legislative power became clear during the presidency of Ronald Reagan, who used military force repeatedly. He introduced U.S. troops into Lebanon, invaded Grenada, carried out air strikes against Libya, and maintained naval operations in the Persian

Gulf. In none of those actions did he ask Congress for authority. In all of the cases he could argue that the operations were completed within the sixty- to ninety-day window. With regard to Lebanon, Congress eventually passed legislation in the fall of 1983 to authorize military action for a period of eighteen months. Long before that deadline, Reagan removed the U.S. forces.

During his administration, executive officials gave assistance to the Sandinista rebels in Nicaragua in violation of the Boland Amendment enacted by Congress, named after its sponsor, Eddie Boland of Massachusetts, a close friend of Speaker Tip O'Neill's. This covert action led to congressional hearings in 1987 on what became known as the Iran-contra affair. Had there been evidence that Reagan had sanctioned this assistance, he would have been vulnerable to impeachment proceedings. Instead, he claimed to have no knowledge of the operations, implicitly acknowledging that crucial national security decisions had been made and carried out without his consent or awareness.

One of the by-products of the WPR is the frequency with which the lawmakers turned not to their colleagues to challenge presidential wars but to the courts. Four times during the 1980s, members of Congress went to court to charge President Reagan with violations of the WPR. When he sent military advisers to El Salvador in 1981, he did not report under the WPR because, he said, the U.S. forces were not introduced with the intent to engage in hostilities. Twenty-nine members of the House claimed in court that he had violated the WPR; arrayed on the other side of the lawsuit were sixteen senators and twelve representatives who urged that the case be dismissed. In *Crockett v. Reagan* (1982), a federal court held that it lacked the "resources and expertise" to resolve the questions of fact concerning the military situation in El Salvador.

Two years later eleven members of Congress charged in court that President Reagan's invasion of Grenada violated the power of Congress to declare war. A federal court, in *Conyers v. Reagan* (1984), refused to provide judicial relief because the lawmakers had failed to exploit the institutional powers available to Congress. The message from the courts was clear: if Congress wants to confront the president, it must do so by exerting legislative powers, not by turning to the courts. Similarly, when members of Congress went to court to challenge Reagan's activities in Nicaragua, a district court in *Sanchez-Espinoza v. Reagan* (1983) spoke about the "impossibility of our undertaking independent resolution without expressing a lack of respect due coordinate branches of government." If Congress failed to defend its prerogatives, it could not expect to be bailed out by the courts.

The War Against Iraq, 1991

A weakness in the WPR is the assumption that presidents, at some point, must go to Congress for authority. Instead, they have gone to the U.N. Security Council or NATO. The former technique had been pioneered by President Truman, in Korea. In 1990, after Iraq invaded Kuwait, George H. W. Bush adopted the Truman model by encouraging the Security Council to authorize the use of force, which it did on November 29. In testimony before the Senate Armed Services Committee on December 3, Secretary of Defense Dick Cheney testified that the president did not require "any additional authorization from the Congress" before attacking Iraq. Reacting to this claim, the House Democratic Caucus on the following day adopted a resolution stating that the president must first seek authorization from Congress unless American lives were in danger. The resolution passed, 177–37.

Fifty-four members of Congress brought a case in federal court, challenging the constitutional authority of the president to initiate war in the Persian Gulf without legislative authority. The Justice Department argued that President Bush could order offensive actions in Iraq on his own, independent authority. In *Dellums v. Bush* (December 13, 1990), the district judge Harold H. Greene ruled that the issue was not ready for judicial determination since the military operation had not begun. In relying on the lack of ripeness to avoid ruling on the merits, he nonetheless took the opportunity to decisively reject many of the sweeping claims of presidential power advanced by the Justice Department. Judge Greene forcefully rejected a unilateral presidential power to wage war. If the president "had the sole power to determine that any particular offensive military operation, no matter how vast, does not constitute war-making but only an offensive military attack, the congressional power to declare war will be at the mercy of a semantic decision by the Executive. Such an 'interpretation' would evade the plain language of the Constitution, and it cannot stand."

On January 8, 1991, Bush asked Congress to pass legislation "supporting" his policy in the Persian Gulf. Congress proceeded to pass legislation *authorizing* him to take offensive action against Iraq. The bill passed the House handily, 250–183. The Republican support was almost unanimous: 164–3; Democrats opposed the measure, 179–86. Bernie Sanders, an Independent from Vermont, voted against the bill. The vote in the Senate was much closer: 52–47. Again, the Republican support was nearly unanimous: 42–2; Democrats voted in opposition, 45–10.

In signing the bill, President Bush said that "my request for congressional support did not, and my signing this resolution does not, constitute any change in the long-established positions of the executive branch on either the president's constitutional authority to use the armed forces to defend vital U.S. interests or the constitutionality of the War Powers Resolution." Of course, what counts legally is language in the public law, not remarks in a presidential signing statement.

During the 1992 presidential campaign, Bush revealed his attitude about the legislative branch and constitutional limits when he was asked why he couldn't bring the same kind of purpose and success to domestic policy as he did to the war in Iraq. He answered: "I didn't have to get permission from some old goat in the United States Congress to kick Saddam Hussein out of Kuwait. That's the reason." Of course he did, in the end, receive permission from Congress, but his response indicates the extent to which he thought that presidents may act independently in external affairs.

Initiatives by Clinton

President Clinton also relied on the U.N. as an authorizing body. On July 31, 1994, the U.N. Security Council adopted a resolution "inviting" all states, particularly those in the region of Haiti, to use "all necessary means" to remove the military leadership on that island. In a nationally televised address on September 15, Clinton told the American public that he was prepared to use military force to invade Haiti, referring to the U.N. resolution and his willingness to lead a multinational force "to carry out the will of the United Nations." He said nothing about carrying out the will of Congress. The invasion became unnecessary when the former president Jimmy Carter negotiated an agreement in which the military leaders in Haiti agreed to step down to permit the return of the elected president, Jean-Bertrand Aristide.

House and Senate debates were strongly critical of Clinton's position that he could act militarily against Haiti without legislative authority. Both houses passed legislation stating that "the President should have sought and welcomed congressional approval before deploying United States Forces to Haiti." The measure passed the House by voice vote; the Senate's vote was 91–8. Even legislators who voted against it agreed that Clinton should have gotten approval from Congress. Of the eight senators who voted against the legislation, at least four — Max Baucus (D- Montana), Bill Bradley (D-New Jersey), Robert C. Byrd (D-West Virginia), and Russ Feingold (D-Wisconsin) — agreed that Clinton should have first obtained approval from Congress. Baucus, even though from

Clinton's party, remarked: "The President did not seek my approval for occupying Haiti. And he will not get my approval now."

President Clinton twice relied on NATO to authorize military action, the first time in Bosnia in 1994–1995, and the second in Kosovo in 1999. On neither occasion did he seek authority from Congress. His decision to use air strikes against Serbian military targets was taken, he explained, in response to U.N. Security Council resolutions operating through NATO's military command: "the authority under which air strikes can proceed, NATO acting out of area pursuant to U.N. authority, requires the common agreement of our NATO allies." In other words, he needed agreement from England, Italy, and other NATO allies but not from Congress. On September 12, 1995, he said the bombing attacks were "authorized by the United Nations." Congress did not challenge his authority to conduct air strikes in Bosnia.

In 1995 President Clinton ordered the deployment of 20,000 American ground troops to Bosnia without obtaining authority from Congress. He approved NATO's plan for sending ground troops to Bosnia (IFOR) and followed that with the successor plan, Stabilization Force (SFOR). He welcomed NATO's decision to approve the plan and the "Activation Order that will *authorize* the start of SFOR's mission." Authority would come from allies, not from Congress. The House and the Senate considered a number of bills and resolutions to limit Clinton, but none was enacted. Typically, the lawmakers would vote overwhelmingly for a nonbinding resolution that U.S. troops could not be deployed without congressional consent. Later, when they considered resolutions that would have a legal effect, the votes in favor would decline.

The actions in Bosnia combined Security Council resolutions and NATO. When Clinton could not get U.N. support for military action in Kosovo, he relied entirely on NATO. At a news conference on October 8, 1998, he stated: "Yesterday I decided that the United States would vote to give NATO the authority to carry out military strikes against Serbia if President Milosevic continues to defy the international community." The decision to go to war against another country was in the hands of one person, exactly what the framers thought they had prevented.

Although the administration did not give Congress a formal role in deciding on the use of military force against the Serbs, legislatures in other NATO countries took votes to authorize military action in Yugoslavia. The Italian parliament had to vote approval for the NATO strikes. The German supreme court ruled that the Bundestag, which had been dissolved with the election that ousted Chancellor Helmut Kohl, had to be recalled to approve the deployment of German aircraft and troops to Kosovo. The

U.S. Congress, supposedly the strongest legislature in the world, was not asked to vote authorization. Representative Ernest Istook (R-Oklahoma) remarked, "President Clinton asked many nations to agree to attack Yugoslavia, but he failed to get permission from one crucial country: America."

On March 11, 1999, with Clinton close to unleashing air strikes against Serbia, the House voted on a resolution to support U.S. armed forces as part of a NATO *peacekeeping* operation. Members were not supporting military action; they expected a peace agreement between the Serbs and Kosovars. Eventually the Kosovars accepted the plan, but the Serbs did not. By the time the Senate voted on March 23, negotiations had collapsed and air strikes were imminent. The Senate voted, 58–41, in support of military air operations and missile strikes against the Federal Republic of Yugoslavia (Serbia and Montenegro). The Senate resolution never became law. The war against Yugoslavia began on March 24.

On April 28, after the first month of bombing, the House took a series of votes on the war. It voted, 249–180, to prohibit the use of appropriated funds for the deployment of U.S. ground forces unless first authorized by Congress. A motion to direct the removal of the U.S. armed forces from Yugoslavia failed, 139–290. A resolution to declare a state of war between the United States and Yugoslavia fell, 2–427. A fourth vote, to authorize the air operations and missile strikes, lost on a tie vote, 213–213. The Senate voted on a series of resolutions to either authorize the war or require Clinton to seek approval from Congress. All of those resolutions were tabled. Clinton thus operated against the Constitution and without any statutory support. Military operations continued until June 3, when Yugoslavia agreed to accept NATO's terms for an end to the war. The agreement was signed on June 9.

Once again, legislators went to court. Representative Tom Campbell (R-California) and twenty-five other members of the House brought an action in 1999, seeking a declaration that President Clinton had violated the War Powers Clause of the Constitution and the War Powers Resolution by initiating an offensive air operation against Yugoslavia without first obtaining authorization from Congress. In *Campbell v. Clinton* (1999), a district court ruled that the lawmakers did not have the standing to raise their claims in court. As in other cases, the court emphasized the importance of Congress's acting as an institution to defend its prerogatives — through a majority of its members — rather than having a few legislators bring a dispute to the judiciary. Only after Congress acted against a president to create a true "constitutional impasse" or "actual confrontation" between the two political branches would there be a basis for legislative standing. The district court's ruling was affirmed by the D.C. Circuit in 2000.

The Response to Terrorism

Some of Clinton's military actions were directed toward nations that supported terrorist acts or were able to develop weapons of mass destruction. His first military action occurred on June 26, 1993, when he ordered air strikes against Iraq in response to what the administration concluded was an Iraqi-planned assassination of the former president George Bush during a visit to Kuwait. He said that the purpose of the attack on Baghdad was "to send a message to those who engage in state-sponsored terrorism."

In September 1996 he ordered the launching of more cruise missiles against Iraq in response to an attack by Iraqi forces against the Kurdish-controlled city of Irbil in northern Iraq. Cruise missiles also struck air defense systems in southern Iraq. When President Saddam Hussein refused to give U.N. inspectors full access to Iraqi sites to examine them for possible nuclear, chemical, and biological programs, Clinton in December 1998 ordered military operations against Iraq.

In August 1998 Clinton ordered cruise missiles into Afghanistan to attack paramilitary camps and into Sudan to destroy a pharmaceutical factory. He justified these actions as a retaliation for bombings earlier in the month against U.S. embassies in Africa. The administration claimed that Osama bin Laden was behind the embassy attacks, that he used the training complex in Afghanistan, and that he was somewhat related to the pharmaceutical plant. It also stated that the plant was involved in the production of materials for chemical weapons, but questions were raised about whether the plant was producing a precursor chemical for a nerve gas or an agricultural insecticide. The Pentagon later conceded that it was not aware that the plant produced a large share of the medicine used in Sudan.

The terrorist attacks of September 11, 2001, continued to shift military power to the president. The stunning collapse of the World Trade Center buildings, the attack on the Pentagon, and the loss of three thousand lives created a strong consensus in Congress and the public for decisive action. Acting within a week, Congress passed a joint resolution authorizing President George W. Bush to use all "necessary and appropriate force" against nations, organizations, or persons that he determined planned, authorized, committed, or aided the terrorist attacks of September 11, or harbored such organizations or persons, "in order to prevent any future acts of international terrorism against the United States by such nations, organizations or persons." Bush proceeded to direct military action against the terrorist structures in Afghanistan.

The administration next considered military force against Iraq to remove Saddam Hussein. In terms of the legislative prerogative to take the country from a state of peace to a state of war, and also to exercise the legislative power of the purse, a commitment of that magnitude would require advance congressional authority. A possible legal argument to justify military force against Iraq is that when Congress passed the authorization bill in response to the invasion of Kuwait in January 1991, it simultaneously sanctioned future military operations authorized by the U.N. Security Council. Such a claim would mean that Congress had surrendered its constitutional power to an international body and that the future scope of American military commitments in Iraq would be determined by U.N. resolutions, not congressional statutes. There is no evidence that Congress intended such a result or could intend such a result.

What factors help explain the loss of congressional power over military operations? It is frequently argued that lawmakers decide that acquiescence on their part is the best of all worlds: if the military action goes well, they can take credit for not opposing it; if it turns out badly, they can blame the president. This interpretation does not explain why the legislators from 1789 to 1950 were willing to fight for congressional prerogatives. What accounts for the decline of legislative power in the past half century?

Part of the reason lies in the emergence of the U.N. Security Council and NATO as alternative sources of presidential "authority." The U.N. Charter and NATO did not contemplate that a president could circumvent Congress, but it has turned out that way, and Congress has never effectively challenged the presidential misuse of these treaties. Without legislative and judicial checks, the president is at liberty to engage in military operations until they backfire.

Other developments have played into the hands of the president. One is the volunteer army. During the Vietnam years, citizens engaged in mass demonstrations to protest presidential initiatives; parents understood that the draft threatened their sons and daughters. With the current volunteer army, public participation has markedly declined. During the four days of bombing Iraq in December 1998, there was not a single U.S. or British casualty despite some 650 sorties against nearly a hundred targets. In 1999 President Clinton waged war against Yugoslavia for eleven weeks of heavy bombing. There was not a single combat casualty from any of the NATO countries. American combat deaths and casualties in Iraq after March 2003 have been modest compared to those in earlier wars, but substantial enough to cause deep concern among U.S. citizens.

In disputes about the war power, lawmakers frequently complain that the administration has failed to consult them. No doubt policymaking by the federal government works better when the president and executive officials consult regularly with members of Congress, on domestic issues as well as matters of foreign affairs and national security. However, consultation is no substitute for congressional authority. Congress is a legislative body and discharges its constitutional duties by passing statutes that authorize and define national policy. Congress exists to legislate and legitimate, including military and financial commitments. Consultation may improve executive-legislative relations, but the authority in a public law is the act that satisfies the Constitution.

For most of U.S. history, federal courts decided the legality of a number of war power disputes. Only in recent decades, beginning with the Vietnam War, did the judiciary begin to lean on a variety of threshold doctrines to avoid these kinds of cases. With Congress unwilling to confront the president with legislative restrictions and the courts loath to decide the merits of these cases, it appears that presidents may initiate and conduct wars whenever they like. In this fundamental respect, the framers' belief in a system of checks and balances, with each branch able and willing to fight off encroachments from other branches, has failed. Patterns over the past half century regarding the war power point to a collapse of constitutional principles and a decline in representative democracy.

— LOUIS FISHER

BIBLIOGRAPHICAL NOTES

For constitutional studies on the war power that emphasize congressional prerogatives, see Francis D. Wormuth and Edwin B. Firmage, *To Chain the Dog of War: The War Power of Congress in History and Law* (Urbana, Ill., 1989); Louis Fisher, *Presidential War Power,* 2nd ed. (Lawrence, Kans., 2004); David Gray Adler and Larry N. George, eds., *The Constitution and the Conduct of American Foreign Policy* (Lawrence, Kans., 1996); and William Michael Treanor, "Fame, the Founding, and the Power to Declare War," *Cornell Law Review 82* (1997): 695–772. Studies that emphasize presidential prerogatives include Robert F. Turner, *Repealing the War Powers Resolution: Restoring the Rule of Law in U.S. Foreign Policy* (McLean, Va., 1991); John C. Yoo, "The Continuation of Politics by Other Means: The Original Understanding of War Powers," *California Law Review 84* (1996): 167–305; and H. Jefferson Powell, *The President's Authority over Foreign Affairs: An Essay in Constitutional Interpretation* (Durham, N.C., 2002). A rebuttal to Yoo's position appears in Louis Fisher, "Unchecked Presidential Wars," *University of Pennsylvania Law Review 148* (2000): 1637–72. An analysis of recent presidential wars appears in Gary R. Hess, *Presidential Decisions for War: Korea, Vietnam, and the*

Persian Gulf (Baltimore, 2001). Studies mentioned in this article include Richard H. Heindel et al., "The North Atlantic Treaty in the United States Senate," *American Journal of International Law 43* (1949): 633–65; Sherman Adams, *First-Hand Report: The Story of the Eisenhower Administration* (New York, 1961); and Dwight D. Eisenhower, *Waging Peace: The White House Years* (Garden City, N.Y., 1965). Other details on the War Powers Resolution, the United Nations, and mutual security treaties are included in Louis Fisher, "Sidestepping Congress: Presidents Acting Under the U.N. and NATO," *Case Western Reserve Law Review 47* (1997): 1237–79; Louis Fisher and David Gray Adler, "The War Powers Resolution: Time to Say Goodbye," *Political Science Quarterly 113* (1998): 1–20; and Louis Fisher, *Congressional Abdication on War and Spending* (College Station, Tex., 2000). Thoughtful studies on the role of Congress in foreign policy are James M. Lindsay, *Congress and the Politics of U.S. Foreign Policy* (Baltimore, 1994), and Stephen R. Weissman, *A Culture of Deference: Congress's Failure of Leadership in Foreign Policy* (New York, 1995).

40

When Republicans Become Revolutionaries: Conservatives in Congress

IN 1994 the Republicans, led by Newt Gingrich (R-Georgia), won control of Congress in the greatest midterm gain by either political party since 1946. This election was a bloodbath for the Democrats. Almost 37 million people voted Republican, adding 52 GOP seats in the House. In the Senate they captured 8 seats. It was not just the numbers that astounded the spectators but those who fell in the massacre, including Speaker of the House Thomas S. Foley (D-Washington) and longtime Chicago politico and chair of the House Ways and Means Committee Dan Rostenkowski (D-Illinois). The Democrats lost Senate races in Pennsylvania and Tennessee. In the states, the Republicans won 484 additional legislative seats. Not a single incumbent Republican governor, senator, or member of the House was defeated in the general election.

Following this Republican sweep, a political analyst from the conservative Heritage Foundation, David M. Mason, declared, "The radicalism of this class is difficult to overstate. They want to question the very basis on which existing programs operate."[1] Republican congressional candidates had run under the banner of a Contract with America, a legislative program devised by Gingrich and a small group of insurgent conservatives. Issued shortly before the elections, the contract offered "the chance, after four decades of one-party control, to bring to the House a new majority that will transform the way Congress works." It called for an end to the "politics as usual" under liberal Democratic rule, pledged support for an eight-point program to reform the House in the first day of the 104th Congress, and offered a ten-point legislative program to be passed in the first hundred days to restore fiscal responsibility, reduce crime and out-of-wedlock births, strengthen defense spending, undertake tort reform, and enact term limits in Congress.[2]

This revolutionary legislative program was designed to overturn what conservatives saw as a half century of liberal rule in which an ineffective and, indeed, a destructive welfare state had been created. The Gingrich Republicans saw themselves as GOP firebrands out to stop their party from aiding and abetting the liberal Democratic agenda. As the head of the Republican National Committee and a Gingrich ally, Haley Barbour declared in his rich Mississippi drawl, "Compromising with the Democrats is like paying the cannibals to eat you last."[3] Robert L. Livingston (R-Louisiana) expressed the sentiments of many of his colleagues when he declared, "We are going to be revolutionary. This is not patty cake, this is not pick-up sticks. This is serious. We're going at their [the Democrats'] throats."[4]

The GOP in Congress had been transformed from an opposition party to a party in power, a role the Republicans were not used to playing. They had united around a legislative program, but fissures in their ranks had become apparent even in the drafting of the Contract with America: differences between those social conservatives who sought to overturn legalized abortion and libertarian Republicans who did not want to touch the issue; budget-cutters who aimed to balance the budget and hawks who wanted to increase defense spending.

Demographics lay at the heart of these ideological tensions. As the political scientists Earl Black and Merle Black observe, GOP strategists built the Republican party in the South by mobilizing evangelical Christian voters around such social and cultural flash points as abortion, gun control, school prayer, and gay rights. The Christian Right established a core constituency for the Republican party, including nearly two-fifths of core Republican voters in the South. Yet this base, even when fully mobilized, was not large enough to win a national election or even state elections in the South, presenting Republicans with a dilemma: Republican politicians who sought to rally white religious voters risked being viewed as extremists by other core Republican voters, swing voters, and white male voters who still identified with the Democratic party. For any GOP candidate running for a statewide or national office, this dilemma was especially acute. Republican presidents, with a broader base in the electorate, proved much more comfortable in carrying the antigovernment and free market message of the GOP than they were in calling for new policies on abortion, prayer in schools, and homosexual issues.

These ideological tensions paled when compared to the even greater fissure that threatened to disrupt the conservative coalition: ideology versus reelection. The Republicans soon confronted a simple question: how could conservatives who distrusted the federal government use their power in government to gain reelection? This question underlay many of the policy debates in the Reagan presidency, but Reagan smoothed over both ideological and policy differences through his ability as the Great

Communicator. Furthermore, in the context of the Cold War and Reagan's resolve to challenge Soviet power, GOP conservatives endorsed a buildup of the American military, which entailed huge increases in budget expenditures and the expansion of the corporate-military complex. The conservatives who came to power in the midterm elections of 1994, however, confronted this paradox of conservatives in power immediately. They were the revolutionaries who had gained power but distrusted the very power they had gained. They wanted to cut programs. Yet in order to win election and reelection, the politicians needed to show that they had served the needs of their constituents by bringing tax dollars home to the district through enlarged federal programs and services. This dilemma continued to dog the GOP throughout the 1990s.

Conservative ideology manifested itself in various ways in Congress during the post-Nixon period. Although most pronounced in the Republican party, conservatism also expressed itself in foreign and defense policy among Democratic hawks. Adding to the partisan muddle, the meaning of "conservatism" itself changed over time, thereby giving it a fluid quality in Congress. For example, Everett Dirksen (R-Illinois), the Senate minority leader during the Johnson administration, was considered a conservative in his day, although his support of the arms control agreements with the Soviet Union and the Civil Rights Act of 1964 and the Voting Rights Act of 1965 makes him appear more moderate in light of the conservatism of the 1990s. Senator Robert Dole (R-Kansas) represented conservative Republicanism throughout most of his career, but by the late 1980s Newt Gingrich could label him "tax collector for the welfare state" with impunity.

In the course of conservatism in Congress, one single observation can be made with certainty: after 1972, partisanship between the parties increased, and as it did, the Republicans and the Democrats became more ideologically divided as the GOP swung to the right and the Democrats to the left. One result is that some political species such as a "liberal Republican" became extinct, while other species such as "conservative Democrats" became endangered.

The history of conservatism since 1972 can be summarized in several phases: disappointment and defeat in the Nixon administration; the revival of the right in the early 1970s over issues such as the Equal Rights Amendment and abortion; the first signs of political triumph by the New Right in the midterm elections of 1978; the Reagan triumph in 1980; disappointment in the George H. W. Bush administration; and the resurgence of congressional conservatism under Newt Gingrich beginning in 1994 and subsequent battles with Bill Clinton in the rest of the decade. We shall look at each in turn.

The Conservatives' Disappointment with Nixon

Divisions among the conservatives became evident during Richard Nixon's administration. While Nixon epitomized right-wing Republicanism for many liberals, many on the right distrusted him. This opposition framed much of the context for the continued shift of the Republican party rightward beginning in the 1970s.

At the Republican convention in Miami in 1968, many conservatives rallied behind Ronald Reagan. Although Nixon won the nomination, large numbers of conservatives continued to distrust him. Once in office, Nixon did little to reassure his conservative base, and as a consequence, conservatives were soon complaining that Nixon had forgotten who had elected him.

Nixon's Family Assistance Plan (FAP), his wage and price controls, and the growth of federal domestic expenditures bitterly disappointed conservatives. Social expenditures rapidly increased, even though Nixon had campaigned on the promise "to clean up the welfare mess." His foreign policy proved even more disturbing to conservatives. His appointment of Henry Kissinger, a longtime associate of Governor Nelson Rockefeller of New York, a liberal Republican, was taken as an insult. Rockefeller was the pariah of conservatives because he (and anyone associated with him) represented the liberal eastern wing of the Republican party, which the conservatives claimed supported internationalism and globalism in foreign policy and big government and welfare in domestic policy. Feelings were so high that Representative John Ashbrook of Ohio challenged Nixon in the 1972 primaries and William Rusher, publisher of the *National Review,* tried unsuccessfully to form a third party.

Nixon moved right with the approach of the election. George Wallace's dramatic showing as a third-party candidate in 1968 convinced him that the northern ethnic Catholic vote — the backbone of the Democratic party in urban areas — was vulnerable. Further evidence was revealed when James Buckley, the brother of William Buckley, editor of the conservative *National Review,* won a Senate seat in New York in 1970 with a plurality of 38 percent, running on a third-party ticket, the Conservative party, against two liberals, the Republican incumbent Charles Goodell and the Democrat Richard Ottinger. Buckley won the support of many disgruntled white voters who were upset with high taxes, runaway social programs, urban decay and crime, union strikes, and racial division. He had previously run in 1968 and received 16 percent of the vote while spending little on his campaign. In 1970 he spent $1.8 million, a huge sum at the time.

Reading the political winds, Nixon saw that shifting to the right on social issues was critical in the 1972 election, for through such a strategy he could win the Catholic vote. With this in mind, he spoke in favor of federal funding for parochial schools and in opposition to abortion. Nixon's "Catholic strategy" paid off. That November he captured 60 percent of the Catholic vote, 59 percent of the working-class vote, and 57 percent of the union-household vote. His victory was made easier — and larger — by a weak rival, George McGovern (D-South Dakota), but for the first time since the Eisenhower victories of 1952 and 1956, a Republican had won the Catholic swing vote.

The 1972 election brought one bright spot for conservatives when Jesse Helms, a fierce anticommunist and social conservative, was elected to the Senate from North Carolina. Helms, a former executive for the Capitol Broadcasting Company of Raleigh, North Carolina, joined James Buckley in Congress to promote conservative policies. These new senators refused to play the humble understudy role traditionally assigned to freshmen. Both men championed the Soviet dissident writer Alexander Solzhenitsyn and opposed détente with the Soviet Union and legal abortion. Helms became known for his outspoken style and his mastery of the Senate's arcane parliamentary rules.

Although he appeared to be an old-fashioned southern politician who denounced communism, federal power at the expense of state power, crime, the breakdown of social mores, and federal involvement in civil rights, Helms represented the transformation in southern politics that would be integral to changes in the Republican party.

The election of Helms (and Nixon's 1972 presidential electoral sweep) encouraged Republican strategists to believe that the South could be won regularly by the GOP. Moreover, social conservatives believed that they could overturn abortion rights in the halls of Congress. The Supreme Court's decision supporting abortion in *Roe v. Wade* (1973) transformed American politics, polarizing the electorate and the two major political parties. On the federal level, the opponents of abortion in Congress sought to repeal *Roe* through constitutional amendments and to prevent the federal funding of abortion. On the state level, antiabortion groups tried to limit legal abortion through restrictive regulations. By early 1976, more than fifty different constitutional amendments to ban or limit abortions had been introduced in Congress. At the same time, antiabortion congressional leaders sought to withdraw federal funding for abortions under Medicaid unless they were deemed "medically necessary."

The Watergate scandal consumed Nixon's second term. By the time Nixon resigned from office in 1974, the Republican party was in shambles and the conservative movement was in disarray. As a result, the GOP gains in the South came to a halt temporarily. The Democrats gained

43 seats in 1974 and controlled the House, 291–144; in the Senate, they picked up 3 seats, adding to their already large majority.

Watergate changed the political landscape. The Democratic party united while the Republicans fell apart. In this political vacuum, the congressional Democrats continued their march to the left. In 1972 the House majority whip, Hale Boggs (D-Louisiana), a foreign policy hawk and an old-fashioned wheeler-dealer, was killed in a plane crash while campaigning in Alaska. Replacing him was Thomas P. "Tip" O'Neill (D-Massachusetts). O'Neill was an Irish Catholic politician from the old school who took care of his constituents first, but he had come out against the war in Vietnam in 1967, which endeared him to House liberals. He joined forces with the liberal Philip Burton (D-California), a loud, bullying politician who stood righteously as a defender of the downtrodden. Under O'Neill and Burton, the House Democrats shifted to the left at the time that the Republican minority stood in disgrace.

The House leadership under O'Neill and Burton benefited from a new generation of Democrats after Watergate. The 75 Democratic representatives elected in 1974 entered Congress anxious to reassert its power over the executive branch. In 1973 Congress had overridden Nixon's veto to pass the War Powers Act, which limited the president's power to involve the United States in prolonged military conflicts. In 1974 Congress reasserted its power of the purse in the Budget Control and Impoundment Act. Yet while the House was able to impose new oversights and means of obstructing the executive branch, it appeared increasingly unable to forge a national consensus on most areas of public policy.

Changes in the financing of congressional campaigns after the Federal Elections Campaign Act (FECA) in 1974 forced candidates to rely more on fund-raising from small donors and political action committees (PACs). These PACs, dominated by organized labor and large business interests, tended to favor incumbents. As a result, the reelection levels for incumbent members exceeded 90 percent during the 1980s. The liberal Democratic majority became more entrenched, even as the electorate shifted to the right during presidential elections. At the same time, the Democrats in the House became increasingly arrogant in exercising their privileges and exerting their power with little regard for the GOP minority.

Matters for conservative Republicans did not get any better when Gerald Ford succeeded to the presidency in 1974. Ford, having been chosen vice president by Nixon when Spiro Agnew resigned in disgrace, picked Nelson Rockefeller as his own vice president and retained Kissinger as his secretary of state. The two appointments cost Ford heavily among GOP conservatives. Moreover, he continued Nixon's engagement policies toward the Soviet Union and Communist China. On domestic policy, Ford sought to hold down federal spending and taxes and prevent the expansion of government, but he faced a Democratic majority in both houses of Congress so huge that theoretically the Democrats could override any veto without a single Republican vote. Ford vetoed more bills than any president since Harry Truman, but any credit he might have received from conservatives for his fiscal restraint was diminished by his continuation of the "Rockefeller-Kissinger" foreign and defense policies they despised. In Congress, Ford relied on moderates such as Paul McCloskey Jr. of California, Gilbert Gude of Maryland, and Ronald A. Sarasin of Connecticut. In the Senate, he found support among moderates including Robert W. Packwood of Oregon, Richard S. Schweiker of Pennsylvania, Jacob K. Javits of New York, and Charles McC. Mathias of Maryland.

The New Right Emerges

Yet, in this period of discouragement, stirrings on the grass-roots level marked a revival of the right. The rise of this movement, labeled the New Right and supported by conservative Republican donors such as Joseph Coors and the Pittsburgh millionaire Richard Scaife, had profound consequences in the ultimate reshaping of conservative forces in Congress. Critical to the New Right was its capacity to raise money through direct mailing and its emphasis on moral issues. Richard Viguerie, a longtime conservative activist, pioneered computerized direct mailing, while one campaign strategist, Terry Dolan, electrified the right wing with his fundraising skills and his relentless attacks on liberals. By interjecting social issues into the political arena, these GOP workers mobilized Protestant evangelicals, who were important in southern and midwestern congressional districts.

Two issues energized the right wing: abortion and the Equal Rights Amendment. The antiabortion wing of the Republican party did not trust Gerald Ford. Even though Ford had served in the House for more than twenty-five years, representing a strongly Republican district in Michigan, as a party leader he had a reputation for moderation. His presidency came under attack from both liberal Democrats in Congress and grassroots conservatives in his own party. He tried to take a moderate stance on abortion but to little avail. Antiabortion crusaders found their hero when, in 1976, the freshman representative Henry J. Hyde (R-Illinois) successfully attached a crucial rider to an appropriations bill. The so-called Hyde Amendment banned federal funding for abortions for any reason. The Senate responded with a similar measure, adding the critical qualifier that federal funds could be used to save a woman's life. After a series of intense conference meetings, an agreement was reached to reconcile the two versions of the bill with less restrictive language. When the bill reached Ford's desk, however, he vetoed the entire appropriations measure, ostensibly for budgetary reasons.

The vote to override Ford's veto presents an interesting example of "strange bedfellows" coming together for their own interests. Representative Bella Abzug (D-New York), a strong supporter of abortion rights, voted to overturn the veto because she wished to maintain the spending levels in the appropriations bill. Hyde voted to overturn the veto on antiabortion grounds, even though he (like many other antiabortion congressmen) was a fiscal conservative. With enough congressional interests intersecting, Congress overrode Ford's veto, and the Hyde Amendment became law.

The congressional opposition to abortion turned Ford. First, he supported a constitutional amendment to allow individual states to regulate abortion policy. Then, when the Hyde Amendment was challenged in the courts, he instructed his solicitor general, Robert H. Bork, to file an *amicus curiae* brief with the Supreme Court in support of it.

Hyde became a symbol for antiabortion activists. The tall, heavyset congressman, a committed conservative, represented Chicago's western, GOP-oriented suburbs. Yet, having grown up as an Irish Catholic Democrat in Chicago, he knew how to get along with members from the other side of the aisle. First elected to the Illinois house in 1966, he rose to majority leader on the strength of his debating and legislative skills. In 1974 he succeeded a longtime GOP incumbent in the Sixth District, winning with 53 percent of the vote.

Having failed on the issue of abortion, Ford encountered a grass-roots revolt over another social issue, the Equal Rights Amendment (ERA). Backed by the recently formed National Organization for Women (NOW), the amendment simply stated, "Equality of rights under the law shall not be denied or abridged by the United States or by any State on account of sex," and that Congress shall have the power to enforce provisions of this article.

The chair of the House Judiciary Committee, Emanuel Celler (D-New York), who supported women's protective labor legislation, held up the ERA in his committee. In the summer of 1970, Representative Martha Griffiths (D-Michigan) rallied a majority of her colleagues to have the ERA discharged from the Judiciary Committee. On August 10, 1970, after only one hour of debate, the House approved the amendment, 352–15. Supporters in the Senate, including Birch Bayh (D-Indiana) and the majority leader, Mike Mansfield (D-Montana), brought the ERA directly to the floor. In an attempt to subvert support for the bill, Sam Ervin (D-

North Carolina) attempted to attach a series of riders to the amendment to protect women from the military draft, alimony and child custody rights, and unfair labor practices, which failed to gain support in the Senate. Differences arose about limiting the time for state ratification, however, and as a result the Ninety-first Senate adjourned without taking action. In 1972 the House voted, 354–23, and the Senate voted, 84–8, to pass the ERA.

Congress gave the ERA until 1979 for thirty-eight states to ratify it. In its first year, thirty states ratified the ERA, leaving only eight more states needed. In late 1973, however, the ERA's proponents had lost control of the ratification process. A longtime Republican party activist, Phyllis Schlafly, started a movement called STOP ERA, declaring that the ERA meant the drafting of women into the military, the loss of the statutory rights of wives and mothers, and the federalizing of laws that conservatives perceived as properly in the jurisdiction of the states. This movement spread like wildfire among traditional women.

Schlafly entered the ERA fight as an experienced organizer with a network of supporters throughout the country. Few political observers believed the chances of defeating the ERA were good. Leaders of NOW, ERAmerica, and other supporters at first dismissed Schlafly and her grass-roots crusade. Three more states ratified in 1974, one in 1975, and another in 1977, bringing the total to thirty-five states. At this point the ERA came to an abrupt halt. Meanwhile, five states rescinded their previous ratification. By 1976 the ERA's proponents were taking Schlafly seriously, admitting that they had failed to win over the average homemaker.[5] Simply put, Schlafly outmaneuvered her opponents, although she was opposed by President Ford and President Carter, as well as by Republican leaders. Her major supporter in Congress was Senator Ervin. She won support in critical state legislatures, primarily in the South and Midwest, from conservatives in both parties and on certain occasions from old-time labor union Democrats.

As her movement gained momentum, Schlafly tapped into a new constituency that had not been previously involved in politics: fundamentalist Christians. Most of these women were traditional mothers without political experience, but their church activities had given them skills in public speaking. Equally important, they brought an evangelical enthusiasm to the cause.

Gerald Ford and his wife, Betty, actively lobbied for the ERA, leading Schlafly at one point to picket the White House. The 1976 Republican platform endorsed the ERA, but it was clear that the ranks were increasingly rebelling against the Republican establishment. Ronald Reagan rode this resurgence by challenging Ford for the Republican nomination. Ford narrowly won, but he was deserted by the right in the general election.

In the presidential campaign of 1976, both Ford and the Democratic nominee, Jimmy Carter, endorsed the ERA while agreeing implicitly to treat the abortion issue gingerly.[6] In the end, Carter narrowly won the election with 49.9 percent of the popular vote to Ford's 47.9 percent. Carter, a self-described "born-again" Christian, swept the South (except Virginia), drawing evangelical Christians to the Democratic party. Once in office, he actively campaigned for ratification of the ERA, and the Democratic Congress extended the deadline three years, to 1982. Nonetheless, the ERA died when Florida, Missouri, Oklahoma, North Carolina, and Illinois refused to ratify it. It was clear by 1980 that Schlafly and the grass-roots right, now called the "pro-family" movement, had won.

Witnessing the success of Schlafly's ability to mobilize the evangelical Christians, Republican activists reckoned that this vote could be harnessed in support of the party by tying social issues such as school choice, abortion, and prayer in schools to long-standing Republican causes — free market economics and hard-line defense and foreign policy. These conservatives took their political skills into the congressional election of 1978 by using the abortion issue as a wedge to separate liberal Democratic representatives from their more socially conservative constituents. Conservative strategists took advantage of the election reform laws to establish PACs, as well as larger focused fund-raising conduits such as the National Conservative Political Action Committee. In the House, the Democratic seats declined from 292 to 277, and in the Senate from 61 to 59. The loss in numbers was marginal, but it was politically significant because the Republicans now had enough Senate votes to sustain a filibuster. More important, for the first time there were signs of a Republican resurgence that was sparked by a right-wing move in the ranks of the GOP.

The emergence of the pro-family movement, consisting of evangelical Protestants and Catholics, and a revitalized conservative movement in the Republican party set the stage for the 1980 election between Carter and the hero of many conservatives, Ronald Reagan. Antiabortion activists rallied at the grass-roots level as the election approached. The Pro-Life Action Committee reported that it had sent fourteen "specially selected" men and women from campaign staffs to a week-long day training school run by the Committee for the Survival of a Free Congress to learn "every aspect of political management."[7]

Reagan overwhelmed Carter at the polls, receiving 51 percent of the vote against Carter's 41 percent (8 percent went to the GOP representative John Anderson of Illinois, who ran as an Independent). Gaining 12 Senate seats, the Republicans won control of the Senate for the first time since 1952. It was the largest net gain in the Senate for any party since 1958, when the Democrats took over 15 seats. The Senate was not only more Republican but also more conservative, as leading liberal Democrats went down in defeat, including George McGovern (South Dakota), Warren G. Magnuson (Washington), Birch Bayh (Indiana), John Culver (Iowa), and Frank Church (Idaho). Moreover, the Republicans introduced a new class of largely dedicated conservatives, including the representatives Charles E. Grassley (Iowa), Steven D. Symms (Idaho), James Abdnor (South Dakota), Robert W. Kasten Jr. (Wisconsin), and John P. East (North Carolina). Republican conservatives also replaced GOP liberal senators with conservatives: Alfonse M. D'Amato replaced Jacob Javits in New York and Don Nickles, backed by fundamentalist groups, took Henry Bellmon's seat in Oklahoma. These and other conservatives were joined by GOP moderates such as Warren Rudman in New Hampshire and Arlen Specter in Pennsylvania.

Nonetheless, the grass-roots right took deserved credit for having changed the temper of Congress. The Moral Majority, formed by Jerry Falwell several years before the election, had supported the conservatives running for Congress. Taking advantage of a loophole in FECA which allowed unlimited "independent expenditures" for a PAC supporting or opposing candidates, the National Conservative Political Action Committee (NCPAC) targeted six liberal Democratic senators with hard-hitting ads and defeated four of them — Bayh, Culver, McGovern, and Church. In the 1980 campaign, NCPAC spent nearly $1 million in independent payments, primarily for negative radio and television ads. An NCPAC target often faced as many as 72 radio ads a day and 200 television commercials a week. In later elections, this loophole would also be exploited by liberal PACs.

In the House, the Republicans gained 33 seats and won more votes outside the South than the Democrats for the first time since 1968. The Republicans were 26 seats shy of controlling the House. Any desertion by southern Democrats meant that the Republicans could score legislative victories.

Reagan Leads a Revolution (Almost)

At the onset of his administration, Reagan placed social issues on the back burner in favor of economic and fiscal issues. In doing so, he encouraged economic conservatives in the GOP to take the lead in policy initiatives, but at the same time he wanted to hold social conservatives in line. Through his Office of Management and Budget (OMB) director, David

Stockman, Reagan proposed a package of $64 billion in budget cuts and the Kemp-Roth income tax cut of 30 percent. The Budget Act of 1974 and the Congressional Budget Office made Congress an effective participant in the budget process, but the absence of a consensus between a Democratic House and a Republican Senate and president created political acrimony. During the next decade, appropriations bills often failed to pass on schedule, and the federal budget process degenerated into threats of government shutdowns and the passage of stopgap "continuing resolutions" to keep the federal government going.

Few Washington insiders thought that Reagan's agenda had much of a chance in Congress. The new chairman of the Senate Budget Committee, Peter Domenici (R–New Mexico), raised doubts with the White House about reaching a balanced budget while cutting taxes and increasing defense expenditures. Elected to the Senate in 1972, Domenici was not a natural ideologue but an old-fashioned budget-balancing fiscal conservative. He did not buy into the administration's "supply-side" economics, which claimed that tax cuts would stimulate the economy and thereby generate enough revenues to pay for both lost revenues and increased defense spending. Reagan and his team, however, put together a masterful strategy. The seventy-year-old president drew both sympathy and admiration for his courage and grace when he was shot by John W. Hinckley Jr. Even while he was recovering, he made telephone calls to members of Congress to support his budget cuts. When he returned to the White House on April 11, 1981, he continued lobbying, ultimately meeting with 467 members of Congress. In the end, he put together a coalition that supported his tax cuts, winning even Pete Domenici by an appeal to party loyalty.

Stockman's plan for cutting the budget focused on the Gramm-Latta bill. It had been sponsored by the Texas Democrat Phil Gramm, a free-market economics professor from Texas A&M, and Delbert Latta, a partisan Republican from northern Ohio. Gramm had been placed on the Budget Committee by the majority leader, Jim Wright, the highly partisan Democrat from Texas. With the support of southern Democrats, the so-called Boll Weevils, Gramm-Latta passed, 253–217, winning all but one Republican vote. A few days after this triumph, the Senate overwhelmingly endorsed the budget cuts, although Domenici and Robert Dole (R-Kansas), chairman of the Senate Finance Committee, warned that the cuts were not large enough to create a balanced budget. The contradictory fiscal policy represented Stockman's desire to cut the budget and Reagan's goal of cutting taxes.

In the fall of 1981 the American economy turned downward, government revenues dropped, and budget deficits grew. Leading Republicans in Congress, including Dole and Domenici in the Senate and the ranking Republican on the House Ways and Means Committee, Barber Conable (New York), called for increased taxes to compensate for the lost revenues. In the Senate, Dole crafted a tax bill to increase revenues, pushing it through the chamber in July 1982 in a session that lasted until three in the morning. He even prevailed on Jesse Helms, who represented a tobacco state, to support the bill, which included a tobacco tax increase. Despite his focus on tax cuts, Reagan allowed it to happen as well.

Many in the conservative movement were outraged by the Reagan administration's retreat on taxes. The July 1982 issue of the *Conservative Digest* openly attacked Reagan for having sold out the conservative agenda by raising taxes $280 billion through 1987. In an open letter to the president, the publisher and direct-mail wizard Richard A. Viguerie cajoled, "Seize the moment, Mr. President, and restore the faith of people throughout the world who look with hope and excitement to you."[8] In the same issue, the New Right leader Paul Weyrich, director of the Committee for the Survival of a Free Congress, asked whether the tax hikes had subverted the 1980 election. He answered, "As bad as things now stand within the Reagan administration, I am convinced that the President and his conservative supporters can turn the situation around, provided Ronald Reagan himself has the political will to do so."[9] An angry Reagan privately wrote to the journal's editor, John Lofton, "I can't conclude this letter without telling you I believe the July *Conservative Digest* is one of the most dishonest and unfair bits of journalism I have ever seen."[10]

As early as 1981, Tip O'Neill decided that his party should fight Reagan's budget cuts and not compromise with the administration. He felt that Republicans were vulnerable on the issue of Social Security as well and wanted to make it a campaign issue. The Republicans saw O'Neill as a political hack. Their feelings were summarized by New York's Representative John LeBoutillier, who described O'Neill as "fat, bloated, and out of control."[11] At the same time, Tony Coelho (D-California) set out to raise unprecedented contributions from PACs. He visited hundreds of PAC offices and told them that "we have every committee chairmanship and every subcommittee chairmanship in the House, and we keep score."[12] In the midterm 1982 election, the Democrats made a net gain of 26 seats.

The Democratic hold on the House continued even with Reagan's easy reelection victory over Walter Mondale in 1984. Much of Reagan's second term was caught up in foreign policy: *glasnost* with the Soviet Union, opposition to the Sandinistas in Nicaragua, terrorism in the Middle East, and the Iran-contra scandal. During these years of Democratic domination in the House, the Republican representatives were ignored and often rudely treated by Speaker O'Neill and his successor, Jim Wright

(D-Texas). This attitude angered many of the young Republicans who had come of age in the Reagan years.

The administration, however, pushed through a major tax reform bill in 1986. Republicans had long been committed to tax reform, and Reagan had made it the centerpiece of his campaign in 1980. When Donald Regan became secretary of the Treasury in Reagan's second term, he took up this issue to ensure his own legacy in office. Many Democrats had turned to support tax reform. "New" Democrats, such as Senator Bill Bradley (D-New Jersey), felt the party's image for supporting the "common man" could be revived through tax reform. At the same time, old-time Democratic politicians such as the Ways and Means Committee chair Dan Rostenkowski saw a political advantage in supporting tax reform. In securing the bill's passage, Rostenkowski rode roughshod over many Democratic legislators, but he compromised with members from high tax states such as New York by including state and local tax deductions. During the drafting of the bill, Rostenkowski excluded lobbyists from "Gucci gulch." In the Senate, Robert Packwood (R-Oregon) joined forces with Bill Bradley to push through a tax reform bill. The final measure was passed into law in September 1986.

Reagan's success thus came from working with Democrats. He often had an easier time with hard-boiled centrist Democrats such as Rostenkowski than he did with the social conservatives in his own party. He also learned that relations with the antiabortion movement created its own difficulties.

Republican Insurgents in the House

Whatever difficulties Reagan experienced with the antiabortion activists and evangelical Protestants, he left office a hero for conservatives. At the same time, his era marked the emergence of a strong Republican party in the South. By the time Reagan left office, more southern whites were calling themselves Republican than Democratic. As conservative and many moderate southern whites turned to the GOP, the Democrats became the party of African Americans as well as liberal and some centrist whites. The rise of the Republican South also coincided with profound demographic changes. During the 1990s the South's population grew by 19 percent, faster than the national average. By 2000 more than 84 million people, three of every ten Americans, lived in the eleven states of the old Confederacy. Moreover, much of this growth occurred in the suburbs around such cities as Dallas and Houston, Atlanta, Birmingham, Orlando, Raleigh, Richmond, Charlotte, and Greenville. There voters supported the so-called conservative values of low taxes, low union support, a strong work ethic, and a strong commitment to family and community.[13]

Reagan was the standard against which all other conservatives were to be judged. His successor, George H. W. Bush, fell far short of this standard for most conservatives. Bush defeated the liberal governor Michael Dukakis of Massachusetts in 1988 with a pledge not to raise taxes and to support conservative measures, but the next four years were characterized by growing alienation among many conservatives, including Republican insurgents in the House. Although the Bush administration's foreign policy was successful, its domestic program left conservatives disappointed and frustrated. Bush supported the Clean Air Act of 1989, the Americans with Disabilities Act of 1990, and the Civil Rights Act of 1991. In response to deficits that reached $141 billion, Bush supported reductions in defense expenditures, which angered many Southerners and Westerners who relied on defense contracts. Despite the military cuts, the annual deficit still increased to $220 billion, and the national debt reached $3.2 trillion.

Under pressure, Bush hoped to control the 1990 budget in a way that was acceptable to both Democrats and Republicans. The resulting compromise between the White House and Congress promised to reduce the deficit by $500 billion over five years. Conservative Republicans, however, were outraged because, as part of the deal, Bush broke his "no new taxes" pledge, and Congress passed a package that included tax increases.

In particular, a group of young insurgent Republicans in the House were angered by Bush. They were led by the upstart Newt Gingrich, who had began to rally the younger conservatives in the House to oppose the conciliatory tactics of the House Republican leadership.

The son of a career soldier, Gingrich spent his youth on military bases in the United States and Europe, a formative experience to which he credits his adult political aspirations. After receiving his bachelor's degree in 1965 from Emory University, he went on to earn a master's and doctorate from Tulane in Modern European History in 1971. During the 1970s he taught Environmental Studies and History at West Georgia College.

Gingrich joined the Republican party and made two unsuccessful runs for Congress in 1974 and 1976. In 1978 he was elected to the first of eleven terms as the representative of Georgia's Sixth District. In 1984 he drew the ire of Speaker Tip O'Neill for his use of the new C-SPAN television network. Every evening, Gingrich and other conservatives went on television to attack the Democrats on foreign policy. An angered O'Neill instructed the cameras to pan the empty House to show that these Republican upstarts were talking only to themselves and their television audience.

Gingrich was intent on undermining the established order in the House. In 1987 he initiated ethics charges against the Speaker of the House, Jim Wright. By the spring of 1989 the House had become mired in partisanship. Shortly after the House Ethics Committee issued a five-count indictment against Wright, the newspapers disclosed that the House Democratic whip, Tony Coelho of California, had been involved in a questionable junk bond deal. Coelho resigned on Memorial Day; shortly thereafter Wright announced his resignation after an emotional, hour-long speech on the floor. Embittered Democrats blamed Gingrich for what Wright called this "mindless cannibalism." After Wright's resignation, Representative Jack Brooks (D-Texas) declared, "There's an evil wind blowing in the halls of Congress today that's reminiscent of the Spanish Inquisition." He added, "We've replaced comity and compassion with hatred and malice."[14] Following Wright's resignation, the House Democrats chose non-Southerners as leaders: Tom Foley (D-Washington) as Speaker, Richard Gephardt (D-Missouri) as majority leader, and William Gray, an African American from Philadelphia, as party whip.

Gingrich was a man of ideas, committed to taking the House away from the Democrats. To do so he formed the Conservative Opportunity Society, which attracted a small team of young Republican conservatives: Vin Weber of Minnesota, Robert Walker of Pennsylvania, Daniel Lungren of California, Judd Gregg of New Hampshire, Dan Coats of Indiana, Duncan Hunter of California, Tom DeLay of Texas, and Connie Mack of Florida. While Gingrich provided the ideas for the insurgency, Dick Armey from Texas provided the tactics necessary for the revolution to succeed. Gingrich's strategy called for not only questioning the ethics of individual Democrats but also denigrating Congress as an institution. He pursued a scandal in which many members of the House, including Republicans, had kept large overdrafts at the House bank.

In fact, a series of scandals aided Gingrich's efforts to nationalize a House election by showing that the institution had become corrupt under Democratic rule. The reputation of Congress had been tarnished by the bitter fight over Bush's nomination of Clarence Thomas to the Supreme Court in 1991 and the ensuing allegations of sexual harassment against Thomas by his former aide Anita F. Hill. Two years later, this image of a tawdry Congress was reinforced when more than twenty women brought sexual harassment charges against the senior senator Robert Packwood (he resigned). By the early 1990s, public support for Congress had fallen to an abysmal level.

At the same time Gingrich began to rally Republican conservatives to his cause. He worked with the Republican national chair, Haley Barbour, to recruit and train a cadre of new Republican candidates for state and national office. To further these goals, Gingrich launched the National Empowerment Television network, which broadcast programs outlining the new Republican agenda. Gingrich also used the development of conservative talk radio programs. At the same time, he took control of GOPAC, which became a major source of funding, campaign support materials, and strategy outlines for young conservatives seeking election. Gingrich sought to replace interest group liberalism in the House with a Republican majority committed to an ideological agenda.

In 1989 Gingrich succeeded Richard Cheney as House minority whip when the Wyoming representative became secretary of defense. From this position he battled the Bush administration over what he and other young Republicans considered the sellout of the Reagan presidency by the Dole wing of the party. When Bush announced a budget deal with the Democrats that included almost $134 billion in new taxes over five years, Gingrich denounced the deal as "the fiscal equivalent of Yalta."[15] When Bill Clinton defeated Bush for the presidency in 1992, Gingrich and his fellow Turks secretly cheered. The party was better off without Bush and his moderate Republicans.

Despite Bush's defeat, the House Republicans gained 10 seats, and nearly all the freshman House Republicans had benefited directly from GOPAC and Gingrich's support. Bob Michel, the Republican minority leader and a moderate, announced that he would step down in 1994. That same year the Gingrich Republicans removed Jerry Lewis of California as the chair of the Republican Conference and installed Dick Armey in his place. The revolution had begun.

The Republican Revolution That Failed

The first two years of Clinton's administration aided this revolution in unexpected ways. Clinton's complex, ill-fated national health insurance plan frightened Republicans and independents alike. His economic package raised taxes. His long debates over a policy for gays in the military (resulting in the "don't ask, don't tell" compromise) stoked conservative resentment. These and other issues energized southern Republicans and set the stage for the approaching midterm elections.

The next step was to create a Republican majority in the 1994 midterm elections. The Republicans had seized on the perceived failure of the Clinton presidency, the effects of the 1990 reapportionment, the unusually large number of Democratic retirements in 1992–1994, the recruitment of excellent Republican candidates, and the Gingrich-inspired legislative covenant with the voters, Contract with America. The strategy paid off: Republicans captured both houses of Congress with a 230–204 majority in the House and 8 new Senate seats. More important, the voters who called themselves conservative constituted a larger share of the electorate than they had in 1992 and they voted Republican. Republicans won on issues such as crime, welfare reform, and immigration. When this Republican majority elected Gingrich as the new Speaker of the House, it appeared to many observers that the revolution had begun.

The election showed the emergence of a powerful Republican party in the South. For the first time since the Civil War, a thoroughly national two-party system existed. Republicans won majorities in the House and Senate in both the North and the South. Yet while the Republicans had emerged as a viable national party, the Republican leadership in the House fell to southern Republicans: Speaker Gingrich of Georgia, Dick Armey of Texas as majority leader, and Tom DeLay of Texas as whip. These men represented overwhelmingly white, suburban, middle-class districts near important southern cities — Atlanta, Dallas, and Houston.

Even before the new Congress convened in January 1995, Gingrich called for monumental changes in the way the House conducted business, cutting three House committees and many subcommittees. Gingrich also made other procedural reforms, including the ending of "proxy voting," in which committee chairs controlled the votes of absent members. In addition, more committee and subcommittee meetings were opened to the public, and the first independent audit of the House's books took place. In addition, the Congressional Accountability Act was enacted, making Congress subject to the federal laws on workers' rights and conditions. Gingrich also appointed new chairs to these committees, often ignoring seniority.

The Contract with America became the Republicans' agenda for the first hundred days of the 1995 congressional session. The new majority initiated bills on crime, congressional term limits, welfare reform, the federal budget, Social Security, defense, illegal drugs, and taxation. A major piece of legislation was entitled the "Taking Back Our Streets Act," which included a limit on death penalty appeals in federal courts, mandatory minimum sentences for drug-related offenses, increased funds for states for building prisons, and the relaxation of rules for securing search warrants. The House also passed a major welfare bill, the Personal Responsibility Act, which transformed Aid to Families with Dependent Children from an entitlement to a block grant to states and barred teenage mothers under the age of eighteen from receiving welfare aid, food stamps, or public housing. The bill passed the House in a close party-line vote, 234–184. In addition, a tax reduction bill was passed.

All in all, the 104th House's record was impressive. With the exceptions of term limits and a space-based missile defense, the House approved each item of the Contract with America. In the Senate, however, many of the major proposals stalled. In the end, only two of the least politically controversial measures, the prohibition of unfunded mandates and the

Congressional Accountability Act, were approved by the Senate and signed into law by Clinton.

Gingrich and his colleagues felt that critical to the fulfillment of the contract was balancing the budget. Having failed to get a constitutional amendment passed, Gingrich focused on the budget itself. This issue rallied both those Republicans who believed that a balanced budget was essential to fiscal responsibility and those who believed balancing the budget meant downsizing government. Gingrich vowed to bring a balanced budget to government in seven years. John Kasich (R-Ohio), chair of the House Budget Committee, produced a budget in early 1995 that proposed around $1 trillion in spending cuts over the next seven years. It called for the elimination of more than 280 federal programs, including the executive departments of Energy, Education, and Commerce. It also called for a $228 billion, or 50 percent, reduction in the projected rate of growth. The bill passed the House by a 238–219 party-line vote.

In the meantime, Clinton had reacted to the GOP takeover of Congress by moving to the right in policy matters while still maintaining his rhetorical commitment to people who "work hard and play by the rules." Flush with success, the Republicans underestimated his and other Democrats' ability to portray the proposed Republican budget cuts as serving the interests of the rich at the expense of the poor and the elderly. Late in 1995, amid intense maneuvering, Congress failed to fund ongoing programs, which led to a shutdown of all but essential government offices. After concentrated negotiation in the Senate, the final reconciliation bill passed both houses in mid-November, in the middle of the government shutdown. When Clinton refused to sign the bill, the House leadership decided to confront the president with another shutdown by holding up appropriations to keep the government running.

The shutdown backfired. In a well-orchestrated counterattack coordinated from the White House, Social Security and Medicare became flash points in the battle over the national budget for fiscal year 1996. The polls indicated that the public blamed the GOP for the government shutdowns and the hardships they created. When a beaten Congress returned after the New Year, Senator Dole made it clear that enough was enough. He pushed through a new budget resolution in the Senate, and after a bitter debate in the House Republican Conference, a similar resolution was passed in the House in early January. By late April the battle over the 1996 budget was over, with Clinton emerging as a clear victor.

The government shutdowns were a critical misstep by conservatives. Gingrich had underestimated the strength of a president armed with the veto and the weakness of a House Speaker presiding over a tiny Republican majority. He did not help matters by pushing his agenda in what was widely considered a harsh, argumentative style. The defining image of congressional Republicans appeared to many Americans as a southern-led party bent on telling them how they should live and willing to shut down the government to get their way.

The House Republicans never regained the momentum of those first hundred days of the 104th Congress, even though, under Gingrich's leadership, Congress passed welfare reform, a balanced budget, and the first tax cuts in sixteen years. Following the government shutdown in 1995, the Republicans proved increasingly anxious to compromise on many issues. At the same time, Clinton also sought compromise by pursuing a centrist strategy, which he felt necessary to win reelection. Clinton, by supporting this legislation, gained equal credit for these measures in the eyes of the voters.

By 1996 a surging economy and a falling federal deficit were seen by the majority of voters to be a vindication of Clinton's economic program. In November, Clinton was reelected with a little less than 50 percent of the vote while his opponent, the Senate majority leader, Robert Dole, received nearly 42 percent; the Reform party candidate, Ross Perot, garnered 8 percent. Although Congress remained in Republican hands, Clinton's considerable political skills had foiled the GOP's opportunity to win both branches of government.

Congress Impeaches Clinton

During his second term, Clinton planned to balance the federal budget by 2002. Supported by a good economy, he presented a balanced-budget proposal for the 1998 fiscal year, and at the end of the year he announced a surplus for the 1998 fiscal year. This good news, however, was marred by further scandal. In 1997 the Republicans charged that the Clinton-Gore campaign had participated in illegal campaign fund-raising activities in 1996. Further difficulties arose over a sexual harassment suit against Clinton by a former Arkansas employee, Paula Jones, when he had been governor. On May 27, 1997, the Supreme Court unanimously rejected Clinton's request to delay the Paula Jones lawsuit until he left office.

In the months that followed, the hostility between the White House and Kenneth Starr, the independent counsel appointed by the attorney general to investigate these charges, increased dramatically when new charges arose that Clinton had encouraged a former White House intern, Monica Lewinsky, to lie under oath in the Jones suit. On January 16 Starr received authority from a grand jury to investigate these charges. In his testimony the next day before the grand jury, Clinton relied on narrow definitions and legal technicalities to deny that he had engaged in sexual relations with Lewinsky. On January 21 Clinton denied the affair to the media, a denial he repeated in more forceful terms five days later. He issued similar denials to his cabinet, his staff, his family, and members of Congress.

As other incriminating evidence was brought to light over the next few weeks, Clinton's statements were clearly shown to be false. On August 17, 1998, in a nationally televised address, Clinton admitted that he had engaged in an inappropriate relationship with Lewinsky but strongly denied that he had done anything illegal.

Starr delivered his report on the Lewinsky matter to the House of Representatives on September 9, 1998. The report concluded that Clinton's actions "may constitute grounds for impeachment," a conclusion that the president's allies disputed. Others believed that impeachment was too severe a penalty, given the nature of the offenses. The diverging views of Clinton's character, the merit of the charges, the manner of the investigation, Clinton's conduct during the investigation, and the appropriate penalties for Clinton's action led to a deep rift in the public and stirred further partisan acrimony. In the midst of the national debate over impeachment, charges reached the press that the leader of the House investigation — none other than Henry Hyde — had engaged in a lengthy adulterous affair and another critic, J. C. Watts (R-Oklahoma), had fathered a child out of wedlock. Charges of hypocrisy rang through the press.

In December a divided House approved two articles of impeachment, charging the president with perjury and obstruction of justice. The Senate convened the impeachment trial on January 7, 1999. Those supporting the president's removal argued that Clinton was guilty of the charges, that he had disgraced his office, and that a failure to punish him would be applying a different standard to the president than that applied to average citizens. Clinton's defenders maintained that the crimes he was charged with were rarely prosecuted and that the alleged offenses did not meet the definition of impeachable crimes described in the Constitution. With public support clearly against impeachment, the Senate voted against removing Clinton from office, acquitting him after five weeks of testimony and deliberation.

The impeachment crisis had a profound effect on Clinton's second term by consuming the attention of the White House and Congress for more than a year. Furthermore, during this time the partisanship in Congress intensified. In January 1997 Gingrich was reprimanded by the House for ethics violations that included giving the Ethics Committee false information and using tax-exempt donations for political activities. Gingrich was fined $300,000. Following the Republican losses in the November 1998 elections, he resigned his position as Speaker and his seat in Congress.

Then, shortly before the next Congress, his elected successor as Speaker, Bob Livingston (R-Louisiana), also resigned amid charges that he too had committed adultery. Dennis Hastert (R-Illinois), a popular (and scandal-free) choice, became Speaker.

The 2000 election brought no relief from partisanship. The presidential contest between Clinton's vice president, Al Gore, and the Republican governor of Texas (and son of the former president), George W. Bush, deadlocked over a razor-thin margin and ballot miscounts in Florida. Although Bush had lost the popular vote, eventually the Supreme Court in effect threw Florida's electoral votes to him, and he took office. Similarly, the 2000 congressional elections resulted in some of the closest in American political history. The GOP retained control over the House, but the Senate was tied, 50–50. Only Vice President Dick Cheney's vote kept the Senate in Republican hands. Then in May 2001 Senator James Jeffords (R-Vermont) bolted the party, became an Independent, and delivered the Senate to Democratic control.

President Bush was able to get his priority, a tax-reduction plan, through the closely divided Congress, but soon the terrorist attacks of September 11, 2001, against New York and Washington changed the agenda. Instead of budget issues, suddenly Congress's attention was focused on terrorism, civil rights versus homeland security, and America's role in a dangerous world. At the same time, the Internet-engendered economic bubble of the late 1990s popped, and an economic recession and slow recovery reduced Congress to bickering about economic policy again. Republicans and Democrats remained divided along conservative and liberal lines, with the GOP recommending further tax cuts and Democrats favoring more government support for workers hurt by the recession. The Democratic opposition, however, was fractured by the support on the part of many Democrats for President Bush's war against terrorists in Afghanistan and other antiterrorist measures.

The 2002 midterm elections surprised many pundits when the Republicans retained the House and regained control of the Senate, although with the slightest of margins. Many Democrats believed that Congress had been lost because they had not challenged the president enough on economic issues. The partisanship flared yet again when the incoming Senate majority leader, Trent Lott of Mississippi, was forced to resign following comments at the hundredth birthday party for South Carolina's Strom Thurmond that appeared to praise his segregationist campaign for president in 1948 under the States' Rights party banner. Further accusations came from leading Democratic congressional leaders including now-Senator Hillary Clinton (D–New York) that Lott's alleged racism reflected the personal beliefs of many Republicans. Although the polls revealed that the vast majority of Americans were tired of this kind of partisan bickering and gamesmanship, Congress on both sides of the aisle appeared insistent on maintaining party warfare.

In many ways, party politics in Congress in the twenty-first century appeared quite similar to those in the late nineteenth century. With support in the electorate for each party equally divided and "swing" votes taking on greater importance in national elections, partisanship inevitably intensified in order to maintain core supporters while not alienating those with no affiliation. Yet such similarities should distract from fundamental differences in politics in the late nineteenth and the late twentieth centuries. Fundamental in this regard was the decline of the distrust Americans expressed in the late twentieth century about their political leaders and institutions. Paradoxically, this distrust coincided with the emergence of a well-organized conservative movement that proclaimed its faith in Republican government. The conservative movement and its leaders had shifted the GOP to the right and in doing so shifted much of the policy debate in a conservative direction. Yes, they had undertaken a revolution and had enjoyed much success, but what followed appeared less a revolution than an ideological civil war that remained unresolved as the United States entered the twenty-first century.

— Donald T. Critchlow

BIBLIOGRAPHICAL NOTES

With the general shift to the right in American politics, a rich and still growing body of scholarship on the history of conservatism has developed over the last decade. For understanding conservatism in Congress, a number of biographies of Barry Goldwater are a good place to begin. These include Robert Alan Goldberg, *Barry Goldwater* (New Haven, Conn., 1995); Rick Perlstein, *Before the Storm: Barry Goldwater and the Unmaking of the American Consensus* (New York, 2001); and a conservative perspective, Lee Edwards, *Goldwater: The Man Who Made a Revolution* (Washington, D.C., 1995). Other conservatives in Congress have attracted biographies of varying worth, including Edward L. Schapsmeir, *Dirksen of Illinois: Senatorial Statesman* (Urbana, Ill., 1985); Ernest B. Furguson, *Hard Right: The Rise of Jesse Helms* (New York, 1986); and Nadine Cohodas, *Strom Thurmond & the Politics of Southern Change* (New York, 1993).

For a general perspective on the conservative movement, see Godfrey Hodgson, *The World Turned Right Side Up: A History of Conservative Ascendancy in America* (Boston, 1993). Also worth reading are Jeffrey Isaac, *The Poverty of Progressivism: The Future of American Democracy in a Time of Liberal Decline* (Lanham, Md., 2003), and Joseph Scotchie, *Revolt from the Heartland: The Struggle of an Authentic Conservatism* (New York, 2002). The transformation of white voters in the South from Democrat to Republican is critical in understanding conservatism since 1980. A good starting place is Merle and Earl Black, *The Rise of Southern Republicans* (Cambridge, Mass., 2002), and Augustus Cochran, *Democracy Heading South: National Politics in the Shadow of Dixie* (Lawrence, Kans., 2001). Also useful but needs to be read with caution is Ronald Radosh, *Divided They Fell: The Demise of the Democratic Party, 1964–1996* (New York, 1996). The limits of conservatism in practice are discussed by David Frum, *Dead Right* (New York, 1994). The rise of the so-called Christian Right is discussed by Clyde Wilcox, *Onward Christian Soldier? The Religious Right in American Politics* (Boulder, Colo., 1996).

Reagan's fiscal policy is captured through two biographies of Dan Rostenkowski, Richard E. Cohen, *Rostenkowski: The Pursuit of Power and the End of Old Politics* (Chicago, 1999), and James Merriner, *Mr. Chairman: Power in Dan Rostenkowski's America* (Carbondale, Ill., 1999). An excellent study of the Senate and the Reagan tax cut is Richard Fenno, *The Emergence of a Senate Leader: Pete Domenici and the Reagan Budget* (Washington, D.C., 1991).

Congressional politics in the Clinton years is found in Pete Baker, *The Breach: Inside the Impeachment and Trial of William Jefferson Clinton* (New York, 2000); Nina Easton, *Gang of Five: Leaders at the Center of the Conservative Crusade* (New York, 2002); Elizabeth Drew, *Showdown: The Struggle Between the Gingrich Congress and the Clinton White House* (New York, 1996); David Maraniss, *Tell Newt to Shut Up!: Prizewinning Washington Post Journalists Reveal How Reality Gagged the Gingrich Revolution* (New York, 1996); Donald R. Wolfensberger, *Congress and the People: Deliberative Democracy on Trial* (New York, 2000); and Herbert Weisberg and Samuel Patterson, *Great Theater: The American Congress in the 1990s* (New York, 1998).

NOTES

1. Quoted in Janet Hook, "New Congress Poised to Turn Tradition on Its Head," *Congressional Quarterly*, Dec. 31, 1994, 3591.

2. Specifically, the Contract with America pledged Republican candidates to the following program:

> On the first day of the 104th Congress, the new Republican majority will pass the following major reforms:
>
> 1. Require all laws that apply to the rest of the country to also apply equally to Congress.
> 2. Select an independent auditing firm to conduct a comprehensive audit of Congress.
> 3. Cut the number of House committees; and cut committee staffs by one-third.
> 4. Limit the terms of all committee chairs.
> 5. Ban the casting of proxy votes in committee.
> 6. Require committee meeting to be open to the public.

7. Require a three-fifths majority to pass a tax increase.
8. Implement zero base-line budgeting.

Thereafter in the first 100 days the Republican majority would bring to the House Floor the following bills:

1. A balanced budget amendment.
2. An anti-crime package.
3. Welfare reform to discourage out-of-wedlock births.
4. Tax incentives for adoption.
5. A $500 per child tax credit.
6. No U.S. troops under U.N. command bill.
7. Raise in Social Security earning and repeal of 1993 tax hikes on Social Security benefits.
8. Small business and capital gain incentives.
9. Loser pay liability legal reform.
10. Term limits on Congress.

3. Quoted in Dan Balz and Ronald Brownstein, *Storming the Gates,* 30.

4. Quoted in Jon Healy, "Jubilant GOP Strive to Keep Legislative Feed on Ground," *Congressional Quarterly,* Nov. 12, 1994, 3210–11.

5. The view that women's groups had failed to connect with "homemakers" is found in Bonnie Cowan to Jane Wells (National Coordinator ERAmerica), March 19, 1976, ERAmerica, Box 1, Library of Congress, Washington, D.C.

6. The Republican party platform declared that "the question of abortion is one of the most difficult and controversial of our time." The platform went on to say that the party urges "a continuance of the public dialogue on abortion and supports the efforts of those who seek enactment of a constitutional amendment to restore protection of the right to life for unborn children." Both the Democratic and Republic planks on abortion are quoted in full in Karen O'Connor, *No Neutral Ground? Abortion Politics in an Age of Absolutes* (Boulder, Colo., 1996), 73.

7. Campaign staffers selected from antiabortion candidates including Representatives Robert Dornan (R-California); Dan Quayle (R-Indiana), who was challenging Senator Birch Bayh; Charles Grassley (R-Iowa), running against Senator John Culver; and Steve Symms (R-Idaho), up against Senator Frank Church. In addition, pro-life political activists from Louisiana, Pennsylvania, Oregon, Connecticut, Oklahoma, Wisconsin, and Massachusetts were sent to school to make them into "pro-life political experts to help bring them over the top next November." See "1980 Elections Start Now!" *The Pro-Life Political Reporter,* September 1979, I:4, in Dee Jepsen papers, Box I, Ronald Reagan Library.

8. Richard A. Viguerie, "An Open Letter to President Reagan," *Conservative Digest* (July 1982): 46–47.

9. Paul Weyrich, "The White House, the Elections, the Right," *Conservative Digest* (July 1982): 45.

10. Ronald Reagan to John Lofton, July 30, 1982; Draft, July 30, 1982, Presidential Handwritten File, Series II, Presidential Records, Box 3, Folder 46, Ronald

Reagan Papers, Reagan Library. The author would like to thank Robert Collins for bringing this to his attention.

11. Quoted in Michael Barone, *Our Country* (New York, 1990), 624.

12. Ibid., 625.

13. Quoted in Earl Black and Merle Black, *The Rise of Southern Republicans* (Cambridge, Mass., 2002), 7.

14. Quoted in Dan Balz and Ronald Brownstein, *Storming the Gates of Heaven, Protest Politics and the Republican Revival* (New York, 1996), 133.

15. Ibid., 139.

Barry Goldwater

January 1, 1909–May 29, 1998

Barry Goldwater

Early in his thirty-year career in the Senate, Barry Goldwater emerged as a leading figure in the Republican party with the enthusiastic reception among conservatives of his book *The Conscience of a Conservative* (1960). A Draft Goldwater group, led by the conservative activist F. Clinton White (who later advised Ronald Reagan, Richard M. Nixon, Gerald Ford, and Jesse Helms), sought national support for the senator in the 1964 presidential election. Goldwater was not enthusiastic about running against the popular Democratic president John F. Kennedy nor, after Kennedy's assassination, Lyndon B. Johnson, a seasoned Texas politician who appealed to the voters of the South and Southwest. By the end of 1963, however, the Arizona senator agreed to run — possibly the worst political move of his career.

Born in Phoenix, Arizona, Goldwater was the son of a successful businessman and retailer who packed the underachieving teenager off to a Virginia military school in 1928. The young Goldwater graduated first in his class and returned home to enroll at the University of Arizona. After his father's death the following year, however, he joined the family business and, for two decades, thrived as a businessman. Unlike the flinty conservative he later seemed to be on Capitol Hill, Goldwater provided his employees with benefits that included profit-sharing and health insurance, and his stores were the first in Phoenix to hire African Americans as clerks. Usually generous and gregarious, Goldwater was also known as a workaholic who, under pressure, was temperamental and relied on alcohol to alleviate the stress. He suffered two nervous breakdowns before entering public life, a fact political opponents liked to mention.

Goldwater married in 1934 and settled into family life (his son Barry Jr. later served in the House of Representatives). In World War II he served as a pilot in the army air corps, rising to lieutenant colonel. Goldwater entered politics in 1949 when he was elected to the Phoenix City Council, where he served two terms and established a reputation for integrity and candor. In 1950 he managed the successful gubernatorial campaign of the Republican Howard Pyle (1906–1987), who convinced him to run in 1952 against the incumbent Democrat and Senate majority leader Ernest McFarland (1894–1984). McFarland may not have recognized his state's gradual transition from Democratic populism to Republican conservatism and did not bother to campaign for reelection. Riding the coattails of Eisenhower's election to the presidency, Goldwater squeaked out a close victory.

Although he captured the 1964 Republican presidential nomination, his political liabilities were many. Goldwater's off-the-cuff remarks, considered straight talk by his right-wing supporters, proved highly controversial on the national stage. His conservative voting record included opposition to federal civil rights laws (Goldwater considered them a state issue), the United Nations, the minimum wage, and the censure of red-baiting Senator Joseph R. McCarthy (1908–1957). The civil rights leader Martin Luther King Jr. (1929–1968) and the labor leader George Meany (1894–1980) compared Goldwater to Adolf Hitler. In the presidential campaign, Goldwater refused to temper his remarks, and his infamous one-liners — that the United States should lob nuclear bombs into the Kremlin men's room or that the nation's poor suffered economically merely because they were stupid or lacked ambition — served only to motivate Democrats and alienate moderate Republicans, who gave Johnson a landslide victory. Goldwater did receive 38 percent of the popular vote, however, showing that conservative ideals struck a chord with many voters and presaging the ascendancy of later conservative candidates. The defeated Goldwater was reelected to the Senate in 1968, where he served three more terms but never again gained the popular support that led to his presidential run.

If Goldwater's first senatorial stint ended in his political comeuppance, his second illustrated his vigor as a political idealist. He played a decisive role in the Watergate drama, informing President Richard M. Nixon (1913–1994) that his impeachment was imminent. Having lost any support the conservative Goldwater might have been able to offer, Nixon realized that he had to resign from office. Goldwater was also critical of the Reagan and Bush administrations, which he felt were overly influenced by the religious right. Even in retirement, the independent Goldwater spoke out in support of gay rights and abortion rights and even supported the embattled Clinton administration, to the consternation of other conservatives. At the end of his life, however, many conservatives considered him a godfather of the modern conservative movement, a man who represented their views years before the modern conservatives came to power.

References

"Goldwater, Barry." *Contemporary Authors Online,* Gale, 2003. Reproduced in *Biography Resource Center.* Farmington Hills, Mich.: Gale Group. 2003. Retrieved July 3, 2003, from http://www.galenet.com/servlet/BioRC.

Rae, N. C. 2000, February. "Goldwater, Barry." *American National Biography Online.* Retrieved July 3, 2003, from http://www.anb.org/articles/07/07-00746.html.

Index

Illustration Credits

JOHN QUINCY ADAMS: Portrait by George Caleb Bingham, ca. 1844, courtesy National Portrait Gallery, Smithsonian Institution/Art Resource, New York. NELSON ALDRICH: U.S. Senate Historical Office. JAMES BUCHANAN: Portrait by John Chester Buttre, ca. 1857–1870, Library of Congress. AARON BURR: U.S. Senate Historical Office. JOHN C. CALHOUN: Library of Congress. JOSEPH GURNEY CANNON: Library of Congress. HATTIE CARAWAY: Library of Congress. SHIRLEY CHISHOLM: © Bettmann/Corbis. HENRY CLAY: Library of Congress. EVERETT DIRKSEN: U.S. Senate Historical Office. STEPHEN DOUGLAS: Library of Congress. BARRY GOLDWATER: Library of Congress. RUFUS KING: Portrait by Gilbert Stuart, 1819–1820, courtesy National Portrait Gallery, Smithsonian Institution/Art Resource, New York. ROBERT MARION LA FOLLETTE: Library of Congress. ROBERT MARION LA FOLLETTE JR.: Library of Congress. HENRY CABOT LODGE: U.S. Senate Historical Office. HUEY PIERCE LONG: © AP/Wide World Photos. JAMES MADISON: Portrait by James Sharples Sr., 1796–1797, courtesy Independence National Historical Park. THOMAS P. O'NEILL: Library of Congress. ADAM CLAYTON POWELL: © Bettmann/Corbis. JEANNETTE PICKERING RANKIN: U.S. Senate Historical Office. SAM RAYBURN: Library of Congress. HIRAM RHOADES REVELS: Library of Congress. RICHARD RUSSELL: Library of Congress. THADDEUS STEVENS: Portrait by Brady Studios, ca. 1868, National Archives and Records Administration. WILLIAM HENRY SEWARD: U.S. Senate Historical Office. CHARLES SUMNER: Library of Congress. DANIEL WEBSTER: Library of Congress. *FEDERAL HALL, THE SEAT OF CONGRESS:* by Amos Doolittle, 1790, Library of Congress. U.S. CAPITOL, CA. 1846: © Corbis. U.S. CAPITOL, CA. 1905: © Corbis. U.S. CAPITOL, 1999: © Joseph Sohm/Corbis.